Sociological Theory

CLASSICAL FOUNDERS AND
CONTEMPORARY PERSPECTIVES

Sociological Theory

CLASSICAL FOUNDERS AND CONTEMPORARY PERSPECTIVES

Doyle Paul Johnson
UNIVERSITY OF SOUTH FLORIDA

JOHN WILEY & SONS

New York • Chichester • Brisbane • Toronto • Singapore

Library of Congress Cataloging in Publication Data

Johnson, Doyle Paul.
  Sociological theory.

  Bibliography: p.
  Includes indexes
  1. Sociology—History. I. Title.
HM19.J64   301'.01   80-23441
ISBN 0-471-02915-7

Printed in the United States of America

10 9 8 7 6 5 4

To my students

Preface

This is an upper-level, undergraduate textbook in sociological theory. It can also help to organize the field of sociology for graduate students, and it can be used in conjunction with courses in social thought and social change.

For students who do not intend to become professional sociologists, the study of social theory can provide stimulating new insights and be a valuable aid in interpreting experiences and events in the real world. Throughout this book I have explained the key distinctions between the major underlying assumptions of the various theorists and schools of theory and have demonstrated their empirical and practical importance.

Anyone who writes a book on social theory faces a dilemma. It is tempting to try to include everyone who has contributed to its development; however, the field is so broad that the end product could easily become a list of superficial encyclopedic sketches. The alternative is to go into great depth on a severely limited number of theorists, such as two or three of the major founders of the discipline. There is also the dilemma of whether to emphasize the classical pioneers or contemporary theories.

These problems can never be resolved to everyone's satisfaction. My choice reflects an intermediate position. The first two chapters discuss the nature of sociological theory and some strategies for developing and evaluating it. Next, a major portion of the book is devoted to five of the classical pioneers whose contributions laid the foundations for the sociological discipline: Comte, Marx, Durkheim, Weber, and Simmel. This is followed by a section on five contemporary schools of theory: symbolic interactionism, exchange theory, functionalism, conflict theory, and open systems theory. The shift from individual theorists to schools of theory reflects the changing state of the discipline. In its early days sociology was dominated by outstanding individual theorists. Many of their contributions are still considered significant. Today, however, the dominance of individual theorists has passed, and most of the work done in the field can best be treated within the context of alternative schools of theory. This shift reflects the growth of sociology and its establishment as a recognized academic discipline. Because of this dual emphasis on classical and contemporary theory, this book is appropriate for a two-term sequence of social theory as well as to a single-term course.

Most of the classical theorists covered are European, and most of the representatives of the contemporary schools are American. There are some exceptions, however. The chapter on Comte includes an extended discussion of Sorokin's model of the dynamics of sociocultural systems. Although the beginning of the field is often traced to Comte, modern sociology reflects the overshadowing influence of Durkheim and Weber more than that of Comte. Nevertheless, contrasting Comte's general model of sociocultural change with Sorokin's allows the exploration of some issues involved in the study of broad-scale cultural change.

Similarly, some material is offered in the section on contemporary schools of theory that is not derived from contemporary Americans. The chapter on symbolic interactionism, for example, includes an extended discussion of George Herbert Mead and more limited discussions of Charles Horton Cooley and William I. Thomas. Although these pioneers were twentieth-century Americans, they are not contemporary. Also, the presentation of alternative conflict theories briefly discusses critical theory, many of whose representatives were from Frankfurt, Germany. Ralf Dahrendorf's conflict theory and Percy Cohen's analysis of the contrast between functional theory and conflict theory are also covered; their contributions have become important ingredients of American sociology.

Several other figures, both classical and contemporary, are touched on briefly when appropriate. The classical figures include, for example, Herbert Spencer, Ferdinand Tönnies, and Vilfredo Pareto. Among the contemporary schools, the phenomenological perspective is discussed in Chapter 2 in terms of sociologists' efforts to construct a model of social reality that is congruent with the scientific perspective and in Chapter 11 in a brief comparison with critical theory. Neopositivism is represented by a short introduction to the strategies and goals of theory construction in Chapter 2. Sociobiology is incorporated in Chapter 12 in connection with the influence of biological factors on social behavior and social systems.

The theorists and theoretical schools that are discussed in depth were selected for their focus on alternative levels of social reality. I believe that a major difference among alternative theories is the level of social reality on which they focus. Thus Comte and Sorokin center on the cultural level of social reality. Parsons also dealt extensively with this level. Marx and Durkheim concentrated on the social structural level, as do contemporary functionalism and conflict theory. Weber began at the individual level, but most of his substantive analyses were at the social structural level. An emphasis on the interpersonal level is represented by Simmel in the classical stage and by symbolic interactionism and exchange theory in contemporary schools. Modern systems theory, discussed in Chapter 12, can encompass the cultural and interpersonal levels, but the emphasis is on the social structural level.

The classical theorists covered represent a shift from the cultural to the social structural to the interpersonal level. In contrast, the contemporary schools are presented to show a progression from the micro level of interpersonal relations to the macro level of large-scale institutional structures. This is a logical progression and does not reflect the actual historical sequence of theory development in American sociology.

The distinction between different levels is an analytical one; in many cases it is arbitrary to say that a theorist or theoretical school deals with one particular level. A major reason that the contributions of the theorists discussed are significant is that they did not limit themselves to one level; they explored and analyzed the linkages among the culture, the social structure, interpersonal relations, and the individual.

The theorists and theoretical schools that I have selected for in-depth presentations represent a significant portion of the mainstream of modern social theory and the major alternative approaches. This book will give students a basic understanding of the most significant classical founders of the discipline and of the dominant contemporary schools of theory. The study questions at the end of each chapter provide an opportunity to review some of the basic principles discussed and to make appropriate applications. An instructor's manual with test questions, discussion questions, and detailed chapter outlines is also available.

Doyle Paul Johnson

Acknowledgments

Although it is impossible to acknowledge all the people who helped me in developing this book, some of them must be named. Robert Lilly at Northern Kentucky University, Valerie Malhotra-Hammond at Carthage College, John Petras at Central Michigan University, and Roger Sennott and Alan Wells at the University of Rhode Island reviewed drafts of the manuscript at various stages and provided valuable suggestions. Roy Hansen, Caroline Kaufmann, and Stephen Turner at the University of South Florida provided constructive comments on particular chapters or parts of chapters while I was writing the book or shared their knowledge of a particular area. Roy Francis, chairperson of the Sociology Department, provided unfailing encouragement throughout all stages of the project and was always a reliable source of critical and creative ideas on standard sociological interpretations of the material. Travis J. Northcutt, Dean of the College of Social and Behavioral Sciences, demonstrated his faith by not allowing the distractions of other important college matters to intrude on my schedule.

I also thank both the graduate and undergraduate students I have taught over the past several years. Their reactions have aided me considerably in sharpening and clarifying this material and in developing contemporary applications of many of the highly abstract principles included in this subject matter.

Also, I am conscious of the continuing influence of the faculty members with whom I came in contact in the graduate program at the University of Illinois in Urbana. I was especially fortunate to have been exposed there to the crosscurrents of symbolic interaction theory and functionalism. In particular, I learned a great deal from the late Lou Schneider and from Harry Johnson and George McCall.

I am indebted to Richard Baker, formerly my sponsoring editor at Wiley, and Carol Luitjens, my present sponsoring editor. Special thanks go to Vivian H. Kahane, senior editor at Wiley, for performing the tedious and time-consuming task of final copy editing.

My wife Sharon and my sons Tim and Alan were supportive and understanding when I was often preoccupied and my participation in cherished family activities had to be kept to a minimum. Finally, Robin Kester performed heroically in typing the manuscript. Her diligence, patience, and ability to decipher my last-minute changes in the earliest rough drafts are sincerely appreciated. Maureen Hersey assisted in typing a portion of the manuscript; I also thank her for her help at a crucial time.

D. P. J.

Contents

One

SOCIAL THEORY AS SOCIAL CONSTRUCTION WORK

1

The Social Context of Sociological Theory

"Who needs theory? Just give me the facts!" is a common attitude among men and women of affairs. In the absence of adequate facts, an idea is often dismissed as unworthy because it is "only a theory." Even students have questioned the need to study abstract ideas that seem to have, at best, a tenuous relation to the "real world." The assumption is that if all the facts were known, they would speak for themselves and no theory would be needed.

However, all the facts we need are seldom available. Even if they were, we would still have to interpret them in order to deal with them in the light of our own needs and plans. Since the meaning of facts is seldom self-evident, we must rely on a variety of theories to help us interpret and evaluate them. A good theory can aid our understanding of the facts, helping us to explain them and to make valid predictions from them; this is essential to planning for the future, both in our personal lives and in public policy planning.

Social scientists and other academicians are sometimes accused of being detached from the real world and of living in an "ivory tower" world. Their theories therefore often seem impractical or irrelevant to us. Even everyday realities seem clouded by the jargon they use to explain them.

Although excessive use of abstract jargon may be unfortunate, specialists in all fields, from physicians and lawyers to automobile mechanics and construction workers, have their own, specialized vocabularies. This promotes precision in communication, making it possible to share and reinforce technical ideas and to cooperate in performing specialized tasks. Moreover, it also defines the boundaries of a profession, enhancing the status of its members and separating those who belong from those who do not.

Students of any academic discipline or profession (or new recruits to various groups) are expected to learn the appropriate vocabulary. This should never be an end in itself, however; it is equally important to be able to relate the vocabulary to the phenomena to which it refers. This is why medical students, for example, are required to do laboratory work and to serve as interns in addition to their purely theoretical work. Making the connection between concepts and experience is one of the major ways that academic study becomes relevant.

Applying sociological terms and ideas to real-life social events can be especially rewarding. Social science students, perhaps more than those in other disciplines, bring to their academic studies many experiences to which the sociological perspective can be applied. Also, because of the mass media, students today have access to information about significant social events around the world. These provide ample opportunities to demonstrate the relevance and practical significance of sociological theory.

GENERAL PLAN OF THIS BOOK

There is a tradition that students who major in sociology should be exposed to the main ideas of the pioneering classical social theorists who established the foundations of modern sociology. These include Durkheim, Weber, Simmel, Marx, Spencer, and Comte in Europe and Sumner, Mead, Cooley, Thomas, and Znaniecki in America. Contemporary theorists such as Merton, Parsons, Homans, Blau, and Goffman, or contemporary schools of theory, such as functionalism, symbolic interactionism, conflict or critical theory, exchange theory, phenomenological approaches, or ethnomethodology are also usually emphasized.[1] This book introduces the key ideas of some of these theorists and shows how they can be applied to improving our understanding of our personal social experiences and contemporary issues.

The classical theorists to be covered include primarily Comte, Marx, Durkheim, Weber, and Simmel. Others, such as Spencer, are discussed briefly when appropriate in connection with the five who are emphasized. Sorokin, although not among the classical European theorists, will also be introduced in order to contrast his model of sociocultural change with Comte's. The section on contemporary theories will include five major schools of theory: symbolic interactionism, exchange theory, functionalism, conflict theory, and general systems theory. The shift from individual theorists in the classical stage to schools of theory in the contemporary stage reflects changes that have taken place in the discipline. Although outstanding individual theorists can certainly be identified in contemporary sociology, the field is no longer dominated, as it was in the beginning, by such individuals. Instead, with the growth of the field and with its institutionalization as a major academic discipline, the field can best be described in terms of major schools of theory, not in terms of individual theorists. Before the classical and contemporary theories are introduced, some attention will be given (in the next chapter) to strategies of theory construction and to the underlying implications of alternative theoretical approaches. Although theory construction reflects an effort to be as explicit as possible in stating assumptions, defining terms, and so on, there are always implicit philosophical assumptions that can be identified.

The selection of theorists to be discussed and the overall organization of Parts two and three of the book are guided by the classification of theories according to primary level of analysis and basic underlying assumptions and emphases. In general, social theories can be classified according to whether the primary level of analysis is broad, cultural patterns (values and norms, world views, meanings, symbol systems, etc), social structure (size, division of labor, degree of consensus, type of power or authority structure, etc.), interpersonal relations (intensity, frequency, degree of cooperation or conflict, etc.), or the individual (motivational patterns, personality characteristics, subjective orientations, etc.). (Most sociologists do not deal with the individual level except in relation to one of the other levels.) Among the theorists discussed in Part Two, Comte and Sorokin concentrate on the cultural level, Marx and Durkheim on the social structural level, and Simmel on the interpersonal level. Among the contemporary schools of theory discussed in Part three, symbolic interaction theory and exchange theory stress the micro level of interpersonal relations, and functional theory and conflict theory deal with macro-level social structure. General systems theory also relates primarily to the social structural level, although allowance is made for input from other levels.

Any effort to classify complex theories runs the risk of oversimplifying and distorting certain aspects. At the least, the differences among theories in the various categories are likely to be exaggerated, but some classification seems essential. The distinctions among these different levels of social reality are analytical and abstract and are made only for convenience in analysis. In reality, *cultural patterns* are institutionalized in the *social structure; individuals* internalize these patterns in their subjective orientations and express them as they *interact* with one another. In other words, these various levels are both interdependent and interpenetrating in real life.

Each of the preceding categories includes important differences among theorists in their basic assumptions and in the specific concepts and processes that they emphasize. These will be discussed later. However, to anticipate with one example, at the social structural level one may emphasize processes that promote *harmony* and *cooperation* among various individuals or groups, or one may emphasize instead the processes that promote *competition* and *conflict*. Among the classical theorists Durkheim, for example, emphasized the processes that promote social integration, while Marx stressed the importance of class divisions and conflict.

The theories are not to be taken as unchangeable dogma. Learning sociological theory means much more than simply memorizing the ideas of a group of people known as social theorists, as though their ideas were final or conclusive truths. There is nothing final or conclusive in any of the theories. They should be learned because some of them may be useful in helping us understand our social worlds. By becoming familiar with the ideas of others who struggled to make sense out of their social worlds we can build on their ideas as we attempt to understand our own social worlds. We should not be content just to learn the ideas of the various theorists; instead, we should continually evaluate their relevance as we apply them to our analysis of the social world today.

Furthermore, no one theory should be expected to provide a complete picture or total explanation of social reality as we experience it. Each theory should offer clear insight into a particular facet or aspect of social life, while perhaps distorting or ignoring other aspects. This is to be expected because of the complex and multifaceted nature of social life. Perhaps at some time in the future a comprehensive sociological theory will be developed that deals adequately and comprehensively with this reality. But with social theory at its present stage of development, our understanding of social reality is best served by using a variety of theories to help us understand its different aspects.

THEORY AND EVERYDAY LIFE

The formal study of sociological theory does not begin in the classroom. All human beings theorize, whether we realize it or not. Even the most practical person, such as the defense attorney admonishing the jurors to stick to the facts, must interpret the facts for them to have any relevance. This is a theorizing process.

Interpretive theorizing is crucial because of the need to explain events. Whatever our current circumstances, be they good or bad, we must explain why, to ourselves and to others. We do this by relating our present situation to past experiences or decisions, social influences or pressures of others, the general crises of the times, or the limitations and opportunities of our environment. Parents try to explain why their children turned out as they did; students attempt to explain to themselves why they did not get the grades they felt they deserved; and teachers, police officers, and political leaders justify to themselves and to others why they do what they do.

Planning for or predicting the future also requires that we go beyond existing facts and theorize. No one can predict the future with 100 percent accuracy. We do, however, make educated guesses and adjust our present behavior in view of our expectations and hopes. Young people choosing careers, parents coping with their children's behavior, customers planning major purchases, salespersons developing new sales tactics, political leaders debating foreign policy dilemmas, and students attempting to "second guess" their professors as they study for examinations all demonstrate our need to go beyond available facts and theorize.

People vary greatly in the degree to which they consciously plan for the future. Young people in our society probably are expected to plan for the long-range future to a greater degree than senior citizens (who supposedly live in the past). There are also cultural differences among various societies in terms of their emphasis on developing goals for the future versus maintaining past traditions. But, to the extent that present actions are guided by images of the future, whether short range or long range, vague or explicit, people must go beyond the facts and theorize.

I am not implying that human behavior involves simply acting out the logical implications of their theoretical perspectives. For most of us our actions are frequently inconsistent with our theoretical understanding. For example, a teacher may firmly believe that the most effective learning occurs when students pursue topics of their own choosing and at their own pace; however, in practice the teacher insists that all students learn the standard material according to a preestablished schedule. Similarly, a person in a family conflict situation may be theoretically aware that showing a willingness to compromise could defuse a quarrel but may be unwilling emotionally to do so because of the fear of momentarily losing face. Nevertheless, a great deal of human behavior does reflect, at least generally, some theoretical perspective.

IMPLICIT VERSUS EXPLICIT THEORIES

People are not always conscious of the theoretical assumptions that are the bases for their explanations and predictions or of the logical structure of their inferences from the available, everyday facts. Instead, everyday theories are usually *implicit,* not *explicit.* Often they are embedded in tradition and commonsense folk wisdom. Underlying theoretical assumptions may be reflected in old maxims such as "Birds of a feather flock together." Or they may be symbolized in highly developed beliefs about human nature or society, such as the religious belief that people have special, divinely implanted qualities that distinguish them from other animals or the belief that, in the long run, "good" behavior will be rewarded and "bad" behavior will be punished.

Such implicit theories color our general attitudes toward other people and society. We all know cynical individuals who believe that people are interested only in their own welfare and optimistic persons who continually look for good or positive qualities in others and often see them when others do not. I am not suggesting that all persons are always consistent in their theoretical assumptions. Since many of these assumptions are implicit (or beneath the level of consciousness), people may not even be aware when there are inconsistencies.

For many persons their theories are likely to remain implicit. For various reasons, however, other persons experience a "consciousness raising" whereby certain aspects of their implicit theories become explicit and subject to objective or critical analysis. This process does not necessarily mean that implicit theories will be rejected; on the contrary, they may even be reinforced. In either case, the point is that individuals become consciously aware of some of their underlying theoretical assumptions and are willing to examine them objectively, at least to a degree. Many students find that this consciousness raising is enhanced through the study of the sociological perspective.

CHALLENGES TO IMPLICIT THEORIES AND THE EMERGENCE OF EXPLICIT THEORIES

Individuals vary greatly in terms of the degree to which their implicit theoretical assumptions become explicit or emerge to the level of consciousness, just as they vary in terms of how critical or defensive they are toward these beliefs and assumptions. What stimulates some persons to become consciously aware of their underlying assumptions and to examine them objectively? More specifically, what motivates persons to study human behavior and society through the sociological discipline? The following suggestions are offered in response to this question.

It is likely that people's implicit theories would remain implicit as long as they are unaware of alternative perspectives and traditional customs or beliefs are not challenged. With the appearance of alternatives or challenges, individuals may feel obliged to justify or revise their customs and beliefs, and this may help bring to consciousness previously implicit and unarticulated beliefs and theoretical assumptions.

Challenges to implicit assumptions may come from several sources. Increasing contact among societies with divergent cultures may lead each one to justify itself. Rapid social change may make established beliefs and customs seem irrelevant or obsolete and may stimulate the development of new theories while coping with change. Higher rates of deviance or challenges to the status quo by oppressed subgroups within a society may stimulate self-conscious efforts by dominant groups to justify existing customs and norms. These experiences do not eliminate the implicit, taken-for-granted assumptions that exist in everyday life.[2] The challenge to implicit theories would normally involve only a portion of all the assumptions that comprise a person's world view.

In a highly stable society that is well insulated from other societies, we might expect that most people would be unlikely to think through, on a conscious level, the underlying assumptions of their world view or the theoretical implications of the customs and habits they follow. Because they are not required to justify or defend their customs and beliefs, such persons do not conceive of the social reality in which they are embedded as an intellectual problem. Instead, there is an obvious and matter-of-fact quality to social reality that does not demand conscious justification.

The self-conscious effort to develop a theoretical explanation of social reality is likely to be seen as a trivial exercise in explaining the obvious.[3]

On the other hand, in a society characterized by rapid social change or extensive exposure to many cultures or subcultures, we might expect many persons to view the customs and beliefs of those in their immediate social milieu with some intellectual detachment and objectivity. Such persons may fully accept these customs and beliefs, but this acceptance is more likely to reflect a conscious choice than when society is stable or cultural alternatives are not available.

For example, when traditional family forms are accepted unquestioningly, it may never occur to young people that there is any realistic alternative to getting married (after an appropriate courtship) and having a family. But, in a society such as ours, where traditional family forms and sex roles are undergoing rapid change, young people may feel the need to choose among several alternatives, each of which has its own advantages and disadvantages. Some individuals will respond to the expectations and pressures of family and friends without consciously thinking through the available alternatives, but the alternatives are available for those who wish to consider them.

There are exceptions to these generalizations. Some people who live in stable or sheltered social environments do *not* maintain a nonreflective or noncritical attitude toward their social reality. Stable village communitites may have their free-thinking skeptics and nonconformists who question what others never did. Young people often question established customs and beliefs; in the process of trying to provide answers their parents may become more reflective and critical themselves. On the other hand, persons in a rapidly changing social environment with numerous subcultural alternatives may not see their social milieu as a source of intellectual puzzles; they may go through life without reflecting seriously on anything more than how to cope from day to day, perhaps experiencing some personal satisfaction and having a little fun in the process.

Rapid social change is almost always accompanied by the emergence of strains and cleavages in the social structure and by cultural lag and discontinuity. These are usually experienced as social problems for which the established traditions do not provide ready-made solutions. The search for solutions may eventually result in questioning traditional assumptions and establishing new social forms. Alternatively, efforts may be made to defend traditional assumptions, perhaps by reinterpreting their meanings to fit the new situation. In either case, many social or cultural forms lose the obvious, matter-of-fact quality that individuals automatically accept and follow; instead, they become contrived and arbitrary and are quite variable for persons with different cultural or subcultural backgrounds.

Recognition of the contrived and variable character of social reality does not apply to all social forms or to all aspects of individuals' world views. Some traditional forms may lose their taken-for-granted character and subsequently be questioned or challenged, but others will continue to be accepted implicitly. Moreover, in place of the traditional forms that are rapidly changing, new forms will emerge; many of them will no doubt eventually be accepted implicitly and unquestioningly. However, the process of social change will rarely be so pervasive that *no* established traditions continue to be accepted and followed implicitly.

The experience of social marginality can also trigger conscious reflection on social reality. *Marginality* means that a person is on the margin of some group or cultural setting; he or she is involved, but not fully, and is capable of carrying on interaction with those inside, but as an outsider who does not fully accept the social reality implicitly accepted by full-fledged insiders.

Almost everyone has probably had this experience at some time. The new member of a club or organization or the new resident (or tourist) in a community will experience at least a phase of marginality. The new person's attitude toward various customs and beliefs accepted by insiders will be more objective or detached than theirs; the marginal person often understands, as insiders might not, that the accepted cultural patterns are not inevitable but are socially contrived and quite arbitrary. Insiders may be unable or unwilling to view established customs and beliefs in this way because, to them, the facts are obvious and inevitable, or beyond questioning.

The differences among people's willingness to examine their social world objectively and analytically cannot be accounted for solely in terms of social milieu. Regardless of the influence of the social environment, self-conscious reflection or intellectual analysis of social or cultural forms is promoted by exposure to the scientific attitude of detachment and objectivity, particularly as applied to human behavior and society. Increased interest in the social sciences may itself be stimulated by the various social experiences just discussed, but social science education also promotes a willingness to examine social forms objectively and analytically, especially for those who study the issues raised by the social scientific perspective.

Education in the social sciences explicitly encourages a questioning and objective attitude toward social reality and an awareness of a wide range of cultural alternatives. The effect presumably decreases ethnocentrism or parochialism. In this process social customs and beliefs become relativized, and individuals become more aware of competing cultural alternatives. This is why education in the social sciences can be a consciousness-raising experience; it encourages the awareness of implicit assumptions regarding social reality and of cultural alternatives.

IMPLICIT VERSUS EXPLICIT THEORIES AND THE SOCIAL CONSTRUCTION OF REALITY

The effects of individuals' social or intellectual experiences on their orientation toward their social milieu is heavily influenced by Berger and Luckmann's perspective on the social construction of reality.[4] Berger and Luckmann emphasize that social systems and their associated world views are socially contrived and maintained, not grounded in an ultimate or absolute reality. However, in a highly stable society that has one dominant cultural world view, people *experience* the social reality in which they are involved, and its justifying or legitimating world view, as based on an ultimate and unchanging reality that is independent of their cultural beliefs and ideas. In contrast, in societies that are more fluid or pluralistic in social structure or cultural ideas, such a monolithic and unchanging world view is implausible. Instead, there develops a multiplicity of competing world views and cultural patterns, each based on alternative social definitions or beliefs, among which individuals must make choices.

Berger and Luckmann's perspective helps us to understand the distinction between social environments that encourage self-conscious reflection on social and cultural forms and those that encourage passive, nonreflective acceptance of these forms. This is consistent with the contention that self-conscious theorizing about social reality will be more common in an open, pluralistic social environment.

To summarize, we all theorize in the process of creating or maintaining social reality, even though we may not think of ourselves as social theorists. As human beings, we go beyond our immediate experience or the facts of our situations in order to interpret, explain, predict, and plan our everyday lives. But we are not always aware of the implicit assumptions that these inferences rest on, nor do we always appreciate that these assumptions are socially contrived.

Our conscious awareness of our theoretical assumptions and their precarious and socially contrived character will probably be aroused by any experience in which established customs become inappropriate or irrelevant and must be changed or in which we are obliged to justify or defend these assumptions or make unaccustomed choices between alternatives. Several such experiences have been identified: mobility or cross-cultural exposure, whereby a person's range of social experiences is broadened; rapid change, which frequently demands conscious choices of a type not covered by established tradition; and marginality, which frequently results in a certain degree of detachment from particular customs and beliefs.[5]

Such experiences, especially when combined with the scientific perspective, stimulate the process of explicit or conscious theorizing, Indeed, those who are committed to scientific methods and values and who have the opportunity to explore various social issues through the scientific perspective may develop an interest in sociological theorizing, even in the absence of the various broadening social experiences just identified. Considered in this way, sociological theory is not simply the esoteric jargon that results from the abstract speculations of academicians; it is an essential human activity that raises our consciousness regarding the social environment. Through exposure to sociological theory we become more aware of the various ways in which our social and cultural world is created and maintained or changed through human activity and interaction. Our capacity to choose among alternatives and our ability to plan realistically and creatively for the future should be enhanced by the consciousness-raising experience of studying social theory.

HISTORICAL CONTEXT OF THE BIRTH OF THE SOCIOLOGICAL PERSPECTIVE

As a distinctive academic discipline, sociology is less than 200 years old. Auguste Comte coined the term "sociology," and he is often considered the father of the discipline. His first major work, *The Course of Positive Philosophy*, published between 1830 and 1842, reflected a strong commitment to the scientific method. This method was to be applied to the discovery of natural laws governing *social* phenomena. Social reality was to be distinguished from the individual level. Social institutions and the general direction of social change could be explained only in terms of principles or laws that transcend the individual or individual psychological principles. Although Comte's theories have long since been superseded, his general concept of sociology as the scientific study of social structure or social reality is still a basic tenet of the sociological perspective.

For most of his life Comet was an academic outsider, however, and the new discipline that he promoted was not an established and respected academic discipline. It was not until the end of the nineteenth century that sociology became institutionalized as an academic discipline under the influence of Emile Durkheim.

Social Thought Prior to the Development of Sociology

There was intellectual concern with sociological-type questions and issues long before sociology was established as a scientific discipline. The eighteenth-century Enlightenment philosophers had emphasized the potential role of reason in understanding human behavior and in providing a foundation for laws and the organization of the state.[6] Their stress on reason and the discovery of natural laws marked a major break with the scholastic or dogmatic style of medieval thought, in which human behavior and the organization of society had been explained in relation to religious beliefs.

But even though medieval European thought was dominated by church dogma instead of the scientific style of open and objective inquiry, a solitary figure appeared in the fourteenth century in the Arab world who foreshadowed to a remarkable degree the emergence of sociology as a scientific discipline. About 400 years *before* Auguste Comte developed his sociological perspective in France. Ibn Khaldun had formulated a model of the contrast between tough nomadic tribes and soft, sedentary-type societies.[7] Khaldun's effort to explain the historical process of the rise and fall of civilization made use of this contrast. The cultural refinements of highly developed civilizations are the product of sedentary societies; however, the flowering of civilization is accompanied by an increased love of luxuries and pleasure, a more centralized political authority system, and a resulting gradual erosion of solidarity, or *esprit de corps*. Thus civilizations are destined not to endure and grow indefinitely but to become more vulnerable to conquest by tough and hardy nomadic peoples whose courage is fortified by high levels of solidarity. Eventually, however, these conquerors imitate the soft and refined life-style of the people they conquered, and the cycle is repeated.

Khaldun's model of societal types and social change was colored by the distinct heritage of the Arab experience in the desert world. However, his goal was not simply to provide a historical description of Arab societies but to develop *general* principles or laws that govern the dynamics of societies and the overall process of social change. He recognized the difficulties of being objective in analyzing social phenomena, but he was nevertheless committed to this goal. The general spirit, or attitude, of his analysis was remarkably close to the modern scientific mode of inquiry, and its substantive content would compare favorably with modern social theory. Nevertheless, Khaldun's work has been neglected by European and American social theorists, perhaps partly because the Arab world was declining while Western Europe was gaining dominance.

The history of the emergence of Western social thought could be carried as far back as the ancient Greeks, such as Plato and Aristotle. Many specialists in the traditional social science disciplines and in other fields of knowledge recognize the contributions of the Greeks to our intellectual development. Their speculations on human nature and the organization of the state were closely intertwined with their concern for promoting the "good" life. The substantive details of these contributions are often overlooked and forgotten, but it is important to recognize that the concern for understanding and explaining human behavior and society did not begin with the emergence of the modern Western world.

Rapid Social Change and the Emergence of Modern Society

This book will not trace the entire history of modern Western social thought.[8] The sociological perspective as we recognize it today is of fairly recent origin.[9] This is not because humans did not have any social life earlier. As far as we know, people have always lived in some sort of group, and they have always interacted with one another, influenced one another, loved one another, fought with one another, helped one another, envied one another, and exploited one another. From time to time throughout history people have even been able to establish large-scale and far-flung social systems (e.g., great empires). This must have required some practical sophistication in social organization or social engineering.

Why, then, was the sociological perspective not established sooner? Perhaps part of the answer lies in the unprecendented and complex social changes that Western societies had recently experienced and were still experiencing at the time of sociology's birth. As noted, rapid social change seems likely to increase the extent of people's conscious deliberation about social forms. In France, the French Revolution and its aftermath provided the historical background for Comte's efforts to explain all of history according to his particular theoretical model of social change and progress and for his proposals for reorganizing society according to scientific principles as he conceived them. Although the French Revolution was primarily a change in political structure, it reflected profound shifts in economic patterns and social stratification.

In England, the Industrial Revolution stimulated social theorists as diverse as Herbert Spencer and Karl Marx (who came to England from France and to France from his native Germany) to develop explanations of the new type of social order that was being brought into existence as a consequence of the growth of factories and factory technology. The Industrial Revolution, both in England and elsewhere, helped to undermine traditional social relations and created new cleavages in the social structure; it also formed the potential basis for a new type of social order. In Germany, also, industrialization and political upheavals promoted an increased concern with understanding society and social change. A major aspect of social change that preoccupied German theorist Max Weber was the growing dominance of rational forms of hierarchical social organization.

The various social, political, and economic changes referred to here began before the nineteenth century. Technological development and industrial growth, the awakening of national consciousness, geographical exploration and colonial expansion, shifts in class structure, and rapidly increasing urbanization were well underway long before Comte launched the new science of sociology. Moreover, these major social changes coincided with profound shifts in the dominant world view by which people attempted to interpret and explain their environment. Traditional religious beliefs and modes of explanation seemed to be declining steadily in the face of the inevitable advance of scientific explanations and a scientific mentality.[10]

In spite of the steady progress of scientific knowledge and technological development, the exuberant and optimistic eighteenth-century faith in human reason dimmed considerably during the nineteenth century. In the eighteenth century the power of reason to discover basic natural laws was enthusiastically celebrated; it was believed that such laws could be implemented in the reorganization of society to insure steady social progress in the future. In contrast, the nineteenth century was characterized by a growing awareness of the limits of reason and of the numerous nonrational foundations of human motivation and social institutions.

By the middle of the nineteenth century Comte saw that intellectual understanding of the laws that govern society could not generate the altruistic sentiments on which social order is based. Traditionally, such sentiments had rested on religious beliefs and rituals. Since religion was being eroded by the growth of the scientific mentality, Comte felt that it was necessary to establish a new religion that would be compatible with science.

By the end of the nineteenth century and the beginning of the twentieth century, there was a fuller appreciation of the importance of the sources of human motivation that lie at a deeper level of our consciousness than the level that is involved with intellectual understanding or rational analysis. Social institutions rely heavily on these nonrational foundations and thus are not readily amenable to rational reorganization. The foundations of modern sociology grew mostly out of an intense effort to deal with the limits of reason in human motivation and human conduct and to understand the nonrational elements of human consciousness as they are expressed in social institutions and the organization of society.[11]

The establishment of sociology as a discipline concerned with social structure (as opposed to interpersonal interaction or individual behavior) was a European, not an American, enterprise. The revolutionary leaders and founders of America were concerned with political structures, of course, but their basic ideas in this regard were borrowed from the Enlightenment social theorists of the eighteenth century. (This precedes the birth of the sociological perspectives as defined here.)

Throughout the nineteenth century American social thought was basically individualistic. Even though America was a dynamic and rapidly changing society, this did not promote the same kind of preoccupation with broad questions of social order that it did in Europe. This may reflect the fact that Americans were not conscious of being involved in a process whereby an old, established social order was being replaced by a new one (although, or course, the Indian tribes would have had good reason to disagree). It may also reflect the optimistic faith that if a particular social structure became oppressive, unresponsive to new needs or, for any reason, undesirable, it was always possible to move West. (Perhaps in more recent times the flight from the inner city to the suburbs or, even more recently, from urban to country areas, reflects this same attitude.)

Western Europe, then, was the birthplace of modern sociology. Moreover, the rapid social changes just referred to were interrelated and interdependent. Changes in each society "spilled over" into other societies. More important, changes in the political, economic, and religious institutions were interdependent with each other and with changes in the class system and general social relations. Furthermore, these changes affected and were affected by the development of science and technology and by the growth of various secular belief systems and world views that competed with and partially displaced the previously dominant religious world view.

This simplified description of the birth of sociology is not meant to be historical; the intention is to form an appreciation for the way in which massive social and cultural change stimulated the kind of intellectual concerns from which sociology eventually developed. No intellectual or scientific breakthrough occurs in a vacuum, and sociology, perhaps more than many other sciences, is affected by its social context.

It would be an oversimplification to claim that sociology is an effort to understand and cope with social change. After all, during numerous periods of rapid social change prior to the late eighteenth and early nineteenth centuries rulers were overthrown and replaced, empires were expanded and then broke down and were conquered, and new technologies occasionally were developed. What is distinctive about the social changes that immediately preceded and accompanied the rise of sociology is that they thoroughly permeated all the major social institutions. Change in each institution stimulated and was stimulated by changes in other institutions.

For example, the immediate background of the French Revolution included massive shifts in the economic structure that propelled the *bourgeoisie* into a position of prominence. The political attacks on the traditional aristocracy and monarchy and their eventual overthrow resulted largely from this new bourgeois power. But not only were economic and political institutions involved. Because the church was so closely aligned with the traditional power structure, the pressures for revolutionary political change included opposition to the church, its representatives, and its beliefs. The ideology developed by the leaders of the French Revolution would soon be modified to legitimate the political struggles of the proletarian class against the eventual conservatism of a bourgeoisie that had been successful in its revolutionary struggles. These considerations suggest the complexity of the social changes in the period under consideration. Not only were the changes in the different institutions interdependent, but they unleashed a dynamic force in which each facet of change stimulated additional change.

Growth of Scientific Mentality

The social changes previously mentioned were accompanied by the emergence of a new way of looking at the world and gaining knowledge about it. Specifically, a scientific orientation was replacing a religious orientation. The accumulation and analysis of empirical data replaced the faith in supernatural revelation and established traditions as the major source of truth and knowledge. (The word "positivism" represents this new approach to knowledge; more will be said about it later.)

By the beginning of the nineteenth century, the scientific method had already made great advances in the physical sciences. In physics and astronomy it was recognized that uniformities in the movements of physical objects, such as stars and falling rocks, could be explained in terms of natural forces. These forces could be discovered by applying human intellect to the analysis of carefully and systematically gathered empirical data. The result would be the discovery of deterministic laws that could sometimes even be expressed as mathematical equations.

The early conflicts between the scientific and the religious perspectives will not be discussed in depth. However, one result of the early work in astronomy was to call into question the medieval world view with its earth-centered cosmology; recall that both Copernicus and Galileo were condemned by the church. I will not trace the growth of the scientific attitude in the various other fields, either. This new attitude emerged later in biology; in fact, perhaps the most dramatic conflict between religion and biological science was stimulated by Darwin's 1859 publication of his theory of biological evolution. This date is well into the time period under discussion. The entire nineteenth century was marked by the extension of scientific methodology into the human and social realms.

A major outcome of the growth of the scientific attitude was the encouragement of technological development. The Industrial Revolution relied greatly on the growth of new technology. The validity of the scientific approach was proven by the fact that it worked, in the sense that it provided people with knowledge that they could use in adapting more effectively and more efficiently to the environment.

Technological development was not an unmixed blessing. The Industrial Revolution caused numerous serious social dislocations and powerful new social forces that had to be dealt with. But could these various social problems themselves not be dealt with by applying the principles and techniques of science? After all, science had proven its worth in stimulating the rise of new material technology; could not a scientific understanding of society provide the basis for solving social problems, even to the point of reforming or reorganizing society if necessary so it would be in accord with natural laws discovered by scientific investigation?

As noted, by the end of the nineteenth century, social theorists had a more sensitive understanding of the difficulties and obstacles of rational reorganization of society than did the eighteenth-century Enlightenment social philosophers. In various ways the pioneers of modern sociology expressed their ambivalence to the breakdown of tradition and the emergence of a modern, urban-industrial society that seemed to have no solid moral foundations in a stable community. But the clock could not be turned back; for all their ambivalence, the founders of modern sociology were convinced that the methods of science and the insights derived from scientific analysis were important both for understanding and for influencing the course of social change in the future.

The increasing influence of the scientific mentality involved a new concept of human nature and society. However, the specific meaning of "a science of society" varied in different countries. One of the sharpest contrasts is between the French and the German theorists. The emphasis of the French social theorists (including Comte and Durkheim) leaned clearly toward the view of people and society as part of nature, with human behavior subject to natural laws that could be discovered by the same type of scientific techniques of empirical investigation that had been successful in the physical sciences. The German theorists were also interested in the establishment of sociology as a science, but they saw it as different from the natural sciences.

This distinction between the sciences of nature and the sciences of society and culture is reflected in Weber's ideas on the nature of social science. Since the social and cultural sciences involve human meaning and human will, different techniques or methods of understanding are required. The natural sciences deal with necessity and deterministic laws, but the social and cultural sciences deal with freedom and creativity. Weber's methodological stress on understanding (*verstehen*) of subjective meaning versus Durkheim's emphasis on external social facts as "things" partially reflects the dilemma. More will be said later on this.

Those who tended toward the natural law viewpoint of human behavior were optimistic about the promise of reorganizing society on an enlightened scientific basis. In this way the social sciences could emulate the success of the physical sciences in creating the foundations for technological development. It was felt that once the laws governing human behavior could be discovered through scientific investigation, they could be implemented through reorganization of the legal and political structures of society. In this way reliance on force, superstition, or ignorance in controlling behavior would be eliminated, and society would be organized on sound scientific principles.

The rapid and extensive changes in social structure and the profound cultural shift in intellectual orientation regarding human behavior and society helped set the stage for the emergence of the sociological perspective. These changes generated conscious reflection on sociological issues and encouraged dealing with these issues by scientific analysis.

These internal social changes were not the only influence. For several hundred years Europeans had been absorbing stories brought back by traders, missionaries, and adventurers of social life and customs in far-off and exotic places. These accounts helped to demonstrate that the way of life taken for granted in Western European societies was apparently not grounded in some principle of ultimate reality, since other societies seemed to function quite satisfactorily with a different world view and a different basis of social order.

Also, the increasing knowledge of other societies, especially so-called primitive societies, led to questions and extensive speculation about the sources and the limits of cultural variation and, more important, about how societies might have evolved from one form to another. In fact, this seems almost to have obsessed the early social theorists; Comte in France and Spencer in England developed models of social change based on evolutionary principles. Essentially, these principles were intended to show that modern, complex forms of society (such as Western societies) represented the culmination of a long evolutionary process that began in simple, primitive societies.

The use of evolutionary principles to explain social evolution preceded the turning point represented by Darwin's model of biological evolution. Darwin's model provided major reinforcement for the general principles of evolution, however, and the last half of the nineteenth century and the opening decades of the twentieth century were dominated by the evolutionary framework in Europe and America.

Several other important influences that stimulated conscious interest in sociological questions and helped to shape the development of sociology could no doubt be identified.[12] The main point, however, is that the dynamic, even turbulent, pace of social change was part of the stimulus for conscious concern with sociological questions. Rapid social change meant that traditional, implicit theories of human behavior and society no longer seemed appropriate as an adequate source of guidance for the future or of justification of existing social patterns. With old social forms breaking down or being seen as barriers to be overcome, it was necessary that new ones be developed. This required conscious concern with sociological questions.

Sociological questions involve areas of concern such as forms or patterns of human social behavior, sources and directions of social change, alternative types of social structure, and underlying bases of social order. Concern with these questions does not necessarily lead to sociology as a scientific discipline (e.g., these questions could be dealt with from a religious or purely philosophical perspective). The development of sociology as a scientific discipline rested just as much on the rise of the scientific mentality as on the massive changes in social structure.

In short, the pioneers who developed the foundations of sociology were convinced that they were living during a major turning point in history. The old social order had crumbled and was being swept rapidly away, and it was not clear what would take its place. The traditional belief system that previously had given meaning to life and helped direct and control behavior was undermined by the emergence of the scientific approach and by numerous new ideologies. Various economic, political, and national interest groups began to pursue their own particular goals, limited not so much by tradition or by shared moral commitments as by the countervailing pressures of opposing groups. Although the specific social context varied in different countries and at different times, all of the pioneer sociological theorists saw their societies undergoing rapid change, often without any clear direction. Of course, their image of the past overestimated its stability and tranquility; nevertheless, this provided a basis of comparison with the present.[13]

Perhaps because these early social theorists knew that the changes they were living through could never be reversed, they also attempted to make plausible projections of the future. The classical theorists differed in terms of how definitive they were in these projections. They also varied in how optimistically or pessimistically they contemplated the future and in how much they believed people could control the future of society by applying sociological knowledge in making social reforms and in social planning. Some envisioned continued technological progress, scientific enlightenment, and human control of the directions of social change. Others looked nostalgically at the past. Whatever their attitude, almost without exception, they developed models of social change that showed how the present had emerged from the past and that projected from present patterns and trends the shape of the future society. In sum, the whole enterprise of sociological theory development represented a new, scientifically insipired view of social reality that was being constructed in the wake of the breakdown of the traditional implicit theories of social reality.

CONTEMPORARY SOCIAL CHANGE AND SOCIOLOGICAL THEORY

Social change is still a major concern for many social theorists. As we move into the latter part of the twentieth century, it is obvious, in retrospect, that both the speed and the complexity of social change in modern industrial societies are far greater than envisioned by the early social theorists. The statement that we live in an age of rapid social change is commonplace and seems almost trivial. Consider how different the world of today's typical, college-age people is from the one that their parents knew when growing up. No wonder intergenerational communication is often strained and that many students see events of 30 years ago as ancient history. Of course, in discussing contemporary social change it is easy to exaggerate and to overstate the case for its uniqueness. Also, students often overestimate its magnitude simply because their personal lives have undergone major changes as a result of their increasing age. But these considerations need not prevent us from affirming that we live in a dynamic, rapidly changing society.

Many modern social scientists are concerned with various aspects of social change, and some are attempting to identify trends that will allow projections of the future to be made. Some believe there are indications that we are at a kind of crossroads that may be just as significant for the long-range future of our society and the Western world as the Industrial Revolution was in the past. For example, Daniel Bell analyzed the emergence of ''postindustrial'' society.[14] The very term suggests the end of one era (the one initiated with the beginning of the Industrial Revolution) and the beginning of a new one.

The transition from industrial to postindustrial society occurs when over 50 percent of the labor force is engaged in service occupations instead of production and related areas. One indication of this transition is the proportion of the labor force engaged in white-collar occupations, a point reached in our society in 1956.[15] In Bell's view, this point is important because the values, attitudes, and life-styles of persons in service occupations are qualitatively different from those in production. They are more likely to be people oriented instead of interested strictly in technical efficiency because their occupations involve working with people, not things. The emerging postindustrial society is also characterized by the ascendance of professional and technical occupations, the primacy of theoretical knowledge and its use in social planning, and the development of rational techniques for developing new knowledge.

A different type of juncture that involves different dynamics is suggested when we consider the effects of our highly successful industrial order in depleting our planet's natural resources and polluting its air, water, and soil. These developments cause us to question the previously held assumption of continued and indefinite material progress and force us to recognize that a constantly rising standard of living is not inevitable and, perhaps, is no longer possible.

In a book written before the recent oil shortages and energy crisis, Burch argued that the unprecedented material abundance brought about by technological progress is really an aberration from the dominant pattern of most of history; he suggested that we are now nearing the end of this age of abnormality.[16] The new strains in our relationship with our physical environment are dramatically revealed by the depletion of cheap energy resources and the emergence of frequent political struggles among promoters of economic progress (e.g., nuclear power plant builders) and environmentalists. These struggles suggest a new consideration of the physical environment and natural resources that will challenge the established attitudes. This new consciousness recognizes the limits of economic progress and environmental resources and the fragile balance of nature on which human life depends.

Numerous other contemporary social changes are taking place, such as the loss of faith in established social institutions (especially political and economic ones), the questioning of authority in major social institutions, the decline of the traditional work ethic, and the widespread repudiation of "technocracy" and many aspects of bureaucratic organization. Many of these changes were associated with the youth movement of the late 1960s and early 1970s. Opposition to the Vietnam war was perhaps the major stimulus for the crystallization of the youth subculture into a political movement. By the middle 1970s, the youth subculture lost the sharpness of its identity and political interests, but its influence has permeated the consciousness of a large segment of our society, even though it has mellowed in the process.

International changes include the decline of American and Western influence in international affairs, the "revolution of rising expectations" in developing third and fourth world countries, the threat of nuclear terror and the spread of nuclear weapons technology with all the risks it entails, and the rapidly rising economic power of the Islamic OPEC countries on which the Western world relies for oil. Whether or not such changes reflect a major turning point depends on the viewpoint of the social analyst.

This discussion is not intended to arouse amazement at how different or how bad things are now compared to the way they used to be, nor is it meant to suggest that sociological theory is occupied exclusively with questions of social change. Many other equally important sociological questions concern us. However, the experience of living in times of rapid change and concern for our personal and collective future should stimulate us to reflect on the implications of social change. If sociology is to have meaning and relevance for students today, it must be capable of aiding us in understanding such issues.

Sociological theory does not provide a magic formula for interpretation of social reality or prediction of the future, or even a solution to the intellectual issues and problems with which it deals. However, the conceptual and intellectual framework of the sociological prespective and the analytic styles that specific theories offer can help us understand our own social world and, in turn, can enhance our objectivity, sensitivity, and perhaps even effectiveness in dealing with people.

In addition, we achieve the intellectual satisfaction that results from learning new strategies to analyze and understand social reality.

HISTORICAL ROOTS OF SOCIOLOGICAL THEORY

The major historical sources of sociological theory may be identified in general terms as follows.

1. *English-Scottish Laissez-Faire Political Economy and British Utilitarianism.* These theories are very individualistic and view human beings as essentially rational, always calculating, and making choices that would maximize individual pleasure or profit and minimize pain or costs. The most obvious application of this view is in the economic marketplace where the classical economists' view of "economic man" emphasizes the type of calculating choices just mentioned. The same assumption also underlies the classical theories of crime and punishment; the pain of punishment must outweigh the profit or pleasure derived from the commission of a crime.

    When these theorists move beyond the level of the individual and seek to explain society or social structure, some form of a "social contract" assumption is involved. That is, they assume that human beings, acting out of their rational self-interest, voluntarily enter into a conscious agreement whereby they limit their individual autonomy, establish a government, and agree to abide by rules developed to control unbridled competition and insure at least minimal cooperation.

    However, the controls imposed must not be too great because, as individuals are encouraged to pursue their own personal interests, the welfare of the society is insured. Adam Smith used the metaphor of the "invisible hand" to describe in almost mystical fashion this paradox in which individuals' greed for gain becomes transformed, as though by the guidance of an invisible hand, into the welfare of society as a whole. In *The Wealth of Nations,* Smith argued that the overall, long-range welfare of society is best served by allowing or even encouraging individuals to pursue their private, selfish interests.[17] Presumably, individuals would contribute the greatest good to society by trying to meet other people's needs through actions that also promote their personal interests.

    Individuals need not necessarily be aware of how their actions contribute to the public good. Most of the time they are probably not aware. In fact, Smith contended that those who claim to wish to advance the public welfare actually do not do so as much as those who give themselves wholeheartedly to the pursuit of their own individual interests.

    The laissez-faire public policy implications of this approach survive to some degree in the private enterprise arguments of conservative Republicans. Also, the paradoxical theoretical point—that individuals' actions contribute to larger social outcomes of which they may not even be aware and that may even be the opposite of the outcomes intended—is a basic argument of contemporary functional theory. The individualistic approach and the assumption that people consciously make rational choices so as to maximize their payoffs are also basic ingredients of contemporary exchange theory.

2. *Postrevolutionary French Positivism.* This approach was represented by St. Simon and Comte in the first half of the nineteenth century and by Durkheim in the latter part of the nineteenth and early twentieth centuries. The word "positivism" denotes an empirical approach to knowledge. According to this approach, all that we know derives ultimately from our sensory experience or empirical data. This reflects a shift away from the traditional acceptance of revelation or tradition as a source of knowledge that was more profound than sensory data. To positivists, however, revelation and religious beliefs were mere superstitions that they were convinced would be replaced by science. Science involves a systematic approach to gathering empirical data with the goal of discovering natural laws. A natural law is simply a statement of a uniform relationship among empirical phenomena.

The growth of sociology in France reflected the conviction that society, or social life, is a part of nature and is governed by natural laws that can be discovered by applying the same scientific techniques of investigation as used in the other sciences. Furthermore, once these laws are discovered, they can be used as a basis for social reform and reorganization of society. Social order and progress would then rest on scientifically established principles, and peace, harmony, and enlightenment would eventually replace war, conflict, superstition, and ignorance.

The national government would play a major part in this program of social reorganization. Government officials, however, would have to act in accordance with the natural laws discovered by sociologists. This dream of the sociologist as a counselor to the ruler was held in exaggerated form by Comte, whose personal vision was to occupy a dominant position, comparable to that of Pope, in the positivist industrial society of the future. The same dream was also held later by Durkheim, albeit in a less grandiose fashion, and was expressed in his commitment to establish firm scientific grounding for moral education. A version of that dream is still held today by those who believe that science can save us by providing solutions to our various social problems or can provide guidance in helping us find fulfillment as human beings.

This vision of the role of government in social reorganization differs from the laissez-faire emphasis of British political economy. While the laissez-faire emphasis survives in modified form in the ideological justification of the free enterprise system, the positivist ideal of enlightened reforms is expressed today in numerous "people-oriented" social programs in which a serious effort is made to take the latest findings of social science into account. One example is the use of behavior modification techniques in juvenile delinquency rehabilitation.

3. *German Historicism.* In contrast with French positivism, the German historicist tradition emphasized the distinction between the natural sciences and the social sciences. Natural laws determine events in the physical world, but the human world is a world of freedom and voluntary choices, not deterministic physical or natural laws. To assume that human beings are subject to the same kinds of laws as natural phenomena is to deny human freedom.

Not only do human beings transcend the realm of scientific determinism, but understanding human behavior and human culture involves a different kind of insight from understanding laws in the natural sciences. To understand or explain human behavior requires more than merely describing its external manifestations. Instead, it is necessary to penetrate its meaning, which means being aware of the subjective orientations and intentions of the individuals involved. To understand the dynamics of a society, it is necessary for the social analyst to penetrate its culture from the inside, subjectively experiencing its particular world view, its ideals and values, and its meanings.

This emphasis reflects a strong idealistic tradition in German social thought, expressed perhaps preeminently in Hegel. As a philosophical position, idealism stresses the reality of the realm of ideas and their importance in human life. Insight into subjective meanings or cultural world views is not needed to understand and explain the movements of physical objects, but to understand human behavior, it is essential.

Related to this emphasis on culture, the German historicists regarded each society as unique and as understandable only in terms of its own cultural traditions. This differs from the French positivist assumption that universal natural laws that could be discovered through scientific methods govern all societies. Instead of searching for universal laws, the German historicist tradition advocated understanding a society's particular "spirit" by a thorough study of its particular culture and the various historical stages through which it had passed. This does not preclude comparative studies; however, such studies should not gloss over important differences among societies.

Both Marx and Weber were heirs to the German historicist tradition. However, Marx ultimately rejected the notion that cultural values and

ideals exert an influence on human behavior independently of their materialistic foundations. Many of the major methodological strategies developed by Weber reflected his efforts to preserve the emphasis on historical and cultural phenomena as unique while dealing comparatively with
cross-cultural phenomena in order to promote sociology as a generalizing
discipline.

4.   *American Pragmatism and Social Psychology.* A large part of contemporary American sociology reflects the European roots just discussed. The
European theories were introduced into the American sociological
perspective by Talcott Parsons[18] and others. The distinctive American
contribution involved the development of social psychology, specifically
the symbolic interactionist perspective. This development was associated
with the Chicago school in the first 20 to 30 years of the twentieth century.

One distinctive characteristic of the American mentality is impatience with highly speculative ideas that have no practical value. Instead,
ideas and human intelligence are closely linked with action. Ideas are
developed or learned in making decisions to cope with real-life problems.
This viewpoint was at the basis of John Dewey's well-known reforms in
educational philosophy and technique. Dewey was critical of traditional
education practices because they artificially separated the world of learning from everyday living. Students were expected to memorize or learn
facts and ideas without being able to see the connection between learning
them and solving real-life problems. As an alternative, Dewey advocated
arranging classroom learning experiences so that they would reflect life as
closely as possible, providing students with opportunities for realistic
problem solving as a basis for learning. Thus, for example, the principles
of democracy can be more effectively learned by participating in democratic decision making in the classroom than by memorizing the Declaration of Independence or other abstract propositions. To this day, education
principles and practices reflect the profound influence of Dewey's emphasis on learning by doing.

Dewey is remembered as a philosopher of education, not a pioneer in
sociology. However, his fundamental insight regarding the close link
between thought and action was shared by George Herbert Mead, who
helped lay the foundations of the symbolic interaction perspective in social psychology. Mead stressed that the emergence of the human mind as a
critical stage in the evolutionary process makes distinctively *human* problem solving possible. This close linkage between thought and action is
consistent with American pragmatism and impatience with "irrelevant"
speculation.

A second distinctive characteristic of the American mentality that
affects American sociology is the strong emphasis on individualism. From

the very beginning, individualistic values were promoted against the conflicting claims of a strong central government. More recently, it has become popular to criticize the loss of individualism and various threats to its expression. Our concern here is not the validity of such criticisms or the wide range of ways in which individualism can be expressed in modern American society. Instead, we note that because of this emphasis on individualism, it is not surprising that a distinctive contribution of the American pioneers in sociology was a micro-level view of social reality. For the most part, the image of massive social institutions that are reinforced by a long-established tradition, regardless or individuals' desires or decisions, was not characteristic of the American orientation toward social reality. Instead, social reality consisted of individuals' social actions and interaction patterns, and social structures or social institutions were established or changed by negotiated agreements among individuals or groups. An emphasis on large-scale social structures with their own distinctive dynamics was eventually developed in American sociology, but this development was heavily influenced by the European pioneers.

The American mentality also optimistically believed in progress and the promise of planned social reforms. This is related to the pragmatic emphasis mentioned earlier. Not all the American sociologists believed that planned social reforms were necessary to promote progress. Social Darwinists such as Sumner believed that progress resulted from a natural evolutionary process and that planned reforms were not necessary to assist this process.[19] In fact, he was doubtful that such reforms could be successfully implemented as planned, particularly if they are contrary to the folkways and norms of society.

For many early American sociologists, however, a concern with social problems and a desire for social reforms were the entreé into sociology. The problems were primarily those of inner-city ghettos which repeatedly had experienced an influx of various immigrant groups. These groups usually started their lives in their new country at the bottom of the socioeconomic hierarchy. Regardless of the specific immigrant groups involved, these inner-city areas experienced high crime and delinquency rates, unemployment, social disorganization, deleterious housing, and the challenge of assimilation into the mainstream of American society. The reforms that were anticipated or advocated were not nearly as extensive as the French positivists had envisioned, however. American reformers were not interested so much in social reorganization as in ameliorative reforms directed at specific problems.

In summary, American sociology was, from the start, characterized by pragmatism, individualism, and optimism. The contemporary sociological perspective reflects both its indigenous American roots and also ideas transplanted from Europe. Among these, special attention has been given to British utilitarianism and political economy, French positivism, and German historicism.

Neither these early sources nor the various contemporary perspectives provide any final answers, however. Perhaps in view of the continually changing nature of social reality, a definitive sociological theory that adequately describes and explains social reality in all its complexity and that achieves intellectual closure is not possible. The pioneering outlooks represented serious efforts to grapple with and understand the rapidly changing social reality being experienced by the pioneers. Contemporary theory represents the same type of effort as well as the additional social dynamics that have emerged as a result of the establishment of sociology as an academic discipline with its own professional reward system, prestige hierarchy, and the like. In succeeding chapters, as the major ideas of classical and contemporary theorists are presented and discussed, the most appropriate strategy for students is to take these ideas not as final truth but as sources that may be more or less useful in developing and evaluating theories and in understanding the social world.

Before presenting the ideas of the various theorists to be covered, we will examine somewhat more formally and systematically what a social theory is and how social theory differs from "social thought," social philosopy, empirical generalization, and so on. Some strategies whereby a sociological theory is constructed are discussed in Chapter 2.

Footnotes

1. Textbook writers vary considerably in terms of the range of classical and contemporary theorists covered, the depth of treatment given to each one, and the overall organization of the field. For some examples, see Theodore Abel, *The Foundation of Sociological Theory* (New York: Random House, 1970); Ernest Becker, *The Structure of Evil* (New York: Free Press, 1968); Randall Collins and Michael Makowsky, *The Discovery of Society* (New York: Random House, 1972); Lewis A. Coser, *Masters of Sociological Thought,* 2nd edition (New York: Harcourt Brace Jovanovich, 1977); Anthony Giddens, *Capitalism and Modern Social Theory* (London: Cambridge University Press, 1971); Clinton Joyce Jesser, *Social Theory Revisited* (Hinsdale, Ill.: Dryden, Press, 1975); Dan Martindale, *The Nature and Types of Sociological Theory* (Boston: Houghton Mifflin, 1960); Nicholas S. Timasheff and George A. Theodorson, *Sociological Theory: Its Nature and Growth,* 4th edition (New York: Random House, 1976); and Jonathan Turner, *The Structure of Sociological Theory,* revised edition (Homewood, Ill.: Dorsey Press, 1978).

2. In their phenomenological approach to explaining social reality, Schutz and Luckmann

emphasize that the distinctive characteristic of human beings' everyday life worlds is its taken-for-granted character. This characteristic can never be eliminated completely. The willingness of individuals to suspend doubt in the reality of their everyday worlds or to refrain from questioning its validity is essential for human action and interaction. Decisive action in coping with the environment is inhibited by a doubting or questioning attitude. Similarly, joint action or interaction is undermined by a breakdown in the implicit consensus in basic world views that underlies communication. See Alfred Schutz and Thomas Luckmann, *The Structures of the Life-World* (Evanston, Ill.: Northwestern University Press, 1973), especially pp. 8 ff.

3.   See Daniel Lerner, *The Passing of Traditional Society* (New York: Free Press, 1958), especially Chapter 1 and Part 1 of Chapter 2, for a discussion of this distinction between the relatively nonreflective, traditional personality type, who has difficulty in imagining himself or herself in a different position in a different social environment, and the "mobile personality" type.

4.   See Peter L. Berger and Thomas Luckmann, *The Social Construction of Reality* (Garden City, N.Y.: Doubleday, 1966). Berger and Luckmann's ideas are generally recognized as an important development in the phenomenological perspective. Readers interested in going into more depth in this area may consult, in addition to Berger and Luckmann, Schutz and Luckmann, op. cit., and Alfred Schutz, *The Phenomenology of the Social World,* translated by George Walsh and Frederick Lehnert (Evanston, Ill.: Northwestern University Press, 1967).

5.   Pursuing the kinds of question raised in this section could lead into the substantive area of a sociology of sociology. In some cases, readers may be able to recognize the kind of social experience that promoted an interest in sociology. Also, for the theorists discussed herein, it is assumed that *their* personal experiences, reflective of the social and intellectual environment in which they lived, were not irrelevant to the type of sociological theory that they developed.

6.   For a brief overview of eighteenth-century thought see, for example, Carl L. Becker, *The Heavenly City of the Eighteenth-Century Philosophers* (New Haven, Conn.: Yale University Press, 1932); Isaiah Berlin, ed., *The Age of Enlightenment,* Vol. IV in *The Great Ages of Western Philosophy* (Boston: Houghton Mifflin, 1956); and Nicholas Capaldi, ed., *The Enlightenment—The Proper Study of Mankind* (New York: Putnam, 1967).

7.   This brief discussion of Ibn Khaldun's early contributions is drawn primarily from Rollin Chambliss, *Social Thought* (New York: Dryden Press, 1954), Chapter 12, "Ibn Khaldun," pp. 285–312.

8.   For a brief survey of premodern forms of social thought, see Chambliss, op. cit. For a more comprehensive and wider-ranging analyses, see Howard Becker and Harry Elmer Barnes, *Social Thought from Lore to Science,* 2nd edition, 2 volumes (Washington, D.C.: Harren, 1952).

9.   The treatment of Comte as the founder of the discipline is consistent with conventional practice in the field. Martindale, for example, touches on the contributions of the ancient Greeks as well as the foundations of modern thought in the seventeenth and eighteenth centuries, but he treats Comte as providing the intellectual breakthrough that culminated in the development of the sociological perspective. See Martindale, op. cit.,

pp. 62–65. See also Coser, op. cit., pp. 3–41; Collins and Makowsky, op. cit., pp. 21–32 and Timasheff and Theodorson, op. cit., pp. 15–30.

10. The influence of the social and intellectual context within which the classical theorists developed their views is widely recognized. See, for example, Coser, op. cit. and Collins and Makowsky, op. cit. for textbook-type treatments of this influence.

11. See H. Stuart Hughes, *Consciousness and Society* (New York: Vintage, 1961).

12. By way of comparison, Patricia Lengermann, in her recent text, identified the following significant social consequences of the Industrial Revolution that affected the development of sociology in its formative years: population growth, U.S. immigration, urbanization, emergence of new social classes (both bourgeois and proletariat), and colonial expansion overseas. She also noted the importance of the French Revolution, political tensions and instabilities, and the rise of nationalism. See Patricia M. Lengermann, *Definitions of Sociology: A Historical Approach* (Columbus, Ohio: Charles E. Merrill, 1974). Martindale, op. cit., Chapter 2, noted the importance of the influence of eighteenth-century rationalism (with its stress on natural law), the growth of the new capitalistic economic system, and the rise of nationalism.

13. See Robert A. Nisbet, *The Sociological Tradition* (New York: Basic Books, 1966) for an analysis of the way in which the fundamental "unit-ideas" of sociology emerged from the efforts of the nineteenth-century classical theorists to contrast the rapidly developing new social forms with their image of premodern or traditional social forms.

14. See Daniel Bell, *The Coming of Post-Industrial Society* (New York: Basic Books, 1973).

15. Ibid., p. 17.

16. See William R. Burch, Jr., *Daydreams and Nightmares: A Sociological Essay on the American Environment* (New York: Harper & Row, 1971), Chapter 7.

17. Adam Smith, *The Wealth of Nations* (New York: Random House, 1937), p. 423.

18. This was one of the major contributions of Talcott Parsons, *The Structure of Social Action* (New York: McGraw-Hill, 1937).

19. See William Graham Sumner, *Folkways* (Boston: Ginn, 1940).

Questions for Study and Discussion

1. Does exposure to the scientific perspective stimulate any changes in people's behavior in their interpersonal relations? Why or why not?

2. What kinds of implicit beliefs and values are *least* likely to be questioned or analyzed objectively as a result of exposure to the scientific perspective on human behavior?

3. Why does exposure to the scientific perspective or the study of explicit theories of human behavior lead to feelings of psychological insecurity for some people?

4. Identify some examples of inconsistencies in people's implicit theories of human behavior or society. Would it be possible to correct these inconsistencies? Why or why not?

5. What are the arguments for and against the positivist view on universal deterministic laws governing human behavior as opposed to the historicist views on the freedom of people to express unique cultural values or beliefs in their behavior?

CHAPTER 2

Explicit Theory Construction and Implicit Images of Social Reality

Scientific theories differ in several respects from the implicit, unconsciously held assumptions of everyday life. A major goal of this chapter is to move beyond a simple awareness of these everyday theories to an appreciation of theory development as part of a scientific enterprise. In making this transition we become conscious of explicit theory building. We also become more objective, more self-critical, and more abstract than we are in everyday life theorizing. An elementary understanding of how theories are developed can help us to grasp the essential ideas of the various theories presented in subsequent chapters.

Regardless of how explicit and objective a theorist might try to be, implicit, taken-for-granted assumptions cannot be eliminated entirely. The process of building a theory never begins from scratch. It would be impossible for a social theorist to eliminate the influences of personal social experiences or the effects of these experiences on how the social world is viewed. The theory-building process rests on certain fundamental images of social reality. These images may include basic philosophical assumptions regarding human nature and society or, at the very least, the notion that there is a certain orderliness or predictability in the social world. A second major goal of this chapter, therefore, is to explore the *implicit* images of social reality that underlie different types of scientific theory.

One difference among these implicit images of social reality is the level of social reality on which they focus. Thus a third goal of this chapter is to distinguish among these levels of social reality. This distinction will be used in subsequent chapters to help organize the discussion of the various theories and theoretical schools.

All theorists would probably agree that a scientific theory is more rigorous than implicit everyday life theories, but they would not all agree on the best procedures for developing a theory that conforms to the scientific model. Perhaps the most pervasive conflict is between those who concentrate on *objective* measurement of empirical data and those who include *subjective* processes. The "objectivists" argue that the social sciences should resemble the natural sciences as much as possible in terms of basic assumptions and methodological techniques. To them the essence of any scientific theory is that it is firmly grounded on objective empirical data. According to this school, subjective processes cannot be incorporated in a scientific theory unless they are manifested in some form of observable behavior. Priority is given to measuring overt behavior or various environmental conditions instead of to understanding subjective processes.

The "subjectivists" emphasize the importance of the crucial qualitative differences between the natural sciences and the social sciences. Failure to recognize this difference gives rise to a superficial analysis of social behavior that ignores the subjective realm of human meaning. The subjectivists maintain that observations of overt behavior without an awareness of its subjective meaning fails to provide an adequate understanding or explanation of such behavior. Antecedents for the objectivist versus the subjectivist points of view can be found in French positivism and German historicism, as discussed earlier.

These opposing positions were debated in a classic interchange in the late 1930s between George Lundberg, a major representative of the objectivist position, and Robert MacIver, who stressed the subjective process of "dynamic assessment." Lundberg, seeking to show the continuity between the natural and the social sciences, asserted that there is no essential difference between a paper flying in the wind and a man running from a pursuing crowd. MacIver countered that "there is an essential difference, from the standpoint of causation, between a paper flying before the wind and a man flying from a pursuing crowd. The paper knows no fear and the wind no hate, but without fear and hate the man would not fly nor the crowd pursue."[1]

Lundberg, after quoting this reference, rejected the use of terms such as "fear" and "hate" as metaphysical and animistic. He explained: "I merely point out that possibly I could analyze the situation in a frame of reference not involving the words 'fear' or 'hate' but in operationally defined terms of such character that all qualified observers would independently make the same analysis and predict the behavior under the given circumstances. . . . The principle of parsimony requires that we seek to bring into the same framework the explanation of all flying objects."[2] Lundberg evidently feared that it would not be possible for observers to agree that the running man is exhibiting fear or, at least, they could not agree on the degree of fear or any objective and precise measurement thereof. For MacIver, on the other hand, the action is unexplainable without reference to its subjective meaning or the emotion it manifests.

The position taken here is that there are both objective and subjective dimensions to social reality, and both must be dealt with in sociological theory. Social reality differs from the reality of the physical world in that it is not part of the natural or physical environment but is socially constructed through symbolic communication. It is imperative, therefore, that social scientists develop their own distinctive strategies to deal with the symbolic and socially constructed nature of much of social reality instead of simply attempting to imitate the strategies of the other natural sciences.

Being rigorous, systematic, and parsimonious need not involve elimination of concern for the subjective aspects of behavior. It is possible to take a disciplined and objective stance in trying to understand covert subjective processes, even while recognizing the elusive, hard-to-measure character of such phenomena. Ease of measurement should not be the principle criterion by which sociologists define their subject matter. Instead, this should be determined by the character of the subject matter. The elusive, unobservable, and symbolic character of subjective processes simply means that the challenge for objective scientific understanding is greater. Certainly, part of the challenge is to be as disciplined, logical, and systematic as possible.

THEORY CONSTRUCTION

The commitment to establish sociological theory as a set of systematically stated, logically interrelated propositions firmly grounded on empirical data dominates the contemporary efforts of the sociologists involved in formal theory construction. Most of those involved in theory construction reflect a neopositivist orientation. This means that they see a close resemblance between the social sciences and the natural sciences in terms of basic assumptions, methodological techniques, logical form, and empirical grounding. Because of their commitment to establish sociology as an empirical science, many of them reflect a strong determination not to rely on elusive and nonempirical subjective concepts.

Also, many of them insist that the logical form of theory be deductive. In particular, deductive logic is used in deriving specific empirically researchable hypotheses from more abstract and general theoretical propositions. Indeed, there may be several levels of abstraction involved as one moves from a highly general level down to more specific propositions and, finally, to a hypothesis (or set of hypotheses) in which a relationship among empirical indicators (operational measures of variables) is predicted.

In general, those involved in theory construction insist on explicit and formal definitions of concepts, variables, and classificatory systems; explicit and formal procedures for relating concepts and variables in propositional statements; strict adherence to procedures of formal logic in stating propositional statements in such a way that new propositions can be derived; and explicit and formal procedures for operationalization and empirical measurement (typically statistical) of the concepts and variables.[3] In some cases symbolic logic notation and mathematical models rather than everyday language are used to express key relationships. In all cases, there is a commitment to cut through discursive argumentation, exposition, and rhetorical appeals to subjective plausibility in order to lay bare the key relationships and logical structure of the theory. The result is a lean, highly parsimonious set of logically interrelated propositions that are intended to describe and explain empirical phenomena, ideally in such a way that empirical predictions can be made and assessed and the results lead to acceptance, rejection, or modification of the theory.

Whether we agree or not with these objectivist or neopositivist assumptions about sociology as a science, we can accept the general goal of being as explicit and systematic as possible in developing sociological theory. Recognizing measurement difficulties, subjective processes, or the distinction between the subject matter of sociology and the natural sciences need not justify a vague or sloppy approach to the discipline. Instead, our ideal is to be as rigorous, disciplined, and systematic as possible in developing sociological theory as a set of logically interrelated propositions formally developed to describe, explain, and interpret social life. The techniques of those involved in formal theory construction today can help us considerably in this process.

As we move toward a better understanding of theory, we must recognize that not just any kind of speculative thought about social life will qualify as a theory. The term ''theory'' will have a more restricted definition whereby we will be able to distinguish theory from, for example, social philosophy, abstract speculation, or the kind of common assumptions used in everyday life. In order to develop this more rigorous and restricted definition, we might begin by briefly identifying and describing the basic components or elements of theory and indicating how these ''parts'' are put together to form a theory. After this, we will suggest briefly some alternative strategies for initiating the process of theory development, relying on very elementary logical procedures and our inquisitive common sense. This whole discussion of theory construction is extremely elementary and nontechnical. The interested reader may consult any of the literature cited in the footnotes for a more thorough and technical presentation.

Components of Theory

Concepts and Variables. Concepts are the most elementary or fundamental building blocks of any theory. A concept is a word (or other symbolic expression) that stands for some phenomenon or class of phenomena; it is a label that we use to name and classify our perceptions and experiences. To attach a specific label to an object, experience, or event is the essential first step in analyzing and understanding it. Young children go through a stage in which the simple need to label the objects in their environment is evidently a compelling one, as their parents could readily testify after responding to questions such as "What is this?" and "What is that?" over and over again. In the same way, when scientists discover some new phenomenon, whether it is a chemical compound, a star, or a subatomic process, the first response (once it is established that the phenomenon does not fit in an existing, already named class) is to decide what label to attach to it.

But the relationship between experience and concept formation is more complex than is implied in the simple idea that new facts lead to new concepts. Among "old" (long-experienced) facts, new relationships or new patterns may be observed, and these may have to be labeled with a new concept (if stretching the meaning of an existing concept does not suffice). This implies the possibility of intellectual creativity in the process of perceiving and conceptualizing, a possibility that has been much debated by philosophers.[4] Although we need not concern ourselves with this philosophical issue, we might question what it is in the "facts" of social life that gives rise to concepts such as *alienation, solidarity, authoritarianism, institution,* or *social class,* for example. Terms such as these result more from a particular way at looking at the "data" of social life than from the nature of this data. Therefore, new ways of "seeing" the data of experience develop from the creation of new concepts.

Furthermore, once concepts are developed they serve to structure one's perception of the facts. Thus, for example, wide fluctuations in one's emotions or temperament that are unconsciously accepted as part of life may be "seen" by a psychiatrist as a manic-depressive syndrome; thereafter that person's relatives and acquaintances may "see" their own much milder shifts in temperament in similar symptomological terms. Similarly, a person trained in Marxist social criticism will "see" obvious exploitation in the relations between employees and employers. Part of the learning process for students in sociology (or any other discipline) involves becoming familiar with a set of concepts whereby they will be able to see things that previously had escaped them, even though all the appropriate "facts" may have been available.

Part of the reason that concepts do not *merely* mirror the facts of our perceptual experience is that they typically represent abstractions from that experience and they enable us to generalize from particular experiences. It is customary to distinguish between concepts that are *observables* and concepts that are *constructs.* An observable is a concept that points to a particular object, event, or other kind of entity that can be apprehended directly by the senses. A word used to refer to a particular object (e.g., a building) would be considered an observable. Even here, however, abstraction and generalization are involved. To label an object as a building is to put it in the general class of buildings, to distinguish it from all objects that are "not buildings," and to imply that it shares certain properties with all other objects in the class of buildings.

In contrast to observables, constructs are concepts that refer to some entity or process that cannot be observed directly but whose existence is *inferred* from an observable or set of observables. For example, psychologists are likely to regard *intelligence* as a construct, while an IQ test score would qualify as an observable. However, at least a low-level inference is likely to be involved even with observables. As McKinney has pointed out, "All concepts are constructs that have been *developed* out of experience."[5] Concepts do not just mirror experience in its uniqueness or its totality; they point to the features of a perceptual experience that are similar to other experiences. McKinney explains that "all concepts are generalizations and all generalization implies abstraction."[6]

The lowest possible level of abstraction characterizes concepts that are *primitive* and *concrete*. A primitive concept is one that cannot be defined in terms of any other concepts; its meaning can be made evident only by pointing to empirical instances so that the observer can experience the sensory impressions directly.[7] A concrete concept (as opposed to an abstract one) is one that is specific to a particular time and place; as such, it points to the unique aspects of a phenomenon instead of including it as a member of a class.[8]

Sociological concepts vary considerably in terms of abstractness and generality. The concept of *role,* for example, is less abstract than that of *institution.* In fact, at first it may seem that role is an observable concept used to describe actual behavior patterns. But, as Skidmore pointed out, to define concrete behavior as a manifestation of a role requires an inferential interpretation of that behavior.[9] Thus, for example, removing one's clothes does not necessarily imply that a person is performing the role of patient in submitting to a physical examination by a medical doctor. The same overt behavior could be a manifestation of the role of sexual partner or of customer in a store trying on new clothing. Such an act would normally not lead to ambiguity or confusion because the setting and the shared meanings would provide clear cues as to what role is being performed. Nevertheless, even though the behavior itself may be observable, the role it manifests is a construct.

Many of the concepts used in the social sciences represent a combination of several observables or constructs. As noted by Larson, development of a "constructed type" such as this involves a high degree of creative synthesis.[10] The patient role, for example, does not involve just undressing at the doctor's request; it also includes a manifestation of symptoms of illness, typically experienced subjectively as unpleasant or painful, a willingness to submit to the doctor's authority, and a temporary suspension of normal activities (in many cases).[11] In short, a number of "observables" or less abstract concepts are combined in the construct "patient."

Another example of an even more abstract "constructed type" is that of *bureaucracy.* The contemporary perspective on bureaucratic organization is heavily indebted to Max Weber's pioneering work in which he delineated its various specific characteristics, such as the hierarchy of rational-legal authority, the stress on formally enacted rules, and impersonality. It is the combination or synthesis of these lower-level concepts that makes up the constructed type. As we will see later, Weber's emphasis on the development of ideal types involves basically the formulation of constructed types. Weber recognized that such ideal types may not exist empirically in their pure form, but they are nevertheless useful for analytical and comparative purposes.[12]

A distinction should be made between concepts that identify what some object or event is and those that describe some property or characteristic thereof that may vary in different cases. For example, the concept ''man'' identifies a recognizable organism that is distinct from ''woman'' and from other kinds or organisms, while the concepts ''tall'' or ''short'' applied to man indicate relative position in terms of the variable ''height.'' Similarly, the term ''group'' may be used to designate any set of individuals who are in face-to-face communication with one another as opposed to an ''aggregate'' who are not in communication; within the general class of ''group'' different groups will vary widely in terms of characteristics such as size, leadership, structure, communication patterns, and solidarity.[13] Sociologists focus a great deal of their attention on identifying crucial *variables* and attempting to explain why they assume the values they do in different cases. Knowing the right label to attach to a phenomenon is an essential first step in scientific understanding, but the real challenge comes in trying to understand why the variable properties of that phenomenon assume the values that they do in particular instances.

Classification Systems. Concepts form an elementary basis for classification. At the very least, a concept implies a distinction between ''things'' that belong in the class named by the concept and everything else. By using variables it is also possible to categorize different cases of the phenomenon named by the concept according to the crucial differences that they exhibit. Let us say that we have named a particular type of object with the label X. This enables us to distinguish between objects that are X and all others (which could be classified as ''not X''). Then we observe that all Xs are not alike; they differ in terms of some particular characteristic. That characteristic would be a variable and, by measuring a series of Xs in terms of this variable, we could classify them as, say, ''X_1, X_2, and X_3.''

For example, most people are probably interested in personality differences between individuals. Without getting into a technical discussion of personality, we note that Riesman's popular distinction among ''tradition-directed,'' ''inner-directed,'' and ''other-directed'' people comprises one simple classification system.[14] There are many others, of course. Or let us say that we wish to analyze membership growth patterns in a voluntary organization; we might begin by developing an elementary classification system that distinguishes among those with ''declining'' (for a designated time period), ''stable,'' and ''expanding'' memberships.

The variables represented in classification systems differ according to whether they represent discrete categories or an underlying continuum.[15] The variable "sex," for example, is represented by two discrete categories: "male" and "female." Similarly, persons can be classified in terms of their citizenship into one of the various nationality groups in the world. On the other hand, variables such as individuals' height or weight represent a continuum with no discrete categories. The same is true for properties of groups such as solidarity, for example, even assuming that a precise definition of solidarity were being used. This distinction is important because it helps us to recognize that the dividing lines between categories of a variable with a continuous distribution are somewhat arbitrary, especially if there are no natural breaks in the distribution. Both the number of categories and the breaks between them will reflect a subjective judgment and the degree of precision possible with available measurement techniques.

Regardless of the number of categories or the techniques of measurement, the categories of a classification system should be mutually exclusive and exhaustive. Being mutually exclusive means that the basis for distinguishing one category from another is sufficiently precise that any given case can fit into one and only one category. Without mutually exclusive categories, there could be ambiguity as to the category in which a given case really belongs. Being exhaustive means that the categories cover all cases of the phenomenon in question; no cases are left unclassified. The catchall category "other" is not really a bona fide category, although it is frequently used to cover all cases that cannot be meaningfully classified.

Concepts, variables, and classification systems are the building blocks of theory, but they do not constitute a theory themselves. This is true regardless of the extent of speculative discussion that is involved in establishing these basic building blocks, even though some provocative insights may emerge from conceptual analysis. At the very least, concepts have to be defined. Since so many of the concepts used by sociologists are borrowed from our everyday language, the theorist must cut through the vagueness, ambiguity, and welter of shifting and multiple meanings to develop a clear, precise definition. Beyond this, it may be useful to elaborate on the significance of a particular concept, to develop its implications, to enumerate examples, and so on. Consider the concept "alienation," which has been used widely in sociological analysis and popular thought. What does it mean? Are there some assumptions about human nature built into the meaning of the concept? What are its psychological components? Its behavioral manifestations? Some of these questions go beyond mere definition and are suggestions for developing a theory.

In the same manner, establishing a set of categories, or demonstrating that a particular case belongs in one category and not another, is not to be confused with developing or testing a theory, even though both of these processes are important stages in the process. Zetterberg distinguished between the taxonomic approach and the theoretic approach in social analysis.[16] The taxonomic approach involves categorization of phenomena. For example, to note that a particular group is a primary group rather than a secondary group is simply to categorize it with no explanation as to why it exhibits primary group characteristics. In brief, naming and classifying helps us to answer the question of "What?" rather than "Why?"

Propositions. The next level in our elementary effort to establish the basic components of theory is the proposition. (The term is used more broadly and loosely here than in the works of many of those involved in theory construction.) A proposition is a statement of a relationship between two or more concepts. Typically, the relationship is between variables. In such statements we have a tentative beginning of an effort to answer the question "Why?" (as opposed to "What?").

Specifically, we want to know why a particular variable takes the value that it does. Why do some juveniles become delinquent? Why do some students consistently get superior grades? Why do some voluntary organizations thrive while others disintegrate? Or, why do some cases (of a particular phenomenon) fit in one category of a classification system, while others fit in other categories?

The standard scientific method for seeking answers to such questions is to search for some other variable that influences the first variable. The statement of this relationship is a proposition, and it can be symbolically expressed as: $X \rightarrow Y$ (Y represents the variable whose value we want to explain and X represents the variable that we think will explain it). A statement expressed in such a form means that as the value of X changes, the value of Y also changes (in either the same or the opposite direction).

Reconsider one of the examples previously mentioned. Why do some juveniles become delinquent? This question will not be answered here; only the basic logic of theory development will be illustrated. Based on common sense and everyday observations we might tentatively hypothesize that inadequate family experiences help explain juvenile delinquency. In itself, this statement begs the question of what constitutes an inadequate family experience. Is it divorce or separation of the parent? High conflict? Emotional deadness? Excessive punishment? Parental rejection? Or some combination of these and other variables (all of which would have to be defined precisely)? The term "juvenile delinquency" must also be defined precisely. While it may not seem as problematic as "inadequate family experience," it also has multiple meanings (ranging from disobedience of teachers to commission of a felony). But assuming that the definitional problems were resolved, the basic proposition that might emerge would follow the $X \rightarrow Y$ form (i.e., "inadequate family experience"→"juvenile delinquency" or, better, the higher the inadequacy of a juvenile's family experience, the higher the probability that the juvenile will get involved in delinquent behavior).

Once the argument linking family experience and juvenile delinquency is put in this form, it can be evaluated on the basis of available evidence or other theoretical arguments. Such a statement obviously oversimplifies considerably; one could easily identify negative cases that do not fit this pattern, and one could point to other factors, such as peer group relations, that seem to be just as crucial on the basis of theoretical argument or empirical evidence. These additional variables could readily be incorporated into the theory of delinquency being developed by simply extending the logic already developed. Schematically, this would be represented as follows. If

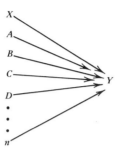

the original $X{\rightarrow}Y$ relationship seems to be important only under certain conditions (identified by these additional variables), this theoretical formulation could be represented as follows: "If $A_1, B_1, C_1, \ldots n_1$, then $X{\rightarrow}Y$." Similarly, time order could be indicated by $A{\rightarrow}X{\rightarrow}Y$.

The Problem of Causal Explanation

Ideally, the effort to develop propositional statements should move toward *causal* explanation. However, we have carefully avoided making the statement that X causes Y, even though when we wish to explain variation in Y we really want to know what *causes* such variation. Causal statements are extremely difficult to prove, as many theorists and philosophers of science have shown. Certainly it is not sufficient merely to show that two variables are significantly correlated, since correlation could result from the fact that both variables are independently related to a third variable. Furthermore, the concept of "cause" itself has multiple meanings. For example, Aristotle distinguished between the notion of cause as a stimulating factor that produces a subsequent effect and the notion of cause as the purpose for which some effect exists.[17]

The time order of the cause-effect sequence differs for these two meanings of cause. In the first case, the effect follows the cause in temporal sequence; in the second case, the cause seems to follow its effect. Although philosophers have had difficulty conceptualizing causes following their effects in temporal sequence, this notion of cause makes sense in the case of goal-directed action. Thus, for example, a student's desire for a good grade can be the cause of studying hard for an exam, even though the grade is not received until *after* the studying has taken place. At the same time, the effective stimulus for studying hard would normally have occurred *prior* to the exam. Such a stimulus might be provided by the teacher's warning that the exam will be a hard one.

Another distinction made by philosophers is the one between *necessary* and *sufficient* causes. Briefly, a statement of a necessary causal relationship is a statement of a condition or factor (variable) that must be present (or change in a specified way) for a second condition or factor to be present (or change in a specified way). However, such a change in the first condition may occur without a change in the second. In contrast, a statement of a sufficient cause asserts that if a given variable changes (by its presence or by a change in its value), this will inevitably bring about a change in a specified second variable. In other words, no changes occur in the first variable without changes occurring in the second.

In applying these elementary notions of different types of causation to the preceding example, it is easy to see that inadequate family structure (however defined) is neither a necessary nor a sufficient cause of juvenile delinquent behavior. To show that it is not a necessary cause, we need only find empirical examples of cases of delinquency by juveniles whose family relations are not inadequate. To show that inadequate family experiences are not a sufficient cause of delinquency, we need only show that some juveniles whose family relations are inadequate do not become delinquent.

In spite of this demonstration that inadequate family experiences are neither a necessary nor a sufficient *cause* of delinquency, we are likely to persist in our conviction that family experiences have a bearing on juveniles' behavior and influence the probability of delinquent behavior. We may even want to go further by including family experiences as one component of a multicausal model that also includes peer group relations, school experiences, community structure, social class, and perhaps some social psychological concepts such as self-concept.

Whether a set of numerous variables would constitute a necessary or sufficient cause is an open empirical question, but it is likely that there would be empirical exceptions even to a multicausal model such as this. At the very least, these exceptions would demonstrate that the relationship is probabilistic (or stochastic) and not deterministic. As Zetterberg pointed out, stochastic relationships are far more common in sociology than deterministic ones, and a strict definition of cause seems incompatible with probabilistic relationships.[18] As an analogy, could we imagine a physicist arging that the density of a gas is *probably* associated with it temperature? These two variables in physics are causally related in a deterministic manner; in contrast, most sociological propositions are probabilistic, not deterministic.

A good theory, however, should include propositions that express highly probable relationships. A common strategy for improving the probability of a proposition is to specify the conditions under which the relationship it describes is likely to hold. This is what Zetterberg refers to as a *contingent* rather than a *sufficient* relationship.[19] To use the delinquency example again, the following proposition might be developed. Given a lower-class position, residence in a high-crime area, poor academic performance, and association with delinquent peers, there is a higher association between inadequate family relations and delinquency than when these conditions do not hold. In other words, inadequate family relations is not *the cause* of delinquency, but it may be a contributing factor along with others, and the strength of its influence may be affected by these additional variables.

The difficulty in establishing causal relations applies more to sufficient causes than to necessary causes. In many cases necessary causes can be easily established, but they seem trivial when stated formally. For example, a necessary condition for drug abuse is gaining access to a supply. Such a statement appears obvious. Sufficient causes, however, involve a stronger claim and are thus more difficult to establish. As noted, propositions stating sufficient causes are not as common as statements of contingent relationships, and even these are likely to be probabilistic, not deterministic.

Part of the difficulty in establishing deterministic causal relationships is our lack of knowledge of all the appropriate variables that are operative in social life, and part of the difficulty is lack of precision in measuring the variables that we have identified. Also, some sociologists would argue that their subject matter differs from that in the physical sciences because there is a greater element of uncertainty. This view reflects the notion that human behavior reflects a realm of freedom instead of deterministic laws. Without getting into the philosophical debate that this issue raises, we might simply note that the claim for the uniqueness of the subject matter could hardly be substantiated unless we were far more certain than we are that all the critical variables have been identified and adequately measured. Certainly, to identify variables that influence our choices as human beings is not to deny that we may experience ourselves making choices, even in terms of manipulating crucial variables.

In spite of the difficulty in establishing strict causal relationships, we will probably continue to use language that implies causation, at least in the loose sense of contributing factor. This is because of our goal of providing explanations of social phenomena (although not all explanations need be causal explanations). Our judgments regarding causal relationships (in the absence of absolute proof) are likely to be influenced by factors such as the strength of the correlation between the variables, especially when the correlation is established under a variety of conditions, the logic and strength of the argument linking the variables in a causal relationship, and the meaningfulness and subjective plausibility of the process implied in the proposition.

Independent versus Dependent Variables

Our discussion of propositions has thus far implied a dependent variable as the focal variable. That is, we have assumed that we wish to explain the variation in some variable, and this leads us to identify the independent variable(s) that we think explains this variation. However, it would also be possible to start with the independent variable as the focal variable and then explore what other variables are affected by this particular variable. Schematically, this could be expressed as follows: $X \rightarrow ?$; in contrast, the form of analysis with the dependent variable as the focal variable would be as follows: $? \rightarrow Y$.

With the independent variable as the focal variable, attention can be directed toward its effects or consequences. Often this type of analysis begins by noting change in some variable, and questions are then raised as to the effects this change will have. To note some examples, we might wonder what effects the proliferation of premarital cohabitation arrangements will have on the family institution. What will be the effects of a new economic policy on our society? What are the consequences of increased leisure time? What effects will the increasing costs of energy resources have on our economy, our political institutions, and our life-style? The basic logic is the same as when the dependent variable is the focal variable in that it involves a proposition of the following form: $X \rightarrow Y$. However, when the dependent variable is focal, we try to identify the "X" variables that affect it or influence its value; when the independent variable (X) is the focal variable, our interest is in seeing how it affects or influences one or more other variables (Y).

In some propositions, the decision as to which variable is independent and which is dependent is arbitrary. This would be true when the relationship is one of mutual interdependence. That is, each variable both affects and is affected by the other; both actually operate as both independent and dependent variables. Schematically, this would be represented as $X \leftrightarrow Y$. One example is the proposition from Homan's analysis of small group processes that links interaction frequency and the sentiment of liking.[20] Essentially, the proposition tells us that people who like each other interact frequently. As a formal proposition, this would be expressed as "High degree of mutual liking↔High interaction frequency."

We can think of exceptions to this proposition, as when two people are obliged to interact even though they may hate each other, or when "Absence makes the heart grow fonder." However, the proposition hold frequently enough in our experience to serve as an example, and the point to note is that the two variables are mutually interdependent. In other words, interaction leads to the development of positive sentiments of liking; this leads to increased interaction, which leads to increased liking, and so on. The values of both variables go up (or change) in small increments rather than suddenly, and they do so as a result of the mutual escalation cycle, as described.

Zetterberg emphasized the gradual evolutionary nature of the process of incremental change in relationships of mutual interdependence. He explains, "Thus, in an interdependent relation, a small increment in one variable results in a small increment in a second variable; then the increment in the second variable makes possible a further increment in the first variable which in turn affects the second one, and this process goes on until no more increments are possible."[21]

Conflict between nations and between individuals often seems to take the form of an interdependent relationship. Consider, for example, the arms race between the

United States and the Soviet Union, especially during the height of the Cold War. Each side observes the other increasing its military capability; this stimulates a response in kind; this reponse stimulates an additional buildup on the other side, and so on. Similarly, bitter enmity between two individuals often results not from a single dramatic confrontation, but from a gradually escalating cycle of mutual exchange of more and more hostile or aggressive messages. Interdependent relationships of this type are very common in social life.

Types of Propositions

Propositions differ from each other in several important ways. They vary in terms of their abstractness and generality, their testability, and the degree to which they have been empirically supported. Those involved in theory construction commonly distinguish between different types of propositions, such as axioms, postulates, and laws. Propositions are frequently distinguished from hypotheses in that the latter are empirically testable statements of expected relationships that are derived from more abstract propositions. Typically, the terms of a hypothesis are indicators (i.e., operational measures) of variables and not the variables themselves.

A whole series of different types of propositions may be formulated prior to the derivation of an empirical hypothesis. Zetterberg, for example, distinguished between postulates (i.e., propositions not derivable from other propositions) and theorems, which are derivable from the postulates.[22] Similarly, an axiom would be a widely accepted statement (comparable to a postulate) that forms the foundation for additional propositions. If a proposition has been repeatedly confirmed in a variety of different circumstances so that it is generally accepted as a true proposition, it could be considered a law. A law, then, is at the other end of the spectrum from a hypothesis, which is a predictive statement rather than a repeatedly confirmed one and one on which there is not yet sufficient evidence.

Reynolds distinguished among five different types of theoretical statements: laws, axioms, propositions, hypotheses, and empirical generalizations.[23] In such a listing, the term ''proposition'' is used in a narrower sense than we have used in this section. All of these statements express relationships between two or more concepts (or variables), but they differ in terms of their generality, abstractness, and degree to which they have been supported empirically. Additional theoretical statements may be needed to explain the laws. Although statements of laws are the most general and abstract in Reynolds' series, explanation need not stop with this level. As Campbell insists, the laws themselves must be explained, and providing the explanation is the highest function of theory.[24]

Theory: A Set of Propositions

So far we have identified concepts, classification systems, and propositions as the components of theory. Concepts are the most elementary building blocks, and theoretical work at the conceptual level involves definitions, conceptual analysis, and existence statements (i.e., statements that assert the empirical existence of a phenomenon referred to by a concept). At the classification level, theoretical work involves establishing categories and classifying empirical phenomena.

The next level is the proposition, which is a statement relating two or more concepts (or variables). We have considered how propositions are developed and the different types of propositional statements that can be developed. We now move to the final step in developing a theory, which involves linking a series of propositions together in a logical and systematic way. A theory is a set of logically interrelated and systematically stated propositions that describes (at a high level of generality) and explains some set of empirical phenomena.

Those involved in the technical and philosophical aspects of theory construction have been concerned with the form that the set of propositions constituting a theory should take. One major school of thought states that the basic logical form of theory should be deductive or hierarchical.[25] Such a model was implicit in the earlier discussion of the derivation of hypotheses from more general propositions and in the discussion of Zetterberg's distinction between postulates and theorems. Zetterberg is a major advocate of this form, which he and others refer to as the axiomatic form of theory construction.

The deductive or axiomatic form of theory construction essentially involves arranging propositions in a hierarchical fashion, from the most general laws down to specific hypotheses. The lower-level propositions are logically derived from the higher-level and more general propositions, or they represent specific instances of the more general propositions. The deductive form may be represented diagrammatically as follows.

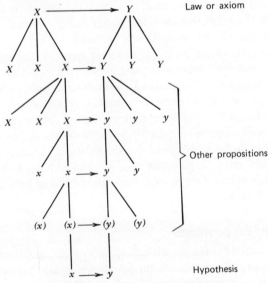

Diagram of the deductive form of theroy.

As can be seen from this diagram, the high-level concepts and propositions can subsume (or include in their definition) several lower-level concepts and propositions. Therefore a hypothesis is never a full and complete test of the proposition(s) from which it is derived. For simplicity, the preceding diagram is limited to two concepts; however, more concepts could be introduced through additional laws or lower-level propositions. As long as there is at least one common term to two or more propositions, the propositions could be related through the standard rules of logic. This may be illustrated as follows.

$$\begin{array}{c} A \to X \\ \underline{X \to Y} \\ A \to Y \end{array}$$

The diagram in this case is that of the standard logical syllogism.

Is the deductive or hierarchical form the only legitimate form to use in developing theories? Clearly, it is the preferred form for many of those involved in theory construction.[26] However, as Warshay points out, a number of critics take exception to this view, arguing that it leads to unfortunate and unnecessary constraints on the theorizing process and that its biases in favor of an objectivist world view like that of the natural sciences do not do justice to human experience or human consciousness.[27]

One alternative to the ''hypothetico-deductive'' model is the ''pattern'' or ''concatenated'' model, as described by Kaplan.[28] Kaplan's distinction between ''deductive'' and ''pattern'' theories is sensitive to the actual process of theorizing in the social and behavioral sciences as opposed to being an abstract and idealized view of the form that theory *should* take. A pattern-type theory involves a kind of ''cognitive map'' or intellectual representation of some set of empirical phenomena in terms of concepts that are related to each other at the theoretical level. In this type of theory relationships are seen between theoretical constructs that mirror (to a degree) relationships in the empirical world.

Unlike the deductive theory, pattern theory does not necessarily involve a hierarchy of statements that range from the most general and abstract down to more specific statements. Instead, there are essentially two levels: the theoretical and the empirical. The empirical level is seen and interpreted in light of the pattern established at the theoretical level. *Interpretation,* not prediction, is the key to empirical application. An empirical phenomenon might be seen as a specific instance of the theoretical concept, and this empirical phenomenon would be seen as related to other phenomena identified by additional theoretical concepts. Schematically, this might be represented in terms of the following diagram.

The theory provides an intellectual model of the empirical level. In this diagram, the letters in parentheses and the dotted lines indicate variables and relationships that are assumed to exist but that may not be obvious or observable in a specific instance. The lines connecting the letters at the two levels indicate that empirical application involves pointing to the empirical manifestation of the theoretical concept; however, this manifestation would not necessarily be recognized as

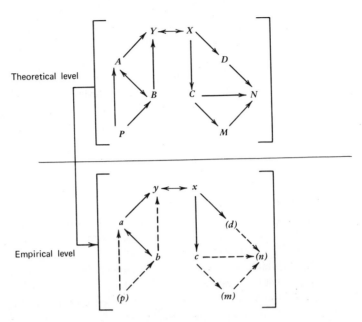

Theoretical level

Empirical level

Diagram of the pattern form of theory.

such without the theoretical concept to point to it. In other words, there would be no "*a*" in the diagram without "*A*".

For example, in Freud's psychoanalytic theory, the "id" does not exist in the same sense that a tree exists for a botanist. Yet this concept may be used by the psychoanalyst in explaining certain aspects of many different types of behavior, including violent aggression and highly controlled, nonaggressive behavior. In the former case, the id is inadequately socialized; in the latter, it is repressed. This concept of the id only makes sense in terms of its relationship to the theoretical concepts of the "ego" and the "superego." These concepts are related to one another in such a way that their very definition is meaningful only in the total framework, which includes all the other concepts.

Disproving a pattern theory is difficult. The test of the theory involves assessing the congruence between the concepts and relationships identified in the theory and the facts of experience or data at the empirical level, not deriving specific hypotheses that can be falsified by the data. A pattern theory may be regarded as fruitful if the interpretation it leads to is meaningful or adds new insight in understanding some aspect of the empirical world.

Kaplan's treatment of the two types of theory is balanced; he does not reject either type. He does, however, indicate that the formal elegance of the deductive theory is often an *ex post facto* reconstruction of the actual process of theorizing. That is, the theory-building process often starts with a pattern theory and then progresses toward a deductive theory. In retrospect, however, scientists often insist that the deductive type is the only proper way to develop scientific theory.

Kaplan's distinction between hypothetico-deductive and pattern or concatenated theories was utilized by Skidmore in his discussion of two contemporary theories.[29] Skidmore apparently did not see irreconcilable differences between the two types; he argued that one form could be translated into the other form.[30] For example, the concepts and relationships identified in the pattern theory could become part of a deductive theory simply by showing how they follow from, or are entailed by, a smaller set of even more general principles. Similarly, it should be possible to develop descriptive (if not predictive) hypotheses from the pattern theory that would be directly applicable to a specific set of empirical data.

UNDERLYING ASSUMPTIONS AND VALUES

Regardless of how many different types of propositional statements are developed or the logical form in which they are presented, all theorists would agree that a theory is a systematically arranged set of such statements (and definitions and classificatory systems). But there is more to theory than this. Sociological theory, like any other scientific theory, rests on a massive foundation of unspoken assumptions. These assumptions need not be taken as part of theory in a narrow sense, but they do influence the way that theory is developed. We might identify these underlying assumptions as metatheory; however, by differentiating them in this way we do not mean to underestimate the crucial influence they have on the development of theory in the narrow sense.

These assumptions include the fundamental image sociologists have of their subject matter, the choice of concepts used to describe and analyze this subject matter, the selection of specific problems for investigation, and the strategies used in the process of analysis. For example, in all of the sciences there is an assumption that natural phenomena manifest some type of order (as opposed to occurring haphazardly or at random) and that through various techniques of empirical investigation this orderliness can be documented. Yet, except for the opening chapters of introductory textbooks, working scientists do not necessarily concern themselves with articulating or defending these assumptions.

Metatheory may also include the fundamental value premises of the theorist. Although a scientific theorist strives for objectivity and value neutrality, a scientist's values inevitably affect his or her work as a scientist. If in no other way, values affect the choices a scientist makes as to what particular problems or areas are worth studying.

Values may have even more profound effects than this, as many radical critics of so-called "establishment sociology" are quick to point out. Friedrichs has distinguished between the opposing value orientations of "prophetic" sociology versus "priestly" sociology,[31] which differ in their attitudes toward and implicit support for the status quo. The prophetic mode takes a critical stance toward the status quo, arguing that an appropriate role for sociology is to identify deficiencies and inconsistencies in the social structure and to provide enlightenment regarding more humane possibilities. The priestly mode operates comfortably within the framework of the established structure. Because of the problems they deal with and the general style of their work, sociologists representing this orientation accept the overall parameters of the social structure and devote their energies to understanding the dimensions and dynamics of the social processes that operate within this structure.

Priestly sociologists need not be aware of the value implications of their work. Indeed, they may strive for objectivity, and their analyses may be cloaked in the language of value neutrality. However, their critics among the "new" or radical sociologists would charge that by failing to provide a critique of the status quo, the priestly, or establishment, sociologists are providing tacit support for it by default. In other words, the critics, or prophetic sociologists, claim that neutrality and impartiality are really impossible and that unless a sociologist is devoted explicitly to promoting a more humane social structure, he or she is basically accepting the legitimacy of the status quo.

Gouldner's *The Coming Crisis of Western Sociology* is an example of a critical analysis of establishment sociology.[32] Gouldner criticizes the dominant modes of social thought from Plato to Parsons for an uncritical and accepting stance toward the status quo. This conservative orientation is revealed in the fact that the existing social and political structures are taken as given, and problems for social investigation or analysis are defined within their framework. In Gouldner's judgment, this is especially true of Parsons' functional theory because of its focus on social system needs and requirements and its tendency to analyze existing social structural patterns in terms of their contributions toward fulfilling these needs and requirements. Gouldner and other critics of establishment sociology argue that human needs, not system needs, should have a much higher priority. They insist that such a reordering of priorities would lead to a much more critical orientation toward the existing structure. Gouldner urges sociologists to recognize their political role. He argues for a "reflexive" sociology in which individual needs and humanistic values would provide a basis for criticizing and reforming the social structure.

A more moderate stance was taken by Shils, who earlier had advocated a "consensual" sociology (rather than a proestablishment or critical sociology).[33] This approach would include an explicit political orientation; however, the sociologist would not presume to impose his or her own particular values. Instead, the sociologist would work with the various groups of society, helping them to articulate their own particular version of our basic democratic values, but only as long as they are not incompatible with the freedom of other groups to do the same. The sociologist also could play a vitally important role in a pluralistic society such as ours by using the sociological perspective to promote mutual understanding and respect between different groups with heterogeneous subcultural traditions.

Whether the value orientations or political leanings of social theorists are explicit or implicit, we must be aware of these commitments and be sensitive to how they may influence sociological analysis. This is especially important when we evaluate sociological analyses in which the language of objectivity and value neutrality masks the underlying value commitments. At the very least, the fact that a sociologist chooses to investigate one particular aspect of social reality and not another may reveal something about underlying value commitments.

In addition, scientific theories rest on implicit intellectual assumptions about the nature of the subject matter that may not be formally stated. They are not likely to be fully articulated even by those who seriously attempt to make explicit all underlying assumptions in terms of axiomatic statements. Specifically, those involved in axiomatic theory construction assume that there is something about the social reality with which they deal that can be adequately represented in the form of logically interrelated axiomatic statements and theoretical propositions. They may cautiously insist that they really have no way of determining the nature of the underlying social reality and that, at best, the empirical grounding of their theoretical propositions is provided by operational measures of indicators and their relationships to each other (with indicators being distinguished from genuine variables).

Yet, with all due respect to such cautious qualifications, sociological analysis and empirical research proceed as though the axioms and propositions of the theory were sufficiently congruent with the social reality that they are intended to explain that no metatheoretical or epistemological problem remains. Without this faith, social analysis and theorizing would lose much of its purpose and meaning. As with implicit values, we do not claim that implicit assumptions can be eliminated from formal theoretical analysis; we merely caution the reader to be sensitive to the unstated assumptions on which all theories rest.

The Paradigm Concept

In a provocative and highly influential analysis of revolutions in science, Kuhn refers to the underlying intellectual assumptions scientists make about their subject matter as a *paradigm*.[34] Although Kuhn is not consistent in his use of this term, the definition implied in his original work is that a paradigm consists of the fundamental world view (*Weltanschauung*) shared by scientists in a particular discipline. For example, the world view implied by Newtonian physics would constitute a paradigm, as would the contrasting world view of Einsteinian physics. The idea of a paradigm as an overarching world view was identified by Masterman as a *metaphysical* paradigm; this definition was one of several implicit definitions that Masterman identified in Kuhn's work.[35] Friedrichs' analysis of the opposing political orientations of priestly versus prophetic sociologists is based on the paradigm concept; he broadly defines a paradigm as "A fundamental image a discipline has of its subject matter,''[36] but his use of the terms really focuses on self-images and political orientations rather than basic world views.

Kuhn uses the concept of the paradigm in his analysis of scientific revolutions. Briefly, he distinguishes between the preparadigmatic stage, the paradigmatic stage, transitional revolutionary stages during which one paradigm is challenged by increasing numbers of anomalies and, eventually, by a competing paradigm, and the ascendancy stage of the new paradigm. Most of the time scientists work within the framework of the dominant paradigm without challenging it; however, as anomalies (or negative cases) gradually accumulate, it becomes more difficult to account for them within the prevailing paradigm, and so there is a need to develop a new competing paradigm.

However, the conflict between representatives of opposing paradigms is not carried out on a purely rational, scientific basis. Instead, there is a political dimension to the conflict that reflects scientists' indoctrination during their training and their scholarly commitments and sources of prestige within the discipline. This means that a nonrational dimension characterizes scientists' acceptance or rejection of fundamental world views. In a science dominated by a single paradigm, the underlying assumptions of the shared world view are likely to be implicit, unstated assumptions.

Sociology as a "Multiple-Paradigm" Science

Is sociology dominated by a single paradigm? On a general level perhaps this question could be answered positively by noting that all sociologists share the basic assumption that individuals' fundamental attitudes, needs, values, and behavior patterns are powerfully shaped by their social milieu. In addition, they would probably insist that the social milieu itself exhibits fundamental patterns that are more or less recurrent. The idea that there is a more or less unified perspective in sociology seems clearly implied in theoretical syntheses such as Nisbet's *The Sociological Tradition*.[37] This same conclusion is supported by the fact that Timasheff can conclude his encyclopedic survey of numerous theories by identifying a common core of basic sociological principles to which the various theorists have contributed.[38] At the very least, sociologists' emphasis on the social dimension distinguishes them from those in neighboring disciplines who may choose a different focus.

Beyond this general world view, however, sociologists' fundamental assumptions regarding their subject matter and, by implication, their methods of research, differ markedly. Using Kuhn's concept of the paradigm, Ritzer developed a useful and parsimonious analysis of sociology as a multiple-paradigm science.[39] He distinguished among three different fundamental paradigms: the social facts paradigm, the social definition paradigm, and the social behavior paradigm. Basic to these distinctions are differences in fundamental assumptions regarding the nature of social reality. The *social facts* paradigm, represented eminently during the classical stage of theory development by Durkheim and at the present time in both functionalism and conflict theory, emphasizes the idea that *social* facts are real or, at least, should be treated as real, just as fully as facts about the *individual*.[40] Furthermore, social facts are not reducible to individual facts; they represent a reality of their own. Social structures and social institutions are included among the social facts of particular concern to sociologists.

The *social definition* paradigm emphasizes the subjective nature of social reality rather than its existence independent of the individual. This paradigm was represented during the classical stage of theory development by Weber;[41] later it was represented by social action theory as developed by Parsons early in his career (with Weber's perspective as a major influence).[42] Also, symbolic interaction theory, from its beginnings in the works of Mead, Cooley, Thomas, and others to the present embodies the fundamental premises of the social definition paradigm.[43] These different theories share the view that social reality is based on individuals' subjective definitions and evaluations. Social structure refers to the common definitions individuals have regarding appropriate modes of relating to one another. Individuals' actions and interaction patterns are guided by such shared definitions, which are themselves constructed through an interaction process.

The *social behavior* paradigm emphasizes an objective, empirical approach to social reality. Of the three paradigms, this one comes closest in its image of social reality to the implicit assumptions that underlie the theory construction approach previously described. For the social behaviorist the approach represented by the social facts paradigm is excessively abstract, while the approach represented by the social definition paradigm is excessively subjective. Both approaches prevent the establishment of sociology as a science firmly grounded in measurable empirical data. According to the social behavior paradigm, the empirical data of social reality are simply the overt behaviors of individuals. Moreover, explanations of individuals' overt behavior are possible in terms of specific environmental stimuli that can also be empirically measured. This approach is developed most fully in behavioral psychology, not sociology, and is represented preeminently by Skinner.[44] However, the basic principles of behavioral psychology were incorporated into Homans' theory of elementary social behavior; by expanding the behavioral psychologist's explanations of behavior into a theory of interpersonal exchanges, Homans attempted to bridge the gap between the individual and the social levels.[45]

The differences among these paradigms seem to be profound, leading to disagreements and debates over fundamental assumptions. Although the principal conflict is about the basic image of the subject matter of sociology, disagreements extend beyond this to include different value orientations and different strategies and techniques of research.

On the other hand, perhaps the differences in basic assumptions are more apparent than real. Typically, the differences are most sharply drawn when a representative of a particular paradigm attempts to define his or her particular position as opposed to that of others who have differing emphases. Establishing one's own point of view as it is distinguished from that of others always leads to an exaggeration of the differences and an undermining of the areas of agreement. For example, Durkheim's "social facts" emphasis was established to distinguish sociology from psychology and from the social theorists who sought to explain society in terms of rational, contractual agreements based on individuals' self-interests. Similarly, Weber attempted to establish his particular image of social reality in opposition to German idealists (who often ignored the constraining influence of the environment) and to Marx (who overemphasized society's materialistic base, in Weber's judgment). Finally, the contemporary exchange theorist, George Homans, developed his theory of elementary social behavior in opposition to the functional approach, which he felt to be too abstract and ignored individuals' motives.

However, if we go beyond the polemical level, in which a theorist is seeking to establish the fundamental groundwork in opposition to those with whom he or she disagrees, to look at the substantive analyses and their implications, we find a much higher level of agreement. It is as though the nature of the subject matter forces theorists in their substantive analyses to make concessions to their opponents. In other words, although representatives of the opposing paradigms start from different positions, they gradually converge at many crucial points.

Specifically, those who represent the social facts paradigm are obliged, in the end, to concede that social facts are not merely external but are also represented (at least to a degree) in individuals' subjective consciousness. This is clearly manifested in Durkheim's work, even though Durkheim's emphasis on the reality of social facts has influenced others working within this paradigm to ignore the subjective dimension. Durkheim himself, however, in discussing nonmaterial social facts such as the "collective consciousness," clearly did not intend to eliminate individuals' subjective consciousness but to refer to the kind of social climate that emerges when there is a sharing of consciousness by the members of a group or society. Also, his later works, especially his analysis of religion, emphasized the social processes whereby individuals internalize the moral and cognitive patterns shared by the group in their individual subjective consciousness.[46] Indeed, the emphasis on the subjective dimension is so strong that Ritzer treated Durkheim as a paradigm bridge builder who actually combined certain aspects of the social facts and the social definitions paradigm.

Similarly, those working within the framework of a social definition paradigm must finally acknowledge that people do not live in a world of make-believe where there is no more to social reality than their subjective definitions. At the very least, in order to communicate with others, individuals must learn a language that they did not invent as individuals but that confronted them initially as an external reality. There are other external realities, including the world of physical objects and the presence, if not the demands and expectations, of others that individuals are obliged to take into account in developing their subjective definitions. These external or objective realities are the main concern of those who work with the social facts paradigm.

Weber's work provides an important example of the transition from the social definition paradigm to the social fact paradigm. Even though he stressed the individual and his or her subjectively meaningful social action as the basic element of social reality, his substantive analyses frequently dealt with the social structural level and seemed to neglect subjective meanings. His analysis of bureaucracy is an example, as are his speculations regarding the long-range social consequences of the Protestant work ethic, which went far beyond the subjective intentions or meanings of the early Protestant capitalists. Like Durkheim, Weber is treated by Ritzer as a bridge builder between these two paradigms.

Finally, those who wish to establish sociology as an objective, empirical science within the framework of the social behavior paradigm inadvertently find themselves dealing with concepts and insights from the other two paradigms. Homans, for example, was obliged to deal with concepts that transcend the individual, such as the concepts of norms, authority, and prestige. In the same way, concepts that refer to subjective phenomena are also utilized, at least implicitly if not explicitly. Such concepts include value, reward expectations (based on previous reinforcement experiences), and comparison level. In fact, Homans is explicit in discussing the subjective experience of the anger (which, of course, has behavioral manifestations) that results when individuals' rewards are less than they are accustomed to or than their peers are receiving. In the last chapter of his work on elementary social exchanges, Homans provides a tantalizing glimpse of the possibilities for linking elementary social behavior (or subinstitutional behavior) with institutional behavior and, by extension, with social institutions (which the social fact advocates emphasize).[47]

These areas of implicit agreement are not intended to suggest that it would be a fairly easy matter to develop a single more comprehensive paradigm that would command widespread acceptance. Ritzer underscores the differences among the three opposing paradigms and, in his concluding assessment of the status of the paradigms, predicts that although some paradigmatic reconciliation may occur, establishment of a single, dominant paradigm is not likely.[48] Nevertheless, the idea of reconciliation is a promising one simply because of the inadequacies of each of the paradigms when they stand alone. At this stage in the development of sociology, all three paradigms are needed to help us understand social reality. As Ritzer says, *"In fact, no aspect of social reality can be adequately explained without drawing on insights from all of the paradigms."*[49]

The possibilities for convergence between theorists who start from different premises are also discussed by Abel in his analysis of the pioneering works of Weber, Durkheim, and Simmel.[50] Weber's emphasis on subjective definitions and Durkheim's emphasis on social facts have already been mentioned. Simmel's primary focus was on various *forms of interaction* but, as Abel shows, he also had to deal with the subjective level and with the external or objective nature of social structures.

In short, sociological theory includes not only explicitly stated concepts and systematically interrelated propositions, but also a rich, complex maze of underlying, unstated assumptions and perhaps even some implicit value premises. But because these assumptions and value premises are unstated, it is necessary to "read between the lines" to determine what they are. Understanding and interpreting a theory involves learning the ideas that are explicitly stated and also being sensitive to their broader intellectual and ideological implications, including the basic world view underlying them.

Kuhn's concept of the scientific paradigm helps us focus on the underlying assumptions and basic world view shared by a scientific community. But, in using this concept, we have noted that, as Ritzer demonstrates, sociology is a multiple-paradigm science. That is, sociologists do not agree on their basic underlying assumptions or world view. As a result, continuing debates over basic assumptions and political conflicts within the sociological discipline prevent the cumulative development of sociology as a science. In spite of these debates and conflicts, possibilities for convergence have been noted, and the work of some prominent pioneers in the field has been shown to involve bridge building between competing paradigms.

In the following section we suggest that the various paradigms really represent alternative *levels* of social reality. Preference for one paradigm over another therefore really represents a choice to focus on one level of social reality instead of on another. Once this choice is made (and it is not necessarily a conscious and deliberate choice), it affects the theorist's perception of social reality so that it becomes very difficult for the theorist to admit the intellectual value or scientific usefulness of concentrating on an alternative level. As Kuhn suggests, once a scientist develops a stake in a particular paradigm, commitment to that paradigm is much more than a rational or merely intellectual commitment.

MULTIPLE PARADIGMS AND MULTIPLE LEVELS OF SOCIAL REALITY

Students, once they are introduced to the sociological perspective, often become impressed with how complex social reality is and how difficult it is to provide any simple explanations in the human and social realms. Numerous social scientists would concur. In spite of the zeal of many sociologists in supporting one particular paradigm over another, probably no sociologist would presume to have a theory that adequately describes and explains people's social behavior or social structure in all of its complexity.

Probably most sociological theorists would find no reason to quarrel with this stance of intellectual modesty, at least in principle. Even Parsons, perhaps the most comprehensive social theorist in American sociology, recognized that he would have to leave to others the task of filling in the empirical details of his abstract intellectual model. But this recognition of the inadequacy of any one theory implies that competing theories may be just as valid for their particular purposes. This is consistent with the point emphasized by Ritzer that insights from all three of the paradigms he identified are essential for helping us understand social life. Thus we should not assume that it is always essential to make a choice as to which theory is right or which is wrong; instead, alternatives theories provide alternative insights into different aspects of social reality. Of course, some theories are superior to others but, of two equally compelling theories, we should not assume that one *must* be right and the other wrong.

One of the basic premises underlying the approach in this book is that there are several analytically distinct levels of social reality on which a theorist may concentrate. In many cases, the differences between alternative theories are about their reality levels. Conflicts between theories or paradigms that emphasize different levels are probably inevitable, since the social reality that each attempts to explain is not the same as the social reality that others attempt to explain. A good analogy is the difference in levels of analysis between a chemist and an ecologist in explaining animal behavior. A chemist might describe the chemical interchanges and transformations in the cells and organs of an animal as they affect the animal's behavior; the ecologist would describe how the animal adapts to its physical habitat and to other life forms in its environment. Both explanations could be correct, but the validity of each would not negate the validity of the other.

Several different ways of classifying the various levels of social reality can be identified but, in this book, the following levels, mentioned briefly in the last chapter, should be noted.

1. *Individual Level.* This level can be further subdivided into the *behavioral* versus the *subjective* level. In either case, it involves a concentration on the individual as the most elementary unit of analysis. Often the focus is not so much on the individual as such, but on units of behavior or social actions of the individual. Many social psychologists emphasize this level, as do reductionist sociologists such as Homans.

2. *Interpersonal Level.* Social reality at this level involves interaction between individuals, with all that this means in terms of symbolic communication, mutual adjustment, negotiation of appropriate interdependent lines of action, interpersonal cooperation or conflict, and joint or interlocking patterns of adaptation to the larger environment. Again, this level is the domain of social psychologists. Two major theoretical perspectives that focus on this level are symbolic interaction theory and exchange theory (although both discuss the individual level as well).

3. *Social Structural Level.* The reality of the social structural level is more

abstract than either of the two preceding levels. Its focus is not the individual or individual actions or interactions but the *patterns* of action and the *networks* of interaction that are inferred from observation of regularities and uniformities over time and space. The most elementary units of social reality at this level can be seen as social *positions* (defined in terms of more or less stable linkages with other positions) and social *roles* (defined in terms of the shared behavior expectations for persons occupying the various positions). The focus may be small social structures (friendship groups, athletic teams, etc.), but the concern is frequently with bigger social structures such as large-scale associations, social institutions, and total societies. Concentrating on the social reality of a total society will inevitably require broad generalizations that ignore the intricacies and complexities of the dynamics of face-to-face interaction between unique individuals. Two major theoretical schools that deal with this level include functional theory and conflict theory.

4. *Cultural Level.* This level is represented by the meanings, values, symbols, norms, and overall world view shared by the members of a society (or a segment thereof). In the broadest sense of the term culture consists of the enduring products of human action and interaction,[51] including the realm of material artifacts produced by human beings and the realm of nonmaterial culture. Several major components of nonmaterial culture were listed by the anthropologist Tylor, in his often quoted definition that culture is ''that complex whole which includes knowledge, belief, art, morals, law, custom, and any other capabilities and habits acquired by man as a member of society.''[52] The items that could be listed as material culture are equally broad, ranging from the creations of artists to the technology represented on a factory floor.

Whether one concentrates on material or nonmaterial culture, the reality of culture can be studied independently of the social structures or interpersonal relations involved in its creation or diffusion. Thus one may trace the growth of transportation technology, for example, from the invention of the wheel to modern space rockets (although a shorter range of development would probably be more fruitful). Similarly, one may compare and contrast different societies, or different stages in any one society, in terms of differences in value orientations or underlying world views.

In a way, this book will build on the notion of alternative levels of social reality by treating various theoretical perspectives according to the level of social reality on which they center. However, these distinctions do not represent empirically discrete categories; they are analytical. *Empirically,* individuals act and interact with one another. From this action and interaction certain regularities or patterns may emerge that become built into individuals' expectations and subsequently guide and con-strain their future interaction. Also, individuals' actions and interactions generate and maintain (or change) certain shared meanings, values, norms, symbols, and material artifacts. *Analytically,* one may choose to concentrate on the individual or individuals' actions, on the dynamics of interpersonal relations, on the structure or patterns of interaction that emerge, or on the cultural products that are created, and recreated, through interaction.

Although the sociological enterprise is concerned primarily with the social structural level, some sociologists are constrained by their commitment to a positivistic or scientific-empirical approach to focus on the individual or individual behavior. Social structure is an abstract, nonobservable concept. Only individuals and individual behaviors are observable. How, then, can an empirical science be built on an abstract and elusive concept such as social structure? The answer to this question requires us to recognize that even though the concept of social structure is abstract, its reality is still inferred from empirical phenomena. However, the concept points not to the empirical phenomena of individuals and their actions as such, but to the *organization* of actions and interaction into more or less stable patterns. This is fundamental to modern systems theory, as we will see in the final chapter, even though the proponents of systems theory are clearly committed to an objective, empirical approach.

Even though sociology is largely concerned with social structure, many specific areas of study deal with more than one level. For example, we noted that social psychology is concerned with both the individual and interpersonal relations. Also, the area of study broadly termed "culture and personality" is concerned with both the individual and the culture, particularly the formation of personality patterns in terms of prevailing patterns of culture. The same thing is true for "social structure and personality." Finally, "social movements" is about both interpersonal relations (particularly those that emerge outside established institutional forms) and social structure (particularly structural deficiencies that stimulate the emergence of noninstitutionalized forms of action and interaction).

Conflict between those who focus on different levels is not likely to erupt as long as those with different intellectual preferences work within their own particular subject matter. But for those who wish to work with a broader view of their subject (such as social theorists often do), the differences in scope can easily become transformed into differences in fundamental images of the subject matter. In this way the conflicts between competing paradigms, which were discussed earlier, may be born.

If we look again at Ritzer's three fundamental paradigms we see that the differences among them may partially reflect differences in the level of social reality on which each focuses. For example, the social facts paradigm relates mostly to the social structural instead of the individual level. The social definition and social behavior paradigms both involve a lower-level focus. Both emphasize the individual; the social definition paradigm deals with the subjective dimensions of human behavior, while the social behavior paradigm concentrates on overt behavior.

This possibility of correspondence between alternative paradigms and alternative levels of social reality should not be pushed too far. Conflicts between competing paradigms or competing theoretical perspectives are not due solely to the differences in level of social reality on which each concentrates. There are also significant conflicts *within* levels. Within the social structural level, for example, a major conflict exists between functionalism and conflict theory; the difference between them is so basic and so profound that Friedrichs and Kinloch treat them as opposing paradigms.[53] In contrast, Dahrendorf simply juxtaposes the fundamental images of society provided by these two perspectives as the "two faces" of society, thereby implying that each model presents only a partial picture of social reality and that both models are needed for a well-rounded theoretical perspective.[54]

Ritzer suggests that the differences between functional (or consensus) theory and conflict theory are exaggerated by elevating these theories to the status of paradigms. He treats them as opposing theories within the social facts paradigm. That is, both theories discuss social structures external to individuals that exert a constraining influence on individuals; in this image of social reality, both theories differ from Ritzer's other two paradigms. The difference between functional theory and conflict theory lies not in their fundamental image of social reality but in the dimensions and dynamics of social structure that they emphasize.

Various efforts have been made to integrate or reconcile functional theory and conflict theory in a more sophisticated way than Dahrendorf has. Coser, for example, emphasizes the integrating functions of conflict; van den Berghe points out that both perspectives rest on the notion of social equilibrium; and Friedrichs suggests the possibilities of a dialectical snythesis between the two perspectives.[55] The various efforts at integration have not really been very convincing thus far, but belief in the possibilities of ultimate reconciliation is consistent with Ritzer's analysis of these two persepctives as sharing the same fundamental paradigm—a paradigm that stresses the social structural level of social reality.

Other differences within levels can be cited. As noted earlier, theories that focus on the individual level can be divided according to whether they emphasize overt behavior patterns or subjective processes. Those who emphasize overt behavior maintain that subjective processes are not amenable to empirical observation or measurement, while those who take a subjectivist approach insist that the objectivist approach is superficial and that the distinctive character of human action can only be understood in terms of its subjective meanings. Similarly, at the cultural level, one may emphasize material culture or nonmaterial culture, or patterns of change that are linear or cyclical, or mass culture versus elite culture, or cultural creativity as reflective of social structure, as influential on social structure, or as compensations for inadequacies of social structure. These distinctions point to the importance of alternative or conflicting approaches *within* levels of social reality as well as *between* levels of social reality.

Why does a theorist focus on one level of social reality as opposed to another? Also, why does a theorist choose to emphasize one particular approach within that level as opposed to another? A thorough answer to these questions is beyond our primary purpose here and is more properly dealt with in the "sociology of sociology" instead of sociological theory as such.[56] However, as noted in Chapter 1, theory development represents one form of response to the universal human need to understand and explain experience. Thus theorists whose individual social experiences differ may be expected to differ in the approach they take to theory.

Another possible approach to explaining a theorist's preference for one level over another or one emphasis within a particular level over another has to do with the dynamics of the struggle for prestige within the normative patterns of the intellectual or academic community. Individuals establish reputations in the intellectual community as they develop their distinctive theoretical perspectives. But, as a theorist develops his or her perspective, it is also necessary to demonstrate its value and validity against competing alternative perspectives.

Typically, a proponent of a new theory will argue that it represents an improvement on existing theories, perhaps correcting their deficiencies and inadequacies and providing a superior, more comprehensive, or more scientific picture of the subject matter. Naturally, the differences between theories are accentuated in this process. This underscores the point made earlier that there is a polemical dimension to most theories, particularly in their early days.

This is all consistent with the normative patterns that govern the intellectual community. These norms call for a self-consciously critical stance toward existing explanations, thereby encouraging, at least to a degree, theoretical innovation. As we examine the contributions of several major theorists in the chapters that follow, it will be important to indicate the intellectual context within which these theorists worked and to show how the theoretical advances that they made were developed, in part, in opposition to already existing theoretical approaches.

SOCIAL REALITY CONSTRUCTION AND THE DEVELOPMENT OF SOCIAL THEORY

Whatever the specific approach a theorist takes, the development of a theory represents one form of reality construction. (The word "construction" is used here in a much broader sense than when the goals of those involved in "formal theory construction" were being considered earlier.) *Reality construction* is a term used by Berger and Luckmann to describe the process whereby people continuously create, through their actions and interactions, a shared reality that is experienced as objectively factual and subjectively meaningful.[57] We must resist the temptation to get embroiled in a philosophical discussion of what is reality or whether there is any reality other than a socially constructed reality that we can comprehend. Whatever philosophers may say about ultimate reality, sociologists working within the philosophical tradition of phenomenology (such as Berger and Luckmann) insist that all of our knowledge of objective facts in the real world is conditioned or colored by the social matrix in which it is acquired, transmitted, or learned. In other words, we can never comprehend reality except within the framework of the social processes in which we are involved.

These social processes profoundly affect our cognitions, or forms of knowledge about reality, and also the very structure of our subjective consciousness. A primary strategy of phenomenologically oriented social theorists is to bracket (or withhold judgment on the truth value of) the statements of belief or knowledge that purport to describe reality and to focus instead on the structure of consciousness, particularly intersubjective (or shared) forms of consciousness. Quite bluntly, perhaps we cannot pretend to understand reality as such, but we can study the *beliefs* people have about reality, and we can relate the forms of their knowledge and beliefs to the patterns of interaction in which they are involved and the type of society in which they live.

Even though the phenomenologist's stress on subjective consciousness conflicts sharply with the objectivist (or positivistic) orientation of many of those involved in formal theory construction, both approaches recognize the tentativeness of any statements we might make about social reality. The phenomenologist insists that we cannot know reality except through the form in which it is manifested in intersubjective consciousness; the theory-constructing positivist concedes that our knowledge of social reality is based on measurements taken of empirical indicators that may or may not adequately reflect the underlying social reality in which the theorist is really interested.

Yet the differences in fundamental assumptions about social reality are profound. The objectivist or positivist assumes that there is a more or less stable objective world of social facts external to individuals' consciousness that can be apprehended through appropriate measurement techniques. The phenomenologist focuses on the social processes whereby that which *seems* to be objective social reality is socially created and experienced as objectively factual in individuals' subjective consciousness.

Regardless of the degree of correspondence that might exist between objective reality and subjective consciousness of that reality, a major part of the reality that we experience in everyday life is socially constructed. This reality is largely symbolic in nature. Even the hard facts of the physical environment are represented to our consciousness through symbols. These symbolic representations indicate to us the meaning of the various objects we encounter in the physical environment and suggest appropriate responses. The ability to create and manipulate symbols enables human beings to transcend many of the limitations imposed by their physical environment and biological endowments. For example, by using symbols, human beings develop a technology that allows them to use resources of the physical environment to construct an aircraft whereby they can partially transcend the limitations of gravity and space.

Although constructing an aircraft or a bridge or a flower garden or other material artifacts out of various physical resources obviously expresses human creativity, the development of legal codes, social organizations, family customs, literature, religious beliefs, and philosophical systems is equally representative of human creativity. Much of the reality that we experience every day is nonmaterial symbolic reality that is constructed through human action and interaction.

This emphasis on the symbolic nature of social reality and on its creation and maintenance through communication is the central theme of Duncan's analysis of social reality.[58] He insists that symbols are not merely the reflection or manifestation of some other type of reality that is nonsymbolic. Instead, the essential nature of social reality is that it is symbolic. Symbols are not merely the medium of social reality; they are its essence. The very nature and characteristics of social relations and social order are defined through symbolic communication.

Berger and Luckmann emphasize both the objective and the subjective dimensions of social reality, but their views on its symbolic nature are essentially similar to those of Duncan. For Berger and Luckmann, society itself and its various institutions are created and maintained or changed through human action and interaction. Even though society and social institutions may seem to be objectively real, their reality is based on subjective definitions created in the process of interaction. The apparent objectivity of social reality results from the social reinforcement provided by others who share similar subjective definitions. At the highest level of generality, human beings create symbolic universes of meaning (or overarching world views) that order and legitimate their social forms and give meaning to the various facets of their everyday experiences.

This process may break down for various reasons; when it does, the result is widespread anomie or, literally, feelings of meaninglessness. Preventing this breakdown and the resulting meaninglessness and disorganization depends heavily on maintaining the belief that our world view is not merely a humanly or socially contrived one. People generally desire a world view based on something more substantial or certain than mere shared social definitions. This feeling of certainty results when there is widespread consensus that our world view is grounded in some objective ultimate reality whose existence does not depend solely on social definitions. This ultimate reality may be seen as transcendent (as in many of the great religious traditions) or as empirical (as in various materialistic world views). In any case, this belief in the objective reality of our world view helps to overcome the precariousness of our social definitions and give stability to the social order and ultimate meaning to our individual lives.

Actually, Berger and Luckmann are interested in the reciprocal relationship of people and society. Understanding this reciprocal relationship helps us to see how society is both objective and subjective. Through their creative activity, human beings construct society and various other aspects of social reality; the social reality thus created then confronts the individual as an external, objective reality; individuals then internalize this reality so that it becomes a part of their consciousness. In other words, people create society, but society, in turn, creates people. Berger and Luckmann use the terms *externalization, objectification,* and *internalization* to describe the dialectical relationship between human beings and society.[59] Externalization refers to the creative activity of human beings; objectification to the process whereby the results of this creative activity confront individuals as objective reality, and internalization to the process whereby the external reality becomes a part of individuals' subjective consciousness.

The interdependence between human beings' creative activity and social reality is sometimes overlooked, however. Lack of insight into this interdependence can lead to the view that people are constrained and coerced by various social forces over which they have no control. Efforts to explain alienation from society can be found in this deterministic view. From Marx to contemporary students of alienation, human beings are seen as suffering from a malaise that results from the obligation for them to conform to the demands of a social world that is beyond their capacity to control or to change and that stifles their creativity and inhibits their development as human beings. Yet, in spite of all the coercion and exploitation that individuals might be obliged to endure, given the unequal distribution of power and of resources needed for survival, power structures are created by human beings and, in principle, can be changed as a result of changes in people's definitions of how they should relate to one another. Power structures and social classes are not part of the objective environment in the same sense that a river or a mountain range that might divide two groups is part of the natural environment.

Failure to appreciate the reciprocal interdependence between human beings' creative activity and social reality can also lead to distortions and limitations in developing sociological theory. The stress on external social facts by the theorists identified by Ritzer as representative of the social facts paradigm might easily lead to failure to appreciate their origins and maintenance in subjective definitions and their socially contrived or constructed character. Similarly, the emphasis of those involved in formal theory construction is based on the notion that there is some objective social reality, external to and independent of individuals' subjective definitions and beyond their control, that the sociologist must measure and analyze. In Berger and Luckmann's terms, perhaps this emphasis could be seen as a one-sided emphasis on objectification.

To be sure, some recognition is given by objectivists to the process of internalization; that is, they acknowledge the profound influence of the various social facts they identify on the formation of the human personality and on individual behavior. But the process of externalization, of human creation of social reality, is largely ignored. The result is a one-sided emphasis on the objectivity of social facts and a minimizing of the importance of the subjective definitions on which the reality of objective social facts depends.

This emphasis on the objectivity of social facts is understandable, given the commitment to develop sociology as a science. The basic underlying world view of science is that its subject matter constitutes an objective reality external to the individual that exhibits a degree of orderliness because it is governed by deterministic laws that can be discovered through various techniques of empirical investigation. Both in the early days of sociology and today, many sociologists identify so strongly with the natural sciences that they assume that social reality is of the same nature as the reality of the physical world. This means that they forget that social reality is essentially symbolic, created continuously through subjective definitions developed in interaction.

But science itself, in any field, is a product of human creativity; that is, it involves the process of social construction of reality, as discussed earlier. Essentially, a science is a highly systematized set of symbols whereby scientists represent to themselves some aspect of reality in order to understand or explain it. In the natural sciences this reality may exist apart from the symbolic representation of it. Nevertheless, the symbols used in this representation are not part of that objective reality; they are socially constructed. In the social sciences the reality itself, not just the symbolic representation of it in a scientific discipline, is socially constructed and consists mostly of shared subjective definitions. Thus sociological theory represents an effort to construct a science of subject matter that is itself socially constructed. Some social theorists, however, borrowing the goals and techniques of the natural sciences, seem to forget the socially constructed nature of social reality and assume that social reality is objectively real, like natural phenomena, independent of individuals' intersubjective social definitions.

In summary, the position taken here is that Berger and Luckmann's perspective on the social construction of reality can be applied to sociological theory just as to any other cultural creation. As we examine several dominant theories in the chapters that follow, remember that they represent alternative ways of representing the major elements of social reality so as to conform to the ideals of science while, at the same time, being true to the nature of social reality as a product of human creative activity. There has been considerable tension between these goals of being both scientific and humanistic, tension that is hardly resolved to this day. On the one hand, the ideals of science dictate that social reality be regarded as objectively real; on the other hand, recognition of the socially contrived nature of social reality, its subjective dimension, and its symbolic character make conformity to the patterns of natural science difficult and, to some, suspect. Considering this alternative and those discussed earlier regarding the various levels of reality on which a theorist may focus, it is not surprising that sociology has a multitude of theories.

Summary

This chapter has explored some of the issues involved in the development of sociological theory. Sociological theory differs from the implicit, taken-for-granted theories of everyday life in that it reflects a deliberate self-conscious effort to be objective and systematic in attempting to analyze or explain social reality. This commitment is clearly manifested in the efforts of those involved in formal theory construction.

The general strategy of formal theory construction was examined briefly to help us identify the formal properties of a scientific theory. The major components of theory that were identified included concepts, variables, classification systems, and propositions. Propositions were identified as statements that relate two or more variables, including either an independent and a dependent variable or two or more mutually interdependent variables. A theory consists essentially of a set of propositional statements. The ultimate goal in developing a theory is to explain variations in one or more dependent variables with sufficiently high probability that predictive statements can be made that can be tested empirically. However, even if clear-cut predictive statements cannot be derived, a theory can still aid our understanding by providing an intellectual model that can be used to interpret some phenomenon.

Even though scientific theories are more explicit and objective than everyday life theories, they also rest on a foundation of implicit, taken-for-granted assumptions. These assumptions include the underlying image that scientific theorists have of their subject matter and their basic value commitments. The concept of *paradigm* was used to portray these underlying images and assumptions. Sociology was shown to be a multiple-paradigm science. The three dominant paradigms discussed included the *social fact* paradigm, the *social definition* paradigm, and the *social behavior* paradigm. Although fundamental disagreements exist among these three paradigms, there are possibilities for reconciliation because of the nature of the subject matter of social reality.

Opposing paradigms may be seen as focusing on different *levels* of social reality. Four different levels of social reality were identified: the individual, the interpersonal, the social structural, and the cultural. Regardless of the level of social reality that a theorist analyzes, it must be recognized that social reality is symbolic in nature, it is socially constructed through the actions and interactions of human beings, and it must be dealt with at the subjective as well as objective level.

In the chapters that follow the reader is invited to examine some selected alternative theories seriously in the light of the specific intellectual purposes that the various theorists set for themselves and to discover what new insights might be gained by applying these theories to social reality as we experience it today.

The selection and organization of theories in these chapters are designed to represent alternative emphases within levels. Our strategy for discussing the theorists will be to indicate their basic assumptions about social reality and to identify the major concepts and propositions that can be derived from their theories, particularly as they have been incorporated into the contemporary sociological perspective. This will necessarily be a highly selective process that will be guided by the commitment to be both systematic in covering the major ideas of the theorists and relevant in making applications of these ideas to our contemporary social experiences. The commitment to being systematic owes a great deal to the approach of those involved in formal theory construction, but without their objectivist assumptions about social reality; the concern for their basic assumptions and underlying world views is based heavily on Kuhn's and Ritzer's uses of scientific paradigms. Above all, sociological theory is seen as the product of the social construction of reality as this process has been analyzed by Berger and Luckmann.

Footnotes

1. Robert M. MacIver, *Society: A Textbook of Sociology* (New York: Rinehart, 1937), pp. 476–477.
2. George A. Lundberg, *Foundations of Sociology* (New York: Macmillan, 1939), p. 13.
3. See, for example, Jack P. Gibbs, *Sociological Theory Construction* (Hinsdale, Ill.: Dryden, 1972). Gibbs describes the essentials of formal theory construction as follows: " Reduced to its essentials, a mode of formal theory construction stipulates: (1) major divisions or parts of a theory, (2) basic units of a theory (for example, statements in the form of empirical assertions), (3) criteria by which basic units are distinguished as to type and identified, (4) rules by which statements are derived from other statements, (5) the procedures for tests of statements derived from the theory, (6) rules for the interpretation of tests, and (7) criteria for assessing theories" (op. cit., pp. 7–8).
4. In the opening chapter of his book on sociological theory, Larson touches on this debate by contrasting the views of William Whewell (who stressed the creative contribution of the mind in conceptualizing phenomena) and John Stuart Mill (for whom conceptualization is merely recognizing and naming what is in the facts themselves). See Calvin J. Larson, *Major Themes in Sociological Theory* (New York: David McKay, 1973), pp. 6–12ff.
5. John C. McKinney, *Constructive Typology and Social Theory.* (New York: Appleton-Century-Crofts, 1966), p. 9.
6. Ibid., pp. 9–10.
7. See Paul Davidson Reynolds, *A Primer in Theory Construction* (Indianapolis: Bobbs-Merrill, 1971), pp. 45–58, for a brief overview of the distinction between *primitive* and *derived* concepts.
8. Ibid., pp. 49–51.
9. William Skidmore, *Theoretical Thinking in Sociology* (London: Cambridge University Press, 1975), pp. 13–14.
10. Larson, op. cit., pp. 14–16.
11. The patient role has been succinctly analyzed from a sociological perspective by Parsons, and we need not dwell further on this example. See Talcott Parsons, *The Social System* (New York: Free Press, 1951), p. 285. Parsons discussed the role of the sick person as a type of deviant behavior that includes the elements of dependency and a claim on the services of others.
12. See McKinney, op. cit., for an analysis of the use of constructed types in sociological theory and research. Reichenbach also recognized the importance of distinguishing between different levels of concepts in his threefold distinction among *concreta, abstracta,* and *illata. Concreta* are concepts that refer to actual physical things or phenomena that are directly observable. *Abstracta* are concepts based on the aggrega-

tion of individual phenomena. For example, an individual birth or an individual move from one geographical area to another will qualify as *concreta,* while birthrates or mobility rates would be examples of *abstracta.* A *rate* for any phenomenon is, by definition, based on the compliation of individual events for a particular population. *Illata* are concepts that are not directly observable, but their existence is inferred from observable phenomena. The concept of intelligence, as opposed to IQ test scores, noted previously, might serve as an example. See Hans Reichenbach, *The Rise of Scientific Philosophy* (Berkeley and Los Angeles: University of California Press, 1962), pp. 263-264.

13. In popular usage the distinction between a group and an aggregate is often overlooked. Thus people often speak of a set of persons as a group, regardless of whether or not there is any interaction or shared activity.

14. See David Riesman, *The Lonely Crowd,* written in collaboration with Reuel Denney and Nathan Glazer (New Haven, Conn.: Yale University Press, 1950).

15. This distinction is typically emphasized as crucial by research methodologists and statisticians. For an example, see Hubert M. Blalock, *Social Statistics* (New York: McGraw-Hill), pp. 11-16. See also Janet Saltzman Chafetz, *A Primer on the Construction and Testing of Theories in Sociology* (Itasca, Ill.: F.E. Peacock, 1978), p. 55.

16. See Hans L. Zetterberg, *On Theory and Verification in Sociology,* 3rd edition (Totowa, N.J.: Bedminister, 1965), pp. 5-10.

17. Aristotle, *Organon: Posterior Analytics,* Book 2, Chapter 11, in Richard McKeon, ed., *Basic Works of Aristotle* (New York: Random House, 1941), pp. 170-171ff.

18. Zetterberg, op. cit., p. 15.

19. Ibid., p. 17.

20. See George C. Homans, *The Human Group* (New York: Harcourt, Brace and World, 1950), pp. 110-113.

21. Zetterberg, op. cit., p. 17.

22. Ibid., pp. 32-33.

23. Reynolds, op. cit., pp. 76-82.

24. See Norman Campbell, *What is Science?* (New York: Dover, 1952), especially Chapter V.

25. See Leon Warshay, *The Current State of Sociological Theory* (New York: David McKay, 1975), Chapter 6, for a discussion of the contrast between this and opposing views.

26. In addition to Gibbs, op cit., and Zetterberg, op. cit., see Hubert B. Blalock, *Theory Construction: From Verbal to Mathematical Formulations* (Englewood Cliffs, N.J.: Prentice-Hall, 1969); Robert Dubin, *Theory Building* (New York: Free Press, 1969); Jerald Hage, *Techniques and Problems of Theory Construction in Sociology* (New York: Wiley, 1972); and Arthur L. Stinchcombe, *Constructing Social Theories* (New York: Harcourt, Brace and World, 1968).

27. Warshay, op. cit., pp. 108-127.

28. See Abraham Kaplan, *The Conduct of Inquiry* (San Francisco: Chandler, 1964).

29. Skidmore, op. cit., pp. 55-71 and Chapters 4 and 5. Skidmore treated exchange theory as an example of a deductive theory and functionalism as an example of a pattern theory. We will consider both theories in subsequent chapters, although not necessarily with Kaplan's distinction in mind.

30. Ibid., pp. 64-65.

31. See Robert A. Friedrichs, *A Sociology of Sociology* (New York: Free Press, 1970).

32. Alvin W. Gouldner, *The Coming Crisis of Western Sociology* (New York: Basic Books, 1970).

33. Edward Shils, "The Calling of Sociology," pp. 1405–1448 in Talcott Parsons et al., eds., *Theories of Society,* 1-volume edition (New York: Free Press, 1961).

34. Thomas S. Kuhn, *The Structure of Scientific Revolutions,* 2nd edition (Chicago: University of Chicago Press, 1970).

35. See Margaret Masterman, "The Nature of a Pardigm," pp. 49–89 in Imre Lakatos and Alan Musgrave, eds., *Criticism and the Growth of Knowledge* (Cambridge: Cambridge University Press, 1970).

36. Friedrichs, op. cit., p. 55.

37. Nisbet identified the following "unit-ideas" as the fundamental themes with which most of the major figures in the early history of sociology were concerned in one form or another: community, authority, status, the sacred, and alienation. Each of these terms is contrasted, respectively, with the following opposing concepts; society, power, class, secular, and progress. See Robert Nisbet, *The Sociological Tradition* (New York: Basic Books, 1966).

38. See Nicholas S. Timasheff, *Sociological Theory: Its Nature and Growth* (New York: Random House, 1966), pp. 313–322. These basic sociological principles include the idea that social phenomena are not entirely reducible to nonsocial facts, an emphasis on interaction as the basic unit of sociological analysis, the notion that stable patterns of interaction can be considered as a system, concern for the functions performed within such systems in satisfying needs, sensitivity to the numerous alternative social processes manifested within social systems, and recognition of culture as a major source of influence on individuals.

39. See George Ritzer, *Sociology: A Multiple Paradigm Science* (Boston: Allyn and Bacon, 1975).

40. Perhaps the best single source in which Durkheim articulated and developed this perspective on the objective reality of social facts is in his *Rules of Sociological Method,* translated by Sarah A. Solovay and John H. Mueller and edited by George E. G. Catlin (New York: Random House, 1964). This perspective was basic to all of his other works as well, as we will see in a subsequent chapter.

41. Although it can be argued that Weber did not always adhere to this principle in his substantive analyses, his image of the subjective nature of social reality as the foundation for sociological analysis is clearly revealed in his methodological writings and in his definition of sociology and its domain. He defines sociology as "a science which attempts the interpretive understanding of social action . . . " and he defines social action to include "all human behavior when and in so far as the acting individual attaches a subjective meaning to it." From Max Weber, *The Theory of Social and Economic Organization,* translated by A. M. Henderson and Talcott Parsons (New York: Free Press, 1964), p. 88.

42. See Talcott Parsons, *The Structure of Social Action* (New York: McGraw-Hill, 1937).

43. Symbolic interaction theory will be dealt with in detail in a subsequent chapter.

44. See B. F. Skinner, *Science and Human Behavior* (New York: Free Press, 1953).

45. See George C. Homans, *Social Behavior: Its Elementary Forms* (New York: Harcourt, Brace and World, 1961).

46. See Emile Durkheim, *The Elementary Forms of Religious Life,* translated by Joseph Ward Swain (New York: Free Press, 1947).

47. Homans, op. cit., 1961, Chapter 18.

48. Ritzer, op. cit., p. 211.

49. Ibid., emphasis in the original.

50. See Theodore Abel, *The Foundation of Sociological Theory* (New York: Random House, 1970).

51. I am indebted to Roy G. Francis for this succinct definition of culture.

52. Edward B. Tylor, *Primitive Culture* (New York: Brentano, 1924), Vol. 1, p. 1.

53. See Friedrichs, op. cit., and Graham C. Kinloch, *Sociological Theory: Its Development and Major Paradigms* (New York: McGraw-Hill, 1977).

54. See Ralf Dahrendorf, *Class and Class Conflict in Industrial Society* (Stanford, Calif.: Stanford University Press, 1959), pp. 157–165.

55. See Lewis A. Coser, *The Functions of Social Conflict* (Glencoe, Ill.: Free Press, 1956); Pierre L. Van den Berghe, "Dialectic and Functionalism: Toward a Theoretical Synthesis," *American Sociological Review,* Vol. 28, October 1963, pp. 695–705; and Friedrichs, op. cit., Chapter 2. See Warshay, op. cit., pp. 60–66, for a cryptic overview of these various reconciliation attempts.

56. See, for example, Friedrichs, op. cit., and Gouldner, op. cit., for explicit concern with such questions.

57. See Peter L. Berger and Thomas Luckmann, *The Social Construction of Reality* (Garden City, N.Y.: Doubleday, 1966).

58. Hugh Dalziel Duncan, *Symbols in Society* (New York: Oxford, 1968). See also Hugh Dalziel Duncan, *Communication and Social Order* (New York: Bedminster, 1962) and Hugh Dalziel Duncan, *Symbols and Social Theory* (New York: Oxford, 1969).

59. Berger and Luckmann, op. cit.

Questions for Study and Discussion

1. Identify a social issue in which you are particularly interested; what specific concepts and propositions could you develop to explain or interpret that issue?

2. To what extent do the efforts of those involved in theory construction rest on an underlying implicit paradigm? What are some of the implicit assumptions in such a paradigm?

3. What is meant by the argument that social reality is symbolic in nature? How does this distinguish social reality from the physical reality of the so-called natural sciences?

4. In what ways does the strategy of theory construction make possible the empirical testing of theories?

5. Do you agree or disagree with the argument that sociology will continue to be a multiple-paradigm science for the foreseeable future? Why or why not? Are there any underlying similarities among the three paradigms identified by Ritzer?

TWO

CLASSICAL EUROPEAN SOCIAL THEORISTS: CULTURAL, SOCIAL STRUCTURAL, AND INTERPERSONAL LEVELS OF ANALYSIS

3

Auguste Comte Versus Pitirim Sorokin and the Problem of Cultural Progress

To what extent does the structure of society reflect fundamental beliefs about ultimate reality? Do different forms of social organization result from differences in basic beliefs or values or styles of thought? For example, do the differences between a religious sect and a scientific research institute result from differences in their intellectual underpinnings or in their methods of gaining knowledge? More broadly, if the basic beliefs and values and dominant world view of a society change, do predictable changes occur in the organizational and institutional forms of that society? Furthermore, to what extent do major historical turning points manifest fundamental shifts in the underlying world view or forms of knowledge? And do such changes in cultural orientation constitute progress, so that modern society can legitimately be seen as superior in some ways to medieval society, for example?

Efforts to answer such questions help us to evaluate the influence of culture on the structure of society. All social scientists agree that it would be impossible to have a social structure without some type of culture (at least a set of symbols for communication), but they do not all agree on the influence that cultural values and ideals may have in determining the nature of the social structure. Subsequent chapters will bear out this conflict. Here, however, we examine the major theoretical ideas of Auguste Comte, considered by many to be the ''father of sociology,'' who believed that the fundamental character of a society's social organization was heavily dependent on the dominant thought patterns or intellectual style of that society; in Comte's perspective, social structure greatly reflects the dominant epistemology.

Consistent with this position, Comte also believed that as our intellect grows and our knowledge expands, society itself progresses (or its potential for progress is expanded).

Beginning our overview of the classic stage of sociological theory with Comte is somewhat arbitrary. Many of his ideas had already been developed by his predecessors. Also, contemporary sociology is probably not indebted to Comte as much as to Emile Durkheim, who followed him by approximately 50 years; Durkheim established sociology as the kind of empirical science that Comte envisioned.

Nevertheless, Comte's contributions to the development of sociology are more significant than often realized; he managed to synthesize creatively many of the opposing currents of thought that others had developed, and he argued forcefully for establishing the science of society on a firm empirical (or positivist) basis. His work, seen in its totality, reflects many of the dilemmas and tensions that still exist in the sociological enterprise: the tension, for example, between stability and progress and between a deterministic scientific perspective and a humanistic moral perspective. Comte even coined the term ''sociology'' to replace his earlier term ''social physics,'' which he rejected when Quetelet began using this term to describe his own pioneering statistical studies.

Comte's focus was on the cultural level of social reality. Thus we will explore the possibilities and limits of this type of approach. After our discussion of Comte, we will examine the work of a major twentieth-century sociologist, Pitirim Sorokin, who also concentrated mainly on the cultural level but whose model of sociocultural change contrasted sharply with Comte's. In spite of their differences, both Comte and Sorokin saw cultural ideas and world views as the key to understanding society.

Finally this emphasis on ideas and forms of knowledge in the realm of *nonmaterial* culture will be contrasted briefly with the work of persons such as Ogburn, who focused on changes in the realm of *material* culture, (i.e., technological development). Briefly, this chapter does more than just present Comte's major ideas; it assesses the fruitfulness of focusing on the cultural level of social reality and examines some of the issues involved in cultural level analysis.

COMTE'S LIFE AND TIMES

To understand the major emphasis of a theorist's ideas, we must know something about the social and intellectual context in which the theorist lived. Auguste Comte was born in Montpellier, France, in 1798. His family was Catholic and monarchist, but young Comte did not maintain these loyalties. He was educated at the *École Polytechnique* in Paris and spent most of his life in Paris, where he experienced its turbulent social, intellectual, and political climate. Comte was a recalcitrant and rebellious student who left the *École* after a student uprising in support of Napoleon was put down.

Comte began his professional career by tutoring in mathematics. Although he had been trained in mathematics, his true interests were human and social affairs. These interests began to be nourished under the influence of Saint Simon, who employed Comte as his secretary and with whom Comte collaborated closely in developing his own early work. The personalities of the two men complemented one another; Saint Simon was an activist, impulsive, energetic, and undisciplined, while Comte was methodical, disciplined, and reflective. After 7 years, however, the partnership broke up as a result of a dispute over the authorship of a collaborated work, and Comte thereafter repudiated his mentor.[1]

In his brief biographical overview of Comte, Coser emphasized Comte's marginal status among French intellectuals.[2] Comte's early career under Saint Simon's tutelage seemed promising; he had the intellectual brilliance and the discipline to establish himself as a respected figure in the French intellectual world. Yet, after the break with Saint Simon, he remained an outsider. This was probably partly because of certain personality quirks; he suffered from paranoia and an overbearing sense of his own importance. Periodically, his paranoiac madness would be violently directed against both friends and adversaries. At one point, soon after beginning a series of lectures in a privately subscribed course, he suffered a severe mental collapse and was hospitalized for "mania." Shortly after his release (without being cured), he unsuccessfully attempted suicide by throwing himself in the Seine and, afterward, continued in a despondent state.

Also, Comte's economic condition was frequently marginal, and he lived in almost continual poverty. He was never able to secure an adequately paid professorial position in France's higher education system. Most of his career was spent in giving private lessons, offering his developing theoretical ideas in a private course paid for by subscriptions, and holding (for a time) the minor academic post of examiner. In later life his livelihood depended on offerings from admirers and followers of his Religion of Humanity.

Comte's involvements with women were equally disastrous,[3] but they are relevant for understanding the evolution of Comte's thought, particularly the shift in emphasis in the later stages of his life from positivism to love. While Comte was developing his comprehensive positivist philosophy, he was married to a former prostitute named Caroline Massin, a long-suffering woman who put up with the emotional and economic hardships of life with Comte. After his hospital release, she patiently attempted to tend to his needs and nurse him back to health, in spite of his lack of appreciation and periodic violent outbursts. However, after several short separations, she finally left him to his misery and madness.

In 1844, 2 years after he had completed his ambitious six-volume *Course of Positive Philosophy*, Comte met Clothilde de Vaux, the woman who was to change his life. Several years younger than Comte, she had been deserted by her husband when she first met Comte, who immediately knew that this was not just another woman. Unfortunately, Clothilde de Vaux was not quite as overwhelmed as Comte; although they exchanged numerous romantic letters, she kept the relationship platonic. Finally, she consented, in writing, to allow the relationship to be physically consummated; she was persuaded by the concern Comte expressed for his own cerebral hygiene (for the sake of which, incidentally, he had earlier radically reduced his reading). The physical consummation apparently did not take place; however, tender feelings continued to be exchanged in the couple's letters. But this romance was not to last long. Clothilde de Vaux suffered from tuberculosis and, just a few months after meeting Comte, she died. Comte's world was shattered; he vowed to devote the rest of his life to the memory of his "angel."

The general tone of Comte's writing changed markedly after his relationship with Clothilde de Vaux. He had already begun work on his second project, the *System of Positive Politics,* which was to be a comprehensive statement of a strategy for practical implemention of the insights of the positive philosophy set forth earlier in *Course of Positive Philosophy.* Instead, the *System of Positive Politics* became a celebration of love, but with the same passion for comprehensive system building that the earlier work reflected.

Intended as a memorial to the memory of his "angel," Comte's "positive politics" was predicated on the idea that the real motive force in people's lives was sentiment, not the steady growth of human intelligence. He proposed a reorganization of society, with numerous rituals designed to arouse pure, unselfish love for the "great being of humanity." His goal was to develop a new religion—the Religion of Humanity—that would tap the fundamental sources of people's emotions and transform them from selfishness and egoism to altruism and love but, at the same time, would not require intellectual assent to supernaturalistic tenets of traditional religion. In other words, the Religion of Humanity was to be compatible with the intellectual standards and requirements of positivism.

The urgency for establishing a positivistic religion was particularly acute in view of the breakdown in the traditional social order, which had earlier culminated in the French Revolution and which Comte feared would lead to anarchy.

While humanity was to be the ultimate object of worship in the new religion, the concept of humanity is too vague for people (especially the masses) to identify with. In order to make this concept tangible, woman or womanhood would be worshipped as the embodiment of the life of the sentiments and as the fullest expression of love and altruism. Repeatedly, Comte argued that feminine sentimentality and altruism are superior to masculine intellect and selfishness in terms of their social value.

In his own life, it seems that Clothilde de Vaux had replaced the Virgin Mother Mary, and had become the symbol and embodiment of "ideal woman." In Freudian terms, Comte's own emotional reaction to the physically unsatisfactory relationship with Clothilde de Vaux involved sublimation of a high order. Their relationship had been a purely platonic one (much to Comte's frustration); after her death this spiritual relationship was transformed by Comte into worship of the feminine spirit that he had found so beautifully and fully incarnated in Clothilde de Vaux's body. In fact, Comte became so enamored by his vision of the positivist society of the future that he even envisioned·the time when perhaps men and women would develop to the point where the sexual act would no longer be necessary and "birth would emanate from woman alone."[4]

The change in emphasis in Comte's writings was distressing to the few admirers he had acquired among the intellectual circles of France and elsewhere. To them, much of his glorification of sentiment and love at the expense of reason and intellect was a repudiation of the positivist ideas espoused in the *Course of Positive Philosophy* and his belief in the steady progress of the human mind, with its promise for a more enlightened society in the future. Comte's acquaintances also found his proposals for extensive regulation of innumerable details of life distasteful and repulsive.

Proposals for such regulation nevertheless continued to pour forth. Even scientific research projects would have to be subordinated to the test of whether or not they contributed to the overriding goal of increasing human happiness and love. Comte was so authoritairan that he seemed unable to imagine an enlightened "positivist" society emerging without him, the self-proclaimed "Founder of Universal Religion, Great Priest of Humanity," showing the way in meticulous detail.[5] To compensate for the lack of intellectual support from his few admirers, Comte eventually tried broadening his appeal to the masses and to various political leaders. He wrote a *Positivist Catechism* for women and workers and an *Appeal to Conservatives* for political leaders. Once the new social order with its new Religion of Humanity was established, Comte expected that other sociologists would follow his lead by serving as moral guardians and priests, providing guidance to industrial and political leaders, and promoting sentiments of altruism and emotional identification with humanity. This was Comte's conception of his mission when, in 1857, he was stricken with cancer and died.

To understand Comte's place in the history of social thought and in the establishment of the sociological discipline, it is necessary to understand the social and political climate in the years after the French Revolution. Many intellectuals who were heirs to the eighteenth-century Enlightenment belief in reason and progress were optimistic, especially in the early days of the Revolution, that the turbulence and destructiveness of the Revolution were only a prelude to a new society that would be based on natural law principles of equality and liberty.

The faith of these Enlightenment philosophers in the power of human reason to reform society according to scientific principles was unbounded. This optimism was manifested in the writings of the various French *philosophes* such as Condorcet and Turgot. Comte's mentor, Saint Simon, reflected this Enlightenment optimism, and Comte himself absorbed much of it. The vision of these rationalists was of a society in which hereditary aristocracy would be replaced by equality, superstition and fear by enlightenment and confidence, coercion by spontaneous cooperation, and religious dominance by the dominance of science. Although the transition would be difficult, the key provided by human reason and scientific progress insured that a new, enlightened, and more humane society established on the basis of equality and liberty was attainable. The ancient traditions that could not stand up to the test of reason and usefulness would be overthrown.[6]

While many intellectuals continued to hold to this optimistic Enlightenment faith in the first half of the nineteenth century, others began to have second thoughts as they viewed the excessive violence of the Revolution and experienced the social turbulence and moral anarchy that followed in its wake. As so often happens after a revolution, a conservative reaction set in, with a renewed appreciation for the resiliency of cultural traditions and their value in helping maintain the very foundation of the social order. This was accompanied by increased skepticism of the naive notion that social institutions can be changed at will simply by applying human reason to reform them to conform to natural laws.[7] Although Comte was heavily influenced by the Enlightenment faith in science, he was equally influenced by the conservative distrust of Enlightenment individualism and the conservative emphasis on the importance of the maintenance of social order against the threat of social anarchy.

Comte's specific creative contribution to the establishment of sociology is seen by Martindale as that of a comprehensive synthesis between two opposing perspectives on the social order: positivism and organicism.[8] As noted earlier, positivism involves wholehearted acceptance of the scientific or naturalistic world view and a strategy for instituting societal reforms. The positivist belief was that the natural laws governing human and social phenomena could be used as a basis for instituting social and political reforms so as to bring society's institutions into conformity with them. The result would be a society in which enlightened reason would lead to cooperative behavior and in which superstition, fear, ignorance, coercion, and conflict would be banished. This viewpoint was basic to Comte's ideas on the steady progress of positivism.

The organic perspective stresses the image of society as an organism, the whole of which is greater than the sum of its parts and that can only be understood as a totality. The parallel to biological organisms should be obvious, although the analogy should not be pushed too far. In any case, the reality of society surpasses the reality of the individual, and the dynamics of society are beyond the power of individuals to control or change significantly. In the organic perspective, the individual is submerged by the overwhelming reality of society and its traditions. Society manifests its own laws, and these laws cannot be improved by various artificial and piecemeal reforms such as those advocated by the positivists.

In the organic perspective there is a danger that the effort to institute reforms may interfere with the natural organic wholeness of society in such a way that society is, in effect, weakened or destroyed. Those who accepted this perspective greatly feared the specter of a society that was not really a true society but simply a mass of individuals with no moral bonds. They feared that the positivist stress on reform, rational self-interest, and individualism would actually destroy the foundations of the social order by undermining the moral consensus that bound individuals together. The conservative organicists saw great value in the accumulated wisdom of a society's traditions, a wisdom to which many generations had gradually contributed and that far surpassed the limited knowledge of those who would destroy these traditions for the sake of promoting scientific rationality and progress.

The organicists even preferred the traditional hierarchical organization of society to the positivist emphasis on liberty and equality, since the organic wholeness of society rested on interdependence between persons whose stations in life differed. This organic system would be undermined, they feared, if everyone acted solely on the basis of self-interest. In short, the conservatives, with their organic image of society, feared that the effort to cure society's ills would destroy the foundations of society.

The political and social climate was equally turbulent. Comte lived in the aftermath of the French Revolution; this included a seemingly continuous series of political upheavals, such as the Napoleonic regime and a succession of monarchical, revolutionary, and republican periods. With such a tumultuous social and political environment, no wonder Comte put a heavy emphasis on the importance of social order. In his judgment, his society was threatened with intellectual and sociopolitical anarchy, and the restoration of order on the basis of sound positivist knowledge of the laws of society was absolutely essential to insure continued progress.

COMTE'S POSITIVIST PERSPECTIVE ON SOCIETY

Although Comte coined the term "positivism," the ideas that this word conveys were not original with him. The positivist beliefs that society was part of nature and that empirical methods of investigation could be used to discover its laws were widespread in Comte's intellectual climate. However, while many of the positivists were progressives, thoroughly committed to overthrowing irrational traditions and reforming society according to natural law so it would be more rational, Comte believed that the discovery of natural laws would disclose certain limits inherent in social reality beyond which reform efforts would be disruptive and counterproductive. Comte's skepticism regarding wholesale reform efforts and his appreciation for traditional pillars of social order categorizes him as a conservative.

Comte saw society as an organic whole whose reality was greater than the sum of its interdependent parts but, to understand this reality, methods of empirical investigation must be utilized in the conviction that society is just as much a part of nature as physical phenomena. Andreski maintains that Comte's insistence that society is part of nature and that gaining knowledge of society requires using the methods of empirical investigation of the other natural sciences is his most valuable contribution to the development of sociology.[9] Certainly it is this conviction, and not any of Comte's substantive theories about society, that pervades the sociological enterprise today.

Comte saw his development of a naturalistic science of society as the logical culmination of a process of intellectual progress through which all the other sciences had already passed. This progress involves movement from primitive *theological* modes of thought, through *metaphysical* explanation and, finally, to establishment of *positive* scientific laws. The field of sociology (or "social physics") was the last to go through these stages because its subject matter was more complex than that of the physical and biological sciences.[10]

Overcoming the absolutist modes of thought of the prepositivist stages, recognizing the relativity of our knowledge, and continually being open to new facts are the distinguishing characteristics that Comte ascribed to the positive approach. He wrote:

> If we contemplate the positive spirit in its relation to scientific conception . . . we shall find that this philosophy is distinguished from the theologico-metaphysical by its tendency to render relative the ideas which were at first absolute. . . . In a scientific view, this contrast between the relative and the absolute may be regarded as the most decisive manifestation of the antipathy between the modern philosophy and the ancient. All investigation into the nature of beings, and their first and final causes, must always be absolute; whereas the study of the laws of phenomena must be relative, since it supposes a continuous progress of speculation subject to the gradual improvement of observation, without the precise reality being ever fully disclosed; so that the relative character of scientific conceptions is inseparable from the true idea of natural laws, just as the chimerical inclination for absolute knowledge accompanies every use of theological fictions and metaphysical entities.[11]

This point of view, expressed rather pompously by Comte, is so common in the sociological discipline today that is difficult to appreciate just how significant a shift it represented in Comte's time.

Having established the general epistemological tone (or mind set) of the positive approach, Comte then describes the specific methods of empirical investigation common to all the sciences: observation, experiment, and comparison. Comte recognized, however, that it is not possible to wait until all the facts are available before formulating a theoretical law, at least tentatively. Even observation, the least sophisticated of these methods, cannot involve simply a registration of all the facts; instead, observation is guided by some implicit theory that directs the observer as to which empirical phenomena are worth noting.

Experimentation as a method is more limited than the other two because of the difficulty of conducting scientific experiments in the social realm. However, the experimental method does not necessarily depend on actual intervention in social processes; natural experiments may occur, such as when some pathological social development interferes with the normal laws of society. Revolutionary political developments would be a case in point.

Comparative analysis can include comparisons between human and subhuman species, between different coexisting societies, and between different stages of a given society. This last type of comparison leads to a fourth method, historical analysis, which is a method especially well suited to social phenomena in that it leads to an understanding of the basic laws of social development.

The idea of using the same methods of empirical investigation as are used in the physical and biological sciences to analyze social phenomena is consistent with Comte's vision of the philosophical unity of all the sciences. Indeed, one of his major purposes in the *Course of Positive Philosophy* was to demonstrate this unity by analyzing the basic philosophical underpinnings of all the sciences, from mathematics and astronomy to sociology.

The unity of the sciences is also demonstrated, according to Comte, in that all the sciences exhibit the same law of intellectual development as they evolve through the three stages of theological, metaphysical, and positive thought. While the basic idea that human and social phenomena are part of nature and can be analyzed by natural science methods was not original with Comte, Comte's contribution was to provide a comprehensive analysis of the underlying philosophical and methodological unity between the so-called natural sciences and social science. The *Course of Positivist Philosophy* is an encyclopedia of the philosophical evolution of all the sciences and a systematic statement of the positivist philosophy that they all manifest in their final stage of development. The topics covered include mathematics, astronomy, physics, chemistry, biology, and social physics (sociology), which are broken down into their various specialties; for example, under physics Comte covers barology, thermology, acoustics, optics, and electrology. For each of the different specialties Comte introduces a basic subdivision between the *statics* and the *dynamics* of the phenomenon in question. Our concern here is limited to his theoretical perspective on society.

The Law of the Three Stages

Although Comte's theoretical perspective included both social statics and social dynamics (or, as sociologists would say today, structure and change), his major interest in the first part of his career was in explaining the dynamics of social progress. Despite the social and intellectual anarchy of his day, he was convinced that European societies, specifically France, were on the threshold of a new social order. Understanding the nature of this new order was essential for overcoming the prevailing anarchy. But establishing reliable predictions of the future requires an understanding of the laws of social dynamics, and this, in turn, depends on historical research, which will reveal and illustrate the operation of these laws. Firmly committed to the belief that historical research would reveal steady human progress,

Comte explained that his overall goal was "to *explain,* as precisely as possible, the great phenomena of the development of the human race, under all its essential aspects, that is to discover by what necessary chain of successive transformations the human race, starting from a condition barely superior to that of a society of great apes, has been gradually led up to the present stage of European civilization."[12] This belief in the inevitability of human progress was consistent with later evolutionary thought. It also reflected the influence of eighteenth-century Enlightenment ideas.

The law of the three stages is Comte's effort to explain the evolutionary progress of the human race from primitive times to the highly developed civilization of nineteenth-century France. This law, perhaps the most famous of Comte's substantive theoretical ideas, is no longer accepted as an adequate explanation of historical change. Also, it is so broad and general that it could not really be subjected to the rigorous empirical testing that Comte claimed to be necessary for establishing sociological laws.

Briefly, the law states that societies (or the human race) evolve through three major stages. These stages are defined in terms of their dominant intellectual style: the *theological,* the *metaphysical,* and the *positive.* (Recall that each of the various sciences also goes through these stages.) Furthermore, the influence of these different modes of thought extends to the institutional patterns and social organization of society. Thus the character of the social structure of society depends on its epistemological style or world view, or the dominant modes of knowing and explaining phenomena.[13]

Comte explains the law of the three stages as follows.

> From the study of the development of human intelligence, in all directions, and through all times, the discovery arises of a great fundamental law. . . . The law is this:—that each of our leading conceptions—each branch of our knowledge—passes successively through three different theroretical conditions: the Theological, or fictitious; the Metaphysical, or abstract; and the Scientific, or positive. In other words, the human mind, by its nature, employs in its progress three methods of philosophyzing, the character of which is essentially different, and even radically opposed. . . . The first is the necessary point of departure of the human understanding; and the third is its fixed and definite state. The second is merely a state of transition.[14]

The distinguishing characteristics of these stages are tersely presented as follows.

> In the theological state, the human mind, seeking the essential nature of beings, the first and final causes (the origin and purpose) of all effects—in short, Absolute knowledge—supposes all phenomena to be produced by the immediate action of supernatural beings.
>
> In the metaphysical state, which is only a modification of the first, the mind

supposes, instead of supernatural beings, abstract forces, veritable entities (that is, personified abstractions) inherent in all beings, and capable of producing all phenomena. . . .

In the final, the positive state, the mind has given over the vain search after Absolute notions, the origin and destination of the universe, and the causes of phenomena, and applies itself to the study of their laws—that is, their invariable relations of succession and resemblance. Reasoning and observation, duly combined, are the means of this knowledge.[15]

This idea of progressive evolution through three intellectual stages was not Comte's alone. The beginnings of Comte's formulation of the law of the three stages were developed while he was associated with Saint Simon, and the basic model was undoubtedly the product of their collaboration. Also, Jacques Turgot had suggested a similar notion of historical progress from primitive modes of thought to modern scientific modes of thought in the eighteenth century.[16] Comte comprehensively systematized and developed the model and linked with it the emphasis on positivism.

For persons today whose world view is shaped by the scientific mentality, the resilience of prescientific modes may be difficult to comprehend. To illustrate the difference that Comte was emphasizing, imagine that we wish to explain a natural phenomenon such as a hurricane. In the theological stage such a phenomenon would be explained as the result of the direct action of a storm god or a supreme deity (depending on the period in the theological stage). In the metaphysical stage the same event would be explained as a manifestation of some immutable law of nature. In the positive stage the hurricane would be explained as a result of a particular combination of air pressures, wind velocity, humidity, and temperature—all variables that can be measured, that change continuously, and that interact to produce the hurricane. Or imagine that we wish to explain someone's violent or antisocial behavior. In the theological stage this might be explained in terms of possession by ᕼome evil spirit or as a result of original sin; in the metaphysical stage it would probably be explained as a result of some violation of a law of nature; and in the positive stage it would be explained in terms of the conditioning effect of the environment in reinforcing or extinguishing various behavior patterns.

The theological stage is the longest period of human history and, for more detailed analysis, Comte subdivides it into the periods of fetishism, polytheism, and monotheism. Fetishism, the dominant mode of thought of primitive societies, involves the belief that all objects are endowed with their own life force. This is eventually superseded by the belief in numerous supernatural beings who, even though they are distinct from objects in nature, nevertheless continue to control all natural phenomena. As the human mind continues to progress the belief in many gods is replaced by belief in one supreme being. Medieval Catholicism represents the culmination of the monotheistic stage.

The metaphysical stage is primarily a transitional stage between the theological and the positive stages. It is marked by a belief in fundamental laws of nature that can be discovered through reason. Protestantism and Deism represented successive accommodations of the theological spirit to the steady rise of the metaphysical spirit. One familiar manifestation of this spirit is expressed in our own country's Declaration of Independence: "We hold these truths to be self-evident. . . ." The idea that there are certain fundamental truths of natural law that can be made self-evident to human reason is basic to the metaphysical mode of thought.

The positive stage is characterized by reliance on empirical data as the ultimate source of knowledge. However, knowledge is always tentative, not absolute; the spirit of positivism manifests a continual openness to new data on the basis of which knowledge is revised and expanded. Reason is important, as it is in the metaphysical period, but it must be guided by empirical data. Rational analysis of empirical data will eventually enable human beings to discover laws, but laws are seen as empirical uniformities rather than metaphysical absolutes.

Relation Between Intellectual Stages and Social Organization

In addition to tracing human intellectual development, Comte wanted to show the social contribution of each stage. When reading the *Course of Positive Philosophy*, one cannot help but note Comte's view that even though prepositive modes of thought were inferior to modern positive modes, in their day these earlier stages performed a valuable contribution to the social order in which they were dominant and contributed in the long run to the continued evolution of the human race. In this evaluation Comte parts company with the progressives who seemed ready to write off most of the history of human thought as a story of one grievously erroneous myth or superstition after another whose cumulative effect was to impede human progress. Thus, for example, even in the earliest days of fetishism, efforts to explain phenomena through primitive superstitions helped to arouse speculative thought and promoted the transition from a nomadic to a settled agricultural way of life. Later, in the polytheistic stage, the emergence of a priesthood promoted the establishment of a speculative class of people who could devote their energies to elaborating and transmitting traditions. In the monotheistic stage under Catholicism, the elaboration of an abstract and transcendental belief system facilitated the separation of the spiritual and temporal power (a development that was of the utmost importance to Comte) which, in turn, promoted the ascendancy of morals over politics.

Above all, prepositive modes of thought promoted consensus on a common set of opinions and beliefs. Such consensus was essential as the primary basis of social order. The evolution of these various modes of thought into more and more general and comprehensive systems was associated with a corresponding enlargement in the size of the group bound together as a social unit, from the earliest extended family and tribe up to the modern nation-state and, ultimately, to all of humanity.

In addition to the contributions the previous stages made to social evolution, each stage also had a particular supportive affinity with the kind of social organization in which it dominated. In other words, in each of the various stages, the dominant patterns of social organization reflected the influence of their respective beliefs and intellectual style. Specifically, Comte felt that the theological stage was supportive of a military type of social organization, while the final positive stage was supportive of an industrial type of social order. The intermediate metaphysical stage was associated with the social dominance of "legists," a term Comte used to designate those who sought to derive social and political doctrines from an understanding of the laws of nature.

Comte's elaborate arguments in support of these relationships emphasize that in the theological stage the legitimating support of religious authority was necessary to inculcate the social discipline necessary for military activity. Military activity was pursued simply because it was the most attractive and simplest way of meeting material needs. Also, both the theological and the military mentalities, as analyzed by Comte, were absolutist.

The rise of an industrial society is stimulated by the growth of positive philosophy and science and, in turn, stimulates additional scientific growth. Scientific knowledge underlies the technological advances that make industrial development possible. Beyond this, both the positive and the industrial mentalities are experimental, not dogmatic, and are continually seeking human progress. The replacement of military with industrial dominance means nothing less than that societies shift their attention from exploiting other societies to exploiting nature.[17] The major social contribution of the metaphysical period was the ideological support it provided for the emergence of the nation-state.

During the theological period, the family was the dominant social unit (although larger groupings would be established for military activities or as a result of military conquest). In the metaphysical period the nation-state became a dominating type of organization. Comte was optimistic that with the emergence of the positive phase, nationalism would be superseded by a social order embracing all of humanity. Implicit in this discussion of the social contribution of the three stages is their effect on human sentiments. Corresponding to intellectual evolution, there is an evolution of sentiments defined by the ever-widening circle with which individuals form emotional bonds. In the earliest stage people identified primarily with the family; later, emotional bonds were extended to the nation-state; finally, people would feel bound to all of humanity.

Comte recognized that the shift from one stage to another is never an abrupt one that represents a clean break with the past and initiation of a completely new stage. Instead, in all periods of history, all three intellectual modes are present to a degree. The difference among stages is in the relative dominance of one mode over the other two. Even in the earliest days of the theological stage, the rudiments of both metaphysical and positive thought were present; primitive positivism was partly represented in the everyday practical knowledge that primitives acquired in the course of coping with their environment. Similarly, even in the most advanced stage of positivism, remnants of the earlier theological and metaphysical modes of thought survive.

Comte would probably explain the persistence of religious explanations of various phenomena among large segments of our modern population in this way. However, most sociologists of religion today would argue that modern religious thought is oriented toward a qualitatively different realm of knowledge than science; for example, science deals with explanations of empirical phenomena, but religion deals with questions of the meaning and purpose of life of the type that scientific methods are not equipped to answer.[18]

The speed of change from one intellectual stage to the next varies in different historical periods. Some periods are marked by fairly high stability, when consensus on basic beliefs and opinions is relatively high and the social organization, political structure, moral ideals, and material conditions exhibit a high degree of harmonious interdependence. In contrast, the periods in which rapid evolution from one stage (or substage) to another is taking place are marked by intellectual and social anarchy. The greater the disruption of the transitional period and the longer it lasts, the more significant is the shift from one evolutionary stage to the next.

Even though the laws of progress insure the long-range evolution from one stage to the next, various secondary factors can accelerate or impede this evolutionary progress. Population growth, for example, can accelerate the process, partially by promoting an increased influence of human intellectual and moral life, which is necessary to control the increased threat of individualism, and partially by stimulating an increase in the division of labor.[19] The evolutionary process can be impeded by the prolonged dominance of a regressive philosophy that results from the conservatives' efforts to cope with anarchy of a transitional period by reimposing the type of mentality appropriate to an earlier period. It can also be impeded by efforts to promote change that are so radical that they destroy the underlying social order necessary for intellectual or social progress to occur.

Comte was extremely bitter in his denunciation of those who would remake society without sufficient awareness of the limitations imposed by the basic laws of progress or of the socially valuable contributions made by earlier evolutionary stages. Both order and progress are essential. Those who would promote progress without being aware of the requirements of order actually contribute to the perpetuation of the transitional state of anarchy.

Principles of Social Order

Consistent with his organic perspective, Comte had a keen appreciation of the harmonious interdependence of the various ''parts'' of society and their contribution to the maintenance of social stability. Although social order could be threatened by social, moral, and intellectual anarchy, it was always ultimately reestablished. Indeed, long periods of history had been characterized by remarkable stability, and part of the task Comte set for himself was to discover the sources of this stability.

Comte's analysis of social order can be divided into two phases. The first is the effort to explain social order empirically, using positivist methods. The second is an effort to promote social order as a normative ideal, using methods that would not be incompatible with positivism but that would touch the sentiments as well as the intellect.

Overall, Comte was more concerned with explaining evolutionary progress than with explaining the stability of a social order, especially in the first part of his career. However, one of the important social contributions of prepositive stages of development was that they promoted intellectual consensus. Such consensus on basic beliefs and opinions is always a primary basis of solidarity in society. Since most of human history was under the dominance of the theological mode of thought, it is not surprising that religion was seen as a major source of social solidarity and consensus. Beyond this the content of religious beliefs motivates individual discipline in the service of goals that transcend individual interests and nourishes the development of emotional attachments that bind individuals together in the social order. This emotional bond is supported by common beliefs and by joint participation in cultic practices.

The importance of religion in supporting social solidarity can be seen in the fact that political and religious authority are usually closely aligned. Even after the institutional separation (or differentiation) between the temporal and spiritual powers, the support of the spiritual power is generally sought to reinforce and legitimate the temporal power. In short, religion has traditionally been the major institution that promotes altruism rather than selfishness. Its past influence in molding opinion stimulated individuals to act spontaneously in the ways that are demanded for the maintenance of the social order.

Indeed, in Comte's view the individual is so completely shaped and molded by the social milieu that the fundamental unit of society is not individuals, but families. It is within the family that the individual is introduced to society. Because the degree of intimacy in the family is so high, the individual's basic instincts are molded by the social sentiments dominant in the family. The family offers in microcosm the experience of dominance and submission, cooperation, and the emergence of altruistic sentiments. Relationships between parents and children link the past to the future, while that between spouses subordinates one of the most powerful natural instincts to social convention and moral codes. Except in rare situations, nobody has escaped the overwhelming socializing influence of the family. For this reason Comte feels justified in treating the family, not individuals, as the fundamental unit of society and as a major foundation of social order.

Social order is also dependent on the division of labor and the economic cooperation that this involves. Individuals undertake economic activity in order to meet their individual needs. However, as a division of labor emerges, individuals' participation in economic activity leads to cooperation, awareness of interdependence, and the emergence of new social bonds on this basis. The division of labor increases with industrialization, and the corresponding growth of specialization promotes individualism. At the same time, the degree of interdependence increases. Thus the stable order of a complex society, in contrast to the episodic and loosely structured character of primitive society, relies on the interdependence fostered by a highly developed division of labor.

On the other hand, there is a danger that the individualism promoted by a high division of labor will be emphasized too strongly at the expense of social solidarity. In view of the inadequacy of the division of labor by itself to bring about a sufficiently high degree of integration, government is necessary to regulate the various "parts" of society and to insure a sufficiently high degree of unity to overcome the disintegrating consequences of the division of labor. Government itself, with its implied division between leaders and followers, is one manifestation of the division of labor.

Comte argues that government is a natural social phenomenon that can be observed in rudimentary form even in primitive societies. However, the scope and power of government is bound to expand as society becomes more complex through the increase in the division of labor. This expansion of government is necessary to compensate for the increased individualism brought about by the increase in the division of labor. In his analysis of the division of labor, as in his analysis of the integrating functions of religion, Comte anticipates some of the major contributions of Durkheim.

The Religion of Humanity

Comte's insight into the beneficial consequences of religion and his prediction regarding the coming of a postreligious, positive stage in human evolution presented him with a perplexing problem. Unlike the radical and revolutionary thinkers of his day, Comte was committed to social order. He feared that the social and intellectual anarchy of his day would destroy the basis for orderly progress. As he looked at history, he recognized that religion had, in the past, been one of the major pillars of social order. It provided the basis for the "universal consensus" in society, and it inspired people's emotional identification with society, helping them to overcome their individual eccentricities and selfishness and promoting altruism. But, in light of the scientific (or positive) perspective, religion was based on fundamental intellectual errors developed initially in the infancy of human intellectual development. The perplexing question Comte faced, then, was that of how social order could be maintained in the positive society of the future, with one of the major traditional bases of social order undermined by positivism.

With characteristic modesty, Comte set out to solve this problem in the second major stage of his career by founding a new religion—the Religion of Humanity—and declaring himself its high priest. This is the second aspect of Comte's concern with social order mentioned earlier. The first aspect involved an objective analysis of the sources of stability in society; the second phase involved promoting social order through the Religion of Humanity as a normative ideal. This was a major subject of Comte's *System of Positive Politics.*

Most scholars agree that Comte's *System of Positive Politics* is not of the same intellectual quality as the earlier *Course of Positive Philosophy.* Some critics maintain that Comte had gone mad by the time he commenced this work. Remember that Comte's ill-fated relationship with Clothilde de Vaux had occurred just before Comte started *Positive Politics.* Coser illustrates the view that a profound change had occurred in Comte's emotional state that adversely affected the intellectual quality of his work. After describing the initial encounter with Clothilde de Vaux, Coser writes: ''Suddenly the cool and methodical mask that Comte had presented to the outside world seemed to dissolve. Comte in love was a Comte transformed. All the previously repressed passionate elements of his nature now come to the fore.''[20]

In describing the *System of Positive Politics,* Coser writes: ''In its pages, Comte now hailed the primacy of emotion over intellect, of feeling over mind; he proclaimed over and over again the healing powers of warm femininity for a humanity too long dominated by the harshness of masculine intellect.''[21] In this same vein, Manuel describes the shift in emphasis by pointing out that Comte went so far as to consider humanity's spiritual well-being threatened by ''excessive absorption in rationalist analysis.''[22] Manuel contrasted the two stages bluntly: ''Between the *Cours* and the *Systeme de politique positive* he had arisen from the depths of misery to a mystical love so overpowering that true disciples looked on in dismay and outsiders scoffed.''[23]

Certainly the shift in emphasis and tone is undeniable. The shift cost Comte dearly in terms of the respect of intellectual admirers and followers. John Stuart Mill, for example, had been impressed with the breadth of the *Positive Philosophy,* but he found the *Positive Politics* antiscientific and authoritarian. Comte attempted to defend himself by insisting that the latter work was not a repudiation of the former but a development of ideas that were latent in the former but had to await the establishment of a firm intellectual footing before they could be expanded. He pointed out that his writings *prior* to the *Course of Positive Philosophy* had stressed the importance of sentiment instead of reason in maintaining the social order. In spite of Comte's efforts to defend himself, his work in the second stage of his career was generally rejected, both by his contemporaries and by many intellectuals since then, as the work of a mad man.

In contrast with this view, Becker defends Comte's *Positive Politics* as a serious effort to develop a system of morals on a scientific foundation (that foundation having been laid in the *Positive Philosophy*). He states unequivocally:

... [C]ontrary to the opinion of many superficial commentators, Comte was well aware of what he was doing—the two ''phases'' of his work were one integral whole. The first period was a systematization that he undertook on a positivistic, scientific basis in order to avoid charges of mysticism which he knew might be leveled against his guiding ideas. The second period was a frank predication of his life work on feeling, love, and morality, which he felt were the basis of his whole position.[24]

Becker goes on to show that Comte's whole position, including the necessary stress on sentiment and morality, were outlined very early in Comte's career.

Becker's purpose, however, was not to defend Comte's elaborate Religion of Humanity; instead, he was concerned with the subordination of science to morals and sought to show that many of the nineteenth-century pioneers in the social sciences actually had incorporated this humanistic moral dimension, which later social scientists have often forgotten, into their work. Becker explains the repudiation of Comte's later work as a result of the fact that it was incompatible with the emerging mechanistic and materialistic view of society.

Comte's Religion of Humanity was a utopian proposal for the complete reorganization of society. Sociology would be the queen of the sciences (just as theology was in the Middle Ages); it would provide a comprehensive explanation of the progress of human knowledge (thereby subsuming all the other sciences) and of the laws of social order and progress. In addition, it would promote an all-embracing system of morals that would unite all people in the worship of humanity and insure the social order necessary for continued progress.

Sociologists would be the intellectual and moral guardians of the new order, and their role would include providing guidance to industrialists and government leaders to insure that their actions are guided by scientific knowledge and moral principles. In short, sociologists would be the spiritual priests of the new social order; under their wise leadership, the members of society would learn that their happiness and well-being, as well as orderly social progress, depends on the development of altruistic sentiments and performance of duties in the service of humanity.

Comte's proposals for a positivist society under the moral guidance of the Religion of Humanity gradually became more and more elaborate. For example, a new calendar was proposed with special days designated to honor great scientists and others who had labored on behalf of humanity and human progress. There would be various rituals and prayers designed to bring about the sublimation of individual desires and absorption into the ''great being of humanity.'' There would be a cult of womanhood with feminine altruistic sentiments celebrated. Comte himself, humanity's high priest, knelt before his own altar (a red plush chair) contemplating a lock of hair from the head of Clothilde de Vaux, and he proposed her grave as a site for sacred pilgrimages.[25]

These details may reflect Comte's compulsive and authoritarian personality.

Remember, however, that he perceived the social and intellectual climate of his day as threatened by anarchy and, like many other intellectuals with an organic perspective, he abhorred and feared anarchy. Also like many other conservatives, Comte admired the unity and the social and intellectual synthesis and harmony that he perceived in the medieval world. Although the conservatives' views of medieval history were distorted, reflecting a nostalgic longing for a harmonious and meaningful past that had never really existed, this image was the basis for comparison with the turmoil of the present.

Whatever the deficiencies and excesses of Comte's elaborate proposals for reorganizing society and founding a new religion, the problems that he faced are indeed crucial from both an intellectual and a moral standpoint. These problems involve the perennial dilemmas of reason versus emotion, intellectual understanding versus moral commitment, and order versus progress. To what extent does the growth in our rational understanding of society erode the moral commitments that make society possible? Can the scientific perspective legitimately be used to guide political decisions and promote progress? It is popular today for philosophers of science to insist that "ought" statements cannot be derived from "is" statements (i.e., values or moral commitments cannot be inferred from an objective scientific analysis), but is this stance an appropriate one considering the grave crises that we face today? Or, on the contrary, is it a way of avoiding responsibility?

Many social scientists today are involved in promoting the practical implementation of the policy implications that they derive from their scientific analyses. Such efforts range from the application of behavior modification strategies in juvenile rehabilitation centers to the use of public opinion sampling techniques to inform political leaders (or would-be leaders) of their constituencies' attitudes and opinions on various issues of public policy.

Even if the broad questions of morality and social values raised in the second stage of Comte's career cannot be answered from within a strictly scientific (or positivist) perspective, they certainly can be broached from a humanistic perspective. The social scientists today who are committed to the ideal of a social science that is objective, analytical, grounded on empirical data, and informed and inspired by humanistic moral values are faithful to the dream of the "father of sociology."

COMTE'S THEORY OF PROGRESS VERSUS SOROKIN'S CYCLICAL THEORY OF CULTURAL CHANGE

One might argue that the various social reorganization proposals made by Comte in the second part of his career reflect loss of faith in the inevitability of evolutionary progress insured by the scientific laws of social dynamics. Certainly he seemed to shift to the view that the evolutionary process must be helped along by human effort. Nevertheless, Comte's faith that the development of positivism would lead to continued progress was firm. His theory implied that history is moving toward a terminal goal and that previous stages of history were important mainly for the contribution they made toward this end. The final stage will be a society in which the intellectual and moral guidance provided by sociologists-priests will enable political leaders to establish policies that insure that people will live together harmoniously and in which humane industrialists will provide the means for people to meet their material needs adequately. Comte shared this model of linear progress toward some final end-state with many eighteenth-century Enlightenment thinkers.

This optimistic faith in the future seems naive today because of events in this century and the prospects for the future. Social scientists today do not share Comte's faith that the future guarantees continued progress, nor do they see human history as manifesting a broad pattern of linear movement toward some ultimate or final stage. Limited areas of linear progress can be discerned, such as the steady advance of technology. But twentieth-century history offers little reason to believe that moral progress has kept pace with material or technological progress.

To provide a contrast with Comte's model of linear progress, we will examine the model of sociocultural change provided by Sorokin, a prophetic twentieth-century sociologist. Sorokin's views on the nature of social reality (i.e., his fundamental image of the subject matter of sociology) correspond closely with Comte's. Both focused on the cultural level of analysis, and both emphasized the crucial importance of intellectual style, world view, or forms of knowledge on patterns of social organization and human behavior.

However, while Comte argued for a linear model culminating in the emergence of the positivist society, Sorokin developed a cyclical model of social change; that is, he believed that historical stages tend to repeat themselves in terms of their dominant cultural mentality, with no ultimate final stage envisioned. These cycles do not involve simple duplications, however; instead, there are numerous variations in the specific forms in which the broad cultural themes are expressed.

Pitirim Sorokin was born in 1889 in Russia and was educated at the University of St. Petersburg. Later he accepted an academic position there, eventually founding and becoming chairman of the Sociology Department. His early academic career was disrupted by the Communist Revolution and, as a result of his involvement in the struggle against communism, he was arrested and sentenced to death. The sentence was commuted to exile and, after several years in Czechoslovakia, he came to the United States in 1924. He began his academic career in this country at the University of Minnesota but, in 1930, accepted a position at Harvard, where he remained for the rest of his professional life. Some indication of his value commitments can be seen in his founding of the Center for Creative Altruism at Harvard; this concern for promoting altruism also characterized Comte's work, it will be recalled.

Sorokin's works reveal a wide-ranging and creative mind, and his writing style is engaging, perceptive, and persuasive. His reputation was international, as revealed by the numerous translations of some of his major works. Nevertheless,

Sorokin's overall theoretical approach does not fit neatly into any of the dominant schools of contemporary sociology. Indeed, he subjects most of the major schools of sociological theory to penetrating and devastating criticism.[26]

Sorokin's Views on Social and Cultural Integration

Sorokin's focus is clearly at the cultural level, emphasizing meanings, values, norms, and symbols as the key to understanding sociocultural reality, but he stresses the interdependence between cultural patterns, society as an interaction system, and the individual personality.[27] The highest possible level of integration of social systems is based on a central set of meanings, values, and "law-norms" that are logically and meaningfully consistent with each other and govern the interaction of the participating personalities. The lowest level at which sociocultural reality can be analyzed is at the level of meaningful interaction between two or more persons.

Even though logico-meaningful integration at the cultural level is emphasized as the foundation for the highest form of social integration, Sorokin made no claim that most action or interaction is integrated in this sense. In fact, he explicitly identified *congeries* at both the cultural and social levels as aggregates or collections of elements that are not integrated in either a causal or a logico-meaningful sense but are simply adjacent in space and time. He pointed out that much of the sociocultural world is made up of just such congeries.

Sorokin's perspective is classified by Martindale as representative of a "purified organicism."[28] This is the final stage of the school of "positivistic organicism" started by Comte. As analyzed by Martindale, Comte's synthesis between the positivistic approach and the organic approach eventually broke down because of the opposing implications of these schools of thought. The result was that the organic perspective was purified of positivist assumptions and implications.

One probable reason that Martindale treats Sorokin as an organicist is Sorokin's emphasis on understanding total sociocultural systems. The organic perspective stresses the independent reality of society and its cultural traditions as an integrated system. Sorokin's analysis of the dynamics of large-scale integrated sociocultural systems in his four-volume masterpiece, *Social and Cultural Dynamics,* is consistent with this approach. Another important reason for considering Sorokin as an organic theorist without positivist assumptions is Sorokin's refusal to limit his conception of truth to empirical data; instead, he indicated a willingness to accept a multidimensional concept of truth and knowledge, with empirical data providing partial knowledge at best. This, along with Sorokin's stress on subjective meanings, sets him apart from the positivist emphasis on empirical data as the only valid source of knowledge.

Sorokin himself denied that Martindale's classification of his approach as an organicist perspective is appropriate. Instead of assuming total integration, Sorokin emphasized the importance of recognizing different levels of integration and of specifying the level at which different aspects of sociocultural reality can be said to be integrated. For example, two elements of culture may be integrated merely because of their link with some third element; this would be a lower level of integration than logico-meaningful consistency between these two elements themselves. In addition, Sorokin insists that many elements of sociocultural reality may represent mere congeries.

For example, religious bookstores and churches in the area of a theological seminary would represent logico-meaningful integration of these particular elements, while the presence on a particular urban block of an adult movie theater, a church-sponsored nursery school, and the city library would probably represent congeries (unless, of course, the parents of the nursery-school children go to the library after dropping off their toddlers and then to the theater when they tire of reading; in this case these elements would be related merely by being linked to their common clientele).

Also, in contrast to the organicists' emphasis on invariable patterns of growth and decline that cultural systems go through, Sorokin emphasizes the high degree of variability that they exhibit. Basic cultural themes may be repeated, but their repetition exhibits variable patterns. Each stage of a society's history thus reveals some elements that are recurrent (i.e., repetitious of a previous stage) and some that are unique. Sorokin refers to patterns of long-range cultural change as "varyingly recurrent." As he explains such patterns:

> ... [S]ince there is no one permanent linear trend, and since the directions change, historical and social processes incessantly undergo ever new variations of the old themes. In this sense they are filled with surprise and are seldom predictable in their totality. In this sense history as a whole never repeats itself, and the entire historical process has a unique aspect at any point of its existence, an aspect which is perhaps predictable only in its unpredictability.[29]

Sorokin's emphasis on the recurrence of basic themes is intended to refute the idea that historical change can be represented as a linear process involving movement in just one direction; in this Sorokin differs from Comte's belief in steady progress in human intellectual development.

Instead of classifying his work as an organic theory, Sorokin prefers to consider his approach an "integralist" perspective. As far as the development of sociological theory is concerned, this means that the *valid* parts of divergent and opposing theories are seen as complementary, while only their invalid parts are irreconcilable. Sorokin attempts to demonstrate this complementarity in his summary evaluations of the major types of theory that he criticized: the singularistic-atomistic type, the cultural system type, and the social system type.[30] Sorokin's own approach hinges on recognizing the analytical distinctions among, and the interdependence of, the cultural level of superorganic reality, the social structural level, and the individual level and on distinguishing clearly between *systems* (at these levels) and *congeries* (or unintegrated elements that are adjacent in space or time or are linked to some third element).

Sorokin's "integralist" approach leads him to criticize severely the idea that all of our knowledge derives ultimately from empirical data. Instead, he argues that empirical data represent only one type of truth, that of the senses. There is also the truth of reason and a third type, the truth of faith or intuition, which is beyond sensory data and rationality.

The validity of each of these is demonstrated in Sorokin's mind by the fact that huge civilizations have been built and endured for long periods on the fundamental foundation provided by the affirmation of each type of truth. In Sorokin's view, a comprehensive epistemology would have to recognize that reality is multidimensional and can be apprehended in part by the senses, in part by reason, and in part by faith or intuition.[31]

One of Sorokin's major criticisms of theories of total cultural or social systems is that they overstate their degree of integration and organic unity by ignoring congeries of elements that are not really part of the overarching system, even though they are spatially or temporally present. But, while Sorokin insists that his approach is not the same as these organic approaches, his emphasis is clearly on large-scale cultural supersystems and on the cyclical shifts they exhibit in history. Large-scale cultural systems do exhibit an organic unity, but the totality of a society's culture at any stage in history may include congeries that are not meaningfully integrated into this dominant organic system.

Types of Cultural Mentality

The key to understanding an integrated cultural supersystem is its *cultural mentality*. This concept refers to the basic world view that is the foundation of the sociocultural system. The fundamental world view of a sociocultural system consists of the answer it provides to the question of the nature of ultimate reality. There are three logically possible answers to this basic philosophical question. One is that ultimate reality consists entirely of this material world that we experience with our senses. Another is that ultimate reality consists of some realm or level of existence that is beyond this material world; that is, ultimate reality is transcendent and cannot be fully experienced through our senses. The third possible answer is intermediate between these extremes and states simply that ultimate reality includes both the material world and a transcendent world.

Related to this question are some additional questions regarding human nature and the satisfaction of basic human needs. Essentially, these questions have to do with whether the basic needs of human beings are physical or spiritual, the extent to which these needs should be satisfied, and whether satisfaction of human needs should involve modification of the self (so that needs themselves are reduced) or modification of the environment (so that they can be satisfied).[32]

Building on this foundation Sorokin identifies three cultural mentalities and several subtypes that are the basis for three distinct sociocultural supersystems.[33]

1. *Ideational Culture.* This type is based on the premise that ultimate reality is nonmaterial, transcendent, and cannot be apprehended through the senses. This world is seen as an illusion, as temporary, as dependent on a transcendent realm, or as an imperfect and incomplete aspect of reality. Ultimate reality consists of the realm of God, or Nirvana, or some other conception of eternal and nonmaterial being. This stage is broken down into the following subtypes.

   a. *Ascetic Ideational Culture.* This mentality represents a commitment to minimize as much as possible human material needs to facilitate ultimate absorption into the realm of transcendent being.

   b. *Active Ideational Culture.* In addition to minimizing sensual needs, this type seeks to transform this material world to bring it into harmony with the transcendent realm.

2. *Sensate Culture.* This type is based on the premise that this material world that we experience with our senses is the only reality there is. The existence of a supersensory or transcendent reality is denied. This mentality is broken down as follows.

   a. *Active Sensate Culture.* This culture encourages an active and energetic effort to promote as much as possible the fulfillment of human material needs by transforming the physical world so it will yield resources for human satisfaction and enjoyment. This mentality underlies the growth of technology and scientific and medical advances.

   b. *Passive Sensate Culture.* The passive sensate mentality involves an eagerness to experience life's sensual pleasures to the fullest. Sorokin describes this approach as a "parasitic exploitation" based on the motto, "Eat, drink, and be merry, for tomorrow we die." The pursuit of pleasure is not tempered by any kind of long-range goals.

   c. *Cynical Sensate Culture.* In terms of its primary goals, this mentality is similar to the passive sensate except that the pursuit of sensate goals is justified in terms of ideational rationalizations. In other words, it represents basically a hypocritical effort to justify pursuit of materialistic or sensual goals by reference to a transcendent value system that is not really accepted.

3. *Mixed Cultures.* This category involves the affirmation of basic premises

from both the ideational and the sensate mentalities. There are two basic types of mixed cultural mentality.

a. *Idealistic Culture.* This culture consists of an organic fusion of the ideational and the sensate mentalities so that both are seen as valid definitions of certain aspects of ultimate reality. In other words, the basic premises of both types of mentality are systematically and logically related.

b. *Pseudo-Ideational Culture.* This type is typically dominated by the sensate approach, but the ideational elements coexist with the sensate as an opposing perspective. Unlike the previous subtype, the two opposing perspectives are not systematically integrated but merely coexist in juxtaposition to each other.

These basic types of cultural mentality are objectified in innumerable material vehicles and in the social norms that govern individuals' behavior. Analysis of large-scale sociocultural systems basically involves determining the cultural theme that underlies various areas of cultural creativity and legitimates the dominant patterns of social organization. To the extent that a society's sociocultural system is integrated, there will be logico-meaningful consistency in the various elements that make up this system, reflecting the dominant cultural mentality. Although there may be cultural or social congeries that are not a part of this logico-meaningful unity, Sorokin emphasizes the tendency for sociocultural systems to become integrated in terms of the dominant cultural mentality they express into massive sociocultural supersystems.

Sorokin discusses at length the way in which basic cultural themes are expressed, or objectified, in various forms of art such as painting and sculpture, music, and architecture.[34] In painting, for example, the ideational mentality is expressed in the symbolic representation of transcendental or nonempirical subjects. Much of the religious art of medieval times would fit this pattern. In sharp contrast to this depiction of transcendental or other-worldly themes, the "visual" style of painting expresses the sensate type of mentality. As treated by Sorokin, the essential feature of this style is that it represents the artist's effort to portray a particular sensory experience without regard to established or conventional forms. In particular, momentary impressions, not lasting characteristics, are accentuated. The school of impressionism in the visual arts fits Sorokin's notion of sensate visual art.

Idealistic styles of painting are intermediate between the symbolic patterns of the ideational mentality and the visual patterns of the sensate mentality. The subject matter is likely to be empirical, but the representation of this empirical subject emphasizes the enduring ideal form and not secondary or accidental characteristics. Idealistic paintings of human figures, for example, would not include deficiences or blemishes; instead, the emphasis would be on portraying human forms as perfect or ideal representations of humanity. The vulgar or profane aspects of human nature would have no place in such forms of art. Although additional subtypes of visual art forms are identified, this description of the three major forms demonstrates Sorokin's style of analysis, in which forms of art or other material artificts objectify the dominant cultural mentality.

It is not only in works of art or music or architecture that dominant cultural themes are expressed. In addition, the great philosophical and ethical systems, the ideologies legitimating particular forms of political organization, the nature of social relationships in the family, the economy, and other social institutions, and many other components of the total sociocultural system form an integrated whole by virtue of the underlying cultural mentality that they express. The comprehensiveness of Sorokin's treatment of cultural systems and the alternative bases for their integration are cogently expressed as follows.

> The basic vast cultural systems are: language, science, philosophy, religion, the fine arts, ethics, law, and the vast derivative systems of applied technology, economics, and politics. The bulk of the meanings-values-norms of science or of great philosophical, religious, ethical, or artistic systems are united into one consistent ideological whole. When grounded empirically, this ideological system is, to a tangible degree, realized in all the material vehicles, or the material culture, and in the behavior of the creators, bearers, agents, or members of each of these systems. . . .
>
> Besides these vast cultural systems there are still vaster cultural unities that can be called cultural supersystems. As in other cultural systems, the ideology of each supersystem is based upon certain major premises or certain ultimate principles whose development, differentiation, and articulation makes up the total ideology of a supersystem.[35]

Even though the emphasis here is on the integration of *cultural* systems and supersystems, identifying the dominant cultural mentality is equally important for understanding the integration of *social* systems as well. (It must be remembered that this distinction is an analytical one.) Thus Sorokin writes:

> To sum up, whether a real social group (in contrast to a nominal plurel of individuals) is a social system or a social congeries is decided, as in cultural systems and congeries, by the fact of the consistency or inconsistency of the central meanings-values-norms because of which and/or for the sake of which the individuals interact. This means, among other things, that each of the organized or unorganized real social groups is built around and contains a set of cultural meanings-values-norms as its "heart and soul," as its main unifying bond and the very reason for its existence. Thus, in any real group—be it a social system or a social congeries or an intermediary type—its "social" form of being is always inseparable from its "cultural" meanings-values-norms.[36]

Sorokin's analysis of the various cultural mentalities may be compared and contrasted with Comte's depiction of the three stages in the evolution of human intellectual development. As noted earlier, both theories have a strong ''mentalis-tic'' cast; that is, they both see the basic ideas embodied in dominant world views or thought styles as the key to understanding sociocultural reality. However, while Comte argued that human history represents unilinear progress, based on the growth of science, which will continue indefinitely into the future, Sorokin maintained that the three fundamental types of cultural mentality repeat themselves in a cyclical fashion. In other words, the ideational period is followed by the idealistic period, which is followed by the sensate, which is followed by some mixed form (usually not idealistic), which is followed by a new ideational period, and so on. Instead of foreseeing continued growth of science based on a materialistic world view. Soro-kin's prophetic forecast was for an end to the sensate period and the eventual rebirth of a new stage of the ideational mentality.

Major Cycles of Western History

The bulk of Sorokin's four-volume *Social and Cultural Dynamics* consists of an overview of the history of the West from ancient Greece up to the twentieth century (concluding with the aforementioned prognosis for the future) in the light of the fluctuation of dominant cultural mentalities from one historical stage to the next. The dominant cultural mentality of a historical stage is determined by identifying the basic underlying themes reflected in the various areas of cultural creativity and other significant human actions.

Sorokin's analysis involves essentially classifying cultural works or major historical events in terms of the various types (or subtypes) of cultural mentality enumerated earlier, computing the proportions classified in each category in this manner, and noting the proportional shifts in dominant categories from one time period to the next. In some cases the results are summarized in tabular form with the various historical stages presented in terms of 20-year time periods from 580 to 560 B.C. to 1900 to 1920 A.D. Data of this type provide the basis for a century-by-century analysis of the dominant cultural mentality reflected in the various areas of the sociocultural system.

Thus, for example, Sorokin analyzes fluctuations in systems of truth and knowledge (after appropriate weighting to reflect the varying degrees of influence of the different writers covered) as follows.

> The truth of faith, represented by the ideational or religious rationalism, until about 460 B.C. amounted in our system of indicators to about 90 percent of all the systems of truth. It was only after 460 B.C. that the truth of senses (empiricism) began notably to rise and grow with minor fluctuations. It remained comparatively strong until 20 B.C., when it weakened again, and was low up to about A.D. 160, when it flared up again and stayed comparatively high until about A.D. 480. After that date it sharply declined and after A.D. 540 disappeared from the ''highway'' of the thought, being submerged by the

rising truth of faith of Christianity. It remained hidden until about 1100, roughly some six centuries, then emerged again and began, with minor fluctuations, to climb; and in the twelfth, thirteenth, and the fourteenth centuries again attained considerable influence, notable but not dominant, somewhat approaching its influence in the fifth and the fourth centuries B.C. in Greece. In the fifteenth century, and for some sixty years it disappeared again (1400–1460), then re-emerged and rose rapidly, and with minor fluctuations grew steadily up to the present time, reaching in the nineteenth century the extraordinary and unique indicator of 42 percent (for the whole century) and for the twentieth century a still higher indicator of some 53 percent! For the last four centuries we have thus had a rising tide of the truth of senses, the contemporary scientific truth. This extraordinary domination of this system of truth at the present time explains why we are inclined to identify truth generally with the truth of senses, why other truths appear to us as "superstitions," why we believe that from now on the truth of senses is destined to grow further and further until it will eliminate forever all the other systems of truth. Such a mentality is but natural for this period.[37]

Comte's predictions regarding the continued progress of positivism would be included in this description of the sensate mentality. Sorokin's analysis of the various other aspects of culture follow a similar vein. The social structure likewise reflects the prevailing cultural mentality. Thus Sorokin classifies social relationships as familistic, contractual, and compulsory and tries to show that these forms are correlated roughly with the dominance of ideational, idealistic, or sensate cultural mentalities, respectively. These relationships are somewhat erratic, however, and there are some notable exceptions. Overall, Sorokin is not as convincing in dealing with the social structural level as with the cultural.

Why do the different types of cultural mentality exhibit these cyclical fluctuations? To answer this question, Sorokin develops the principle of "immanent change" and the principle of "limits."[38] The first principle states that the sources of change of a sociocultural system are to be sought within the system itself, not in external factors, although the latter may accelerate, retard, or otherwise modify the change process in secondary aspects. (Of course, with the sociocultural system defined as broadly as Sorokin defines it, it is difficult not to accept his thesis of immanent sources of change.) Sorokin argues that sociocultural systems are living, ongoing systems and, as such, it is impossible for them to remain static. Instead, they continually change as their inherent potentialities are unfolded and developed through the creative activities of the individuals involved. This process can be seen as a long-term development of the implications of the basic underlying cultural mentality as it is expressed in more and more material forms and extended to more and more areas of life.

To be sure, different areas of the sociocultural world proceed at different rates in this process, but the implications of a developing cultural mentality gradually are extended to pervade all the major areas of the sociocultural system. This process continues until all the potentialities of the system are developed, at which time the system will have reached its maximum level of logico-meaningful integration. After a period of high integration, the process of disintegration will set in as an alternative cultural mentality (dormant during the earlier stage) begins to be developed and ultimately replaces the earlier dominant cultural mentality as a result of the same kind of process. (This model of growth and decay is no doubt one of the reasons that Sorokin can be classified as an organicist.)

The principle of *limit* is implicit in this process. Sociocultural systems do not continue indefinitely in the same direction. After a given cultural mentality is developed to its maximum, the direction of change is reversed, and an opposing cultural mentality is subsequently developed to its maximum level; after this there is another reversal in direction, with the theme from the earlier stage repeated.

Why can the system not continue indefinitely in the same direction? Any why is it necessary for earlier stages to be repeated when the direction does change? The principle of limit helps to provide answers to these questions. On the first question Sorokin appeals partly to an organic analogy, arguing that a living system is bound ultimately to reach a stage of disintegration. Sorokin also appeals to his ''integral'' conception of truth. In his view, a comprehensive picture of reality would have to recognize its multidimensional character. The dominant cultural mentalities fail to do this, however. Instead, as a particular cultural mentality unfolds, it exaggerates one aspect of reality and suppresses other equally valid aspects. In the long run, Sorokin argues, a sociocultural system cannot endure on such a limited or distorted foundation. The most comprehensive world view is provided by the idealistic cultural mentality, but this type tends to be relatively short lived, partly because of the built-in tension between the opposing sensate and ideational mentalities. Sorokin is particularly concerned to show the limits of the sensate cultural mentality as the basis for a permanent, highly integrated system.

On the question of why the different cultural mentalities repeat themselves, Sorokin argues that it is because the possibilities for change are limited. This means that each stage of history should not be expected to manifest a completely new cultural mentality. For example, on the basic question of the nature of ultimate reality, the only answers that are logically possible are that it is either nonmaterial, material, or both, or that one or both of these opposing dimensions is unknown or unknowable. This notion of limited possibilities of change also applies to social and political systems. In short, since sociocultural systems (and the various elements thereof) are not infinite and do not have unlimited possibilities, there is bound to be a repetition of basic themes from one historical stage to another.

The Crisis of the Twentieth-Century Sensate System

The principle of limits applies to both of the opposing cultural mentalities, but special emphasis is given to the limits of the sensate supersystem. These limits are discussed in a prophetic vein as Sorokin attempts to forecast the future of Western civilization for the remainder of the twentieth century and beyond. From the towering vantage point provided by his historical survey, Sorokin concluded that the first part of the twentieth century was witnessing the end of the road for the sensate supersystem that had more and more dominated the Western world for the previous 400 years. As he surveyed the turmoil and the crises during which he lived, he saw them as symptoms of a deep and profound cultural disintegration. This disintegration would continue until it would ultimately be replaced by a new ideational system (perhaps after going through a mixed stage).

Sorokin describes "the crisis of our age" as follows:

> The organism of the Western society and culture seems to be undergoing one of the deepest and most significant crises of its life. The crisis is far greater than the ordinary; its depth is unfathomable, its end not yet in sight, and the whole of the Western society is involved in it. It is the crisis of a Sensate culture, now in its overripe stage, the culture that has dominated the Western World during the last five centuries. It is also the crisis of a contractual (capitalistic) society associated with it. In this sense we are experiencing one of the sharpest turns in the historical road, a turn as great as any of the other few made by the Graeco-Roman and Western cultures in passing from Ideational to Sensate, and from Sensate to Ideational, phases.[39]

Sorokin's analysis of this fundamental crisis extends our understanding of the principle of limits as applied to the sensate system. This analysis hinges on the close connection between the dominant cultural mentality and its stage of development on the one hand and social solidarity on the other. Briefly, Sorokin argues that as the sensate cultural mentality unfolds and develops, it gradually dissolves the intellectual and moral consensus that is the underlying foundation of social solidarity. Unlike the ideational mentality, the sensate mentality in its advanced stage carries relativism to the extreme with respect to knowledge or world view as well as ethics and morals. The result is that there is no overarching intellectual or moral framework that is accepted as ultimate or absolute and that can unite individuals in a way that enables them to transcend their own narrow, individual perspectives and interests.

Added to this intellectual and moral breakdown is the fact that the sensate mentality focuses attention on human material and sensual needs and desires and encourages the maximum possible fulfillment of these needs. Along with this material self-indulgence there is a downplaying or denying of human spiritual nature or any other supraindividual bonds that link individuals on a basis other than self-interest. As a result, competition for scarce material goods and conflict between people is bound to increase. This threat of intellectual and social anarchy is one of the major reasons why the sensate mentality cannot develop indefinitely but must face the end of its road.

The prophetic tone of Sorokin's description of the moral bankruptcy of this "overripe" and dying sensate stage is clearly illustrated in the following.

1. Sensate values will become still more relative and atomistic until they are ground into dust devoid of any universal recognition and binding power. The boundary line between the true and false, the right and wrong, the beautiful and ugly, positive and negative values, will be obliterated increasingly until mental, moral, aesthetic, and social anarchy reigns supreme. . . .

5. Rude force and cynical fraud will become the only arbiters of all values and of all interindividual and intergroup relationships. Might will become right. As a consequence, wars, revolutions, revolts, disturbances, brutality will be rampant. *Bellum omnium contra omnes*—man against man, class, nation, creed and race against class, nation, creed and race—will raise its head. . . .

11. In the increasing moral, mental, and social anarchy and decreasing creativeness of Sensate mentality, the production of the material values will decline, depressions will grow worse, and the material standard of living will go down.

12. For the same reasons, security of life and possessions will fade. With these, peace of mind and happiness. Suicide, mental disease, and crime will grow. Weariness will spread over larger and larger numbers of the populations.

13. Population will increasingly split into two types: the Sensate hedonists with their "eat, drink and love, for tomorrow we die"; and, eventually, into ascetics and stoics indifferent and antagonistic to Sensate values.[40]

This last prediction must be expanded. Although Sorokin is pessimistic about the immediate future as he foresees the growing disintegration of the sensate supersystem, he is optimistic that a new and more hopeful age will emerge in the long run. Thus he writes:

We are seemingly between two epochs: the dying Sensate culture of our magnificant yesterday, and the coming Ideational or Idealistic culture of the creative tomorrow. We are living, thinking, acting at the end of a brilliant six-hundred-year-long Sensate day. The oblique rays of the sun still illumine the glory of the passing epoch. But the light is fading, and in the deepening shadows it becomes more and more difficult to see clearly and to orient ourselves safely in the confusions of the twilight. The night of the transitory period begins to loom before us and the coming generations, perhaps with their nightmares, frightening shadows, and heart-rending horrors. Beyond it, however, the dawn of a new great Ideational or Idealistic culture is probably waiting to greet the men of the future.[41]

If Sorokin were alive today, as we enter the closing years of the twentieth century, he would interpret diverse phenomena such as the continual threat of annihilation in a nuclear war, the eruption of international flash points in numerous places around the world, the growing environmental catastrophes, the widespread feelings of anomie or meaninglessness, the continued insatiable appetites for material goods and sensual pleasures, and the widespread interest of many in various new forms of religious experience as manifestations of the disintegration of the sensate cultural mentality and of the birth pains of a new mentality struggling to be born. The contrast with Comte's vision of continued scientific and materialistic progress could hardly be more pronounced. Although Comte recognized the need for a binding moral authority in the positivist stage, Sorokin would say that such an authority could hardly be maintained in the face of sensate relativism and self-indulgence.

A Critique of Sorokin's Model

Sorokin might be criticized for overstating the case for his prophetic picture of the impending doom of Western civilization. Certainly, his predictions involve interpreting empirical events in light of his general model of sociocultural change instead of analyzing these events on their own terms. A theorist starting from different premises could well analyze the same events from a different vantage point or could choose different sets of events as significant and worthy of careful analysis.[42]

Sorokin's overall model of sociocultural change and his effort to provide empirical support (limited though it may be) for his model must be considered one of the most ambitious sociological projects ever undertaken. But on the negative side, Sorokin's historical analysis involved superimposing his theoretical model on the data and interpreting the data in relation to this model. It is difficult to imagine that the data could not be used to support alternative interpretations. One result of using a set of data to support a particular, already established theoretical model is that the data may be distorted somewhat to fit the model. Thus there is a tendency in Sorokin's analysis for the degree of cultural integration in relatively stable periods to be overemphasized and for the breaks between different stages to be overdrawn. Sorokin recognizes this danger, of course (as indicated by his discussion of congeries), but the shortcomings of his emphasis are still discernible.

Specifically, for example, Sorokin's stress on logico-meaningful integration downplays the fact (which Sorokin recognized) that different areas of culture and society proceed through the cyclical changes at somewhat different rates and times. Therefore, in a given century, the significant literature may be rapidly approaching the climax of the sensate stage while the dominant political ideologies still reflect an ideational or idealistic mentality and are changing rather slowly. Considering the scope of Sorokin's analysis and the number of different elements of the sociocultural system that he analyzed, the problem of unequal rates of change in these different areas should be obvious. An alternative approach would be to consider the different "parts" of the sociocultural system separately so as to delineate the specific dynamics of each particular area in the sociocultural world. In short, while the attractiveness of Sorokin's model is in the comprehensive perspective that it provides, such a perspective suffers from overgeneralization and oversimplification.

Another limitation in Sorokin's analysis of culture is apparent in the type of data used. In analyzing literature, paintings, philosophical systems, or music, Sorokin had to rely on the works that survived and were recorded. Are these works representative of the total cultural creations that were produced? Or are they more representative of the works of a cultural elite who had the time, resources, and skills to be involved in creative activities? If the latter is true, perhaps the works analyzed survived precisely because they stand out from the ordinary. Even so, one might offer the counterargument that even though these cultural works are outstanding, they still reflect the widely shared mentality. For example, not everyone could design or build a cathedral in medieval times, but the fact that the creative minority did so provides an indication of the mentality that prevailed and, in fact, symbolizes this mentality.

But whether creative cultural works merely reflect the general cultural mentality or transcend it, the creation of cultural works cannot be the major concern of the general, ordinary population. In all periods of history, most people have to be concerned with mundane, everyday affairs such as making a living and surviving. Because of the pressure of universal biological and social needs and the universal necessity to adapt to a physical environment in which resources are not unlimited, we should expect the everyday lives of most people to be much more similar in different stages of history than Sorokin's theory implies, regardless of which high-level cultural mentality is dominant. Other than his discussion of different types of social relations and the cyclical fluctuations in intergroup relations, Sorokin's model has very little to say about the ongoing life-styles of ordinary people in different sectors of society or in different historical periods. In short, by focusing on the implicit themes expressed by the elite minority involved in cultural creativity, Sorokin probably exaggerated the differences between the different types of sociocultural systems. Differences between people in terms of their day-by-day concerns would probably not be nearly as great.

The major similarity between Comte and Sorokin is that both focused on forms of knowledge as the key to understanding social reality. Knowledge, beliefs, ideas, intellectual style, world view—any of these terms would be appropriate in identifying their primary focus, which is obviously at the cultural level. This approach enabled them to deal with large-scale processes of long-range sociocultural change and to develop a theoretical perspective in terms of which innumerable specific historical events could be interpreted. Although such perspectives can be criticized for being too general or overly simplistic, it is difficult to imagine how a more microscopic approach, focusing on a lower level of analysis, could possibly have been used to accomplish the goals that Comte and Sorokin set for themselves. Whether these goals are the most fruitful to pursue is a different question; the point is that their concentration on the cultural level enabled them to provide an overview of the history of the Western world that would probably not have been possible if they had focused on a lower level of analysis such as, say, the dynamics of face-to-face interaction.

Similarly, if we were asked to give a macroscopic overview of the major differences between a business firm and a church, for example, or between American society and Russian society, our descriptions would probably center on differences between the general cultural values of these different systems. We would probably not focus on differences in the personalities of the American president and the Russian premier, for example, or on the specific interaction patterns in which these political leaders are involved. Indeed, analyses of the dynamics of large-scale bureaucratic societies suggest that American and Russian societies exhibit many sociological similarities because of their bureaucratic structures. The essential difference between these societies is in their fundamental value premises and general world view.

In short, the advantage of analyzing the cultural level is that it can provide a macroscopic picture of a social system; the disadvantages are that it can lead to oversimplification, exaggeration of cultural unity and consistency, or errors in interpretation of specific events or projection of future developments. Comte's vision that industrialism would eventually displace militarism is an obvious example of such an error in prediction; the dominance of the military-industrial complex in industrial societies shows that industrialism has been used to enhance military power and not as an alternative to militarism. Similarly, Sorokin's sweeping generalizations regarding the decadence of an advanced sensate culture can lead to a cynical misinterpretation of the actual motives and values of individuals or groups that do not fit this overall pattern. Whether or not the general cultural themes that seem to dominate a particular society are actually the operative themes in each of its various "parts" is always an open question.

NONMATERIAL VERSUS MATERIAL CULTURE

Both Comte's stages of intellectual progress and Sorokin's types of cultural mentality consider the nonmaterial realm of ideas, modes of thought, or world view as the major keys to understanding social structure and individual behavior. In the next chapter we will see that this idealistic approach is thoroughly repudiated by Marx's historical materialism, in which ideas or modes of thought are seen as *reflections* of material conditions instead of being the major key to understanding a society. In the remainder of this chapter, however, we suggest that advances in *material* culture provide an alternative focus to our previous emphasis on changes in *nonmaterial* culture.

The materialistic aspect of culture was implicit in both Comte's and Sorokin's theories. Comte's views on the transition from military to industrial society has obvious implications concerning changes in material culture. Specifically, the rise of industrialism depends on technological progress, and advances in technology represent changes in material culture. Sorokin also dealt with technological progress and the increased material abundance that it made possible; he saw these developments as a manifestation of the sensate mentality. But Sorokin generally treated material culture as the vehicle whereby the nonmaterial cultural mentality is objectified. This suggests that analysis of material culture should concentrate on the cultural meanings that are symbolized or objectified in material forms. This approach is appropriate in understanding works of art and architecture. But, in spite of the fact that material culture was not ignored, Comte and Sorokin clearly treated it as dependent on nonmaterial culture.

A previous chapter suggested that part of the stimulus for the rise of the sociological discipline was that the Industrial Revolution had led to numerous major social changes that the pioneers in sociology were attempting to understand. Since the Industrial Revolution rested on technological progress, the implication is that technological progress (which represents a change in material culture) provides the key to understanding social change. The crucial effect of technological progress and industrial development in stimulating major social change was obvious to the classical theorists; in one form or another Comte, Spencer, Marx, Durkheim, Weber, Töennies, and others developed their theories against the backdrop of the Industrial Revolution and related social changes. Indeed, Comte's interest in the steady advance of positivism can be seen as an effort to explain why the Industrial Revolution had come about and would continue to advance.

Technological Development and Cultural Lag

Another theorist who even more explicitly felt that technological progress was the key independent variable in explaining social change was the American sociologist, W. F. Ogburn (1886-1959). Ogburn was educated at Columbia University and spent most of his professional academic life at the University of Chicago. His most famous contribution to the field is his concept of culture lag. This concept refers to the tendency for social customs and patterns of social organization to lag behind changes in material culture. The result is that social change is typically characterized by strain between the material and nonmaterial cultures.[43]

The contrast with Comte and Sorokin should be obvious. For Ogburn, the leading edge of social change is advances in material culture, including inventions and technological developments, while Comte and Sorokin stressed changes in forms of knowledge or world view as the major stimulus of social change, with material culture changes reflecting changes in these nonmaterial aspects of culture.

Ogburn also different from Comte and Sorokin in his fundamental definition of culture. As Martindale pointed out, both Comte and Sorokin had organismic concepts of cultural reality; that is, they stressed the organic unity of cultural phenomena and the notion that the sociocultural level should be analyzed independently of the individual level.[44] Ogburn, on the other hand, took more of a behavioral approach to cultural phenomena. Material artifacts result from human activity. In addition, culture includes the accumulated customs and institutional patterns that are part of the social heritage and that are transmitted from generation to generation and imitated as a result of the social influence process.

Ogburn's real concern was to show that human behavior is a product of this social or cultural heritage and not of biological factors transmitted through heredity.[45] Thus Martindale classifies Ogburn as a representative of pluralistic behaviorism; this school includes many different specific approaches, but the basic notion underlying all of them is that social reality consists essentially of individuals' overt behavior patterns and their consequences.[46]

Overt behavior patterns exhibit a high degree of regularity because people tend to imitate the behavior of others and repeat their own behavior patterns over time, especially those that are successful. The aggregation of established behavior patterns over large segments of the population and the interdependence of these standardized behaviors among the various segments of society constitute social or cultural reality. Although changes do occur as a result of occasional social inventions and innovations, Ogburn emphasized the widespread tendency for changes to be resisted, either because of habit or differential advantages that result from maintaining the established customs.

Inventions and innovations occur most frequently in the realm of material culture. These changes range from early inventions such as the wheel and primitive hand tools to modern high-speed computers and communications satellites. The nonmaterial culture—the customs, mores, and patterns of social organization—must eventually *adapt* to changes in material culture but, because of the various sources of resistance to change, this adaptive process always lags behind changes in material culture. The result is malintegration, or strain between the material culture and the nonmaterial culture.

Changes in material culture have occurred from time to time throughout history, but the pace of change accelerated sharply with the advent of the Industrial Revolution and the continued emphasis on technological development. Thus the nonmaterial culture is unable to "catch up," because the rate of change in the material culture continues to grow. The result is a constantly increasing strain between the material culture and the adaptive or nonmaterial culture. Many modern social problems can be traced to this failure of social customs and institutional patterns to keep pace with technological advances in material culture.[47]

Ogburn's thesis is provocative and popular; it is frequently mentioned in introductory textbooks, along with examples of the kind of cultural strains that this theory explains. In collaboration with M. F. Nimkoff, Ogburn demonstrated the relevance of this theory in explaining strains in the family institution as a major proportion of the American population has shifted from a rural-agricultural environment to an urban-industrial one.[48] While this shift has taken place, many of the traditional functions of the family have been taken over by other institutions, limiting the family to the task of maintaining affective bonds between family members and providing individual happiness. But fulfilling these tasks is not easy because of the lack of other necessary functions and the increasing stress on individualism in the urban environment. In the same vein, Ogburn and Nimkoff analyzed the social effects of aviation by predicting its effects on population distribution, organizational patterns, and the like.[49]

The failure to provide adequately for the economic and social needs of workers displaced by mechanization and automation; the growth of large-scale computerized information storage and retrieval systems without corresponding safeguards against misuse of personal information or violation of individuals' rights to privacy; the development and spread of nuclear weapons with insufficient protection against international misunderstanding or miscalculation; the widespread resistance in developing countries to modern birth control techniques—these and other examples of lag not cited here illustrate the strain that Ogburn analyzed and provide evidence of the validity of his theory.

But, as provocative and insightful as Ogburn's thesis is in helping us understand numerous cases of strain, the notion that nonmaterial culture *always* lags behind material culture provides, at best, a partial picture of the sources of social strain or of the dynamics of social change. In some cases the answer to a strain induced by a technological innovation is not adaptation in the realm of nonmaterial culture, but additional technological innovation. For example, in many cases breakthroughs in medical technology are initially available on only a limited basis. Naturally, persons who live in scattered or isolated locations who become aware of these advances and who could benefit from them experience their lack of access as a strain. The obvious resolution to such strain is additional innovation, whereby the innovation can be routinized and made widely available. Similarly, the tremendous increases in agricultural productivity brought about by technological advances are not matched in some of the developing countries by comparable developments in distribution mechanisms. Finally, the massive loss of human lives in automobile accidents perhaps could have been reduced by changes in nonmaterial culture such as in attitudes toward cars or driving customs and earlier development of driver education courses. However, in recent years this challenge has been tackled at the level of new technological developments: seat belts, passive restraint systems, and automobile design changes. Even so, one might argue that widespread use of these innovations will depend on appropriate changes in nonmaterial attitudes and values. Nevertheless, it seems that there is often a lag between the development of a technological innovation and the diffusion of that innovation, with the diffusion dependent on additional technological advances.

Lags in Material Culture

In some areas it might be useful to reverse the sequence of cultural change hypothesized by Ogburn—that is, to note situations in which advances in nonmaterial culture are ahead of material culture. This reversal might apply in the area of science fiction, where dreams of technological innovations are entertained long before it is possible to bring them to fruition. For example, people dreamed of flying long before the airplane was developed. Contemporary developments in the exploration of space were foreshadowed in the writings of science fiction writers several years prior to their achievement. In short, a completed technological development does not emerge suddenly on the social scene; it is always preceded by the *idea* that certain possibilities are worth pursuing. We are not suggesting that the crucial ideas that stimulate change should always be sought in science fiction; developments in science, not science fiction, are more likely to be the crucial ones.

Even more important, certain cultural ideals and values have been part of the cultural heritage for thousands of years and are still regarded as the most enlightened and advanced products of the human mind and spirit, even though the means—or the technology—to implement these ideals must still be developed. Sorokin points out in his critical evaluation of materialistic theories such as Ogburn's that the moral teachings of the great religions of the world, such as the Ten Commandments and the Golden Rule, have never been surpassed as ideals or guidelines for ordering human life.[50] Indeed, in most areas of life the high ethical ideals of the great religions of the world are not even regarded as realistic goals that can be pursued without a great deal of compromise. No multiplication of technological gadgets will make such basic and transcendent ideals obsolete. These ideals do not represent cultural lag; they are far ahead of developments in material culture or behavioral or organizational adaptations to material culture changes.

Specifically, for example, all of the major universal religions have entertained the vision of the fundamental unity of humanity, stressing the brotherhood (and sisterhood) of all people and seeking to inspire the kind of self-transcending love that will ultimately embrace all of humanity. But this vision could be nothing but a vague abstraction as long as the technology of communication could serve only to unite people in a particular limited territory. Only with the advent of modern communication and transportation technology does the vision of a true worldwide community seem remotely feasible.

Even in our national society it would be difficult to imagine the current level of national consciousness being maintained without the mass media and other means of communication whereby the various regions of the country share certain common experiences. In recent times the development of communication satellites provides this same capability on a worldwide scale. The widespread, vicarious participation in events such as the first landing of men on the moon or the Olympic games provides the foundation of common experiences without which the ideal of the worldwide human community is merely an abstraction.

We are not suggesting that global communication or extensive worldwide travel is *sufficient* to unite the various nations of the world into a genuine international human community. On the contrary, increased communication and travel have magnified international tension and conflict, thus producing an illustration of cultural lag of the type Ogburn identified. However, the ideal of a universal human community is one element of the nonmaterial culture that has endured for thousands of years prior to the development of the basic material culture technology that makes the realization of this ideal remotely feasible. This reverses the sequence of cultural change and lag postulated by Ogburn.

An adequate model of the differential rates of cultural change would have to deal with the situations in which nonmaterial cultural change seems to be the leading edge as well as those where material culture change seems to be the leading edge. In the preceding example of the dream of a worldwide community, we might suggest that the transcendent cultural ideals are the most advanced. The material culture technology necessary for moving toward the practical realization of the ideals is developed much later and in response to a totally different set of stimulating factors (such as scientific advance). Then the specific nonmaterial customs and patterns of social organization that must be developed to enable the material culture advances to be used in promoting the realization of the enduring transcendent ideals lag behind the material culture innovations. During this lag period, there is the risk that the material culture advances may actually be used to undermine realization of the enduring transcendent ideals.

This example also illustrates the type of situation in which certain aspects of the nonmaterial culture (operative customs and norms, patterns of organization in international relations, etc.) lag behind other aspects of nonmaterial culture (such as the transcendent ideals of a universal human community). In short, sociocultural change is more complex and exhibits more variations than Ogburn's culture lag thesis recognizes. The thesis is valid in certain limited situations, however.

Linear versus Cyclical Models of Cultural Change

Perhaps the basic conflict between theories of linear cultural change and cyclical theories can be analyzed by making use of the distinction between nonmaterial culture and material culture. If we examine material culture changes since the beginning of the Industrial Revolution, an argument can be made for a linear model. Support for such an argument would involve noting the steady increase in technological inventions and innovations developed in the last few hundred years. Even a broader historical view would probably be consistent with such a model since new inventions, no matter how rare, are accumulated or added to the already existing material and technological base.

Numerous instances could be cited of the effects of materialistic progress. We already cited the increased speed and range of communication and transportation methods. We might also note the decreasing reliance on human energy in material production, the increased number of products available to make life easier or more enjoyable for larger and larger segments of the population in our society, and the steady improvements in agricultural productivity or increased life span. In short, material or technological progress seems to follow a linear pattern. However, the fact that it has followed a linear pattern in the past is no guarantee that it will do so indefinitely into the future. Contemporary developments such as depletion of readily available energy sources or environmental pollution suggest that there may be limits to this pattern of indefinite materialistic progress.

If we examine nonmaterial culture change, the case for linear progress is much less convincing. It is popular for critics to point out that in spite of all the materialistic progress from which we currently benefit, many of the customs and mores involved in intergroup or international relations are essentially the same as they have been for a very long time. We no longer use clubs or bows and arrows to fight one another; we use bombs or missiles (or the threat of them), but the underlying psychological and sociological dynamics of intergroup or interpersonal relations still involve mutual hostility.

How might we account for this apparent lack of progress in the realm of nonmaterial culture? Schneider[51] pointed out that culture is always superimposed on the substratum of physical and biological reality and, therefore, its development is necessarily constrained by the limits imposed by this reality. The result is that regardless of the wide range of variation that cultural systems may exhibit in time and space, it is unlikely that any cultural system can continue to develop indefinitely in just one direction; instead, it can develop only to the degree that it is not in gross disharmony with physical or biological reality. For example, achievement of the dream of a universal human community is limited in part by human cognitive and affective limitations. Individuals would find it almost impossible, because of logistical and time constraints, to maintain the relationships required for a genuine community with more than a few hundred individuals. This limitation holds regardless of how far modern communication technology may advance.

Schneider also pointed out that physical and biological factors do not necessarily pose absolute or unchangeable limits.[52] Through technology, human beings can transcend many of the constraints imposed by physical or biological reality. From the earliest use of primitive tools to the development of elaborate life-support systems for surviving in space, human beings have repeatedly demonstrated that they are not completely bound by their biological nature or physical environment. Nevertheless, biological and physical limitations do provide parameters within which cultural systems must develop.

Another reason for the lack of progress of nonmaterial culture is provided by Sorokin's notion of limits.[53] Sorokin developed this idea in his argument against continued linear change. Briefly, the argument is that sociocultural systems have certain inherent limits beyond which they are unable to develop, and they must shift directions as they approach these limits.

Recall that the key to understanding a sociocultural system in Sorokin's model is the dominant cultural mentality; in turn, this is based on certain fundamental philosophical assumptions regarding the nature of ultimate reality. But there are only a limited number of logical possibilities as far as these philosophical assumptions are concerned. Thus, as a particular cultural mentality approaches its limit, the only alternative is to repeat the basic theme of an earlier stage, albeit with variations. The idea of limits to a given trend and the idea of limited possibilities of change are basic to Sorokin's theory of varyingly recurrent cyclical change.

Moreover, since the dominant cultural mentalities of different stages frequently are mutually contradictory, the development of one mentality will depend somewhat on demolishing the opposing mentality. Thus, unlike the realm of material culture, the realm of nonmaterial culture does not exhibit to the same degree the pattern of steady and uninterrupted accumulation in one direction.

Summary

This chapter focused on the cultural level of social reality. The initial objective was to present the basic principles of Comte's pioneering perspecitve. Comte's contributions included a strong emphasis on the importance of establishing sociology on a firm empirical (or positive) basis and a general model of social order and social change. His theory of the three stages of intellectual development provided the key to his understanding of social evolution. Specifically, as a society moves from the theological to the metaphysical to the positive stage, these changes in fundamental modes of thought, or world view, stimulate corresponding changes in forms of social organization. Overall, Comte attempted to explain how the growth of science generates social and industrial progress, even to the point that an industrial social order will eventually replace a military social order. Steady progress depends on social order, however. In addition to attempting to analyze the foundations of social order in society, Comte attempted to promote the development of altruistic sentiments as an essential ingredient of social order instead of relying solely on reason and the growth of science.

Comte's theory of linear progress based on the steady growth of science was then contrasted with Sorokin's cyclical model of cultural change. Sorokin was similar to Comte in his emphasis on basic world views or dominant styles of thought as the key to understanding social reality. Sorokin identified three major cultural mentalities: the ideational, the idealistic, and the sensate. They are manifested as the basic underlying themes expressed in the various fine arts, in philosophical systems, in legal codes and political organization, and in social relations in various social institutions. In line with his cyclical model of cultural change, Sorokin did not anticipate continued scientific or material progress. Instead, he believed that twentieth-century Western civilization was nearing the end of a long sensate stage and was destined ultimately to return to some form of ideational system. The reasons for this lie in the breakdown of intellectual consensus and moral commitments and an excessive emphasis on material indulgence.

Both Comte and Sorokin felt that changes in nonmaterial culture are the key to understanding the dynamics of social change. An alternative would be to focus on changes in material culture, such as technological or industrial development, as the leading edge of social and cultural change. This was manifested in Ogburn's notion that the customs and normative patterns of society lag behind changes in technology. Ogburn's cultural lag theory was criticized, however, for its failure to recognize situations in which material culture lags behind developments in nonmaterial culture.

The problem of cultural change is considerably more complex than is implied in the linear or cyclical models of cultural change. It was suggested that perhaps the linear model would be more applicable to material culture than to nonmaterial culture, while the cyclical model would be more applicable to nonmaterial culture. Material culture follows a pattern of cumulative growth. In contrast, nonmaterial culture often follows a pattern in which the growth of one dominant pattern requires the decline of an opposing pattern.

Comte's pioneering emphasis on the cultural level of social reality has not been maintained as sociology developed. Sorokin's place in modern American sociology is unique in the sustained analysis of cultural systems that he attempted. He does not clearly fit into any established school in the American mainstream, even though his contributions and influence are readily acknowledged. Instead, the American mainstream reflects a shift to the social structural or interpersonal levels rather than the cultural level. The social structural level was also the primary focus of Marx and Durkheim, and contemporary sociology is more indebted to their work than to that of Comte.

This is not to deny that many contemporary theorists recognize the importance of dealing with the cultural level and of relating it to the social structural level. Parsons, for example, who was a student of Sorokin's, dealt extensively with different aspects of the cultural level and its interdependence with and control over the social structural level. Even so, his explicit emphasis is on the *social,* not the *cultural,* system. Also, many specialized areas within contemporary sociology concentrate on cultural-level issues, although not on the same global scale as Comte. For example, sociology of knowledge, sociology of religion, or sociology of science, art, or literature all involve subject matter that is at the cultural level, and all involve an effort to understand the social dynamics involved in these various areas. Outside of these specialized fields, many mainstream sociologists leave it to others to specialize explicitly in cultural-level analysis. These others include cultural anthropologists and social psychologists who work in the culture-and-personality area. The general pattern for mainstream sociologists is to deal with culture as it pertains to the social system or interpersonal relations instead of stressing the dynamics of the cultural system as such. This emphasis on the social system or on lower levels of social reality will be reflected in the remaining chapters of this book.

Footnotes

1. See Frank E. Manuel, *The Prophets of Paris* (Cambridge, Mass.: Harvard University Press, 1962), Chapter VI, "Auguste Comte-Embodiment in the Great Being," especially pp. 251–260, for a description of the relationship between Henri Saint-Simon and Auguste Comte. See also Frank E. Manuel, *The New World of Henri Saint-Simon* (Cambridge, Mass.: Harvard University Press, 1956), Chapter 29, "The Master Denied."

2. Lewis A. Coser, *Masters of Sociological Thought,* 2nd edition (New York: Harcourt Brace Jovanovich, 1977), pp. 35–40.

3. This description of Comte's relations with the women in his life is drawn from Manuel, op. cit., pp. 260-263.

4. Auguste Comte, *System of Positive Polity,* 4 volumes, translated by Richard Congreve (New York: Burt Franklin, 1877), Vol. IV, pp. 276-277.

5. Coser, op. cit., p. 19.

6. This optimistic faith in reason as the key to establishing a new social order was the major theme of Carl Becker's *The Heavenly City of the 18th Century Philosophers* (New Haven, Conn.: Yale University Press, 1959).

7. This conservative reaction was manifested in Edmund Burke's *Essays on the French Revolution,* which he composed from his relatively isolated position across the channel in the British parliament. Other contemporaries who reacted similarly included de Bonald and de Maistre, both of whom Comte admired greatly.

8. See Don Martindale, *The Nature and Types of Sociological Theory* (Boston: Houghton Mifflin, 1960), pp. 62-65.

9. Stanislav Andreski, ed., *The Essential Comte* (New York: Barnes and Noble, 1974), "Introduction," p. 16.

10. Auguste Comte, *The Positive Philosophy of Auguste Comte,* freely translated and condensed by Harriet Martineau (New York: Calvin Blanchard, 1858), p. 452. Reprinted by AMS Press, Inc., New York, 1974.

11. Ibid., p. 453.

12. Auguste Comte, *System of Positive Polity,* Vol. IV, translated by Richard Congreve (New York: Burt Franklin, originally published 1877), General Appendix, Fourth Part, p. 599.

13. This emphasis was clearly stated by Comte: "[T]his is why, since the birth of philosophy, the history of society has been regarded as governed by the history of the human mind." *The Positive Philosophy of Auguste Comte,* p. 521.

14. Ibid., pp. 25-26.

15. Ibid., p. 26.

16. See Frank E. Manuel, *The Prophets of Paris,* Chapter 1, "Turgot, Baron de l'Aulne: The Future of Mind," especially p. 32ff.

17. This notion of evolutionary progress from a military to an industrial type of social order was also an important ingredient of Herbert Spencer's comprehensive evolutionary theory. See *Selections from Herbert Spencer's Principles of Sociology,* edited and with an introduction by Robert L. Carneiro (Chicago: University of Chicago Press, 1967). especially pp. 53-62.

18. Even a casual perusal of most contemporary sociology of religion texts would bear this out. See, for example, Louis Schneider, *Sociological Approach to Religion* (New York: Wiley, 1970).

19. See *The Positive Philosophy of Auguste Comte,* op. cit., pp. 519-520.

20. Coser, op. cit., p. 19.

21. Ibid.

22. *The Prophets of Paris,* p. 268.

23. Ibid., p. 265.

24. Ernest Becker, *The Structure of Evil* (New York: Free Press, 1968), p. 44.

25. Manuel, *The Prophets of Paris,* pp. 265-268.

26. See Pitirim Sorokin, *Fads and Foibles in Modern Sociology and Related Sciences*

(Chicago: Regnery, 1956), and *Sociological Theories of Today* (New York: Harper & Row, 1966).

27. See Pitirim Sorokin, *Society, Culture, and Personality* (New York: Harper & Row, 1947), where this perspective is systematically developed.
28. Martindale, op. cit., p. 115.
29. Pitirim Sorokin, *Social and Cultural Dynamics,* 1-volume edition (Boston: Porter Sargent, 1956), p. 63.
30. Sorokin, *Sociological Theories of Today,* Chapter 18.
31. Sorokin, *Social and Cultural Dynamics,* 1-volume edition, pp. 683–692.
32. Ibid., pp. 24–27.
33. This overview of the major types and subtypes of cultural mentality is adapted from ibid., Chapter 2, "Ideational, Sensate, Idealistic, and Mixed Systems of Culture."
34. Ibid., Chapter 7, for example.
35. Sorokin, *Sociological Theories of Today,* pp. 22–23.
36. Ibid., pp. 27–28.
37. Sorokin, *Social and Cultural Dynamics,* 1-volume edition, p. 243.
38. See ibid., Part Nine, "Why and How of Sociocultural Change."
39. Ibid., p. 622.
40. Ibid., pp. 699–701.
41. Ibid., p. 625. Sorokin's analysis of the crisis of our times and his prognosis for the future appeared initially in the closing chapters of his *Social and Cultural Dynamics,* but subsequently were published in an abbreviated volume entitled *The Crisis of our Age* (original publication date, 1941). In his foreword to a 1957 edition of this work, Sorokin asserted that the events that have transpired since the original publication of his predictions confirm these predictions. See Pitirim Sorokin, *The Crisis of our Age* (New York: E.P. Dutton, 1941).
42. Parsons, for example, argues that traditional Christian values have been more fully institutionalized in the structure of modern American industrial society than is often realized by those who criticize the secularization process. Parsons suggests that even though the church as an institution no longer wields the power it once did, many of the basic values of Christianity are actually incorporated into the social and political structure of American society. For example, the democratic form of government can be seen as a political manifestation of the traditional Christian belief in the equality and dignity of all people. See Talcott Parsons, "Christianity and Modern Industrial Society," pp. 33–70, in Edward A. Tiryakian, ed., *Sociological Theory, Values, and Sociocultural Change* (Glencoe, Ill.: Free Press, 1963). For another critical assessment of Sorokin's model, see Louis Schneider, "Toward Assessment of Sorokin's View of Change," pp. 371–400, in George K. Zollschan and Walter Hirsch, eds., *Explorations in Social Change* (Boston: Houghton Mifflin, 1964).
43. See William F. Ogburn, *Social Change with Respect to Culture and Original Nature* (Gloucester, Mass.: Peter Smith, 1964), especially Part IV, pp. 199–280. Although Ogburn did not insist that nonmaterial culture must always necessarily lag behind material culture, his emphasis was clearly on the types of situations in which it does. According to his terminology, much of the nonmaterial culture is adaptive culture; that is, it must be adapted to the material culture. Rapid changes in material culture, such as represented by technological development, necessitate some type of eventual adaptation

of nonmaterial culture but, before this adaptation is made, the "lag" of the nonmaterial culture creates a condition of cultural strain.

44. Martindale, op. cit., pp. 62–65, 116ff.

45. See Ogburn, op. cit., Part I, "The Social Heritage and the Original Nature of Man," pp. 3–51.

46. Martindale, op. cit., pp. 324–327.

47. In addition to his analysis of strain between material and nonmaterial cultures, Ogburn also discussed the strain between the biological makeup of human beings and the demands of the culture. Obviously, biological evolution lags far behind cultural evolution. The result is that modern persons are obliged to cope with the complex pressures of a rapidly changing society endowed with the primitive biological makeup of the caveperson. Contemporary problems such as widespread anxiety and mental illness may have their source in this discrepancy between cultural demands and biological nature. (See Ogburn, op. cit., pp. 283–365.)

48. See William F. Ogburn and Meyer F. Nimkoff, *Technology and the Changing Family* (Boston: Houghton Mifflin, 1955).

49. See William F. Ogburn and Meyer F. Nimkoff, *The Social Effects of Aviation* (Boston: Houghton Mifflin, 1946).

50. See Sorokin, *Sociological Theories of Today,* pp. 304–322, especially p. 316.

51. See Louis Schneider, *The Sociological Way of Looking at the World* (New York: McGraw-Hill, 1975), especially Chapter 3, "The Heritage of Culture."

52. Ibid., especially pp. 61–69.

53. See Sorokin, *Social and Cultural Dynamics,* 1-volume edition, Part IX, "Why and How of Sociocultural Change," especially Chapter 39, pp. 647–663.

Questions for Study and Discussion

1. In what ways did Comte fail to follow his own idea that sociology should be based firmly on a careful study of empirical data?

2. What are the arguments for a linear view of sociocultural change as opposed to a cyclical view?

3. Would Comte's views that conventional religious beliefs and institutions are an obstacle to continued scientific and social progress be relevant and valid today? Why or why not? In what ways does religion in America today differ from religion in the historical context in which Comte lived?

4. Do you agree or disagree with Sorokin's argument that the emphasis on materialistic values leads to increased selfishness and social anarchy? Why or why not?

5. What are the advantages and disadvantages of focusing on the cultural level of analysis as opposed to the social structural or interpersonal level?

4

Economic Structure, Class Conflict, and Social Change: The Social Theory of Karl Marx

Imagine that your income were five times what it is now. What effect would this have on your way of looking at the world? Would your political ideas and your views on who should pay more taxes and who should be given tax relief be the same? What changes would there be in your basic values and life-style? What kinds of people would you see as similar to you in economic position, cultural tastes, and world view? Such questions may help to sensitize us to the crucial effect that position in the economic hierarchy has on our values and ideological commitments, our cultural patterns and social relations, and our material well-being and life-style. Recognizing the importance of the material conditions to which individuals must adapt by virtue of economic position is a key foundation of Marx's theory.

Our individual lives and our society are based on an economic foundation. This means, among other things, that the institutions of politics, education, religion, science, the arts, family, and the like, depend on the availability of economic resources for their survival. It also suggests that these institutions cannot develop in ways that contradict the requirements of the economic system. The creation and maintenance of libraries and museums as repositories of cultural creations, the achievements of an athletic team, the implementation of a political policy, a family's enjoyment of a vacation trip, a scientist's laboratory research, the mobilization of a crowd to take part in a demonstration—these and innumerable other activities could not be carried out without economic resources and the material base provided through economic activities. This economic base is referred to by Marx as the "infrastructure" on which the rest of the social and cultural "superstructure" is erected and to which it must adapt.

Activities in the noneconomic sectors of society are not always consciously oriented toward the requirements of the economic foundation; indeed, there may be considerable autonomy in other social institutions. But in the final analysis activities in the various noneconomic institutions must operate within the limits established by economic requirements, and the specific social dynamics of other institutions cannot be greatly incompatible, in the long run, with the dynamics of the economy. Individuals and families recognize the importance of economic factors in their determination to "live within their income." Also, as Marx emphasized, the requirement of earning a living to insure biological survival may consume so much time and energy that it is almost impossible to develop other human potentialities.

In terms of our perspective here Marx's focus is on the social structural and not the cultural level of social reality. The contrast with Comte's and Sorokin's images of social reality and analytical focus should be apparent. They saw dominant ideas or world views as the key to understanding social reality; Marx concentrated on the way people adapt to their material environment. He also dealt with the social relations that emerge from this adaptation and the subordination of other aspects of social and cultural reality to this economic foundation. While dominant ideas or basic world views may *seem* to be the key to understanding a society, in reality ideas are "epiphenomenal"; that is, they are *reflections* of the material conditions of life and the economic structure through which people adapt to these conditions. Thus, to center on major intellectual themes as manifested in art, science, philosophy, and so on is to mistake an idealized or distorted reflection of reality for reality itself. In these and other noneconomic areas of life, people may experience a limited degree of independence and autonomy, but they cannot transcend the limitations imposed by their material condition or their economic resources and position.

For Marx, the key to understanding social reality is not found in abstract ideas but on factory floors or in coal mines, where workers toil at dehumanizing and dangerous jobs to keep from starving to death; in unemployment lines, where persons find their worth as human beings set by their inability to sell their labor power on the market; in capitalists' offices, where calculating analysis of the financial ledger leads to a decision to increase capital investment instead of wages; and, ultimately, in revolutionary confrontations between the leaders of workers' organizations and those representing the dominant capitalist class. Such events comprise social reality, not the naive and idealistic dream that science, technology, and industrial growth will lead to increased cooperation and steady improvement in the material well-being of all. As we will see, Marx also had a vision of a future utopian society, but this could only come about through revolutionary struggle, not as an organic growth of the social organism. Before discussing Marx's theoretical ideas, we will note briefly some crucial features of his social and intellectual environment.

MARX'S LIFE AND TIMES

Karl Marx was born in Trier, Germany, in the Rhine region in 1818.[1] Both his father Heinrich and his mother Henrietta came from families of Jewish rabbis. Heinrich Marx had received a secular education, however, and attained a relatively prosperous bourgeois life as a successful lawyer. When the political climate became unfavorable for his continued success as a Jewish lawyer, he and his family converted to Protestantism and were baptized into the Lutheran church. It is impossible to avoid the parallel between Henrich Marx's conversion to Protestantism for political and social expediency and Karl Marx's own emphasis later in his life on the idea that religious beliefs do not exert a major independent influence on behavior but, instead, reflect underlying social and economic factors. In any case, from his father and from Ludwig von Westphalen, a family friend and neighbor, Marx acquired an appreciation of eighteenth-century Enlightenment thought. Young Karl did not share his father's monarchical political beliefs, however.

At 18 years of age, after studying law for a year at the University of Bonn, Marx transferred to the University of Berlin. There, as a result of his association with the Young Hegelians, some of the basic ingredients of his social theory started to form. Although Hegel was dead when Marx entered the University of Berlin, his spirit and philosophy still dominated philosophical and social thought there. The Young Hegelians took a critical and irreverent stance toward many of Hegel's ideas and his followers, particularly their preoccupation with the past as opposed to the future and their increasingly conservative tone.

Hegel had propounded an idealistic philosophy by which he attempted to explain the broad patterns of historical change and progress. The key to his model was dialectical analysis. The usual elementary understanding of dialectical analysis hinges on the notion of opposition between a *thesis* and an *antithesis* and their ultimate reconciliation in a new *synthesis;* this, then, becomes the new thesis, in opposition to which a new antithesis emerges, and these are eventually combined in a new, higher-level synthesis. Although this model is rather abstract, it might be illustrated in a limited way in our own society's traditions by the opposition between ideas that have been used to justify various forms of social ranking and egalitarian ideas. It would be difficult to imagine such a fundamental dilemma ever being completely reconciled, however.

Historical progress, according to Hegel's abstract model, thus involves the negation of existing ideas and their replacement by new, opposing ideas. However, the new ideas are not final; they will eventually be negated also. Through this process the spirit of reason unfolds in succeeding historical stages as a series of opposing ideas are reconciled at ever higher levels. As it does, self-consciousness, which is really the consciousness of reason as it manifests itself, also increases. In other words, social progress reflects the unfolding of the spirit of reason as it discloses itself in history. A continuing struggle between existing ideas and social forms and those that are coming into being is a basic element of Hegel's model of sociocultural change. In the course of this struggle, individuals and societies gradually transcend themselves and achieve greater degrees of self-consciousness.

Hegel's views were idealistic; that is, he believed that the driving force of historical change is the unfolding of ideas whereby the spirit of reason becomes more fully manifested. Also, in his old age Hegel and some of his followers assumed that the social and political structure of the Prussian state was a full embodiment of the spirit of reason. In other words, there was a shift to a more conservative political position. This increasing conservatism led the Young Hegelians to criticize and reject the teachings of their acknowledged master. Thus Marx's reaction to Hegel was influenced as much by his exposure to the critical ideas of the Young Hegelians as by Hegel's ideas. Later, in developing his own theoretical and philosophical position, Marx would retain the dialectical mode of analysis (which involved sensitivity to internal contradictions and to the struggles between old and new ideas and social forms), but he would reject the philosophical idealism and substitute his version of a materialistic approach.[2]

After completing his doctoral dissertation at the University of Berlin, Marx intended to enter an academic career. However, his sponsor, Bruno Bauer, was dismissed from his academic post because of his leftist and antireligious views, leaving Marx without sponsorship. With the door to the academic world blocked, Marx accepted an invitation to write for the new liberal bourgeois paper, the *Rheinische Zeitung*. The paper's liberal-radical stance reflected bourgeois opposition to the remnants of the old feudal-aristocratic system. Marx became editor-in-chief of this paper; instead of confining himself to espousing bourgeois causes, he championed the cause of peasants and the poor. Marx's editorship was short; the paper was soon repressed and, after his marriage to Jenny von Westphalen (whose family had long been a friend of the Marx family), Marx and his young bride moved to Paris.

During his Paris years (1843–1845), Marx was in the thick of radical activity. Paris at that time was a major European center of social and intellectual liberalism and radicalism, and Marx became acquainted with the leading thinkers in French socialist thought, including St. Simon and Proudhon, and with even more revolutionary figures such as Blanqui. Marx's response to these ideas was affected by the convictions he had developed in association with the Young Hegelians. These convictions would eventually lead him to oppose the assumption that the abuses of the expanding capitalist system could be eliminated by a socialist transformation promoted solely by the intellectual elite. This approach ignored the actual material and social conditions and the degree of class consciousness of the working class. Similarly, Marx's understanding of the dialectical contradictions pervading the emerging capitalist society led him to oppose the idea that its deficiencies could be eliminated without a total transformation of the social structure and of people's consciousness.

Also while in Paris Marx became acquainted with the writings of the British political economists such as Adam Smith and David Ricardo. Recall from Chapter 1 that British and Scottish political economic theory argued that individuals' rational self-interest was the foundation for both the market and the social order, and that *laissez-faire* political policies were the best guarantee that individuals' rational self-interests would contribute to the public good. Marx took issue with the individualism of this approach, insisting that human *social* nature was ignored thereby. But, more important, Marx saw the extension of the impersonal market mentality to social relationships and social structure as a profound source of alienation.

Perhaps the most decisive event of Marx's Paris days was his encounter with Friedrich Engels, with whom he would be a close collaborator for the rest of his life. Since Engels' father was a textile manufacturer, Marx's acquaintanceship with him provided him firsthand information on the bourgeois life-style and also on the conditions of the proletariat. Engels had experience as a manager of one of his father's firms, but his involvement with Marx suggests that he had transcended his bourgeois class consciousness. Specifically, Engels impressed on Marx the fruitfulness of economic analysis; this, combined with Marx's own reading of the British political economists, led him to attempt to integrate economic and philosophical analysis. This attempt was reflected in Marx's *Economic and Philosophical Manuscripts*.[3]

Also, while Marx was still in Paris, he and Engels began work on a comprehensive interpretation of historical change and development that would be an alternative to Hegel's idealistic interpretation of history. In their interpretation, material conditions and the social relations resulting from them, not the unfolding of ideas or the growth of reason, are the foundation of intellectual developments and the driving force in historical change. This work eventually was published as *The German Ideology;* later, Engels would describe it as setting forth the principles of historical materialism.

Marx was expelled from Paris in 1845 by the government, partly as a result of pressure from the Prussian government, which was agitated by Marx's socialist writings. From Paris Marx went to Brussels, where he quickly became immersed in international socialist activities. His contacts in Brussels included workers as well as intellectuals; some were German refugees like himself. Many of these new acquaintances had been involved in the dissolved League of the Just, an international revolutionary organization.

In 1846 Marx and Engels traveled to England. Shortly after, they helped to establish corresponding committees to enable French, German, and English socialists to maintain contact. Soon Marx and Engels were invited to join the Communist League, a revolutionary organization headquartered in London and intended as an enlarged successor to the League of the Just. After an internal struggle between Marx and Weitling on the timing of the proletarian revolution and the preparatory role of the bourgeoisie, Marx was commissioned to write a statement that would be a theoretical platform for the organization. The result was *The Communist Manifesto,* published in 1847 and, for many years, the most widely read of Marx's writings. Unfortunately, the popularity of this work, combined with Marx's failure to get his *Economic and Philosophical Manuscripts* published, contributed to a one-sided picture of Marx's views. A more balanced perspective would see the *Manifesto* for what it was: a propaganda statement intended as a platform to unite and inspire the revolutionary members of the fledgling Communist League.[4]

In 1848 Marx was invited back to Paris by a new government. These were turbulent days, as revolutionary movements rapidly gained momentum throughout Europe. After a short stay in Paris, Marx returned to Germany to edit the *Neue Rheinische Zeitung* and, in this way, to influence the course of the revolution. Marx saw this period as the beginning of a crucial historical turning point that would soon lead to a culmination of the process of basic social transformation that had been initiated by the French Revolution in 1789. Both in 1789 and in 1848 the attacks on the traditional aristocratic dominance were spearheaded by the rising bourgeois class. But the 1848 revolutions included a better organized, more self-conscious, and potentially more influential contingent of working-class people than did the French Revolution over 50 years earlier. In view of his faith in the ultimate outcome Marx, unlike some working-class revolutionaries, supported an alliance between the bourgeois and the proletariat until the dominance of the aristocracy was overthrown; this phase of the revolution, in turn, would prepare the material and social conditions for the ultimate triumph of the proletariat over the bourgeoisie.

But Marx's expectations proved to be ahead of the times. While the bourgeois debated on how to proceed and some segments of the proletariat demanded an immediate proletarian revolution in spite of the inadequacy of the material and social conditions, the conservative forces managed a comeback, with the bourgeoisie in a much more powerful position. With the return of more prosperous times in the early 1850s, the fires of revolution had burned out. *The Neue Rheinische Zeitung* ceased publication in 1849, and Marx was again expelled from Germany. He returned to Paris but was not allowed to remain there; he went into exile in London, where he remained for most of the rest of his life.

Marx's own economic position in his early years in London was precarious. At first, he probably anticipated that his stay would be a short one, pending the renewal of revolutionary activity on the continent. He continued writing, most notably *The Class Struggles in France* and *The Eighteenth Brumaire of Louis Bonaparte.* These essays apply Marx's method of historical materialism by attempting to reveal the underlying social and material conditions beneath the surface of the ideological battles but expressed through them.

Marx's own desperate and insecure material condition meanwhile left him unable to provide adequately for his family. This situation was relieved somewhat through financial help provided by Engels, who had returned to work in one of his father's cotton firms. Also, Marx himself was able to earn some money when he made arrangements with the foreign editor of the *New York Daily Tribune* to send regular weekly articles on European events. In the middle 1850s, Marx received a small legacy as a result of a death in his wife's family; this gave the family temporary reprieve.

The most important work that Marx produced during his London years was *Das Kapital,* his *magnum opus.* In it he developed and systematized on a large scale many of the ideas that had been sketched earlier in the *Economic and Philosophical Manuscripts, The German Ideology,* and other writings. Overall, the focus of *Das Kapital* was on the internal contradictions within the capitalist system. These contradictions contribute to the expansive dynamism of the system but, at the same time, they provide the seeds for its ultimate radical transformation. The tone of this analytical work is quite different from that of *The Communist Manifesto.* Written some years after the 1848 revolution had failed, *Das Kapital* is Marx's effort to provide an objective and longer-range historical analysis of the dialectical forces within capitalism that will insure its ultimate demise. Above all, it was intended as a criticism of the orthodox theories of political economy, such as Smith's and Ricardo's, with their individualistic assumptions, their *laissez-faire* political implications, and their naive optimism regarding the long-range beneficial consequences of a free-market, capitalist economy.

Marx intended *Das Kapital* to be one part of an even larger, multivolume work on economics. However, the project was more forbidding than he had anticipated. Even though his preliminary plans were formulated in the early 1850s, he did not get his first volume published until 1867. By this time he had already completed rough drafts of Volumes 2 and 3 (which were not published in his lifetime). He did publish some preliminary works, however, including an *Outline of the Critique of Political Economy* (1857), *A Contribution to the Critique of Political Economy* (1859), and an *Introduction* (1859).[5] Marx's difficulties in producing his planned comprehensive treatise resulted partly from his recurrent financial worries, partly from declining health, and partly from periodic involvement in the political issues and conflicts of the revolutionary socialist movement.

The economic prosperity of the early 1850s was punctuated by a serious slump in 1857, but the 1848 revolutionaries were still disillusioned, and their ranks were plagued by internal disagreemnts. Thus no serious revolutionary threat erupted in the late 1850s in spite of the economic crisis. Marx meanwhile continued his studies, utilizing the resources of the British Museum to do the research necessary for his laborious project and remaining somewhat aloof from (although no doubt still interested in) practical political activities of the socialist movement.

By 1863, however, Marx was ready to end his political detachment. A group of French workers visiting an industrial exhibition in London discussed with the English workers they met there the possibility of organizing an international worker's organization. Representatives from various other countries were invited, and the fledgling federation was launched, representing a wide assortment of ideological persuasions. Marx became involved in this First International from the beginning and soon managed to become its dominant figure. He delivered the inaugural address and, for the remainder of the 1860s, attempted to steer the International between those who would compromise with bourgeois ideas in the interest of expediency and those who would promote anarchy without a practical understanding of what was realistically possible.

— Marx's goal during these years was to promote an understanding of the shortcomings and inevitable collapse of the capitalist system among the workers so they would understand the underlying dynamics of the historical stage in which they were involved and be confident in their own ultimate triumph. Marx's ideas had an impact; the International was a potent social and political force during the 1860s. The publication of the first volume of *Das Kapital* in 1867 solidified Marx's influence and intellectual dominance. The book was widely recognized as a definitive theoretical and historical analysis of the dynamics of capitalist society and of its eventual collapse from its own internal contradictions. Along with *The Communist Manifesto, Das Kapital* continued to be the most widely recognized of Marx's works, especially in America, until after World War II.

But the success of the International was short. Its climax was reached with the working-class seizure of power in Paris, a movement known as the Paris Commune, which was put down in a bloody confrontation. Shortly after, the ideological tensions within the International threatened to break out and divide the organization. Marx, sensing that the International had become a lost cause, proposed transferring its headquarters to New York. Even though the challenge of the International was more serious than the challenge of the Communist League, it was not the decisive historic catalyst that Marx anticipated. By the middle 1870s, it ceased functioning.

By this time Marx was an old man. He continued to write (no major new works were produced during these post-International days) and to correspond extensively with socialist leaders from throughout Europe. His financial situation improved significantly, thanks to an annuity provided by Engels, and he spent much time with his family. In 1883 (following the death of his wife by 2 years), Marx died.

Marx's career is inseparable from the development of the mid-nineteenth-century socialist movement. Like Comte, he was a marginal man, but for different reasons. Comte' marginal status stemmed from various personal eccentricities; Marx's marginality was related to his extensive involvement in radical causes.

Perhaps partly because of his marginality, Marx was a catalyst for three very different intellectual orientations. His theoretical contributions drew extensively from Hegel's dialectical method and German historicism, from British political economic theory, and from French socialist thought. However, all three orientations were changed significantly in Marx's work, and Marx's central ideas, although repetitiously stated over the course of his life, represent an important creative contribution to the development of modern sociology.

MARX'S HISTORICAL MATERIALISM

Historical materialism (a term Marx did not use) is useful as a label for the underlying assumptions of his theory, provided it is correctly understood. From *The Communist Manifesto* and *Das Kapital* it has traditionally been assumed that Marx's major emphasis was on human materialistic needs and the class struggle that results from efforts to satisfy these needs. In this view, ideas and human consciousness are nothing more than distorted reflections of material conditions. Additionally, attention has focused on Marx's promotion of a socialist revolution so that the proletariat could enjoy a greater share of the material abundance provided by industrialism.

These traditional assumptions are somewhat distorted. Marx did emphasize the importance of material conditions in opposition to Hegelian idealism, but he did not deny the reality of subjective consciousness or the crucial role that it may play in social change. Certainly he did not agree with the philosophical materialists who insisted that all of reality is nothing more than matter in motion. Nor did he agree with the positivist notion that the techniques of empirical investigation used in the natural sciences were adequate to explain human behavior or social change. To Marx, an acceptable scientific understanding of social phenomena requires the scientist to be true to the nature of the subject matter. This involves recognizing that human beings are not merely material organisms; instead, they are endowed with self-consciousness. That is, they have a subjective awareness of themselves and their material situations.[6]

Shortcomings of Traditional Abstract Philosophy

Marx's materialistic emphasis should be understood as a reaction to Hegel's idealistic interpretation of history. This philosophy of history ascribes a major determining role to the progressive evolution of ideas.[7] Marx rejected Hegel's philosophy of history because it attributed to the evolution of ideas a primary independent role in historical change without regard to the constraints and limitations of the material situation or to the social relations established by people in adapting to this material situation. In his view, idealistic theories such as Hegel's ignored the obvious fact that ideas do not exist independently of real people in a real-life material and social environment. Ideas are products of individuals' subjective consciousness, but consciousness is not separate from the material and social environment; it is always consciousness *of* this environment.

Marx expressed this emphasis as follows.

> In direct contrast to German philosophy which descends from heaven to earth, here we ascend from earth to heaven. That is to say, we do not set out from what men say,

imagine, conceive, nor from men as narrated, thought of, imagined, conceived, in order to arrive at men in the flesh. We set out from real, active men, and on the basis of their real life-process we demonstrate the development of the ideological reflexes and echoes of this life-process. . . . Morality, religion, metaphysics, all the rest of ideology and their corresponding forms of consciousness, thus no longer retain the semblance of independence. . . . Life is not determined by consciousness, but consciousness by life.[8]

The reason for the unwarranted attribution of independent power to ideas divorced from practical material conditions grows out of the division between material and mental labor or, in other words, from the emergence of a speculative class of people. Separated from practical, everyday activity, members of the speculative class can specialize in the elaboration of ideas, to which they then mistakenly attribute an independent influence in human affairs. To quote Marx:

Division of labor only becomes truly such from the moment when a division of material and mental labor appears. From this moment onwards consiousness *can* really flatter itself that it something other than consciousness of existing practices, that it is *really* conceiving something without conceiving something *real;* from now on consciousness is in a position to emancipate itself from the world and to proceed to the formation of "pure" theory, theology, philosophy, ethics, etc.[9]

The reciprocal interdependence between practical experience in the material world and the realm of consciousness and ideas is revealed in Marx's views on *Praxis*.[10] Although conventionally translated "practice," the German word really carries more meaning than the English word. By *Praxis* Marx refers to human activity that is carried out within the context of existing material and social conditions but is informed by an enlightened awareness of both material interests and basic human needs. *Praxis* is opposed to pure intellectual speculation and involves a willingness to examine dominant ideologies and existing social conditions critically.

Philosophical criticism is only a first step, however. The ultimate goal is to break through the mystifying effect of philosophy divorced from real human life and to realize the goal of philsophical criticism in practical political activity. The union of philosophical criticism and practical political activity must have the centrality of people as its basic guiding premise. As long as human beings are obliged to endure oppressive and dehumanizing material and social conditions, revolutionary overthrow of these conditions must be the goal of *Praxis*.

Marx's materialist conception applied to historical change was first elaborated in *The German Ideology,* coauthored with Engels. A major theme of this work is that changes in forms of consciousness, ideologies, or philosophical assumptions *reflected* instead of *caused* changes in human social and material life. The material conditions of life depend on both the natural resources available and the productive activity of human beings. Human beings are differentiated from animals in their ability to *produce* the material conditions of their lives; they do not simply fit into an ecological niche in nature or use material resources in their "natural state."

Nor do people adapt to nature or produce their material environment as isolated human beings; instead, they enter into social relations with other people in the course of attempting to satisfy their basic needs (for food, shelter, clothing, etc.). These elementary relations of production give rise to a division of labor. Closely related to the division of labor is the emergence of property relations involving differential ownership and control of basic resources and the various means of production. This differential ownership and control of property is the fundamental basis for the emergence of social classes. Since the material resources needed for the satisfaction of human needs are scarce, the relations between the different classes are bound to be competitive and antagonistic.

Also, unlike animals, human needs are insatiable. Humans do not limit their productive activity to the minimal level necessary for survival. As soon as elementary biological needs are met, new needs emerge, and the satisfaction of these new needs gives rise to new forms of material production and to new kinds of social relations. The result is a complex set of interdependent productive activities that reflect the existing level of technology. Each individual's specific productive activity and overall life-style are determined by his or her position in the division of labor and by the extent of his or her access to the material resources it provides.

In an ongoing society, the material conditions and accompanying social relations exist prior to the individual and are independent of any individual's will or conscious intentions. On a larger scale, each generation confronts an already existing material and social environment that includes various natural resources, tools and techniques of production, a division of labor with established patterns of social relations, and a class structure that reflects, in the final analysis, differential ownership or control of the means of production. The activities of individuals, whether oriented toward mere biological survival or toward fulfillment of various other human needs, are limited for them by the specific social position in which they happen to be in this social and material environment.

Also, individuals' ways of looking at the world (their subjective consciousness) are conditioned by their particular position in their material and social environment. As Marx repeatedly emphasized, consciousness is not divorced from people's actual experience in the real world; it is fundamentally consciousness *of* this real-world experience. This same close connection between individuals' real-life experiences and subjective mental states also applies to the whole realm of culture, including ideas and ideology, knowledge, ethics and morals, and aesthetic standards. None of these various aspects of culture is independent of its base in the material world.

However, the realm of subjective consciousness and cultural ideas is not *simply* a reflection of the material and social environment. There may be distortions that obscure its material and social basis. Indeed, the naive assumption that ideas or ideology are the major moving force in history is a good example of such a distortion, a distortion that is explainable, however, as a result of the aforementioned division of labor between the speculative class and classes involved in material production.

Materialistic Explanation of Historical Change

As applied to broad patterns of historical change, this materialistic emphasis focuses on changes in the *mode* or techniques of material production as the major source of social and cultural change. This would encompass the development of new technology, the discovery of new resources, or any other new development in the nature of productive activity. Changes such as these may result from efforts to improve existing strategies of coping with the material environment, to satisfy existing needs more efficiently, to fulfill new needs that emerge, and so forth. As the mode of production and the resulting material conditions change, contradictions emerge between the *modes of production* and the *social relations of production*. When this imbalance becomes sufficiently acute, it leads to changes in the relations of production, such as in the division of labor, with resulting shifts in class structure, changes in class or property relations, emergence of new classes or decline of old ones, or other kinds of related social changes.

For example, in the early days of the Industrial Revolution, the development of large-scale manufacturing machinery and related factory technology contradicted the social relations involved in the traditional system of handicraft production, carried out on a household basis, and stimulated the development of new types of social relations to take their place. Specifically, the old small-scale and highly personal kinds of relations that were possible and appropriate in household production were replaced by the highly impersonal market-type social relations of large-scale factory enterprises.[11]

In *The German Ideology* Marx and Engels traced the major changes in material conditions and modes of production, on the one hand, and social relations and property norms, on the other, from the primitive tribal community to contemporary capitalism. The primitive tribal community was one in which property was owned collectively and the division of labor was minimally developed. This stage was followed by the ancient communal type of social structure that is marked by increased size and division of labor and by the beginnings of private property. The next major stage is the feudal system, which involves further developments in the division of labor and strengthened patterns of ownership of private property. The feudal stage eventually gave way to the bourgeois mode of production and accompanying social relations.

The tragedy of the bourgeois stage is the undermining of communal life under the influence of individualistic ideologies and the reduction of human relationships to property relationships. In this capitalist stage, the proletarian wage earner is related to the bourgeois employer solely as a seller of labor power whose productive activity is consumed in making products to be sold in the impersonal market system. This stage is destined to be followed by the communist stage, which Marx idealizes as a stage in which private property will be abolished and individuals will be able to interact in communal, not merely economic, relationships. Moreover, the constraining and dehumanizing aspects of the division of labor will be replaced by a system that allows individuals to develop the full range of human potentialities instead of being limited to a narrow occupational specialty.

῀ The purpose of *The German Ideology* was to show that people create their own history as they struggle to cope with their material environment and engage in definite social relations in this process. However, the ability of people to make their own history is limited by the nature of the already existing material and social environment. Throughout their analysis Marx and Engels are sensitive to the internal contradictions that emerge during the various stages of history. Thus they identify the conflicting interests of opposing tribes whose relations are determined by military conquest, for example, of slaves and freemen, of landowners and those without land, of rural and agricultural people and town dwellers, and of manufacturing and commercial interests. The specific tensions and contradictions that are salient will vary according to the historical stage and its material and social development. But in all stages the struggles of individuals in different classes to cope with their particular material and social environment in order to survive and fulfill their needs is the major source of change to the next stage.

Marx's vision of the future communist society is extremely idealistic and seems to suggest an end to the internal contradictions and class conflicts that had been the major stimulus for social change in the past. However, the attainment of this stage depends on the material contributions of the̦ capitalist stage in promoting the maximum development of the productive forces of society. These productive forces would comprise the foundation for the future communist society by providing the material resources for the fulfillment of basic material needs. This would free individuals from the need to use all their time and energy for mere physical survival and enable them to devote time and energy to their full development as human beings.[12] Marx did not advocate destruction of the material base provided by bourgeois capitalism; instead, he envisioned communal ownership of the productive forces of society and a more equitable distribution based on human need, not bourgeois greed.

ECONOMIC INFRASTRUCTURE AND SOCIOCULTURAL SUPERSTRUCTURE

As noted in the previous section, individuals are obliged to transform their material environment through productive activity to survive and meet their various needs. But the means of production are not distributed equally among all members of society. This means that those who do not have access to the means of production must enter into social relations with those who do. The result is a differentiation of society's members into socioeconomic classes. The totality of all the various social relations of production, together with the associated means (or mode) of production, constitute the economic structure of society.

A consistent emphasis throughout all of Marx's writings is that the economic structure of society (i.e., the *means* and *social relations* of production) constitutes its real foundation. All other social institutions are built on this foundation and conform, to a greater or lesser degree, to the constraints and requirements imposed by the economic structure. Specifically, for example, the state and legal system must be supportive of the class system that emerges from differential ownership of the means of production. As Marx tersely asserted in *The Communist Manifesto,* ''The executive of the modern state is but a committee for managing the common affairs of the whole bourgeoisie.''[13]

While Marx repeatedly emphasized this dependence of politics on the economic structure, the same type of analysis would also apply to education, religion, family, and all other social institutions. Similarly, the culture of a society, including standards of morality, religious beliefs, philosophical systems, political ideologies, and patterns of artistic and literary creativity, also reflect the real-life experiences of people in their economic relations. This link between the economic infrastructural base and the social structural and cultural superstructures erected on this foundation is a direct corollary of the position of historical materialism discussed in the preceding section. People's adaptation to their material environment is always mediated through specific economic relationships, and these relations are so pervasive that all other social relations, as well as basic forms of consciousness, are molded by them.

To assert that the economy is the foundation of society is not to claim that there is a simple deterministic influence of the economy on the rest of society. Nor can all social processes in other institutions or all aspects of culture be neatly or simply explained as a result of economic necessity. The relations between the economy and the rest of society are more complex than that. Marx himself seemed to shift in his views on the degree of freedom afforded other institutions from the controlling influence of economic necessity or material conditions. Other institutions may acquire limited autonomy, as a result of which the dynamics of their own internal logic can be developed. They may even exert a limited influence on the economic base.

For example, in the area of religion, priests, theologians, or devotees may expand and embellish their beliefs according to the central theme and the ideals they express to the point where any connection between the religious consciousness and economic realities is quite obscure. This is similar to the point noted earlier that philosophers may develop their philosophical models to the point where they are convinced that philosophical ideas and not material forces determine the historical development of society. These examples illustrate the possibility that some aspects of culture may become partially detached from their economic base and develop in ways in which hard economic necessity or constraints cannot readily be discerned.

Nevertheless, *in the final analysis*, economic necessity always reasserts itself. For example, the limited opportunities that priests or philosophers might have to develop their beliefs or ideologies is dependent on sufficient economic resources to free them from the necessity of material labor. Presumably, the greater the freedom from economic constraints and limitations, the greater the possibility that noneconomic institutions may develop a massive and complex overlay of beliefs, attitudes, and ideologies that may obscure the economic foundation.

Effects of "False Consciousness" in Reinforcing Economic Structure

One reason for the difficulty in seeing the close connection between material and economic conditions and cultural ideologies is that cultural ideologies provide illusions to compensate for deficiencies and inadequacies in the material conditions of life. The result is that although the cultural ideology reflects the material conditions and economic relations of people's real lives, this reflection is often highly distorted. To the extent that these cultural ideologies are internalized in individuals' subjective consciousness, individuals find themselves unable to grasp what their true interests are. That is, they fail to see the close connection between their lack of human fulfillment, their dissatisfaction, and their suffering, on the one hand and, on the other, the economic and social structure and material conditions in which their lives are involved. The result is false consciousness.

The compensating and distorting function of ideology is most evident in Marx's analysis of religion. Marx argued that the traditional religious emphasis on a transcendental, nonmaterial realm and the hope for a life after death in this realm helped divert people's attention from their physical suffering and material hardship in this life. Furthermore, traditional religious ideals actually reverse natural priorities by suggesting that suffering and hardship have positive spiritual value if endured patiently, perhaps even increasing individuals' chances for rewards in the hereafter. Material wealth, worldly status, and power are viewed in the religious consciousness as illusionary, transitory, and as posing grave dangers with respect to individuals' spiritual well-being and rewards in the next life. Thus poverty is transformed into a virtue and wealth into a spiritual liability. This is the basis for Marx's famous quip regarding religion being the "opiate of the people." Such a religious ideology would probably not be accepted with equal fervor by all social classes, but its serious acceptance by the lower classes of society would tend to encourage their passive acquiesence and willingness to endure the hardship associated with lower-class status rather than revolt.

Besides holding out hopes of future rewards that will compensate for the deficiencies of this physical life, religious ideologies typically provide tacit support for the existing social, political, and economic arrangements of society. The ancient belief in the divine right of kings is a blatant example of religious legitimation for the political structure, as was the occasional medieval practice of acquiring the support of the church to help bolster the legitimacy of the "temporal" political ruler. In American society the traditional, widely accepted idea that our society has divine support is a similar source of political legitimacy. More generally, religious support for various norms that underlie the social order (norms of private property, etc.) legitimate the status quo and motivate individuals to act in accordance with the requirements for maintaining the existing social order.

The same type of analysis is also used in Marx's critique of political ideologies and the structure of the state. In *The German Ideology* Marx treats the state as a compensation for the tensions that result from the division of labor. The political system of the state and its supporting ideology offer the illusion of a human community. This masks the conflicts between the opposing classes of society and provides the framework within which the dominant class is able to protect its interests. Moreover, in its power to establish the legal framework for economic and other kinds of social transactions, in its monopolization of the right to exert coercion on its citizens, and in its function of setting national policies vis-à-vis other nations, the state serves the economic interests of the social classes that are strong enough to control it for their own purposes.

Marx did not deal with other social institutions as extensively as the economy, the political system, and religion. However, his basic premise regarding the primacy of the economic system could readily be extended in analyzing other institutions. Marx and Engels do provide some comments on the family, for example, pointing out the effects of the proletarian class position on family forms. Specifically, the economic status of the working-class individual was so precarious that wives and children were obliged to work long hours in factory jobs in order to provide sufficient income for their families to survive. Thus the husbands and fathers were reduced to treating other family members as sources of family income just as they were treated as commodities with labor power to sell in the impersonal market. In other words, the quality of relationships established in the economy "spills over" into family relationships.

Not only specific institutions with their own supporting ideologies but the overall world view dominant in a society will reflect, with varying degrees of clarity, the material conditions of life as mediated through the economic structure and will support the positions of the dominant class within that structure. As Marx said, "The ideas of the ruling class are in every epoch the ruling ideas... "[14] Marx's position on this point is that of a complete relativist for whom ultimate or absolute knowledge or moral standards do not exist. Instead, all forms of human creative, intellectual activity are conditioned by the material and social environment and reflect a specific historical stage in human development of this environment.

Changes in Socioeconomic Structure and Changes in World View

It is not the unfolding of ideas that explains the historical development of society (as Hegel and Comte would have argued), but the development of the social structure in response to changing material conditions that explains the emergence of new ideas. Even the development of revolutionary ideas depends on the formation of new material forces that generate changes in social relations; thus the apparent struggle between revolutionary ideologies and conservative (or reactionary) ideologies is a reflection of the material struggle between the social classes that represent the new material and social forces and the social classes whose dominance rests on perpetuating the existing social and economic structure.

As an example of the relationship between the overall ideological world view and the economic structure, in the preindustrial feudal society the social divisions between landowners, serfs, and peasants were thought to be part of the divinely ordained plan for this temporal world. However, the intellectual world view supporting this type of social structure, with its aristocratic dominance, was not consistent with the economic interests of the emerging bourgeois class, whose rise to economic prominence was brought about by the growth of industrialization and commercial expansion. Just as the traditional aristocratic social order was supported by an appeal to eternal abstract principles, so also were the bourgeois ideological attacks on this social order justified by an appeal to eternal natural law. Traditional inherited privileges of the aristocratic class were attacked as gross violations of natural law, and support for individual liberty and political equality were seen as being derived from natural laws that any reasonable person could discern. In reality, Marx suggests, the demand for "liberty, equality, and fraternity" (the rallying cry of the French Revolution) was a demand that the rising bourgeois class be freed from traditional constraints and limitations on their rights to pursue their bourgeois interests.

In the same way, British political economic theories, in their justification of the impersonal *laissez-faire* market system, also served the interests of the expanding bourgeois capitalist class. Starting from an extremely individualistic view of human nature (which Marx rejected), the British political economists argued that the impersonal market system of the capitalist economy freed individuals from traditional artificial social constraints to pursue their own private interests, while at the same time providing assurance that the overall welfare of the society was best served through this pursuit. In opposition to the argument that the impersonal market system was grounded in some immutable natural law of political economy or was consistent with basic human nature, Marx offered the counterargument that the impersonal market system of the capitalist economy is specific to a particular historical stage and reflects the social relations of that stage. However, just as previous ideologies are eventually superseded, so also will the ideological support that political economy offers capitalistic development eventually be transcended when changing social relations make it obsolete.

The relevance of this prediction is borne out by even a cursory examination of the history of the *laissez-faire* ideology in our own society. As our society has grown more complex and as independent small businesspeople have been replaced by giant corporations that require more of government than a simple "hands-off" policy, the extreme form of *laissez-faire* political policies has lost much of its credibility. Many students, when exposed to this idea for the first time, wonder how such an ideology could ever have been seriously entertained as a way to promote the public welfare. In our own times the support of Republican party spokespersons for the free enterprise system is an echo of the old doctrine that business people contribute to the well-being of society as they selfishly pursue their own interests. But even the most conservative of them do not envision the kind of unregulated economy that Adam Smith did in the eighteenth century or Herbert Spencer in the nineteenth.

Marx's basic contention regarding the pervasive influence of the economic system on other institutions and patterns of culture can readily be extended to provide a comprehensive critique of modern industrial societies. Such a critique need not be limited to an analysis of the state or dominant ideologies. The various institutions could be analyzed to show their dependence on the material resources that are provided through the economic system and their subservience (whether conscious or unconscious) to the requirements of the economic system. The educational institution, for example, might be seen as serving the needs of the economy by indoctrinating individuals with norms and values that support the status quo and by training them to fill occupational positions in the economic system. The mutlifaceted entertainment industry can be seen in a critical perspective as providing diversion and pacification that help individuals endure their lack of personal fulfillment and their subordination to the demands of the economic system; it is also a major economic institution in its own right.

Again, Marx did not consistently argue for crude economic or materialistic determinism. Even though the economy is the foundation of the whole sociocultural system, other institutions may acquire a limited degree of autonomy and even exert a limited influence on the economic structure on which they ultimately depend. Like many other writers, Marx sometimes overstated his case in order to establish his point against competing viewpoints. With these qualifications in mind, Marx's analysis of material conditions and economic structure as the foundation of the rest of the sociocultural system provides a note of hard realism that is sometimes lacking in more idealistic theories of society. Certainly, however, Marx recognized that human needs and aspirations go far beyond mere economic survival, even though economic realities and material conditions may be such that other kinds of human needs may be left unfulfilled. The relation between human activity, especially economic activity, and the opportunity to find fulfillment as a human being will be explored more fully in the following section.

ACTIVITY AND ALIENATION

Central to Marx's overall theory is the proposition that human survival and the fulfillment of human needs depends on productive activity in which people actively engage in transforming their natural environment. Productive activity has an ironic and paradoxical result, however, As individuals express their creative energy in productive activity, the products of this activity take on the character of objective entities that become independent of their human producers. Since productive activity involves an expenditure of human energy and creative ability, the products created actually embody a portion of the "human essence" (a favorite Marxist expression). Thus human beings confront their own essence (i.e., the results of their energy and creative ability) in an alienated or estranged form, or as objects in the external world that are beyond their control and to which they must adapt. Subsequently, individuals' freedom to continue to express their creativity and to develop their potentialities as human beings is severely constrained.

In other words, individuals must adapt to a world of objects that limits their freedom as human beings but that they themselves have created. Of course, they are not aware that the limitations and constraints from which they suffer are of their own making. Like Scrooge in Dickens' Christmas classic, they are bound by chains that they, themselves, have unwittingly forged. This is the most general statement of the dialectical process leading to alienation or self-estrangement, and Marx's critical analysis of social institutions and forms of consciousness relies heavily on an understanding of it.[15]

For example, Marx wrote on the alienating consequences of the mechanized system of production in the factory. Machines are made by people, of course, and so represent human creative activity. Moreover, they have a *potential* liberating influence in freeing people from physical toil. But the *actual* effect of the development of machine technology in the early days of the Industrial Revolution was to enslave workers, limiting their opportunity for creative activity. Submission to the discipline of machine production, Marx argued, dehumanizes workers, requiring that they serve the machine instead of making the machine serve them.

This same process applies not only to material artifacts in the physical environment but also to the nonmaterial culture created through human activity. For example, in formal organizations individuals create rules and regulations as a means of coordinating their activities to achieve their collective goals; then, as students of formal organization such as Merton[16] have frequently pointed out, they allow themselves to be so dominated by the rules and regulations they have established that the rules and regulations become an end in themselves, not a means to an end. Numerous other institutional patterns also have this character. Social institutions are, in the final analysis, the products of human beings' creative activity; yet these institutions often appear to individuals' consciousness as objective and alien powers to which they must submit.

Influence of Feuerbach

Marx's theory of alienation and self-estrangement borrows heavily from Ludwig Feuerbach's inversion of Hegelian philosophy. Feuerbach was even more consistent than Marx in insisting that the realm of human consciousness and ideas is *merely* a reflection of material forces, a position that, like Marx's, reverses Hegel's philosophy. Feurerbach had developed his perspective in *Essence of Christianity,* his critique of religion. Briefly, his argument was that religion represents the human projection of essential human qualities—human potentialities and aspirations—onto a supernatural being. This projection leaves people psychologically emptied of these qualities and, in order to regain them, people must approach a supernatural being as a supplicant, pleading for the return of the qualities that will make them fully human—but that were really theirs in the first place. Thus, in Feuerbach's analysis, religion represents human beings' estrangement from their own nature.

Feuerbach also extended this analysis to Hegelian idealistic philosophy. According to him, Hegel's philosophy was nothing more than an abstract and philosophical form of theological thinking. It ascribed an independent role to the unfolding of the universal spirit of reason, interpreting human behavior and human history as manifestations of the self-disclosure of the spirit of reason independent of human activity. Feuerbach's inversion of this approach in his own materialistic philosophy provided the Young Hegelians with an attractive ideological alternative to Hegel's philosophy.

Although Marx's theory of alienation was influenced by Feuerbach, Marx was also critical of Feuerbach. Specifically, he attacked Feuerbach's one-sided materialistic emphasis and his abstract ahistorical view of the passive individual isolated from the social context. In opposition to Feuerbach, Marx emphasized the importance of understanding the specific social and historical context within which specific forms of consciousness and specific religious or ideological illusions emerge. Marx also emphasized the active role that individuals may play in the historical process. Instead of accepting Feuerbach's one-sided materialistic emphasis in which a person is a passive object acted on by material forces, Marx emphasized the *dialectical* relationship between a person as an object and a person as an active subject. Through *Praxis,* people make their own history while, at the same time, their creative activity is conditioned and constrained by the specific material and social environment already established. Marx's most terse and cogent criticism of Feuerbach is contained in his famous *Theses on Feuerbach*; its concluding statement is: "The philosophers have only *interpreted* the world, in various ways; the point, however is to *change* it."[17]

Marx's commitment to changing the world through practical activity is based on his own idealistic belief that alienation can ultimately be overcome. Feuerbach's insight regarding religion as a source of alienation was only the first step for Marx; the next was to identify the specific material and social conditions that are the sources of alienation and illusions. Once the real-life conditions that create the need for alienating illusions are uncovered through social criticism, the next step is revolutionary activity, which will abolish the need for illusions by enabling people to act creatively for themselves.

Marx agreed with Feuerbach that the most profound form of alienation is the one expressed in religious and philosophical ideologies. Acceptance of such ideologies helps to compensate human beings for the deficiencies and deprivations that are left unfulfilled in their real lives as a result of the internal contradictions within the social structure. However, this is not the only area in which alienation can be observed; it is also expressed in economic relations and in political institutions and ideologies.

Alienation of Labor in Capitalist Society

Marx's 1844 *Economic and Philosophical Manuscripts* was intended as a criticism of the established political economic theories developed in England by Smith, Ricardo, and others. British political economy was based on a very individualistic view of human nature. The existence of society was explained as a result of contractual agreements that individuals entered as a result of a rational assessment of how best to pursue their own individual interests. Another basic doctrine was that the overall welfare of society is best served by allowing individuals as much freedom as possible to pursue their selfish interests. This *laissez-faire* approach was promoted and celebrated as a significant advance in human freedom.

With his background in Hegelian dialectical philosophy, Marx drew conclusions from his study of the *laissez-faire* capitalist system that were far less benign than those of the British thinkers. Specifically, he lamented the effects of increased individualism and the free market associated with it in dissolving the traditional social bonds that had, in the past, helped to humanize economic relationships. He saw these effects as reducing people to mere commodities on the market whose labor was bought and sold like any other commodity without any concern for the human needs of those involved in this process. The result is alienation of human beings from each other and from their own social nature. Marx pressed this point in his famous *Communist Manifesto*. "The bourgeoisie, wherever it has got the upper hand, has put an end to all feudal, patriarchal, idyllic relations. It has pitilessly torn asunder the motley feudal ties that bound man to his "natural superiors," and has left remaining no other nexus between man and man than naked self-interest, than callous cash payment.''[18]

Alienation also results from individuals' loss of control over their own creative activity and over the products they produce. Work is experienced as a necessity for mere survival and not as a means for human beings to develop or express their creative potentiality. Individuals find they are unable to fulfill themselves, in the broadest sense of this term, through their productive activity.

Similarly, loss of control over the products of their activity means that they cannot use the products they produce for meeting their own needs, even though these products actually embody their own life energy in objective form. Instead, workers produce commodities to be exchanged in an impersonal market system. The result is that they confront the products of their own labor and life's energy in an alien form, or as objects in the external world of the market over which they have lost control. In short, workers in the capitalist system are obliged to perform unfulfilling and dehumanizing work from which they are unable to benefit except in the narrow sense of providing for their mere physical needs.

This philosophical critique of political economy is set against the background of an analysis of capitalist economic processes. Contrary to the optimistic views of the political economists, Marx showed that the normal operations of the impersonal economic laws of supply and demand reduced the wages of labor to the level at which workers were barely able to survive by working the maximum number of hours possible. Since capitalists obviously have an economic interest in keeping the cost of producing commodities as low as possible, the wages they offer are barely high enough to attract workers to offer their labor for sale. The workers, however, hardly have a choice in the matter inasmuch as they do not own the means of production; thus their only option is to offer their labor at wages set by the capitalist employers in order to survive.

Since the supply of human beings as workers exceeds the demand of capitalists for their services, the economic laws of supply and demand insure that wages are kept at the lowest possible level. This relationship between capitalist employers and workers is a purely economic one, devoid of any moderating or humanizing influence of noneconomic social ties. The worker becomes, in effect, a commodity on the labor market whose job is dictated by the desires of the capitalist employers for maximum profits and by the demands of machine production. The worker serves the machine instead of the machine serving the worker; in a larger sense, the worker serves the capitalist employer.

Paradoxically, the more productive laborers are in producing commodities, the more they find themselves impoverished and unable to control their own life activities. As Marx said:

> The worker puts his life into the object, and his life then belongs no longer to himself but to the object. The greater his activity, therefore, the less he possesses. What is embodied

in the product of his labour is no longer his own. The greater this product is, therefore, the more he is diminished. The *alienation* of the worker in his product means not only that his labour becomes an object, assumes an *external* existence, but that it exists independently, outside himself, and alien to him, and that it stands opposed to him as an autonomous power. The life which he has given to the object sets itself against him as an alien and hostile force.[19]

Alienation is inherent in any system with a division of labor and private property, but its most extreme form is found in capitalism, in which the impersonal mechanisms of the market, with its reduction of human beings to commodities, is seen as an expression of natural law and human freedom. This extreme form of alienation results from the expropriation of the products of labor by their capitalist employers. Marx developed this point as follows. "If the product of labour is alien to me and confronts me as an alien power, to whom does it belong? If my own activity does not belong to me but is an alien, forced activity, to whom does it belong? To a being *other* than myself. And who is this being?"[20] The obvious answer is that it is the capitalist employer.

Moreover, there is no valid defense of such a system in the argument that since the capitalists own the means of production, they have the right to control the products that labor produces using these means. The means of production are themselves the objectification and embodiment of prior labor. Machines and other technology do not exist in nature; they are produced by people. This means that capitalist control of the means of production is really control over the objectified labor power of the laborers involved in capital goods production. The rules that defend the rights of capitalists to control the products produced by labor because they own the means of production reflect the efforts of capitalists to solidify and reinforce their "right" to exploit the labor power of the working class.

The solution of the problem of working-class exploitation and misery is not simply to raise wages. Increased wages might alleviate the material hardship faced by workers, but it would not overcome the alienating consequences of the division of labor and private property. Workers would still be essentially a commodity, without the opportunity to develop the human nature they share with other human beings (what Marx refers to as their "species life") or their human potentialities, and the products of their labor would still be controlled by others and would confront workers as alien objects. This estrangement from the products of individuals' creative activities is a much more profound problem than the problem of inadequate wages; it requires not just increases in wages but a radical transformation of society for its resolution.[21]

Political Alienation

Another manifestation of alienation is expressed in Marx's theory of the state. In an article written early in his career entitled "On the Jewish Question" and in his criticisms of Hegel's philosophy of the state, Marx analyzed the distinction between the state and civil society. The distinction corresponds to the distinction between people as *individuals* with basic biological needs and egoistic interests and people as *social* beings who share a common "species life." The state represents, in objective form, people's "species life," or the communal side of human nature. However, since people project this side of their dual nature onto the external institution of the state, their real life is dominated by the egoistic side of their human nature. Indeed, the opposition is so great that in bourgeois political revolutions the state is seen as giving individuals certain rights as citizens—as though the state were in some way independent of the members of civil society who make it up, and as though individuals as *citizens* were somehow different from individuals as *real men and women*. This analysis of the state parallels Marx's analysis of religion; in both cases one dimension of human nature is projected onto an external entity that, although created by people, comes to confront people as an alien power to which they must become subject.

Marx's analysis of the state changed somewhat as he developed his views. For example, in *The German Ideology* Marx treated the state as a compensation for the tensions in society resulting from the division of labor. The dialectical conflict between individuals' private and public lives is masked by the illusions that the state provides of a genuine human community that transcends the real conflicts between the opposing classes of society. But in *The Communist Manifesto* Marx's emphasis shifts somewhat to the view that the state serves primarily to protect the interests of the dominant classes of society. These two views are not necessarily contradictory, but the shift in emphasis from the state as a source of illusions regarding human communal life to the state as a tool used by the dominant classes should be apparent.[22]

Alienation seems to be virtually inevitable in view of the paradoxical nature of human activity. On the one hand, human beings express their creative human potential in their activity; on the other hand, the products of their creative activity become objects that are beyond human control and that dominate their creators, inhibiting their continued creativity. This fundamental human paradox is exacerbated in societies with a division of labor and private property. Although most historical societies have included these alienating features (except for the stage of primitive tribal communism), they are far more highly developed in bourgeois capitalist societies, so that the degree of alienation is much higher than in previous stages of society. Indeed, overcoming the alienation inherent in the structure of capitalist societies will require nothing less than a total revolution that will abolish all the internal contradictions in society by transcending the division of labor, private property, the state in its traditional form, and all exploitation and oppression. This will bring an end to alienation, Marx believed, enabling people to express their full human nature in activity for themselves.

SOCIAL CLASSES, CLASS CONSCIOUSNESS, AND SOCIAL CHANGE

One of the most profound and far-reaching contradictions inherent in any society with a division of labor and private property is the opposition between the material interests of different social classes. The crucial role that the concept of class plays has been implicit in our discussion of economic relations, political structure, and alienation. In this section we turn to a more explicit analysis of social classes and of the significance of class conflict in generating social change.

Marx was not the first to discover social classes in society. In spite of his frequent use of the concept, nowhere does he provide a systematic and comprehensive analysis of it. Yet the concept of class is so pervasive in almost all of his major writings that it would be safe to say that he considered it the most basic category of social structure. The most significant divisions within society are the divisions between different classes; the most important factor influencing an individual's life-style and consciousness is class position; the greatest tensions and conflicts in society, whether latent or open, are those between different classes, and one of the most potent sources of social change is that provided by the victory of one class over another. As Marx said early in *The Communist Manifesto:*

> The history of all hitherto existing society is the history of class struggles.
> Freeman and slave, patrician and plebeian, lord and serf, guildmaster and journeyman, in a word, oppressor and oppressed, stood in constant opposition to one another, carried on an uninterrupted, now hidden, now open fight, a fight that each time ended, either in a revolutionary re-constitution of society at large, or in the common ruin of the contending classes.[23]

Economic Relations and Class Structure

How do social classes originate? What determines their relationship to each other? The answers to these questions are closely connected with Marx's materialistic conception of history discussed earlier. Recall that human beings' ability to meet their various needs depends on their entering into social relations with others to transform the material environment through productive activity. These elementary social relations constitute the economic infrastructure of society. In the beginning these relations are influenced by the natural differences between people in terms of strength, size, energy, abilities, and the like. But very early in the emergence of a society's economic structure, a division of labor is developed, and this necessitates a system of exchange. These social processes, coupled with the natural differences between people, soon give rise to differences in ownership or control of natural resources and of the tools of production. This differential ownership or control of the means of production, which Marx emphasizes much more strongly than the natural biological differences between people, is the primary basis for the formation of different social classes.

Because of the scarcity of natural resources and the natural interest of each individual in maximizing personal material well-being, the relations between classes must be antagonistic. This fundamental antagonism may be masked by the development of ideologies that provide the illusion of a harmonious community of interests and by various noneconomic social bonds, but the antagonism still persists, even though it is not necessarily visible to the members of society.

Ownership or control of the means of production is the primary basis for social classes in all types of society, from the earliest class-differentiated society that emerged from primitive tribal communism (in which, presumably, the division of labor and private property were only minimally developed, if at all) to modern capitalism. However, there are important differences in class structures between different types of society or different stages of history, largely because of the variations in the resources and means of production.

The most significant impetus for class changes is expansion in the means of production represented by technological development. The effect of the development of new tools and techniques of production is that these productive forces eventually become inconsistent with the social relations of production as represented by existing class relations. Technological development may lead to the emergence of new occupational groups, it may undermine the economic basis for a group's dominance, or it may alter in other ways the nature of the social and material environment in which individuals are involved. For example, the growth of large-scale machine production in the early days of the Industrial Revolution provided a significant alternative to land as a resource and means of production and propelled the bourgeois capitalist class into a position of economic dominance that undermined the aristocratic class. At the same time, the proletariat emerged as part of the same process and, in Marx's theory, was destined to play the major role in eventually transforming capitalist society into the next historical stage (which he believed would be the final stage).

Even though ownership or control of the means of production is always the ultimate source of class divisions, the specific characteristics of the different classes and the nature of the social relations between them will differ in different societies or different historical stages. For example, the social relations between the landed nobility and the serfs in feudal times differed substantially from the social relations between the capitalist employer class and the proletarian worker class. For one thing, noneconomic social bonds were more richly developed in the former type. Similarly, the class relations in feudal society differed in important ways from the earlier stage involving slavery.

Along with the differences in class relations in various stages of history, there are also internal differences in life-style and modes of consciousness wtihin the major classes. Even though the landed nobility and the bourgeois capitalists each dominated their respective stages of history, there are major differences between these classes. Indeed, the bourgeois capitalist class had to engage in revolutionary struggle against the aristocratic class in order to establish its dominance. Similarly, the urban proletarian class differs substantially from the rural peasantry, even though both are subordinate classes.

Primary versus Secondary Class Distinctions

Our discussion so far has presupposed a two-class model of society. Although the quotation from *The Communist Manifesto* on p. 140 emphatically asserts this model, Marx was not always consistent in this regard. In a section of the third volume of *Das Kapital*, Marx began a systematic treatment of the concept of class in which he identified three major classes in capitalist society: wage laborers, capitalists, and landowners. These classes are distinguished primarily by the differences in their principal sources of income, which are wages, profits, and ground rent, respectively. The sharp divisions between these primary classes may be obscured by various intermediate or other secondary groups. In England, for example, which was the most highly developed capitalist society, Marx conceded that the primary three-part class system was not apparent in its pure form.

Moreover, as the capitalist system develops, Marx anticipated that the three-class system would gradually be replaced by a two-class system as intermediate strata are eliminated and, apparently, as the capitalist mode of operations is extended from industrial to agricultural enterprises. The idea that the capitalist societies of Marx's times were in the process of moving toward a simplified two-class system is also suggested in *The Communist Manifesto*: "Society as a whole is more and more splitting up into two great hostile camps, into two great classes directly facing each other: Bourgeoisie and Proletariat."[24]

While the three-class model or perhaps the two-class model (depending on the specific historical stage) might describe the most basic class divisions in capitalist society, other classes can also be identified. The bourgeois class, for example, can be subdivided into the dominant bourgeois and the petty bourgeois. The dominant bourgeois would consist of the large capitalists with giant enterprises who employ large numbers of workers; the petty bourgeois would consist of small shopkeepers, small manufacturers, and the like, whose operations are much smaller. Among the dominant capitalists, a distinction can also be made between finance capitalists and industrial capitalists.[25] Marx predicted that the development of capitalist society toward the two-class system would eventually result in the elimination of the petty bourgeois class and the proletarianization of its members.

Marx also identified the "lower middle class, the small manufacturer, the shopkeeper, the artisan, the peasant" who are engaged in a fight against the bourgeois.[26] From another standpoint, however, the peasants should be considered as a category distinct from the others. They do not clearly fit into the three-class system, even though they most closely resemble the proletariat in the three-class listing. However, their ideology is reactionary, and their level of organization as a class is nonexistent.

Also, below the level of the proletarian wage earners in a capitalist society, there are the social "dropouts" and "ne'er-do-well's," which Marx refers to as the *Lumpenproletariat*; this category is "a recruiting ground for thieves and criminals of all kinds, living on the crumbs of society, people without a definite trade, vagabonds, people without a hearth or a home."[27] Intellectuals also form an intermediate class that does not fit neatly into the two- or three-class model. On the whole, however, they support the bourgeois class by their development of ideologies that reinforce the economic and social structure. In *The Communist Manifesto* Marx asserts that "the physician, the lawyer, the priest, the poet, the man of science" have been converted into the "paid wage-labourers" of the bourgeoisie.[28] (Marx would no doubt consider himself an exception, and his own personal economic hardship would prove it.) As a final indication of how Marx departed from the simple two- or three-class system, his analysis of the class struggles in France identified seven different classes: "the financial bourgeoisie, the industrial bourgeoisie, the mercantile bourgeoisie, the petty bourgeoisie, the peasants, the proletariat, the lumpenproletariat."[29]

Marx's refusal to be bound by his own two- or three-class model is consistent with his view of social structure as continually undergoing change and as varying in different historical periods. The specific constellation of classes that can be identified in different societies or in different historical periods cannot be analyzed adequately by any static model that ignores these variations. The productive forces that are differentially distributed between dominant and subordinate classes will vary, as will the array of secondary or intermediate classes. Nevertheless, in spite of these historical variations, the most fundamental basis for class divisions is access to the means of production and, in the crucial historical turning points, this fundamental criterion reveals itself more and more clearly.

Objective Class Interests and Subjective Class Consciousness

The basic underlying source of the major class distinctions—differential access to the means of production—may not be apparent to the members of society, particularly in relatively stable periods. This is due to the emergence of various secondary or intermediate classes and also to the development of ideologies that provide illusions that actually hide individuals' true class interests. The result is that individuals may not even be aware of their own class interests, which they share with others who are in a similar position.

The question then arises as to whether a mere aggregate of people who share a similar position in the productive system but who do not communicate with each other or are not aware of their common interests should be considered a class. In

The Communist Manifesto Marx suggests that the organization of the proletarians into a class was being disrupted by their competition with one another. This implies that their common proletarian position itself is not sufficient to consider them a class. Similarly, capitalists themselves do not always act in a united fashion; in fact, their normal mode of activity is to compete with each other. To the extent that their relations are competitive, they do not fully qualify as a class. Yet, as noted earlier, a person's class is objectively determined as the position that person occupies in the existing social relations of production and the access it provides to the various means of production. Marx recognized both an objective and a subjective aspect to the concept of class, and the fullest meaning of the term must include both aspects.

Marx contrasted the two dimensions and specified the importance of the subjective dimension most clearly in his analysis of nineteenth-century French peasants.

> In so far as millions of families live under economic conditions of existence that separate their mode of life, their interests and their culture from those of the other classes, and put them in hostile opposition to the latter they form a class. In so far as there is merely a local interconnection among these small-holding peasants, and the identity of their interests begets no community, no national bond and no political organisation among them, they do not form a class.[30]

Related to the distinction between the objective and subjective dimensions of class is the distinction between class interests and class consciousness. The latter involves a subjective awareness of objective class interests shared with others in similar positions in the productive system. The concept of "interests" refers to the actual material resources needed to fulfill individuals' needs or desires. Thus, for example, the class interests of the capitalists are in increased profits; the interests of the proletarian class, if defined narrowly, include wage increases but, if defined more broadly, would include greater control over the productive process.

Lack of full awareness of class interests is due mostly to the acceptance of ideologies developed to support the dominant class and the existing social structure. The effect of these ideologies is to create "false consciousness." False consciousness might include the belief that one's present and future material well-being lies in supporting the political status quo, that one's material interests are compatible with the interests of the ruling class, or that the ruling class is genuinely concerned about the welfare of all segments of society. Whatever the specific belief, false consciousness creates illusions that obscure the real interests of a segment of society and support the interests of the dominant class.

An example will clarify the distinction between true class consciousness and false class consciousness. Factory workers at the bottom of the organizational hierarchy who believe that if they work hard they will eventually be promoted to high positions in the firm and who, therefore, see their own personal success as linked with the success of the firm would probably be exhibiting false consciousness, particularly if actual promotion rates are very low. In opposition to this "company person" ideology, factory workers who realize that their chances for promotion are very slight and who, therefore, work to help organize fellow workers into a union to pressure management for higher wages, better working conditions, greater automony, and so on, would probably be exhibiting true class consciousness.

Emergence of Class Consciousness and Class Struggle

What causes false class consciousness to be replaced by true class consciousness? Marx's answer to this question centered on developments within the proletarian class of capitalist society. One important factor is the increasing concentration of proletarian workers in urban industrial areas. As they work together in common dehumanizing conditions in the factory and live adjacent to each other in blighted urban neighborhoods, the protetariat become aware of their common misery and economic plight. In short, concentration leads to the establishment of communication networks and resulting shared consciousness. Indeed, this is one of the major distinctions between the urban proletarian class and the rural peasantry, whose members live isolated from each other and who seldom communicate on any sustained basis.

Also, Marx envisioned that the oppressed condition of the proletarian class would gradually become more and more miserable as the capitalist society approached its impending demise. It is not entirely clear whether this prediction of increasing immiseration of the working class is to be taken in an absolute or a relative sense. If taken in an absolute sense, it would mean that working-class individuals find it more and more difficult to survive in a merely physical sense. If taken in a relative sense, it would mean that the gap between the owners of the means of production and the workers would continue to widen, even though the actual material resources available to the typical working-class individual might actually improve.

Marx was certainly aware of the significance of relative deprivation; at one time he wrote that a small house among other small houses may be sufficient as a dwelling place but, if a palace is erected next to it, it becomes a hut.[31] In any case, whether increasing proletarian deprivation is absolute or relative, this process makes it more difficult for the working class to sustain the illusions created by false consciousness. Instead, the working class gradually becomes aware of the fundamental antagonism between its interests and the interests of the capitalists.

Once a communication network is established and common interests become apparent, the stage is set for organizing the proletarian class against its common foe. This organization may involve the establishment of labor unions or other associations of workers to exert pressures for higher wages, improved working conditions, and the like. Ultimately, however, the organization of the working class will be strong enough for them to push for the complete overthrow of the capitalist social structure and its replacement by a social structure that will recognize the needs and interests of all of humanity.

Along with this process of political organization, an ideology is developed that reveals the true interests of the working class and provides an explanation of its historic role in transforming the social structure. Development of the ideological side of the struggle is enhanced by the proletarianization of the petty bourgeois, whose social background equips them for this role. Remember, however, that the *ideological* struggle between revolutionary and conservative viewpoints is only a mirror of the *real* struggle taking place.

The preceding process described the proletarian class in capitalist society, but the same general process of class struggle also occurred in the bourgeois revolutionary struggles against the traditional, aristocratically dominated social system. In its struggle against the old feudal system, the bourgeois class had exhibited the same general process of growth in communication, increased class consciousness, political organization, and development of a supporting ideology. The crucial difference, however, was that the bourgeois class represented its own special interests, while the proletarian class was destined, in Marx's utopian vision, to represent all of humanity.

Class Struggle and Dialectical Analysis of Social Change

Obviously, not all revolts of oppressed classes lead to a successful revolution or total reorganization of society. What determines whether or not a class will be successful in transforming society as it asserts its interests? Marx's answer to this question relies on his overall perspective on historical change. Recall that changes in the means of production (such as new technology) lead to imbalance between these material forces and the social relations of production (including property relations). The existing social relations of production eventually become an obstacle to continued development of the productive forces of society. The class whose interests are advanced by the specific developments taking place in the productive forces is able to play the decisive role in bringing about the revolutionary transformation of society. Thus it was that the bourgeoisie struggled successfully against the feudal aristocratic system, and thus it will be that the proletariat will eventually revolt against the bourgeoisie. In both cases, however, the revolutionary class had its origins within the matrix of the social structure that it eventually transformed.

The dialectical irony of this can be seen in the fact that in the early days of the bourgeois transformation, the emerging proletariat was enlisted to aid the bourgeoisie in the struggle against the aristocracy. By mobilizing the proletariat in this way as a political force, the bourgeoisie was unwittingle preparing the way for its own ultimate demise. In any case, the success of an oppressed class in mobilizing revolutionary political action to promote its interests is dependent on an appropriate development of the material forces of production. The level of development of these material forces determines whether the revolutionary class will serve as the catalyst to bring about the next historic stage in the development of society or whether it will be merely an abortive revolt. Briefly, a revolutionary class is successful if it is able to link its own class interests with the social requirements of society as a whole in advancing to the next historic stage.

The dialectical mode of analysis is central in this model of how class conflict contributes to social change. In general, dialectical analysis involves a view of society as consisting of temporarily balanced opposing forces. Dialectical analysis is sensitive to the internal contradictions within society whose resolution advances a new stage of history. In Marx's view, the most significant contradictions are those between the material forces of production and the relations of production and those between the interests of different classes. Because of these contradictions, each historical stage in the development of society can be thought of as preparing the way for its own eventual dissolution, with each new stage negating the previous stage in which, paradoxically, it had its beginnings.

The development of a given historical stage depends the emergence of forces that, in the end, cannot be contained within the structure in which they were born. As these social forces develop, they eventually burst out of the structure within which they first came into being; in the process, they transform it into a radically new structure representing the next historical stage. Those social classes representing the emerging new forces are destined historically to be successful in transforming the existing structure as they assert their class interests.

The dialectical movement of history is not independent of human will or effort, however. Marx did not advocate a view of history in which individuals are merely passive. People create their own history, even though their creative activity is conditioned and constrained by the existing material and social environment. Although people make their own history, they cannot make it just as they please. Marx repeatedly insisted on this point in his opposition to the utopian socialists who assumed that they could design practically any type of society they chose, regardless of existing material and social conditions.

Marx's own career certainly demonstrates his unwillingness to trust the impersonal dialectical forces of history to bring about the kind of social change that he envisioned. He was an activist and, although his analytical writings suggest that general historical processes unfold according to their own impersonal dynamics, his political writings, such as *The Communist Manifesto*, are virtually a call to arms. Specifically, he urges the working class to seize the historically appropriate moment provided by the appearance of economic crisis to transform society through their own revolutionary activity.

The appearance of economic crises within the capitalist system were taken by Marx to signify that the internal contradictions within capitalism were coming to a head and that the time was right for the proletarian class to launch a successful revolution. In contrast, during times of prosperity Marx felt that the capitalist system had considerable potential for continued development and thus could not be overthrown immediately. In the absence of realistic possibilities for a successful revolution, political activity could take the form of organizing the working class.

CRITIQUE OF CAPITALIST SOCIETY

Although Marx's overall theoretical approach is applicable to any historical stage, his major concern was with the capitalist stage—its development from its beginnings in the late feudal period, its internal strains and contradictions, and its ultimate dissolution and transformation into the future communist society through the revolutionary activity of the proletarian class. Many of the key ideas needed for a Marxist analysis of capitalist society have already been discussed. This section summarizes some of these key ideas and indicates the additional concepts and ideas developed primarily in *Das Kapital* that are needed for a well-rounded Marxist critique.[32]

Marx's purpose in *Das Kapital* was to reveal the underlying dynamics of the capitalist system as the system actually operates, as opposed to the naive and idealized version of its operations presented by the political economists. He perceived the dynamics of the system as centering around the production of commodities and the accumulation of capital. The production of commodities for the market, and the production of capital goods to be used as a means for additional production, both involve human labor.

Like most of the political economists of his time, Marx accepted the labor theory of value. According to this theory, the market value of a commodity is determined by the amount of labor that went into its production. This value is a major factor in determining the price of commodities. Thus, if the labor required to produce a desk lamp, for example, is the same as the labor required to produce a pair of shoes, these two commodities should sell for the same price. In both cases the total labor involved would include the labor used in a direct sense in manufacturing these specific items, the labor that went into the manufacturing of any capital goods (i.e., machinery) used in their production, and even the labor of the scientists or engineers who developed techniques for processing animal hides into leather and using electrical power to produce light. There may be complicating factors that prevent commodities from being sold at their true value, but the natural tendency is for their exchange value in the market to be determined by the total amount of labor power that they represent.

Production of "Surplus" Value and the Exploitation of Labor

In their idealistic view of the market system, political economists such as Smith and Ricardo had argued that economic transactions that take place in the market are beneficial to all concerned; otherwise, individuals would not choose to engage in them. Thus, for example, if one farmer has a surplus of ham and another has a surplus of eggs, obviously both benefit by the exchange of ham and eggs. The benefit derives from the fact that after the exchange, both will have something to consume that they did not have before.

However, such an exchange differs from the type of exchange that takes place in the impersonal market system, where commodities are exchanged for money or money for commodities. The difference in these exchanges lies in the distinction Marx makes between "use value" and "exchange value." The mutual benefits that exchange partners receive from a transaction are most apparent with respect to exchange of use values. Furthermore, the terms of such exchanges are likely to be set on an ad hoc basis determined by the particular needs and resources of the exchange partners. In contrast, exchange values are determined not on an ad hoc basis such as this, but on the basis of the amount of labor power that they embody. The difference between use value and exchange value can readily be appreciated by anyone who drives an old car that would be worth only a small fraction of its new car price on the market (exchange value), but that serves its owner as a thoroughly reliable means of transportation (use value) that could not be replaced without a substantial investment of money over and above what the old car's market value would be.

The distinction between exchange value and use value is especially critical in transactions involving the sale or purchase of labor. Labor can be considered a source of both use value and exchange value. As a source of use value, labor consists of activity directed toward the production of some specific item to be used. As a source of exchange value, labor is considered as a general input into the process whereby commodities are produced not for the worker's own personal use or even for the use of an employer, but for sale in the impersonal market system in exchange for money. Although money is the general medium used to facilitate the exchange of commodities in the market, their monetary value actually reflects the amount of labor that went into their production.

As seen earlier, labor itself is treated in the capitalist system as a commodity to be bought and sold in the impersonal market like any other commodity. However, labor is able to produce more exchange value than is required for its maintenance. That is, a worker is able to produce quantities of commodities with a total exchange value greater than the exchange value of the food, clothing, shelter, etc., necessary to survive and reproduce more workers. This increment over the worker's survival and reproduction requirements is "surplus value," and an understanding of how it is created is essential for grasping Marx's theory of capitalist exploitation.

For example, let us say that a worker can produce in 6 hours of work each day enough commodities to provide the money needed for the survival of himself and his family; however, the length of the working day is set at, say, 12 hours. The value of the commodities produced during the second 6-hour period becomes surplus value. This value is realized when the capitalist employer sells the commodities in the market. The money earned can be used by the employer for buying more raw materials, for example, for expansion of the productive capacity of the enterprise, or even for personal consumption. Thus, the surplus value is expropriated by the capitalist employer. As a result, workers are alienated from their own productive labor. They confront the products of their own labor as objective and alien commodities in the impersonal market that are subject to general laws of exchange beyond their understanding, let alone their control.

The capitalist stage of history is distinguished from previous stages partly because of the high development of its productive forces. Large-scale machine production replaces the old handicraft system of production, and this leads to increasing specialization in the division of labor and major qualitative changes in the nature of productive work. Individual workers become virtual appendages of machines, submitting to the rigorous discipline of machine production instead of fulfilling themselves through their work.

Also, the heavy financial investment required for machine production means that large amounts of capital must be accumulated to finance a productive enterprise. The expropriation of surplus value provides this capital but, obviously, fewer and fewer people will be in a position to own or control the essential means of production. Small-scale handicraft producers find themselves unable to compete successfully with their small-scale hand tools against the capitalist mode of machine production. As a result, they, too, are reduced to a position of having to sell their labor power to the capitalists. Gradually, the capitalist mode of production replaces all other forms.

A major reason that the capitalist is eager to invest in machinery that expands productive capacity is the desire to earn more profits than competitors. Increased productive capacity represented by machinery means that more commodities can be produced for sale in the market, and the reduction in labor power requirements that labor-saving machinery makes possible means that labor costs per commodity are reduced. However, machines cannot produce value; only human labor can produce value. Of course, human labor is involved in the production of the machine that is used in subsequent productive activity, and the capitalist must pay for this labor in the price invested in the machine. The labor value embodied in the machine is then gradually given up in the commodities produced by the machine; ultimately, the machine will have to be replaced (or, in other words, its value will be used up). Nevertheless, in the short run a capitalist may increase profits by expanding production through the introduction of labor-saving machinery.

Capitalist Expansion and Economic Crisis

The introduction of labor-saving machinery disrupts the equilibrium between productive capacity and demand and thus precipitates periodic economic crises in the capitalist system. Specifically, as labor-saving machinery is installed, large groups of workers are put out of work, even while the productive capacity is being expanded. However, unemployed workers are unable to buy the commodities being produced in increasing quantities and, without any markets for their products, the capitalist's profits are threatened. The capitalist's response to this threat is to increase the length of the working day to try to extract more surplus value from the workers. But the continued shrinkage of the markets relative to productive capacity means that more workers will have to be laid off, and this has additional depressing effects on the market. Also, with the total supply of workers exceeding the demand for their labor power, wages are reduced to an even lower level, thus increasing the misery of the working class and depressing the market for commodities even futher.

In short, in their competitive struggles for profits, capitalists introduce labor-saving machinery that increases their productive capacity; this disrupts the equilibrium between productive capacity and demand, and the result is a downward spiral, with reduced market demand (relative to productive capacity) leading to reduced profits, reduced investment, and reduced employment, which leads to further reductions in market demand, and so on. The vulnerability of capitalism to these periodic economic crises lies in its tendency to overexpand productive capacity; this tendency results from competition between capitalists for increased profits.

As this downward spiral continues to develop, it eventually creates the conditions necessary for its own reversal. For one thing, after a period of stagnation involving underutilization of the means of production, the excess of commodities is gradually reduced. Also, the expansion of the length of the working day and the reduction in the wages of labor increase the proportion of the value produced by labor that can be expropriated by the capitalist as surplus value and used to maintain the enterprise during the crisis. However, not all capitalists can afford to maintain their enterprises during the economic crisis while awaiting the eventual return of economic prosperity. These unsuccessful capitalist enterprises will be bought out by the larger capitalists.

The overall result is a tendancy for capital to be concentrated and centralized among fewer and fewer capitalists. Their enterprises expand to a gigantic scale that dwarfs the capitalist enterprises of an earlier stage of capitalism. This particular prediction is borne out by the fact that in our own society, the economic system is dominated by a few hundred gigantic, multinational corporations whose growth has dwarfed the economic significance of independent, small-time capitalist entrepreneurs.

The basic contradictions in the structure of capitalist society are seen by Marx as coming to a head in the economic crises with which the capitalist system is periodically afflicted. Capitalists compete with each other for profits; the resulting overproduction undermines the basis for profits, and small capitalists are eliminated in the resolution of this conflict. Workers compete with each other for jobs; the result is that wages are depressed, the collective misery of the working class is increased, and their potential class solidarity is obscured. On a more abstract level there is the opposition between workers and the products of their labor that confront them as alien objects in the impersonal market and that they may be unable even to purchase during the crisis. There is also the opposition between use value and exchange value, with human activity dominated by the requirement to produce exchange value. These contradictions exist in addition to the obvious conflict of interests between the capitalist employer and the wage-earning laborer. The ultimate resolution of these contradictions will require transformation of the structure of capitalist society, with the division of labor, capital accumulation as private property, and the resulting class antagonism abolished.

Marx does not offer a detailed blueprint of postcapitalist society, but he envisions a society in which the gains in productive capacity brought about by capitalism will be collectively instead of privately owned, thereby freeing individuals from having to spend all of their time in labor for the sake of survival and enabling them to develop more of their potentialities as human beings. The appearance of economic crises contributes to the ultimate transformation of capitalist society by revealing its underlying contradictions, making the ideological illusions that obscure these contradictions more difficult to sustain. In such a situation, the possibilities for the emergence of class consciousness on the part of the proletarian class are strengthened. These possibilities are offset by the competition between workers for scarce jobs and increased wages. Overcoming this competitiveness and developing class consciousness requires that workers be enlightened as to the nature of the historical process in which they are involved. As an activist, Marx considered this to be one of his primary roles.

MARX'S CRITICS

Marx's critique of capitalist society and his predictions regarding its future development have been subjected to numerous criticisms. No doubt part of the criticism is a reaction to Marxism as a political ideology, not as an objective sociological or economic theory. However, the use of the Marxist perspective as a political ideology in Communist countries in the twentieth century involves considerable distortion and simplification of Marx's theory. Thus criticisms directed at Marxist ideology as propounded by contemporary political leaders to support their particular society's economic and political and international policies may or may not represent valid criticisms of Marxist theory seen in its totality. Marx himself once disclaimed the ideological uses to which his theory was being put by asserting that he was not a Marxist. This section will examine briefly some of the various criticisms that have been directed against Marx's theory and the counterarguments offered in rebuttal.

A major criticism is that Marx did not adequately foresee the magnitude of the increase in productive capacity that continued industrial development would bring about. This increase means that a given amount of labor time produces far more value in a highly developed industrial system than in a minimally developed system. Consequently, it is possible for the wages of labor to be increased far above the level that Marx seemed to feel was possible. In brief, his prediction regarding the more and more oppressive economic conditions of the proletarian class does not seen to have been realized, even granting his suggestion that the degree of oppressiveness must be seen in relative and not absolute terms.

In American society the increased productivity of labor and the related increase in wages means that members of the proletarian class have not been obliged to struggle to overthrow the basic structure of the capitalist system in order to assert their class interests. The social and political organization of workers in labor unions and political parties clearly reflects the availability of options other than revolutionary struggle for asserting class interests. In short, labor unions have been able to wage their struggles for increased wages and improved working conditions within the context of the capitalist structure, and they have been relatively successful, at least in American society. As a result, labor unions tend to be far less radical than Marx envisioned. It is doubtful that Marx could have envisioned the high level of national patriotism of American labor union leaders and members in supporting a political system associated with an advanced stage of capitalism.

It is also charged that Marx failed to envision the growth of a large, politically dominant middle class. Such a development undercuts his argument that as capitalism advances, its social structure is more and more split into two hostile classes: the capitalist owners of the means of production and the proletarian laborers. Actually, Marx did mention the growth of the middle classes intermediate between the capitalist and the worker,[33] but he did not develop this idea systematically. His overwhelming emphasis was on the tendency for class relations to be simplified into a two-class system as the capitalist system develops.

The growth of the middle class is partly related to the increase in the wages of labor mentioned earlier. It is also related to changes in the nature of work resulting from continued technological development. As automation has been added to mechanization and as technology has become more complex in many other ways, many forms of industrial work have become less oppressive.

Furthermore Marx's evaluation of labor as dehumanizing actually reflects his own subjective evaluation of it and not the evaluation attached to it by the workers themselves.[34] In this evaluation Marx really reveals his own rather conservative, bourgeois attitude. He assumed that industrial work, or work required for mere physical survival, cannot be fulfilling or satisfying. This evaluation is valid as a subjective evaluation reflecting Marx's own preferences, but we should be aware that it is *his* evaluation, not the evaluation of the workers themselves. Work that may be dehumanizing to one person may be satisfying to another. In any case, the various changes in the situation of the working class means that workers, instead of being forced into a more and more precarious situation as capitalism advances, are actually able to achieve middle-class status in terms of their consumption patterns and life-styles.

Also, the widespread ownership of the means of production through investments in stocks was not anticipated by Marx and offers an alternative to his prediction regarding the increasing concentration of capital in fewer and fewer capitalists' hands.[35] Marxists could readily counter that highly dispersed ownership does not amount to collective control and that the controlling shares of stocks of most large corporations continue to be held in a concentrated and centralized form.

More generally, critics of the Marxist interpretation of capitalist society argue that he underrated its flexibility and adaptability in weathering crises and its potentialities for continued long-term growth and development. Actually, Marx alternated in his assessment of the potentialities inherent in capitalism that remain to be unfolded before the final collapse. In his 1859 *Outline of a Critique of Political Economy,* he seems to assume that the capitalist system will endure for some time before it exhausts its possibilities of development, especially in view of the increased productive capacity which it stimulates. On the other hand, during times of economic crisis, Marx assumes that the stage was almost set for the transformation to a postcapitalist society.

In any case, Marx's overall evaluation of capitalist society and its future development did not envision governmental policies designed to redistribute wealth more equitably or to offset the socially harmful effects of economic crises. In this connection, Marx's *Communist Manifesto* calls for "a heavy progressive or graduated income tax," among other things, as part of his revolutionary program. Highly developed capitalist systems have adopted this specific policy without undergoing a revolution, mostly because of their acceptance of the necessity for government to play an active role in income redistribution. Marx did not anticipate this development.

A committed Marxist would be able to offer a counterargument to each of these criticisms. For example, the increased wages of the working class, the growth of the middle class, widespread dispersion of stock ownership, and the adoption by government of countercyclical fiscal policies and basic welfare responsibilities could be seen as strategies whereby the dominant capitalist class seeks to insure the continuation of the illusions whereby individuals identify their interests with the maintenance of the capitalist system. These strategies undermine the potential for revolt and revolution and help preserve the status quo. In addition, such policies are necessary to protect and enlarge the market for commodities on which the maintenance and enhancement of capitalist profits depends.

Furthermore, the political conservatism of labor unions can be readily explained as a result of co-optation of their leadership by the capitalist class; because of this, they also develop an interest in maintaining the social and political system within which they have been able to achieve the power and prestige associated with their position. Finally, a Marxist might point out that the unanticipated material well-being of the working class and the overall continuing prosperity widely shared among most major segments of the mature capitalist society is made possible by exploitation of the material resources and labor of less developed societies. Thus the conflict shifts from capitalist versus proletarian classes *within* the capitalist society to capitalist versus underdeveloped *societies*.

Whether Marx and his followers or Marx's critics offer the most valid interpretation of the basic dynamics of capitalist society probably cannot be determined on any purely objective basis. Instead, which interpretation is most plausible or most convincing will probably be determined largely on the basis of the fundamental assumptions and underlying attitudes with which one approaches the alternative interpretations. Our discussion of Marx shows that his theoretical perspective offers one provocative type of insight into social reality. This insight is not necessarily more "valid" or "correct" than that provided by alternative theoretical perspectives. We now reiterate the major points of Marx's theoretical perspective and relate them to contemporary theoretical developments.

Summary

Marx's theory has been presented as a major example of a theory that deals primarily with the social structural level of social reality and that emphasizes the high interdependence between the social structure and the material conditions to which individuals must adapt in order to survive and fulfill their various needs. His emphasis on the necessity of adapting to the material environment and on the scarcity of resources needed for the satisfaction of human needs and wants provides a major note of practical realism in his theoretical analyses.

The relationship between individuals and their material envrionment is mediated through the economic structure of society. Marx may have overstated his case for the determining influence of the economy on the rest of the sociocultural system, but the importance of the economy as a key cornerstone of social structure is generally recognized today, even though the relationship between the economy and other institutions may be more variable and more complex than he indicated.

The internal structure of the economic system consists of social classes that come about from the inequality in access to the means of production and the resulting incompatibility in economic interests. The social relations between the opposing classes are characterized by periodic social and political conflicts that result in internal pressures for change. This emphasis on social class as a basic category of social structure, on inequality in economic resources, on incompatible interests, on conflict as the most pervasive social process, and on social change generated from internal pressures and forces are key elements in the general contemporary perspective that is referred to broadly as conflict theory. Alternatives of this perspective will be presented in Chapter 11.

Marx's emphasis on how ideologies and other aspects of culture reinforce the economic and social structure by providing legitimation for dominant groups' interests is a major proposition emphasized in the contemporary area of sociology of knowledge. Mannheim, for example, who is one of the major figures in the development of the sociology of knowledge, stressed the point that ideologies are developed and used to protect or promote the interests of various groups in society.[36]

Also, Marx's insight regarding the dialectical relationship between human activity and the products of this activity is a key element of the contemporary approach, developed by Berger and Luckmann, that is known as the "social construction of reality" perspective.[37] Marx and Berger and Luckmann noted that while individuals express their human nature in creative activity, the results of this activity take on the character of an objective reality to which individuals must adapt. For Marx this objective reality created by human beings then confronts its human creators as an alien reality that limits and constrains their subsequent activity and to which they feel subservient. Marx's theory of alienation is based on this insight. Contemporary sociological approaches referred to as humanistic or critical sociology draw heavily from Marx's theory of alienation in the effort to create a sociological perspective that is centered around the needs and potentialities of human beings and that can be used to criticize the social structures that dehumanize or enslave human beings or prevent their full development.[38]

Marxism and other theoretical approaches that emphasize the process of conflict are generally seen as being opposed to functional theory. In Chapter 5 we will examine the contributions of one of the major pioneers in functionalism, Emile Durkheim. At this point, we might note that functional approaches stress value consensus and harmony instead of conflict in society. However, Marx's basic assumption regarding the interdependence between the various institutions of society is also emphasized in functionalism, as is his insight regarding the importance of unintended outcomes of action that are actually the opposite of the effect intended. An example of this can be seen in the unintended effects of capitalist investment in machinery that is intended to enhance profits but that unintentionally precipitates economic crises.

In our overall evaluation of Marx's theoretical perspective it is important to remember that Marx was not a detached academician but was heavily involved as a political activist. As such, he directly experienced being in conflict with the political power structure and being in a precarious economic situation. This career pattern and the life-style associated with it undoubtedly helped to determine what Marx saw as the essential features of social reality. In Chapter 5 we turn to the theoretical contributions of a person who, starting with a different "vision" of social reality and a different set of basic assumptions and attitudes, developed a markedly different theoretical perspective.

Footnotes

1. For a brief overview of the major events in Marx's life and of the social and intellectual influences that affected his thought and his career, see Isaiah Berlin, *Karl Marx: His Life and Environment* (New York: Oxford University Press, 1959).
2. This approach was different from the materialistic philosophies, reflected in positivism, for example, that fail to deal with the realm of subjective consciousness and that insist that all reality is simply some form of matter in motion. See Berlin, op. cit., Chapters III and IV.
3. This set of manuscripts was not published in Marx's lifetime, however; indeed, these

writings did not become available in English until after World War II. Thus the older, traditional interpretation of Marx did not reflect the strong humanistic and philosophical emphasis that these manuscripts reveal. Nevertheless, many Marxist scholars today generally recognize the fundamental continuity in Marx's thought between his early *Economic and Philosophical Manuscripts* and his mature work in *Das Kapital*. In addition to the *Manuscripts*, Marx's publications in Paris included some articles for the short-lived *Deutsch-Französische Jahrbücher;* he and Engels also collaborated in writing *The Holy Family*, in which they sought to demolish the idealistic theories of Hegel's followers.

4. Although the basic theme of the *Manifesto* is not incongruent with Marx's other writings, its emphasis is not consistently maintained in his other writings and its tone is not nearly as analytical. It does not reflect the post-Hegelian humanistic philosophy of the *Economic and Philosophical Manuscripts,* nor does it present a historical analysis as full as that in *The German Ideology.*

5. The first of these works was intended as a comprehensive overview of Marx's planned *magnum opus* on economics, while the second was a preliminary statement. The main ideas of these works were later incorporated into *Das Kapital,* while the *Introduction* was simply a brief restatement of the principles of historical analysis developed earlier in *The German Ideology.* This interpretation of Marx's publications in the late 1850s is based heavily on David McClellan's analysis in *The Thought of Karl Marx* (New York: Harper & Row, 1971). According to him, all three of these working manuscripts can be seen as providing a bridge between Marx's earlier post-Hegelian philosophical writings in Paris and his economic analysis in *Das Kapital.*

6. See Z. A. Jordon, ed., *Karl Marx: Economy, Class, and Social Revolution* (London: Michael Joseph, 1971), pp. 36–39, for a brief discussion of this point as it contrasts with the one-sided view of materialistic or economic determinism.

7. Unlike many other philosophers, Hegel recognized that the dominant ideas of any historical epoch are not absolute but must eventually give way to more progressive ideas which express more fully the spirit of reason. Standards of truth or error, right or wrong, are limited by the particular historical stage and are bound eventually to be superseded as the dialectical process unfolds. This relativizing approach was thoroughly accepted by Marx.

8. Karl Marx, from *German Ideology,* pp. 197–216 in Erich Fromm, *Marx's Concept of Man* (New York: Frederick Ungar, 1961), p. 198.

9. Ibid., p. 204. This separation between thought and practice, between philosophical ideas and material and social conditions was, Marx thought, especially marked in Germany. Germany had not experienced the kind of radical political transformation that the French had in the Revolution of 1789, nor was Germany as advanced as England in industrial development. Germany's social and political structure was still heavily influenced by the feudal system of the late Middle Ages; yet German philosophy had kept pace with—or perhaps even led—philosophical developments in other countries. But this philosophical development, in the absence of corresponding developments in social, economic, and political conditions, resulted in a highly idealistic form of philosophy divorced from real-life conditions. In *The Critique of Hegel's Philosophy of Right,* Marx criticized this inconsistency, pointing out that Germany had only *thought* what other nations had *done.*

10. See Henri Lefebvre, *The Sociology of Marx* (New York: Random House, 1968), Chapter 2, "The Marxian Concept of Praxis," for a discussion of this concept in Marx's writings.

11. On a more contemporary note, this same dialectical relationship between the modes of production and the relations of production might be seen in the effect that development of computerized registration and record systems might have on the social relations between students and university administration officials.

12. This theme is developed more fully in Marx's *Outline of the Critique of Political Economy,* in which the freeing of time by capitalist modes of production is the potential means for the development of human beings beyond the level of mere survival.

13. Karl Marx, "Manifesto of the Communist Party," pp. 335–362 in Robert C. Tucker, ed., *The Marx-Engels Reader* (New York: Norton, 1972), p. 337.

14. Marx, from *German Ideology,* in Fromm, op. cit., p. 212.

15. The dialectical process is operative in this analysis of alienation in the opposition between the needs of the living and active human being and the demands or the logic imposed by the external objects previously produced.

16. See Robert K. Merton, "Bureaucratic Structure and Personality," *Social Forces,* Vol. 18, 1940, pp. 560–568.

17. Karl Marx, *Theses on Feuerbach,* quoted in Tucker, op. cit., p. 109.

18. Quoted in Tucker, op. cit., p. 337.

19. Karl Marx, "Alienated Labour," in *Early Writings,* translated and edited by T. B. Bottomore (New York: McGraw-Hill, 1964), pp. 122–123.

20. Ibid., pp. 129–130.

21. This problem was discussed in a section of the 1844 *Economic and Philosophical Manuscripts* entitled "Alienated Labour." (See footnote 19.)

22. See McClellan, op. cit., pp. 180–181, for a discussion of Marx's changing views on the nature of the state.

23. Quoted in Tucker, op. cit., pp. 335–336.

24. Ibid., p. 336. See also McClellan, op. cit., pp. 151–156.

25. David McClellan, *Karl Marx* (New York: Viking, 1975), p. 44.

26. Karl Marx, *The Communist Manifesto,* in Tucker, op. cit., p. 344.

27. Quoted in McClellan, *Karl Marx,* p. 44.

28. Quoted in Tucker, op. cit., p. 338.

29. Lefebvre, op. cit., p. 121.

30. Karl Marx, "The Eighteenth Brumaire of Louis Bonaparte," reprinted in *Karl Marx and Friedrich Engels: Basic Writings on Politics and Philosophy,* edited by Lewis S. Feuer (Garden City, N.Y.: Doubleday, 1959), pp. 338–339.

31. McClellan, *The Thought of Karl Marx,* p. 153.

32. Although Volume I of *Das Kapital* was not published until 1867, its major ideas had been developed in a preliminary way in the 1844 *Economic and Philosophical Manuscripts* and further refined in Marx's writings in the late 1850s, especially in the *Outline of the Critique of Political Economy.* According to McClellan, the development of Marx's thought can be seen in the shift in emphasis that these three works reveal. In the 1844 manuscripts, Hegelian philosophical analysis and political economic analysis are juxtaposed but not well integrated; by the late 1850s, Marx was able to synthesize these two modes of thought and relate them to specific historical conditions and, in Volume I

of *Das Kapital,* Marx mostly dropped the explicit concern with Hegelian philosophy and concentrated instead on economic processes. See Ibid., pp. 69-79.

33. McClellan, *The Thought of Karl Marx,* p. 153.

34. I am indebted to Roy G. Francis for pointing out to me in a personal communication this subjective bias inherent in Marx's evaluation of industrial work as dehumanizing. Marx's ideological evaluation of industrial work rules out the possibility that some factory workers may be satisfied with their work. Certainly, for many of them, factory work was a more attractive alternative than other options.

35. This is an essential feature of "postcapitalist" society as analyzed by Ralf Dahrendorf in *Class and Class Conflict in Industrial Society* (Stanford, Calif.: Stanford University Press, 1959).

36. See Karl Mannheim, *Ideology and Utopia* (New York: Harcourt, Brace and World, 1936).

37. See Peter Berger and Thomas Luckmann, *The Social Construction of Reality* (Garden City, N.Y.: Doubleday, 1966).

38. See Erich Fromm, *Marx's Concept of Man* (New York: Frederick Unger, 1966), and Adam Schaff, *Marxism and the Human Individual* (New York: McGraw-Hill, 1970).

Questions for Study and Discussion

1. Why did Marx emphasize the economy as the infrastructure or foundation for all other social institutions? Do you agree or disagree with this emphasis? Why or why not?

2. To what extent do people's basic beliefs and values change as a result of change in their economic position? Cite examples or research findings to support your point.

3. Do you agree or disagree with Marx's view of the political system as an instrument of bourgeois capitalists in American society? What kinds of evidence would you use to support your argument? What evidence does not support it?

4. Is the concept of "false consciousness" a valid scientific concept? Why or why not? What is the scientific basis for Marx's assertion that workers should not be happy or satisfied with their jobs?

5. In what ways does Marx's strong emphasis on human fulfillment differ from the political policies followed in so-called Marxist countries today?

CHAPTER 5

Emile Durkheim: Establishing Sociology as a Science of Social Integration

Have you ever found yourself in a group that seemed emotionally dead, in which members were unwilling to invest any more energy in the group's activities than absolutely necessary? Have you ever tried to improve a group's morale or get its members excited about a project? Have you ever been in a group in which there was constant bickering or such serious conflict that it threatened to destroy the group? Have you ever wondered why some groups exhibit high morale while others are characterized by apathy or continual conflict?

Consider, for example, a college basketball team that has just won the national championship with a well-distributed scoring pattern and highly coordinated team-work. In the euphoria that follows such a victory there will be a strong feeling of togetherness, partly because of shared pride in the team's victory. This is expressed immediately after the game in displays such as mutual hugging, backslapping, and lifting the coach high and carrying him off the floor.

In contrast, there are many voluntary associations in which the commitment and ego involvement of members are apparently so low that many of them would forget to attend the meetings unless reminded immediately beforehand. Promoting commitment and involvement is a perennial problem for the leaders; even they may be serving in this capacity reluctantly, only after having been promised that it would not be too demanding. The group's decisions and activities seem to be guided by the rule that the less energy and time demanded by the group the better. Members are not willing to become involved in the group's activities above the minimum possible level unless it is convenient for them or they are guaranteed a personal payoff.

Solidarity of a group may also be undermined by conflict. For example, with the end of the rapid expansion of higher education of the 1960s, university departments and programs found themselves competing more and more for the scarce available funds. Thus, beneath the superficial appearance of mutual professional respect, academic colleagues in different departments unfortunately may feel resentment and envy of one another and may attempt subtly to undermine one another. The unwritten rule is that each department will look out for itself instead of for the whole school. This will certainly undermine or inhibit feelings of togetherness and solidarity of the school as a whole.

Athletic teams, voluntary associations, and universities are very different types of social organizations. In all types, however, there is likely to be common concern about issues such as encouraging commitment to group goals and activities, promoting group morale, and dealing with conflicts. Group members vary in terms of how much they are consciously aware of such concerns and how much they deliberately plan strategies to promote solidarity.

From a practical standpoint it is important to know something about how to motivate members of a group to get involved in the group's activities, how to promote morale, how to cope with conflicts, and so on. But these issues are part of a larger, more general problem that social scientists have long considered crucially important. This is the problem of social integration and solidarity, considered not only in relation to specific groups and organizations but also in relation to society as a whole. For some sociologists, both in the early days of sociology and today, the central issue in sociological analysis is to explain the underlying social order of society in terms of social processes that promote integration and solidarity. This was the key issue for Durkheim, and it is also one of the major issues of the contemporary functionalist perspective, especially as represented by Parsons and his followers.

Parsons was explicit in this regard.[1] He felt that the fundamental sociological problem is explaining how societies manage to avoid the hypothetical "state of nature" postulated by Hobbes as the "war of all against all." This unfortunate state would presumably result from individuals pursuing their selfish interests, unrestrained by consideration of the expectations of others or the common good. However, there are innumerable ways whereby individual motivations are shaped and their behavior regulated to prevent this state of nature from developing and to preserve social order.

The phrase "social order" is not to be taken in the narrow sense of "law and order," as some conservative politicians use this term to mean preservation of the status quo and getting tough with lawbreakers. Instead, it refers to the underlying sources of support for the dominant institutional patterns of society. It would encompass the society's shared value system and ideas of morality. It could also include the shared beliefs that legitimate or support the major institutional patterns and give direction and meaning to individuals as they participate in society. Understanding social order involves knowing what "holds society together" in a very broad sense.

Even though existing societies may never exhibit the anarchy of Hobbes' state of nature, they do vary in terms of degree of social integration or strength of social order. Similarly, any given society may vary along this line over time. Some commentators on the contemporary social scene in America express fear and apprehension that we are witnessing a gradual erosion of the underlying basis of the social order and breakdown of the bonds of social integration. Phenomena such as widespread alienation, growing cynicism (especially toward our political institutions), rapidly changing standards of personal morality (e.g., in work, sex, family patterns), and the more and more strident insistence of various groups on pursuing their economic interests regardless of the costs to other groups indicate that the fabric of our social order is threatened by various forms of disintegration.[2]

We are not concerned here with the question of whether the critics or the alarmists are right or wrong in their pessimistic analysis of our society. The point for us to recognize is that social integration and solidarity are important to study at the level of the overall society as well as the group or organizational level.

Social solidarity and integration were the key substantive issues with which Durkheim was concerned in his major works. Some of the specific questions he dealt with were: What are the principle forms or patterns of social solidarity? How and why do societies change from one form to another? What are the empirical indicators of various forms and degrees of solidarity? What happens when solidarity is threatened or breaks down? What are the social processes that promote solidarity or reinforce it? In grappling with these and related questions, Durkheim also insisted that his analyses be scientifically grounded in empirical data and that these data be about the society or the social structure itself, not individual data. This was important for establishing sociology as an empirically based science separate and independent from psychology. This advocacy of empiricism and the scientific method is in line with the French positivist tradition discussed in Chapter 1.

In terms of the different levels of social reality identified in Chapter 2, Durkheim's focus was on the social structural level, although many of his substantive ideas also concerned the cultural and the individual levels. However, Durkheim's focus on social solidarity and integration is in marked contrast to Marx's emphasis on dialectical contradictions and class conflicts discussed in the last chapter.

Unlike Marx, Durkheim became a well-established and highly influential academician. Perhaps more than any other person, he succeeded in getting sociology institutionalized as a legitimate academic discipline. Prior to Durkheim, sociology had been a maverick field, not clearly distinguished from philosophy in terms of theoretical ideas or from history or psychology in terms of substance and methods.

Durkheim's influence on the development of contemporary American sociology has been enormous, in terms of both methodology and theory. His insistence on the reality of social phenomena distinct from individual phenomena, his analysis of alternative types of social structure and of their differing bases of solidarity and integration, his concern for tracing the social functions of social phenomena independently of individuals' conscious purposes or motivations, his sociological insights regarding phenomena such as deviance, suicide, and individualism, and his careful statistical study of suicide rates as an example of how to analyze social phenomena empirically—in all of these areas Durkheim made significant contributions to the development of the modern sociological perspective.

His influence is perhaps most pronounced in the functionalist school of contemporary sociology. Functionalism also stresses integration and solidarity, as well as the importance of separating analyses of social consequences of social phenomena from analyses of individuals' conscious purposes and motivations. Before we discuss Durkheim's specific substantive contributions, we will review some significant points in his life and in the social and intellectual context in which he lived.

DURKHEIM'S LIFE AND TIMES

Emile Durkheim was born in 1858 in Epinal,[3] a small Jewish enclave on the eastern edge of France that was somewhat insulated from the larger society. Durkheim's father was a rabbi, like his father before him, and if Durkheim had followed the traditional path he, too, would have become a rabbi. However, he was deflected from this course partly, perhaps, as a result of a mystical experience and temporary conversion to Catholicism under the influence of a Catholic teacher. He soon gave up Catholicism and became an agnostic, but basic questions of morality and promotion of society's moral foundations were a major interest throughout his life. Probably part of his concern with solidarity and integration grew out of his awareness that the decline in the influence of traditional religion undermined one of the major traditional supports for the shared moral standards that had helped to hold society together in the past.

Durkheim was admitted at age 21 to the *École Normale Superieure* (Superior Normal School). Twice earlier he had failed the stiff competitive entrance exams, although his earlier educational experiences had been outstanding. He had come to Paris to prepare for admission at the Lycée Louis-le-Grand (a distinguished high school) after having been strongly supported and encouraged by his teachers in Epinal.

Durkheim established himself at the *École Normale Superieure* as a very serious student. Like many students today, Durkheim was highly dissatisfied with the curriculum. Its traditional dominant emphasis was the literary classics, including Latin and Greek. Newer developments in science seemed, for the most part, to be downplayed. Even at this early stage in his life, Durkheim desired a more thorough grounding in science, which he felt could help provide a basis for the moral reconstruction of society. This faith in science as the key to social and moral reform was characteristic of positivism (as already noted) and of the earlier work of Comte in particular.

At least two of Durkheim's professors at the *École Normale*—Fustel de Coulanges and Emile Boutroux—had a major impact on him.[4] From de Coulanges, a historian famous for *The Ancient City,* Durkheim learned the value of scientific rigor in historical research. Also, de Coulanges' emphasis on intellectual consensus and religion as the foundation of social solidarity evidently made a lasting impression on Durkheim; when Durkheim began to grapple, much later in his career, with the question of how society's moral demands are internalized in idividuals' subjective consciousness, he turned his attention to religion and the contributions it makes in maintaining the integration of society.

From Boutroux, a philosopher, Durkheim learned the importance of recognizing that there are different levels of reality and that higher levels of reality may exhibit emergent properties not explainable solely in terms of lower-level phenomena. In other words, the whole is greater than the sum of its parts. This insight was fundamental to Durkheim's overall approach to social phenomena. His insistence that social facts exist at their own level, distinct from the individual level, is an important sociological application of Bourtroux's philosophical premise. As developed by Durkheim, this principle is an argument against psychological reductionism. (Psychological reductionism is the idea that social phenomena can be adequately explained in terms of psychological principles at the individual level.)

After finishing his education, Durkheim began to teach. For 5 years he taught in a series of *lycées* (secondary schools) in the Paris area. For 1 year during this period he received a leave of absence for further study, most of which he spent in Germany. There he became acquainted with the Psychological Laboratory of the experimental psychologist Wilhelm Wundt and was impressed by the commitment to the scientific-empirical study of human behavior that it represented. Also, he was undoubtedly exposed to the idea of the *Gemeinschaft-Gesellschaft* distinction that was soon to be made famous by Tönnies' book, *Gemeinschaft und Gesellschaft,* which Durkheim later reviewed.

From the beginning of his teaching career Durkheim was determined to emphasize practical scientific and moral instruction instead of the traditional philosophical approach that he perceived to be irrelevant to the crucial social and moral questions facing the Third Republic. In spite of this faith in the practical value of sociology for dealing with questions of morals and social policy, as a scholar Durkheim was firmly committed to dispassionate objective analysis firmly based on facts. His own personal involvement in various social or political issues and his ideological commitments never became a substitute for the disinterested or objective quest for knowledge.

Durkheim's own personal ideological stance was that of a liberal. Yet it is easy to detect some major conservative implications in his theoretical work, partially because of the stress on the overriding importance of the social structure and the complete subordination of the individual to society for his or her development. In practice, however, he defended individual rights against unjust or excessive claims made on behalf of society.[5]

Institutionalizing Sociology as an Academic Discipline

By 1887, when Durkheim was 29 years old, his teaching performance and several articles he had written distinguished him as a promising young social scientist; he was rewarded for this by being appointed to the pedagogy and social science faculty of the University of Bordeaux. The explicit inclusion of social science among his teaching responsibilities was in recognition of his commitments and achievements as a social scientist. This was the first official academic recognition given to the new discipline of sociology in the French university system. Half a century earlier Comte had failed to establish sociology as a legitimate discipline and had remained virtually an outsider from the academic-intellectual world.

The necessity of teaching education courses permitted Durkheim to develop his sociological perspective regarding how the human personality is molded and shaped by society through its representatives in the educational system. By teaching these courses, serving on numerous committees, and personally influencing members of the academic community, Durkheim was a major force on the French educational system. He had a strong faith in education and believed that training in the science of society could contribute significantly to establishing and reinforcing the moral foundations of society.

In 1896 Durkheim was promoted to full professor in social science. Again, this represented a breakthrough; it was the first full professorship in social science in France. Two years later, another significant milestone was reached when Durkheim established *L'Anée Sociologique,* the first scholarly journal devoted to sociology.

The journal was successful and influential from the start. It provided Durkheim with a forum for some of his pioneering papers; in addition many other leading French scholars and the German Simmel also published in *L'Anée.* The journal was a focal point for those promoting the scientific study of society; it gave them a sense of community, if not complete unity, and helped to consolidate the sociological enterprise, specifically the Durkheimian school. It promoted appreciation and respect for the rapidly expanding discipline of sociology. Unfortunately, publication of *L'Anée* was terminated with the outbreak of World War I after only 12 impressive annual issues. To this day, however, the Durkheimian approach dominates sociology in France.

In 1899 Durkheim was called to the Sorbonne. He was promoted to full professor in the science of education in 1906. Sociology was not yet established at the University of Paris; naturally, here at the pinnacle of the higher educational system in France, the decision whether or not to establish a place for sociology could not be made hastily or lightly. In 1913 Durkheim's chair was changed to science of education and sociology.[6] At last, sociology was officially established at the most prestigious educational institution in France.

Durkheim continued to be active in scholarly and academic pursuits but, with the outbreak of the war, part of his energy was deflected into promoting the French cause in the war. His son, André, was fatally wounded in 1915, and Durkheim never really recovered from this loss. In 1917, at the age of 59 he died, having earned the respect of his contemporaries for a productive and significant career and having established the foundation of scientific sociology.

Social and Intellectual Influences on Durkheim

Durkheim's lifelong concern with social solidarity and integration occurred partly because of the precarious state of the social order of the Third Republic during his youth.[7] Briefly, the long-term aftermath of the French Revoluation included continuing tension and periodic conflicts between the monarchists and the left-wing republicans that persisted throughout most of the nineteenth century. At one point, the president of the Third Republic actually dissolved the Chamber of Deputies as part of his effort to establish a strong presidency. Then, too, France's defeat in 1870 by Prussia had left poignant memories and deep wounds in French pride.

In spite of the precarious and unstable political situation, the Industrial Revolution continued to advance, promoting profound changes in economic structure, social relations, and basic cultural orientations. Traditional values, beliefs, customs, social relations, and patterns of earning a livelihood were steadily being undermined or destroyed, and a new urban-industrial social order was emerging. Although this process was not as dramatic in France as in England, the underlying dynamics still promoted a profound break with the traditional social order. However, the foundations of the new social order seemed shaky.

Unlike some of his conservative contemporaries, Durkheim did not advocate trying to turn the clock back to a more stable and secure past. He was more interested in trying to understand the foundations of the emerging social order. Durkheim recognized the difficulties of the transitional period in which he lived, but he was also optimistic that scientific knowledge of the laws of society could contribute to the consolidation of the moral foundation of the emerging new social order. To this end he was a determined advocate of educational reforms that would inculcate in the citizenry a strong sense of civic morality and a feeling of solidarity with the nation as a whole.

Durkheim's preoccupation with civic morality coincided with a period of transition in France's educational system. Because of the strong anticlerical feeling in the Third Republic, most of the Catholic educational system was replaced by a secular educational system. Durkheim felt that in making this transition, it was necessary to develop an alternative to the traditional religious foundations of moral training. In short, what was needed was a secular ideology or system of beliefs that would provide the underpinnings for morals and ethics in a secular society. Quite clearly, Durkheim viewed the teaching of civic morality to future citizens in their formative years as extremely important for strengthening the foundations of society and promoting its integration and social solidarity.

In his desire to establish an empirically grounded science of society that was coupled wtih a commitment to social and moral reconstruction, Durkheim followed the same path as Comte had. He did not go along with Comte's effort to found a new religion, but his commitment to the cause of civic morality developed from the same kind of concern for social order and solidarity.

Durkheim recognized Comte as the founder of the discipline of sociology (and also acknowledged St. Simon's influence), and he shared Comte's organic image of society. This image, as noted, stresses the interrelatedness of social phenomena and the idea that social reality transcends the individual level. Also, Durkheim's views on the functions of the division of labor in promoting social integration were supported by reference to Comte; although Durkheim's sociological analysis is more sophisticated and more significant for contemporary sociology than Comte's, Durkheim nevertheless found general reinforcement for his theoretical ideas in the work of the "father of sociology."

Opposition to Spencer's Individualism

Durkheim defined his distinctive sociological approach in opposition to Herbert Spencer's individualistic perspective. Spencer was a British social theorist who was highly influential in nineteenth-century England and, later, in America for his ideas on social evolution and progress. Spencer was primarily a journalist, not an academician, but his social theory was comprehensive and convincing enough at the time for him to have had a marked influence on the early development of the sociological perspective. Like Comte and Durkheim in France, Spencer was interested in the long-range evolutionary development of modern societies and, like them, he developed an organic perspective. However, Spencer's organic image of society differed in some crucial respects from Comte's and Durkheim's, and Durkheim's particular focus was no doubt sharpened in opposition to the basic assumptions of Spencer's approach.

For Spencer, the key to understanding social phenomena or any other natural phenomena was the universal law of evolution.[8] Physical, biological, and social phenomena are all subject to this basic law. One reason for considering Spencer an organic theorist is his effort to extend evolutionary principles that operate at the biological level to social institutions. The major manifestations of this universal law of evolution, evident in both the biological and the social realms, are gradual increases in size and complexity. Size and complexity are themselves related, of course. As a biological organism or a society increases in size, it must develop differentiated parts that can perform specialized functions in order to survive. Evolution in the biological realm from simple or undifferentiated unicellular organisms to large and complex mammals with various differentiated and interdependent organs is comparable to the evolution from simple, primitive societies with a minimal division of labor to large and complex societies with a high division of labor and extensive interdependence.

Although Spencer was not indebted to Comte for his views on evolutionary progress, his faith in progress was similar. Also, like Comte, he anticipated the possibility of evolution from a military society to an industrial society. He differed from Comte, however, in focusing on social structural change in society and not on intellectual development.

Spencer's social evolutionary model of increasing social complexity through increases in the division of labor closely parallels Durkheim's analysis of the division of labor. Spencer, however, was less specific than Durkheim in identifying the mechanisms whereby the division of labor is increased; to him, this development was simply a manifestation of the universal law of evolution.

The crucial difference between Spencer and Comte and Durkheim was Spencer's individualistic image of social reality. Although an individualistic image of social reality and an organic model of society might, at first glance, seem incompatible, Spencer attempted to reconcile these two views by pointing out the main differences between biological and social "organisms." Unlike a biological organism, a society is not enclosed within a skin and does not have a central source of intelligence or control that is analogous to the brain. Instead, the various "parts" of society are dispersed, and each part has its own intelligence and self-control. Society does not exist independently of the individuals who are its "parts." It comes into existence as a result of contractual agreements that individuals negotiate with each other in order to pursue their individual interests.

Spencer's image of the ideal, or most progressive, society was one in which individuals have maximum freedom to pursue their interests and promote their happiness without being directed or controlled by any central authority. This point of view, which can be used (and was) to justify a *laissez-faire* approach to government, is highly congruent with the theoretical perspective that had been developed earlier by the British political economists (discussed in the last chapter) and the British utilitarians such as Jeremy Bentham. Eventually, when coupled with the Darwinian principles of struggle for survival and survival of the fittest, which were extended from the biological to the social realm, these ideas could provide potent ideological support for the ruthless competitiveness, the harsh individualism, and the resistance to governmental welfare or reform measures associated with the rapidly expanding capitalist economic system.[9]

Spencer's views on the proper role of government differed from Comte's and

Durkheim's.[10] Comte's vision of the ideal positivist society of the future was one in which sociologically enlightened leaders would maintain firm control in regulating many details of social life to insure that the basic laws governing social order and progress were maintained. Durkheim's views were less grandiose, but he, too, saw government as the guardian of the moral foundations of society.

Also, Spencer's individualistic image of social reality differed sharply from Durkheim's emphasis that social facts transcend the individual. Spencer assumed that society results from contractual agreements between individuals that they enter in order to pursue their individual interests; Durkheim insisted that the very possibility for negotiating contractual agreements presupposes an already existing society. People do not enter contractual relations with those with whom they do not already share a social bond. At the least, there is the already existing moral consensus regarding the binding nature of contracts.

Moreover, in Durkheim's perspective, individuals' perceptions of their personal interests are not formed in isolation from other human beings but are shaped by the common beliefs and values shared with others in society. On the question of how society is formed, Durkheim's criticism of Spencer and other individualistic theories is that they do not explain the primordial social bonds or the moral consensus on the basis of which contractual agreements between individuals are possible. Simply, Spencer saw society as formed by individuals, while Durkheim saw individuals formed by society. This stress on the primacy of the social level is one of the basic foundations of Durkheim's overall theory.

THE REALITY OF SOCIAL FACTS

The most fundamental general assumption underlying Durkheim's approach to sociology is that social phenomena are real and exert an influence on individuals' consciousness and behavior distinct from that of psychological, biological, or other individual characteristics. Furthermore, since social phenomena are real facts, they can be studied by empirical methods, thereby allowing a genuine science of society to develop. Both of these assumptions—the reality of social phenomena and the view of sociology as a science—may seem obvious today, especially for students with even minimal training in the sociological perspective. Remember, however, that in Durkheim's time neither the domain nor the methodology of sociology was yet established.

Many of those interested in developing a naturalistic or scientific explanation of human behavior and even social institutions based their analysis on individual characteristics, such as instincts (or some variation thereof, such as Pareto), will (Tönnies, to some extent), imitation tendencies (Tarde), or self-interest and rational choice (both British utilitarianism and Spencer's evolutionism). All such theoretical perspectives imply that social reality and social structure are simply the result of the aggregation of individual characteristics and behaviors. For example, the individualism built into Spencer's theory is manifested in his assumption that the social and political structure of society is based on contracts that individuals voluntarily enter into in order to protect or enhance their self-interests. This view ignores both the normative consensus that underlies rational contractual relations (strongly emphasized by Durkheim), and the social origins of what individuals define as their self-interests (also implied in Durkheim's perspective).[11]

Durkheim's emphasis on the objective reality of *social* phenomena was opposed not only to this excessive individualism but also to those theorists whose approach was overly speculative and philosophical. In the past, philosophical speculation had been the major mode of thought about human behavior and about society. Even in Durkheim's time, there were those who were skeptical about the possibility of an objective science of human behavior or social phenomena. These skeptics held that social phenomena reflect subjective mental process that are not amenable to objective measurement, or that the effort to explain human behavior in terms of scientific laws would, in effect, deny the possibility of freedom in making choices.[12]

Perhaps one of the reasons that criticisms of the objective, scientific approach have been so attractive is that this approach seems to imply a deterministic position that limits individuals' freedom in making choices. It is flattering for people to believe that they can control their own future by the kind of choices they make as opposed to being told that choice is an illusion because behavior is controlled by deterministic laws. But this is really a simplisitc and superficial way of stating the issue. Durkheim did not see the issue this way. He felt that knowing how social forces operate can have a liberating effect on individuals because these forces can then be taken into account and perhaps even modified through human action. Instead of arguing for deterministic laws as opposed to freedom, Durkheim's style of analysis leads us to raise questions about the kind of social structure that maximizes the range of choices individuals can make.

Social versus Individual Facts

Another question raised by Durkheim's stress on the objective reality of social phenomena concerns the basic nature of that reality. This is a fundamental question, and Durkheim attacked it directly. He insisted that social facts are not reducible to individual facts but have an independent existence at the social level. In Durkheim's time this emphasis was necessary in order to establish sociology as an independent discipline, but the issue is not dead today. Homans, for example, takes an explicit "reductionist" stance, arguing that any effort to explain social phenomena must ultimately rest on propositions about individual behavior.[13]

To appreciate why this issue is so basic, imagine that you are asked to describe a group in which you are involved. You might, for example, describe it as a cohesive, cooperative, or friendly group. You might even describe the positive atmosphere or spirit that pervades the group when its members get together. But let us go further and ask how you know that the group has these qualities. You may be warned that you could be describing your own attitude toward the group and not the group itself. At this point, you may say that anyone coming into the group can "feel" the solidarity of the group. It is not just your personal feeling; it really does characterize the group.

If the question of how you know is pursued, your justification or proof may involve descriptions of individual members spending a great deal of time with the group, members doing a variety of things together, members indicating in various ways to one another how much they enjoy what they do together, and members expressing approval of or liking for one another. In developing this proof you have made use of observations about individuals: individual attendance at group gatherings, individual actions or reactions toward one another, and so on.

Can you say anything more about the group? Anything that is *not* based on observations about individuals? Perhaps you might describe the high consensus within the group on its values and norms or that elusive feeling of solidarity that cannot be pinned down to any one individual or any one episode in the life of the group. You might note that *all* the group members agree with one another frequently, unite in correcting or expelling deviant newcomers or, in response to your queries, describe strong personal attachment to the group. However, your real goal is not to describe these individual behaviors or attitudes but the group itself, and it may seem naive and simplistic to claim that the group (and its characteristics) is nothing more than the sum of its individual members and their individual attitudes or activities with one another or to one another. Durkheim, in looking at social phenomena, whether in a small group or a total society, would insist that the whole is greater than the sum of its parts.

Even though group characteristics may be more than the sum of the individuals comprising the group, the group cannot exist independently of its individual members.[14] In the final analysis one does not even observe a group as a physical entity; one *infers* its existence by observing activities and interactions of individuals with one another over time or by learning from the individuals involved that they *perceive* the group as real and relate to it as such. The former inference requires that social structure be inferred from observations of an ongoing and constantly changing interaction process; the latter strategy makes the definition of social structure contingent on individual perceptions and definitions. In neither case can the social structure be perceived as a physical entity in the same way that individuals can.

In contemporary sociology there are models available for studying groups or larger social structures scientifically without assuming that they must have an actual physical existence, as such, independently of their individual members.[15] In Durkheim's time, however, under the influence of positivism, science was seen as being concerned with "real" (i.e., factual) phenomena. Without real objective phenomena as its subject matter, a science of society was impossible. This accounts for Durkheim's repeated insistence, especially early in his career (in *The Rules of the Sociological Method*), that social phenomena are *things*.[16] That is, social phenomena are objectively real, with an existence independent of individual biological or psychological phenomena.

Characteristics of Social Facts

How can genuinely social phenomena be distinguished from purely individual (or psychological) phenomena? Durkheim claimed that there are three distinguishing characteristics. First, social phenomena are external to the individual. After giving several examples of such facts (language, monetary system, professional norms, etc.), Durkheim asserts that "Here, then, are ways of acting, thinking, and feeling that present the noteworthy property of existing outside the individual consciousness."[17]

Although many of these social facts are utlimately internalized by the individual through the socialization process (as Durkheim clearly recognized), the individual initially confronts social facts as an external reality. Almost everyone has experienced being in a novel social situation, perhaps as a new member of an organization, and sensing clearly that there were customs and norms being observed that he or she did not fully comprehend or appreciate. In such a situation these customs and norms were clearly perceived as external.

The second characteristic of social facts is that they exert constraint over the individual. It was obvious to Durkheim that individuals are constrained, guided, persuaded, induced, coerced, or otherwise influenced by various types of social facts in their social milieu. As Durkheim says: "These types of conduct or thought are . . . endowed with coercive power, by virtue of which they impose themselves upon him, independent of his individual will."[18] This does not mean that the individual necessarily experiences the constraints of social facts in a negative or limiting way, as somehow forcing one to behave contrary to one's will. Indeed, if the socialization process is successful, the individual will have so thoroughly internalized the appropriate social facts that their dictates will seem natural, not at all opposed to the individual's will. Of course, socialization is seldom so thorough that there is no tension at all between social facts and individual will. However, if the individual's reluctance to be guided by the appropriate social facts should lead to serious violation, the constraining power of these facts would become apparent, either informally (e.g., in public disapproval) or formally (e.g., in expulsion or arrest).

The third characteristic of social facts is that they are general or widespread throughout a society. In other words, social facts are shared; they are not unique individual characteristics. This generality does not result simply from the summation of numerous individual facts. Social facts are genuinely collective in their nature, and their effect on the individual results from this collective property.

Durkheim wanted to establish the primacy of the social level instead of deriving social reality from individual characteristics.

These three characteristics—externality, coercion, generality—describe the type of phenomena that Durkheim sees as sociology's subject matter. He sums up sociology's domain as follows.

> We thus arrive at a point where we can formulate and delimit in a precise way the domain of sociology. It comprises only a limited group of phenomena. A social fact is to be recognized by the power of external coercion which it exercises or is capable of exercising over individuals, and the presence of this power may be recognized in its turn either by the existence of some specific sanction or by the resistance offered against every individual effort that tends to violate it. One can, however, define it also by its diffusion within the group, provided that . . . one takes care to add . . . that its own existence is independent of the individual forms it assumes in its diffusion. . . .[19]

What kinds of facts qualify in terms of these criteria? One consists of an aggregation of individual facts and is expressed as a social rate. Marriage rates, birthrates, suicide rates, and mobility rates are examples. Obviously, such rates cannot pertain to an individual, but only to a plurality. Individuals do not have marriage rates; societies do. To analyze such rates, one can establish trends over time or correlate changes in one rate with changes in another rate, for example. In this way, our understanding of the social level, as opposed to the individual level, can be advanced.

However, a rate, as an aggregation of individual data for some specified population, does not seem to constitute a level of reality that is clearly more than its parts. A rate as such does not have coercive power over an individual. For Durkheim, the importance of social rates is that they are indications of a larger collective reality to which individuals are subject and that accounts for the various rates. Thus he writes:

> Currents of opinion, with an intensity varying according to the time and place, impel certain groups either to more marriages, for example, or to more suicides, or to a higher or lower birthrate, etc. These currents are plainly social facts . . . statistics furnish us with the means of isolating them. . . . Since each of these figures contains all the individual cases indiscriminately, the individual circumstances which may have had a share in the production of the phenomena are neutralized and, consequently, do not contribute to its determination. The average, then, expresses a certain state of the group mind.[20]

"Currents of opinion" or "group mind" are far more elusive concepts than marriage rates, suicide rates, or other types of rates. Nevertheless, they represent the distinctively social reality that Durkheim sees as sociology's domain.[21]

The legal code is another type of social fact. It is an official embodiment of the rules and regulations of society, it is related to the basic values and customs shared throughout society, and it is capable of exerting constraint over the individual. The legal code transcends the individual, and Durkheim's substantive theoretical analysis of social solidarity and social change made use of different types of legal codes as indicators of different types of social structure.

However, the legal code presents only a partial picture of the social realm. There are numerous customs, morals, norms, and thought patterns that are not encompassed in a society's laws. Social facts include phenomena such as norms, moral ideals, beliefs, customs, thought patterns, feelings, and popular opinion. Durkheim used the term ''collective representations'' to refer to these phenomena when they are shared by the members of a society. This aspect of the social realm is close to being equivalent to the concept of culture, discussed at length in Chapter 3.

Strategies for Explaining Social Facts

After establishing the nature of social facts, how does one develop sociology as an empirical science based on these social facts? *The Rules of Sociological Method* is Durkheim's expanded answer to this question. This work is justifiably a classic in setting forth the foundations of methodology in sociology. A few examples of its basic principles will illustrate the point.

One of the basic methodological principles that Durkheim stressed is that social facts must be explained in terms of other social facts. This is absolutely fundamental. The most likely alternative would be to explain social facts in terms of individual phenomena (like will, consciousness, individual self-interest, etc.) such as those advocated by the classical economists and by Spencer. This would empty sociology of its content, reducing it to the psychological (or biological) level. Durkheim wrote that ''The determining cause of a social fact should be sought among the social facts preceding it and not among the states of the individual consciousness.''[22]

A second basic principle (and one that is fundamental to contemporary functionalism) is that the *origins* of a social phenomenon and its *functions* represent separate questions. As Durkheim wrote: ''When, then, the explanation of a social phenomenon is undertaken, we must seek separately the efficient cause which produces it and the functions it fulfills.''[23] This principle is related to the preceding one. If the cause of some social phenomenon were the function or purpose it fulfills, this would imply that conscious intention to achieve such a purpose is what led to the particular phenomenon being established in the first place. Again, this would reduce sociological explanation to individuals' subjective intentions and would undercut Durkheim's earlier insistence on the constraining effect of social facts.

The question of the social effects of individual's actions is independent of the question of what purposes individuals envisioned. Thus, for example, individuals get married for very personal reasons; the result is a given marriage rate. Or individuals make their personal decision to go to college; the result is a certain demand made on the facilities of educational institutions, a rise in the educational level of society, and so forth. This transformation of individual decisions into social outcomes is basic to contemporary functionalism.

Having established that explanations of social facts must be sought in other social facts, Durkheim advocates the strategy of *controlled comparison* as the most appropriate method for developing causal explanations in sociology.[24] This principle will be exemplified in the discussion of Durkheim's analysis of suicide. By the comparative method, however, Durkheim did not mean an indiscriminant mixing of colorful descriptions of exotic practices found in many different societies, nor did he mean comparing different stages of a given society in terms of some cosmic evolutionary scheme. Indeed, Comte's famous three-stage evolutionary model was criticized by Durkheim, partly because of its ultimate foundation on the psychological assumption of the human desire for improvement or progress.

Durkheim's comparative method was more rigorous and more limited. Essentially, the method of controlled comparison involves cross-classification of specific social facts to determine the extent to which they covary. If the correlation between two different sets of social facts can be shown to be valid in a variety of circumstances, this provides an important clue that the two types of facts may be causally related. That is, variation in the value of one type of variable may be the cause of variation in the value of the second variable.

Consistent statistical covariation is not in itself sufficient to *prove* causality, however. There must also be a *logical* connection between the two facts. In the absence of such a connection, the observed statistical correlation may be due to the mutual relation of both types of social facts to a third social fact. Durkheim notes, for example, that the statistical correlation between suicide and education occurs because both variables are affected by "the weakening of religious traditionalism."[25] Contemporary techniques of multivariate analysis, in which the statistical correlation between variables is examined with the confounding effects of extraneous variables controlled, represents an elaboration of the basic logic of controlled comparison as advocated by Durkheim.

SOLIDARITY AND TYPES OF SOCIAL STRUCTURE

Of all the social facts identified and discussed by Durkheim, none is as central as the concept of social solidarity. In one form or another, it underlies all his major works. Closely related terms include, for example, social integration and social cohesion. Briefly, solidarity refers to a state of relationships between individuals and/or groups that rests on shared moral sentiments and beliefs reinforced by common emotional experiences. This bond is more basic than contractual relationships entered into by rational agreement because such relationships presuppose at least a degree of consensus on the moral principles underlying contracts. This point was frequently made by Durkheim in his continuing attack on Spencer, Rousseau, and others who tried to explain the origins of the state in terms of contractual agreements that individuals negotiated to further their private interests. The remainder of this chapter will present Durkheim's analysis of solidarity in terms of: (1) differences in types of solidarity manifested in different types of social structure, (2) threats to solidarity and society's responses to these threats, and (3) the emergence and reinforcement of solidarity through religious rituals.

Mechanical versus Organic Solidarity

The major source for Durkheim's analysis of the alternative types of solidarity and their social structural sources is *The Division of Labor in Society*.[26] Published 2 years prior to the *Rules of Sociological Method,* this book anticipates many of the methodological points made in the latter book. The overall purpose of this classic work is to analyze the effects (or social functions) of increased complexity and specialization in the division of labor on the social structure and the resulting changes in the major forms of social solidarity. Briefly, growth in the division of labor promotes a shift in the social structure from *mechanical* to *organic* solidarity.

The distinction between mechanical and organic solidarity is one of Durkheim's most famous contributions. Before we develop a formal definition, let us consider an example of each type of solidarity in modern society: a church congregation and a business firm. What holds the church congregation together? What is the nature of the social bond that ties the individual to the group? Certainly it is not physical coercion in a free society with church-state separation. Nor is it likely to be the hope of economic gain, although for some this may be an indirect payoff as a result of social contacts established. The primary bond is the common beliefs, ideals, and moral commitments. Persons who share these beliefs and ideals feel that they belong together because of their like-mindedness.

There may be variations in how much unanimity exists or is expected. Large, liberal denominations in American society exhibit considerable variation and tolerance of diversity in terms of specific beliefs, while more conservative or sectarian churches might expect almost complete agreement with the official doctrines.[27] (The strength of integration may be higher in the latter type of church because of the higher consensus.) Differences in degree notwithstanding, at least some sharing of a common religious orientation is the underlying basis of social integration and the bond that links individuals together in the organization. In Durkheim's terms, this exemplifies *mechanical* solidarity.

In contrast, consider a business firm. What holds such an organization together? In all probability, a large part of the members' motivation will be their desire for the economic rewards (salaries or profits) that they receive for participating. But personal economic interests such as this do not fully explain the nature of the social integration that exists in a business organization. Instead, the organization is likely to exhibit considerable interdependence between the various participants, with each person's contribution dependent on the contributions of several others. Thus, for example, in a manufacturing firm there are likely to be machine operators, machine repairers, supervisors, salespeople, accountants, purchasers, managers, public relations experts, secretaries, and so forth, with the specialized activities of these various participants interrelated and interdependent so that the system forms a functioning whole Solidarity based on interdependence was referred to by Durkheim as *organic* solidarity.

In addition to this functional interdependence, the members of the business firm will also share some general common values and norms, particularly if the firm exhibits high morale. But these *common* values and norms cannot regulate or control behavior as closely or specifically as when differentiation and specialization are lower. The interdependence resulting from differentiation and specialization becomes *relatively* more important as a basis of solidarity than the *common* values and norms.

Durkheim used the terms *mechanical* and *organic* solidarity to analyze total societies, not organizations within society. Nevertheless, these examples illustrate some of the key elements of the two types of social structure. Mechanical solidarity is based on a strong common "collective consciousness" (one of Durkheim's terms; it can also be translated as "conscience"), which refers to "the totality of beliefs and sentiments common to average citizens of the same society."[28] It is a solidarity that depends on individuals being alike and sharing the same beliefs and normative patterns. Accordingly, individuality is not developed; it is continually stifled by overwhelming pressures for conformity. The individual does not necessarily experience this as a stifling pressure, since awareness of alternatives may not be developed.

For Durkheim the clearest indicator of mechanical solidarity was the strength and scope of *repressive* laws. Repressive laws define as crimes any behavior that threatens or violates the strong collective conscience. Punishment of criminals expresses the moral outrage of the group against such threats or violations, since they undermine the basis of the social order. Punishment does not necessarily reflect rational deliberation of the amount of damage objectively done to society, nor is consideration given to fitting the punishment to the crime; instead, it reflects and expresses collective passions that are aroused not so much by the objective nature of the deviant or criminal act as by the repudiation of the collective conscience that it represents. The crucial feature of mechanical solidarity is that it rests on a high degree of homogeneity in beliefs, sentiments, and the like. Such homogeneity is possible only when the division of labor is at a minimum.

In contrast, organic solidarity emerges as the division of labor advances. It rests on a high degree of interdependence. Such interdependence increases as a result of increasing specialization in the division of labor, which allows and even encourages the development of individual differences. The emergence of individual differences undermines the collective conscience which, in turn, becomes less important as the basis of the social order than the growing functional interdependence between specialized and relatively more autonomous individuals. As Durkheim says, "It is the division of labor which, more and more, fills the role that was formerly filled by the common conscience,"[29]

Durkheim maintains that the strength of organic solidarity is indicated by the relative importance of *restitutive* instead of repressive laws. The purposes of the two types of laws are quite different. Repressive law expresses strongly felt collective passions; restitutive law functions to maintain or protect the complex patterns of interdependence between the various specialized individuals or groups in the society. Correspondingly, the nature of the punishment meted out to a criminal differs under the two laws. As Durkheim says of the restitutive type of sanctions: ". . . it is not expiatory, but consists of a simple *return* in state."[30]

In the organic system, collective passions are less likely to be aroused by deviant behavior, since the collective conscience is not as strong. As a result, punishment is more rational, suited to the seriousness of the offense, and its purpose is to restore or protect the rights of the aggrieved party or insure the maintenance of the complex patterns of interdependence that underlie social solidarity. This restitutive pattern is evident in property laws, contract laws, commercial laws, and administrative and procedural rules.

This idea of a transition from repressive to restitutive laws, which parallels the increase in social complexity resulting from growth in the division of labor, is somewhat oversimplified. Durkheim apparently recognized this, since he did not develop this idea beyond the initial statement early in his career in *The Division of Labor*. As Nisbet points out, Durkheim's image of primitive moral outrage, which is collectively aroused in reaction to the slightest degree of deviance and expressed in harsh punishment of the deviant, exaggerates both the moral unity of primitive societies and the degree of interest in individuals' deviations.[31] Except for a limited number of major moral rules, primitive deviance and punishment are more likely to be private matters that are dealt with by the party, family, or clan that is wronged.

It is generally recognized that private justice is the typical mode for dealing with most cases of deviance in primitive societies and that the involvement of society as a whole in reacting to deviance, expressed through political or law enforcement functionaries of the state, is a comparatively recent development. Indeed, it is not difficult to show that the very concept of the *general* welfare of society as a whole, plus the development of repressive laws designed to prevent deviance from undermining the general welfare, emerged with the development of the modern nation-state. This superseded the earlier system of private or family justice.

As Nisbet suggests, it would probably be more accurate to reverse Durkheim's description of the types of law dominant in mechanical and organic society, that is, to associate mechanical solidarity with restitutive laws and organic solidarity with repressive laws.[32] Nevertheless, the general implication that laws in complex societies that have a high degree of interdependence are likely to reflect the process of deliberate and rational enactment instead of traditional customs is valid.

The Collective Conscience in Organic Societies

Not only do repressive laws continue to be important (or even more and more important) in an organic society, but the common collective consciousness also continues to contribute to social solidarity, reinforcing the bonds that emerge from increased functional interdependence. Growth in the division of labor (and the organic solidarity that results) does not destroy the common collective conscience; it simply reduces its importance in the detailed regulation of everyday life. This leaves more room for individual autonomy and social heterogeneity, but it does not necessarily result in individuals becoming completely detached from the social bonds that are based on moral consensus. This point is crucial; the continuing influence of the moral rules shared throughout society is necessary as an underlying noncontractual basis for the increased number of contractual relationships that people enter as a result of increased specialization and interdependence. The collective consciousness provides the noncontractual moral foundations that underlie contractual relations. In Durkheim's mind, this underlying collective conscience is ignored by theorists such as Spencer, who saw the fundamental basis of the social order in contractual relations.

Durkheim relates this continuing influence of the collective consciousness to the increased individualism of organic societies.

> This is not to say, however, that the common conscience is threatened with total disappearance. Only, it more and more comes to consist of very general and very indeterminate ways of thinking and feeling, which leave an open place for a growing multitude of individual differences. There is even a place where it is strengthened and made precise; that is the way in which it regards the individual. As all the other beliefs and all the other practices take on a character less and less religious, the individual becomes the object of a sort of religion. We erect a cult in behalf of personal dignity.[33]

For example, in our modern, organic society, a person is not required to choose a marriage partner from a particular family or clan or from any other particular group, nor is one required to accept the decision of one's parents in the choice of a spouse. Individuals have a wide range of freedom in choosing their marriage partners, but the overall majority still generally expect that their marriages will be heterosexual, not homosexual. And even though sexual norms and family forms have undergone drastic changes, there is probably still the general expectation that individuals who wish to form an enduring sexual union will get married (at least eventually). These areas where there is a broad degree of unanimity or consensus reflect the influence of the common collective consciousness.

On a more general level, we might say that moral consensus in modern, complex societies is at the level of abstract values rather than specific norms. That is, there is a wide degree of agreement on abstract principles but considerable heterogeneity in the interpretation and application of these general principles among the various diverse groups in a complex, organic society.

The collective consciousness also exists in a more limited form in various specific groups within society. As noted earlier, a church whose members are united by a common faith is one example of such a group. In addition to the mechanical solidarity manifested within religious groups, there are numerous other primordial, "mechanical" social bonds, such as kinship, ethnicity, and community. These bonds obviously cannot unite all members of a complex society, but they are important sources of solidarity for the innumerable primary groups that honeycomb the overall society. Membership in such groups is probably far more important for the development of individuals' values, norms, and overall world view than membership in the overall society in an abstract sense.

Durkheim also emphasized the importance of the common collective conscience that may exist in various occupational and professional groups. Similarity in occupational activities and interests results in an internal homogeneity that makes possible the development of common customs, beliefs, sentiments, and moral principles or ethical codes. Consequently, the members of these groups are guided and constrained in their behavior just as surely as the members of a primitive tribe with a minimal division of labor are guided and constrained by their strong collective conscience. Durkheim felt that this mechanical solidarity within various occupational and professional groups should become more and more important, as the division of labor expands, as a vital mediating link between the individual and the overall society.[34]

> The rules of occupational morality and justice, however, are as imperative as the others. They force the individual to act in view of ends which are not strictly his own, to make concessions, to consent to compromises, to take into account interests higher than his own. Consequently, even where society relies most completely upon the division of labor, it does not become a jumble of juxtaposed atoms, between which it can establish only external, transient contacts. Rather, the members are united by ties which extend deeper and far beyond the short moments during which the exchange is made.[35]

Social Evolution

Implied in Durkheim's analysis of mechanical versus organic solidarity is a general model of social change. Writing in the context of the rapidly expanding Industrial Revolution, Durkheim took as his point of departure the growing specialization and complexity of the division of labor. Unlike those nostalgic conservatives who saw the disintegration of society in this development, Durkheim saw the basis of social integration being transformed into a new form, that is, from mechanical to organic solidarity. This new form of organic solidarity, based on genuine interdependence between specialized "parts," can be a more thorough, more potent, and more profound source of social integration than the older form of mechanical integration, which is based primarily on similarities in beliefs and values.

The collective conscience that underlies mechanical solidarity is most strongly developed in simple primitive societies. In such societies all members have essentially the same beliefs, opinions, and values, and all share roughly similar life-styles. This homogeneity is feasible in view of the fact that the division of labor is only minimally developed. Of course, there may be some specialization along age and sex lines. Older persons may be expected to serve as leaders, or at least as wise counselors, while women may be expected to specialize in domestic activities. But this elementary division of labor does not result in such high social heterogeneity that the *common* ways of thinking and acting are seriously undermined.

As the division of labor begins to expand, the common collective conscience gradually begins to dissolve. People whose occupational activites become more specialized and dissimilar find themselves becoming more dissimilar in beliefs, opinions, and life-styles as well. This is to be expected, since people's social experiences are so heavily influenced by their occupation. As people's experiences become more heterogeneous, so do their beliefs, attitudes, and general consciousness.

But this growing heterogeneity does not destroy social solidarity. Instead, as the division of labor expands, individuals and groups in society find themselves becoming more and more interdependent rather than self-sufficient. Persons who devote themselves to an occupational specialty must depend on others with different specialized occupations for many of the goods and services that they need for surviving and meeting their various needs. The gradual increase in the functional interdependence between the various specialized and heterogeneous parts of society provides an alternative to the common collective conscience as a basis of social solidarity.

Although a comprehensive model of linear evolutionary development was not as important in Durkheim's theory as in many other nineteenth-century theories of social change, his analysis of the growth of the division of labor and increasing social complexity nevertheless is such a model. The broad historical trend in Western societies has been toward increasing specialization and complexity in the division of labor. This development had two major effects. First, it undermined the collective consciousness, thereby making possible the growth of individuality. Second, it promoted organic solidarity based on functional interdependence. Durkheim saw modern urban-industrial societies as the fullest embodiment yet of organic solidarity. We see the same development in the history of our own society, with its gradual transformation from a primarily rural-agricultural society to a predominantly urban-industrial one.

Durkheim did not stop with analyzing the *effects* of the growth in the division of labor; he also tried to determine its *causes*. Why does the division of labor increase? Durkheim's answer to this question focuses primarily on demographic changes and their effect on interaction frequency between persons and on the competitive struggle for survival. Specifically, growth in the size of a society's population leads to an increase in its "moral density"; this term signifies increasing rates of interaction among the various members of society. This increased interaction promotes increased cooperation and stimulates the emergence of new ideas.

But, as the population grows, the struggle for existence also increases. The effect is that individuals gradually increase their degree of specialization as they seek some means of livelihood in which competition or conflict with others is less acute. Furthermore, as individuals specialize, they become more efficient, which enables the larger population to be maintained. Equally important, specialization encourages the growth of interdependence and contractual exchanges as individuals limit themselves to their specialty and rely on other individuals for other goods or services needed.

We may summarize this section by juxtaposing the major characteristics of societies based on mechanical solidarity with those of societies based on organic solidarity.

Mechanical	*Organic*
Low division of labor	High division of labor
Pervasive collective conscience	Weakened collective conscience
Repressive laws dominant	Restitutive laws dominant
Low individuality	High individuality
Consensus on specific normative patterns important	Consensus on abstract and general values important
Community involvement in punishing deviants	Specialized social control agencies punish deviants
Relatively low interdependence	High interdependence
Primitive or rural	Urban-industrial

This general dichotomy between premodern and modern forms of social structure was not unique to Durkheim. Perhaps the closest parallel is Tönnies' famous distinction between *Gemeinschaft* and *Gesellschaft* societies.[36] Translated *community* and *society,* these terms correspond roughly to mechanical and organic solidarity, respectively. For Tönnies, the *Gemeinschaft* society reflects a *natural* will and represents a social structure characterized by organic unity, strong traditions, diffuse relationships, and seeming spontaneity in behavior. In contrast, the *Gesellschaft* society is characterized by *rational* will, a more contrived character, and greater predominance of specialized, segmental social relations. Maine's distinction between status and contract is a similar dichotomy,[37] as is Redfield's much later delineation of folk versus urban cultures.[38]

THREATS TO SOLIDARITY

Whether the social structure of a society reflects mechanical or organic solidarity, the maintenance of a minimum level of social integration is never automatic. In a society based on mechanical solidarity, social solidarity is threatened by the possibility of segmentation of functionally autonomous subgroups and by any kind of deviant behavior that violates the strong collective consciousness. Punishment for deviation is a deterrent to future deviation and, more important, provides an opportunity for the community to reaffirm the normative demands of the collective consciousness and reestablish the dividing line between socially approved and disapproved behavior. There is the clear implication here that this collective reaffirmation serves a vital social function in maintaining commitment to the collective consciousness on which the social order rests.

The transition from mechanical to organic solidarity is not necessarily a smooth and harmonious process without accompanying strains. As the old primordial social bonds of religion, kinship, and community are undermined by the increase in the division of labor, there may be a failure of other social bonds to replace them. The result is a fragmented or atomized society in which individuals are cut loose from their social moorings and in which intermediate groups that might link the individual to the larger society are not well developed. Indeed, this was one of the major problems that Durkheim perceived in his own society, and his promotion of the importance of occupational and professional groups was intended to help remedy this situation.

Sources of Strain in Complex, Organic Societies

In a society with a highly developed division of labor and complex patterns of interdependence, integration may be undermined by inadequate coordination of highly specialized persons whose activities fail to mesh together. In this situation, various specialized institutions become more or less autonomous in the short run, developing in ways that may or may not be compatible with the welfare of the overall society.[39] One modern example of this is the tendency of schools of education to continue to train new teachers for the elementary and secondary levels long after the teacher shortage has passed and a surplus exists.

An even more important threat to organic solidarity develops from the increasing heterogeneity and individuality associated with a high division of labor. With high heterogeneity, the common bond uniting the various members of society becomes attenuated. Individuals start to identify with more limited groups within the general population, such as their occupational groups, instead of the overall society. Solidarity within such groups is, of course, based on mechanical solidarity.

As noted earlier, Durkheim saw great value in occupational or professional group solidarity. Through such groups, individuals may be linked to the larger social order. However, if strong solidarity at this level is combined with loss of identification with the larger society, the stage is set for possible conflict, with these specialized groups pursuing their particular interests at the expense of the welfare of society as a whole.

Durkheim does not imply that conflicts over particular group interests can or should be eliminated; however, for the sake of integration at the level of the total society, it is important that there be agreement at a higher level between the parties to the conflict. This agreement may be in terms of a common commitment to the rules that govern the conflict or to basic values that are shared by all parties to the conflict. Nevertheless, there is the possibility that commitment to the *common* values and norms will be undermined by the *particular* values and interests of the various different groups in society. The willingness of unions to engage in strikes, for example, which sometimes represent a serious threat to the public welfare, might well reflect inadequate organic solidarity.

The rationale behind punishment for deviant behavior that threatens organic solidarity differs from that for deviance that threatens mechanical solidarity. Since the common collective consciousness is less highly developed or less uniform, there is not the same need to express collective outrage at its violation. Instead of expressing such emotions, punishment restores the patterns of interdependence that may have been disrupted by the deviance. For example, if a person fails to live up to contractual agreements, social control agents simply intervene to correct this failure.

On the whole, punishment of deviants in an organic society tends to be more rational and suited to the seriousness of the violation. Also, dealing with offenders is more likely to be assigned to specialized professionals instead of the community as a whole. But the important point is that the different forms of solidarity will be reflected in different responses to deviance. Furthermore, society's reaction to deviance serves a broader purpose for society itself than that of simply punishing the deviant or deterring future deviance. This broader purpose is that of reaffirming the basic normative structure that underlies the social order.

Organic solidarity can also be undermined by an excessive emphasis on individualism. As noted previously, organic solidarity is characterized by heterogeneity; individuals become more differentiated from one another as the division of labor increases and the common collective consciousness is reduced in importance. Consistent with this trend, individualism flourishes as people become more dissimilar. That is, they are encouraged to be independent and to develop their own unique abilities.

This may weaken the social bonds that unite individuals to various social groups or to society at large and may result in the loss of adequate social anchorage for a meaningful life. In Durkheim's perspective, the individual is dependent on society (or at least on particular groups within it) for the beliefs and values that give meaning and purpose to life and for norms to guide and regulate behavior. Any weakening of social bonds undermines the shared beliefs, weakens the moral values, and erodes the normative structure. The result is anomie, or a state of meaninglessness and normlessness in which individuals are adrift, cut loose from the social bonds through which normative regulation is exercised.

Subjectively, individuals may experience such a state as one of uncertainty and insecurity or as one in which their personal desires and ambitions rise out of all proportion to realistic opportunities of attainment. At its most profound level, anomie is manifested in widespread feelings of meaninglessness, that gnawing suspicion that life really has no purpose or makes no sense in the final analysis. Given Durkheim's strong emphasis on the dependence of the individual on society, the rise of anomie is one of the unfortunate consequences of the strong cultural emphasis on individualism.

Social Integration and Suicide Rates

Changes in the level of integration in a society are manifested empirically in various ways. A major manifestation that Durkheim analyzed intensively was changes in suicide rates. For instance, when organic solidarity declines and the level of anomie in society rises, suicide rates are likely to increase. Durkheim referred to suicides resulting from anomie as *anomic* suicide.

The general question of how changes in suicide rates reflect changes in the state of solidarity in society was the subject of Durkheim's classic research monograph, *Suicide*.[40] This work was intended to demonstrate the validity of Durkheim's basic methodological premise that social facts must be explained by other such facts. If such a proposition could be demonstrated for suicide, an act that seems preeminently personal, then surely its value would be established. Durkheim's primary interest was not in suicide as an individual act but in fluctuation in suicide rates. Suicide rates qualify as social and not individual facts and, as such, should be expected to be affected by other social facts such as degree and type of social integration.

The basic proposition supported in *Suicide* is that suicide rates vary with the degree of social integration. Durkheim identified three different types of suicide, reflecting three different types of relationship. The three types are egoistic, anomic, and altruistic. For the first two types suicide rates vary inversely with the degree of social integration; that is, the lower the integration, the higher the suicide rates. Egoistic suicide results from an excessive emphasis on individualism or a lack of sufficiently strong ties to social groups. Thus Protestants have higher suicide rates than Catholics, since their beliefs encourage greater individualism and the communal bond in Protestant churches is weaker. Similarly, unmarried persons have higher suicide rates than married persons, and married persons without children have higher rates than those with children. These examples demonstrate that egoistic suicide may result either from the cultural emphasis on individualism or from the lack of personal bonds to significant primary groups.

Anomic suicide results from partial deregulation of individuals' goals and aspirations. Under normal or stable conditions, individuals' desires are held in check by appropriate norms supported by general moral principles. These regulative norms insure that individuals' desires and aspirations are roughly proportional to available means. Thus individuals strive for and receive the rewards that they have been taught to anticipate as appropriate. When these regulative norms break down, the effect is to remove the constraints on individuals' desires; these desires then explode beyond any realistic possibility of attainment, and the individual is doomed to perpetual frustration. As Durkheim argued, human wants and desires are insatiable but are normally constrained by established norms. When these constraints are removed, the basic insatiability of human appetites becomes manifest. Because of the increased frustration resulting from unfulfilled desires, suicide rates rise.

In support of this proposition, Durkheim showed that sudden changes in society, such as acute economic crisis or periods of unusual economic expansion and prosperity, are generally associated with an increase in suicide rates. The rise in suicide rates in times of unusual prosperity may seem surprising, but it makes sense in terms of the effects of this prosperity on people's desires and aspirations. Briefly, when people's economic status dramatically improves, the constraints of poverty are removed and their expectations of further improvement rise even more dramatically.[41] Similarly, divorce and suicide are positively correlated because divorce removes the social constraints and normative regulations associated with family life.

While egoistic and anomic suicide both reflect a breakdown in social integration, altruistic suicide results from an excessively *strong* level of social integration. Such a high level of integration depresses individuality to the point where the individual is regarded as unworthy or insignificant in his or her own right. Instead, the individual is expected to submit totally to the needs or demands of the group, subordinating any individual desires that detract from the life or welfare of the group. If the level of solidarity is sufficiently high, the individual does not resent this subordination to the group but, instead, finds great satisfaction and personal fulfillment in sacrificing for the larger good of the group.

Altruistic suicides may result from either of two conditions. First, the norms of the group may demand sacrifice of an individual's life. An example would be the suicide missions of Japanese Air Force pilots during World War II. Another example is manifested in the ancient custom in some societies whereby a man's wife and servants are ceremonially killed and buried with him at his death in order to meet his needs in the next world. Second, the norms of the group may demand the performance of tasks that are so difficult to achieve that individuals experience failure in spite of their most heroic efforts. If their identification with the group and with their task is sufficiently strong, this experience of failure may result in severe demoralization and loss of a sense of self-worth at having let the group down. Suicide may be chosen as an alternative to continuing to live with such disgrace. Thus, for example, military officers who have suffered defeat have high suicide rates, higher, in fact, than that of the soldiers under their command, since their identification with the military is greater.

The relationship between social integration and suicide rates is shown in the following diagram.

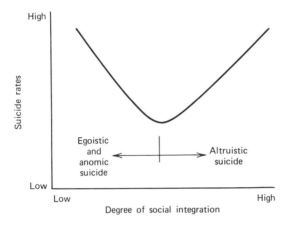

Suicide rates and social integration.

As noted, egoistic and anomic suicide rates are high when the level of social integration is low, and altruistic suicide rates are high under certain conditions when the level of social integration is high.

Change in suicide rates is not the only empirical manifestation of a change in the level of social integration (although this was Durkheim's major focus). Changes in crime and delinquency rates, alcoholism rates, divorce rates, and rates of mental illness also reflect changes in the type or degree of social integration or other sociological variables. Durkheim explored briefly the relationships between different forms of insanity and suicide and between homicide and suicide and concluded that these relationships are too inconsistent to be caused by the same social processes. Instead, each phenomenon results from different causal processes, even though all serve as indicators of some aspect of the overall state of social integration in society.

Durkheim did not accept the popular view that such phenomena necessarily reflect a pathological state of society or that such phenomena could be eliminated by appropriate reform measures. In his view, all societies exhibit phenomena such as suicide, deviance, crime, and so forth (to varying degrees); therefore their occurrence should be considered "normal," not pathological, at least as long as a given rate is maintained.

A pathological state of society would be manifested by rapid fluctuations in the rates of phenomena such as those just listed. These fluctuations would signal a change in the degree or type of social integration and perhaps the development of a social crisis. But if rates of suicide or deviance are stable for long periods, this would indicate a state of normalcy for the particular society under consideration.

Moreover, deviance is really inevitable, given the natural variability of human behavior and individual characteristics. Since society rests on a foundation of shared moral commitments, it is necessary for moral distinctions to be made between acceptable versus unacceptable, normal versus deviant behavior. The natural variability in human behavior provides the opportunity for making these moral distinctions in line with a society's particular normative system. These moral distinctions are reinforced through punishment of the deviant. Thus, Durkheim suggests, not only is deviance inevitable, but it actually serves a positive social function for society by providing an occasion for reinforcing the moral values on which the solidarity of society rests. The specific nature of this reinforcement will vary, depending on whether the society is based on mechanical or organic solidarity.

This perspective on deviance has been further developed by contemporary labeling theorists.[42] Labeling theorists insist that society creates deviants by making the rules whose infraction constitutes deviance. Durkheim would add that society *has* to make such rules and punish those who deviate therefrom, since the basic structure of society rests on a moral foundation that must be continually reinforced.

EMERGENCE AND REINFORCEMENT OF SOLIDARITY

Durkheim's concern with society's moral foundations stimulated the development of his classic sociological perspective on the social functions of religion. His analysis of the close interrelation between religion and society, developed in detail in *The Elementary Forms of the Religious Life,* was the last major part in the development of his overall theoretical perspective on social solidarity.[43]

Implicit in this work is a subtle shift in Durkheim's emphasis. As noted previously, in the early stages of his career Durkheim promoted the position that social facts are external to the individual and exert constraint over the individual, as exemplified in legal codes, for example. By the time of *The Elementary Forms,* the emphasis seems to have shifted to the processes whereby individuals actually create and internalize social facts (norms, values, etc), so that they exert their control from *within* the individual.

This shift from external to internal control makes sense in terms of our individual experience. For most of us much of the time, we accept various normative expectations as right and proper and we conform to them voluntarily because they express the basic personality patterns we have developed, not in response to external coercion. But with this shift in Durkheim's emphasis, we are faced with the basic sociological question of what social processes cause the internalization of society's norms and the development and reinforcement of motivations to conform to them. Like Comte before him, Durkheim sensed that religion traditionally had made a major contribution toward fulfilling these particular functions because of its traditional emphasis on moral obligations.

For Durkheim, sociological analysis of religion must start with recognition of the close interdependence between religion and society. He chose to study religion in a primitive society because he felt that this interdependence would be more apparent there than in advanced societies, with their richly developed cultural patterns that may overlay and obscure this interdependence. Also, in more advanced societies, religious institutions develop a certain degree of autonomy that may also obscure the essential relationship between religion and society.

Collective Experiences and the Emergence of the Idea of the Sacred

The Elementary Forms of the Religious Life is a detailed analysis of the beliefs and rituals of the totemic religion of the Arunta, primitive tribes of Australia; it also contains supplementary material on some North American Indian tribes. The social organization of these tribes is based on the clan as the primary social unit. Durkheim's analysis, interwoven with extensive descriptive detail, is intended to demonstrate the close link between this type of social organization and the totemic type of religion.

The central feature of any religion, in Durkheim's view, is concern with a sacred realm. He defined religion as:

> . . . a unified system of beliefs and practices relative to sacred things . . . things set apart or forbidden—beliefs and practices which unite into one single moral community called a Church, all those who adhere to them.[44]

Although this definition can be criticized, the emphasis on the sacred is valid and understandable as a broad definition. The concept of the sacred refers to a realm believed to be set apart from and totally different from the ordinary, everyday world of the profane.

Given this emphasis, one major part of Durkheim's analysis involves searching for the source of the idea of the sacred. In other words, what is there in human experience that gives rise to the idea of a realm of the sacred that is wholly different from the ordinary, everyday realm? Durkheim reviewed and rejected several prevailing theories that explained beliefs in a sacred realm as mere superstitions or illusions needed by persons in a prescientific age to explain natural phenomena. Such views are too rational in assuming that primitive religious beliefs represent the efforts of primitive peoples to explain the natural phenomena around them on an intellectual level. They are also too individualistic in the assumption that these intellectual questions are posed and answered on an individualistic basis without considering the overriding influence of the social group. Besides, Durkheim argued, it is inconceivable that such a pervasive and powerful a social institutions as religion could be based on nothing more than illusion or imagination. The idea of the sacred, he felt, must reflect or correspond to something that is real. The basic question, then, is: What is the reality that underlies the universal concept of the sacred?

Durkheim's answer is not surprising, considering his theoretical framework. Briefly, the idea of the sacred emerges out of group life and, in fact, represents the reality of the group in symbolic form. In developing this argument, Durkheim pointed out that primitive totemic clans identified themselves by the names of their particular totems. Whatever the totem was (a kangaroo, a crow, etc.), the name of the totem was the name or emblem of the clan, and the totemic object was believed to embody the sacred totemic principle, or *mana*. Since the clan members believed themselves to be related to the totem in a special way, they also shared in this sacred power. Thus a close kinship existed between the clan and its totem, and this kinship was represented by a common name. As Durkheim wrote, the totem is:

> . . . the symbol of the determined society called the clan. It is its flag. . . . The god of the clan, the totemic principle can therefore be nothing else than the clan itself, personified and represented to the imagination under the visible form of the animal or vegetable which serves as totem.[45]

He goes on to show that the relationship people feel with a supernatural divine power is similar to their relationship with society. For example, in both cases the individual has a dependency relation, and in both cases the individual's behavior is guided and controlled, sometimes in opposition or indifference to his or her private interests. Most important, in both cases the individual has a feeling of being in the presence of a transcendent power that is greater than the individual and that cannot simply be ignored.

Durkheim's explanation of how individuals become aware of such a power is based on a model of interaction and mutual stimulation comparable in some ways to the dynamics of crowd psychology. Individuals come together on ceremonial and ritual occasions and, through their intense interaction with one another while concentrating on a common object, there is a gradual emotional buildup that is reinforced for each person by the awareness that all of the others are sharing the same experience. Each person's actions contribute to the shared experience, but the total collective experience transcends any one individual. The ultimate effect of this collective process of mutual stimulation is the creation of an emotional climate in which individuals lose their individuality and self-control and get swept along on a kind of emotional "high." This can stimulate behavior that would never be indulged in on private or ordinary occasions.

Such a process can readily be documented in many contemporary sects and cults. New recruits typically find themselves overwhelmed by the intensity of the collective emotional experience generated within the group. The opportunity to share such an experience often moves members to give up their personal possessions and to commit their lives to the mission of the group. In many cases personal hardships are gladly endured, compensated by the feeling of being part of a great cause that transcends any one individual. This feeling on the part of each member is reinforced by intense and frequent interaction with fellow members.

As Durkheim writes, in his description of primitive totemic rituals:

> When they are once come together, a sort of electricity is formed by their collecting which quickly transports them to an extraordinary degree of exaltation. Every sentiment expressed finds a place without resistance in all the minds, which are very open to outside impressions; each re-echoes the others and is re-echoed by the others. The initial impulse thus proceeds, growing as it goes, as an avalanche grows in its advance. . . . The passions released are of such an impetuosity that they can be restrained by nothing.[46]

> So it is in the midst of these effervescent social environments and out of this effervescence itself that the religious idea seems to be born.[47]

In such a collective experience, individuals feel themselves to be in the presence of an extraordinary power to which they are very intimately linked. Sensing the importance of this transcendent or sacred power, the members of the clan have a need to represent it to themselves in some visible way and to explain it to themselves. Essentially, this is the purpose of the totemic object. The totem symbolizes the collective life and power of the group and is seen by the clan members as the source of the extraordinary power they experience. Thus the distinction in Durkheim's definition of religion between the sacred and the profane corresponds to the distinction between individuals' collective life and their private lives.

Relationship Between Religious Orientations and Social Structure

The religious experience and the idea of the sacred are *products* of collective life; religious beliefs and rituals also *reinforce* the social bonds on which collective life rests. In other words, the relationship between religion and society is one of close mutual interdependence. Essentially, Durkheim argued that totemic beliefs (or other types of religious beliefs) express the reality of society itself in symbolic form. Totemic rituals (or rituals in other religious forms) unite individuals in common activities with a common goal and reinforce the beliefs, sentiments, and moral commitments that are the foundation of the social structure. Thus the very idea of the sacred is reinforced as members of the group repeatedly experience the reality of the group itself. This reality is manifested in the common sentiments and joint activities associated with the repeated performance of religious rituals or reaffirmation of shared beliefs about the sacred.

We might go beyond Durkheim's concerns by noting that once religious beliefs and rituals emerge from collective life in this way, they may be subjected to extensive intellectual or aesthetic elaboration that may obscure their social foundations and their correspondence to a particular social structure.[48] Elaborate doctrinal systems may be developed that explain the nature of the sacred power and the relationship between this power and the ordinary, everyday world. Complex ritual forms may gradually be developed as a way of arousing and channeling the primeval collective emotions, and these ritual forms may or may not continue over the course of many generations to correspond to the emotional state of the group or the structure of relationships among its members. But the linkage between religious beliefs and rituals and the collective life is nevertheless still present, even though it may gradually be obscured or attenuated. Even in modern American society, many people who attend church services are aware that their social relationships are strengthened as a result of their attendance, and their commitment to the basic values and norms shared by the group are reinforced.

The challenge for those who take Durkheim's perspective on religion seriously is to show as precisely as possible how specific religious beliefs or rituals reflect or reinforce the social structure and the moral principles on which it rests. Swanson attempted to do this in a comparative analysis of numerous primitive societies.[49] As one general example to illustrate his analysis, we might note that as societies expand in number and in territory controlled, their concept of the supernatural power expands in a parallel fashion. Thus limited tribal deities that must coexist with other tribal deities gradually become dominant as the tribe expands, perhaps ultimately becoming national gods. The final stage is the development of the concept of a universal deity. This has occurred in the various world religions, even though a genuine, worldwide social order has not yet fully emerged. Nevertheless, such a development reflects the growth of a worldwide perspective.

Another example of the correlation between religious orientation and social structure is the development of highly personal forms of religious commitment that parallels the growth of individualism in a society based on organic solidarity. In our own society, for example, a person's religious orientation and commitment are likely to be considered very personal, even private. In contrast, in the primitive clan society based on totemism, where individualism was not developed, religion was essentially a public affair.

Religion in Modern Society

Durkheim's analysis of the emotional excitement associated with collective rituals might seem somewhat out of place in today's society. Indeed, many religious leaders are critical of typical church services as being mere ritualistic forms that do not carry the meaning or arouse the emotions they think they should. Certainly the church service in a typical American denomination cannot be accused of generating much "collective effervescence" or emotional enthusiasm.[50] Many people probably attend church services out of habit or a sense of duty and with a rather low level of emotional intensity. They may be inspired or experience a sense of euphoria or satisfaction as a result, but the intense emotional excitement that Durkheim describes would be rather unusual in many church services. There are exceptions, of course; some churches pride themselves on the high level of emotional enthusiasm they generate, as opposed merely to going through set ritual forms.

Durkheim recognized that the traditional religious forms of his day did not exhibit the vitality that he attributed to the religion of the Arunta of Australia. This was partly because of the rapid changes in his time; old forms were in the process of decline, but new forms had not yet emerged to replace them. He also felt that the lack of vitality of religious forms in his day was symptomatic of the low level of solidarity in his society; yet he believed this would one day change as new kinds of collective experiences give birth to new forms of solidarity and new forms for reaffirming this solidarity. As he wrote:

> If we find a little difficulty today in imagining what these feasts and ceremonies of the future consist in, it is because we are going through a stage of transition and moral mediocrity. The great things of the past which filled our fathers with enthusiasm do not excite the same ardour in us. . . . But a day will come when our societies will know again those hours of creative effervescence, in the course of which new ideas arise and new formulae are found which serve for a while as a guide to humanity; and when these hours shall have been passed through once, men will spontaneously feel the need of reliving them from time to time in thought, that is to say, of keeping alive their memory by means of celebrations which regularly reproduce their fruits.[51]

In the meantime, we must recognize that the kinds of dramatic collective experiences that Durkheim believed to be the basis for the idea of the sacred occur today in many places outside established religions. Indeed, this ''collective effervescence'' may be manifested in athletic contests, perhaps in rock concerts such as Woodstock and, usually to a lesser degree, in political or patriotic rallies. It is interesting to analyze professional football contests in terms of Durkheim's perspective on religion. There is the totemic emblem (e.g., the dolphin, the cowboy, and the eagle), the emotional identification with a geographical place (e.g., Miami, Dallas, and Philadelphia) and, most obviously, the collective emotional excitement of the crowd of spectators, with live television coverage enabling the entire country to share the experience of the ceremonial celebration of basic American values such as competition and aggressiveness.[52]

Similarly, although the degree of emotional excitement is probably less, political rallies or Fourth of July celebrations can readily be understood in terms of Durkheim's perspective on rituals. On such occasions, members of the community gather together to reaffirm basic values or commemorate important events in their collective history. The medium through which this reaffirmation and commemoration take place is largely ritualistic.[53]

In fact, any of the national holidays, whether religious or civil, can be seen in this light. The Christmas season, for example, commemorates the birth of the Christ child into the holy family; it also provides an occasion for families to get together, often over great distances in our highly mobile society. Furthermore, the ritualistic exchange of gifts symbolizes the interdependence and the mutual moral obligations of individuals to each other. Other, more cynical interpretations are certainly possible, such as the view that the basic dynamic underlying our commercialized Christmas season reflects pervasive economic exploitation. Yet it is instructive to apply Durkheim's perspective to such phenomena.

Durkheim's theory may be criticized because of its one-sided emphasis on solidarity. This emphasis is built into the definition (i.e., "religion... unites people into a single moral community...''); thus it is not surprising that Durkheim sees religion as promoting social cohesion and solidarity. Indeed, considered in this way, the argument is tautological. This perspective also ignores the numerous occasions thoughout history of bitter religious conflict. To be sure, conflicts between religious groups often reflect basic political, economic, or social differences; however, the religious element may exacerbate the conflict and provide ideological support.

In defense of Durkheim one might offer the counterargument that cohesion and solidarity should be expected only within the religious in-groups. When conflicts between groups are seen in the context of the dynamics of in-group versus out-group relations, it should be obvious that the cohesion and solidarity of the religious in-group can hardly be extended to include the out-group whose members do not share the same religious orientation.[54] Conflicts may occur within the in-group as well, of course, but these should be seen as reflecting social control processes whereby the group attempts to reinforce its moral foundations and normative structure against the threats represented by deviant behavior. Certainly, however, Durkheim's model should not be expected to apply to a society marked by sharp cleavages and disagreements between different religious groups except *within* these various groups.

In America at the present time, the established pattern of religious pluralism does not generally reflect such sharp cleavages. In fact, observers of American religion have pointed out that the various major established religious groups are essentially united in support of America's "civil religion."[55] The civil religion basically represents a sacralization of the American way of life, which corresponds closely to Durkheim's concept of civic morality as a basis of social cohesion on a national level.

Social Origins of Forms of Knowledge

Toward the end of *The Elementary Forms* Durkheim expanded his major point by stating that not only religious thought but knowledge in general rests on, and reflects, its social base. For example, all knowledge depends on language for social transmission, and language is social product, not a creation of any individual. On a more profound level, Durkheim suggests that the basic categories of thought (time, space, class, force, cause, etc.) emerge from social life and reflect the social structure.[56] The concept of time, for example, emerged initially in the primitive world because of the need to regulate the cycles of individual and collective life. Space, as a general category of the mind, grows out of and reflects the spatial distribution of the members of the group in a particular geographical territory. The concept of class or category emerged from the social divisions within the group. Without the shared experience of various social categories, in terms of which members of the group may be sorted and selected according to some relevant criteria, the possibility of classification of natural phenomena would not occur to the human mind. Durkheim suggests that the concept of force is based, in the final analysis, on the subjective awareness of the compelling power of the group over each of its members that the members of the group share. Related to this, the concept of cause grows out of the common experience individuals have of perform- ing actions that produce certain effects in their collective emotional life. Without such an experience of cause and effect in social experiences, natural phenomena in the physical and biological worlds would be perceived simply in terms of the succession of one event after another, without any causal relation between such events.

In view of this analysis of the social origins of knowledge, it is clear that both religious and scientific thought are conditioned by, and reflect, the type of social structure in which they emerge. The categories of thought just discussed are essen- tial parameters within which scientists must work in their search for knowledge. Based on this insight of Durkheim's, we might speculate that the scientist's faith in the orderliness of natural phenomena reflects the experience of orderliness or regu- larity in social life. Although Durkheim did not develop this perspective in the sociology of knowledge fully, it reflects his basic assumption regarding the priority of society to the individual and the fundamental proposition that the development of the individual personality or the subjective life of the individual profoundly reflects the influence of the social milieu.

Summary

We have treated Durkheim as the major classical representative of a theoretical approach that focuses on the social structural level of analysis and emphasizes the social processes that promote solidarity and integration in society. However, no classification of Durkheim's work into one or another school of sociological thought can really do justice to his contributions to the development of the contemporary sociological perspective.

Social solidarity or integration may be seen as an example of a social fact that exists external to the individual and that cannot be explained in terms of individual characteristics.

To understand the degree and type of solidarity existing in society, it is necessary to analyze its social structure. Two different types of social structure were identified in Durkheim's theory, reflecting differences in the extent of the division of labor and in the major forms of solidarity. A society based on mechanical solidarity has a minimally developed division of labor and a strong collective conscience. A society based on organic solidarity has a highly developed division of labor. The resulting high level of interdependence largely replaces the strong collective conscience as a source of solidarity. In general, societies evolve from mechanical to organic solidarity; however, the collective conscience does not disappear entirely in the organic society.

We also examined various sources of strain that threaten to undermine social solidarity. Intergroup conflicts, deviance, excessive individualism, and anomie were identified as potential threats, particularly during the period of transition to a new type of social structure. One major consequence of breakdown in solidarity is an increase in suicide rates. Durkheim's analysis of suicide rates was examined as a demonstration of the importance of focusing on the social structural level of analysis, particularly the state of social integration in society. Paradoxically, however, even though deviance of various types may threaten solidarity, the public reaction to deviance reinforces the moral foundations of society.

The moral foundations of society have their origins in collective religious experiences. We examined Durkheim's theory of religion, concentrating on how religious beliefs and rituals reflect and reinforce the social structure of society. The loss of religious influence in modern society may readily be seen in Durkheim's perspective as an indicator of a breakdown in social solidarity.

Durkheim's emphasis on the social structural level of analysis and on the reality of social facts, social structure, and the like is rejected by some equally influential theorists such as, among the nineteenth-century classical theorists, Max Weber. As we will see, Weber contended that the fundamental unit of sociological analysis should be meaningful action of the acting individual, not social facts that transcend the individual, even though, like Durkheim, he was concerned with large-scale trends and patterns.

Durkheim's emphasis on solidarity and integration and the underlying image of social harmony that this emphasis portrays is obviously inconsistent with the Marxist perspective as developed in Chapter 4. Marx concentrated on the internal strains and conflicts that inevitably pervade all societies and that are expressed primarily in the antagonistic social relations between opposing classes. In contrast, Durkheim did not deal with social classes extensively. Marx's predictions regarding the growing conflict between social classes and the ultimate revolutionary overthrow of the capitalist system contradicts Durkheim's image of steadily advancing organic interdependence and solidarity in urban-industrial societies. These opposing images of social reality are still matters of disagreement among twentieth-century sociologists, especially functionalists and conflict theorists.

In spite of these differences, Marx and Durkheim both focused their attention on the social structural level of social reality. They did not ignore the cultural or the individual levels, but they treated these levels primarily in terms of their relations to the social structure. For instance, Durkheim's analysis of the collective consciousness and Marx's analysis of ideologies and false consciousness each concern the cultural level. However, the cultural level was not analyzed on its own terms in Marx's or Durkheim's theories as extensively as in Comte's or Sorokin's theories. In many ways Durkheim's theory builds on Comte's pioneering work. But while Comte's primary concern was the stages of intellectual development, Durkheim's primary focus was forms of social integration or solidarity. Nevertheless, Durkheim shares with both Comte and Sorokin the basic idea that intellectual and moral consensus are necessary as foundations for a harmonious or integrated social order.

Durkheim's stress on the social structural level of analysis, his emphasis on analyzing objective social outcomes independently of subjective motives, and his concern for investigating the foundations of the social order are major elements of contemporary functional theory. Furthermore, the general idea that individuals' subjective consciousness, personality patterns, attitudes, values, and the like are largely a product of the social milieu is one of the most basic propositions of practically all schools of sociology. Indeed, if sociology has a single paradigm, this would probably be its major theoretical principle.

In addition to these general theoretical contributions, there are other areas also in which contemporary sociology is indebted to Durkheim. In the area of methodology, his statistical analysis of suicide rates and their correlation with other measurable characteristics of the social environment is justifiably a classic. His detailed study of the Arunta clans in Australia is an excellent early example of the use of the case study method as a source for sociological generalizations. In addition, contemporary students of deviance are indebted to Durkheim for his analysis of the social structural sources of deviance and his recognition that punishment of the deviant is a major mechanism for reaffirming the normative structure of society. Finally, contemporary sociologists of religion still find Durkheim's analysis of the social functions of religion and the interdependence between religion and social structure to be an indispensable ingredient of their field.

Footnotes

1. See for example, Talcott Parsons and Edward A. Shils, eds., *Toward A General Theory of Action* (New York: Harper & Row, 1962), Chapter 4 of Part 2, "Values Motives, and Systems of Action," especially pp. 197ff.; Talcott Parsons, *The Social System* (New York: Free Press, 1951), especially pp. 26ff.; and Harry M. Johnson, *Sociology: A Systematic Introduction* (New York: Harcourt, Brace and World, 1960), pp. 51–56.

2. Sorokin's predictions regarding the future of Western society that were discussed in Chapter 3 could be considered an example of this type of analysis. See Pitirim Sorokin, *The Crisis of Our Age* (New York: Dutton, 1941).

3. For a brief overview of the major biographical highlights of Durkheim's life, see Harry Alpert, *Emile Durkheim and His Sociology* (New York: Columbia University Press, 1939), Part I, "Emile Durkheim: Frenchman, Teacher, Sociologist," pp. 15–78; Henri Peyre, "Durkheim, The Man, His Time, and His Intellectual Background," pp. 3–31 in Kurt H. Wolff, ed., *Emile Durkheim, 1858–1917* (Columbus: Ohio State University Press, 1960); and Robert A. Nisbet, *The Sociology of Emile Durkheim* (New York: Oxford University Press, 1974), pp. 3–24. For a comprehensive study of Durkheim's intellectual biography set in its historical context, see Steven Lukes, *Emile Durkheim: His Life and Work* (Harmondsworth, Middlesex, England: Penguin, 11973).

4. Alpert, op. cit., pp. 22–24.

5. Later on Durkheim's willingness to defend the rights of the individual was revealed dramatically in his position in the then-famous Dreyfus affair. Captain Alfred Dreyfus

had been accused of providing intelligence to the Germans and, after much publicity, was found guilty and exiled for life. Subsequently, he was found not to be guilty, but his case was not reexamined until pressure was brought to bear through a public appeal on his behalf. Durkheim justified his partisan position as a "Dreyfusard" by arguing that recognition of the dignity and the sacredness of the individual is an essential element of the moral foundation of modern society. See Lukes, op. cit., pp. 332–349.

6. Alpert, op. cit., pp. 61–62.

7. For brief summary discussions of the major influences that affected Durkheim, see Robert A. Nisbet, *Emile Durkheim* (Englewood Cliffs, N.J.: Prentice-Hall, 1965), Chapter 1, "Social Milieu and Sources," pp. 9–28; Peyre, op. cit.; Nisbet, *The Sociology of Emile Durkheim*, pp. 24–30, and Lukes, op. cit.

8. See Herbert Spencer, *The Evolution of Society: Selections from Herbert Spencer's Principles of Sociology*, edited and with an Introduction by Robert L. Carneiro (Chicago: University of Chicago Press, 1967).

9. For a well-known account of these ideas transferred to the American scene, see Richard Hofstadter, *Social Darwinism in American Thought* (Boston: Beacon Press, 1955).

10. Spencer's views on the proper role of the state and the dangers of excessive government are contained in Herbert Spencer, *The Man Versus the State* (Caldwell, Idaho: Caxton, 1965, Copyright © 1940 by Caxton Printers, Ltd.; copyright © 1892 by D. Appleton & Co.).

11. See Talcott Parsons, *The Structure of Social Action* (New York: McGraw-Hill, 1937), for an extensive analysis of the contrasts between utilitarianism and other individualistic theories on the one hand and Durkheim's emphasis on social structural limitations and constraints on individuals' actions on the other; see especially pp. 344–368.

12. As noted in Chapter 1, this view was especially characteristic of the German historicist position.

13. See George C. Homans, *Social Behavior: Its Elementary Forms* (New York: Harcourt, Brace and World, 1961).

14. See William Skidmore, *Theoretical Thinking in Sociology* (London: Cambridge University Press, 1975), pp. 24–30, for a brief discussion in which the argument is made that those who are committed to an objectivist position are obliged to focus on the individual as the fundamental unit of analysis.

15. One such model, systems theory, will be discussed in Chapter 12.

16. Emile Durkheim, *The Rules of the Sociological Method*, translated by Sarah A. Solovay and John H. Mueller and edited by George E.G. Catlin (New York: Free Press, 1964, copyright © 1938 by University of Chicago). This is Durkheim's basic statement of the nature of social reality and the methods appropriate for studying it scientifically. The following discussion of the nature of social facts and of strategies for explaining them is based primarily on this early work.

17. Ibid., p. 2.

18. Ibid.

19. Ibid., p. 10.

20. Ibid., p. 8.

21. Durkheim has been criticized for seeming to argue for the existence of some sort of "group mind" that is somehow empirically independent of the individual members of the group. It is clear that this emphasis on the *social* level was intended to differentiate

his approach from various individualistic perspectives such as Spencer's. His polemics may have led him to overstate his case, but his real purpose was to show that the subject matter of sociology is real empirical phenomena that can be studied scientifically.

22. Ibid., p. 110.
23. Ibid., p. 95.
24. Ibid., pp. 125–140.
25. Ibid., p. 132.
26. Emile Durkheim, *The Division of Labor in Society,* translated by George Simpson (New York: Free Press, 1964; copyright © 1933 by Macmillan).
27. See Charles Y. Glock and Rodney Stark, *Religion and Society in Tension* (Chicago: Rand McNally, 1965), Chapter 5, "The New Denominationalism," for a description of the wide variation in belief patterns in the major American denominations.
28. Durkheim, *The Division of Labor in Society,* p. 79.
29. Ibid., p. 173.
30. Ibid., p. 111.
31. Nisbet, *The Sociology of Emile Durkheim*, pp. 128–132.
32. Ibid.
33. Durkheim, *The Division of Labor in Society,* p. 172.
34. See Nisbet, *The Sociology of Emile Durkheim,* Chapter 4, "Political Sociology," for a discussion of the importance of various intermediate groups between the individual and the state. Durkheim's views in this regard were consistent with the ideas of Alexis de Tocqueville on the importance of various intermediate groups or associations for maintaining a pluralistic power structure. See Alexis de Tocqueville, *Democracy in America* (New York: Knopf, 1945).
35. Durkheim, *The Division of Labor in Society,* p. 227.
36. See Ferdinand Tönnies, *Community and Society,* edited and translated by Charles P. Loomis (New York: Harper & Row, 1963).
37. Henry Sumner Maine, *Ancient Law* (New York: Henry Holt, 1906).
38. Robert Redfield, *The Folk Culture of Yucatan* (Chicago: University of Chicago Press, 1941), and *The Primitive World and its Transformations* (Ithaca, N.Y.: Cornell University Press, 1953).
39. This idea was developed at some length by Karl Mannheim in his discussion of the functional rationality of large-scale bureaucratic organizations. The concept of functional rationality might be compared to Durkheim's concept of organic solidarity based on interdependence. Functional rationality refers to a situation in which the various "parts" or subsystems of a large-scale bureaucratic organization are well integrated in a purely technical sense; however, the degree of specialization in such a system may be so high that no one is fully aware of, or even accountable for, the overall direction of the organization's policies or activities. See Karl Mannheim, *Man and Society in an Age of Reconstruction* (London: Routledge and Kegan Paul, 1940). This type of situation will be discussed more fully in connection with Weber's theory of bureaucratic organization.
40. Emile Durkheim, *Suicide,* translated by John A. Spaulding and George Simpson and edited by George Simpson (New York: Free Press, 1966, copyright © 1951).
41. This type of situation is explained in contemporary sociology in terms of the concept of *relative deprivation.* According to the theory of relative deprivation, people evaluate

their own situation or their own achievements not in terms of some absolute or ultimate standard but in terms of their particular expectations. These expectations, in turn, are influenced by the individual's reference group(s). Thus, if individuals' expectations rise faster than their achievements, their level of frustration will increase. Rapid increases in economic prosperity can, therefore, lead to increased frustration because of the effect of the rapid improvement in stimulating enlarged expectations. Regardless of the *actual* level of achievement, the degree of frustration will increase as the gap between actual achievements and expectations increases. See Robert K. Merton, *Social Theory and Social Structure* (New York: Free Press, 1968), Chapters X and XI.

42. See, for example, Kai Erikson, "Notes on the Sociology of Deviance," pp. 9–21 in Howard Becker, ed., *The Other Side: Perspectives on Deviance* (New York: Free Press of Glencoe, 1964), and David Matza, *Becoming Deviant* (Englewood Cliffs, N.J.: Prentice-Hall, 1969).
43. Emile Durkheim, *The Elementary Forms of Religious Life,* translated by Joseph Ward Swain (New York: Free Press, 1947, copyright © 1915 by George Allen & Unwin Ltd.).
44. Ibid., p. 62.
45. Ibid., p. 236.
46. Ibid., p. 247.
47. Ibid., p. 250.
48. See Louis Schneider, *A Sociological Approach to Religion* (New York: Wiley, 1970), pp. 73–78ff., for a discussion of this tendency for intellectual elaboration to take place, as a result of which religious beliefs lose their intrinsic connection with a particular social structure.
49. See Guy E. Swanson, *The Birth of the Gods* (Ann Arbor: University of Michigan Press, 1960).
50. See Thomas F. O'Dea, "Five Dilemmas in the Institutionalization of Religion," *Journal for the Scientific Study of Religion,* Vol. 1, 1961, pp. 32–39, for a discussion of the difficulty in maintaining congruence between shared emotional experiences and ritual forms.
51. Durkheim, *The Elementary Forms of the Religious Life,* p. 475.
52. One might argue that football does not fit Durkheim's model of a religious ritual because of its emphasis on competitiveness and local identification instead of national solidarity. Moreover, if there is any relationship between football and national values, the charge might be made that football expresses national values in a limited and distorted form.
53. See W. Lloyd Warner, *The Living and the Dead,* Yankee City Series, Vol. 5 (New Haven, Conn.: Yale University Press, 1959).
54. The dynamics of in-group versus out-group relations will be considered in more detail in Chapter 7 on Georg Simmel.
55. See Will Herberg, *Protestant, Catholic, Jew* (Garden City, N.Y.: Doubleday, 1955), and Robert Bellah, "Civil Religion in America," pp. 350–369 in Joseph E. Faulkner, ed., *Religion's Influence in Contemporary Society* (Columbus, Ohio: Charles E. Merrill, 1972), for a discussion of America's "civil religion." This notion of the national civil religion would not apply to the various sects and cults that have emerged on the American scene in recent years.

56. Durkheim's perspective on the social origins of the categories of thought has profound philosophical implications. Refuted by this perspective is Kant's famous assertion that there are certain innate, a priori categories of the mind in terms of which we order and interpret the empirical data of experience. Also, the argument of empiricists such as David Hume must be modified in the light of Durkheim's recognition of the social origins of our patterns of thought. According to the empiricists, all our knowledge is derived from the empirical data of our experience, which is recorded in our minds as on a cerebral blank sheet. In Durkheim's perspective empirical data are organized and interpreted in terms of preexisting categories of thought, but these categories of thought are not innate or a priori (as in Kant); instead, they are formed by social experience and reflect the social structure of the group.

Questions for Study and Discussion

1. In what ways does Durkheim's emphasis early in his career on objective and external social facts differ from his emphasis on shared subjective experiences later in his career? Are these emphases contradictory or compatible? Why?

2. Do you agree or disagree with Durkheim's suggestion that a high division of labor threatens moral consensus? Why or why not? What kinds of evidence would you need to support your position?

3. To what extent are Durkheim's views on religion and social integration, derived from a simple primitive society, relevant to modern, complex societies? Does secularization undermine Durkheim's argument for modern societies? Why or why not?

4. Consider Durkheim's argument on the growing importance of shared values within occupational groups in modern society. What are the shared values that promote social integration in a university community? Are these values reaffirmed periodically through rituals? Do the members of a university community identify more strongly with the overall university or their own discipline? How would you support your answer?

5. Do you agree or disagree with the argument that devaince is necessary for providing an opportunity for society to reaffirm its normative patterns? Does punishment of deviants help reinforce solidarity in modern society? Why or why not?

CHAPTER 6

Max Weber and the Problem of Rationality

So far we have concentrated on broad cultural themes (Comte, Sorokin) and economic or social structure (Marx, Durkheim). With Weber, problems of individual motivation and subjective meaning become important. One of his primary goals was to analyze the necessary linkage between subjective motivational patterns and the broad institutional patterns of society. Weber's interest in social institutions (or social structure) and social change was equal to Durkheim's, but his starting point was different.

Any social theorist who wishes to base an analysis of the institutional patterns of society on individuals' subjective orientations or motivational patterns is faced immediately with their variety and complexity. Where should one begin? What aspect of individuals' subjective orientations and motivations will prove most fruitful in understanding the dynamics of social institutions?

Weber chose the concept of *rationality* as his primary focus; it plays the same central role in his theory that solidarity does for Durkheim, class conflict for Marx, stages of intellectual development for Comte, and cultural mentality for Sorokin. Weber saw the development of modern Western society as involving a steady increase in one particular form of rationality. This increase is reflected in individuals' everyday economic actions and in forms of social organization; it is even manifested in the evolution of Western music.[1] Even though music is often considered the language of the emotions, Weber shows that it, too, was subject to the rationalizing trends that pervaded the development of modern Western culture.

Since criteria of rationality provide a common frame of reference, the problem of the uniqueness of individuals' subjective orientations and motivations can be partially overcome. Shared also by the scientific perspective, criteria of rationality thus provide a logical and objective basis for establishing a science of social action and institutions while at the same time helping to establish the link with subjective meaning.

Several problems are likely to be encountered in analyzing social action from this point of view. Social philosophers, poets, and other observers of the human scene differ profoundly in giving priority to the head (intellect, reason, logic) or the heart (emotion, sentiments, feelings) when explaining human behavior. To what extent is human behavior rational? No one does anything without a reason, but the reason may be simply the desire to express some sentiment, not a conscious, logical calculation.

Most of us have wondered at the occasional powerlessness of our intellect to arouse our motivations or to energize us into action. We have probably also sometimes thought another person's action completely unreasonable, only to have it make sense when that person explains the reason for the action—although the criteria we use for such judgments may be rather loose. For example, it may seem reasonable that a person pay a high price for a large automobile with low gas mileage when we learn that a friend was killed while driving a small, underpowered vehicle. But then, when persons offer such justifications, we are likely to wonder if they are, in fact, *ex post facto* rationalizations of actions undertaken for quite different reasons. Pareto, for example, saw most action as nonlogical (springing from sentiments) and subsequently rationalized in terms of socially acceptable motives.[2]

The questions that can be raised about rationality become even more complex when we consider its role in social institutions. To what extent do social institutions and organizations reflect some type of rationality? One of Weber's most famous contributions to sociology is his classic analysis of modern bureaucracy as the most rational (technically efficient) form of social organization ever devised. In what sense is a bureaucracy a rational type of social organization? In our modern, bureaucratically dominated society we often experience certain aspects of bureaucracy as irrational, particularly when we are obliged to interact with its representatives as consumers or clients. What are the limitations on rationality? Is the rationality of a social organization of a different type or at a different level from that of the individual?

We know, for instance, that individuals in low positions in a bureaucratic organization may not even be aware of how their particular contribution is linked with that of hundreds of others in a highly rational system of interdependent and closely coordinated activities. Rationality at the individual level and at the organizational level may reflect different criteria, with rationality at neither level implying rationality at the other.

A simple "yes" or "no" answer to the question of whether human action is rational or not is impossible. Certainly, there is a rational or intellectual aspect to much human behavior. The use of implicit theory in reflecting on one's past experience and in developing plans for the future (as discussed in Chapter 1) is obviously an intellectual process. But there is more to human behavior. An affective aspect (feeling state) is also involved in action, as are values and goals that go beyond criteria of rational calculation. Analysis of the place of rationality in human action requires that we define, in the course of this chapter, what specifically is meant by *rationality* and the level, individual or institutional, to which this term applies. Before doing that and discussing Weber's contributions to sociological theory, we will briefly review Weber's life and the social and intellectual context in which he lived.

WEBER'S LIFE AND TIMES

Max Weber was born in Erfurt, Thuringia, in 1864, but grew up in Berlin, where his family moved when he was 5 years old. His family was upper-middle-class Protestant, steeped in bourgeois culture. Weber's father was a magistrate in Erfurt and, when the family moved to Berlin, became a city councillor and later a member of the Prussian House of Deputies and the German Reichstag. He was also involved in the National Liberal Party; his social circle included many leading intellectuals and politicians of Berlin. His political stand was generally proestablishment in the time of Bismarck, but he was not willing to make any substantial sacrifices for idealistic causes. Apparently without deep convictions or high ideals, the elder Weber seemed to be at home in the world of political compromise and bourgeois comforts.

Weber's mother, Helene Fallenstein Weber, had an altogether different temperament. Her religious convictions and Calvinist sense of piety and duty were much stronger than her husband's. Considerable family tension resulted from this marriage of a devoutly religious and duty-bound woman to a pleasure-loving and compromising politician who ruled his family with an iron hand, even to the point of mistreating his wife. This background may well have been an element in the intense inner conflicts that Weber suffered much of his adult life; it certainly invites psychoanalytic analysis of the sort found in Mitzmann's biography.[3]

As a child Weber was shy and sickly but intellectually precocious, reading widely and writing scholarly material by adolescence. He rebelled against the authority of his teachers, finding school routine boring and the intellectual interests of his peers frivolous. At 18, Weber began to study law at the University of Heidelberg. By this time he seemed to have established a strong identification with his father.

Weber's Heidelberg studies were interrupted by a year's military service in Strasbourg, where he established a close relationship with his uncle, Hermann Baumgarten, and his maternal aunt, Ida. Hermann Baumgarten had not modified his youthful liberalism for political expediency. Ida shared her sister's piety, sense of duty, and strong humanitarian concerns, but she was able to express these values more effectively in her life than Weber's mother. In both ideology and temperament the Baumgartens seemed much more compatible with one another than Weber's own parents were. Hermann Baumgarten's own idealism, coupled with the respect he showed for his wife's piety, demonstrated to Weber that practical success does not necessarily require complete sacrifice of principles of conscience. The Baumgartens treated young Weber with intellectual respect and emotional warmth and, perhaps because of this supportive climate, Weber was strongly influenced by them. Partly as a result, Weber came to identify more strongly with his mother.

Weber's later theoretical concerns with the influence of ideas (or ideals) versus interests in governing people's behavior were therefore represented in his family. His father gave priority to his political and economic interests, while his mother and the Baumgartens gave priority to their Protestant-ethic ideals. Eventually, Weber rejected his father's amoral attitude and domineering behavior toward his mother.

Weber continued his academic studies in Berlin and began serving in the law courts there while living with his parents. He finished his doctoral thesis ("History of Commercial Societies of the Middle Ages") in 1889. After completing his postdoctoral thesis (required for a university teaching position) on Roman agrarian history, he began teaching at the University of Berlin while still working at the bar. His work load during these years was heavy, and his style was rigorous and methodical; this hectic pace may have been a way to divert his attention from his negative attitude toward his father.[4] In any case, he continued living with his family until 1893, when he married Marianne Schnitzer.

Weber's Interrupted Academic Career

Weber began devoting his whole time to his academic life when he accepted a position as professor of economics at Freiburg University in 1894. Two years later he returned to the University of Heidelberg as a professor of economics. His scholarly productivity was extensive during this early stage of his academic career.

This promising early start was to be interrupted. In 1897 Weber's parents came to Heidelberg and, during the visit, father and son had a violent argument. Weber, Jr., accused his father of brutally mistreating his mother and ordered him out of the house. About a month later, the senior Weber died. This tragedy apparently left Weber so overcome with guilt that his physical and psychological health suffered for many years; in 1899 he spent several weeks in a mental institution. Travel or intensive work provided temporary relief, but he was unable to keep up a regular teaching schedule. (Fortunately, university policy did not require termination of employment.) In spite of repeated efforts, not until 1918 at the University of Vienna was Weber able to get through an entire semester of a full teaching load.

Weber was not inactive during the years of turmoil and anxiety. Following travel in Italy and elsewhere, in 1903 he joined Sombart in editing the *Archiv für Sozialwissenschaft und Sozialpolitik,* which was to become the leading social science journal in Germany. In 1904 he published the first part of his *Protestant Ethic and the Spirit of Capitalism*[5] and also went to the United States to deliver a highly successful paper for a Congress of Arts and Sciences in St. Louis. He then traveled in America for 3 months, observing the influence of Protestant sects, the role of bureaucracy in a democratic society, and the pattern of voluntary associations. In 1910 he worked with Tönnies and Simmel in founding the German Sociological Society.

An ardent nationalist who admired Bismarck's goal of developing a strong and unified Germany, Weber was critical of Bismarck's intolerance of independent-minded leaders and his neglect of the East German peasants who were being displaced by the growth of the Junkers' estates. (His real concern was that the Junker policy, which relied on imported Polish seasonal laborers, would undermine German unity.) Ultimately, he shifted leftward from his father's National Liberal Party to the Social Democrats but, throughout his life, he remained somewhat detached from any single party or ideology. During the political and foreign policy crises that preceded World War I, Weber became more and more despairing of the state and destiny of the nation and of the blind and bungling incompetence of its leadership and administrative structure.

Yet, when war began, Weber was at first an enthusiastic supporter, calling it "a great and wonderful war."[6] He even volunteered for service (although he was 50) and, as a reserve officer, was put in charge of running nine military hospitals, a position that gave him an insider's view of bureaucracy. In time, Weber opposed further expansion of the war, particularly at sea, because he saw that America would be brought in and Germany defeated. He tried desperately but unsuccessfully to exert his political influence.

After an honorable retirement from his reserve commission, Weber continued to be productive. His series of monographs on comparative religion[7] were published shortly after his retirement from military service, and he continued to work on his masterpiece, *Wirtschaft und Gesellschaft (Economy and Society),* which had been started earlier. Unfortunately, however, Weber was not to complete this work. On June 14, 1920, he died of pneumonia, leaving a large part of his life and career tragically unfulfilled.

Social and Political Climate

Germany's social and political structure in Weber's time was as full of tension and contradiction as his family life. Because of his intense political interests and nationalistic fervor, these tensions and contradictions no doubt also had an effect on Weber's own internal struggles.[8] Germany was at peace for the 43 years prior to the outbreak of World War I in 1914, although it was a precarious peace at times. After Bismarck's rule ended, German foreign policy deteriorated, becoming erratic and drifting toward a policy of colonial and military expansion. In spite of his strong nationalism, Weber opposed such unrealistic expansion, sometimes experiencing despair over the direction of Germany policy.

The complex social and political climate of Weber's Germany was partially a result of the fact that the Industrial Revolution and related changes in economic structure occurred later in Germany than in England or even France. Nevertheless, during Weber's youth and the early stages of his career, industrialization was proceeding at breakneck speed. England was the model of a powerful industrial society with global colonial interests; it was natural that the political power structure in Germany would strive to prove that Germany was no less a major world power. The development of Germany's power was thought important to prevent British and Russian cultural-political domination.

While industrial development and bourgeois economic power were rapidly expanding in the western part of Germany, the eastern part was still dominated by the traditional feudal pattern in which the values of an aristocratic life-style prevailed.[9] Germany had not experienced as thorough and decisive a revolution as the French Revolution; therefore the traditional value system was still very influential. The political structure, especially the civil service, was heavily influenced by these conservative values. Many of the rapidly rising bourgeois class hoped that they or their descendants might some day enter the ranks of the aristocracy or at least enjoy comparable status.

But the economic base for the aristocratic life-style was rapidly being eroded, partially because of the growing economic dominance of the bourgeoisie and changing patterns of foreign trade. Thus Germany's social and political structure was characterized by a sharp cleavage between its economic structure and its political structure and value system. The economic structure was more and more dominated by the industrial system and the bourgeoisie, while the cultural value system and political structure were still dominated by traditional semifeudal values and bureaucratic conservatism.

Superimposed on this basic internal contradiction was the strong nationalistic emphasis of the political leaders, which was made possible largely by the elaborate bureaucracy of the government and the army, both dominated by Prussian conservatism and devotion to duty. In the Prussian administrative system and army and in the organization of industrial enterprises, Weber observed many of the characteristics of bureaucracy (which he analyzed) and its stultifying effects on individual personalities (which he feared). On a more abstract level, the basic contradictions within German society among its emerging economic system, value system, and political structure provided Weber with a contemporary illustration of his insight into the distinctions among class, status, and power as alternative bases for social stratification, so important for many of his historical studies.

The role of intellectuals in Germany also deserves mention. University professors enjoyed high esteem and good pay and naturally felt no great need to be overly critical of the political status quo. These establishment academicians tended to share the political ideology of the power structure and to be supportive of the political goal of a strong, united, and culturally dominant Germany. Although some scholars remained aloof from politics, their general acceptance of the *status quo* was *de facto* support for those who were actively involved. There were circles of intellectuals not officially connected with the universities among whom critical thought could emerge. Members of this intellectual counterculture, like those in relatively low-ranking university positions, did not have real political influence and were unable to challenge the political influence of the prestigious university professors. Unlike the situation in France, social and political life was not stirred very deeply by intellectual criticism.

Weber's interest in political affairs was moderated by his insistence on intellectual objectivity. Nevertheless, in both his personal life and his writings there is a keen sense of the overriding importance of *Realpolitik* (practical politics). Following his brief involvement with the Christian-Social movement, Weber became a strong supporter of democratic policies. One of the major reasons was his belief that a democratic political system could stimulate the emergence of strong political leaders who could promote the cause of national unity. He was impressed by the strong urban political machines in American politics.

Although Weber was sympathetic to the problems of the urban working class, his primary concern was that it (and all major interest groups) be involved in supporting the cause of German nationalism. Yet he did not have much faith in the Social Democrats, the party promoting proletarian interests. In his later years he helped organize the German Democratic Party, the party of the liberal bourgeoisie. He was also a member of the commission that drafted the Weimar Constitution. If he had lived longer he probably would have become heavily involved in the politics of postwar Germany.[10]

Weber's sociology must be understood against this social and political background of German society, a society in rapid transition and full of internal contradictions. Within Weber's lifetime Germany experienced the transition from a primarily agrarian society to a heavily industrialized, urban society. This transition was accompanied by increasing rationalization of all areas of life, economic and political.

INDIVIDUAL ACTION AND SUBJECTIVE MEANING

Weber was very interested in broad sociological questions about social structure and culture, but his view was that social reality consists fundamentally of individuals and their meaningful social actions. He defines sociology as:

> a science which attempts the interpretive understanding of social action in order thereby to arrive at a causal explanation of its course and effects. In "action" is included all human behavior when and in so far as the acting individual attaches a subjective mean-

ing to it. . . . Action is social in so far as, by virtue of the subjective meaning attached to it by the acting individual, . . . it takes account of the behavior of others and is thereby oriented in its course.[11]

Weber's Image of Social Reality versus that of Durkheim

The emphasis in Weber's definition differs from Durkheim's insistence that sociology is the study of social facts that are external to and exert constraint over the individual and that such facts must be explained in terms of other social facts. Durkheim saw social reality as transcending the individual, existing on an independent level; Weber saw social reality as grounded in individuals' motivations and social actions.

The difference between Durkheim and Weber corresponds to a basic distinction between two opposing images of social reality. Durkheim's position is generally referred to as *social realism*. That is, society is seen as real, existing independently of the individuals who happen to belong to it and operating according to its own distinctive principles, which do not necessarily reflect individuals' conscious intentions. The realist position is reflected in various organic theories of society. Such theories compare societies to biological organisms in that they constitute a reality that is more than just the sum of their individual parts.

In contrast, Weber's position is referred to as the *nominalist* position. The nominalists insist that only individuals are objectively real and that society is merely a name to refer to a collection of individuals. The concept of social structure or other types of social facts that are more than individuals and their behaviors and transactions is regarded as a speculative abstraction without any fundation in the empirical world. Such a position seems congruent with an individualistic view of social structure. The individualism of the British political economists and utilitarians are an example; in their view society and social institutions result from contractual agreements between individuals that they enter into in order to pursue their interests. The idea that there are general laws that govern society independently of the individuals who comprise society is a pure chimera in this view.

Weber's substantive analyses did not reflect such an extreme individualistic position. He recognized the importance of the dynamics of broad historical trends and their influence on individuals. Nevertheless, all general statements regarding broad historical trends are, in the final analysis, statements regarding trends or patterns of individuals' actions or interactions. Weber's position might be referred to as *methodological individualism*. That is, the only admissible social scientific data refer ultimately to individual actions.

Another key difference between Durkheim and Weber is their treatment of subjective processes. Durkheim's emphasis on social facts as things reflected an effort to be factual and objective and thus to eliminate subjective orientations from analysis as much as possible, except to the extent that these orientations reflected objective facts shared throughout the social milieu. In contrast, subjective meanings were essential in Weber's definition. He was just as committed as Durkheim to being scientific, but this meant something slightly different for him because of the differences in their intellectual backgrounds.

Weber's position is clearly stated here.

> Interpretive sociology considers the individual (*Einzelindividuum*) and his action as the basic unit, as its "atom"—if the disputable comparison for once may be permitted. In this approach, the individual is also the upper limit and the sole carrier of meaningful conduct.... In general, for sociology, such concepts as "state," "association," "feudalism," and the like designate certain categories of human interaction. Hence it is the task of sociology to reduce these concepts to "understandable" action, that is, without exception, to the action of participating individual men.[12]

Weber's goal was to penetrate the subjective meanings associated with various "categories of human interaction," to use them to distinguish between different types of social structure, and to understand the broad directions of social change in Western societies.

Why did Weber emphasize the individual and the subjective meaning of his or her actions as he did? To answer this question it is necessary to remember that the intellectual background of Weber's time included a strong emphasis on idealism and historicism. (Marx's writings repudiated the idealistic position, but it continued to be an important intellectual strand.) This emphasis was expressed, for example, in Hegel's view that the universal spirit of reason is being realized more and more in historical progress. Such a view necessarily involves a focus on the cultural realm—on human ideals and values and their progressive realization in history.

The cultural realm was not considered amenable to being understood in terms of purely natural scientific laws, which express relationships of causal necessity; it was seen as a realm of freedom and in terms of experience and internal understanding whereby subjective meanings are grasped. Purely objective knowledge of the type sought in the natural sciences is not sufficient. This view of the distinctive character of the social and cultural sciences was developed by Weber's mentor, cultural historian Wilhelm Dilthey, and was incorporated into Weber's approach. It obviously differs from French positivism as reflected by Comte's and Durkheim's search for universal scientific laws governing human behavior in an external or objective sense.

Explaining Social Action Through Subjective Understanding

Probably the most famous aspect of Weber's thought that reflects the idealist tradition is his emphasis on *verstehen* (subjective understanding) as a method of gaining valid insight into the subjective meanings of social action. For Weber this term does not mean simply introspection. Introspection may give a person insight into his or her own motives and subjective meanings, but it is not sufficient for understanding the subjective meanings of the actions of others. Instead, what is required is empathy—the ability to put oneself in the frame of mind of those whose behavior one wishes to explain and to see their situation and goals from that perspective. The process is what symbolic interactionists refer to as "role taking."

Failure to consider individuals' subjective meanings and orientations can lead the social theorist to impose his or her own perspective and values on the behavior of others. The result may be an insightful social philosophy or a biased misinterpretation of human behavior, but it certainly is not scientific sociology grounded in empirical data. The social philosophy of idealists such as Hegel, who interpreted all of Western history as an unfolding of the spirit of reason, was based on this type of nonempirical introspection. For him, since all human beings share this universal spirit, one could adequately understand others through introspection.

In contrast, Weber insisted that sociology must be an *empirical* science; it must analyze the actual behavior of individual human beings in terms of their own particular subjective orientations. This emphasis, which Weber shared with the German historicists, is opposed to the idealistic strategy of merely interpreting individuals' behavior, or a society's historical development, in terms of broad, *a priori* assumptions. This empirical emphasis was also consistent with positivism; however, it does not mean eliminating subjective aspects of behavior and dealing only with overt objective aspects. Taking account of the subjective elements of behavior is essential to prevent the distortion in interpretation that would result if a theorist were simply to impose his or her own value judgments on others' behavior.

Weber went even further in separating values from scientific analysis. Besides guarding against bias through the method of *verstehen,* Weber also maintained that scientific knowledge can never provide a basis for making value judgments. Science is neutral with respect to evaluating opposing moral positions. In this, Weber differed from French positivists such as Comte and Durkheim in that the latter *did* believe that adequate empirical knowledge of the laws of society could provide a basis for moral reconstruction and education. Weber recognized that values affect scientific work, particularly in the choice of phenomena to analyze or questions to research. (Weber's own intellectual interest in politics was influenced by his ardent nationalism.) However, once the facts are in on a particular question, they cannot be used to establish conclusive proof of the legitimacy of a particular moral position. Objectivity and value neutrality are still recognized as part of Weber's legacy for contemporary sociology.

Ideal-Type Analysis: From Unique Events to General Propositions

In addition to idealism, the German historicist school also influenced German social thought. In economics, for example, the historicists rejected British classical economics (with its general assumptions about universal characteristics of "economic man" from which universally applicable propositions about economic behavior could supposedly be deduced). To the German historicists, such propositions could not do justice to the various social and cultural factors that limited economic rationality. They chose to emphasize the particular institutional setting of economic behavior. Similarly, they believed that all social institutions could only be understood in terms of the unique historical background and particular culture of a society. Weber agreed that social and economic behavior should be related to their institutional setting. For the historicists, however, this emphasis on institutional uniqueness led to a preoccupation with amassing historical data with little concern for theoretical generalization beyond a particular society or historical period. Against this approach Weber developed the ideal type as a way to make comparison and theoretical generalization possible.[13]

Earlier social scientists had used ideal-type analysis implicitly. Formal clarification of it as a deliberate methodological technique is considered one of Weber's most important methodological contributions. In the context of his overall theory, the ideal type should be seen as a counterbalance to his emphasis on the individual, providing the key for generalizing beyond the individual level to larger social units.

The use of ideal types is common in everyday life. For example, we speak of the *typical* citizen, the *typical* politician, the *typical* college student, and so on, when we wish to describe the general instead of the unique characteristics of those in a particular category.

Weber wrote that "An ideal type is formed by the one-sided accentuation of one or more points of view and by the synthesis of a great many diffuse, discrete, more or less present and occasionally absent *concrete individual* phenomena, which are arranged according to those one-sidedly emphasized viewpoints into a unified *analytical* construct."[14]

In other words, the analyst selects the aspects of some phenomenon that seem to belong together by logical consistency and constructs a unified and coherent whole from them. The intellectual construct may ignore or distort certain aspects of the empirical phenomenon, but this is inevitable, since social reality is far too complex to be grasped in all its complexity. Once the ideal type is constructued, it can be used as a measuring rod to assess the extent to which phenomena conform and as a theoretical concept in the development of research hypotheses.

Construction of ideal types does not imply any value judgment about the phenomenon under consideration. One can develop an ideal type of a criminal as well as of a saint. Ideal types are used for analysis, not for evaluation.

Probably Weber's most famous ideal type is that of bureaucracy. The various characteristics of bureaucracy—division of labor and specialization, hierarchy of authority, recruitment on the basis of technical expertise, emphasis on formal rules, and impersonality—constitute the ideal type of a bureaucratic organization.

Ideal types can be constructed at various levels and with various degrees of generality. One can develop ideal types of personality patterns, social relations, groups, or larger collectivities. Similarly, one can develop an ideal type that applies to a specific historical situation (an American urban machine politician) or to a more general pattern ("economic man"). What determines the level and the degree of generality is the analytical interest of the theorist. Certainly it is appropriate to analyze a unique individual or a unique historical event in sociological terms if one chooses to do so. It is equally appropriate to generalize, to establish uniformities in numerous situations, and this is possible with the ideal type method.

In his acceptance of both of these approaches as valid, Weber disagreed with the neo-Kantian philosophers Rickert and Windelband. They had distinguished between the *idiographic* sciences, which focus on describing unique events, and the *nomothetic* sciences, which seek to establish general or universal laws, and had insisted that human culture and history belong in the idiographic category.

In any case, the ideal-type method allows the theorist to ignore the unique characteristics of some social phenomenon and to focus on characteristics that are typical. In this way Weber was able to deal with larger social units, even while holding to the assumption that social reality is, in the final analysis, based on the *typical* actions of *typical* individuals in *typical* social situations.

TYPES OF SOCIAL ACTION

If social action is to be understood in terms of the subjective meaning attached to it, one needs to develop some method for dealing with subjective meaning objectively and analytically. In the absence of such a method, the critics of various subjective approaches would surely be right in claiming that such unobservable aspects of individuals' experiences could not be incorporated into a scientific analysis of human behavior. For Weber, however, the concept of rationality provides the key for objective analysis of subjective meanings as well as a basis for comparison of different kinds of social action.

In view of the traditional conflict between objectivists and subjectivists[15] "objective analysis of subjective meaning" may seem to be a contradiction in terms. A common assumption underlying this debate is that "objective" approaches deal only with observable phenomena (physical things or overt behavior), while "subjective" approaches try to deal also with elusive and unobservable phenomena such as individuals' feelings, thoughts and motives. Another way of looking at the objective-subjective distinction is in terms of the extent to which an individual's personal subjective experience is shared by a social group. A subjective experience that can be understood because it is widely shared can be treated as objective, while a subjective experience that can be neither communicated nor understood remains elusive as a private subjective experience, even though it may be very real to the person involved.

Rationality and ordinary rules of logic provide a widely shared frame of reference in terms of which subjective aspects of behavior can be evaluated objectively. For example, when a person chooses the less expensive of two otherwise equivalent products, we understand that behavior as rational because it conforms to the objective criteria of rationality that we accept. Not all behavior can be understood as a manifestation of rationality. Passions such as anger or love or fear may be expressed in overt behavior in ways that superficially seem irrational. However, one can understand (*verstehen*) such behavior if one knows the underlying emotions being expressed.

Rationality is the basic concept Weber utilized in his classification of types of social action. The major distinction made is between *rational* and *nonrational* action. Briefly, rational action (for Weber) has to do with the extent of conscious deliberation and choice that the action expresses. Within the two major categories of rational and nonrational action there are two different subclasses.

Instrumental Rationality (*Zweckrationalität*)

This highest degree of rationality involves conscious deliberation and choice with respect to both the *ends* of action and the *means* used to attain them. The individual is seen as having a variety of possible desired ends and, on the basis of some criterion, as making a choice among these competing goals. The individual then assesses alternative means that might be used to attain the chosen end. This may include gathering information, taking note of opportunities and obstacles in the environment, and attempting to predict the probable consequences of alternative lines of action. Finally, a choice is made of the means to be used that presumably reflects the individual's judgment on their efficiency and effectiveness. After completion of the action, the individual can determine objectively the extent to which the ends were achieved. Weber explains:

> Action is rationally oriented to a system of discrete individual ends (*zweckrational*) when the end, the means, and the secondary results are all rationally taken into account and weighed. This involves rational consideration of alternative means to the end, of the relations of the end to other prospective results of employment of any given means, and finally of the relative importance of different possible ends.[16]

Economic action in impersonal market systems is perhaps the prototype of instrumental rationality. This type of action is also reflected in bureaucratic organizations. Weber saw both impersonal market systems and bureaucratic organizations increasing in the modern Western world.

Value-Oriented Rationality (*Wertrationalität*)

In comparison to instrumental rationality, the major distinguishing characteristic of value-oriented rationality is that only the means are the object of conscious deliberation and calculation; the ends are given in terms of the individual's absolute or ultimate values. Ultimate values are nonrational in that a person cannot calculate objectively which ends to choose. Furthermore, commitment to these values is such that rational considerations of utility, efficiency, and the like are not relevant. Nor (if the values are indeed absolute) does the individual weigh them in comparison to alternative values. The individual deliberates about the means for achieving such values, but the values themselves are given.

Religious action is perhaps the prototype of value-oriented rationality. A religious person may value the subjective experience of being in God's presence or feeling at peace with oneself or the universe as an ultimate value in comparison with which other values are insignificant. Given this value, the individual chooses means such as meditation, prayer, and attending church to provide that religious experience. Whether such a value is achieved effectively cannot be ''proved'' objectively in the same way that success in attainment of the ends of instrumental action can be proved.

Traditional Action

Traditional action is a nonrational type of social action. If an individual engages in some behavior out of habit, without conscious reflection or deliberation, such behavior would qualify as traditional action. The individual would justify or explain the action, if pressed to do so, by the simple assertion that he or she has always acted that way or that such behavior is the custom. When groups or total societies are dominated by this orientation, their customs and institutions are legitimated or supported by reference to long-established customs and traditions that are accepted unquestioningly. The only justification necessary is, ''This is the way our ancestors have done, and their ancestors before them; this is the way it has always been and always will be.'' Weber saw this type of action being swept away by the steady increase in instrumental rationality.

Affective Action

This type of action is characterized by the dominance of feelings or emotions (affect) without conscious deliberation or intellectual reflection. A person experiencing an overwhelming passion such as love, anger, fear, or joy and acting spontaneously and unreflectively in expressing that emotion is exhibiting affective action. The action is nonrational precisely because of the lack of an appeal to logic, ideology, or other criteria of rationality.

These four types of social action just discussed should be seen as ideal types. Weber recognized that few, if any, actions conform completely to any of these ideal types. For example, traditional action may reflect a conscious belief in the sacred value of a society's traditions, and this would mean that it shades into value-oriented rationality. Or it may reflect a conscious assessment of alternatives and a decision that the established traditions represent the best way to achieve some goal that is consciously chosen over alternative goals. Similarly, people may consciously deliberate on the best way to express emotions, as with the man in love trying to decide the right gift for his lover or the best way to propose marriage. This deliberation would mean that the action is rational; in this case it is probably value-oriented rationality, since the relationship may be an ultimate value that is not evaluated in comparison to other goals. However, for many actions it should be possible to identify which of the preceding subjective orientations is primary. Making distinctions between different types of action on this basis is crucial for understanding Weber's approach to social organization and social change.

The same specific behavior pattern may fit into different social action categories in different circumstances, depending on the subjective orientation of the individual involved. A handshake may be a spontaneous expression of friendship, may reflect a habit, or may signify agreement on a business arrangement between persons who have no other social involvement with one another. Social action is understandable only in terms of the subjective meaning and motivational patterns associated with it. For rational action the subjective meaning can be grasped in terms of the means-ends schema.

SOCIAL ACTION AND SOCIAL STRUCTURE

Even though Weber's methodological writings stressed the importance of subjective meanings and motivational patterns, his substantive work includes a far-reaching structural and functional analysis. This is to be seen, for example, in his three-dimensional model of stratification, his studies of bureaucratic domination and its effects in modern society, and his predictions regarding the long-range consequences of the influence of the Protestant ethic.

Social structure in Weber's perspective is defined in probabilistic terms instead of as an empirical reality that exists independently of individuals. Thus, for example, a "social relationship *consists* entirely and exclusively in the existence of a *probability* that there will be, in some meaningfully understandable sense, a course of social action."[17] An economic class refers to a category of persons who share similar life chances as determined by marketable economic resources. A legitimate social order is based on the probability that a set of social relationships will be oriented toward a *belief* in the validity of that order.[18] In all these cases the ultimate reality on which these larger social units are based is that of individuals' social actions with their subjective meanings. Since individuals' subjective orientations include an awareness (accurate or otherwise) of the probable actions and reactions of others, these probabilities have a genuine influence on social action, either as a constraint or as a means of facilitating one type of action instead of another.

Stratification: Economic, Cultural, and Political

The hierarchical ordering of persons within a system of social stratification is a basic aspect of Weber's view of social structure. Weber agreed with Marx on this crucial point and expanded Marx's emphasis on the economic basis of social classes by developing a more comprehensive picture of at least three analytically distinct bases of stratification. Marx saw the economy as the foundation of the social structure, and people's positions in this structure were determined primarily by whether or not they own means of production. By extension, property ownership or wealth becomes the primary basis for stratification. The most fundamental division in the social structure is that between the "haves" and the "have-nots" even though, of course, additional subdivisions and secondary criteria may emerge and mask this fundamental cleavage.

Weber also recognized the importance of economic stratification as the fundamental basis for classes. For him, a *social class* consists of all those who share similar life changes as far as their economic fate is concerned. As he put it, "We may speak of a 'class' when (1) a number of people have in common a specific causal component of their life chances, in so far as (2) this component is represented exclusively by economic interests in the possession of goods and opportunities for income, and (3) it is represented under the conditions of the commodity or labor market."[19]

This latter point makes clear that social classes rest on an impersonal and objective basis of stratification. Members of the same class *may* become aware of their common economic interests and engage in organized economic or political action to promote them, just as Marx argued in his notion of class consciousness. Whether this subjective awareness of class interests or class consciousness is or is not present, class position is determined (for both Marx and Weber) by the objective criteria of life chances in the economic realm.

People are ranked also on the basis of honor or prestige, as manifested in a shared life-style. The result is an ordering of persons into *status groups*. Marx had not dealt specifically with this aspect of stratification, but a Marxist perspective would see status as merely reflective of economic interests and class consciousness. Weber disagreed, insisting that status ranking is analytically distinct from economic stratification. Although economic class position and status ranking are often highly correlated, this is not necessarily always the case. The status hierarchy reflects its own particular dynamics, and persons who become economically dominant may deliberately adopt different strategies to enhance their prestige.

Unlike economic classes, status groups *do* rest on a subjective bond between their members, who are bound together by a shared life-style, by shared values and customs, often by intramarriage, and by feelings of social distance from other status groups. They recognize one another as "our kind of people," and they strive to maintain a sense of superiority to those who do not belong to their social circle. The distinction between economic classes and status groups is dramatized in the contrast between the ''new'' wealth of a successful entrepreneur and the ''old'' wealth of long-established, high-prestige families. It is well known that money alone is not sufficient to be admitted to the most highly esteemed social circles in Boston or other old communities. The family background and history are equally important. For example, a Texan rancher who strikes oil and gets rich will find himself excluded from Boston's inner circle of top 400 families if he would be foolish enough to move there and try to buy his way in. The reason lies in the prestige structure, not merely in economic class position.

These dynamics also apply to those at the bottom of the prestige hierarchy. They are bound together by a shared sense of being excluded and looked down on and by the necessity of assuming a deferential role toward their superiors. In other words, they ''know their place,'' even though they may struggle to change it. They may also develop their own internal alternative ranking system in terms of which they can regard themselves as more worthy than those who rank higher. This is a common development in lower-class religious sects, where adherence to rigid moral standards enables their members to see themselves as morally superior in God's eyes to those higher in rank who have more worldly or compromising ethical standards.

In addition to economic position and status group honor, another basis for stratification is political power. This dimension may also overlap one or both of the others in many situations, but it is analytically distinct and may vary independently. For Weber power is the ability to impose one's will despite the resistance of others. Persons may strive to attain power for its own sake or as a means of enhancing their economic position or their status. The *political party* is the type of organization through which the struggle to attain or manipulate power is expressed most clearly at the societal level. All organizations have their political side, however; various component groups compete or negotiate with each other for the ability to control the organization and to define its goals and procedures.

The power structure is not necessarily equivalent to the *authority* structure. Authority is the probability that a person will be obeyed on the basis of a *belief* in the *legitimacy* of his or her right to exercise influence; power is the ability to *overcome* the *resistance* of others in accomplishing one's objectives, particularly when this involves influencing their behavior. An armed bank robber may exert power over a bank official but he or she certainly does not have any authority. In contrast, leaders of voluntary associations who are selected by the members can exert influence because of members' beliefs that the leader has the right to exert influence.

Those who seek to exercise power on a continuing basis usually try to establish a belief in their right to do so; that is, they seek to establish the legitimacy of their power. This is manifested, for example, when the leaders of successful revolutionary political movements seize control of the mass media and attempt to revise the dominant political ideology so as to justify the revolution and their continuation in positions of power. Nevertheless, the dynamics of the struggle for raw power differ from the dynamics of the exercise of established authority, even though persons with authority may wield great power as a result. In modern bureaucratic organizations the power and authority exercised by salaried officials may be a more salient dimension of their position in the overall stratification system of society than their economic class or their status group membership.

Contemporary analyses of social stratification are heavily indebted to Weber. The distinction between status as a dimension of stratification and economic position has become standard fare in contemporary stratification theory and research. Gusfield, for example, studied the history of the Women's Christian Temperance Union, the antidrinking organization whose political activities culminated in the short-lived prohibition amendment to the Constitution, as an example of status politics.[20] In this case, the life-style and value system of established rural and small-town Protestants were perceived as threatened by the rapid expansion of Catholic immigrants into urban areas. In our own time, the involvement of many middle- and upper-middle-class women in the women's liberation movement should probably be seen as reflecting status and power concerns that are at least as important as economic factors. Also, many contemporary organization studies reflect major concern with the power and authority dimensions of organizational processes.[21]

The multidimensional approach to social stratification is now so firmly entrenched in the sociological tradition that it has generated a new perspective involving status inconsistency.[22] (''Status'' is used in a broader sense here than in Weber's theory.) Status consistency refers to the degree to which the various dimensions of a person's position in the stratification system are in line with one another. Some of the research using this concept suggests that degree and type of inconsistency are associated with political ideology. The implication is that in addition to a person's overall position in the stratification system being important, the degree to which positions in several different stratification systems are consistent with one another is also crucial.

Types of Authority and Forms of Social Organization

Individuals' social actions (with their associated meanings) constitute the basic building blocks of larger social structures. In *The Theory of Social and Economic Organization* Weber builds on this foundation by developing a series of typological distinctions that move from the level of a social relationship to the level of economic and political social orders. The concept of the legitimacy of a social order underlies Weber's analysis of economic, political, and religious institutions and his interpretation of social change. The stability of a legitimate social order does not rest primarily on mere *custom* (i.e., uniformities of behavior not enforced by external sanctions) or on the *self-interest* of the individuals involved. Instead, it is based on individuals' acceptance of the *norms* or *rules* underlying the order as valid or desirable. These norms or rules may be based on *convention* or *law*. The dinstinction between them is that law is enforced by a specialized agency, while convention is enforced by general social reaction.

On what basis do individuals accept the rules and norms of a social order as valid? Weber identifies four different bases of legitimacy; they reflect the typology of social action developed earlier.

> Legitimacy may be ascribed to an order by those acting subject to it in the following ways:—a) By tradition; a belief in the legitimacy of what has always existed; b) by virtue of affectual attitudes, especially emotional, legitimizing the validity of what is newly revealed or a model to imitate; c) by virtue of a rational belief in its absolute value, thus lending it the validity of an absolute and final commitment; d) because it has been established in a manner which is recognized to be legal.[23]

Persons' self-interests may be met by conforming with the rules of a social order, but this is not the primary basis for its enduring stability. Instead, its stability rests on one or more of the preceding bases of legitimacy.

Social relationships within the various types of social order just identified exhibit considerable variety. Weber identified several different types, but he was particularly interested in the relationships that emerge in organizations with an established authority structure—that is, a structure in which designated individuals are responsible for enforcing the social order. Such relationships, if they are closed to outsiders unless they are admitted according to rules, are referred to as "corporate groups." If the relationships are associative instead of communal, include an administrative staff, and are devoted to a specific type of continuous activity, they are referred to as "corporate organizations." (*Associative* relationships are based on rational agreement; *communal* relationships involve a subjective feeling of joint belonging.)[24]

Corporate organizations established by contractual agreement may reflect the congruent or convergent interests of those involved, or they may rest on a foundation of force or control of scarce resources. Weber's primary focus, however, was on organizations that are based on the foundation of a legitimate social order. This means that the social order and accompanying patterns of dominance are accepted as right, both by those subject to being dominated and by those who are dominant. The dominance patterns thus reflect primarily a structure of *authority*, not a structure of *power*. Power is the *ability* to carry out one's will despite opposition; authority is the *right* to exercise influence as supported by the rules and norms underlying the social order.[25] The exercise of authority depends on the willingness of subordinates to comply with orders of the authority figure. The degree of willingness varies in different situations. Furthermore, those in positions of authority naturally have an interest in strengthening beliefs in their legitimacy.

Weber identified three primary bases of legitimacy of authority relations; they are built on the typology of social action earlier discussed. Each type is associated with its own distinctive type of administrative structure and its own particular social dynamics. These types, with their respective administrative structures, are as follows.

Traditional Authority. This type of authority rests "on an established belief in the sanctity of immemorial traditions and the legitimacy of the status of those exercising authority under them. . . ."[26] Thus, whatever other reasons people may have for conforming to the authority structure, one important reason is their belief that it has always existed. Those who exercise authority belong to a status group that has traditionally exercised authority or they are chosen in accordance with time-honored rules.

The relationships between the authority figure and subordinates are essentially personal relations. In fact, one key to understanding the dynamics of a traditional authority system is to see it as an extension of family relationships. Subjects or subordinates owe personal loyalty to their leader who, in turn, has certain obligations to care for them. While both the leader and subordinate are bound by traditional rules, there is room for the exercise of personal discretion by the chief in his or her exercise of authority and, in such circumstances, subordinates are obliged to obey.

Weber distinguished among three different forms of traditional authority: gerontocracy, patriarchalism, and patrimonialism. Gerontocracy involves control by the elders of a group; patriarchalism involves control of a kinship unit (household) by a specific individual whose authority is inherited. In neither of these systems is there an administrative staff as such, and the subordinates are not really subjects but members of the group on whose behalf authority is exercised.

In contrast, a patrimonial system of authority does include an administrative staff. Unlike the administrative staff of a bureaucracy (to be discussed shortly), however, a partimonial administrative staff consists of persons who have personal relations with the leader. As Bendix says, "Patrimonialism means, first of all, that the governmental offices originate in the household administration of the ruler. . . . Governmental administrators are originally personal servants and personal representatives of the ruler."[27]

The degree of discretionary authority of the patrimonial chief may vary widely, as may the degree of centralization. Limited authority and wide decentralization occur when members of the administrative staff are chosen from, or develop on their own, a particular status group, or even a corporate group. When this occurs the administrative staff may appropriate their positions as their own personal property and exercise limited discretionary authority within the sphere of their administration. For example, a territorial ruler may establish an agreement with the chief of a mercenary army to control subjects in outlying areas, with the army chief responsible for providing his own supplies, perhaps with booty gained from military expeditions for the ruler. Similarly, the responsibility of collecting taxes may be delegated to members of a particular status group, with the expectation that they will have the right to collect additional revenues for their own use. In both cases the administrative staff is able to enjoy semi-independent status. Ultimately, their rights and privileges may be passed on by inheritance.

There are various reasons for the dilution of the ruler's patrimonial power among various administrative or other semi-independent groups. One of the most important is territorial expansion to the point where the patrimonial ruler is no longer able to govern directly or through members of his own family.

Feudalism is a system of traditional domination in which the dilution of patrimonial authority has developed to the point that relations with military or administrative persons are governed by contract and not by personal subjugation by the ruler. Thus owners of landed estates and military knights were able to maintain their own positions of honor and independence even while entering a relationship of formally voluntary fealty (loyalty) to a ruler. In the developed feudal system, the rights and privileges of the various independent status groups (particularly the landed nobility) were hallowed by tradition and transmitted from generation to generation. Consequently, the ruler found his discretionary authority and power severely curtailed. This type of system contrasts with *sultanism,* which is a patrimonial system in which the power and discretionary authority of the ruler are at a maximum.

Conflicts and change occur in patrimonial systems precisely over the degree of discretionary power and authority, unbounded by tradition, available to the ruler. Naturally, the ruler's interest is in enlarging his personal discretionary power, while subordinates have an interest in enlarging the sphere of their independence. Both sides, however, appeal to tradition as their ultimate basis of legitimacy.

Charismatic Authority. Charismatic authority is based on the extraordinary qualities of the leader as a person. As such, it is outside the realm of established institutional forms of authority. The term "charisma" is widely used to refer to the personal attractiveness of various individuals as leaders. This is related to Weber's usage in that it involves personal characteristics that inspire potential followers. The term originally had theological connotations, referring to the gift of grace that God freely bestows to certain individuals. Again, this is related to Weber's usage in describing charismatic religious leaders in that the basis of their leadership is the belief that they have a special relationship with the divine being, or even embody divine characteristics themselves.

To quote Weber: "The term 'charisma' will be applied to a certain quality of an individual personality by virtue of which he is set apart from ordinary men and treated as endowed with supernatural, superhuman, or at least specifically exceptional powers or qualities.''[28] Such qualities attract disciples who are devoted to the charismatic leader personally and who commit themselves to the normative or moral order that he or she claims to represent. In terms of the typology of social action discussed earlier, compliance of followers rests either on an affective (emotional) identification with the leader as a person or on commitment to the absolute values that he or she embodies or teaches.

Unlike both traditional and rational-legal systems of authority, charismatic leadership is not oriented toward long-lasting stable routines. While traditional authority is oriented toward preservation of the status quo, charismatic leadership usually involves challenging the status quo. The charismatic leader introduces his or her message with the assertion, "It is written, but I say unto you. . . ." The message calls for a break with traditions and a breakthrough to a new and better form of social or moral order.

Sometimes this call to a new order is justified by reference to long-established but forgotten traditions, with the charismatic leader claiming to want to restore these traditions in their pristine purity. This is manifested, for example, in the Ayatullah Khomeini's desire to eliminate Western influences from Iran and to restore the ancient patterns of Islamic culture. It is also illustrated in the efforts of sectarian groups within the Christian tradition to restore the close-knit social relations and high levels of personal commitment that characterized the New Testament church. This appeal to a forsaken or forgotten tradition is particularly likely to be used by religious charismatics as they criticize the present corruption and hypocrisy of the religious establishment for having distorted the true faith. But whether he or she is a religious prophet or a political revolutionary, the charismatic leader's appeal is based on exemplary or heroic personal characteristics. For his or her followers these characteristics legitimate the leader's appeals to break with established routines and to help in the special mission of establishing a new social order.

A charismatically led social movement is inherently unstable and highly fluid. Frequently, those most highly involved in the movement forsake their regular occupations, leave their families, and sell or give away their material possessions in order to devote themselves to the charismatic leader and the cause that he or she represents. These highly committed disciples establish a close, quasi-family relationship with their leader and with one another. They look to their leader for continual guidance and inspiration in coping with obstacles, making decisions, and securing the resources needed for their survival. Resources are obtained on an *ad hoc* basis outside established routines and are shared in common among the inner circle of disciples. The motivation necessary to sustain this high commitment of the members of the inner circle rests on the leader's ability to display, again and again, the extraordinary or heroic personal qualities on which the leadership rests.

Surrounding the inner circle of disciples are varying numbers of fringe members and onlookers. Some of these may be merely curious, but many of them find themselves attracted to the charismatic leader and the message. However, the appeal for them is not so great that they are willing to renounce everyday concerns and become a part of the inner circle (even assuming they would be accepted as such).

Charismatically led social movements usually arise outside the framework of ordinary everyday concerns and are opposed in their spirit to ordinary routine. Not surprisingly, such movements tend to arise during times of great social crisis or rapid social change when traditional norms and patterns seem inappropriate or unworkable. The crisis may result from any one or more of several sources, including for example, economic collapse, military defeat, political instability, or natural disasters. In any case, the charismatic leader's appeal, both to the inner circle of disciples and to fringe members, must be understood against the background of a turbulent and unstable social environment. Indeed, the urgency of the charismatic message results in part from the fear that the established social order is threatened.

Many charismatic social movements fail to endure beyond the lifetime of their leader. The social crisis that helps precipitate the movement gradually passes or the charismatic leader loses his or her charisma (i.e., the ability to continually persuade followers of his or her extraordinary personal qualities). The movements that do endure, however, go through a transformation process referred to by Weber as the "routinization of charisma." This process results from the intrusion of practical, everyday concerns. A key transitional stage occurs when the leader dies (or otherwise abdicates) and a successor must be chosen. The leader may personally choose the immediate successor but, even so, the one chosen must validate the claim in the eyes of fellow disciples who might be envious. Eventually, stable understandings must be developed regarding procedures for choosing leaders, based either on an emerging tradition or on officially enacted legal norms.

Other practical concerns that gradually lead to the routinization of charisma include the need for settling conflicts, the need for a reliable source of economic support, and the need for developing some basis for making decisions regarding recruitment and socialization of newcomers. In addition, if property is acquired by the group, provision will have to be made for its routine care and upkeep. In view of these numerous pressures for routinization, it is not surprising that a pure charismatic movement is, at best, a one-generation phenomenon.

Rational-Legal Authority. Authority that rests on commitment to a formally enacted and impersonally administered set of rules is referred to by Weber as rational-legal authority. This is the type most closely related to instrumental rationality, as discussed earlier. It differs from traditional and charismatic authority in the impersonal way in which it is exercised. Briefly, the person exercising rational-legal authority does so by virtue of occupancy of a social position that established rules define as an authority position. Subordinates submit to this authority because the social positions they occupy are defined by the rules as requiring submission in certain specifically defined areas. In other words, the rules pertain to the positions as such, not to the individual persons who may happen to occupy the positions.

Selection of persons to occupy positions of authority or subordination is also governed explicitly by the formally enacted rules. For example, the rules may specify certain requirements in terms of education or expertise. In any case, individuals' commitment to a relationship involving the exercise of rational legal authority rests on their more general commitment to the impersonal rules that define and govern the relationship. In short, the rules, when enacted by accepted and authorized procedures, are seen as legitimate and binding.

The Bureaucratic Form of Organization

Rational-legal authority is embodied in bureaucratic organizations. Weber's well-known analysis of bureaucratic organizations differs from the popular contemporary attitude focusing on bureaucratic inefficiency, waste, and seemingly irrational red tape. Instead, in comparing bureaucracy with the ancient traditional forms of administration, based on extended family and personal relationships, Weber saw modern bureaucracy as the most efficient, systematic, and predictable form of social organization yet devised. As he witnessed his own society, dominated as it was by the Prussian military and political bureaucracy, and as he viewed the development of industrial and national political administrative systems in other Western societies, it seemed to him that the development of the modern world was characterized by the growing dominance of bureaucracy. The bureaucratic form of social organization, reflecting a high level of instrumental rationality, was able to expand steadily at the expense of traditional forms simply because of its greater efficiency.

A large part of Weber's analysis of bureaucracy involved identifying its distinguishing characteristics as an ideal type. Recall that an ideal type involves selecting those features of some empirical phenomenon that seem logically and meaningfully interrelated, even though these features may never occur empirically in their pure form. For example, the ideal type of bureaucracy stresses the impersonal nature of social relations within it, but real bureaucratic organizations can never completely exclude personal relations or prevent their emergence. (We are all familiar with stories such as that of an executive falling in love with his secretary or of a boss promoting his lazy, incompetent nephew.)

The ideal-type characteristics of bureaucracy are as follows:

(1) A continuous organization of official functions bound by rules. (2) A specified sphere of competence. This involves (a) a sphere of obligations to perform functions which has been marked off as part of a systematic division of labor. (b) The provision of the incumbent with the necessary authority to carry out these functions. (c) That the necessary means of compulsion are clearly defined and their use is subject to definite condi-

tions. . . . (3) The organization of offices follows the principle of hierarchy; that is, each lower office is under the control and supervision of a higher one. . . . (4) The rules which regulate the conduct of an office may be technical rules or norms. In both cases, if their application is to be fully rational, specialized training is necessary. . . . (5) In the rational type it is a matter of principle that the members of the administrative staff should be completely separated from ownership of the means of production or administration. . . . (6) In the rational type case, there is also [usually] a complete absence of appropriation of his official position by the incumbent. . . . (7) Administrative acts, decisions, and rules are formulated and recorded in writing. . . .[29]

Bureaucratic administration consists essentially of the continuous routine application of general rules to specific cases by officials acting in their official capacity and using for this purpose the authority and other resources specifically allocated for this purpose, with a record of the action duly filed.

The superiority of this form of organization is evident.

Experience tends universally to show that the purely bureaucratic type of administrative organization . . . is, from a purely technical point of view, capable of attaining the highest degree of efficiency and is in this sense formally the most rational known means of carrying out imperative control over human beings. It is superior to any other form in precision, in stability, in the stringency of its discipline, and in its reliability.[30]

A major reason for the efficiency of the bureaucratic form of organization is the way that it systematically links the individual's interests and motivational energy with the performance of organizational functions. This is insured by the fact that performance of a specifically designated organizational function becomes the primary occupational activity of the bureaucratic official; in exchange for reliable performance, the official receives a salary and opportunity for promotion along a specific career path.

Weber contrasted the continuous and systematic involvement of bureaucratic officials in performing organizational tasks with those whose positions are assumed on an honorific, part-time, or voluntary basis. Anyone experienced in attempting to recruit and motivate members of voluntary organizations can appreciate the difficulty of maintaining continuous and systematic organizational functioning on a voluntary basis. Similar difficulties are encountered when organizational positions are assigned as a mark of honor. Some examples of this would be the custom of having the U.S. president's wife assume honorary chairmanship of a Red Cross or Easter Seal drive, or appointing a wealthy and substantial donor to the board of trustees of a private college.

Another reason for the high efficiency of bureaucratic organizations is the systematic exclusion of all personal elements, including individuals' emotions and feelings as well as the personal element in social relations. As Weber pointed out:

[The calculability of decision-making] . . .[is] the more fully realized the more bureau-cracy "depersonalizes" itself, i.e., the more completely it succeeds in achieving the exclusion of love, hatred, and every purely personal, especially irrational and incalcul-able, feeling from the execution of official tasks. In the place of the old-type ruler who is moved by sympathy, favor, grace, and gratitude, modern culture requires for its sustain-ing external apparatus the emotionally detached, and hence rigorously "professional," expert.[31]

This exclusion of the personal element means that individuals can establish relations as occupants of organizational positions even though they may be strangers on a personal level. Relationships in the marketplace between buyers and sellers are an example. The operations of a bureaucratic organization would be severely ham-pered if officials were obliged to deal only with those with whom they have personal ties. The exclusion of the personal element also means that the decisions and actions of bureaucratic officials, whether in the area of policy formation or administration, are to be guided by the goals or needs of the organization as such, not by individu-als' personal needs or desires. Thus, for example, if a decline in a company's sales or the development of automated machinery necessitates a layoff, management is not obligated to retain employees who are not needed merely because of personal bonds with them. Consideration of efficiency and organizational needs, not personal feelings and relations, is to have priority.

Even though a bureaucratic organization may exhibit a high level of rationality and predictability, it does not follow that each official in the organization will necessarily be *aware* of how all the different elements of the organization are linked together to form a rational system. The subjective orientation of the individual official will concentrate on his or her own specialized task and perhaps the connec-tion of this task to closely related tasks. Also, the individual may be aware of the probable future path of his or her own career in the organization, but the functioning of the overall system will often be beyond the range of the individual official's knowledge or concern. This lack of awareness may be expected to apply particularly to officials in low-level positions of large bureaucratic organizations. High-level officials must be aware of the functioning of the overall system; however, in very large organizations there may be many aspects of organizational processes in which their knowledge will also be limited.

The rationality of bureaucratic organizations refers to considerations of techni-cal efficiency and predictability, not human needs or ultimate values. In some cases the overall goals of the organization, or the indirect effects of its routine function-ing, seriously frustrate the fulfillment of human needs or undermine the achieve-ment of widely shared values. Even though an organization is highly rational in the formal sense of technical efficiency, it does not follow that it is also rational in the substantive sense of the moral acceptability of its goals or the means used to achieve them. Just as individual officials may not be conscious of the organization's overall operations, they may also be unaware of the moral implications of the organization's activities. The very fact that individual officials have specialized and limited responsibility and authority means that they are not likely to raise basic questions regarding the moral implications of the overall operations of the organization or their own particular activity within it.[32]

Weber had mixed feelings toward the growing dominance of bureaucratic organizations. He did not see their increased efficiency as leading to greater human happiness or promoting clear progress toward any kind of utopian society. In this respect he was more pessimistic than Marx who, as we know, envisioned ultimately a classless society.

Growth in organizational size and the increased control and efficiency made possible by bureaucracy represent a certain kind of progress, but it exacts a heavy psychic or emotional toll. Bonds of personal loyalty that had helped give meaning and purpose to life in the past are undermined by bureaucratic impersonality. The satisfactions and joys of emotional spontaneity are submerged by the demands for rational and systematic devotion to the narrow specialty of one's bureaucratic office. In short, the logic of efficiency crudely but systematically destroys human feelings and emotions and reduces human beings to cogs in a gigantic bureaucratic machine.

In developing and promoting bureaucratic forms of organization, people were, in effect, building themselves an "iron cage" from which they would one day find it all but impossible to escape. This process was not limited to capitalist societies; it would also occur in socialist societies. The only possible escape Weber envisioned was his wistful dream that perhaps one day in a future a charismatic leader would appear who would lead a breakthrough from the stifling hold of the soulless bureaucratic machine and restore the capacity for authentic human feelings and ideals.

Mixed Types of Authority

Since the three different patterns of authority relations are ideal types, we should not expect any of them to be manifested empirically in pure form. Instead, in most cases authority relations in real life are likely to reflect varying degrees of all three types. For example, the late President Kennedy was widely regarded as a charismatic personality. While his charisma and message were less dramatic than those of charismatic leaders who claim supernatural powers and who call for a radical break with the established order, his idealism and leadership abilities were personal qualities that he utilized in his performance as president. Yet, at the same time, the office of U.S. president is defined by legal norms, and the nature of the relationships with the other branches of government is carefully specified. (Note that the constraining characteristics of bureaucracy pertain less to the top level than to lower levels.) Also, the presidency as a component of our political institutions is based firmly in our society's traditions.

Similarly, in the Roman Catholic Church, the positions of the pope, priests, bishops, and other officials are formally defined by enacted church law besides being supported by ancient tradition. However, these traditions include symbolic representations of past charisma in routinized form (as in rituals commemorating the charismatic founder). In addition, individual clerical leaders and church officials use whatever personal leadership qualities they may possess to perform their duties.

Along this line, Etzioni has developed a model of organizational dynamics that discusses explicitly the continuing manifestations of charismatic influence in bureaucratic organizations.[33] He argues that one of the challenges of a bureaucratic organization is to harness the charismatic influence of organizational officials and channel it in ways that contribute to the vitality of the organization instead of allowing it to be disruptive.

Social psychological studies of organizational leadership also recognize the crucial difference that personal qualities make in exerting organizational influence.[34] Even though these studies reject the "trait theory" of leadership (i.e., the view that certain personality traits always characterize the leader) and insist that leadership can only be understood in terms of the nature of the relationship that exists between the leader and followers, personal qualities are still relevant. Mere occupancy of a bureaucratic position provides a *minimum* basis for exerting influence. Effective leaders are those who are able to build on this basis, using whatever personal qualities they have to inspire the loyalty and confidence of their followers.

In addition to charismatic influence, bureaucratic organizations make extensive use of the support that tradition provides. From the highest to the lowest level, decisions are made and influence attempts justified on the basis of precedent. The strength of traditional custom is revealed in the frequency of the claim that "we have always done things this way." Indeed, contemporary organization theorists point out that the search for solutions to new problems frequently begins with examining the organization's past to see if some guiding precedent can be discovered and utilized in coping with the present crisis.[35] In view of the interdependence among the three authority patterns, utilizing these concepts in empirical data analysis should involve attempting to determine the dominant pattern and also the way in which the three types are interrelated and the degree to which they mutually support or undermine one another. Weber's own emphasis in using these ideal-type concepts was to show how rational-legal authority was growing in modern, urban-industrial societies at the expense of traditional authority.

RELIGIOUS ORIENTATIONS, MOTIVATIONAL PATTERNS, AND RATIONALIZATION

The growth of bureaucratic organizations was not the only manifestation of a partial breakdown in tradition and the emergence of a more and more systematic and rational approach to life. This same trend toward rationalization was also stimulated by the development of Protestantism. Weber's analysis of the relationship between the Protestant ethic and the growth of the capitalist economic system is perhaps his most famous contribution.[36] This particular analysis can best be understood and appreciated within the context of Weber's overall theoretical perspective, however. The Protestant ethic reflected and promoted the trend toward increasing rationality and, even more important, demonstrated the crucial role that religious ideas can play in promoting social change. Through this demonstration Weber intended to correct Marx's one-sided materialistic interpretation of history and of the capitalist system specifically.

Weber versus Marx on the Influence of Religious Ideas

Recall that for Marx, class struggle provides the key to understanding historical change and the transition from one type of social structure to another. Class struggle reflects the opposing objective economic interests of the different classes, particularly when the lower class becomes aware of these interests through class consciousness. These interests are determined by the material conditions in which members of the different classes find themselves. The realm of culture, particularly social values and norms, beliefs, ideals, and world view, merely reflect these material conditions. Ideas or ideals exert only a limited independent influence of their own on human behavior or the social structure. Thus, in a stable period, when class consciousness is at a low level of development, religion is seen as the "opiate of the people." Revolutionary change will therefore require the destruction of religious illusions and institutions in Marx's view.

Weber recognized the crucial importance of material conditions and economic class position in influencing people's beliefs and values and their behavior. In fact, he expanded Marx's perspective on stratification considerably, as we have seen. However, Weber felt that Marx's theory was one-sided, recognizing only the influence of material or economic facts and denying that ideas, even religious ideas, could have an independent influence on people's behavior. He stressed that people have ideal as well as material interests. Ideal interests can exert an independent influence on people's motivations, sometimes even in opposition to their material interests. However, he did not accept the position of idealists such as Hegel, who downplayed material forces and instead saw human history simply as a manifestation of cultural ideals. Instead, Weber felt it was important to recognize the *reciprocal* influence of ideal and material interests and to determine empirically in individual cases whether material or ideal interests are dominant.

Protestant Beliefs and the Unintended Promotion of Capitalism

Weber's analysis in *The Protestant Ethic and the Spirit of Capitalism* should be seen in the context of his overall effort to demonstrate the independent influence that ideas play in historical change. Briefly, the major thesis of this work is that certain aspects of the Protestant ethic provided a powerful stimulant in promoting the growth of the capitalist economic system in its formative stages. This stimulating effect was due to an "elective affinity" (logical consistency and mutually supportive motivational influence) between certain ethical demands derived from Protestant beliefs and the economic motivational patterns necessary for the growth of the capitalist system.

Weber's thesis has stimulated a voluminous body of literature, both pro and con. In some cases the criticism results from a misreading of what Weber actually meant. In view of the considerable controversy his thesis aroused, it should be made clear that he did not claim that the growth of capitalism was *caused* by Protestantism. His concept of *elective affinity* clearly avoids the imputation of cause. This concept refers both to logical congruence and to psychological consistency involving mutual reinforcement. To claim that there was an elective affinity between the Protestant ethic and the spirit of capitalism is to argue that the kind of motivations that resulted from acceptance of the beliefs and ethical demands of Protestantism helped to stimulate the type of behavior that was involved in the origins of modern bourgeois capitalism.

Both Protestantism and capitalism involved a rational and systematic approach to life. The Protestant ethic emphasized avoidance of idle or impulsive pleasure and diligence in the performance of one's duties in all aspects of life, including especially one's occupational calling and economic activities generally. Similarly, the development of modern capitalism required limitation of consumption for purposes of reinvestment and capital growth, a willingness to submit to the discipline of systematic planning for future goals, regular employment in an occupation, and the like. This is a much more modest claim than the simplistic assertion that Protestantism caused capitalism. At most, the Protestant ethic acted as a stimulant, or a source of encouragement, but it was not the only factor involved. Weber emphasized the importance of this particular factor, but he would certainly agree that other factors were also important, including material conditions and economic interests.

Although Weber emphasized the influence of Protestantism on capitalist development, he would not have denied that Protestantism was also influenced by the growth of capitalism. His overall approach emphasized that both ideal and material interests govern action, and that the relationship between religious ideals and economic interests was actually one of mutual interdependence. In other words, the relation was reciprocal, involving mutual interdependence of Protestantism and capitalism. His emphasis, however, was deliberately on the influence that the ideas of Protestantism exerted because he wished to correct Marx's one-sided materialist concept of historical change.

Furthermore, Weber recognized that this impact of Protestantism on capitalism would not necessarily be permanent. The notion that Protestantism helped stimulate the rise of capitalism in its formative stages did not mean that capitalism would forever need religious legitimation. Weber recognized that after capitalism was established, it became autonomous and self-sustaining, without any need for religious support. In fact, he noted that this religious support had already died out by the time of Benjamin Franklin.[37] This means that criticisms of Weber that stress the purely secular nature of contemporary capitalism, that argue that the motivations necessary to sustain it are materialistic ones, or that demonstrate that Protestants and Catholics currently show no significant difference in their occupational aspirations or achievements really miss the point.

Indeed, with the establishment of capitalism as a self-sustaining economic system, the "spirit" of this system may, ironically, undermine whatever religious ethic helped support its establishment. Weber recognized this in his discussion of the temptations to forsake an ascetic life-style that wealth offers. The long-term relationship between Protestantism and capitalism is thus seen as a dialectical one, with Protestantism promoting the growth of capitalism in its early days but subsequently being undermined by the materialistic influence of an established secularized form of capitalism.

The Protestant Ethic as a Protest Against Catholicism

What were the distinctive features of the Protestant ethic that were relevant to the emergence of capitalism and that differed from the Catholic ethic? For Weber the Protestant ethic represented an inner-worldly ascetic religious orientation more fully than any other major religion, including Catholicism. *Inner-worldly asceticism* refers to the commitment to deny oneself (or limit severely) the opportunity for indulgence of physical or sensual desires or enjoyment of materialistic pleasures in order to pursue a "higher" or spiritual goal; this spiritual goal was to be achieved through systematic and diligent commitment to tasks to be performed in this world (as opposed to withdrawing from the world to pursue a life of meditation). A contemporary example would be a student who decides not to go out on dates or take part in other social activities in order to devote himself or herself to studying out of a strong sense of moral duty.

The inner-worldly ascetic orientation of Protestantism should be understood as resulting from genuine religious convictions regarding the proper role of the church in mediating the individual's relationship to God. In the traditional Catholic belief system the church served an essential function in linking the individual to God and in providing salvation. It was believed that the church was established to serve as a vast treasury of God's grace, which its priests could dispense to those who took part in the prescribed sacraments. By the time of the great reformer Martin Luther, the system of dispensing grace had evolved to the point that divine grace could be given in exchange for certain financial contributions as well as for numerous other ritualistic acts.

Along with this sacramental system, the traditional Catholic orientation was much more other-worldly than the Protestant orientation. That is, Catholic beliefs and values concentrated individuals' attention on the hereafter; the primary purpose of this life was seen as preparation for the life after death. Even though the pope and many high church officials were very much involved in the temporal political and economic affairs of this world, the effect of their teachings was to downgrade the importance of this earthly life. In the short span of this earthly life individuals were expected to adhere to established traditions and to accept the social position to which they were assigned in life.

In the marketplace, prices of goods were governed by the idea of the "just price," not by the economic law of supply and demand. The just price was one that would enable the seller to maintain his traditional social status. Usury, or the lending of money at interest, was forbidden because of the belief that money cannot produce money. People who had to borrow money did so because of poverty, and the charging of interest in this type of situation obviously made their poverty worse. In general, economic activity was seen as necessary for survival in this earthly life, but it should not be the most important part of one's life. Moreover, no ordinary person involved in the normal mundane affairs of this world could hope to enjoy the high status of those who had given their lives to spiritual matters as ecclesiastical officials or members of a religious order.

The leaders of the Protestant reformation were not aspiring capitalists. Luther, Zwingli, Knox, Calvin, and the other reformers, whatever their individual differences, were not interested in promoting economic activity at the expense of religion. Their religious faith was the most important aspect of their lives, and their concern was to restore the true faith which they felt the Catholic Church had diluted and distorted. Specifically, they attacked the sacramental nature of the Catholic Church, whereby God's grace is controlled by mere human beings (even though priests in the church) and must be earned by participating in various church rituals. Arguing against this mediating function of the church, the reformers believed that the individual could come to God directly through faith in Jesus Christ, and that God's grace and salvation are available as a free gift to all who have this faith. Sacramental works are no longer necessary, and the domination of the institutional church is thereby undermined. The concept of predestination[38] was developed to support the idea that a person's salvation is decided by God's free choice and that this divine decision cannot be affected by ritualistic pronouncements of mere human priests.

Along with this shift in emphasis on the proper role and scope of the church, the Protestant reformers and their followers downgraded the status of church officials and members of religious orders as religiously superior. Instead, they insisted that all are equal before God, regardless of their specific vocation, and all have an equal opportunity and duty to serve God in their various vocations. In this way, secular occupations became sacred callings. The individual's religious obligations were no longer confined to taking part in the sacramental life of the church; they were extended to include one's occupation and, indeed, one's whole life. This is what is meant by the observation that Protestantism helped destroy monasticism but, in turn, transformed the whole world into a monastery. Secular economic activity in one's occupational calling was no longer a matter of indifference, to be engaged in simply as a matter of necessity in this earthly life; instead, as Weber put it, it "was the highest form which the moral activity of the individual could assume."[39]

Combined with the strong emphasis on the duties of one's calling, the Protestant ethic stressed a life-style in which sensual and material pleasures were rigidly and systematically controlled. By no stretch of the imagination did their inner-worldly orientation embrace hedonism. Instead, the early Protestants lived in constant awareness that indulging the appetites and passions of the flesh diverted attention from one's spiritual life and was a continual threat to the soul. The picture of the typical Protestant that emerges is that of a person who is highly devoted to his occupational calling as a religious duty and who systematically disciplines his life to keep his physical desires and passions well under control.

Theoretically, adoption of this life-style has no bearing on a person's eternal salvation. After all, Protestants recognized their unworthiness and the weaknesses of the flesh (at least in the abstract, no matter how self-righteous some of them may have seemed to be). Salvation was a matter of God's eternal decree and was not based on any human works. However, persons who see questions of eternal salvation and damnation as extremely important cannot be content to be indifferent to their own eternal fate, even if it had already been foreordained by God. What the early Protestants really needed was some sign or indication whereby they could be assured that they were of the "elect" (i.e., those whom God has chosen to save).

With secular occupations regarded as a religious duty, it was natural that these early Protestants should come to regard prosperity and success in their occupational calling as a sign of their election for salvation. After all, it hardly seemed likely that God would bless those who were not of the elect. Thus the (theoretically) fatalistic attitude regarding salvation became transformed (in practice) into an overpowering commitment of the early Protestants to prove themselves by economic success. This, in essence, was exactly the kind of motivational pattern required for the establishment of capitalism. Devotion to occupational duties, limitation of consumption, a strong achievement drive, and a highly rationalized and systematic approach to life were the common ingredients of both Protestantism and capitalism. In brief, Protestantism helped to promote capitalism by endowing ordinary economic activity with religious meaning and significance in an age when individuals' most profound and far-reaching motivations were religious in nature.

Also, under the influence of the Protestant idea of stewardship, traditional constraints on lending money at interest were modified. In an age of developing and expanding economic enterprises the idea that money cannot breed money was modified and later abolished. While interest charged on loans made to the poor for their survival could be seen as a form of exploitation, interest on loans made to enterprising young traders for making more money could hardly be seen in the same light. This distinction was gradually recognized and formalized, and the result was the opening up of new possibilities for capital accumulation and financing of large-scale enterprises through credit, all within the framework of the Protestant ethic.

The Protestant Ethic and the Secularization Process

Aside from the specific beliefs involved, Protestantism represented a major break with tradition. Similarly, the emergence of capitalism required the breakdown of numerous traditional constraints on economic activity. Weber's emphasis, however, was that the specific ideas of Protestantism represented a shift from traditionalism to a more rational orientation.

Working within his perspective, one can argue that these effects were not limited to the economic realm. For example, Merton has shown that there was a disproportionate number of Protestants among early scientists, many of whom saw their scientific investigations as a means for discovering the infinite wisdom and power of God.[40] Similarly, the Protestant belief in the equality of all people before God is expressed in the growth of democratic political institutions, especially in America. Also in America, the early stimulus for universal public education was the Protestants' desire for their children to be able to read the Bible for themselves. In all of these ways the early Protestants saw themselves as attempting to fulfill God's will for their lives here on this earth. But in this process everyday secular activities acquired new meaning and significance. Eventually, this would undermine preoccupation with the hereafter and other strictly spiritual or other-worldly concerns and would promote a thoroughly secularized attitude and life-style.

The early Protestants did not anticipate the long-range secularizing effects of their inner-worldly ascetic ethic. This certainly was not their goal. Yet, as Weber pointed out:

> Since asceticism undertook to remodel the world and to work out its ideals in the world, material goods have gained an increasing and finally an inexorable power over the lives of men as at no previous period in history. Today the spirit of religious asceticism— whether finally, who knows?—has escaped from the cage. But victorious capitalism, since it rests on mechanical foundations, needs its support no longer.[41]

Bluntly, the Protestant ethic led to materialistic success; the temptations to enjoy the fruits of materialistic success helped erode the religious motivations to follow the ascetic life-style demanded by Protestantism. In the same fashion, the positive Protestant influence on science was followed by a situation in which the traditional religious beliefs of Protestants were undermined by the scientific approach to the explanation of natural phenomena. Perhaps most important, the Protestant emphasis on the religious importance of activity within this world helped generate a climate in which the world of the supernatural and the hereafter gradually disappeared from consciousness. Analysis of this process led Berger to focus on Protestantism as the fullest manifestation of the dialectical process whereby an inner-worldly religious orientation serves as its own "grave digger."[42] Certainly the process reveals a paradoxical development in which the long-range consequences of a particular pattern of action were far different from those intended.

Weber's ideas on the effects of the Protestant ethic were not based on systematic historical analysis. His goal was not to trace the historical development of Protestantism. Instead, he moves rather freely between various branches of Protentantism at various periods of Protestant history. The major figures or schools of Protestantism from which he draws the central tenets of the Protestant ethic include Luther, Calvinism, Pietism, Puritanism, Methodism, and the Baptist sects. Although the specific emphases of these schools vary, for our purposes (as for Weber) the focus is on the common ethical thread that runs through all of them.

Protestantism Compared to Other World Religions

The case of the Protestant ethic illustrates Weber's major theoretical assertion regarding the independent role that religious ideas can play in promoting social change. However, analysis of this one case, even though persuasive, was not enough for him. He also undertook ambitious studies of the other major world religions, publishing monographs on Confucianism and Taoism in China, Hinduism and Buddhism in India, and ancient Judaism.[43] He died before he was able to complete planned monographs on Islam and early Christianity. One of the major goals of these comparative studies was to demonstrate that regardless of material conditions, the modern, Western type of rational bourgeois capitalism did not emerge anywhere in the absence of an inner-worldly ascetic religious orientation. The motivational effects of inner-worldly asceticism contrast most sharply with *other-worldly mysticism*. This orientation promotes psychological withdrawal from the material world, with motivational energy directed toward contemplation or other activities designed to achieve a sense of subjective or emotional union with a divine being or transcendent realm.

Weber's works on the major world religions are extremely valuable even today. He analyzed religion as a major basis for the formation of status groups and various types of leadership structure in religious groups. He recognized the mutual interdependence between religious beliefs and motivations on the one hand and life-style and material interests on the other. Thus persons in different strata of society or different types of social and material conditions will vary in their religious "appetite." For example, a religion that represents a break with traditional customs in ethics and ritual practices is much more likely to be adopted among urban dwellers than peasants. Also, religious elites will gradually emphasize more and more the aspects of their beliefs that justify their particular status and life-style. At the same time, those beliefs will have an effect in shaping the life-style and patterns of conduct of their devotees.

In comparing the various world religions with Protestantism, the emphasis is on the effects of the belief systems of the different religions on people's motivational patterns and actions in the secular world, specifically in the economic realm. In Hinduism, for example, economic and other types of secular activity are governed by the maxim that individuals should conform to the traditional duties of their caste position. Meticulous adherence to these traditional caste duties may, it is believed, result in reincarnation at a higher level of existence. As a result, there is no religious motivation for breaking out of traditional patterns through increasing rationality. In Buddhism there is a profound rejection of this material world. The religious ideal is to limit physical desires and all forms of materialistic involvements as much as possible. This material world is regarded as a kind of gigantic trap, full of illusions and suffering, and maximum detachment from it is recommended as the only way for ultimate escape to the dreamless sleep of nirvana. Obviously, a rational, bourgeois life-style, reflecting commitment to worldly duties, can hardly be nourished with this kind of religious orientation.

Confucianism, in contrast, is not a world-rejecting religion; the Confucian world view stresses that an ultimate principle of reason and order pervades the entire universe, including the world of nature and the social structure. This order is reflected in the traditions of society, and the major life goal that is stressed is to become properly educated in these traditions so as to cultivate an aesthetic appreciation for the profound rationality of this traditional order. Obviously, considerations of rationality other than traditional rationality are severely constrained.

In ancient Judaism, active involvement in promoting change in the material or social world was strongly encouraged, as it was in Protestantism. However, this involvement was seen in terms of preparation for a coming messianic age that would be initiated by a supernatural intervention. During periods of external threat or internal crisis, messianic hopes would be stressed by the prophets, with the result that ordinary, everyday activity took on a tentative quality that undermined long-range rational planning. More important, the Jewish people's collective self-concept as a distinct chosen people and their particularistic ethical system made it difficult for them to establish long-term, stable relations with persons of other nationalities, even when strict economic rationality might have made it expedient to do so.

In brief, then, the Hindu meticulously conforming to the traditional economic and ritual duties of his caste, the Buddhist monk seeking to disengage himself from the world to live a life of poverty and contemplation, the Confucian gentleman with a well-cultivated sense of traditional propriety, the Jewish prophet calling on his people to forsake the false gods of the heathen and to await the messianic age, and the devout, medieval Catholic faithfully performing the rituals prescribed by the church in the hope of attaining salvation in eternity—all of these religious personality types contrasted sharply with the bourgeois Protestant who is devoted to systematic, rational work in a calling as a religious duty, maintaining a rigid discipline so as not to yield to the temptations of the flesh and believing that his or her religious worth (and maybe even eternal salvation) can be gauged by the degree of success achieved in his or her occupational calling.

Weber's Protestant ethic thesis has generated considerable controversy and a voluminous literature.[44] Among the criticisms, some have noted that many pre-Reformation Italian Catholics were quite involved in nontraditional money-making activities. Also, many recent empirical studies show Catholics to be just as high as Protestants in occupational aspirations and achievements.[45] An alternative interpretation of Protestant accomplishments in the early days of capitalism is offered by Scoville's argument that it was the minority group status of Protestants that motivated them to strive for economic success and occupational distinction.[46] Another perspective is offered by those (such as Sorokin) who see both Protestantism and capitalism as a manifestation of an even more basic cultural change, such as increasing secularization and breakdown of tradition.

Some of the critical literature seems to be based on a misinterpretation of what Weber actually said. He did not claim that acquisitiveness for material goods originated with Protestantism. Nor did he claim that Protestantism was merely a religious rationalization for the pursuit of materialistic success goals. What was distinctive about the Protestant ethic was its capacity to motivate long-term, disciplined, systematic, rational action in secular occupational callings as a religious duty. This orientation helped to legitimate the economic activities of early capitalists, but Weber never maintained that the continuation of an established capitalist system would require continued religious legitimation. As noted earlier, capitalism (and the occupational commitments on which it rested) became self-sustaining; in addition, capitalist consumption patterns actually helped to undermine the ascetic religious orientation of Protestantism.

The Work Ethic in Modern Society

Aside from the pro and con arguments on Weber's Protestant ethic thesis, the issue of the work ethic is still a basic sociological issue today. To what extent is a secularized form of the work ethic, reflected in a high need for individual achievement, operative today?[47] Some social analysts have suggested that the growth of material abundance and increase in leisure time have seriously threatened the traditional work ethic. More dramatically, the young people who, in recent years, have opted for dropping out of "the system" for whatever reason seem to have rejected the form of the work ethic that involves devoting oneself to occupational success in a bureaucratic setting. On the other hand, commitment to work in an occupation still dominates vast segments of the middle-class, middle-aged population, and persons on welfare who seem not to be diligently looking for a job are still widely regarded as morally suspect. Whether the work ethic retains its strength in the future or whether it will assume a lower priority in the wake of some emerging new consciousness will undoubtedly have a profound bearing on our society's future, including its national strength and the material welfare of its citizens.

As Weber himself speculated on the future, he did not see a clear alternative to the continued growing dominance of bureaucratic organizations, with participants' motivational energy supplied by a secularized form of the work ethic, reinforced by the promise of materialistic success and bureaucratic career advancement. In the final analysis, economic necessity picks up where the work ethic leaves off.

The increasing rationality and efficiency that these motivational and organizational patterns represent are bought at a heavy psychic cost, however. In submitting to the demands of highly specialized, systematic, and calculable work routines in impersonally controlled organizations, individuals must sacrifice much in the way of spontaneity, meaningful personal relations, opportunities for emotional expression, and their capacity to become well-rounded human beings. High predictability of people's organizational behavior may be necessary for the sake of efficiency, but a fully predictable and calculable world is an emotionally cold world. Similarly, while bureaucratic organization requires specialization, a highly specialized bureaucrat becomes like a mere cog in a giant bureaucratic machine. The capacity of such a person to experience and respond to life as a complete human being is diminished by the narrowness of his or her bureaucratic role.

In view of the tremendous psychic costs of the secularized compulsive work ethic channeled into narrow bureaucratic roles, it is not surprising that the work ethic has lost its appeal among some segments of our population, or that some segments periodically opt for "dropping out" of a system dominated, as they see it, by narrow bureaucratic and technocratic imperatives. Small wonder, too, that Weber looked to the future with a gloomy eye. Although he did not forsee any sure way out of the bureaucratic "iron cage", with its compulsive work ethic and its overriding concern with technical efficiency, he did allow himself to hope that perhaps one day a charismatic leader would emerge who would rekindle the human spirit, inspiring commitment to values that transcend questions of mere efficiency and rationality. In the absence of this, perhaps the only alternative for some people today is to develop their own personal alternative value system and an appropriate life-style to express their refusal to be absorbed completely by the bureaucratic system.

Summary

The influence of Weber on contemporary American sociology cannot be summarized adequately in a few brief concluding remarks. Although Weber dealt extensively with large-scale social structures and broad patterns of historical change, his fundamental image of social reality focused on individuals' actions, which can be understood only in terms of the subjective meanings that they reflect. This differed from Durkheim's concentration on social facts that transcend the individual. In Weber's perspective various categories of social structure were defined in probabilistic terms, not as objective facts, and the strategy of ideal-type analysis was promoted as making possible a genuinely comparative analysis of different types of social structure or different types of cultural orientation.

Following Weber's emphasis on the concept of rationality, we identified two different types of rational action and two types of nonrational action. Then various aspects of Weber's analysis of social structure were reviewed. Specifically, we discussed his threefold model of stratification and showed how the distinctions among economic resources, prestige, and power gives rise to the distinctions among economic classes, status groups, and political parties. Following this, his three types of authority—traditional, charismatic, and rational-legal—were discussed, with special attention given to the differences in the organizational dynamics associated with each type. The growth of modern urban-industrial society can be seen in terms of a shift from traditional authority structures to rational-legal structures. This is manifested most fully in the growth of large-scale bureaucratic organizations. However, bureaucratic organizations do not eliminate completely the other types of authority.

The roots of individuals' motivations are far deeper than deliberate rational assessment of means and ends or conformity to the demands of authority figures. Weber's analysis of the Protestant ethic and its effect in promoting the growth of capitalism demonstrates his sense of the importance of religious beliefs and values in shaping individuals' motivational patterns and economic actions. The influence of religion on individuals' behavior patterns and forms of social organization was also demonstrated in Weber's comparative analysis of major world religions.

Weber's thesis regarding the effects of Protestantism on capitalism was primarily limited to the early stages of capitalism, and these effects were largely unintended even at that stage. In the long run the Protestant orientation toward worldly activities may have contributed to the growth of a secular mentality that undermines the influence of any religious ethic. Since this long-range consequence was not intended, it demonstrates that Weber's analysis was not limited to conscious motivations, in spite of his insistence on understanding subjective motives.

The earliest work of Weber's with which American social scientists became familiar was *The Protestant Ethic and the Spirit of Capitalism* (translated by Talcott Parsons and published in 1930). However, this particular monograph was only one in a series of comparative studies of the effects of different religious orientations. Moreover, Weber's interests were not limited to religion. The earliest major introduction of Weber's overall theoretical perspective to American sociologists was provided by Parsons' 1937 work, *The Structure of Social Action*.[48] Since the publication of Parsons' work, as more and more of Weber's work has become available in English translation and as more and more scholars have become interested in analyzing Weber's theoretical contributions, the tendency to view Weber's ideas through Parsons' perspective has diminished.

One noteworthy feature of Weber's work is that his theoretical ideas are extensively interwoven with historical analysis. The range of historical knowledge that he was able to use in developing and illustrating his theoretical ideas is probably unsurpassed among the classical theorists and contemporary sociologists. Other classical theorists, such as Comte, for example, fitted historical data into a preestablished theoretical framework. In contrast,

Weber's historical analysis reflected a less biased perspective, with historical data used as the basis for developing theoretical concepts and categories instead of simply confirming or illustrating concepts established on some other basis. The result is a more open-ended, more flexible, and less dogmatic approach to historical analysis.

Perhaps one of the major reasons for Weber's open-minded approach to historical data was his insistence on understanding the subjective meaning represented by historical events. Instead of interpreting historical events by imposing his own theoretical meaning on them, he sought to understand such events in terms of their meaning to those actually involved. This is one manifestation of Weber's value neutrality, and this effort to be unbiased and objective in understanding subjective meanings is an essential ingredient of all contemporary sociological strategies that reflect an attempt to deal with the level of subjective meaning. For example, the participant observation research strategy involves an explicit commitment to understand the subjective point of view of those whose behavior is being analyzed. This emphasis on subjective meaning, along with the strategy of ideal-type analysis, are among the key methodological principles developed with great skill by Weber. Ideal-type analysis enables the theorist to transcend particular events and to engage in comparative analysis using general theoretical categories.

Aside from Weber's influence in the general areas of social theory and methodology, numerous substantive subfields of sociology are indebted to his pioneering analyses. For example, sociologists of religion are still concerned with the theoretical questions that Weber raised concerning the dynamics of social processes in religious institutions (e.g., the routinization of charisma), the influence of religion on other institutions, and the role of religion in promoting social change. Students of social stratification still make use of Weber's distinctions among the three different dimensions of stratification. Sociologists who specialize in complex organizations frequently trace the beginnings of this field to Weber's pioneering analysis of the bureaucratic organization. In addition, the sociology of law, political sociology, sociological analysis of economic institutions, and the general area of social change all draw on theoretical ideas and historical analyses provided by Weber.

Classification of Weber's social theory in terms of the general perspective we are using in this book oversimplifies and distorts his approach somewhat. The starting point for Weber's theory is the acting individual whose actions can only be understood in terms of their subjective meaning. Social reality for him consists essentially of the subjectively meaningful social actions of individuals. In contrast, social reality for Durkheim consisted of social structures or other social facts that transcend the individual, and for Comte and Sorokin it consisted primarily of the basic beliefs that comprise the dominant world view of a society.

Because Weber's fundamental unit of sociological analysis is individual action, we can classify Weber as focusing on the individual level of social reality (as opposed to the social structural or cultural levels). However, Weber's substantive interests carried him far beyond the individual level. He dealt extensively with the social structural level (in his analysis of bureaucracy or the capitalist economic system) and the cultural level (in his analyis of religious orientations). In these macroscopic analyses, the subjectively meaningful social action of individuals seems to be neglected. In some respects Weber's concerns were parallel to those of Durkheim, Marx, and Comte. In various ways all of these theorists were preoccupied with the breakdown of traditional, small-scale social structures and the emergence of modern urban-industrial societies.

Weber's individual-level starting point reminds us that social structures or cultural systems cannot be thought of as existing independently of the individuals involved in them. Social structures consist of particular patterns of social action and interaction (defined by Weber in probabilistic terms), and cultural systems are operative in social life as they affect the subjective orientations and motivations of individuals. Weber's approach demonstrates convincingly that seeing individuals as the primary unit of sociological analysis does not at all preclude analysis of large-scale social systems or broad historical patterns.

Footnotes

1. See Max Weber, *The Rational and Social Foundations of Music,* translated and edited by Don Martindale, Johannes Riedel, and Gertrude Neuwirth (Carbondale, Ill.: Southern Illinois University Press, 1958).
2. See Percy Cohen, *Modern Social Theory* (New York: Basic Books, 1968), Chapter 4, "The Action Approach," especially pp. 81–89, for a brief critical discussion of the contrast between Weber and Pareto on the role of reason or logic in a social action. Some of Pareto's basic ideas, as seen by Parsons, will be discussed in a subsequent chapter on functional theory.
3. Arthur Mitzman, *The Iron Cage* (New York: Knopf, 1970). I have relied extensively on this insightful biography in this section on Weber's life.
4. Ibid., Chapter 2, "In the Father's House," thoroughly discusses how Weber's work pace was related to the constraining situation of remaining in his parents' home for roughly 10 years after his military discharge and being financially dependent on his father.
5. Ibid., pp. 171–175 has a provocative discussion of how Weber's analysis of the Protestant work ethic may be seen as an effort to discover the source of his own earlier compulsive need to work to liberate himself partially from it.
6. Hans Gerth and C. Wright Mills, eds., *From Max Weber: Essays in Sociology* (New York: Oxford University Press, 1958), "Introduction: The Man and His Work," p. 22.
7. In addition to his study of the Protestant ethic, which had been written earlier, these monographs included studies of Hinduism, Buddhism, Confucianism, Taoism, and ancient Judaism.
8. Mitzmann, op. cit., attempts to show a close interconnection among Weber's own intellectual development, his family relations, and national political trends in Germany.
9. Compare Talcott Parsons, *Essays in Sociological Theory* (New York: Free Press, 1954), Chapter VI, "Democracy and Social Structure in Pre-Nazi German."
10. Talcott Parsons, "Introduction," to Max Weber, *The Theory of Social and Economic Organization* (New York: Free Press, 1964), p. 5.
11. Max Weber, *The Theory of Social and Economic Organization,* edited by Talcott Parsons and translated by A. M. Henderson and Talcott Parsons (New York: Free Press, 1964), p. 88.
12. Quoted in *From Max Weber: Essays in Sociology,* translated, edited, and with an introduction by Hans Gerth and C. Wright Mills (New York: Oxford University Press, 1958, copyright © 1946), pp. 55.

13. See Parsons, "Introduction," to Max Weber, *The Theory of Social and Economic Organization,* for a discussion of how Weber's insistence on ideal type analysis enabled him to overcome the deficiencies of the positivists (who could not deal with subjective meaning) and the historicists (who insisted on the uniqueness of events, particularly in terms of the subjective ethos they express), pp. 8–29.

14. Max Weber, *The Methodology of the Social Sciences,* edited and translated by Edward A. Shils and Henry A. Finch (New York: Free Press, 1949), p. 90.

15. See, for example, William Skidmore, *Theoretical Thinking in Sociology* (New York: Cambridge University Press, 1975), pp. 24–47, for a brief discussion of this issue.

16. Weber, *The Theory of Social and Economic Organization,* p. 117.

17. Ibid., p. 118.

18. Ibid., p. 124.

19. *From Max Weber: Essays in Sociology,* edited by Hans Gerth and C. Wright Mills, p. 181.

20. Joseph Gusfield, *Symbolic Crusade* (Urbana: University of Illinois Press, 1963).

21. For an example see Amitai Etzioni, *A Comparative Analysis of Complex Organizations,* revised and enlarged edition (New York: Free Press, 1975).

22. See Gerhard Lenski, "Status Crystallization: A Non-vertical Dimension of Social Status," *American Sociological Review,* Vol. 19, August 1954, pp. 405–413, and *Power and Privilege: A Theory of Social Stratification* (New York: McGraw-Hill, 1966).

23. Weber, *The Theory of Social and Economic Organization,* p. 130.

24. Weber's distinction between associative and communal relationships corresponds to Tönnies' famous distinction between *Gemeinschaft* and *Gesellschaft* organizations, with which he was certainly familiar. See Ferdinand Tönnies, *Community and Society,* edited and translated by Charles P. Loomis (New York: Harper & Row, 1963). The distinction may also be compared to Durkheim's distinction between mechanical and organic solidarity (even though Weber's emphasis is different).

25. See Weber, *The Theory of Social and Economic Organization,* pp. 152–153.

26. Ibid., p. 328.

27. Reinhard Bendix, *Max Weber, An Intellectual Portrait* (Garden City, N.Y.: Doubleday, 1960), pp. 334–335.

28. Weber, *The Theory of Social and Economic Organization,* p. 358.

29. Ibid., pp. 330–332.

30. Ibid., p. 337.

31. Bendix, op. cit., p. 427.

32. This distinction between rationality as it related to technical efficiency versus rationality as it relates to ultimate values was developed more fully by Mannheim in his distinction between *functional* rationality and *substantive* rationality. See Karl Mannheim, *Man and Society in an Age of Reconstruction* (New York: Harcourt Brace, 1940).

33. Etzioni, op. cit., pp. 303–364.

34. For example, see Daniel Katz and Robert L. Kahn, *The Social Psychology of Organizations* (New York: Wiley, 1966), Chapter 11, "Leadership," for a discussion of the inadequacy of formal structure and the need for authority figures to enhance their official authority with their personal influence for maximum effectiveness in organizational functioning.

35. Ibid., Chapter 10, "Policy Formulation and Decision-Making," especially pp. 278–279.

36. Max Weber, *The Protestant Ethic and the Spirit of Capitalism,* translated by Talcott Parsons (New York: Scribner, 1958).

37. Ibid., p. 180.

38. This concept has been widely misunderstood as a harsh doctrine of blind fatalism that says that salvation or damnation in the hereafter is foreordained by God and cannot be changed by a person's good or bad deeds in this earthly life. Although the doctrine may be interpreted as a form of fatalism, in fact the doctrine represented the effort of the early Protestant reformers to make sure that salvation is not dependent on good works (which would leave all human beings without salvation) or on a human priest's decision (which, in effect, takes the decision away from God).

39. Ibid., p. 80.

40. Robert K. Merton, *Social Theory and Social Structure* (New York: Free Press, 1968), Chapter XX, "Puritanism, Pietism, and Science," pp. 628–660.

41. Max Weber, *The Protestant Ethic and the Spirit of Capitalism,* pp. 181–182.

42. See Peter Berger, *The Sacred Canopy* (Garden City, N.Y.: Doubleday, 1964), Chapters 5–7 particularly. Berger's discussion is cast in terms of the general process of secularization, which threatens to undermine a religious orientation that combines an emphasis on inner-worldly activity with the belief that the divine power is not continuously involved in the affairs of this world. See also Louis Schneider, *Sociological Approach to Religion* (New York: Wiley, 1970), Chapter 6, for a discussion of some of the important issues that Weber's Protestant ethic thesis has raised, particularly in connection with the effects of Protestantism on the economy, science, literature, and the polity. Schneider also emphasizes the dialectical relationship between Protestantism and these "secular" areas by pointing out that the Protestant *religious* orientation has ultimately been undermined by the kind of secular involvements that it initially helped to stimulate.

43. Max Weber, *The Religion of China: Confucianism and Taoism,* translated by H. H. Gerth (New York: Free Press, 1951); *The Religion of India: The Sociology of Hinduism and Buddhism,* translated by H. H. Gerth and Don Martindale (New York: Free Press, 1958); and *Ancient Judaism,* translated by H. H. Gerth and Don Martindale (New York: Free Press, 1952).

44. For a brief overview and evaluation of some of the issues involved, not only with respect to Protestantism itself but dealing with Weber's comparative studies as well, see Stanislav Andreski, "Method and Substantive Theory in Max Weber," Chapter 5.1 in Clinton Joyce Jesser, *Social Theory Revisited* (Hinsdale, Ill.: Dryden Press, 1975). See also Robert W. Green, *Protestantism and Capitalism: The Weber Thesis and Its Critics* (Boston: D. C. Heath, 1959).

45. See Gary D. Bouma, "Recent 'Protestant Ethic' Research," *Journal for the Scientific Study of Religion,* Vol. 12, June 1973, pp. 141–155.

46. Warren C. Scoville, *The Persecution of Huguenots and French Economic Development, 1680–1770* (Berkeley and Los Angeles: University of California Press, 1960).

47. For an analysis of the *general* problem of achievement motivation, see David C. McClelland, *The Achieving Society* (Princeton, N.J.: Van Nostrand, 1961).

48. Talcott parsons, *The Structure of Social Action* (New York: McGraw-Hill, 1937). Parsons saw Weber contributing some important ideas to the voluntaristic theory of action that Parsons developed. In Parsons' analysis Weber's theory is linked with an idealistic tradition. This perspective on Weber's work has had a major influence on American sociologists' perception of Weber, and it has probably led them to overemphasize the contrast between Weber and Marx.

Questions for Study and Discussion

1. How does Weber's emphasis on individuals' actions and their subjective meaning differ from Durkheim's emphasis on objective social facts external to the individual? Do you think these two views are contradictory? Why or why not?
2. What is meant by a "probabilistic" definition of social structure? Could you define a college class, a family, or a social club in probabilistic terms?
3. How does the ideal-type strategy help a theorist to move beyond the individual level and make broad generalizations about large-scale social structures? Identify two *general* ideal types and two *historically specific* ideal types.
4. In what ways does the struggle for high status differ from the struggle for a high economic-class position? Can you think of examples of persons who would prefer a high status position instead of a high economic-class position? What about persons who prefer a high economic-class position even at the risk of losing status?
5. To what extent does the work ethic influence people's behavior today and to what extent is it being eroded by a new "leisure ethic?" How does the secularized work ethic in modern society differ from the Protestant ethic as analyzed by Weber?

7

Society as Interaction: The Sociology of Georg Simmel

The social reality that most people experience the most directly is face-to-face interaction. For example, students experience the reality of the educational establishment not as an abstract structure with complex interrelations with other institutions but as a series of encounters and relationships with professors, other students, secretaries, librarians, clerks, and administrators. Each encounter can be described in terms of the underlying social form or pattern that it manifests. An encounter between a professor and a student in an introductory class of 200 students will involve a different form of interaction than an encounter between the same professor and student in a senior seminar of 12 or 15 students. These differences will be evident regardless of the personalities of those involved or the subject matter.

Assuming that these different forms or patterns of interaction could be systematically identified, could we then apply them to different types of situations? Is there likely to be any similarity, for example, between the professor and a large class and a minister with a large congregation or an entertainer with a large audience? Would there be any similarity between the social forms manifested in the small, senior seminar class and a group of corporation executives interacting around the conference table? Such questions lead directly to Simmel's analysis of the significance of the number of persons involved in interaction on the social forms that develop.

We can readily appreciate the importance of the subtle dynamics of interaction processes on a face-to-face level in our individual lives. Some of the major challenges we face, as well as our greatest joys and most bitter disappointments, are closely intertwined with the series of social encounters and relationships through which the drama of our individual lives unfolds. For many persons, however, there seems to be a sharp break between the subtle and intricate dynamics of face-to-face encounters and personal relationships on the one hand and large-scale social structures or institutions on the other. Large-scale structures sometimes seem abstract and distant from the social processes with which we are involved every day. The dynamics of face-to-face interpersonal relations often seem more interesting and exciting to study, probably because this level of social reality seems more immediately relevant than the reality of large-scale social structures.

For Simmel, however, large-scale social structures or institutions and face-to-face encounters and relationships are not at all independent. Social institutions do not have an objective existence of their own, independent of the interaction patterns that make them up. Instead, social structures or institutions are crystalized forms or patterns of interaction that are followed on a fairly broad scale in society. As a result, they may *seem* to confront individuals as an objective reality to which they must adapt. Simmel concentrated on the subtle dynamics that underlie various forms of interpersonal interaction, but these forms are the material, as it were, out of which social structures are formed.

SIMMEL'S MICRO APPROACH AND THE REALISM-NOMINALISM CONTROVERSY

Georg Simmel was the major classical theorist to study interaction processes at the micro level. Comte emphasized the cultural level of social reality, specifically stages of intellectual development. Marx and Durkheim both concentrated on the social structural level, even though they differed substantially in their major emphases.[1] Weber's basic image of social reality emphasized individuals and their subjectively meaningful social actions, but his substantive analyses dealt extensively with both the social structural and cultural levels, including broad patterns of major historical change.

Simmel, however, stressed the interpersonal level of social reality. This was because of his conviction that the development of sociology as a distinctive discipline required steering an intermediate course between the opposing views of the realists and the nominalists (discussed in Chapter 6.) Recall that the realist position (as reflected in Durkheim) asserted that social structures have a real and objective existence of their own, independent of the individuals who might happen to be involved in them. Thus society constitutes a whole greater than the sum of its parts. In contrast, the nominalist position (as reflected in Weber's definition of sociology) insisted that only individuals are objectively real and that society is nothing more than a collection of individuals and their behaviors. In this view social structure tends to be explained in terms of characteristics of individuals or their conscious intentions.

In Simmel's intermediate position society is more than just a collection of individuals and their behavior patterns; however, society is not independent of the individuals who comprise it. Instead, society refers to *patterns of reciprocal interaction* between individuals. Such patterns may become extremely complex in a large society and may seem to individuals to be objectively real. But, without the recurrent patterns of reciprocal interaction, the reality of society would simply dissolve. Although Simmel dealt primarily with small-scale interaction patterns, his perspective can also be extended to large-scale social institutions. Before we discuss Simmel's perspective, let us examine briefly his social and intellectual background.

SIMMEL'S LIFE AND TIMES

Georg Simmel was born in 1858 in the heart of Berlin. His father, a well-to-do Jewish businessman who had converted to Christianity, died when Georg was still quite young, and his relationship with his mother was rather distant. A friend of the family was appointed guardian for Georg after his father's death, and a financial fortune left him by his guardian would later enable him to maintain a comfortable, bourgeois life-style in spite of lack of financial success during most of his career.

Simmel received his doctorate from the University of Berlin in 1881 and began teaching there in 1885. Almost immediately he established himself as a brilliant lecturer, sensitive, insightful, and well versed in a broad range of topics. His lectures were so successful that they attracted not only an attentive audience of students but also the intellectual elite of Berlin.

In spite of the breadth of his knowledge, the acknowledged brilliance of his lectures, and the quantity and quality of his writings, the professional recognition accorded Simmel for most of his professional life was meager. For 15 years he remained a *Privatdozent* (an unpaid lecturer whose remuneration was based on student fees). Then he was given the title of "Extraordinary Professor," but this was a purely honorific title without financial compensation. Simmel finally left the University of Berlin in 1914 to accept a position as full professor at the University of Strasbourg but, unfortunately, academic life was soon disrupted by the outbreak of war.[2]

In spite of the lack of official professional recognition, Simmel's virtuosity on the lecture platform earned him many admirers, and he enjoyed friendships with several leading intellectuals in academic circles. Together with Weber and Tönnies, Simmel helped to found the German Society for Sociology. Weber attempted to get Simmel promoted earlier in his career than he was, but without success. Simmel was certainly not an outsider to the academic community to nearly the same degree as Comte had been in France earlier in the century, but his status was clearly marginal.

Several reasons might be mentioned for Simmel's marginal position. Coser and Spykmann both point out that Simmel's Jewish ancestry probably was partly responsible.[3] In addition to this anti-Semitic attitude in Germany, Simmel himself contributed to his own marginality by refusing to fit comfortably within a recognized academic specialty. His interests were broad and, from the point of view of the dominant academicians of the time, this represented a refusal to carve out a particular niche within a recognized specialty and to devote his life to in-depth scholarship within this area. Simmel was not interested in building any kind of comprehensive philosophical or sociological system. Instead, as Coser points out,[4] he seemed to follow his impulses, ranging from Kant's epistemology to the sociology of meals or fashion or any other topic that might strike his fancy. In the process he developed numerous brilliant analytical vignettes, but the total output was fragmented.

Also, Simmel's association with the fledgling field of sociology did not help his situation. The German historicist tradition seemed to deny the legitimacy of sociology as a distinctive science, particularly as represented by comprehensive system builders such as Comte. It will be recalled that the German historicists emphasized that each society has its own distinctive cultural ethos and that individual behavior and social processes must be understood as a manifestation of this ethos. Moreover, German scholars such as Wilhelm Dilthey, a contemporary of Simmel's, made a sharp distinction between the world of nature and the world of human behavior and culture and insisted that universal deterministic laws do not apply to the human and cultural realm. In short, those influenced by the historicist position did not accept the idea that sociology could provide a comprehensive explanation of the social world according to universal deterministic laws. They feared that such efforts would lead to denial of human freedom and the uniqueness of individuals and societies. Simmel did not agree with the comprehensive system-building approach (à la Comte) either, and his style of work would seem to preclude this type of effort anyway. Nevertheless, Simmel was committed to sociology as a distinct scientific discipline.

Also, as Jesser points out, academic life was rather closed and thus lacking in internal sources of social and intellectual criticisms.[5] As a result, a contracultural, bohemian type of intellectual life emerged on the fringes of the academic establishment. Simmel associated with this subculture, thereby adding to his difficulties with the academic establishment.

In any case, Simmel's urban background and academic status undoubtedly provided him with the sensitivity to the subtleties of social processes that are portrayed in his writings. Perhaps some of these insights would not have been forthcoming if Simmel had been more firmly rooted and hence less detached in his intellectual perspective.[6]

Simmel's Social Environment

Berlin during Simmel's life was an important center for a wide variety of intellectual currents. Simmel's own intellectual development undoubtedly owes much to the fact that for most of his life he was exposed to these currents, and his marginal position enabled him to sort and select without strong partisan attachments. As far as the larger social setting is concerned, during the latter part of the nineteenth century Germany experienced an explosive development of capitalist industrial development and a corresponding rapid increase in urbanization. Berlin was a major center for this economic and commercial activity. Both the bourgeois and proletarian classes had expanded rapidly. Nevertheless, the political climate of Germany strongly reflected semifeudal aristocratic values and the ideals of Prussian military discipline. The rapidly growing ranks of the workers were placated by various welfare measures but, overall, the social structure was characterized by a disjunction between the emerging capitalist ethos in economic affairs and a pre-capitalist set of ideals in political affairs.

Intellectual life tended to be divorced from practical social and political affairs, although established academicians enjoyed high status and were generally supportive of the existing social and political order. However, they were more detached than French intellectuals had been in the period before and after the French Revolution. Simmel himself manifested this pattern of political noninvolvement; when he dealt with contemporary social, political, or economic affairs at all, he did so to illustrate general theoretical points. According to Coser, Simmel's noninvolvement ended with the outbreak of the war, and he became a passionate nationalist. Coser suggests that his inability to maintain a dispassionate stance was a reaction to the accumulated psychic cost of marginality and detachment.[7]

Major Intellectual Influences

Although Simmel rejected the organic model of society (such as Comte had developed in France and Spencer in England), he was influenced to a degree by Spencer's evolutionary model of increasing social complexity. Spencer had used an evolutionary model to attempt to explain the gradual transformation of society from a simple structure with low differentiation and high homogeneity to a more complex structure with high differentiation and heterogeneity. Simmel's first publication, *On Social Differentiation,* clearly reflects this influence, as does his discussion of the changing bases of group formation and individuals' social involvements.

Another major influence on Simmel was that of the famous German philosopher Immanuel Kant. Kant had developed a philosophical perspective based on the distinction between human *perception* of phenomena and the fundamental *essence* of objects as they are in themselves. He had shown that we can never know objects as they are in themselves but only as they appear in terms of certain *a priori* categories of consciousness or thought. This point of view, which has become a basic part of the modern world view to a considerable degree, represented a monumental compromise between the opposing claims of empiricists and rationalists. The empiricists had insisted that all knowledge is based on sensory impressions, the mind being essentially like a blank sheet on which these impressions are simply recorded. In contrast, the rationalists believed that there are important nonempirical bases of subjective experience and that knowledge is not limited to mere empirical data. Kant's position was that there are certain fundamental, *a priori* categories of thought (space, time, cause, etc.) that are not based on sensory stimuli but that, nevertheless, shape our subjective awareness of the external empirical world. Furthermore, we can never know the nature of external things in themselves outside these fundamental categories of the mind.

As Simmel applied this mode of thought to social reality, he realized that the development of sociological knowledge involves more than simply taking note of universal laws that are clearly disclosed by empirical data. Instead, the human mind performs a sorting, selecting, and organizing function as it interprets empirical facts; it uses its own criteria in this process that are not given in the facts themselves. The influence of Kantian philosophy is reflected in Simmel's distinction between *form* and *content*, which roughly parallels Kant's distinction between *a priori* categories of the mind and empirical objects.

Another probable influence on Simmel's approach is Hegel's dialectical mode of analysis. Although Simmel did not build explicitly on Hegel's philosophy of history, he used the dialectical mode of analysis at a different level in his sensitive, insightful analyses of the numerous paradoxes and contradictions that pervade social life. Opposition and contradictions between different groups (such as Marx identified), between opposing forms, between form and content, between individual and society, and between objective culture and subjective experience are dealt with repeatedly throughout his writings. In the final stage of his career Simmel analyzed the dialectical conflict between established social forms manifested in existing institutions and cultural patterns and the life process itself, which must continually create new forms for its own expression.[8]

Simmel's interests were not confined to sociology. He wrote and lectured extensively on philosophy, ethics, history, and general cultural criticism and on art and literary criticism, specifically. His writings were published in scholarly and popular nonscholarly journals. Coser has shown that as Simmel's career developed, he published progressively more in nonscholarly journals, reflecting no doubt the gradual substitution of a lay audience for the professional scholarly audience that failed to reward him adequately.[9] His general style reflects the effort to appeal to this wider audience. In any case, he did not establish a comprehensive sociological system or found a school of sociology, nor could he claim to have attracted devoted disciples as such, even though his work was much admired. In view of these circumstances, acknowledgment of his contributions to the development of modern sociology has been belated.

EMERGENCE OF SOCIETY THROUGH RECIPROCAL INTERACTION

Simmel provides a clear conception of the appropriate subject matter of sociology and a general strategy for developing it as a scientific discipline distinct from psychology on the one hand and from social philosophy or a philosophy of history on the other. Briefly, Simmel's approach involves identifying and analyzing the recurring forms or patterns of "sociation." "Sociation," a translation of the German word, *Vergesellschaftung,* literally means the "process whereby society comes into being."[10] Sociation involves reciprocal interaction. Through this process, whereby individuals are linked together and exert influence on one another, society itself emerges.

This image of the nature of social reality indicates that society is more than the sum of the individuals making it up. In addition, there are patterns of reciprocal interaction whereby they are linked together and influence one another. But, just as clearly, society cannot exist as an objective entity independent of its members. Its reality consists of the reality of the *process* of reciprocal interaction. This approach strikes a balance between the opposing claims of the nominalists (who believe only individuals are real) and the realists or organic theorists (who insist that social reality is independent of the individuals who make it up). As Spykmann stated, Simmel can be credited with shifting the focus of sociological thought from a philosophy of society to a science of association.[11] As a scientific discipline, sociology should have as its major goal the identification and analysis of the various recurrent forms of reciprocal interaction through which society emerges.

Numerous everyday examples may be cited to illustrate the process of sociation. For instance, a number of separate individuals waiting quietly in an airport terminal do not form any kind of society or group. But if an announcement is made that the flight will be delayed several hours because of a crash, several people may start talking to the people next to them, and society thereby comes into being. In this case, the "society" (or the degree of "societalization") that emerges would be extremely fragile and temporary, reflecting the casual and temporary bonds of reciprocal interaction.

The process of sociation is highly variable, ranging from the fleeting encounters between strangers in public places to the enduring bonds of close friendship or family relations. Regardless of the degree of variation, this process of sociation transforms a mere collection of individuals into a society (or a group or association). Society exists (to some degree) wherever and whenever a number of individuals are linked through interaction and mutual influence.

FORM VERSUS CONTENT OF INTERACTION PROCESSES

To understand Simmel's perspective, we must clarify his distinction between *form* and *content.* In a rough sense, this distinction parallels Kant's philosophical distinction between *a priori* categories of thought and their empirical content. Specifically, Simmel was interested in isolating the form or pattern whereby the *process* of interaction can be distinguished from the *content* of the particular interests, goals, or purposes being pursued through the interaction. As an analogy, mathematics is a study of the *formal* relationships between numbers and the logical processes that can be applied to them without any specific *content*. Geometry also deals with various kinds of spatial patterns and their relations independent of any particular material content. Simmel envisioned a kind of geometry of social life, identifying forms that can be abstracted from the ongoing interaction process and analyzed independently of content.

The *contents* of social life include: "Erotic instincts, objective interests, religious impulses, and purposes of defense or attack, of play, of gain, of aid or instruction, and countless others [which] cause man to live with other men, to act for them, with them, against them, . . . to influence others and to be influenced by them."[12] But these various goals and purposes are not themselves social. "They are factors in sociation only when they transform the mere aggregation of isolated individuals into specific forms of being with and for one another—forms that are subsumed under the general rubric of interaction. Sociation thus is the form (realized in innumerable, different ways) in which individuals grow together into units that satisfy their interests."[13] "Pure" or "formal" sociology isolates these forms for analysis, just as a grammarian isolates the accepted forms of language from the contents expressed through language.

The content of interaction and its form may vary independently.

> However diverse the interests are that give rise to these sociations, the *forms* in which the interests are realized may yet be identical. And on the other hand, a contentually identical interest may take on form in very different sociations. Economic interest is realized both in competition and in the planned organization of producers, in isolation against other groups as well as in fusion with them. The religious contents of life, although they remain identical, sometimes demand an unregulated, sometimes a centralized form of community. The interests upon which the relations between the sexes are based are satisfied by an almost innumerable variety of family forms; etc.[14]

Simmel lists the following as illustrations of forms of sociation: "superiority and subordination, competition, division of labor, formation of parties, representation, inner solidarity coupled with exclusiveness toward the outside, and innumerable similar features. . . ." These forms may be manifested in "the state, in a religious community, in a band of conspirators, in an economic association, in an art school, in the family."[15]

The distinction between form and content can be seen in a classroom situation. Assuming constant size, the *form* of interaction in a psychology class will probably be similar to that in a geology class, even though the subject matter is different. Moreover, while both of these examples deal with the content of education, certain features of the same form of superordination and subordination may be manifested in a business firm in the relations between a supervisor and the staff. There may be some important differences between these situations, but they could be analyzed in terms of an alternative form.

Sociability

The relationship between form and content is a dynamic one. Although forms of sociation or interaction are typically the *means* whereby various interests or goals are fulfilled, the forms may become detached, as it were, from their content and subsequently be pursued for their own sake or serve as their own content. When sociation or interaction is divorced from extraneous content (or is its own content), the resulting form is *sociability*. In one sense, all interaction is sociable, or at least social. Sociability as a pure form, however, is interaction engaged in for its own sake and for no other purpose.

Examples of sociability abound; one of the most obvious is interaction at a party. The typical expectation for a party is that people will interact, but their interaction is not limited to practical, everyday concerns. In some cases conversations about everyday concerns are actually considered in poor taste. For example, people may work closely together in an office all year and have many interests in common but, at their annual office Christmas party, the understanding is that no business will be discussed. The person who insists on bringing practical workday concerns into the conversation is likely to be considered a bore, just like the recluse who sits in a corner and refuses to mingle.

This same separation of practical or material contents from the pure form of sociability can also be observed in the interaction of strangers. They do not share any common "contents" in their everyday lives; their only link is their temporary presence in one another's company. They may simply ignore one another if possible but, if they choose to interact, their interaction will probably reflect the pure form of sociability. Thus they may exchange pleasantries about the weather, even though neither needs the information the other has to offer and both know it. The specific subject is not as important as the fact that it serves as the basis for the *form* of sociability.

Sexual Flirtation

Another example of the form-content distinction is provided by Simmel's discussion of coquetry, or sexual flirtation. Just as sociability is the autonomous or "play" form of sociation, coquetry is the autonomous or "play" form of erotic drives or instincts. As a *pure* form, coquetry does not include the sociable interaction that may precede a sexual relationship. Neither does it include interaction that obviously precludes the possibility of sexual consummation. Coquetry is characterized by a delicate balance between these two extremes. Both parties will engage in provocative behavior suggesting their sexual availability while, at the same time, discretely refraining from making or demanding a definite commitment (provided both know the game being played and do not misunderstand one another's intentions). In this way they may enjoy the charming and ego-gratifying *form* of a sexual relationship without actually including the *contents* of such a relationship.

The separation of the *form* of sociability from *content* does not imply that forms alone are trivial. Even though conversations about trivial subjects may be common in the absence of practical concerns, the pure form of sociability may reflect a high degree of aesthetic and ethical refinement and provide a profound degree of mutual involvement of persons with one another. Far from being trivial, the pure form of sociability reveals more clearly than any other kind of interaction the social (or sociable) nature of human beings. As long as form and content are both involved, the form is the *means* whereby some practical purpose or objective goal is fulfilled. But, when divorced from practical content, the form becomes its own end. Individuals express their sociable nature through sociation for its own sake, not for some other purpose.

Significance of Forms for Sociology

The distinction between form and content enables us to see Simmel's conception of the subject matter of sociology as a science distinct from the other social sciences. Sociology is not an encyclopedic study of everything social (as it seemed to be for Comte), nor is it a general philosophy of history or a study of the purely subjective level of social life. Instead, sociology abstracts from the total complex array of social reality according to its own particular focus. This, Simmel suggests, should be the *form* of sociation and reciprocal interaction, including "the identification, the systematic ordering, the psychological explanation, and the historical development of the pure forms of sociation."[16]

Simmel offers numerous sociological vignettes in which particular forms are identified, analyzed, sometimes subdivided or contrasted with related forms, and illustrated with concrete examples from a wide range of settings. The overall goal is to show how the same form may be manifested in various cultural or historical contexts (or with a variety of contents). Many of these vignettes have become famous as brilliant and provocative sociological analyses, but they are not systematically related and so do not form a comprehensive theory as such.[17]

Levine developed an exhaustive listing of the various forms Simmel discussed under three general headings: (1) social processes, (2) social types, and (3) developmental patterns.[18] Under social processes Levine lists forms such as elementary collective behavior, formation of parties, division of labor, isolation, association of three or more members, subordination under a single leader, opposition to the ruler, conflict, competition, unification, rivalry, gratitude, wandering, and conversation. Social types focus not on the total interaction process but on the typical role behavior of an individual involved. Some examples include the mediator, the nonpartisan, the arbitrator, the. superordinate, the subordinate, the middleman, the merchant, the woman, the poor, the stranger, and the aristocrat. Developmental patterns include more complex social processes; some examples are social differentiation, shift from local to functional basis of social organization, shift from external or mechanical criteria as a basis for social organization to more rational criteria, and the separation of form and content and emergence of form as autonomous.

In addition to his emphasis on "formal" sociology, Simmel also identified two additional "problem areas" in sociology: "general sociology" and "philosophical sociology."[19] General sociology is essentially the application of his particular sociological method (i.e., identification of various forms of sociation) to historical development. It may involve, for example, analysis of economic development, political structure, cultural creativity, or other historical patterns as the result of the activities of a particular group or society within which certain types of interaction patterns prevailed. Alternatively, it may involve study of the gradual transformation of society from a simple, undifferentiated structure of homogeneous individuals to a more complex, highly differentiated structure of heterogeneous individuals integrated through increased interdependence.[20]

Philosophical sociology involves two specific areas of study that border, as it were, on the analysis of the empirical forms of sociation: epistemology and metaphysics. As applied to sociology, epistemology is the identification of the basic philosophical foundations of the sociological method, including philosophical or methodological assumptions not amenable to empirical "testing," but that provide the general intellectual framework for empirical sociology. One example might be the basic assumption regarding the sociable nature of human beings, which is central in Simmel's approach. The metaphysical area goes beyond the empirical level in attempting to reach intellectual closure on the basis of fragmentary empirical data. It may involve efforts to interpret the significance of empirical data or to assess its general philosophical meaning or its implications regarding the nature of reality.[21]

SUPERORDINATION AND SUBORDINATION

Simmel's discussion of the forms of superordination and subordination (or dominance and submission) illustrates his strategy of formal analysis.[22] Even though these forms may seem at first to involve a one-way flow of influence from the superordinate to the subordinate, Simmel insists that the key element of sociation, *reciprocal* interaction, is not lacking. Only in rare circumstances does the superordinate have no regard whatsoever for the subordinate. In most cases, the superordinate takes into account the subordinate's needs or desires, even if only for the purpose of controlling the subordinate. To this extent the superordinate is influenced by the subordinate.[23]

At the same time, these forms also clearly reveal that the process of sociation transcends the individual. The behaviors of both the superordinate and the subordinate are not simply a manifestation of their respective personality characteristics or individual wills; they reflect the partial submergence of personality to the influence of the social form.

Subordination Under an Individual and Group Structure

Simmel distinguished among subordination under an individual, subordination under a plurality of individuals, and subordination under a general principle. Subordination under an individual typically has a unifying effect on subordinates. The leader often is able to fuse subordinates into a cohesive group, giving them a sense of common purpose and symbolizing their unity in his or her own person. However, subordination under an individual often stimulates opposition to the leader, and this common opposition may be the source of the group's unity rather than their common identification with the leader. These two seemingly divergent tendencies— unification through common identification with the leader versus unification through common opposition—may actually be combined. Group members may be united in abstract identification with the leader as the symbol of the group and in their willingness to follow his or her direction in certain areas but, at the same time, they may be united in their desire to restrain the leader's power.

Opposition to a ruler does not always unite subordinates. If a group (or a society) is composed of heterogeneous persons, the hostility and antagonism that the leader arouses may be deflected to other members due to fear of the leader or expediency or lack of opportunity for attacking the leader. For example, a child who experiences failure in school may express resentment against fellow students who do well instead of against the teacher. Similarly, frustrated members of the lower-middle or working class may be hostile to those on welfare or to minority group members instead of to the established politcal power structure. This splintering effect may be overcome if the leader can provide some common bond between the heterogeneous individuals or groups subordinate to him or her. For example, opposing ethnic groups may be united by a common religion, and opposing social classes may be united in opposition to a foreign enemy.

Simmel also distinguished between subordination under an individual through leveling and through gradation. The leveling pattern involves eliminating all distinctions in rank and power among subordinates so that all are equal in their subservience to the ruler. Simmel shows that this pattern is conducive to despotic rule in which the ruler's power is absolute. This is because the equalization of subordinates prevents any one of them from having a position of influence for launching a successful opposition movement.

In contrast, subordination through gradation involves establishing (or allowing) various intermediate ranks of power and authority. This is the familiar hierarchical form as it exists in bureaucratic organizations, although it is not limited to the formally structured bureaucracy. The intermediate groups may act as a buffer between the ruler and the lowest-ranking members, and their position of relative dominance and superior rank over the lowest-ranking members may make it possible for them to restrain the ruler's arbitrary exercise of power. Within the gradation pattern, Simmel distinguishes between whether this pattern is consciously established by the ruler or whether it results from the inability of the ruler to eliminate or control the power of intermediate groups.

Simmel also distinguished between whether the subordination of a group is to one of their own members or to an outsider. Historical examples of both patterns abound, and each pattern has its distinctive advantages and disadvantages. Subordination under an outsider is advantageous because of the greater impartiality of the outsider, while subordination under a fellow member is advantageous because of his or her greater understanding.[24] Simmel suggests that the lower the relative status of the group as a whole, the less willing its members will be for one of their own number to rule and the more likely they are to turn to an outsider. Conversely, the higher the relative status of the group, the more likely it is that its members will insist that only one of their own is qualified to rule over them. For example, professionals insist on the right to control and discipline their own members.

Subordination Under More Than One Person: Advantages and Disadvantages

Subordination under a plurality of persons differs in several respects from subordination under an individual. Subordination under a plurality is likely to be more objective and less personal than subordination under an individual. This greater objectivity may result in fairer, more equitable, or less harsh treatment of subordinates. On the other hand, the lower level of personal involvement may permit a degree of exploitation far more severe than with a single individual. Simmel provides examples of both of these opposing patterns and speculates that, in general, if the situation of the subordinate benefits most from impartiality and objectivity, subordination under a plurality is preferable; but if the situation of the subordinate is such that personal tenderness and altruism are important, subordination under an individual is preferable.

As schoolchildren move from the elementary grades to high school, their pattern of subordination typically shifts from being under the supervision of a single classroom teacher to being under the supervision of several teachers in different subject areas. Although several other factors (such as students' increasing age) are obviously relevant, part of the greater impersonality of teacher-student relations in high school compared with elementary school can be accounted for in these terms. On the other hand, the control of a riotous mob over a victim under attack lacks the impartiality and objectivity expected of individuals as individuals. This demonstrates that subordination under a plurality of persons is not necessarily always fairer or more objective than subordination under a single person.

When individuals are subject to the domination of a plurality, the relations between superordinates and subordinates will be influenced strongly by the relations between the superordinates themselves. If the superordinates are involved in conflict, the subordinate may become virtually a pawn in their struggle, with both superordinates demanding total loyalty from the subordinate. The ancient maxim regarding the difficulty of serving two masters reflects this insight. If a subordinate feels a sense of loyalty to both masters, their conflict will be internalized within his or her conscience as a conflict of opposing duties.

On the other hand, in some situations a subordinate might be able to enhance his or her autonomy by having more than one superordinate. If the superordinates are not in conflict or even in contact with each other, and if the subordinate is not completely subjugated to either of them, then the subordinate might be able to use the relationship with one of the superordinates as a buffer in negotiating the relationship with the other so as to gain a greater degree of autonomy. In other words, one can be played against the other.

A special case of subordination under a plurality exists in hierarchical organizations in which individuals are technically subservient to all superordinates up the line, from the immediate supervisor to the president of the company. In general, intermediate levels may serve as a buffer between the top and bottom levels. For all practical purposes, the subordinate is expected to be subservient to the immediate supervisor. It is considered poor management practice for higher-level supervisory or management persons to bypass the immediate supervisor. Nevertheless, the immediate supervisor is, in effect, an intermediary who channels directives from higher levels in the organization to his or her own subordinates.

In many cases policy decisions initiated at the top are distorted or dampened as they are filtered down through the various hierarchical levels of the organization. Thus major policy changes made at the top appear at the bottom levels as rather mild shifts. Perhaps the most notorious example of this process in our society is the apparent imperviousness of much of the federal government bureaucracy to periodic changes in administration. United States presidents come and go with their administrations' policy changes, but the civil service bureaucracy seems to be permanent—and permanently resistant to implementing major changes.

On the other hand, there are cases in which the desires or influence attempts of top-level superordinates are magnified as they are transmitted down the line. The results may be humorous or disastrous. Top-level expressions of irritation or annoyance may be taken by subordinates as a call to action. For example, a U.S. president's expression of negative feelings toward the leader of some foreign country may encourage subordinates to change their mode of operations in that country.

Another common pattern is the process whereby pressures exerted by top-level officials arouse the antagonism and hostility of middle-level personnel to such a degree that they treat their own subordinates in a hostile or aggressive way. The same pattern is reflected when these subordinates, in turn, go home and take it out on their children. This process also involves intensification of power relationships as demands are transmitted down the line.

Low-level subordinates in hierarchical organizations who are subjected to excessively harsh demands by their immediate superiors sometimes succeed in entering a coalition with top-level persons to restrain those in the middle. The "open door" policy of top executives is an invitation to adopt this strategy. By taking up the cause of the lowest-ranking persons, top-level officials can manage to have themselves seen in a very magnanimous light and, if successful, their overall power in the organization may be enhanced considerably by this means. However, this strategy is not always successful. Since top-level persons must rely on those in the middle to implement policies designed to improve the condition of those at the lowest level, the middle-level personnel may, if their interests require, succeed in diluting the improvements intended for those at the bottom or providing them in such a way that their own power and resources are enhanced.

Another example of subordination under a plurality is provided by democratic organizations in which decisions are made collectively by voting. According to democratic ideology, the majority vote is the best way to determine the collective will. Because of the greater power of a majority than a minority and because of the belief that the majority expresses the unity of the group or society as a whole, minorities are expected to accept the decision of the majority as binding. Indeed, it may be that opposition of minorities is considered an indication of their selfishness, while the equal selfishness of majorities is not considered selfishness at all but an expression of the *common* good that will, in the long run, also benefit the minorities. Whether this assumption is valid is another question entirely; the point is that members of democratic organizations often see majority decisions as morally right decisions that can justly be imposed on minorities.

Moreover, the leader of any democratic organization is legally and ethically subordinate to its members. Leaders elected to their post by a democratic process will find their power subject to various contraints that self-appointed leaders of autocratic organizations do not experience. The ancient Christian ideal whereby the master should be the servant of all is an idealistic expression of this pattern. Of course, this ideal is frequently violated. Appointed or elected leaders may become so dominant that they can impose their will despite the objections of those to whom they are morally and legally accountable. (This phenomenon will be examined in more detail in a subsequent chapter in connection with Michel's concept of the "iron law of oligarchy."[25])

Subordination Under an Ideal Principle: The Rule of Conscience

The third major pattern of subordination and superordination, subordination under a general principle, is expressed, for example, in the American concept of government by laws instead of by people. Although men or women are obviously required to administer the laws or to make decisions in areas not covered by the laws, the primary loyalty of people, from the president down to ordinary citizens, is ideally to the laws. This same loyalty and obligation to laws or impersonal rules are also characteristic of bureaucratic organizations.

Subordination to a principle is often considered preferable to subordination to individuals, since it limits the possibility of arbitrary capriciousness by an individual. On the other hand, in groups or societies in which social cohesion rests largely on personal relations, individuals may feel a certain dignity in being bound in loyal subordination to an appreciative person, particularly a high-status person, which would be missing in submission to impersonal rules in which personal reciprocity is not possible. Feudal relations, for example, were based on personal loyalty. Similarly, high-level executives in modern corporations often take top assistants with them when they transfer to a new position, thus indicating the personal loyalty that the executive and assistants have for each other rather than for the organization in which they are involved.

In some cases subordination to an abstract principle or value is seen as the highest expression of personal freedom. In this connection Simmel discusses the subordination of an individual to the moral principles of his or her own conscience. As Durkheim emphasized in his concept of the "collective conscience," an individual's conscience represents the internalized normative patterns of society. In Simmel's perspective these internalized normative patterns may not seem to be arbitrary demands of society but transcendent moral imperatives that are objectively valid regardless of social definitions, or sometimes even in opposition to current social definitions.

The examples set by great moral or religious leaders express this type of subordination. Their commitment to ultimate moral principles motivates them to ignore their practical interests and conventional moral expectations in order to be subordinate to the higher demands of their conscience. History is filled with examples of heroic persons who were faithful to transcendent moral principles even in the face of misunderstanding, hostility, and persecution from their social peers or even superiors.

In some cases the relations between superordinates and subordinates are governed by objective principles or laws to which they are *both* expected to be subservient. Their common subordination to an objective or impersonal principle puts certain constraints on the superordinate's dominance while, at the same time, investing it with a validity that transcends the personal relationship. For example, the police officer who gives a ticket to a speeding motorist may remind the motorist that he or she is also subject to the law and, therefore, really has no choice but to issue the ticket. If the objective principle or ideal to which both superordinates and subordinates are subject is sufficiently transcendent, their relationship might even approach that of peers. For example, ministers are considered the children of God along with their parishioners and equally subject to His transcendent will. In fact, ministers may be considered not so much superordinates over their congregations as instruments of God whose job it is, literally, to minister to their needs.

Subordination and Individual Freedom

Simmel also analyzed the relation between superordination and subordination and individual freedom. Subordination is often experienced as a depressing or oppressive condition that denies subordinates their freedom. To them, achievement of freedom seems to require elimination of the distinction between superordinates and subordinates. This is why social movements representing the struggles of subordinates for freedom are often, at the same time, a struggle for equality. In the ideology of reform or revolutionary movements these two goals are closely linked; equality is seen as the necessary condition for freedom.

As Simmel shows, however, freedom and equality are not necessarily compatible on a long-term basis. For subordinates, freedom means having the privileges of superordinates, but these privileges include the privilege of domination. Thus the real goal of reform or revolutionary movements is not to eliminate the *form* of superordination and subordination but to enable those who were previously subordinate to attain a position of superordination. Historical experience shows that successful consummation of a revolutionary movement is generally not followed by equality but by substitution of one set of dominants for another.

Similarly, as Simmel shows, the demands of a group within society for freedom from dominance by the state is really a demand that the group be able to control its own members. In other words, the real goal of groups demanding freedom is not freedom for the *individual* but freedom for the *group* to dominate its members. Often this domination of individuals by a subgroup within society is far more restrictive than domination by the state would be.

Given the natural and inevitable differences between people, complete equality is not a realistic goal. Moreover, the existence of society presupposes some pattern of superordination and subordination. However, this necessary social pattern can be implemented in such a way that subordinates are not degraded or oppressed. Simmel identifies several patterns of subordination that preserve the subordinate from feeling personally degraded. For example, the separation between social position and personality can enable the subordinate to maintain a sense of personal freedom, even while assuming a position of subordination as a technical or organizational necessity for certain objective purposes. In other words, the form of superordination and subordination expresses a strategy for organizing society rather than a belief about individual differences.

Also, the degrading effects of subordination can be alleviated by having individuals reciprocate in assuming positions of super- or subordination. This means that people would be subordinate in some areas or at some times and superordinate in other areas or at other times. The system of democratic voting and of periodic turnover of leaders expresses this pattern to a degree. Simmel's discussion of these issues implies a great deal of faith in the democratic process and in the wisdom of an open society in which there is wide access to leadership positions.

CONFLICT AND COHESION

Relations between superordinates and subordinates are shot through with possibilities for conflict. In this section we shift to a discussion of conflict as one of the basic forms of interaction.[26] Conflict is inextricably interwoven with various unifying processes in social life instead of being a mere negation of unity. Conflict and unification can be seen as alternative forms of sociation; neither is necessarily more basic or more significant than the other. Both are normal, and both involve reciprocal interaction.

The opposite of unification is not conflict; often social relations characterized by high cohesion are also characterized by latent tensions and periodic conflicts. Without this antagonistic element, individuality would be absorbed by the demands of others or the expectations of the group. Preservation of individual autonomy and personal integrity depends on individuals' willingness to resist demands of others or complete absorption in the group, even though this may lead to conflict.

To assume that the tensions and conflicts are somehow "abnormal" or that they necessarily undermine the unity of the group is to impose a biased perspective not supported by the facts. From a sociological standpoint, the opposite of unity is not conflict but noninvolvement (i.e., lack of *any* form of reciprocal interaction). Indeed, if a social relationship can be destroyed by the eruption of discord, this might be a good indication that the degree of unity was low originally. Simmel's perspective on conflict and unification as alternative but equally important and closely interdependent forms of interaction provides a valuable middle-ground alternative to Marx's concentration on social conflict and Durkheim's emphasis on integration and social solidarity.[27]

To show how natural conflict is in social life, Simmel offers several examples that demonstrate that individuals are not merely willing to engage in conflict; they often seem eager for it. If significant issues are lacking, individuals will engage in conflict over trivial issues. For example, Simmel cites the case of a quarrel between two Irish parties that embroiled the whole country over the color of a cow. Also, the fascination that competitive games have for many people suggests their eagerness for conflict. Just as sociability is the pure form of reciprocal interaction and coquetry is the pure form of erotic attraction, so competitive games can be seen as a pure form of conflict that has become autonomous (serves as its own content). Unlike other forms of conflict in which there is some objective to be obtained by victory, in the competitive game victory is its own reward. (Of course, in professional athletics victory is sought not only for its own sake but also for financial rewards and prestige.)

Not only do relations that are primarily cohesive have some elements of conflict, but relations of antagonism and conflict also have some unifying elements. In competitive games, for example, the competitors must obviously agree on the rules of the game. The rules, then, constitute a common bond between the competitors.

On a broader level, even warfare is governed, at least to some degree, by general international understandings regulating the conduct of war. Also, when two or more parties are in conflict or competition for some prize or other type of material gain, they are, at the same time, unified by their desire for the prize or gain. Still another instance of this close interdependence between conflict and unification is the fact that competitors in the economic marketplace often develop strategies to limit the extent of their competition, thereby creating shared bonds between them.

Alternative Forms of Conflict and Their Social Effects

Conflict can take many different forms. Simmel analyzed several of these, including antagonistic games, legal conflicts, conflicts over basic principles or various objective causes that transcend the individuals involved, conflicts between persons who share certain qualities in common, conflicts in intimate relations, and conflicts that threaten to disrupt a group. In antagonistic games, legal conflicts, and conflicts over basic causes, unity is provided by agreement on the basic rules or principles that regulate the conflict or for which the conflict exists. In the case of conflicts between persons who share common qualities, have an intimate relationship, or are fellow members of the group, the source of unity is obvious. But, in such cases, the conflict is likely to be more intense than when no unifying bonds exist.

Common experience confirms Simmel's observation that conflict with persons with whom we share a great deal in common frequently tends to be more hostile and more bitter than conflict with persons with whom we share nothing but the conflict itself. Traitors are typically punished with far more vehemence than enemies who never belonged to the group, and marital conflicts tend to be far more volatile than conflicts between casual acquaintances. Conflicts between persons who share many things in common are dynamically interwoven with the basis of their unity. The fact that the parties share so much in common means that each is vulnerable to attacks and counterattacks in areas of the personality with which strangers or even casual acquaintances might not be familiar. While intimate relations may be strong enough to include disagreements or even thrive on them, it is not surprising that the intensity of the conflict is often directly proportional to the degree of solidarity or similarity in the relationship.

Simmel also distinguished between direct person-to-person conflict and competition. Competition need not involve person-to-person contact; instead, competitors may each strive independently for a common goal, with their antagonism resulting from the fact that one person's gain means the other person's relative loss. However, in some forms of competition, even the losers may eventually gain indirectly through the victory of the winner. For example, competition between scientists for new discoveries or professional prestige leads to the general advancement of science and, from this advancement, all scientists benefit.

In many cases the beneficiary of competition is not just the victor but a third party. This follows from the fact that the goal of competition is often to influence the actions of some third party. As competitors seek to win the favor of some third party, they must become sensitive to the needs and desires of the third party and prove themselves able and eager to meet these needs. Paradoxically, therefore, competitors' efforts to secure personal victory results in their attention and motivation being directed outward toward the needs and wishes of others. For example, as Simmel points out, a man competing with another man for a woman's love will be stimulated to become more attractive as a companion than his competitor.

Similarly, business firms must become adept at assessing consumer needs and preferences and in trying to provide more attractive goods than their competitors. Thus society as a whole benefits from competitors' efforts to gain the third-party favor of consumers through competition. This is a basic premise of the free enterprise system and is one of the major emphases of eighteenth- and nineteenth-century British political economy. On an even more general level, the pervasive competition in social life for approval or esteem motivates people to be far more sensitive to the needs and opinions of others than direct moral appeals for people to transcend their selfishness.

Competition is not always the best means for promoting the common good. The welfare of some groups seems to exclude competition. For example, families or other groups that are based on a high level of interpersonal intimacy do not include competition as a part of their structure. Indeed, the incest taboo may be seen as a strategy for eliminating the possibility of sexual competition within the family. Also, individuals or groups may work out procedures for limiting or eliminating competition. This is feasible because of the absence of personal antagonism and because of the underlying agreement on the common goal of the competitors. For example, business firms may minimize or eliminate competition through price fixing, product standardization, or other means. Or the competitive pattern may be eliminated externally through socialist organization of the economy. In the American system, laws and regulations that control business competition are designed to prevent ''unfair'' competition (such as through false advertising) and to insure that the competitive pattern itself continues (through prohibitions of combinations such as trusts that eliminate competition).

Conflict and the Relation Between In-Groups and Out-Groups

The interdependent relationship between conflict and cohesion is manifested also in the dynamics of in-group and out-group relations. Those who idealize a cohesive social structure based entirely on love, peace, and harmony easily forget that cohesion tends to disintegrate during times of peace. Just as individuals engaged in conflict have their energy mobilized to strive for victory, so also a group or society is most likely to have its resources mobilized and its solidarity strengthened when it is engaged in conflict with other groups or societies. During times of external threat or conflict, intragroup disagreements or conflicts tend to be either settled or downplayed. Selfish or individualistic pursuits are partially submerged, and the members unite in devoting their energy to the common task of pursuing victory over their common enemy. This increase in in-group solidarity that results from conflict with an out-group was illustrated by the immediate reactions of large numbers of Americans to the seizure of American hostages by Iranian militants at the American embassy in Iran. Courage and heroism often flourish as a result of conflict. This phenomenon has long been recognized; for example, William James noted the moral commitments that war can inspire and called for a search for a "moral equivalent."

The unifying effects of conflict often apply to minority groups within a society. In many cases the social solidarity of minority groups is greatly dependent on their members' common opposition to the larger society. Exclusive religious sects and radical political parties both exhibit this pattern. Such groups actually thrive on the fact that they are rejected by the larger society because it helps justify their opposition to society. As a result of this reciprocal rejection, the minority group develops a highly cohesive internal structure with high *esprit de corps*.

The solidarity of minority groups is likely to be undermined if the opposition of society declines. Lack of opposition may even eliminate part of the justification for the minority group's very existence. It has been observed that radical religious sects have great difficulty maintaining their radical sectarian characteristics in a tolerant and heterogeneous society such as the United States. In effect, they are killed with kindness and tolerance.[28]

Conflict may also lead to the formation of new groups consisting of persons (or groups) who were previously indifferent or even antagonistic to one another. This phenomenon is illustrated when groups of nations form an alliance for their common defense and when numerous trade unions combine into a large labor organization. The larger and more heterogeneous the group that is formed in this way, the fewer but more basic will be the interests that they can share. For example, an alliance of nations may develop no common goal except that of territorial defense. However, once a relationship is established even for such a limited goal, it may be that the parties involved will gradually discover or create other bonds between them. Thus military alliances between nations may lead eventually to economic trade and perhaps even to a degree of cultural assimilation.

Conflict Resolution

Even though conflict may be a natural and inevitable phenomenon in social life, it is not necessarily continuous, at least overtly. Instead, social life at many different levels exhibits cycles of peace and conflict, tranquility and hostility. Motivations for ending conflicts may include exhaustion or a desire to devote energies elsewhere.[29] This leads to the question of how conflicts are resolved or terminated. Simmel analyzes several different forms for the ending of conflict, including removal of the basis of conflict independently of the conflicting parties' actions, victory of one party and defeat of the other, compromise, reconciliation, and irreconcilability.

Victory by one party does not always mean that the defeated party has lost absolutely all power to continue the struggle. The defeated party may make a deliberate choice to give up the struggle and surrender, once he or she senses what the outcome would otherwise be. By making such a choice, the defeated party is spared the necessity of spending all his or her energy and other resources in a futile effort while, equally important, preserving the dignity of being able to make a "free" choice.

Compromise might seem initially to be impossible where the object of the conflict is indivisible (i.e., it cannot be divided between the conflicting parties). However, Simmel points out that even in such cases compromise can be achieved by the victor's awarding some alternative "consolation" prize to the loser. Indeed, conflict might be considerably truncated by one party offering a substitute value to another party in exchange for access to some object for which both would otherwise compete. This leads Simmel to a brief consideration of the general process of exchange whereby parties with conflicting interests exchange items that are substitutable in terms of an objective measure of value instead of attempting to use force to gain what they want from others.

While victory or compromise involve settling a conflict on an objective basis, conciliation and forgiveness involve a subjective element. A relationship that has been reconciled differs in important ways from one that has never been broken. A reconciled relationship may exhibit either greater or lesser intensity than before the break, depending on the nature of the relationship and the issues involved in the break. The increased intensity that sometimes follows reconciliation may be due to the fear that a second rupture could not be reconciled without trivializing the meaning of the first reconciliation.

In some cases reconciliation may not be possible. Irreconcilability of a conflict sometimes leads to termination of a relationship. However, Simmel pointed out that another alternative is for the relationship to be reestablished with the irreconcilable issue not being allowed to contaminate other aspects of the relationship. This pattern is widely recognized when close fiends or relatives "agree to disagree" on some particular issues and then make sure that the relationship is not dominated by this irreconcilable difference. In some cases the subject of disagreement is simply considered not an appropriate subject for discussion.

INFLUENCE OF NUMBERS ON SOCIAL FORMS

Another manifestation of Simmel's concern with social forms is his analysis of the significance of numbers for social relations and social organization. As with the previous forms, the effects of numbers may be exhibited in a variety of contexts and involve a variety of substantive issues. The concern, however, is not with these "contents" but with the "forms." Briefly, the major proposition that underlies Simmel's analysis is that as the number of persons involved in interaction with each other changes, the forms of their interaction also change in regular and predictable ways.[30]

The Dyad versus the Triad

Perhaps the most well-known of Simmel's analyses of the effects of numbers of forms is the contrast between a dyad and a triad.[31] The dyad exhibits certain unique features that do not apply in any larger social unit. These follow from the fact that each individual is confronted by only one other individual instead of by a superpersonal collectivity (i.e., a collectivity that seems to transcend the individual participants). For this reason the potential influence of an individual over the social unit is greater than in any other type of social unit. On the other hand, if an individual chooses to disengage from a dyad, the social unit itself disappears. In contrast, in all other groups the removal of one member does not destroy the entire social unit.

The uniqueness of the dyadic form is recognized in the old adage that "two is company, three is a crowd." The common belief that a secret can safely be shared with one person, but not with more than one, reflects the uniqueness of the dyadic form. Also, because each person in a dyad needs to be concerned with only one other person, the specific needs, desires, and personal characteristics (both strengths and weaknesses) of that other person can be considered much more fully than would be possible in any larger group. As a result, dyadic relationships acquire an emotional intimacy and uniqueness that are not possible in any other social form. This leads to an exclusivistic character—the belief that the life that two persons share can be shared with no other and that no other relationship has the same degree of emotional richness. As love songs affirm over and over, there has never been another like you and probably never will be, nor has there ever been a relationship like ours. In fact, millions of persons in love have experienced similar emotions.

Dyadic relationships are not always dominated by positive feelings. In situations of conflict, no matter what the specific issue or cause, the very intimacy of the relationship often makes the conflict particularly vicious and bitter. Conflict issues that seem trivial to an objective outsider are charged with emotional significance. Indeed, the previous openness of the partners to one another at the deepest levels of their personalities makes them vulnerable to highly personal attacks on one another at these levels. The rejection and humiliation that one or both partners may feel would be far less painful if they had not known each other so well.

Also, even when open conflict is absent, dyadic relations are sometimes vulnerable to gradual atrophy resulting from the gradual elimination from the relationship of all contents that are *not* unique to the relationship but that are shared with others. The very uniqueness of the relationship may lead the partners to exclude all features that either or both of them share in *other* relationships. This pattern is recognizable in emotionally dead marriages in which neither partner seems to have much to talk about with the other, even though both may be eager conversationalists in other relationships. In this type of situation, the features or contents that either or both partners have in these other relationships seem irrelevant to *their own* relationship.

A marriage relationship is perhaps the most obvious exception to the feature just discussed, in which each partner in a dyadic relation is confronted only by the other individual instead of by a superpersonal entity. In a marital relationship the partners are confronted not only with one another but with the societal institution of marriage. Through its power to license, annul, or dissolve, the state as a whole has an interest in recognizing and regulating the dyadic relation between marriage partners. This legal recognition is matched by the customs and standards of morality shared by the public at large.

Regardless of the specific pattern of the dyadic relation, the forms it manifests are not possible in social units of any larger size. Conversely, there are possibilities in larger social units that are impossible in a dyad. To illustrate this, Simmel contrasts the dyad with the triad. The triad is the smallest social unit in which each party is confronted by a plurality and so must take into account not just one individual's unique personality characteristics but those of two individuals. This means that it is impossible for each party to achieve the kind of intimacy possible in a dyad; each person will feel obliged to relate to what the other two have in common.

No doubt most of us have had the experience of having an intimate and stimulating conversation with a close friend interrupted by the intrusion of a third party. The conversation may continue with the third party present, but the form of interaction will definitely change. Initially, the members of the dyad are likely to explain to the third party what they were talking about. If there is a disagreement or latent conflict, each member of the initial dyad will want to present his or her side to the third party, along with the appropriate justification or rationalization, so as to enlist the third party's support. Even if the third party falls silent after the initial greeting to listen to the original two people, the continued conversation of these two will be modified simply by the silent presence of the third party.

Alternative Third-Party Roles

One of Simmel's more famous vignettes is his discussion of the various roles that a third party can take. These roles, none of which are possible in a dyad, include mediator, arbitrator, *Tertius Gaudens* ("third who enjoys"), and "divider and conqueror."

In some situations the mediator role results because the bond between the members of the dyad is based primarily on their common relationship to the third party. That is, the dyadic bond is an indirect one. For example, the relationship between a mother-in-law and daughter-in-law is based on their common relation to the son-husband who is linked with each of them separately. In many other situations, however, the members of the dayd are directly linked to each other as well as to the third person. For example, husband and wife are related to each other directly, and also share a bond with their children. For this reason children often strengthen a marriage; that is, they provide an additional bond between the spouses.

In cases of conflict between two parties, the mediator's nonpartisan role may be an important factor in resolving the conflict. By maintaining a nonpartisan role, the mediator is likely to be perceived by both parties as fair and objective. However, this role does not involve resolving the conflict, but simply serving as a link between the conflicting parties. The mediator can, for example, explain the position of each party to the other in a more objective and less passionate manner than either of the contending parties could do. Moreover, in presenting their positions and their arguments to the mediator, the contending parties themselves are forced to become more objective and dispassionate.

The arbitrator role differs from the mediator role primarily in that the arbitrator makes the final decision that resolves the conflict. As with the mediator role, the parties to the conflict must perceive the third-party arbitrator as objective and fair, and they must present their own case to this third party in as objective a manner as possible. Having done this, however, they must agree to be bound by the arbitrator's decision instead of eventually coming to terms themselves. In contrast to mediation, resorting to arbitration is a confession that the contending parties themselves cannot reach agreement.

The purposes and strategies of the other two third-person roles—the *Tertius Gaudens* and the one who "divides and conquers"—are not quite as benevolent toward the dyadic relation as the previous two. The *Tertius Gaudens* role involves taking advantage of the actual or potential conflict between the members of a dyad for furthering one's personal interests. The conflict may exist independently of the relation of either or both dyad members to the third party, or it may result from competition for favors or support from the third. In either case, the third party's detachment and objectivity means that he or she can choose freely which side to support in the dyadic conflict and, as a result, can make certain demands of the members of the dyad in exchange for their support. The payoff for the third party may be substantial if the two members of the dyad try to outbid one another.

There are exceptions to the pattern of emotional detachment on the part of the third party. For example, a woman whose love is sought by two men can hardly remain emotionally detached, even though she is the third party. In this situation the competition or conflict between the men results from the woman's wavering emotionally between the two and not from her complete impartiality.

In analyzing this role, as with the other third-party roles, Simmel offers numerous examples that extend beyond the situation of three individual persons. For example, consumers as a whole are in a third-person role as they benefit from the competition of business firms for their purchases. Another example is the opportunity that relatively small political parties might have to exert a decided influence in situations where two large-scale political parties effectively prevent one another from gaining dominance. In this situation the third party is able to exert influence far out of proportion to its small size simply by tipping the balance of power between the two dominant parties. Essentially, this is the role that George Wallace was able to play in recent presidential politics.

The divide-and-conquer role is similar to the *Tertius Gaudens* role in some ways; its major difference is that the third party deliberately fosters conflict between the members of the dyad so as to profit from their disagreement (as opposed to simply taking advantage of their conflict when it erupts). Children in families sometimes learn to use this role as they play one parent against another, hoping to profit by their disagreement in gaining increased privileges. Again, Simmel extends the analysis of this role beyond the case of three individual persons. For example, totalitarian governments that forbid unauthorized associations or gatherings of people are, in effect, following the divide-and-rule, third-party strategy.

Growth in Group Size and Emergence of Bureaucratic Forms

The analysis of changes in forms that result from the addition of more persons (or other units) could be extended. For example, a four-person group is the smallest group in which there can be coalition formation of equal size; a five-person group is the smallest in which there can be coalition formation of unequal size. Such internal divisions may not develop; small groups are often characterized by a high degree of consensus and unity.

As groups grow larger, the probability of internal subgroup formation increases. If this occurs, the social forms appropriate to the numbers involved in the various subgroups will be dominant. No doubt many of us have observed the effect of group size on subgroup formation at social parties or other informal gatherings. At small parties (e.g., four to six persons), a great deal of the conversation involves the entire group. When one person talks, everyone listens. At larger parties, however (e.g., twenty to twenty-five persons), it is rare for one person to be able to monopolize everyone's attention for very long. Instead, the party tends to break down into several subgroupings, each with its own conversation. The same kind of centrifugal pressures also operate in other kinds of large-scale social units.

In order to compensate for these pressures and prevent a large unit from segmenting into smaller units, special integrating mechanisms must be developed. For an enduring group the development of a division of labor is one such mechanism. Simmel points out that a complex division of labor results in the kind of interdependence that holds large units together. Also, large groups tend to formalize and objectify their normative patterns as laws. External enforcement of formalized laws partially replaces reliance on the influence of custom.

One of the main differences between the social forms manifested in large groups and dyads is that in the large group the individual is confronted with an objective structure that seems to transcend its individual members, while in the dayd, as noted previously, the individual is confronted only with the other individual. This objective structure might be codified in laws and rules or symbolized in a name or a building. It might even have its own reputation, independent of the individual reputations of its members. For example, most members of the public no doubt have some image in mind of General Motors, the U.S. Defense Department, or Sears Roebuck, even though they might not know the names of any of the individuals who play important roles in these organizations. This jump from dyads to national organizations is dramatic, but the point is that large-scale structures seem to be objective entities that transcend their individual members.

Bureaucratization can be seen as a function of group size. In a small group in which everyone knows everyone else, face-to-face interaction is sufficient to negotiate appropriate rules, roles, and goals for joint action. As groups expand in size, however, this kind of informal structure based on personal relationships quickly becomes inadequate. For one thing, it becomes logistically impossible to establish personal relations with enough members of the group to insure group unity. In a very large and widely dispersed organization, fellow members may not even recognize one another in the absence of some means of identification such as a uniform or insignia. When personal relations are established in a large organization, they are likely to be less intense or intimate. If they are as intense and intimate they are less likely to be relevant for the overall group than personal relations in a small group. (For example, fellow employees of a large firm may fall in love and get married, but this dyadic relationship is not really relevant for their involvement in the firm.) In view of these various difficulties, members of expanding groups must resort to formalizing rules and relationships, procedures for selecting leaders, minimal requirements for membership, procedures for settling conflicts, objective goals, and so on. This process constitutes establishment of a bureaucratic structure.

Both small and large groups have their distinctive advantages and disadvantages. Some groups, such as some religious sects, radical political parties, secret societies, and aristocracies or other kinds of elites, must be small in order to preserve their distinctive character. Such groups are defined in terms of their being distinct from the majority and, if they expand to the point of including the majority, this distinctiveness is obviously lost. The well-known transformation of exclusivistic religious sects into broad-based, church-type religious establishments illustrates the point. If a religious sect is successful in expanding its membership to include a large segment of society, it inevitably loses its distinctive character as a religious sect.

On the other hand, some social units require a large number as their minimal size. A crowd or a mass is a case in point. A gathering of only a few persons is obviously not a crowd. Also, the impersonal social forms established in bureaucratic organizations such as national corporations and armies could hardly emerge in small groups.

ALTERNATIVE FORMS OF GROUP FORMATION AND SOCIAL INVOLVEMENT

One of the inevitable consequences of increased group size is increased differentiation. Like Spencer, Durkheim, and other nineteenth-century classical theorists, Simmel recognized the long-term evolutionary transformation of society from small-scale simple systems made up of homogeneous elements to large-scale complex systems made up of heterogeneous elements. In addition, Simmel was interested in exploring the effect of this development on the dynamics of group formation, the nature of individuals' social involvements, and individual freedom. Briefly, differentiation helps to provide alternative bases of group formation and thereby partially releases the individual from domination by a single monolithic social structure.[32]

Simmel argued that the earliest and most primitive basis for group formation beyond the family is simply geographical propinquity. People who inhabit the same general territory develop social bonds on the basis of their common habitat. However, as heterogeneity increases, alternative bases of group formation emerge because of expansion in group size and development of a division of labor. Individuals can choose to establish social bonds with those whose occupation or interests are similar, thereby separating themselves from others in their common geographical area and making possible the establishment of social bonds that transcend geographical areas. For example, the emergence of a military organization as a differentiated social unit may stimulate its members to unite to pursue their particular interests as military personnel; similarly, farmers may unite as farmers and traders as traders. Although geographical propinquity does not become irrelevant, it must compete with other bases of group formation. Common interests as a basis for group formation require the employment of rational criteria; that is, individuals *choose* others with whom to associate on the basis of a rational assessment of objective interests instead of relating unreflectively to those who happen to be spatially close.

There are numerous alternative criteria that can be used in establishing social bonds in a complex, highly differentiated society. Some seem to be objectively given, such as sex and age. These objective criteria do not require a high degree of social complexity or abstract rationality, but they still represent social choices. Even in primitive societies the tribal elders might be consciously set apart for providing leadership on the basis of age and sex. A more abstract form of rationality is represented by criteria that rest on the sharing of a common point of view or set of values. Simmel discussed the social bonds between Renaissance humanists that rested neither on objective physical criteria, common utilitarian or economic interests, or even a single intellectual ideology, but on a common commitment to the intellectual life generally and intellectual independence.[33] Similarly, universal religions make their appeal to individuals as human beings independently of their family bonds, nationality, ethnic or racial group membership, and economic or occupational interests; the resulting social bonds are thus based on the common religious experience or beliefs. The religious community is, therefore, a socially contrived one as opposed to being based on objective criteria such as age, sex, or geographical propinquity.

As society becomes more and more complex, the alternative bases of group formation become more and more abstract and rational (although they do not replace the earlier, more primitive types of social bonds). For example, in the early days of the labor union movement, workers who had identical occupations in the same factory might join together. Later, persons with *different* occupations who work for the same employer might unite or, alternatively, persons might join with others who have the *same* occupations but work for *different* employers in widely scattered locations. Eventually, all those who work in the same type of industry might unite to pursue their common interests. Finally, perhaps, they might join with others (or at least feel a solidarity with others) who work for wages in any occupation or industry. Thus a specific occupation in a specific place is gradually replaced as a basis for group formation with the abstract idea of wage laborer. In a complex society with a high degree of differentiation and a purposive or rational approach to social organization, there is no limit to the extent to which individuals can devise criteria on the basis of which they can unite to further some shared purpose.

Multiple-Group Involvements and Individual Freedom

The nature of the individual's involvement in society varies according to the degree of its complexity. With the increase in the number of bases for group formation, the probability increases that individuals will belong to a multiplicity of groups. However, each group involves a specific and limited purpose and so claims only a specifically defined aspect of the individual's personality instead of the individual's total personality.

Thus, multiple group membership is accompanied by limited involvement in each group. Although there may be instances of conflicting demands in specific situations, these two patterns—multiple group membership and limited involvement in each group—generally are sociologically compatible and, in fact, define the typical nature of individuals' involvements in a complex society. It is often noted that people today may belong to many different groups, including their family and kinship groups, a neighborhood clique, a social or fraternal organization, a church, a political party, the organization in which they are employed, and their labor union or professional association. Each has its specific claim on the individual, but the claim of each is limited so that the individual can balance these competing claims and integrate them in his or her own personality. This type of social involvement (i.e., segmental or limited involvement in a variety of different groups) is the basis for the image of the modern person as being at the intersection of numerous crosscutting social circles.

Simmel suggested that this type of social involvement contrasts sharply with the patterns of social involvement of earlier historical periods. In primitive societies individuals were immersed in an extremely limited number of primary groups, such as family, clan, or tribe, with their whole personalities. There was little room for deviation from the expectations of these primary groups and little opportunity for the individual to become differentiated from others in the group. Instead, the individual was dominated in most life activites by the shared customs and demands of the group and, because of the high homogeneity within the group, individuality was undeveloped.

By medieval times, patterns of social involvement had become more complex because of the increased complexity in the patterns of group formation. However, the individual was still considered indivisible as a personality; that is, the various groups in which a person might participate were so related to one another that participation in one implied participation in certain others. The idea that an individual could have multiple group involvements that were completely differentiated from one another would not have seemed feasible. A common pattern was for the individual to belong to a local group and, through this involvement, he or she would also belong to a wider association. In other words, the individual's link to large and inclusive associations was mediated through involvement in smaller local groups. Thus the various groups to which a person belonged formed a series of concentric circles, with the individual as their nucleus. A contemporary example of this type of multiple-group involvement would be a person who is a member of a labor union local, through which he or she is simultaneously linked to a regional, national, and even international federation.

Individuality and social heterogeneity differ significantly according to whether the individual's social involvement is based on a small number of homogeneous local social circles (as in the primitive pattern), a series of concentric circles extending from local groups to wider associations (as in the medieval pattern), or a multiplicity of independent social circles that intersect solely within the individual's own personality (the pattern of modern urban society). The latter pattern provides much more opportunity for individuality to develop. As the number of different groups with which individuals may affiliate multiplies, the probability decreases that any two individuals will belong to exactly the same set of groups or associations or hold exactly the same positions in these various groups. The uniqueness of the specific set of social circles to which an individual belongs promotes and expresses the emergence of a unique personality. The resulting social heterogeneity contrasts sharply with the homogeneity of individuals within the small-scale and limited social circles of primitive times.

Moreover, individual freedom and autonomy are enhanced in the modern pattern because the individual is able to resist being completely absorbed in any one group. The demands of each group can be balanced against the demands of all the others. Of course, some groups require a much heavier degree of personal commitment than others; families, occupational groups, and some religious groups are examples of such high-priority groups. Even here, however, the individual may choose many aspects of his or her involvement in such groups as opposed to being assigned on the basis of tradition or spatial proximity. Moreover, one's involvement with local neighborhood or community groups or with extended kin can be as extensive or as minimal as one chooses. Although the family does not reflect the shift to rationally specified and limited objectives to the same degree as various larger special interest associations, even the family's functions are more limited than in the past.

Another consequence of multiple-group participation is the enrichment of the personality that results from the wide range of social experiences provided by the different groups to which an individual belongs. Each group makes possible the unfolding or the development of a different aspect of the personality. There is therefore a fuller development of the various potentialities of the individual than when the range of social involvements is more limited. For example, a person who is a subordinate in one group (e.g., occupation) may be a leader in another (e.g., church or social club). The individual is no longer bound to just one overwhelming type of role in a narrowly circumscribed social circle; instead, one can develop a complex repertoire of different roles that corresponds to the various groups in which one is involved.

The increased functional specificity of various social roles promotes increased impersonality in interpersonal relations. Individuals relate to one another not on a diffuse basis involving their total personalities, but in terms of specific goals and interests. In other areas their knowledge of one another may be quite limited. Perhaps nowhere is this impersonality more pronounced than in the market system in which buyers and sellers may conduct business with one another with practically no personal knowledge of one another.

The Significance of Money for Social Relations

The functional specificity, the rationality, and the impersonality of many modern social relations are symbolized and facilitated by money. Simmel developed this idea in an essay entitled "The Philosophy of Money."[34] As an objective and standardized measure of value, money makes it possible for grossly dissimilar products or services to be compared with one another to establish their relative worth in exchange transactions. As a general medium of indirect exchange, money also makes possible a tremendous expansion in the range of transactions that becomes feasible. No longer are individuals limited, as in the barter system, to exchanging goods or services according to their immediate needs; instead, a product or service can be exchanged for money, which can subsequently be used in another exchange transaction with a different person. Money enables individuals to transcend their immediate needs in their economic transactions and to engage in transactions with numerous others with whom direct exchange or barter would not be feasible.

In addition, since money is an objective measure of value, its use promotes increased rationality in interpersonal transactions. Monetary evaluation of products or services requires that decisions be made as to their worth relative to the worth of other products or services. This encourages conscious calculation of the precise outcomes of exchange transactions independently of the personalities of those involved. In comparison, informal understandings of mutual rights and obligations, which characterized the traditional, diffuse social relations of earlier, less complex social structures, seem extremely vague and unreliable as a basic for complex exchange transactions between persons not well acquainted with one another. Meticulously drawn up written contracts replace informally shared understandings based on custom.

Moreover, the pervasive influence of money in modern life results in a tendency for individuals' worth as persons to be evaluated in monetary terms. Although this is a constant source of criticism of modern life, it is an inevitable consequence of the crucial role that money plays in exchange transactions. In the marketplace a seller may know nothing about a buyer except that the buyer has the necessary money (or equivalent credit). More generally, people who know each other on only a limited personal basis often tend to make superficial summary judgments about one another on the basis of how much money they earn or have saved or how many material commodities they have been able to accumulate. Thus, paradoxically, monetary considerations may inhibit the development of interpersonal relations even while extending their range.

Money may also promote individual freedom—at least for those who have enough of it. In this respect, its sociological effect is similar to limited and multiple-group involvements. In a society dominated by monetary considerations the trend is for every conceivable product, service, or personal experience to be offered for sale. Persons with a lot of money may take advantage of this trend and extend the range of their experiences in whatever way they choose. Individuals' life-styles are set not so much by custom and tradition as by the financial resources they have to purchase the various accoutrements necessary for the life-style of their choice.

In summary, the social forms dominant in modern life differ significantly in a variety of ways from the social forms dominant in earlier historical periods. Part of the difference is due to the increased numerical scale of modern life and, therefore, can be related to the effect of numbers on social forms, as discussed earlier. Simmel was aware of both the advantages and the disadvantages of modern forms of social organization. As he showed, individual freedom has increased, but at the expense of the security of close-knit social bonds. In the same way, the type of culture that develops in a large, complex society also has its distinctive advantages and disadvantages. The next section will examine Simmel's ambivalent view of modern culture.

INDIVIDUAL CREATIVITY VERSUS ESTABLISHED CULTURAL FORMS

In this section we return to the distinction discussed earlier between form and content so as to portray Simmel's dialectical analysis of culture. Stated briefly, culture is the product of human beings' creative activity; paradoxically, however, once cultural forms come into existence, they may inhibit continued creativity. There is thus an inherent tension between the subjective life process as it continually seeks to express itself creatively and the objective cultural forms that necessarily result from this creative activity.

Moreover, the development of individuals' creative potentialities requires them to internalize already existing objective cultural products in their subjective consciousness; yet this subjective appropriation is seldom complete and may, in fact, lead to tension between the ongoing creative life processes of the subjective consciousness and the inherent logic and dynamic of the objective cultural forms themselves. The dialectical interplay between the subjective life process and objective cultural forms gives rise to Simmel's idea of the "tragedy" of culture. The tragedy lies precisely in the fact that the development of objective cultural forms may, by their own intrinsic logic, eventually inhibit the very life process that brought these forms into being.[35]

Simmel's analysis of cultural forms is somewhat more abstract and philosophical than his analysis of social forms. In "The Conflict in Modern Culture," for example, he speaks of the flow of life itself (as opposed to its various contents) creating various channels or boundaries for its development and then immediately struggling to transcend these boundaries. He cites Schopenhauer and Nietzsche as two philosophers who recognized the importance of focusing on life itself as opposed to its various contents or manifestations in art, philosophy, literature, legal and political systems, religion, and science. Simmel seemed to picture the life process as a dynamic, pulsating energy force that cannot express itself except by creating various objective forms for its expression. However, these forms necessarily become static and constrictive. As a result, the life force must continually struggle against the forms that it has created, resisting imprisonment by them and struggling to transcend them.

Although this analysis is more abstract and philosophical than Simmel's analysis of social forms, in one sense it is parallel. As we saw in analyzing the effect of numbers on social forms, large, formalized groups seem to take on the character of an objective entity that transcends and dominates the individuals involved. In the same way, the culture that individuals create as an expression of their subjective consciousness becomes objectified in forms that seem to be independent of and to transcend the individual. Subsequently, these objectified forms mold and shape the subjective consciousness, sometimes constraining and limiting its continued creative expression. For example, just as individuals create organizational rules to which they subsequently subject themselves, they also create literature, art, or music that subsequently becomes reified as a pattern that must be imitated whether or not it corresponds with the creative impulse.

The Struggle to Be Creative

Simmel developed this idea by analyzing numerous examples of the tension between established cultural forms and the subjective creative impulse.[36] In art, for example, the school of expressionism represents a rebellion against the idea that art is merely a representation of fixed objective forms and strives to portray the creative impulses and feelings of the artist's subjective consciousness as independently of fixed forms as possible. In philosophy, Simmel discusses pragmatism as an effort to reunite the search for knowledge with the actual life process; as such, it can be seen as a reaction against the goal of seeking knowledge for its own sake divorced from real-life considerations. In the area of religion, history is filled with numerous instances of the clash between established forms and the "pure" religious feeling or impulse. In sexual relations, the subjective life process expressed in a beautifully spontaneous and intensely personal relationship between a man and woman is expected to be governed by the objective cultural form of the marriage relationship. Finally, in the area of economics, Simmel uses Marx's notion of the "fetishism of commodities" to point out that the material products resulting from human beings' creative activity become objects that seem to follow the impersonal laws of the market, apparently in complete independence of the wishes, intentions, or needs of their human creators. As a result, individuals feel estranged or alienated from their own creative powers.

Creative individuals who feel constricted or artificially constrained by established cultural forms can never simply throw away the existing cultural heritage and start again from scratch. One reason for this, aside from the impossibility, is that the growth and development of the individual's subjective life and its creative potential requires the individual to internalize at least some elements of the existing culture. A creative person may eventually transcend or even reject these internalized cultural forms in the process of creating new ones, but the existing forms are still relevant as the point of departure for creating new forms. In this process of internalizing the existing culture base, a person runs the risk that subjective creativity might be repressed and constrained to fit within these already existing forms.

Probably most students experience this paradoxical aspect of culture. During the college experience, students are introduced to the vast ''intellectual'' world of literature, philosophy, history, art, and science and are told, in effect, that their own intellectual growth and their individual creativity depend on absorbing much of this cultural material. However, as students become devoted to this task of absorbing existing cultural material, their creative impulses are likely to be gradually shaped and modified to fit the already existing forms.

Many highly educated people devote their creative lives to imitating already existing forms. Others, however, refuse to have their creative impulses constrained in this way. For these persons, even though they must begin with the existing cultural base, they actually transcend existing forms and create new forms. In the end, Simmel is optimistic that the vital life energy that is the source of cultural creativity cannot be constrained for long in the stifling boundaries of already existing lifeless forms but will transcend them.

Cultural Alienation

There is another aspect to the tragic paradox of culture that many college students have no doubt experienced. Persons who do not go to college and who have no aspirations for continued intellectual growth may never become aware of the vast ''intellectual'' world of philosophy, literature, history, science, and the arts. For them life consists mostly of coping with immediate, everyday practical concerns. Students, however, do become aware to some extent of the vast world of interesting and stimulating cultural objects beyond their immediate worlds. But the more they internalize of this larger cultural world, the more they realize that there are vast areas of it that they will never be able to internalize fully. In short, the more one learns, the more one realizes how much more there is to be learned.

In comparison to this vast cultural base, any creative contribution that the individual might try to add to it may seem utterly insignificant and trivial. As a result, the individual's own subjective life process with its creative potentiality becomes estranged from the objective cultural world. For many the constant challenge of mastering a portion of the already existing cultural base may deflect or discourage them from ever attempting to develop their own creative potential.

The degree of tension between objective cultural forms and the subjective life process is partly a result of the size and social complexity of society and the length of its history. In a small and simple society there is a good chance that almost all its members will be close enough to one another to share the same basic life experiences, customs and social values, and cultural symbols. Even though individual creativity might not be highly developed or strongly encouraged in such a society, if someone does produce a useful cultural innovation, it can be readily incorporated into the existing cultural base and understood by all.

As society grows, however, this degree of closeness and homogeneity cannot be maintained, just as we saw earlier in discussing the effects of numbers on social forms. With a larger population there will simply be more people adding their various creative contributions to the cultural base. This, in itself, makes it more unlikely that any one person will be aware of or able to absorb the contributions of all members. But beyond this, as the population grows and becomes more heterogeneous, not everyone will share the same social experiences or cultural base. Thus a cultural innovation in one specialized area may be neither understood nor appreciated by persons in other areas. Indeed, many creative contributions to the cultural base are simply unknown outside a narrow specialty.

In some instances, however, there is likely to be a vague and general awareness of creative developments occurring in many different areas, but these developments are simply not understood except by specialists working in the same area. When many persons in our society, even college graduates, read in the newspaper about the discovery of new energy waves from a star in space or a new biological break-through toward creating life in the laboratory, they may be appropriately impressed by these scientific advances but fail to appreciate their significance or even under-stand them fully. For such people, these developments are primarily objective culture, which they can not internalize to any significant degree and from which they therefore feel estranged or alienated.

Simmel's analysis of culture shows that objective cultural forms become dif-ferentiated from subjective life experiences just as, in his analysis of interaction patterns, forms of interaction may be detached from their contents. Both processes are important for grasping Simmel's image of the paradoxes in social life.

Summary

This chapter focused on the various forms of interaction analyzed by Simmel. His starting point was that social reality, including society itself, consists essentially of various forms of reciprocal interaction. In his view the most appropriate subject matter for sociology is the *forms* of interaction as opposed to the *contents* of interaction. Forms such as sociability and sexual flirtation demonstrate the importance of the distinction because these particular forms are pursued for their own sake without regard to content.

Several other types of forms were also discussed, including various forms of superordi-nation and subordination and the dynamic interdependence between conflict and cohesion. The forms of superordination and subordination differ according to whether subordination is under a single person, a plurality of persons, or an ideal principle. Similarly, the forms of conflict differ according to the degree of intimacy or mutual involvement of the parties in conflict.

Moreover, forms change in response to the numbers of persons involved in interaction. This was illustrated by the distinction between the dyad and the triad and by the growth of bureaucratic patterns as groups become too large for personal relations to be maintained between all members. On an even larger scale, as society becomes larger and more complex, there is a shift in the nature of individuals' associations toward limited involvement in many different types of groups; the effect of this is to enhance individuality and individual freedom.

At the cultural level, growth in the size and complexity of society leads to tremendous expansion in the number and type of cultural products created by the members of society. Individuals may feel overwhelmed by their cultural heritage, not fully understanding all aspects of it and yet dependent on at least a portion of it for developing their own individual creativity. Paradoxically, individual creativity may be inhibited by the forms represented in the established cultural base.

Even though Simmel did not create a systematic or comprehensive sociological theory, his emphasis on the forms or patterns of interaction is basic to the contemporary sociological perspective. For example, early in their sociological studies, students learn the importance of *normative conformity*. This simple example illustrates a social form devoid of specific content. Whatever the content of the norm—following correct rules of etiquette at a dinner party, arriving at the agreed time for a tennis match, or filling out income tax forms correctly and mailing them by the deadline—people in the variety of groups and situations exhibit normative conformity. Additional distinctions could be introduced, such as conformity resulting from a strong emotional bond with the group versus conformity out of fear of punishment, but this type of analysis is in the same vein. It involves distinguishing between different types (or subtypes) of forms independently of content.

Although many of Simmel's most famous sociological vignettes were at the micro level, he did not limit himself to this level. For example, his analysis of the formal distinctions between the dyad and the triad apply at the level of face-to-face interaction and also to relations between larger groups and in the market system. His analysis of social differentiation and individuality and of the dialectical conflict between objective cultural forms and subjective life experiences are also at the macro level.

Contemporary macro-level analyses of social structure as a complex set of interrelated and interdependent forms of interaction is consistent with Simmel's approach in the emphasis on general social forms and not specific contents. Many complex organization theorists devote themselves to comparative studies of different types of organizations because they recognize that despite differences in the *content* of the goals and objectives of various types of organizations, organizations can still be compared in terms of the basic underlying sociological forms that they exhibit. For example, business firms, government agencies, universities, and churches can be compared in terms of authority structure or communication flow in spite of the fact that the substantive content of the goals and activities of these organizations are quite different.

No doubt part of the reason that contemporary sociology is so close to Simmel's concept of what sociology should be is that this focus on interaction forms avoids the danger of reifying social structure. Early organic theorists such as Comte assumed that society and its institutions exist on a level separate from individuals and that society conforms to sociological laws of its own independently of the intentions or actions of its individual members. This approach involves the danger of reification, that is, assuming that society (or other social systems) exists as a real entity independently of its constituent members.

Simmel's study of interaction patterns avoids this danger while at the same time recognizing that social reality transcends the reality of the mere sum of the individual members of society. It was noted that Simmel provides a bridge between the realist or the organic image of social reality (such as Comte's and Durkheim's) and the nominalist image (such as Weber's). Sociologists today recognize that social reality consists precisely in the forms or patterns or structures of interaction and the results of this interaction in the creation of enduring cultural products.

In addition, Simmel's dialectical approach also provides a framework for dealing simultaneously with the opposing emphases of Durkheim and Marx. Durkheim's stress on solidarity and cooperation and Marx's emphasis on conflict can both be seen within Simmel's perspective as alternative forms that may exist simultaneously in dynamic tension. The specific mixture will vary in different situations, but Simmel's discussion of how conflict may be magnified in intimate relations or cohesive groups shows that these two forms are by no means independent of one another, or mutually exclusive.

Simmel's influence on American sociology was manifested in the focus of the early Chicago school sociologists on social forms and social processes. Some of his writings were translated by Albion Small and published in the *American Journal of Sociology*, a University of Chicago publication. The areas of study of the Chicago school sociologists were quite varied, ranging from social psychology to ecology to deviance to social organization and disorganization. But a common thread in the works of all of these pioneers was explicit recognition of the dynamic nature of social processes. Simmel's approach provided a strategy for abstracting from these ever changing social processes certain recurrent patterns or forms and analyzing the myriad way in which they occur in the incessant rhythms of social life.[37]

A major difficulty of Simmel's formalistic approach is that there seems to be no logical basis for achieving theoretical closure; the identification of different forms seems to be limited only by the sensitivity and imagination of the theorist.[38] Nor is there any clear-cut basis in the theoretical framework itself, or in the sociological subject matter, for choice of one set of forms over another.

Although identification of various social forms is undeniably a useful strategy for certain purposes, the nature of social reality does not provide any objective basis for developing any one exhaustive and comprehensive set of social forms. Instead, identification and analysis of social forms, like other theoretical strategies, must be seen as one useful option for some purposes, not the definitive key for understanding social reality.

The usefulness of this option is particularly apparent in the effort to abstract general principles from specific and unique interpersonal relations and in the effort to compare similar kinds of social processes in widely varying contexts and with widely varying types of groups. In some instances new areas of sociological study have been opened by the strategy of extending the use of a basic form from one established subfield to a newly emerging subfield. For example, the growth of the women's studies movement has borrowed extensively from the already established sociological studies of minority group–majority group relations, with the result that new insights have been developed in our understanding of male-female relationships in our society.

Simmel's focus on the micro or interpersonal level of social reality was similar to the symbolic interactionist theoretical perspective that developed out of the Chicago school. Moreover, his extensive reliance on widely varied, everyday examples to illustrate recurrent general social processes in a novel way is perhaps best paralleled by the recent development of the dramaturgic approach, represented in the work of Goffman. Symbolic interaction theory and the dramaturgic approach will both be explored more fully in Chapter 8.

Footnotes

1. Marx emphasized the interdependence between the social structure and the material environment. This interdependence is mediated through the economic structure and is reflected in his idea of economic determinism. The social process that he stressed as most basic is the process of class conflict. In contrast, Durkheim emphasized the importance of the common collective conscience as the foundation of the social order. He stressed cooperation, reflecting moral consensus, as the most fundamental social process. Although both Durkheim and Marx obviously recognized the cultural level and the individual level, the primary focus of both was on the social structure.

2. Simmel was 56 years of age at this time; the normal age for promotion to full professor was 40. See Lewis Coser, *Masters of Sociological Thought* (New York: Harcourt Brace Jovanovich, 1971), p. 197, fn. 33.

3. See Lewis A. Coser, ed., *Georg Simmel* (Englewood Cliffs, N.J.: Prentice-Hall, 1965), "Introduction," p. 3, and Nicholas J. Spykmann, *The Social Theory of Georg Simmel* (New York: Russell and Russell, 1964), "The Life of George Simmel," p. xxvi. I have relied heavily on these sources in this entire section.

4. Coser, *Georg Simmel*, p. 3.

5. Clinton Joyce Jesser, *Social Theory Revisited* (Hinsdale, Ill.: Dryden Press, 1974), pp. 188–189.

6. See Coser, *Masters of Sociological Thought,* pp. 195–196.

7. Spykmann offers a different picture of Simmel's reaction to the war; according to him, "Simmel himself remained objective and analytical," even though many contemporary intellectuals became passionate nationalistic chauvinists. See Spykmann, op. cit., pp. xxviii–xxix.

8. See Coser, *Masters of Sociological Thought,* pp. 191–193.

9. Ibid., pp. 212–214.

10. An alternative translated for this term is "socialization"; in this case socialization does not have the usual contemporary meaning of learning the culture of a society; instead, the word refers to the process whereby an individual becomes a part of society through interaction.

11. Spykmann, op. cit., pp. 271–272.

12. Georg Simmel, *The Sociology of Georg Simmel,* translated, edited and with an introduction by Kurt H. Wolff (New York: Free Press, 1950), p. 40.

13. Ibid., p. 41.

14. Ibid., p. 22.

15. Ibid.

16. Ibid., p. 23.

17. In Theodore Abel's interpretation of Simmel's approach, identifying "forms-of-interaction" should not be an end in itself; these forms should be related to other variables in propositional-type statements that portray certain regularities in social life. See Theodore Abel, *The Foundation of Sociological Theory* (New York: Random House, 1970), Chapter 4, "The Contribution of Simmel," especially pp. 78–85.

18. Donald N. Levine, "Some Key Problems in Simmel's Work," pp. 97–115 in Coser, *Georg Simmel*, p. 97–115.

19. Simmel, *The Sociology of Georg Simmel,* pp. 16-25.
20. Simmel's discussion of this historical transformation of society from a simple to a complex structure no doubt reflects the influence of Spencer, who had invoked the universal law of evolution to try to explain this broad historical process. See Herbert Spencer, *The Evolution of Society,* edited and with an introduction by Robert L. Carneiro (Chicago: University of Chicago Press, 1967).
21. Simmel provided an example of philosophical sociology in his discussion of the intellectual history of the eighteenth and nineteenth centuries. He contrasted the individualistic assumptions of eighteenth-century social thought with the collectivist assumptions of nineteenth-century social thought and pointed out the differences in their social and political implications. As he said: ". . . the 18th century doctrine of freedom and equality is the foundation of free competition; while the 19th century doctrine of differentiated personality is the basis of the division of labor." Simmel, op. cit., p. 83.
22. The discussion in this section is drawn primarily from Simmel, op. cit., Part Three, "Superordination and Subordination."
23. The notion that power, authority, or influence is a characteristic of an interactional process and not of an individual personality trait is a key feature of contemporary sociological theories of leadership.
24. Ibid., p. 216.
25. See Robert Michels, *Political Parties* (Glencoe, Ill.: Free Press, 1949).
26. The discussion of conflict in this section draws heavily from Simmel's essay entitled "Conflict," in Georg Simmel, *Conflict and the Web of Group-Affiliations,* translated by Kurt H. Wolff and Reinhard Bendix (New York: Free Press, 1955), pp. 13-123.
27. Marx emphasized the process of conflict as the most basic social process; appearances of unity or social integration were explained away, as it were, as the result of false consciousness in relationships involving inequality. Durkheim, on the other hand, focused on the social processes that promote social integration and cohesion. Although he recognized that conflicts do occur in social life, he tended to treat excessive conflict as an abnormal breakdown in the integration of society.
28. Stimulated by the pioneering analysis by Ernst Troeltsch in *The Social Teachings of the Christian Churches,* 2 volumes, translated by Olive Wyon (New York: Macmillan, 1931), sociologists of religion have been heavily influenced in their analyses of religious organizations by the general proposition that sect-type religious organizations frequently evolve into established church-type or denominational organizations. Being in a tolerant social environment is one of the factors responsible for this change. See J. Milton Yinger, *The Scientific Study of Religion* (New York: Macmillan, 1970), Chapter 13, "Types of Religious Organizations," for a discussion of the various factors that influence the relationship between religious organizations and their social environment.
29. Simmel, *Conflict and the Web of Group-Affiliations,* p. 111.
30. This analysis of the effects of size on interaction forms is drawn primarily from Simmel, *The Sociology of Georg Simmel,* Part Two, "Quantitative Aspects of the Group," p. 87-177.
31. Simmel also considered the case of the isolated individual. The isolated individual is almost never the mythical person on an island whose life is spent in complete solitude. Indeed, a person may experience social isolation even when surrounded by a crowd. Isolation is defined in terms of the absence of social relations or detachment from some

particular group, not physical isolation. Isolation often results from efforts to resist demands of a group that might threaten to engulf the individual's total personality. See also Simmel's essay, "The Stranger," ibid., pp. 402–408.

32. This idea is developed most fully in Simmel's essay, "The Web of Group-Affiliations," in Simmel, *Conflict and the Web of Group-Affiliations,* pp. 127–195. This section draws heavily on this essay.

33. Ibid., p. 135ff.

34. See Spykmann, *The Social Theory of Georg Simmel,* pp. 215–253. See also Simmel's essay, "The Metropolis and Mental Life," pp. 409–424 in Simmel, *The Sociology of Georg Simmel,* for a discussion of the compatibility between the emphasis on money in interpersonal transactions and many crucial features of urban life. The impersonality, the emotional detachment of people from one another, and the high development of individuality are also discussed as characteristic of modern urban life.

35. This analysis is developed in two essays entitled "On the Concept and the Tragedy of Culture" and "The Conflict in Modern Culture," both of which, along with several other essays in cultural analysis, have been brought together in a volume by K. Peter Etzkorn. See Georg Simmel, *The Conflict in Modern Culture and Other Essays,* translated, and with an introduction by K. Peter Etzkorn (New York: Teachers College Press, 1968).

36. Ibid., pp. 15–25, 42ff.

37. One example of this explicit focus on social forms is the distinction made between alternative forms of intergroup relations by Park and Burgess in their famous introductory text. These forms are: competition, conflict, accommodation, and assimilation. They are distinguished on the basis of two criteria: whether they are cooperative or antagonistic, and the degree of personal involvement with the other group. Obviously, the first two are antagonistic and the second two are cooperative. The degree of interpersonal involvement is at a minimum with competition and at a maximum with assimilation. See Robert E. Park and Ernest W. Burgess, *Introduction to the Science of Sociology* (Chicago: University of Chicago Press, 1921).

38. E. A. Ross, for example, identified and discussed thirty-two different forms, including stimulation, personal competition, sex antagonism, class struggle, adaptation, cooperation, stratification, gradation, equalization, selection, individualization, commercialization, professionalization, and ossification. See E. A. Ross, Principles of Sociology (New York: Century, 1920).

Questions for Study and Discussion

1. In your judgment, does Simmel's focus on forms of interaction succeed in resolving the realism-nominalism controversy? Why or why not?

2. If you were asked to serve on a committee, would you prefer serving on a large committee or a small committee? What factors would you consider before making your choice? What are the advantages and disadvantages of being on a large committee versus being on a small committee?

3. Would Simmel's views on alternative third-party roles also apply in larger systems, such as international relations, for example? What would be the similarities and differences between the relations among three interrelated nations and three interrelated individuals?

4. Why is conflict inevitable in social life, even in close, intimate relationships?

5. In what ways do established artistic or literary forms inhibit artists' or writers' creativity and in what ways do established forms promote individual creativity? Is it possible to strike an appropriate balance between mastering an existing culture and creating new cultural forms?

PART THREE

MAJOR SCHOOLS OF TWENTIETH-CENTURY AMERICAN SOCIAL THEORY: MICRO AND MACRO LEVELS OF ANALYSIS

CHAPTER 8

Emergence of Social Reality from Symbolic Interaction

Have you ever observed small children playing? One of the most interesting aspects of children's play is their ability to create a world of their own merely by definition. For example, a strip down the middle of the room may become a busy city street or an automobile racetrack, and adults who intrude are warned not to get in the way of the cars. A space on the floor next to the wall may become a parking lot, and blocks or old boxes might be transformed into stores, hospitals, police or fire stations, or skyscrapers. These definitions may be applied not only to the material objects with which the children are playing but to themselves as well. As they play they may be race car drivers, police officers, store clerks, nurses, or doctors.

These definitions need not necessarily be completely arbitrary. If the children are playing with realistic toys, their definitions may be influenced by the close resemblance between their toys and objects in the adult world. For example, a toy police car is likely to be used in children's play as a police car. However, children are not limited to such established definitions. If the owner of the toy police car decides to take part in an automobile race, the police car may be used as a race car. Similarly, a building block might be used as a toy hammer for pounding something or as a ball for throwing. Children are extremely creative in defining the objects in their environment in whatever way is appropriate for what they want to do.

The world children create for themselves in playing together is very fragile, easily disrupted by outside interference (such as parental interruption) or by disagreements within the group. The reason is that the definitions that create this world emerge through the process of interaction and are based on a minimal level of consensus within the group. Any disruption of the interaction process or any breakdown in consensus threatens to destroy the "reality" that had been created and to undermine willingness to continue playing the particular game. In many cases, even if only one child decides to stop playing a particular game, the whole game collapses.

The real world of adults differs from the make-believe world of children in many ways. It is a much more durable world, not being as vulnerable to breakdown resulting from momentary changes in mood or minor distractions. But this difference is not absolute; the adult world is also subject to disruption and breakdown, although not to the same degree in the short run. Also, the adult world seems not to be quite as arbitrary; definitions of material objects reflect the actual characteristics of such objects to a greater degree instead of reflecting momentary wishes. Again, this difference is not absolute. Probably most objects in the material environment can give rise to multiple social definitions or be used in a variety of ways.

There is at least one sense, however, in which the real world of adults is similar to the make-believe world of children. Both types of worlds largely reflect shared subjective definitions that emerge through the process of interaction. Just as children must negotiate with one another to transform their play area into a make-believe town, so must adults negotiate regarding the zoning of their geographical territory for commercial expansion, residential development, or other land-use patterns. In this way the physical resource of land is transformed by social definition into municipalities, commercial developments, congressional districts, farmland, wildlife preserves, and so on.

The idea that social reality emerges through the *process* of interaction is basic in symbolic interaction theory. In this respect symbolic interaction theory is similar to Simmel's emphasis on the forms of interaction, which we examined in Chapter 7. But symbolic interaction theory goes deeper than Simmel's overt interaction forms. As the name suggests, it deals with the *symbolic* medium through which interaction takes place. In the work of Mead, particularly, this involves analysis of the ability of human beings to create and manipulate symbols.

This ability is necessary for both interpersonal communication and subjective thought. Among all symbolic interactionists, the link between subjective symbolic processes and interpersonal interaction is emphasized, and the social reality that emerges from interaction is viewed as a contrived, symbolic reality. This differentiates *social* reality from the objective physical reality that is the subject matter of the so-called natural sciences (physics, biology, etc.). However, even our awareness of physical reality, plus our ability to communicate about it, is mediated through symbols.

The symbolic interactionist concern for the *subjective* dimension parallels Weber's insistence on understanding the subjective meaning of individuals' social actions. Symbolic interaction theory does not deal with the subjective level in the same way that Weber did, nor is it based explicitly on Weber's perspective. Also, while Weber moved beyond the analysis of individuals' actions and subjective meanings to deal with broad patterns of institutional and cultural change, symbolic interactionists, like Simmel, focus primarily on the micro level of interpersonal interaction.

Symbolic interaction theory can be extended to deal with the macro level. The socially contrived character of large-scale social institutions may not be as obvious as the contrived character of children's play worlds, but all social institutions are socially constructed. That is, they rest on shared subjective definitions developed through interaction. As a result, social institutions undergo change when there is change in the subjective definitions or patterns of interaction on which they are based. Some of the key concerns in symbolic interaction theory are the dynamics of face-to-face interaction, the close interdependence between an individual's self-concept and small group experiences, the negotiation of shared norms and individual roles, and other processes involving the individual and small-scale interaction patterns.

Since many of the key ingredients of symbolic interaction theory are drawn from the pioneering work of George Herbert Mead, major emphasis will be given in this chapter to Mead's contributions. The pioneering contributions of Charles Horton Cooley and William I. Thomas will also be discussed briefly. Contemporary symbolic interactionism is not a unified or comprehensive theory. Nevertheless, it provides a distinct image of the nature of social reality that sets it apart from other major theoretical perspectives. This image will be discussed along with differences of emphasis within symbolic interactionism. In addition, Erving Goffman's contemporary dramaturgic perspective will be reviewed. This perspective is comparable to symbolic interaction theory in that it stresses micro-level interaction processes and emphasizes the close interdependence between the self-concept and interaction strategies.

Role theory and reference group theory are less general theories than symbolic interactionism, but these theories also focus on the individual and micro-level social processes. Phenomenological sociology and the recently developed school of ethnomethodology are also congruent with symbolic interactionism in concentrating on subjective processes and the micro-level interaction processes that generate shared subjective definitions of social reality. Symbolic interactionism, however, is the major and most general contemporary perspective that analyzes the interdependence between subjective consciousness and interaction patterns at the micro level.

MEAD AND THE DEVELOPMENT OF SYMBOLIC INTERACTIONISM

Mead's interests were much broader than sociology or social psychology. He was an important representative of pragmatic philosophy, even though he was perhaps overshadowed as a proponent of pragmatism by John Dewey, his friend and colleague for many years at the University of Chicago. Mead's contributions to the development of the symbolic interactionist perspective in social psychology reflect this broader philosophical background.

As suggested in Chapter 1, pragmatic philosophy seems to be especially congruent with the American experience and culture. Pragmatism emphasizes the close link between knowledge and problem-solving action. This is consistent with American impatience with abstract speculation, which has no direct bearing on real-life problems. Also, the optimism and practical ingenuity that characterized the American heritage during the long phase of geographical, industrial, and commercial expansion is reinforced in pragmatic philosophy through the emphasis on people's abilities to cope successfully with their changing environment through flexible or innovative action. Mead's philosophical and sociological perspective reflects the influence of the larger American culture.

Biographical Highlights of Mead's Life

George Herbert Mead was born in 1863 in Massachusetts, but moved during his childhood to Oberlin, Ohio, home of the Oberlin Theological Seminary, where his father, Hiram, had been called to teach.[1] Hiram Mead had been a Congregational minister in Massachusetts. Through both parents Mead was heir to the legacy of New England Puritanism. Mead entered Oberlin College at the age of 16. According to Coser's biographical sketch on Mead, Oberlin was a socially progressive institution, but its curriculum and intellectual style were extremely traditional and dogmatic reflecting, no doubt, the influence of New England Puritanism.[2] Under the influence of Henry Northrup Castle, an Oberlin acquaintance who became a lifelong friend, Mead gradually rejected much of the religious dogmatism of Oberlin, but he retained the strong social concerns.

Mead's father died prior to his graduation from Oberlin. Mead earned his board at college by waiting on tables. His mother, Elizabeth Storrs Billings, began teaching at Oberlin and eventually became president of Mount Holyoke College. After graduating from Oberlin, Mead taught grade school for a short time, but he was dismissed after 4 months because he sent too many rowdy children home. This brief episode was followed by a 3-year period of employment with the Wisconsin Central Rail Road Company. Mead worked with a surveying crew that laid a line from Minneapolis, Minnesota, to Moose Jaw, Saskatchewan. During these years he read extensively and did private tutoring.

In 1887 Mead enrolled at Harvard University. His main interests at this time were philosophy and psychology. He was especially attracted to Hegelian philosophy through his teacher, Josiah Royce. Mead also became acquainted with the famous pragmatist, William James. According to Miller, Mead took no courses with James,[3] but Coser stated that he lived in James' home for a while and tutored his children.[4] Nevertheless, Miller contends that Mead and James did not become close personal friends, perhaps because of the status differences between them, and that James' pragmatic philosophy did not really have a substantial influence on Mead until much later.

After a year at Harvard, Mead followed the pattern of many students of his time and went to Europe for continued study. Henry Castle and his sister, Helen, had left for Europe several months before Mead, who met them in Leipzig. Although Mead had known Helen Castle for many years, he apparently saw her in a new light in Leipzig, and they were married in Berlin in 1891. While in Leipzig, Mead became acquainted with the work of Wilhelm Wundt, whose concept of the gesture was basic to Mead's own subsequent work. While in Leipzig he also met G. Stanley Hall, the well-known American physiological psychologist.[5]

In 1891 Mead returned to America and took a position as an instructor in philosophy and psychology at the University of Michigan, where he met John Dewey and Charles H. Cooley. Three years later Dewey was invited to head the Philosophy Department at the University of Chicago, newly founded and heavily endowed by John D. Rockefeller. Dewey accepted on the condition that he could bring Mead with him. From 1894 until Dewey left Chicago for Columbia University in 1905, Dewey and Mead maintained a close personal and professional relationship.

Dewey was generally the more influential of the two in his time, no doubt because of his more dynamic personality and prolific writing.[6] However, the Chicago school of pragmatism really stemmed from both men, probably owing as much to their mutual stimulation of one another as to a simple summation of their individual efforts. Mead's publications included only a few articles. His most influential works, however, were not published by him, but by his students posthumously. His students evidently recognized the brilliance and originality of the ideas he put forth so effectively in the classroom.[7]

Mead stayed at the University of Chicago when Dewey left for Columbia in 1905. Dewey maintained contact, occasionally returning to Chicago for a visit. In 1931 Dewey arranged for Mead to join him at Columbia but, before the arrangements for his move to Columbia were finalized, Mead died.[8]

Mead, a modest and unpretentious man, was quite at home in the dynamic urban environment of Chicago. Like the other Chicago pragmatists, he had a strong faith in the possibilities of social reform, and he involved himself in attempting to cope with the mushrooming social problems of a dynamic urban environment. Along with Dewey, he participated in the progressive education movement, even serving for a time as president of the School of Education's Parents' Association.[9] He also took part in many civic projects; he was involved in the City Club of Chicago and served as chairman of its Committee on Public Education and as its president. He was a friend of Jane Addams, and he helped support her work, providing settlement houses for immigrants or others deprived of adequate housing.[10]

Intellectual Influences on Mead

Mead was heavily influenced by Darwin's evolutionary theory. *Social* Darwinism was a major element of the social scientific perspective in America throughout Mead's lifetime. Mead was not a Social Darwinist, however, in the same sense as William Graham Sumner, for example. Specifically, Mead did not advocate a *laissez-faire* approach to the struggles between the strong and the weak, nor did he see social reform efforts as violating natural evolutionary laws. He did, however, accept the Darwinist principle that organisms are continually involved in attempting to adapt to their environment and that through this process the form or characteristics of organisms are subject to continual modification.

Mead's explanation of the mind, or human consciousness, is cast within this evolutionary framework. He saw the human mind as *emergent* in the natural evolutionary process. Its emergence enables human beings to adapt more effectively to nature. Through thinking, individuals can often bypass the trial-and-error procedure that usually occurs over the course of several generations in subhuman species. To use one of Mead's examples, the long evolutionary process whereby herbivorous animals such as cows developed a digestive system to digest grasses and grains is short-circuited in the human realm by the technology of refining mills and cooking. This emphasis on the practical, adaptive functions of human intelligence is consistent with pragmatic philosophy.

Mead's emphasis on progress also reflected the influence of Hegel and other idealistic German philosophers. Hegel's philosophy was based on a view of the dialectical unfolding of ideas, or forms of consciousness. The dominant ideas of each historical stage are not seen as permanent or absolute, but as contributing to the next historical stage, where they will be negated. This idealistic analysis differs greatly from the Darwinian emphasis on the flesh-and-blood biological struggle for survival through which species gradually adapt to their environment. However, in both views there is a strong emphasis on the process whereby old forms are superseded by new ones. For Darwin, the forms in question were biological forms; for the German dialectical philosophers, they were forms of consciousness. Also, even though German idealism differed substantially from American pragmatism, the dialectical view on the relativity of forms of consciousness or knowledge was compatible with the pragmatic notion that forms of knowledge should be expected to change as the environmental problems to which people must adapt change.

Mead's emphasis on *process* and the relativity of existing forms can be summarized as being drawn from three different philosophical perspectives: American pragmatism, Darwinian evolutionism, and German dialectical idealism. Yet Mead's work is not merely a synthesis of these three perspectives; it is a genuinely creative contribution in its own right.

Communication and the Emergence of Mind

Mead considered his perspective as social behaviorism.[11] This position was an elaboration of the behaviorism of Watson, which Mead considered incomplete. In seeking to establish psychology on a firm scientific foundation, Watson had insisted on focusing on overt behavior or measurable physiological processes. Behavior was explained in terms of conditioned reflexes, environmental stimuli, or physiological processes, all of which were capable of empirical measurement in principle.

In this view scientific psychology could not include states of consciousness or mental processes not amenable to empirical measurement. Although individuals may have subjective experiences, such as emotional experiences of fear, anger, and joy, without any obvious behavioral expression, Watson (and others committed to this view) would insist that such experiences must have some empirical physiological basis. The individual's subjective experience can be explained as an awareness of these physiological processes. For example, a person experiences fear when he or she becomes aware of rapid breathing and heartbeat, increased adrenalin flow, and constriction of muscles. Similarly, the thinking process could be the individual's awareness of subliminal vocalizations that perhaps could be empirically measured if instruments could be devised to measure tiny contractions of the muscles of the throat, just as, for example, persons can often be observed moving their lips as they read.

To many idealists, such as the German Hegelian philosophers, this empirically based psychology seemed to imply a superficial view of human beings. After all, much of the empirical work in the area had been done with animals. The idealists would insist that human beings are qualitatively different from subhuman species in that they are endowed with consciousness and mental abilities that are not controlled by, or even very well correlated with, physiological processes or environmental stimuli. Human beings can think, evaluate ideas, plan for the future, and develop moral and aesthetic sensibilities in ways that seem independent of physiological processes or environmental stimuli.

Mead's approach did not affirm or deny either of these two positions. His goal was to show that Watson's simple stimulus-response, or conditioned reflex, model was incomplete. Like Watson, Mead recognized the physiological basis of behavior and referred frequently to neurological processes. Like the idealists, Mead recognized the importance of subjective consciousness or mental processes not directly amenable to objective empirical measurement. He did not, however, see subjective mental processes as being on a level of reality qualitatively different from biological nature or physiological processes. In his view, the idealists failed to explain adequately the processes whereby the external world comes to be represented in individuals' subjective consciousness.

Mead's position was that perception of the external world, physiological processes, and subjective consciousness are all closely interdependent. The classic debate about the existence of a human mind somehow independent of physiological processes, its nature and location with respect to the brain, and the sources of its varying states of consciousness is simply bypassed. Mind or consciousness is not an entity that has to be located. These concerns divert attention from the functional significance of the mind. Mental processes are not reducible to the neurological processes within the brain, even though such processes are necessary for thinking. However, instead of concerning himself with such questions, Mead insisted that mind is a *process* through which individuals adapt to their environment.

Mind or consciousness emerges in the process of action. However, individuals do not act as isolated organisms. Instead, their actions are interrelated and interdependent. The process of communication and interaction whereby individuals influence one another, adjust to one another, or fit together their individual actions is not qualitatively different from the internal thinking process. Overt communication and covert thinking are like two sides of the same coin. In Mead's view both the idealists and the behaviorists neglected this social dimension. Unlike the behaviorists, Mead insisted that individuals' adaptation to the external world is mediated through the communication process, as opposed to being a simple reflexive response of the organism to environmental stimuli. For this reason Mead insisted that his position was *social* behaviorism.

Gestures versus Symbols in the Communication Process. The dynamics of the communication process can be illustrated in the "gestural conversations" of animals.[17] Mead's example of two dogs about to engage in a fight illustrates his point. One dog starts growling, baring its teeth, and bracing its body to lunge at the other. The second dog will respond (if it does not run away) by growling, baring its teeth, and positioning its body for defense or counterattack. The first dog will then adjust to the reaction of the second dog by repositioning its body, perhaps snapping its teeth, and the like. This will stimulate additional adjustive responses by the second dog. This process is a conversation of gestures. A gesture in this context is simply the first phase of a completed act. Each of the various preliminary body movements of the dogs (growling, baring the teeth, bracing the body to lunge, etc.) can be seen as the first phase of the complete act of attack or counterattack. Each dog, therefore, is stimulated by the first phase of an act of the other to make appropriate adjustments in its own behavior.

Human beings also communicate with gestures. For example, the adolescent gang leader involved in a quarrel with a rival gang leader may clench his fist or reach into his pocket for his knife, and this may stimulate a similar response from his opponent. Or an individual may lose interest in a conversation in which he or she is involved and stare off into space absentmindedly or unconsciously start to withdraw. In both cases, the initial phase of the act may stimulate the others to adjust their own behavior. There is no necessary intention on the part of the person to communicate a message. The person simply begins his or her own action, which stimulates the others to adjust their actions. Indeed, in some cases an individual may actually attempt to act surreptitiously; for example, the gang leader may try to conceal his withdrawal of a knife, or the bored conversationalist may attempt to appear interested.

Communication through simple gestures is the simplest and most elementary form of communication, but human beings are not limited to this form of communication. This is because human beings are able to become an object to themselves (as well as an acting subject) and view their actions as others might view them. In other words, human beings can reflect self-consciously on their behavior from the viewpoint of others. As a result, they can deliberately construct their behavior to call forth a particular type of response from others.

In the example of the dog fight, the dog does not growl or bare its teeth with the conscious intention of communicating the message: "I am angry or have hostile feelings." It simply initiates an attack. In the case of human beings, however, people may intend to show anger and hostility by deliberately clenching a fist or raising their voices without intending to follow through with actual physical aggression. Individuals know the response that such behavior will elicit in others because they know the response that they would call forth in themselves. Also, individuals are able to put themselves in the position of others and view their own actions as others view them; in other words, they become objects to themselves.

A gesture that calls out the same response in the person performing it as it does in the person to whom it is directed is a *significant* gesture. This common response is the *meaning* of the gesture, and the emergence of shared meanings makes symbolic communication possible.[13] Thus, the clenched fist becomes a symbol for anger or aggression or hostility, not just the first phase of a physical attack. Political candidates, for example, may clench their fists and raise their voices when describing their determination to beat their opponents, even though their opponents may not even be physically present.

There is an intrinsic connection between the symbolism of the clenched fist, the sentiment of anger or intention to attack, and actual physical aggression. The same connection between a gesture and the complete act that it symbolizes can be seen in other instances, such as opening one's arms to signify a willingness to be open to another person or to embrace, cupping one's hand over one's mouth next to another person's ears to signify a desire to share a secret, or grasping another person's arm in order to solicit his or her undivided attention. Students of body language have become adept at reading the messages that people convey to others, intentionally or unwittingly, by body posture and movements. Those who consciously employ body language to communicate a message are using the body as a medium of symbolic communication.[14]

The distinctive characteristic of human beings' symbolic communication is that it is not limited to physical gestures. Instead, it employs *words,* that is, vocal symbols that carry shared or standardized meanings. In contrast to physical gestures, vocal symbols can be experienced by the person using them in practically the same way that they are experienced by others (i.e., individuals can hear themselves talk). With physical gestures, on the other hand, people do not see their own gestures in the same way others do; for example, people can not be expected to clench their fists to express aggression toward themselves or to express self-satisfaction by embracing themselves.

In Mead's view, because of the fact that persons can experience their own vocalizations in the same way that others do, they can stimulate themselves in the same way that they are able to stimulate others.[15] For example, people crossing a street could not physically push themselves to get out of the way of a rapidly approaching automobile, but they could tell themselves, "That car is coming pretty fast; I'd better hurry." This ability to use vocal symbols enables people to see themselves from the perspective of others. It is crucial for the emergence of shared meanings, or shared responses to these vocal symbols.

The possibility for communication through vocal symbols with shared meanings opens vast possibilities for communication that are not possible through physical gestures or through the limited range of sounds of which nonhuman species are capable. One important reason is that there need be no intrinsic connection between a particular sound and the response that it symbolizes. To illustrate, there is no intrinsic connection between the phonetic sound of the word "anger" and the response it symbolizes as there is between the clenched fist and the response it symbolizes or stimulates. The connection is purely arbitrary. There are some exceptions; the words "buzz" and "pop" seem closely connected to the specific sounds they symbolize, but such instances are relatively rare. Whether intrinsic or contrived, the sharing of symbols and their meanings makes human symbolic communication possible.

Perhaps partly because there need be no intrinsic connection between the sound of a vocal symbol and what it symbolizes, human communication is not limited to the immediate here and now of sensory experience. Instead, human beings can communicate about objects or actions far removed in time and space.[16] Beyond this, they can create symbols that stand for abstract universal categories, in which case specific empirical objects are seen merely as instances or examples of the abstract category in which they are classified.[17] For example, human beings are not limited to pointing to specific chairs, trees, or whatever; they can construct a universal concept of chair, say, as an object for sitting that can be distinguished from tables, or they can construct an even more general category of furniture that includes both tables and chairs and that can be distinguished from machinery, for example. Similarly, the physical action of sitting in a chair can represent any one of a number of different responses, such as relaxation following strenuous activity, intention to remain in a home for a visit, subordination in a social relation (as when a parent commands a child to sit down), or occupancy of a leadership position (such as sitting in a chair at the head of a table), all of which can be symbolically distinguished, even though the same physical action is involved in each case.

In short, the human capacity for using shared vocal symbols makes possible a tremendous elaboration and refinement of communication far beyond what would be possible through physical gestures alone. Indeed, this capacity means that the world in which human beings live is not just a physical world; it is also a contrived symbolic world. It includes not only physical or biological objects such as land, water, trees, and other people; it also consists of residential or congressional districts, forest preserves, and city boundaries; politicians, musicians, business people, and students; traffic rules and legal codes, career paths and organizational structures, artistic styles and philosophical ideas; in short, it is a cultural world. Its creation and maintenance rest on the human capability of creating, manipulating, and communicating through symbols.

The Thinking Process. Just as human communication involves symbol manipulation, so does subjective thinking. In Mead's view, the connection between communication and subjective consciousness is so close that the subjective process of thinking or reflection can be seen as the covert side of communication. It involves carrying on an internal conversation with oneself. This conversation is not isolated from people's social involvements or their overt behavior. For example, in carrying on a conversation, individuals will plan what they are going to say and how they are going to say it prior to the overt utterance in light of the anticipated reaction of the other party. In many cases, they may covertly think through several alternatives, particularly if the others involved are seen as likely to misunderstand a more spontaneous statement. This subjective thinking process involves shifting back and forth between one's own perspective and the perspective of the others involved.

Individuals are not necessarily conscious of going through this process. Also, the expectation that one should say something instead of remaining silent may preclude a thorough evaluation of many alternatives. Persons often say things without thinking that they later regret because of the misunderstandings unintentionally created.

This same kind of process also applies to individuals' efforts to cope with problems in their environment. In line with his pragmatic philosophy, Mead emphasized that the thinking process is initiated or stimulated by the appearance of a problem or, more specifically, an obstacle that blocks individuals' actions to meet their needs or goals. This blockage stimulates a covert process of constructing tentative solutions to the problem. The individual may think through a series of alternative solutions and attempt to evaluate their probable consequences before finally enacting one that is expected to be satisfactory.

People are not always completely rational in thinking through alternative solutions or in selecting the most efficient or most effective alternative. Several factors might undermine rationality, one of which may be the pressure to do something about the problem immediately, before there is sufficient opportunity to identify and evaluate better alternatives.[18] Subsequently, if the same kind of problem or blockage occurs again, the individual may simply repeat the solution that worked earlier, with only a minimal degree of reflection or interruption of the ongoing flow of activity.

The problems that stimulate the thinking process may be extremely varied. Problems may occur in the physical environment that interrupt ongoing behavioral routines, such as when the car fails to start or one discovers that a book he or she was going to read has been misplaced. In addition, the challenge for an artist or a writer to share a particular vision or idea can also be seen as a problem that stimulates conscious thought and eventual overt communication. Moreover, because human beings are reflective, the challenge of organizing one's various experiences and activities into a meaningful whole, expressing a consistent life-style or set of values, might also be seen as a problem requiring conscious reflection or thought.

Does *all* thinking involve symbol manipulation connected with overt communication or problem solving? Or are there other forms of thought that are more private in nature or are not oriented toward problem solving? Certainly there are aspects of individuals' subjective experience that cannot be fully shared with others. If we reflect on our own subjective thought processes, we recognize that these processes are not limited to conscious problem solving. Much of our thought patterns in routine, nonproblematic times probably consists of reverie, a series of unarticulated images that move across our minds in an almost random pattern. This semiconscious thinking may not even involve the use of words, as seems evident by the difficulty many people have in articulating a meaningful response to the challenges "A penny for your thoughts!" or "What are you thinking about?" Nevertheless, Mead's emphasis was on the kind of thinking that involves conscious problem solving or interpersonal communication.

Mind or consciousness emerges from the process of covert manipulation of symbols, particularly language symbols. Alternatively, mind *is* the process of internal or covert symbol manipulation. An essential feature of this model of human intelligence is that it involves self-consciousness. Human beings reflect on potential actions prior to enactment and evaluate them in terms of the anticipated consequences, including the likely reactions of others. This requires them to become an object to themselves (i.e., conscious of self or reflective).

A person's response to an environmental stimulus will vary depending on the particular need or impulse that is salient at the time and the nature of the ongoing activity in which the individual is involved. This is related to the human capability of *selective attention* and *subjective interpretation*. Individuals may focus attention on certain stimuli while ignoring other stimuli in their environment; the stimuli on which they focus will be defined and interpreted in terms of the kind of response that will satisfy their impulses, or latent plans of action. For this reason, the same environmental stimulus may have different meanings for different persons, or for the same person, at different times. That is, different behavioral responses may be elicited from the same stimulus because of differences in impulses, needs, or attitudes.

For example, a student might see a textbook on a desk as a reminder of an exam scheduled in the near future; the student's roommate, who is not taking the same course, might not see the book even when working at the desk on which it lies. After the academic term is over, that same book may become an economic resource for the first student to be exchanged for needed cash. To the teacher the book may be merely a source of exam questions instead of new information. For each alternative, the definition of the book is more than simply its sensory qualities of color, weight, shape, and texture. There is an interpretive phase between perception of the stimulus and the behavioral response that reflects the individual's particular needs and latent plans of action.

The covert symbolic processes that form the basis for subjective consciousness and interpretation of environmental stimuli were not dealt with in the stimulus-response or conditioned reflex models of behavior of Watson and other physiological behaviorists. Such models suggest that behavior is elicited by environmental stimuli in an automatic, nonreflective fashion. Thus, for example, Pavlov's dogs start salivating at the sound of a bell after being conditioned to do so without subjectively reflecting on the meaning of the bell. While human beings may also exhibit such conditioned responses, much of their behavior is symbolically constructed, not simply released automatically. Mead would agree that subjective processes depend on the complex neurological structure of the brain. But mind or consciousness is not to be equated with the brain as a biological entity.

Even though different people may respond to the same stimulus in different ways, social behavior involves establishing a minimal degree of consensus in definitions of objects in the environment so that individuals' attitudes and emerging lines of action can be fitted together in a genuinely social response. The influence of social definitions is crucial in view of the relative lack of specific genetic or instinctual programming of human behavior. Even the identity, or self-concept, of an individual will reflect shared social definitions. In the next section the relationship between social environment and self-concepts will be analyzed.

Self-Concepts and Social Organization

Subjective definitions are not limited to objects in the external environment. One of the most important definitional problems faced by human beings is the need to define themselves, particularly in relation to the others with whom they are involved. Indeed, a person's self-concept is probably the object of more self-conscious reflection than any single object in the external environment, including other people. So important is the self-concept that persons may sacrifice the fulfillment of many other needs, even basic physiological needs, to act in accordance with it.

In spite of the centrality of the self-concept in a person's subjective consciousness, individuals are not born with a self-concept. They gradually acquire a self-concept in the course of interaction with others as part of the same process through which the mind itself emerges.[19] Just as the thinking process consists of an internal conversation, so the self-concept is based on the individual covertly indicating to himself or herself the definition of self, or identity, expressed or implied in the reactions of others to one's own behavior. The thinking process involves self-consciousness; the self-concept involves self-consciousness focused on the self as the object.

The self-concept consists essentially of the individual's answer to the question "Who am I?" This does not mean simply being aware of one's own body or even of one's subjective experiences, feelings, and behaviors.[20] Persons frequently differentiate between their physical bodies and their self-concepts. For example, they may injure their body, but this does not mean that the self-concept is damaged or diminished; they may experience some sensation or feeling, such as pain or fear, without it becoming a component of their descriptions of self; or they may engage in random behavior, such as shuffling their feet absentmindedly, without any consciousness of the self expressing itself through that behavior.

Mead insists that the self-concept consists of the individual's consciousness of his or her particular involvement in a set of ongoing social relations or in an organized community.[21] This self-consciousness results from a covert reflective process in which the individual views personal, or potential, actions from the standpoint of the others with whom the individual is involved. In other words, the individual becomes an object to himself or herself by taking the position of the others and assessing his or her own behavior as they would. This assessment involves an effort to predict the responses of the others and an evaluation of these responses in terms of their implications for the individual's very identity. For example, a sergeant in the military service may not be content simply to have his orders obeyed; instead, his tone and volume of voice and general bearing will be such as to insure that those under him not only obey, but also fear him and recognize him as a tough and demanding sergeant. Similarly, a politician may deliberately refrain from using his usual salty and vulgar language when making a public speech because he does not want the public to see him as a crude person who would use such language.

The "I" and the "Me" as Dimensions of the Self-Concept. The self-concept is not limited to people's passive perceptions of the reactions and definitions of others. Individuals are also acting subjects. An important part of Mead's discussion had to do with the reciprocal interplay between the self as object and the self as subject.

The self as *object* Mead refers to as the "me"; the self as acting *subject* is referred to as the "I."[22] The "I" is the nonreflective aspect of the self. It does not include memories of past actions or anticipations of future ones. It is the actual behavioral response of the individual in the present moment of existence to the demands of the situation considering current needs or plans. As soon as an action is completed, however, the memory of it becomes part of the "me" of the self-concept. The individual looks back to the action just completed and reflects on its implications for his or her identity. In this reflective process, the individual will evaluate the completed action from the standpoint of others. Similarly, in planning future actions, the individual is involved not in overt action, but in covert anticipation of the potential results. Again, this includes efforts to anticipate the reactions of others in terms of their implications for the self-concept. The self as acting subject (the "I") exists only in the present moment of action.

The relationship between the "I" and the "me" is one of dynamic interdependence. To a large degree, an individual's overt actions will express the "me." The individual covertly assesses the environmental situation in terms of the shared attitudes or potential responses common to the group, takes note of his or her own particular position in the ongoing activity, and prepares to call out in himself or herself the responses to the situation that he or she believes will fit in with the anticipated actions of the others. Thus, for example, a high school student who is generally considered a bright and well-behaved student will inhibit the desire to engage in boisterous play during a class period and will exert the discipline to do class assignments because he or she perceives that this is the behavior that the teacher and other students expect. On the other hand, a student who develops the reputation for being the class clown will be attentive to opportunities to live up to this reputation.

But even though the overt behavior of the "I" is heavily influenced by the definitions of others incorporated into the "me," the "I" is not completely determined by the "me." Instead, the "I" is the aspect of the self in which there is room for spontaneity and freedom.[23] Even though an individual may carefully reflect on a given line of behavior prior to its enactment, there will frequently be some aspects of the actual performance that are not completely predictable on the basis of the individual's prior covert rehearsal. This lack of complete predictability may be due to a variety of factors. There may be unforeseen changes in the environment or in the behavior of other people that prevent the individual from carrying out a line of behavior as planned; the individual may make a mistake or may lack the physical skills or mental concentration that would insure a completely flawless (or completely predictable) performance; or, in the excitement of performing some action in a tense situation, the individual may actually surprise himself or herself and others by a more outstanding performance than usual.

Whether better or worse than anticipated, the performance becomes part of the person's memory as soon as it is completed and may lead to modification of the "me" aspect of the self-concept. After its completion, the individual reflects on the performance, and on the reactions of others to it, in terms of its implications for the self-concept. For example, a player on a sports team who surprises himself or herself and others with an outstanding performance will begin revising his or her self-concept upward. One surprising performance will not lead to permanent revision of the self-concept but, if the individual manages to enact a series of surprising performances, he or she will gradually be considered an outstanding or heroic player. Conversely, an outstanding player who is unable to live up to a good reputation will slip from that exalted rank. Certainly Mead's position is not one in which the attitudes and expectations of others influence behavior in a deterministic fashion. Mead's analysis of the "I" provides a large area for freedom and spontaneity. Also, his analysis of how the "I" affects the "me" shows how the novel or unique dimensions of behavior lead to gradual modification of the self-concept.

The spontaneous and unpredictable aspects of individuals' behavior are a major source of innovation and change in the attitudes of the members of the group or community. Another source of social change is provided by persons, perhaps outsiders or newcomers, whose attitudes and responses differ in some respects from those that are dominant within the group. In other words, the "me" dimension of the self-concepts of these persons will be incongruent to some degree with the expectations of the others involved. The result is that the individual opposes or tries to change their expectations.[24]

One of the major reasons for this incongruence may be that a person's attitudes were derived from some group other than the one in which he or she is currently involved. In many cases, the deviant identifies with a wider or more comprehensive community than that of the immediate group. The widest community with which an individual can identify is that formed by rational thought. Identification with the abstract community formed by rational thought leads individuals to evaluate their own responses and those of their associates in terms of criteria of rationality. This means that instead of simply incorporating the expectations and definitions of others in the group in an automatic fashion, individuals may criticize these attitudes and behaviors as irrational and attempt to promote change.

Stages in the Development of the Self-Concept. Although the process of social learning continues throughout life, Mead emphasized the stages through which children move as they gradually acquire a self-concept that links them to the ongoing social life of their families and other groups and, eventually, of the overall community. This process can be readily observed in any typical family with a new baby. Over and over again the proud father will tell his infant daughter that she is "daddy's little girl," and then he will reward her profusely when she repeats the statement or behaves appropriately. In short, the infant is given a social identity by the parents and is then treated in such a way as to call out and reinforce the responses appropriate to this identity. Through this process, the child learns the rights and responsibilities that go along with this identity and the responses of the parents in relation to the child. Thus ''daddy's little girl'' is repeatedly told that children should obey their parents, should not eat candy just before mealtime, should share their toys with playmates, and so forth.

The identities offered to children gradually change as they grow and acquire more physical and social skills and as their social world expands. When the child is old enough to play with peers, the identity of playmate or friend will be added to that of child (or son or daughter). When the child starts kindergarten, the identity of student will be added. As the child advances in age, there will be additional corresponding changes in identity. These various identities influence behavior as a result of the development of the ability to monitor one's impulses and to evaluate one's potential behavior from the standpoint of others. Parents and teachers assist in this process when they urge the child to think of what some other person, such as a friend, would think of some line of behavior (e.g., ''You'd want your friend to share his toys with you, wouldn't you?'').

Mead distinguished among at least three different phases of this process whereby individuals learn to take the perspective of others and look at themselves as objects.[25] First is the *play* stage in which the individual ''plays at'' someone else's social role. For example, children will ''play at'' being a police officer, a doctor, a nurse, or various other roles that they observe others performing. Even this elementary ''playing at'' a role requires children to take the role of the other.[26] Children attempt to adopt the perspective and the attitude of the other in responding to a situation or in evaluating their own behavior, perhaps when playing at another role. For example, a little girl may play at her mother's role in trying to control her imaginary daughter's behavior; then she may play at the role of disobedient daughter, and immediately shift back to being the mother as she scolds the daughter for her disobedience. Or if the little girl has a playmate, the two of them may pretend that one is the daughter while the other is the mother. Even though children are pretending in such behavior, the play stage is important in a person's social development. It contributes to the development of the ability to stimulate one's own behavior from the perspective of someone else in a related role. In addition, children acquire an elementary sense of social organization, or of the way different roles are linked together.

At the play stage of development, children are capable of only a limited degree of social organization. They can engage in simple forms of play in which the number of different roles is limited and the need for overall coordination of different activities is minimal. Forms of play, such as hide and seek, tag, and pitch and catch, would characterize this stage. It is for this reason that large groups of very small children are practically never involved jointly in a common undertaking, particularly a long-term one. In the absence of some external stimulus (such as a teacher), the play of a large "group" of children will tend to be fragmented and disorganized. The corollary of this lack of external social organization is lack of stable internal organization of the self-concepts of those involved.

As children develop more social experience, the *game* stage emerges as the next crucial step in the development of the self-concept. The game stage is distinguished from the play stage in that there is a higher level of social organization. The participants in a game are able to take the role of several others simultaneously and to organize them into a larger whole. They go beyond relating to the others only as individuals and relate to them in terms of the common undertaking in which they are all involved. This identification with the common undertaking is possible in spite of the fact that each person's particular activity or role might be different from those of the others, as would be the case if there is a division of labor in the group.

The self-concept of each participant in the game will consist of the individual's subjective awareness of his or her particular role in the common undertaking, including perceptions of the expectations and responses of each of the others. For example, in baseball, each player must take into account the specific roles of each of the other players on his own team and on the opponents' team. Thus the pitcher and catcher will respond not just to one another, but to the batter, the runner on first, the outfield players, and so on. This distinguishes the pitcher and catcher in a baseball game from the situation of two persons playing pitch and catch.

Beyond this, the participants in a baseball game are also oriented toward the general rules that define the game of baseball, and they control their own actions (or attempt to) in terms of these impersonal rules. These rules determine the ultimate goal of the undertaking (to score more runs than the opposing team) and set constraints or boundaries within which this goal can be pursued. Indeed, the goal would be meaningless without the constraints, as is illustrated by the difficulty a young person may have in adhering to self-imposed rules in an improvised game of hitting the ball and running bases by oneself.

In Mead's terminology, when individuals control their own behavior in terms of general impersonal roles, they are taking the role of the *"generalized other."* This is the third stage in the development of the self. The "generalized other" consists of general expectations and standards, as opposed to the expectations of specific individuals, in terms of which individuals plan and carry out their various lines of action. To quote Mead:

> The organized community or social group which gives to the individual his unity of self may be called "the generalized other." The attitude of the generalized other is the attitude of the whole community. Thus, for example, in the case of such a social group as a ball team, the team is the generalized other insofar as it enters—as an organized process of social activity—into the experience of any one of the individual members of it.[27]

The concept of the generalized other is not limited to small-scale social events such as organized athletic contests. It can also be used to refer to the expectations and standards of the overall community or society. These expectations and standards may include specific customs and normative patterns or highly abstract ideals and values in terms of which people define their overall orientation and life goals. The generalized other may even transcend a particular group or community or even societal boundaries. For example, an artist, philosopher, or religious leader may consciously attempt to construct his or her lines of action in a way that calls out responses in others that will be expressive of their common humanity. Those who succeed are destined to transcend particular societal boundaries or historical periods. Individuals need not create a permanent cultural legacy (art, literature, etc.) to express the generalized other, however. Whenever individuals evaluate their actions or their lives in terms of universal values or the common human condition, they are, in essence, taking the role of the generalized other.

To participate in the common life of a group or society or of all humanity requires the individual to incorporate the shared perspectives and attitudes of this common life. However, individuals will reflect the common attitudes and responses from their own particular perspectives and backgrounds.[28] Individuals each have their own unique way of participating in the common life of the group or community, and it will be reflected in the emergence of certain unique aspects of the self-concept. With any division of labor, there will be, by definition, differentiation in the activities of the various members. As a result, individuals see themselves as unique. If there is a low division of labor, so that the contributions of all members are essentially the same, individuals may still attempt to differentiate themselves from one another in terms of the superior quality of their performance. If they are unable to achieve superiority, they may still take pride in the distinctive style of their performance. A person's distinctive contribution may stimulate greater ego involvement than the behaviors or attitudes that are common throughout the group and that are perhaps taken for granted as a result. For example, a baseball player may be only average in terms of batting ability but still take great pride in being by far the best pitcher on the team.

The effort to express a unique self-concept does not necessarily involve opposition to the common life and goals of the group. Individuals may identify strongly with the group, even to the point of being willing to make personal sacrifices on the group's behalf. As Mead pointed out, people may be able to enhance and enlarge their self-concept by incorporating into it the collective identity of the group.[29] The result is that members consider their group superior and look down on other groups as inferior. When this fusion between the individual and the group exists, the unique contributions of the individual enhance his or her status within the group instead of putting the individual in a position of opposing the group.

However, the unique dimensions of the self-concept do not necessarily always stimulate individuals to act on behalf of the group. Such contributions might be extremely costly, involving greater self-discipline or sacrifice than an individual is willing to make. Individuals may define their interests and needs in narrow or selfish terms and simply refuse to conform to the expectations of others, in spite of the social approval that is foregone as a result. This tendency will be much stronger in groups or societies in which individualism is encouraged than in groups or communities that stress conformity to the common attitudes and behaviors.

Taking the Role of Others as the Basis for Social Organization. In Mead's view, the internal (or subjective) organization of individuals' definitions, attitudes, and self-concepts and the external organization of groups, social institutions, and society itself are intricately interrelated and interdependent, since both internal and external organization emerge from the process of symbolic communication.[30] This distinguishes social organization in the human realm from the forms of social organization in the subhuman world that are biologically determined. In view of the flexibility of human beings' responses to their environment, the development of shared meanings and attitudes is crucial for social organization. Mead repeatedly emphasized the process whereby individuals take the role of others (both specific others and the generalized other) and control their own behavior in such a way that it fits within the framework set by the shared definitions and attitudes.

Moreover, no given form of social organization need be regarded as final. With the emergence of intelligence, human beings can self-consciously guide the course of social evolution. They can develop shared visions and goals for an ideal future society, and they can adjust their responses to one another to move toward such a future.

In short, social organization manifests human intelligence and choice. With the emergence of intelligence (or the ability to create and manipulate symbols), individuals can transcend many of the limitations imposed by their biological nature or the physical environment. They can, for example, construct shelters to protect themselves from weather extremes so that they can inhabit areas that would otherwise be uninhabitable. They can overcome the limitations of physical distance by developing sophisticated transportation technologies. They can build machines to lift loads that would be humanly impossible to life. To a degree, they can influence lower forms of life, such as cattle and crops, to insure an abundant food supply.

Although Mead focused more on the micro level of interaction than on social structure as such, he nevertheless showed how his perspective could be used in analyzing social organization. For example, both the economic institution and the religious institution can be understood in terms of the fundamental process of taking the role of the other.[31] In the case of the economy, the participation of buyers and sellers in the market presupposes that each can take the role of the other. In offering items for sale, sellers put themselves in the perspective of potential buyers. Similarly, the growth of universalistic religions is based on the idea that the religious person is able to take the role (at least to a degree) of any human being and to respond as to a neighbor or member of the same community.

Both economic and religious attitudes tend toward becoming more universal. Economic attitudes tend toward universality because any human being can be a buyer or seller; religious attitudes tend toward universality because of the religious belief that the unity of all people is based on their common human or spiritual nature. The economic attitude will be more superficial, while the religious attitude touches the deepest levels of one's identity as a human being.

Mead dealt with the growth of political democracy in terms of the development of the common attitudes on which it is based.[32] At the very least, democracy requires a willingness to transcend exclusive, castelike attitudes of group superiority within a society, particularly in the political realm. It presupposes a willingness on the part of each member to take the role of any and all other citizens, especially in terms of accepting their right to have an equal influence in the selection of political leaders. Moreover, the citizens must take the role of the political leader to understand the leader's behavior in terms of his or her responsibilities for the welfare of the entire society. The leader must also take the role of average citizens to see their needs and his or her own behavior from their perspective.

In a manner reminiscent of Weber, Mead pointed out that social organizations may be based either on personal relations or on a commitment to some impersonal goal.[33] In the latter case authority and other rights and responsibilities are allocated to individuals on the basis of their technical skills relevant to the shared goal. Like Weber, Mead saw the latter type of social organizations as manifesting a higher level of rationality.

The social psychological and sociological aspects of Mead's thought do not exhaust his intellectual contributions. As noted in the opening section, he was a pragmatic philosopher, and the philosophical position that he developed is worthy of study, even apart from its sociological implications. Mead was perhaps more thorough than any other contributor to symbolic ineractionism in attempting to establish a firm philosophical foundation for his sociological position. Nevertheless, there were other pioneers who contributed substantially to the development of contemporary symbolic interactionism. Some of the crucial contributions of two of them will be discussed next.

OTHER PIONEERS IN SOCIAL PSYCHOLOGY

The contributions of Charles Horton Cooley and William I. Thomas will be discussed in this section. Both of these theorists focused heavily on the individual and micro-level interaction processes and both contributed to establishing the foundation of American social psychology. Contemporary symbolic interaction theory is still indebted to their pioneering contributions.

Cooley: The Looking-Glass Self and the Primary Group

As noted earlier, Cooley and Mead were colleagues for the short time that Mead was at the University of Michigan. Cooley was born in Ann Arbor, Michigan, home of the University of Michigan, in 1864.[34] His family had migrated from Massachusetts to western New York and from there to Michigan. His father became an ambitious and distinguished lawyer who, in 1864, was elected a justice of the Michigan Supreme Court. Charles attended the University of Michigan, but his studies were interrupted by travel, both at home and abroad. Cooley received his bachelor of arts degree in 1887. He worked a short time for the Interstate Commerce Commision and the Census Bureau, but was drawn into academic life by his love of reading, writing, and contemplation. He did his graduate work at the University of Michigan, was eventually appointed to a faculty position there, and spent his entire professional life there. He died in 1929.

Thus, while Mead's ambience was the dynamic Chicago metropolis, Cooley's was the quiet college town of Ann Arbor.[35] This social environment was compatible with Cooley's withdrawn and contemplative temperament.[36] In many respects, Cooley's social theory reflects this temperament. Like Mead, Cooley's own values and ideological position were those of Midwestern progressivism and, like Mead and most other intellectuals in America at the time, Cooley accepted the basic principles of social evolution as the key to social progress. However, Cooley had severe reservations about Spencer's organic approach, partly because of Spencer's playing down of the individual psychological level in his insistence on evolutionary principles that transcend the individual.[37] Also, like Mead, Cooley did not accept the *laissez-faire* political implications of Spencer's theory.

Cooley's approach was organic, but his focus was the organic interdependence of individuals through the communication process as the foundation for the social order. Cooley's image of social reality was strongly idealistic, perhaps partly as a result of his New England heritage. He found much inspiration from the transcendental idealism of Ralph Waldo Emerson.

The title of Cooley's best-known work, *Human Nature and the Social Order,* suggests his basic theoretical approach. In the beginning, Cooley argues that the individual and society are organically interrelated; neither can be understood without the other. An individual's mode of life or patterns of behavior do not result from instincts or biological characteristics transmitted through heredity; instead, the human biological makeup is plastic and indeterminate, capable of being developed in various ways. The human biological heritage may include certain physical characteristics (race, size, etc.) and a limited number of basic unlearned responses (breathing, sucking, etc.), but the development of the individual as a human being with a distinctive personality and distinctive modes of behavior results from the influence of the social heritage transmitted through human communication.[38] Thus Cooley dealt with the dilemma of biological heredity versus social environment by insisting on the dynamic interdependence of both levels, but his major goal was to show how human beings are formed within the context of the ongoing social order. This emphasis on the organic interdependence between the individual and society is comparable to Mead's perspective.

The organic interdependence between the individual and society is revealed in Cooley's analysis of the development of the self-concept (the ''I'' of an individual). Although Cooley felt that human beings were born with a vague and unformed self-feeling, he emphasized that the growth and development of this self-feeling results from the process of interpersonal communication in a social milieu.[39] Its development, like the process of communication itself, rests on individuals' sympathetic understanding of one another. Through their imaginations, individuals can enter into and share one another's feelings and ideas. Particularly important is how people perceive that others see them. This is intimately related to a person's own self-feeling. Whether a person is pleased or disappointed with his or her appearance and behavior is largely a result of whether others are seen as approving or disapproving this appearance and behavior.

Cooley refers to this aspect of the self-concept as the ''looking-glass self.''[40] Each social relationship in which an individual is involved provides a reflection of the self that is incorporated into an individual's own identity. Since most people are involved in a multiplicity of social relations, each providing a particular reflection, people can be thought of as living in a world of mirrors, each providing its own particular perspective or angle. Some mirrors will provide a more accurate or acceptable reflection than others. A clear reflection is provided in the relationships in which people feel that others understand them well, including perhaps aspects of the personality that are not widely shared. Some of the mirrors may provide a cloudy or distorted reflection, such as when people feel that some other person does not really understand them. But individuals cannot escape these definitions of their identities that they see reflected in others.

Here is Cooley's description of the looking-glass self.

> Each to each a looking-glass
> Reflects the other that doth pass.
>
> As we see our face, figure, and dress in the glass, and are interested in them because they are ours, . . . so in imagination we perceive in another's mind some thought of our appearance, manners, aims, deeds, character, friends, and so on, and are variously affected by it.
>
> A self-idea of this sort seems to have three principal elements: the imagination of our appearance to the other person; the imagination of his judgment of that appearance, and some sort of self-feeling, such as pride or mortification. . . .[41]

The metaphor of the mirror is inadequate alone because the mirror cannot approve or disapprove, while the approval or disapproval of others is crucial.

There are numerous variations in the relationship between one's self-feeling and relations with others. People differ, for example, in terms of their sensitivity to the opinions of others; they differ in the degree of stability with which they maintain a particular kind of self-feeling even in the face of contradictory or conflicting reactions from others; they differ in the amount and frequency of social reinforcement that they seek to maintain their self-feelings; they vary in the particular mix of positive and negative feelings associated with their self-concept; and they vary in terms of which aspect of their lives is most closely connected with the self-feeling. Cooley analyzes such variations in his discussion of concepts such as pride, vanity, honor, humility, and other characteristics that are commonly used to describe individuals' personalities.[42]

For example, egotistical persons are not particularly sensitive to the social definitions or sentiments of those around them. Vain persons are overly sensitive and need constant social reinforcement for an exalted self-image. Productive persons must have an assertive self-concept; they need not be regarded as selfish, however, because their achievements may benefit others and earn their approval and respect. Self-depreciating persons are overly sensitive to the negative reactions of others, incorporating them into their own self-feelings to such a degree that positive qualities cannot be asserted.

Persons may find their self-feeling so out of tune with the prevailing reactions and sentiments of others that they withdraw, physically or psychologically, to cultivate an inner life of the self that will not be vulnerable to the discrepant reactions of others. Other persons may become so engrossed in some activity that they seem to lose themselves in it and are not conscious of the impression being made on others or of their reactions. Some persons, such as beauty queen contestants, will attach great importance to their physical bodies, while others seem oblivious to their physical appearance and define the crucial aspects of their self-concepts in terms of, say, their work or their ideological position. In spite of such variations, a self-concept emerging in complete isolation from the social environment without any awareness of the sentiments and reactions of others is unthinkable.

Persons' self-feelings are frequently extended to the various groups of which they are a part. Thus an individual may think or speak of "my family," "my club," or "my neighborhood" or of "our family," "our club," or "our neighborhood." As Cooley stated: "The group self or 'we' is simply an 'I' which includes other persons. One identifies himself with a group and speaks of the common will, opinion, service, or the like in terms of 'we' and 'us.' "[43]

The "we" feeling, the experience of unity between self and others, emerges first within the context of the primary group. Cooley considers the primary group to be the "nursery of human nature"[44] in that each individual actually begins life in the social world within the context of a primary group: the family. Also, it is the earliest and most primitive type of social organization and the only type that can be found universally. No matter how varied and complex the overall institutional structures of different societies might be, all societies have such groups as their nucleus.

Cooley describes primary groups as follows.

> By primary groups I mean those characterized by intimate face-to-face association and cooperation. They are primary in several senses, but chiefly in that they are fundamental in forming the social nature and ideals of the individual. The result of intimate association, psychologically, is a certain fusion of individualities in a common whole, so that one's very self, for many purposes at least, is the common life and purpose of the group. Perhaps the simplest way of describing this wholeness is by saying that it is a "we"; it involves the sort of sympathy and mutual identification for which "we" is the natural expression. One lives in the feeling of the whole and finds the chief aims of his will in that feeling.[45]

Examples of such groups include "the family, the play-group of children, and the neighborhood or community group of elders."[46] Friendship groups and many types of work groups could be added to the list.

Cooley insists that the unity of primary groups does not consist only of harmony and love with a complete absence of conflict.[47] There may be competition, conflict, and self-assertion in opposition to others, as even a cursory observation of most normal families would reveal. However, these individualistic or competitive impulses are tempered and moderated by individuals' sympathetic understanding of one another and by the shared sentiments that provide the unity of the group. Within the context of primary groups, individuals develop and learn to express their social sentiments, such as loyalty and willingness to help and cooperate with others.

Primary groups are also the foundation for larger institutional structures. As Cooley explains, "Primary groups are primary in the sense that they give the individual his earliest and completest [sic] experience of social unity, and also in the sense that they do not change in the same degree as more elaborate relations, but form a comparatively permanent source out of which the latter are ever springing."[48] In many cases, larger social structures will stimulate a simple extension of the primary group feeling to embrace the larger social unit. Thus, for example, patriotic Americans may experience a sense of unity through identification with the nation. Members of a church congregation may refer to their congregation as their "church family."

However, not all larger social units can stimulate this primary group feeling. Many social relations in larger structures will be of secondary rather than primary group quality. Secondary groups or relations are more impersonal in nature, reflecting the much lower level of interpersonal intimacy. In secondary groups, individuals relate to one another on a superficial level, perhaps in terms of specific contractual-type rights and responsibilities, instead of in terms of intimate familiarity with one another. However, when secondary relationships involve frequent or prolonged contact, they may gradually be transformed into primary relationships as the members become more and more acquainted with one another as individuals. Students of formal, bureaucratic-type organizations have repeatedly demonstrated that primary groups emerge and flourish within bureaucratic systems.

Larger social units, such as bureaucratic organizations or large-scale social institutions, rest on shared sentiments and ideas forged through the process of interpersonal communication. This emphasis on the subjective nature of social reality is reflected in Cooley's definition of social institutions. "An institution is simply a definite and established phase of the public mind, not different in its ultimate nature from public opinion, though often seeming, on account of its permanence and the visible customs and symbols in which it is clothed, to have a somewhat distinct and independent existence."[49]

Institutions may take on a seemingly objective character that seems to be independent of public opinion or individual sentiment. Just as an individual may persist in following a habit without reflection, a society may also follow a particular custom or institutional pattern that seems strangely out of accord with current public opinion simply because of tradition. Nevertheless, Cooley's overall emphasis is on the notion that society (its structure, institutions, normative patterns, etc.) exists in individuals' minds and feelings.

The public opinions and sentiments that form the basis for social institutions are not simply a summation of individuals' private opinions and sentiments. Public opinion is an emergent new level of social reality, a whole that is more than the sum of its parts. Public opinion emerges through interpersonal communication and, even though individuals contribute their individual parts to the total public mind, each person's part is shaped, to a considerable extent, by awareness of the opinions and sentiments of others. Cooley states that "Public opinion is . . . an organization, a cooperative product of communication and reciprocal influence. It may be as different from the sum of what the individuals could have thought out in separation as a ship built by a hundred men is from a hundred boats each built by one man."[50] Cooley's dream for modern democratic society was that the public mind of the entire society would be characterized by the same sense of unity and emotional warmth as the group mind of a primary group.

Cooley's emphasis on the organic interdependence between the individual and society, his focus on the social origins of the self-concept, and his stress on interpersonal communication as the foundation of social organization are comparable to Mead's. Nevertheless, Mead had certain reservations about Cooley's basic assumptions.[51] For one thing, Cooley assumed that there is a basic, innate self-feeling with which individuals are apparently born. Its reality is demonstrated by the ease with which first person personal pronouns are learned. Although Cooley's primary emphasis was on the way the self-identity is shaped and expressed in interaction with others, Mead took issue with the notion of an innate self-feeling, insisting instead that the self-concept itself emerges through the communication process instead of preceding it in any form whatsoever.

Mead also objected to Cooley's emphasis on the *feeling* component of the self-concept. In contrast, he emphasized the cognitive component based on individual awareness of one's actual position in the ongoing social process as determined by the definitions and reactions of others. Mead insisted that his perspective is a *behavioral* perspective, as opposed to Cooley's emphasis on the *subjective* level. Specifically, he stressed the ongoing social process in which individuals assess their actions, adjust to one another, and so on. Although this overt process was reflected at the covert or subjective level, the subjective level was not independent of the overt behavioral level. In contrast, Cooley emphasized the self-feeling and subjective sentiments and ideas expressed in overt interaction and behavior; however, he also recognized the influence of the overt social process on subjective sentiments. The issue, basically, is a difference in emphasis; certainly this difference should not be allowed to obscure the overall consistency between Mead and Cooley. Both were important pioneers in micro-level sociological analysis, and both are remembered today primarily for their work on the subtle interdependence between the self-concept and the small-scale social relationships that form the immediate social environment of practically everyone.

Thomas and the Definition of the Situation

Thomas is another important figure among the early American sociologists who focused on the organic interdependence between the individual and the social environment and whose ideas can readily be incorporated into the micro-level style of sociological analysis of symbolic interactionism. He was born in 1863 in rural Virginia.[52] His father was a Methodist preacher and farmer. William was still a child when he moved with his family to Knoxville, Tennessee, where he eventually enrolled at the University of Tennessee. Upon graduation, he taught languages at his alma mater for 5 years; then he went to Germany to study. After returning, he taught English and sociology at Oberlin College for 5 years. He then resigned to enroll at the University of Chicago, where his path crossed Mead's and Dewey's. Most of his career was spent teaching sociology at the University of Chicago.

Thomas' career was seriously disrupted at the age of 55 because of a scandal that led to his dismissal and the blacklisting of his name. The scandal was precipitated by a *Chicago Tribune* story stating that Thomas had been arrested by the F.B.I. for violating the Mann Act by transporting young women across state lines for immoral purposes. Although Thomas was known as a controversial and flamboyant figure, this charge had no basis in fact and, accordingly, was thrown out of court. However, the bad publicity resulted in the decision to terminate Thomas. Thomas then moved to New York. He lectured for a time at the New School for

Social Research, accepted a temporary lectureship at Harvard University (on Sorokin's recommendation), and continued his research. In 1926 he was offered the
presidency of the American Sociological Association (despite "old guard" resistance). He died in 1947 at the age of 84.

Thomas is frequently remembered for the monumental work he did with Florian Znaniecki, entitled *The Polish Peasant in Europe and America*.[53] This classic
research project dealt with the psychological and social adjustment problems of
Polish immigrants in their new environment in Chicago. Its general theoretical
implications are of much wider import, however, as is still recognized by students
of ethnic subcultures and minority group relations. Thomas' major theoretical contribution to the development of symbolic interactionism is his emphasis on the
importance of individuals' subjective definitions of the situation and the basic
principle, sometimes referred to as Thomas' theorem,[54] that "If men define situations as real, they are real in their consequences."

In his earliest work Thomas attempted to identify innate biological and
psychological factors that could explain human behavior. This is reflected, for
example, in the well-known set of four wishes identified in *The Polish Peasant:* (1)
desire for new experience, (2) desire for recognition, (3) desire for mastery, and (4)
desire for security.[55] Eventually, however, Thomas stopped trying to identify or
classify innate predispositions in this manner, and the situational analysis that he
ultimately developed is based on a different strategy that does not require assumptions about innate biological or psychological characteristics.

In developing his situational analysis, Thomas insisted that human behavior
cannot be adequately understood as simple reflexive responses to environmental
stimuli; instead, there is a process of subjective definition that is interposed between
the stimulus and the response. The response, therefore, is to a subjective definition,
not to the physical properties of the stimulus. The same stimulus may elicit different
responses from different persons or by the same person at different times if the
subjective definition of the situation varies. As Thomas said, "Preliminary to any
self-determined act of behavior there is always a stage of examination and deliberation which we may call *the definition of the situation*."[56]

During socialization, individuals gradually learn the standard cultural definitions of the typical situations they are likely to encounter.[57] In this way, individuals' behavior is gradually shaped by their social and cultural environment. There is
always the possibility for tension and conflict between the socially accepted definitions of the situation and the individual's spontaneous definitions. Spontaneous
definitions reflect individualistic desires; social definitions reflect shared values and
purposes. Yet the individual and the society cannot be considered in isolation
because they form an organic whole in which individuals' attitudes and social values
are mutually interrelated.

Thomas' situational analysis represents an improvement over his earlier
biologistic and psychologistic biases and provides an alternative to the simple

stimulus-response model of human behavior propounded by psychological behaviorists. The stimulus-response model does not deal with subjective processes such as definition or evaluation of a stimulus, since these are not amenable to empirical measurement. Once a conditioned response to a stimulus is established, it is released in an automatic fashion whenever the appropriate stimulus occurs. Thomas' analysis of the intervening definitional process is similar to Mead's treatment of the covert rehearsal process in which individuals subjectively evaluate alternative definitions and responses prior to overt behavior. Both Thomas and Mead pointed out that individuals can inhibit or delay customary respones to environmental stimuli instead of reacting automatically. Both also emphasized that the response that individuals make will reflect subjective attitudes (or predispositions to act) formed in the process of social interaction.

Once the importance of subjective definitions for explaining behavior is recognized, it follows that, as Thomas stated, "If men define situations as real, they are real in their consequences." This idea can readily be applied at the level of a person's self-identity. If, for example, a person is treated by others as socially undesirable or intellectually inferior, the person so labeled may have no choice but to behave in a manner consistent with the negative label; if a group is regarded as ethnocentric or intolerant, the behavior of others toward members of that group may insure that they virtually have no choice but to become ethnocentric and intolerant; or, if a particular urban area is defined as an attractive residential area, this definition will have consequences in terms of variables such as tax base, socioeconomic class composition, population density, crime and delinquency rates, and educational quality. Social definitions of situations, even though subjective, have objective consequences.

Thomas' situational analysis can be used to explain why persons who have different attitudes or who have been socialized in different cultural or subcultural environments do not respond to the same stimulus in the same way. The differences in response to a given situation result from differences in subjective definitions. Possibilities for misunderstanding and conflict are magnified across the cultural boundaries of different societies. Thomas' situational analysis contributed to establishing the importance of cultural and subcultural differences in definitions that is well recognized today.

CONTEMPORARY SYMBOLIC INTERACTIONISM

Since the pioneering work of Mead, Cooley, Thomas, and others, symbolic interaction theory has been elaborated and refined considerably. Today it is one of the leading theories that concentrates on social processes at the micro level, including subjective consciousness and interpersonal interaction dynamics. Some of the ideas previously discussed that are basic in contemporary symbolic interactionism include: the organic interdependence between the self-concept and social organization; the image of social reality as emergent from symbolic communication; the stress on the social origins of individuals' self-concepts and attitudes; the idea that responses to environmental stimuli are highly variable and reflect shared subjective meanings; and the extensive use of concepts such as role, role performance, and role taking. These and many other related ideas convey a particular image of social reality that reflects sharp differences from other contemporary perspectives, such as functionalism in sociology and behaviorism (of the stimulus-response type) in psychology.

Symbolic interaction theory is not a fully developed or unified theory. Manford H. Kuhn identified several limited or partial theoretical perspectives for which symbolic interactionism is a kind of umbrella. They are role theory, reference group theory, social perception and person perception perspectives, self theory, and dramaturgic theory.[58]

In addition, there has been a serious debate among symbolic interactionists as to the appropriate research methods to measure the central concepts of symbolic interactionism. Underlying this debate are contrasting images of the nature of social reality implied by symbolic interactionism. One of Kuhn's primary goals was to develop strategies for objective empirical measurement of the major symbolic interactionist concepts. His own work is devoted to measuring and analyzing the self-concept. (In the preceding list, self theory reflects primarily his work.) His best-known accomplishment is the development of the Twenty Statements Test (TST).[59] Essentially, the TST consists of 20 responses that subjects are asked to make to the question, "Who am I?" Kuhn's work (and that of others who have used the TST) demonstrates how responses to this question can be analyzed and correlated with various other sociological variables.[60]

Kuhn's commitment to objective empirical measurement of variables such as the self-concept is criticized by some symbolic interactionists, such as Herbert Blumer.[61] The critics charge that efforts such as Kuhn's ignore or distort the *emergent* quality of social reality. They insist that the self-concept emerges in the process of action and interaction. Any effort to measure the self-concept which is isolated from the ongoing interactional or situational context or implies that it can be measured in a fixed or static manner fails to capture this emergent and fluid quality. This would also apply to most other symbolic interactionist concepts. For any concept or any variable that sociologists might use, its *meaning* is not fixed but emerges and changes in the process of interaction. Therefore researchers must develop strategies that will recognize the dynamics of the interaction process, capturing the meaning of concepts and variables as they are developed in this process and being sensitive to their fluid and always changing character. Not surprisingly, participant observation is a research method highly favored by researchers working in the symbolic interactionist framework.[62]

This emphasis on the emergent and fluid nature of social reality also distinguishes symbolic interactionism as a whole from functionalism, which will be discussed in a subsequent chapter. Symbolic interactionists criticize functionalists for overemphasizing the structural and cultural influences on individuals' behavior and failing to recognize that social institutions or social systems emerge through the process of subjective interpretation and interpersonal communication.

Blumer was a major representative of the symbolic interactionist perspective as opposed to the approaches that emphasize social structural categories. Blumer, a student of Mead's, insisted on preserving and developing Mead's fundamental emphasis on the ongoing interactional process. Through this process, individuals interpret their environment and one another and negotiate shared meanings or shared definitions of the situation. In a highly polemical article Blumer writes:

> By and large, of course, sociologists do not study human society in terms of its acting units. Instead, they are disposed to view human society in terms of structure or organization and to treat social action as an expression of such structure or organization. Thus, reliance is placed on such structural categories as social system, culture, norms, values, social stratification, status position, social roles and institutional organization.[63]

This focus on structural determinants ignores the interpretive process whereby individuals actively construct their actions and the process of interaction in which individuals adjust and fit together their various lines of action through role taking and symbolic communication. Briefly, for symbolic interactionists social organization does not *determine* interactional patterns; social organization *emerges* from the interactional process.

Social structural or cultural variables influence the interaction process only as they affect the situation in which individuals act or are taken into account by individuals in their subjective interpretation or definition of the situation. On the first of these points Blumer states that "People . . . do not act toward culture, social structure or the like; they act toward situations. Social organization enters into action only to the extent to which it shapes situations in which people act. . . ." And again, "Social organization is a framework inside of which acting units develop their actions. Structural features, such as 'culture,' 'social systems,' 'social stratification,' or 'social roles,' set conditions for their action but do not determine their action."[64]

Social organization may become relevant for behavior as it is taken into account by individuals in their subjective interpretation of the expectations of others or their awareness of the interdependence of their various lines of action. To use Mead's example of baseball again, the social organization of a baseball team is relevant for the behaviors of the players because of their common subjective awareness of their shared goal and the interdependence of their individual roles. In the same way but on a broader scale, large-scale social institutions become relevant in influencing individuals' actions as they are taken into account by individuals in their subjective interpretation of their various social situations.

It follows that social institutions cannot persist of their own weight, independently of individuals' subjective definitions. When individuals' subjective definitions and interpretations change on a broad scale, this creates change in social institutions. Although traditional definitions and institutional patterns may persist with minimal change for long periods of time, the emphasis in the symbolic interactionist image of modern society is on the fluid, changing nature of social reality. There is continual flux and change in the ongoing process of interaction as individuals continually reassess their subjective interpretations of their environment and of one another in constructing their various lines of action. For example, the rules of a bureaucratic organization do not enforce themselves automatically; instead, they *may* be taken into account and defined as appropriate or inappropriate for a given situation, or they may be reinterpreted, forgotten, or deliberately ignored.

The Self-Concept: McCall and Simmons' Role-Identity Model

Symbolic interactionists today still follow Mead's lead in emphasizing the centrality of the self-concept in interaction. This emphasis is manifested in McCall and Simmons' model of "role-identities."[65] Role-identities consist of the idealized self-images individuals have as occupants of various social positions. Persons have numerous role-identities that correspond to the various social positions they occupy and that vary in terms of their relative prominence. These role-identities are expressed overtly in role performances, and the degree of social support (or lack thereof) received from others in return will help determine the *prominence* of a given role-identity in a person's overall self-concept.

In McCall and Simmons' model the relative prominence of a given role-identity is also affected by the individual's level of commitment to and investment in that identity and by the level of gratifications received in performing it. If, for example, a person purchases a guitar, invests time and money in learning to play, and ultimately performs so well that others express pleasure in listening, the role-identity of guitar player or musician would probably be fairly high in that person's prominence hierarchy of role-identities. If the person's reputation grows to the point that he or she can actually earn a living by performing at concerts, this identity of musician may become the most prominent or central role-identity in the entire set of role-identities.

Mead emphasized that the self-concept emerges in the course of interaction as individuals take the role of others and view themselves as objects from the perspective of others. However, individuals are not merely passive reflectors of others' momentary opinions and judgments. Mead's concept of the generalized other suggests that the self-concept may incorporate abstract ideals that transcend specific reactions of particular individuals. In some cases the specific reactions of others may fail to support an individual's abstract or idealized self-concept.

Overall, a person would probably have difficulty sustaining a particular idealized self-concept if supportive or approving reactions from others were never received. Consistent lack of support or constant criticism of a particular type of role performance may lead to a decline in the relative prominence of a given role-identity. Other options are possible, however. People may choose the persons with whom to enact a particular identity to insure a supportive reaction. In addition, they may interpret (or misinterpret) the reactions of others so as to see themselves in the most favorable light possible. Or, if the negative reactions of others cannot be ignored, these reactions may be rejected as coming from persons not competent to make a proper evaluation. Through such mechanisms, individuals may sustain a particular self-concept, even if the reactions of others may not be quite as supportive as they might desire.[66]

The idealized self-concept need not necessarily always be a positive or satisfying one. Persons who consistently receive negative reactions from others or experience difficulties in enacting idealized role-identities may ultimately think of themselves in negative terms, even in the face of occasional approval from others.

Our self-concept has a major influence on our actions, on our choice of interaction partners, and on our interpretation of their reactions. Every action we perform is, to some extent, an expression of our self-concept, and every reaction of others has the potential for reinforcing or undermining that self-concept, for enhancing or degrading it. We choose to interact with those whose reactions support our favorable self-concepts, and we interpret their reactions in such a way as to see ourselves in the most favorable light.

Persons cannot enact all of the role-identities that make up their self-concept at once. Instead, they must allocate their time and other scarce resources selectively, and the role-identity that they enact in a given situation will be influenced not only by the prominence of that identity but also by the opportunities provided in the particular situation. McCall and Simmons point out that in contrast to the relatively stable *prominence* hierarchy of role identities, the temporary *salience* of these various role-identities will vary according to the type of situation in which the individual is involved.[67] For example, the role-identity of chess player may not be very prominent in a person's enduring hierarchy of role-identities but, if a friend brings out a chess set and there is time available, this identity may become salient in such a situation. The salience of a particular role-identity is also affected by the person's need for the social support and other kinds of gratifications derived from enacting that identity.

This is not to suggest that human beings are incapable of transcending a narrow self-centeredness. There are times when people become so thoroughly involved in some activity that no conscious thought is given to maintaining or enhancing the self-concept. In Mead's terminology, the behavior of the ''I'' is not necessarily a simple, conscious expression of the ''me.'' No doubt most people have occasionally found themselves caught up in the emotional excitement of some activity to such an extent that they were not consciously aware of how they looked to others or, more

· ·

important, cared what they thought. However, following such activities we invariably reflect on their implications for the kind of persons we like to think of ourselves as being. In this way surprising or spontaneous reactions of the moment may subsequently lead to revisions in the enduring aspects of the self-concept. (In Mead's terms, the "me" is affected by the "I.")

The Symbolic Interactionist Perspective on Deviance

The importance of social reactions on a person's self-concept is revealed in studies of deviance. Perhaps in no other substantive area of sociology is the fruitfulness of the symbolic interactionist perspective more clearly manifested.[68] Some of the most interesting work currently available in studies of deviance borrows explicitly from the symbolic interactionist framework, particularly the emphasis on negotiation of the meaning of situations and behaviors and the responses of individuals to one another in terms of these negotiated definitions.

The symbolic interactionist perspective on deviance starts with the recognition that deviance is not simply a manifestation of some inborn character trait or personality defect. Instead, it is produced as a result of a particular type of interaction process. Moreover, deviance must always be defined with reference to a society's or group's specific normative standards. The definitions of what is deviance or what is conformity will thus vary for different societies or different groups within a society.

The normative standards and rules of a group or society are usually general in nature and must be interpreted in order to be applied to specific situations. Thus there is always the possibility that individuals may differ in their interpretation of whether the normative patterns have been adequately followed in a specific situation. Moreover, the shared normative patterns or expectations of others may be inconsistent with our impulses or interests. That is, others may expect us to follow certain normative patterns in situations in which we do not find it convenient to do so. In view of the differences in interpretation of normative patterns and the frequent tension between normative demands and individual interests and desires, most people probably deviate from the norms from time to time, or at least from someone's interpretation of the norms.

In most cases this occasional deviance is ignored; others make whatever adjustments in their own behavior are necessary, but without the deviation becoming the central defining feature of the interaction or the identities of those involved. But, in some cases, deviation is not ignored. Instead, it triggers a response, often by an official social control agent of society. The deviant behavior thereby becomes the central feature of interaction and ultimately a key element in the self-identity of the deviant.

Violations of criminal law, if detected by a law enforcement officer, are likely to have this effect. The arrest and subsequent processing of a suspect in the court system will usually have a major impact on the way that others perceive and treat that individual. As a result of such an experience and its aftermath, the individual is likely to develop a self-identity as a deviant or criminal, and his or her attitude toward society and other people generally will probably reflect a certain degree of hostility or alienation. Also, persons who are singled out in this way as deviant will often band together and develop their own particular subculture; this reflects their efforts to adapt to a rejecting society and to meet their various needs, both conventional and deviant. In this way, then, deviant identities of individuals and deviant subcultures emerge from the process of interaction as deviants gradually adopt and adapt to the deviant identities with which they are labeled by the representatives of society. This is the basis for the labeling theory idea that society itself creates deviants by making rules whose infraction constitutes deviance and by singling out for special treatment some of those guilty of such violations.

A key question must be raised concerning the criteria used to distinguish between deviance that is ignored and deviance that is singled out for differential treatment. One criterion would be the social disruption or personal harm that results from a particular type of deviance. Thus the criminal law codifies the violations considered disruptive or harmful to society.

In addition, the interests and normative preferences of those who are politically powerful or otherwise rank high in the overall stratification system of society are likely to have an effect on the definition of which forms of deviance are serious enough to warrant differential treatment. Indeed, the argument can be made that those who have sufficient political and economic power may behave in ways that are harmful to many segments of society and still avoid being perceived or punished as deviant. Traditionally, the greater emphasis given to fighting street crimes than white-collar crimes could be used to support this argument. Moreover, as documented in numerous studies, law violators who are at the bottom of the socioeconomic hierarchy are more likely to be singled out and treated as law violators than those higher up.

In short, the criteria used to single out certain forms of deviance for negative sanctioning reflects a complex social process based on subjective definitions and the differential distribution of resources that enables certain groups to impose their particular definitions on other groups. These definitions will inevitably have a major effect on the self-identities and other definitions and attitudes of those labeled as deviant.

GOFFMAN AND THE DRAMATURGIC APPROACH TO INTERACTION DYNAMICS

The influence of individuals' self-concepts on their definitions of situations and their behavior and interaction style is one of the major themes of the contemporary dramaturgic perspective as developed under Erving Goffman's influence. Although Goffman's approach is a novel one for sociological analysis, it reflects the ancient insight of Shakespeare that all the world is a stage and that human beings are merely players on this stage, each with an entry on the stage, a particular role to perform or character to portray and, finally, an exit. The title of one of Goffman's earliest seminal works, *The Presentation of Self in Everyday Life,* suggests his basic approach.[69] Using the language of the theater, Goffman analyzes the various strategies individuals employ in their efforts to obtain social validation of their self-concepts.

According to this mode of analysis, the basic problem that individuals face in their various social relationships is controlling the impressions they make on others. To this end, individuals seek to control their appearance, the physical setting in which they enact their roles, and their actual role behavior and accompanying gestures.

For example, a typical middle-class hostess will prepare carefully for a party she is giving by meticulously cleaning her house, grooming herself, selecting appropriate clothing to wear, and so forth, all of which is intended to convey the impression that she is an attractive person, a gracious hostess, and competent in her routine household duties. During the party, she will attempt to make everyone feel welcome, insure that food and drink are available to all, mingle with all the guests instead of confining herself to conversation with just one person, and attend to mishaps that might occur without acting angry or frustrated. The validity of seeing this as a role performance should be obvious when the guests have all gone and the demeanor of the hostess changes abruptly as she kicks off her shoes to stretch out on the sofa and relax before cleaning up.

The deliberate staging and contrived character of an event such as a party may seem obvious. However, all social occasions have this dramaturgic aspect because all forms of behavior have potential implications for the self-concepts of the actors involved. The effort to convey a particular impression of oneself to others is manifested, for example, in the case of students trying to appear knowledgeable as they take part in class discussion, lawyers who strive to exude confidence in ultimate victory as they argue cases in court, office workers who make sure that they look busy when the office manager comes in, or members of a tavern clique who take their turn buying drinks all around, even though they know that the money is needed for other purposes.

Individuals' concerns with impression management are not limited to their overt behavior. Individuals' appearance and general demeanor are also highly relevant for their identity. Therefore they will attend to their appearance prior to a particular role performance (through personal grooming, selection of appropriate clothing, dieting, etc.) and will attempt to control various inappropriate mannerisms that might detract from the style of the performance.

In addition, the physical setting in which a role performance takes place is often relevant to an individual's self-concept. For example, the self-concept of a high-level corporation executive would be undermined if he or she worked at a small desk in a crowded, noisy office. By the same token, that executive would entertain a prospective client with a business lunch at an establishment that caters to business executives and not at the local hamburger outlet where high school students gather. Because of the importance of the physical setting, individuals must attend to matters such as physical props and selection of sites in which to enact their roles. These concerns with impression management may be seen as attempts to control the general definition of the situation, since individuals' identities are closely linked to the social definition of the situation in which they are involved.

One of the intriguing features of Goffman's dramaturgic analysis is his recognition of the innumerable ways in which people collaborate in protecting one another's various claims regarding the social reality they are attempting to stage or the identities they are trying to enact. This is important, because the contrived nature of social reality makes it very vulnerable and fragile. In other words, the impressions of reality and of self that individuals are attempting to create can easily be disrupted or fall apart. An individual may make a mistake in a crucial part of his or her performance; as a result, the impression being created cannot be sustained. For example, an outstanding athlete may accidentally trip over his or her own shoelace, or the gracious and poised hostess may accidentally spill coffee on a guest's lap. In a less dramatic vein, a person who takes pride in being a witty and intelligent conversationalist, for example, may happen to be in a social situation in which he or she is too tired to participate as fully as usual, or too uninformed to be able to say anything without revealing his or her ignorance.

In innumerable ways, individuals are constantly threatened with the possibility of losing face in their social relationships. However, perhaps since no one is immune to the threat of a disrupted performance, individuals frequently collaborate in helping to support one another's identities and to sustain the impressions being conveyed by others. Indeed, this is the significance of the elementary norms of tact and courtesy. Thus we try to cover for the mistakes of one another or, if this is not possible, we pretend not to notice even while we adjust our own behavior accordingly.

On the other hand, there are some social situations, often involving competition and conflict, in which individuals may seek ways to discredit one another's performance. One example of this is the situation in which a political opponent will seek to discredit the incumbent's performance in office, perhaps by demonstrating that person's incompetence or proving that the incumbent used the office for personal gain. In many cases, however, a person will not want an opponent to be totally discredited but just put in a position of *relative* inferiority. For example, an experienced tennis player will take greater pride in beating an outstanding opponent in a hard fought game than in winning over someone totally inept. For this reason, the opponents will cooperate in creating the reality of the game as a serious match, not an occasion for merely "horsing around."

Teams and Audiences

Collaboration between persons in creating a particular impression or definition of the situation is perhaps revealed most clearly in Goffman's analysis of teams and team performances. A dramaturgic team is a group of persons who cooperate to stage a particular performance. To quote Goffman, "A team, then, may be defined as a set of individuals whose intimate cooperation is required if a given projected definition of the situation is to be maintained."[70]

The dynamics of interaction within a dramaturgic team differ significantly from the patterns of interaction between the team and the audience. The audience is expected to accept the definitions of reality, including the identities of those involved, portrayed by the team. However, the members of the team will be aware, in a way that audience members are not, of the contrived or staged nature of the reality being presented. Members of the team may, for example, cooperate in setting up the props (or at least they will know that they have to be set up deliberately to convey a particular impression). They may even practice their "lines" with one another to determine their effectiveness or appropriateness, and they may invite critical evaluation by others on the team of the performances they plan to enact. Frequently this is done in a very informal fashion with a great deal of camaraderie. After all, since the team members know the staging that is involved in creating a particular reality, they do not have to worry about keeping up appearances. In short, social relations within the team will be characterized by relatively low social distance because of the intimate familiarity that results from sharing secrets regarding techniques used in staging performances.

Numerous examples illustrate the dynamics of the interaction patterns within a team. A professor may try out some new classroom technique on a colleague and invite his or her professional reaction prior to risking this technique before an audience of students (who, after all, may not be regarded as being able to give a fair evaluation). A corporation president may ask his or her secretary and close associates to listen to a draft of a speech before delivering it before a meeting of the corporation stockholders. A group of office workers or factory workers may devise ways to look busy when the boss is present, even though they know that this is staged for the boss's benefit. Ministers may joke with one another about how important it is to have an anthem or a time for silent meditation before they deliver their sermons so as to give them one last chance to go over their notes. Teachers or doctors will deliberately refrain from questioning their colleagues in a critical fashion in the company of students, patients, or other outsiders to sustain the impression of their absolute competence to discharge their professional obligations.

Related to the distinction between team members and audience is Goffman's distinction between "frontstage" and "backstage" regions. Quite simply, the frontstage is wherever the audience is expected to be, while the backstage is typically off limits to the audience or other outsiders. In the backstage region team members can relax by dropping their concerns with appearances or impressions and prepare for or rehearse their frontstage performances. Practically every public establishment has a particular area designated "for employees only."

These distinctions are relative. A backstage area may become frontstage if an outsider intrudes, or it may be a frontstage for a different kind of performance. For example, the kitchen area of a restaurant would be backstage as far as the customers are concerned but, when the sanitation inspector makes an appearance, it may quickly be transformed to a frontstage region as the members of the kitchen crew collaborate to make the right kind of impression about the maintenance of required sanitation standards for the inspector's benefit. Or the teachers' lounge of a high school will be backstage and off limits as far as students are concerned; here the teachers are free to stop acting like teachers for a while; they can relax and vent their frustrations over difficult students in language that would be inappropriate in the students' presence. However, a young unmarried female teacher may see the lounge as an ideal frontstage area in which to display her attractive qualities as a potential dating partner in the course of casual conversation with the male teachers. Similarly, the lounge may become a frontstage area for the school administrators when they wish to demonstrate to an audience of potential union organizers their concern for the comfort and well-being of the teaching staff.

Throughout his work, Goffman is sensitive to the difficulties people experience in maintaining desired appearances and impressions. These difficulties are compounded by the fact that people expect the social reality in which they are involved not to be a contrived or staged reality, but "really real." Thus, for example, medical doctors are not supposed merely to *act* like doctors; they are expected actually to *be* doctors. Similarly, in a church service, the members of the congregation are expected not merely to *act* reverential or worshipful; they are expected to *be* reverential or worshipful. Some "acting" might be considered normal for members of the congregation, but the minister or priest is expected to *feel* the sentiments he or she is expressing and not think about an upcoming golf game. Goffman's style of analysis points to the tenuousness of the distinction between appearances and reality, with explicit recognition of the notion that reality is, after all, socially constructed.

In many cases, the success of a person or team in having a particular definition of the situation or a particular identity accepted without question by the audience will be directly proportional to the degree to which the contrived nature of the setting and the performance is concealed. Thus, for example, a hostess may attempt to wave off a compliment on the elaborate variety of food served at a party by insisting that it really was no trouble or not out of the ordinary. Similarly, a golfer will take a stance and prepare for a swing in a natural and easy style, even though this style may have been privately practiced repeatedly in meticulous detail.

In view of the socially constructed and, therefore, tenuous nature of social reality, ambiguities, contradictions, and threats of breakdown abound in the social world. Goffman analyzes and illustrates several such situations. For instance, he discusses several discrepant roles, such as the informer, the shill, the spotter, the shopper, and the go-between.[71] To illustrate, the spy is an informer who gains access to a team's backstage region by pretending to be a member of the team, but whose real intention is to obtain the team's secrets so as to discredit its performance by sharing the secrets with the audience. A shill is a dramaturgic team member who pretends to be part of the audience, perhaps for the purpose of leading the audience in expressing approval for the team's performance. (An obvious illustration of this is the audience member who is "planted" for the express purpose of laughing loudly and applauding a comedian's performance.)

Another type of discrepancy occurs when an individual or a team acts or says something that is not consistent with the identities or definitions of the situation that are being projected. Goffman discusses several types of communication that are "out of character." For example, a performer may be distracted and make a mistake in the performance or simply forget some part of the planned routine. Or team members may need to engage in "stage talk" while the audience is present in order to cope with unforeseen problems that emerge during a performance. When this occurs, it is likely to distract from the image the team may be trying to present of a natural and spontaneous performance. To illustrate, a musician in a symphony orchestra might accidentally drop the musical score, causing the performance to be halted or slowed down momentarily.

Still another type of out-of-character communication would occur when members of a team make disparaging or otherwise inappropriate comments about the audience without being aware that someone from the audience is within hearing distance. For example, a group of students whose classroom behavior and decorum are quite proper and conventional might make jokes about a professor's mannerisms or refer to the professor by disparaging nicknames while in the local student hangout, only to notice eventually that the professor is sitting nearby. Or a nurse's aide might complain to a nurse in very uncomplimentary terms about a patient's frequent complaints and demands in the hope that more tranquilizers might be given, without realizing that the patient is awake and listening to every word. In many cases, team members make disparaging or cynical comments about an audience because of the audience's lack of sophistication in evaluating a performance adequately or apparent lack of appreciation for the difficulties involved in staging a successful performance.

Communication out of character need not disrupt or destroy a performance, however. Members of a team are often able to maintain the definition of the situation that they want the audience to accept and to stage their performances successfully, even while they act toward one another in terms of a different reality. That is, the team members may be involved in presenting two different versions of reality simultaneously—one to the audience and another one to fellow team members. In such cases, team members' interaction with one another is likely to involve various subtle cues or special code words that will have no meaning to the audience. Such secret codes are common in retail establishments, for example, where clerks will collaborate in dealing with various types of customers.

Interaction Difficulties of the Stigmatized

The difficulties of projecting an identity that will be accepted by others and satisfying to oneself are revealed dramatically in the interaction problems of handicapped persons. A chief social problem faced by the handicapped is that they appear ''abnormal'' to such a pronounced degree that other persons are uncomfortable interacting with them or are unable to interact with them in a way that the handicap itself does not become the focal point of the interaction. As Goffman points out, a visible physical handicap is one of the chief sources of stigma.[72] A stigma is any characteristic that is too obvious to be ignored and that is assumed to have such a pervasive effect on the individual's personality that the individual is incompetent to act in a normal fashion. Physical handicaps are not the only source of stigma. People may be stigmatized by their general reputation (e.g., the reputation of ex-convict or ex-mental patient) or by other characteristics that have a pervasive denigrating effect.

Whatever the source of the stigma, the interaction difficulties of stigmatized persons should be obvious. Nonstigmatized persons are assumed to be competent unless they demonstrate incompetence, but the stigmatized person is assumed to be incompetent (in general or in some specific fashion) unless able to prove competence. Thus the first and probably most important problem for a handicapped person is to overcome the negative assumptions of others by demonstrating that, except for the specific area of the handicap, he or she is able to interact normally with others and to experience the full range of emotions and interests and needs of which human beings are capable. For example, a crippled person must demonstrate that even though unable to walk, he or she can still enjoy good music and stimulating conversation, have dreams and goals for future occupational success, experience joy and grief, and be interested in the needs and problems of others. The basic problem is to project an identify of being a normal and competent human being, except for the specific limitations imposed by the handicap.

Goffman also dealt extensively with the problems of persons in mental institutions.[73] Again, just as handicapped persons are assumed to be incompetent, so are patients in mental hospitals. Moreover, the ideology and organizational structure of mental hospitals are designed to reinforce, in innumerable ways, the image of their inmates as incompetent, unable to make basic decisions in their lives, and irresponsible or perhaps even dangerous in their relationships with others. Beyond this, the mental hospital is organized on the basis of the assumptions that the staff are able to evaluate properly the needs of patients, to structure all aspects of their lives in such a way as to insure their improvement, and to evaluate their behaviors in an objective and benevolent way. Since the inmates themselves have very little control over their environment or the decisions that affect their lives, their only alternative may be to accept the negative definitions of self offered them by the staff (either in appearance of sincerely). Indeed, unless the patient accepts the notion that he or she is sick and belongs in the institution, the staff definition may be that the person is too ill to realize how serious the problem is. Successful adaptation to hospital routines and eventual release thus depend on collaborating with the staff (again, either in appearance or sincerely) in the process of trying to change the self.

Although the interaction difficulties of the handicapped and mental hospital patients offer a dramatic portrayal of the difficulties of having a satisfactory self-concept accepted by others, even "normal" persons face similar problems. These problems are most acute for those whose identity includes some distinctive claim that will distinguish them from the average person. As every hero of the moment knows, one outstanding or heroic performance does not usually guarantee a permanent identity as a hero. Those satisfied with being average persons must control their behavior to insure against being stigmatized as strange or different. Regardless of the specific identity claims being made or the particular definitions of the situation that are projected, the social realities people create are tenuous, fragile, and continually subject to renegotiation or even breakdown.

The Context of Interaction

The activities people engage in are typically subject to alternative interpretations or multiple meanings. The determination of the meaning of a set of activities is set by the context within which such activities occur. There will necessarily be a physical dimension to the context, consisting of the space within which activities occur and various material artifacts that are involved. In addition, there will be a social dimension, a set of conventions whereby individuals involved in some social undertaking will come to an understanding of what sort of undertaking it is. In a recent work Goffman refers to these shared understandings as the "frame" within which social events take place.[74]

An example is provided by a formal meeting being conducted according to parliamentary procedure. The opening statement of the chairperson, "The meeting will come to order," marks the beginning. From this point until the chairperson says "The meeting is adjourned," everything that is said will be considered part of the official meeting and duly recorded as such, unless the frame is broken for a recess or for some remarks that are "off the record." But even during the meeting some members may exhibit various side involvements, such as lighting a cigarette or whispering to one another to make arrangements for some future activity. These side involvements are not officially part of the meeting, even though they may be carried on while the meeting is in process.

In a "real" business meeting of a "real" organization, the official opening and closing statements of the chairperson mark the boundaries of the occasion. Informal conversations before and after the meeting, or even during the meeting, are secondary to the main event and are not included in the frame of the official meeting. But the words spoken to open and close the meeting officially rest on certain implicit understandings regarding the nature of the occasion. For a different occasion these words might be part of a different frame. For example, these same words could be used for purposes of practice in a class in parliamentary procedure or as part of a comedy routine. Or they could be used when the chairperson or some other members provide a narrative account of the meeting to absent members. Thus the meaning of the words in defining the situation and marking its boundaries rests on the implicit understanding among the participants as to the nature of the occasion.

The frame of a set of activities is not always as obvious as in the example of the formal meeting. There are occasions in which some participants may be unsure as to exactly what is going on; even though they may be able to see clearly the activities being performed, they do not know how such activities should be taken. Also, individuals involved together in some undertaking may differ in their understanding of what is going on. Such differences may or may not be known to the participants and may or may not be disruptive of the activities in process. Whether these differences are disruptive or not will depend on the nature of the activity and the importance of informed consensus regarding its meaning. For example, a casual conversation between a supervisor in a bureaucratic organization and a subordinate may be merely a means to fill some free time to the supervisor, while to the subordinate it may be a long-awaited opportunity to become personally known to someone who may be able to help advance the subordinate's career. These differences in frame need not be disruptive, as long as both participants interact according to the general understandings that govern casual sociable conversations.[75]

The frames within which activities occur are subject to transformation, either unintentionally or intentionally, in which case the activities being performed will take on a totally new meaning. One example is provided by puns and other forms of humor. The person telling a pun attempts to lead the audience into implicit acceptance of one meaning of the key words and, at the punch line, the meaning changes radically, leading to a humorous reinterpretation of all that came before. (Thus, as a play on words, a pun is like a volume of Shakespeare placed on top of a dictionary.) Or, in the example of the official meeting previously discussed, the side conversation of two participants may result in loud, uncontrollable laughter that breaks up the meeting, or the chairperson may get a case of the hiccups and thus literally lose control of the meeting. These examples illustrate rapid transformation of the implicit frame that had given meaning to the activities, resulting in a somewhat different meaning being created.

Numerous examples could be cited of instances in which efforts are made to mislead others as to the meaning of a particular set of activities. Such deceptions may be either malevolent or benevolent. A malevolent deception is illustrated by the case of the "con artist." The con artist attempts to get the victim to accept one interpretation of his activities so as to gain the victim's trust; when this objective is achieved and the con man obtains what he wants, the victim discovers that he or she has been "set up" or deceived. An example is the case of the phony "bank examiner" who gets a depositer to withdraw a large sum of money in order to catch a dishonest bank employee and then escapes with the money. In contrast, the surprise birthday party might be cited as an example of a benevolent deception. The "victim" is deliberately kept uninformed as to the nature of the elaborate preparations made on his or her behalf and may actually be diverted from situations that might reveal the truth. Then, when all the guests jump out from behind the furniture and shout "Surprise!", the meaning of the family's secrecy and the evasive answers to the inquiries about what is going on become clear.

  Goffman's focus is primarily on the micro level of social reality. His writing is filled with fascinating examples of the intricacies of interaction processes in a variety of settings, but he does not provide a systematic analysis of large-scale social institutions or the dynamics of social processes at the macro level. (His study of the mental hospital is his most systematic institutional analysis.) However, the social processes that he describes can be related to an institutional or social structural approach if we accept the symbolic interactionist notion of social institutions as shared definitions of situations and roles that are widely understood and accepted and have endured long enough to become more or less standardized. As a result of these definitions, most people have a general understanding of common roles such as businessperson, police officer, teacher, professional baseball player, musician, student, and store clerk. In addition to these occupational roles, there is common understanding of familial roles such as mother, father, son or daughter, and mother-in-law and person-to-person roles such as friend, lover, neighbor, acquaintance, and associate. Numerous other types or categories of roles could be identified, but these illustrate sufficiently that there is a widely shared understanding of the attitudes and behaviors associated with these common roles.

  These various commonly understood social roles are accepted and internalized by individuals as an important part of the self-concept that they seek to project to others. Each person who plays these various roles will have a distinctive style, and each role player might seek to modify the definitions of others in some respects. In spite of such variations, it is through the performing of more or less standardized social roles that individuals's identities and related behaviors fit into a larger social structure. In the next chapter we will examine how individuals are motivated to perform various social roles through rewards obtained on both interpersonal and institutional levels.

Summary

  This chapter has been devoted primarily to the development and the current state of symbolic interaction theory. The social psychological contributions of Mead were emphasized because they provide the basic foundation of this theory. The distinctive ability of human beings to create and manipulate symbols was crucial for Mead's explanation of human intelligence, human conduct, and social organization. The fundamental image of social reality implied in Mead's perspective is that it is symbolically constructed and reflects individuals' efforts to fit together their own actions with the unfolding actions of those with whom they are involved. This process depends on the individuals' ability to see their own actions from the perspective of others, or to be self-conscious. Although social structures emerge from this process, no form of social organization can endure independently of the shared subjective definitions negotiated through symbolic interaction.

The pioneering contributions of Cooley and Thomas were also reviewed briefly. The self-concept was a key part of Cooley's social psychological theory. He emphasized that its emergence is dependent on the intimate and emotionally warm social environment of the primary group. Individuals' behavior reflects their desire for social support for their self-concepts. In addition, it will also reflect their definition of the particular situation in which they are involved. Thomas' situational analysis was reviewed because of his emphasis on the importance of this symbolically mediated process.

The fundamental legacy of Mead has been extended and elaborated by a number of more contemporary symbolic interaction theorists. We looked briefly at Blumer's efforts to defend the symbolic interactionist perspective as opposed to the theoretical perspectives (such as functionalism) that place primary emphasis on structural categories. For Blumer the distinctive characteristic of social reality is that it reflects the symbolically mediated process whereby individuals negotiate shared interpretations of their common situations. Blumer's emphasis on the fluid and emergent nature of social reality is also in opposition to the efforts of others in the symbolic interactionist school to develop clear operational measures of the major symbolic interactionist concepts. We examined Kuhn's development of the Twenty Statements Test to measure the self-concept as an example of such efforts. Although efforts such as Kuhn's have produced some interesting findings, the criticism of Blumer and those in his school is that these findings fail to capture adequately the fluid interpretive process that is the essence of social reality.

A more elaborate analysis of the self-concept is provided in McCall and Simmons' model of role-identities. Although McCall and Simmons' approach reflects a commitment to objective measurement, they also recognize explicitly the idealized nature of individuals' self-concepts as well as their tendency to change from situation to situation. McCall and Simmons' role-identity model analyzes the way in which individuals' self-concepts influence their overt behavior, their choice of interaction partners, and their interpretation of others' responses. Their model also helps to explain why the various role-identities that make up an individual's self-concept vary in their importance to an individual.

The symbolic interactionist perspective today can be seen as providing a general umbrella-type orientation for several more limited perspectives. We examined Goffman's dramaturgic perspective as one example, even though Goffman did not really base his ideas solely on Mead's theory or symbolic interactionism as such. Goffman's major goal was to demonstrate the importance of the processes whereby individuals attempt to stage a particular definition of the situation, with special emphasis given to efforts to obtain social support for the self-concept that individuals attempt to project in their interactions with others. This same concern is central to symbolic interaction theory.

It should be clear from all of the symbolic interactionist theorists discussed that the primary level of social realtiy on which symbolic interactionists focus is the micro level, particularly the interrelation between subjective consciousness and interpersonal interaction. This focus distinguishes symbolic interactionism from the theorists discussed in the last part. As we saw earlier, Comte and Sorokin both concentrated on the cultural level and Marx and Durkheim dealt principally with the social structural level of social reality. In general, most of the European founders of the discipline of sociology were preoccupied with trying to analyze the massive new social forces brought about by the growth of urban-industrial societies. Although they were not uninterested in forms of individual consciousness or personal relations, their major concerns were at the macro level, especially broad-scale historical changes in major institutional structures. Of the theorists discussed in the last part only Simmel concentrated primarily on micro-level social processes. He, too, was interested in the general social processes involved in the development of modern society, but he was especially concerned with forms of interaction at the micro level. However, he did not analyze the complex interdependence between overt interaction processes and forms of consciousness as thoroughly as the symbolic interactionists. The micro level of social reality will also be treated in the following chapter on exchange theory.

Footnotes

1. For the material on Mead's biography, I have relied heavily on David Miller, ''Introduction: Biographical Notes,'' in Miller's *George Herbert Mead—Self, Language and the World* (Austin: University of Texas Press, 1973), pp. xi–xxxviii, and Lewis Coser, *Masters of Sociological Thought,* 2nd edition (New York: Harcourt Brace Jovanovich, 1977), chapter on ''George Herbert Mead.''
2. Coser, op. cit., pp. 341–342.
3. Miller, op. cit., p. xiv.
4. Coser, op. cit., pp. 342–343.
5. Miller, op. cit., pp. xv–xvi.
6. Coser, op. cit., p. 346.
7. The most important of these posthumously published works for establishing Mead's distinctive sociological approach is *Mind, Self, and Society,* edited and with an introduction by Charles W. Morris (Chicago: University of Chicago Press, 1934). Other major works include: *The Philosophy of the Present,* edited and with an introduction by Arthur E. Murphy (LaSalle, Ill.: Open Court, 1932); *Movements of Thought in the Nineteenth Century,* edited and with an introduction by Merritt A. Moore (Chicago: University of Chicago Press, 1936); *The Philosophy of the Act,* edited and with an introduction by Charles W. Morris in collaboration with John M. Brewster, Albert M. Dunham, and David L. Miller (Chicago: University of Chicago Press, 1938); and *Selected Writings,* edited and with an introduction by Andrew J. Reck (Indianapolis: Bobbs-Merrill, 1964). Of these, *The Philosophy of the Present* and *The Philosophy of the Act* have sociological implications, even though they are primarily philosophical.
8. Miller, op. cit., p. xxxvii.
9. Coser, op. cit., pp. 344–345.

10. David Miller, op. cit., pp. xxxi–xxxii.
11. Thus the first part of *Mind, Self, and Society* is entitled "The Point of View of Social Behaviorism." A large proportion of the material in this section is derived from this first part, plus the second major part entitled "Mind."
12. See Mead, *Mind, Self, and Society,* p. 42ff.
13. Ibid., pp. 75–82.
14. For an example of a relevant study along this line, see John P. Spiegel and Pavel Machotka, *Messages of the Body* (New York: Free Press, 1974). See also Edward T. Hall, *The Silent Language* (Garden City, N.Y.: Doubleday, 1959) and *The Hidden Dimension* (Garden City, N.Y.: Doubleday, 1966). Both books are informed by an awareness of the importance of cross-cultural differences in patterns of nonverbal communication. In *The Hidden Dimension* Hall focuses specifically on the patterning of spatial distance and on comparisons of human beings with nonhuman species in this regard.
15. Mead, *Mind, Self, and Society,* p. 65ff.
16. One of the major themes developed in Mead's *Philosophy of the Present* is that the *meaning* of one's present action can only be understood in the light of the individual's memory and interpretation of the past on the one hand and anticipations of the future on the other. Past events are selected and interpreted for explaining the present, while the present is evaluated in terms of the future to which it leads.
17. Mead, *Mind, Self, and Society,* p. 82ff.
18. These covert processes involved in problem solving that Mead analyzed—identification of problem, search for alternative solutions, evaluation of alternative solutions in terms of probable consequences, and selection of a solution to try to implement—are recognized as basic ingredients of the decision-making process in modern decision theory. For a brief review of this process in an organizational context, see Daniel Katz and Robert L. Kahn, *The Social Psychology of Organizations* (New York: Wiley, 1966), pp. 274–299.
19. This discussion of the self-concept is based primarily on Mead, *Mind, Self, and Society,* Part III, "The Self," pp. 135–226.
20. Ibid., p. 136ff.
21. Ibid., pp. 140–144.
22. Ibid., pp. 173–178, 192–200.
23. Ibid., p. 209ff, 214ff.
24. This point is frequently made in *Mind, Self, and Society.* For example, see pp. 167–168.
25. For Mead's discussion of these stages, see ibid., pp. 149–164.
26. The phrases, "taking a role," "playing a role," or "performing a role" are not always used consistently by social psychologists. Mead's usage seems to distinguish between "taking the role of another" and "playing at" or "playing" a role. "Taking the role of another" is the same process just discussed as putting one's self in the perspective of another. Thus, to take the role of parent is to attempt to put oneself in the frame of mind of the parent, or to see a situation or one's own behavior as the parent would. "Playing at" a role, on the other hand, refers to make-believe performances by children with frequent shifting from one role to another; while "playing" a role refers to a more consistent performance of a role that is socially recognized and validated.

27. See Mead, *Mind, Self, and Society,* p. 154.

28. Ibid., pp. 201–207.

29. Ibid., pp. 207–208.

30. The discussion that follows of the larger social or institutional framework that emerges from the interaction process draws heavily from Mead, *Mind, Self, and Society,* Part IV, "Society," pp. 227–336.

31. Ibid., pp. 258–259ff., 281–282, 289ff.

32. Ibid., pp. 284–289.

33. Ibid., pp. 311–317.

34. For a sensitive and insightful biographical overview of Cooley's life, see Edward C. Jandy, *Charles Horton Cooley—His Life and His Social Theory* (New York: Octagon, 1969), Part I, "The Life of Charles Horton Cooley," from which most of the biographical highlights in this paragraph are drawn. See also Robert Cooley Angell's introduction to Albert J. Reiss, Jr., ed., *Cooley and Sociological Analysis* (Ann Arbor: University of Michigan Press, 1968), pp. 1–12.

35. See Lewis A. Coser, *Masters of Sociological Thought* (New York: Harcourt Brace Jovanovich, 1977), pp. 352–354, for a brief discussion of the contrast between Cooley's social environment and Mead's.

36. Cooley turned down an offer from Giddings to join the faculty at Columbia University. See Jandy, op cit., p. 60.

37. Jandy, op. cit., pp. 85–86.

38. Charles Horton Cooley, *Human Nature and the Social Order* (New York: Schocken Books, 1964), Introduction and Chapter 1, pp. 3–50.

39. Ibid., pp. 170–183.

40. Ibid., pp. 183–184.

41. Ibid., p. 184.

42. Ibid., Chapter VI, pp. 211–263.

43. Ibid., p. 209.

44. Charles Horton Cooley, *Social Organization—A Study of the Larger Mind* (New York: Charles Scribner's Sons, 1929), p. 23.

45. Ibid.

46. Ibid., p. 24.

47. Ibid., p. 23.

48. Ibid., pp. 26–27.

49. Ibid., p. 313.

50. Ibid., p. 121.

51. See George Herbert Mead, "Cooley's Contribution to American Social Thought," reprinted in Cooley, *Human Nature and the Social Order,* pp. xxi–xxxviii.

52. For a brief biographical overview of Thomas' life and intellectual development, see Morris Janowitz's introduction to Morris Janowitz, ed., *William I. Thomas on Social Organization and Social Personality* (Chicago: University of Chicago Press, 1966).

53. William I. Thomas and Florian Znaniecki, *The Polish Peasant in Europe and America,* 2 volumes (New York: Dover, 1958).

54. See Robert K. Merton, "The Self-Fulfilling Prophecy," in *Social Theory and Social Structure* (New York: Free Press of Glencoe, 1957), pp. 421–436.

55. Thomas and Znaniecki, op. cit., Vol. 1, p. 73.

56. William I. Thomas, *The Unadjusted Girl* (Boston: Little, Brown, 1923), pp. 41–43. The relevance of Thomas' strategy of situational analysis for symbolic interaction theory is shown in the inclusion of his basic statement on this strategy in Jerome Manis and Bernard Meltzer, eds., *Symbolic Interaction—A Reader in Social Psychology,* 2nd edition (Boston: Allyn and Bacon, 1972), pp. 331–336.

57. One of the major conceptual distinctions which Thomas and Znaniecki made in *The Polish Peasant* is that between *attitudes* and *values.* Both reflect social processes, but attitudes refer primarily to the subjective definitions of individuals, while values refer primarily to the objective cultural patterns as embodied in social institutions external to the individual. Of course, there is reciprocal interdependence between these two concepts, with individual attitudes being gradually shaped by social values, and conversely. Perhaps partly because of this interdependence the distinction is sometimes difficult to maintain, particularly in any discussion of socially shared attitudes.

58. Manford Kuhn, "Major Trends in Symbolic Interaction Theory in the Past Twenty-Five Years," *The Sociological Quarterly,* Vol. 5, Winter 1964, pp. 61–84.

59. See Manford H. Kuhn and Thomas S. McPartland, "An Empirical Investigation of Self-Attitudes," *American Sociological Reivew,* Vol. 19, February 1954, pp. 68–76.

60. For some relevant examples, see Carl J. Couch, "Family Role Specialization and Self-Attitudes in Children," *The Sociological Quarterly,* Vol. 3, April 1962, pp. 115–121; Edwin D. Driver, "Self-Conceptions in India and the United States: A Crosscultural Validation of the Twenty Statements Test," *The Sociological Quarterly,* Vol. 10, Summer 1969, pp. 341–354; and Louis Schneider and Louis Zurcher, "Toward Understanding the Catholic Crisis: Observations on Dissident Priests in Texas," *Journal for the Scientific Study of Religion,* Vol. 9, Fall 1970, pp. 197–207.

61. The debate between those who follow Kuhn's approach and those who follow Blumer's approach is described in more detail by B. N. Meltzer and J. W. Petras, "The Chicago and Iowa Schools of Symbolic Interactionism," in Thomas Shibutani, ed., *Human Nature and Collective Behavior* (Englewood Cliffs, N.J.: Prentice-Hall, 1970), pp. 3–17. Kuhn is representative of the Iowa school, while Blumer is a major spokesman for the Chicago school. For a more detailed analysis, see Jonathan H. Turner, *The Structure of Sociological Theory* (Homewood, Ill.: Dorsey Press, 1978), Chapter 15, "Symbolic Interactionism: Herbert Blumer versus Manford Kuhn," pp. 326–346.

62. For a thorough discussion of the research implication of Blumer's position, see Norman K. Denzin, *The Research Act: A Theoretical Introduction to Sociological Methods* (Chicago: Aldine, 1970).

63. Herbert Blumer, "Society as Symbolic Interaction," in Arnold M. Rose, ed., *Human Behavior and Social Processes—An Interactionist Approach* (Boston: Houghton and Mifflin, 1962), pp. 188–189.

64. Ibid., especially pp. 189–190.

65. See George J. McCall and J. L. Simmons, *Identities and Interactions,* rev. edition (New York: Free Press, 1978), especially Chapter 4, "The Role-Identity Model." Much of the following discussion borrows heavily from this model.

66. See ibid., pp. 92–97, for a discussion of these various "mechanisms of legitimation."

67. Ibid., pp. 79–82.

68. For some examples, see David Matza, *Becoming Deviant* (Englewood Cliffs, N.J.: Prentice-Hall, 1969); Richard Hawkins and Gary Tiedeman, *The Creation of Deviance: Interpersonal and Organizational Determinants* (Columbus, Ohio: Charles E. Merrill, 1975), and Earl Rubington and Martin S. Weinberg, eds., *Deviance: The Interactionist Perspective,* 3rd edition (New York: Macmillan, 1978).

69. Erving Goffman, *The Presentation of Self in Everyday Life* (Garden City, N.Y.: Doubleday, 1959). The following discussion draws heavily from this work. See also Erving Goffman, *Interaction Ritual* (Garden City, N.Y.: Anchor, 1967), and *Encounters* (Indianapolis: Bobbs-Merrill, 1961).

70. Goffman, *The Presentation of Self in Everyday Life,* p. 104.

71. Ibid., Chapter IV.

72. Erving Goffman, *Stigma* (Englewood Cliffs, N.J.: Prentice-Hall, 1963).

73. Erving Goffman, *Asylums* (Garden City, N.Y.: Doubleday, 1961).

74. Erving Goffman, *Frame Analysis: An Essay on the Organization of Experience* (Cambridge, Mass.: Harvard University Press, 1974).

75. Concern with the implicit understandings that underlie interpersonal transactions is a major ingredient of the recently popular ethnomethodological theoretical perspective. One major difference between ethnomethodology and symbolic interactionism is that while symbolic interactionists concentrate on the overt or explicit negotiation of shared definitions of situations, shared meanings, and the like, ethnomethodologists stress the implicit, taken-for-granted character of the assumptions underlying interaction. There may be overt negotiation when the implicit understandings break down, but the major emphasis of ethnomethodology is on trying to understand how people arrive at these implicit understandings, often without explicit negotiation. (The root meaning of the word "ethnomethodology" refers to "methods of people"; this suggests the central concern with methods people use to create a sense of regularity or order in their social lives.) See, for example, Harold Garfinkel, *Studies in Ethnomethodology* (Englewood Cliffs, N.J., 1967), and Aaron Cicourel, *Cognitive Sociology: Language and Meaning in Social Interaction* (New York: Free Press, 1974). For an exploration of the possibilities of convergence between symbolic interactionism and ethnomethodology, see Norman K. Denzin, "Symbolic Interactionism and Ethnomethodology: A Proposed Synthesis," *American Sociological Review,* Vol. 34, December 1969, pp. 922–934.

Questions for Study and Discussion

1. Under what circumstances are the messages that people attempt to communicate through symbolic interaction likely to be undermined by unconscious gestures?

2. Imagine the following scene. A police officer accidentally shoots a person speeding away from the scene of a reported robbery. Upon investigation it becomes evident that the speeding motorist is responding to a call from his pregnant wife by hurrying home. Use Thomas' notion of the "definition of the situation" to contrast the interpretations of the police officer's actions by the police officer, the victim of the robbery, a journalist covering the story, the police chief, the pregnant wife, the real robber who reads of the accidental shooting in the newspaper, the victim's fellow factory workers, and the public at large.

3. Why is the ability to take the role of others and view oneself from their perspective essential for social organization? Are there differences between people in their role-taking ability? If so, what effect does this have on social organization?

4. What is meant by Blumer's emphasis on the emergent and highly fluid or ever-changing nature of social reality? Do you agree that social reality can be changed through changes in subjective definitions? Why or why not?

5. What are the similarities and differences between Goffman's dramaturgic view of the self-concept and Mead's behavioral view? Which of these perspectives corresponds most closely with your own experience?

CHAPTER 9

Interpersonal Exchanges and the Emergence of Social Structures

Do you ever feel that your friends are always trying to get something out of you? Do you feel that you are always being asked for favors or that others are reluctant to do favors for you when you need help? Friends are expected to be interested in one another and concerned about one another's welfare. They are expected to do things for one another, help one another if needed, and provide social support for one another. Having friends is rewarding. There is great satisfaction in knowing that our close friends care deeply about us, consider our company enjoyable, and accept us in spite of our faults.

But there are also certain costs to maintaining a friendship. At the very least, there is the cost of time and energy and the alternative activities that are foregone. There is also the obligation to help our friends when they need it. Even though these costs might not be experienced as costly or burdensome in light of the rewards of friendship, they nevertheless must be taken into consideration when we analyze objectively the various transactions involved in friendship. When costs and rewards seem unevenly distributed, this frequently arouses concern and resentment on the part of those who feel that the rewards are too low for the costs involved.

If we look at friendship in terms of the rewards and costs involved, the frequent failure of persons to maintain friendships for long periods of time when they are geographically separated from one another is understandable. When friends no longer live reasonably close to one another, it becomes impossible for them to continue to interact with each other and engage in shared activities often. This means that the rewards they are able to provide for one another are drastically reduced. At the same time, the cost of maintaining even minimal contact rises significantly. It takes time and energy to sit down and write letters, and this will not be rewarded or reinforced by a response for several days or weeks. For many American families the infrequency and irregularity of correspondence is perhaps one of the most common complaints that geographically distant family members and relatives have of one another. The cost of more intensive or sustained forms of interaction, such as through telephone calls or visits, is usually even higher.

Not all friendships are dissolved because of lack of opportunities for frequent interaction. Close friends may share such a wide range of valued experiences and develop such a profound depth of feeling for one another that their friendship endures in spite of circumstances that prevent frequent interaction. On the other hand, casual acquaintances may fail to develop a deep friendship in spite of the fact that they may interact and share many common activities quite frequently.

Analysis of social relationships in terms of costs and rewards is one of the major features of exchange theory. In this chapter exchange theory will be discussed as our second major example of a contemporary theory that focuses primarily on the micro level of analysis. In terms of the various levels of social reality presented in Chapter 2, exchange theory is particularly appropriate for dealing with the interpersonal level. Major emphasis will be on the exchange theories of Homans and Blau; some attention is also given to Thibaut and Kelley's exchange theory. As we will see, Homans' exchange theory does not really begin with the interpersonal level but with the individual level. More than any other major theorist treated in this book, Homans insists on the necessity of utilizing individual psychological principles in order to *explain* social behavior as opposed merely to *describing* it. Blau, on the other hand, attempts to move from the level of interpersonal exchanges at the micro level to larger (or macro level) social structures. Briefly, he attempts to show how larger social structures emerge from elementary exchange processes. Thibaut and Kelley focus on the contrast between exchange patterns in a dyad and those in larger groups.

In contrast to symbolic interaction theory, exchange theory deals primarily with overt behavior, not subjective processes. Homans insists that scientific explanation must focus on overt behavior, which can be empirically observed and measured. Internal states (subjective feelings and attitudes, etc.) must be defined in behavioral terms for purposes of empirical measurement.[1] Neither Homans nor Blau concentrate on the level of subjective consciousness or the dynamic interrelations between the subjective level and overt interaction as fully or explicitly as symbolic interactionists.

The process of social exchange had been dealt with by numerous earlier social theorists. In the classical economic theory of the eighteenth and nineteenth centuries, British political economists such as Adam Smith had analyzed the economic market as the result of the overall aggregation of untold numbers of individual economic transactions. It was assumed that exchange transactions would occur only when both parties could benefit from the exchange, and that the overall welfare of society is best served when individuals are allowed to pursue their individual interests through such privately negotiated exchanges. This same stress on individual goals and rewards also characterizes contemporary exchange theory in America.

This individualistic emphasis is congruent with the broader tradition of British utilitarianism. The basic premise of utilitarianism is that individuals act to avoid pain and maximize pleasure. This notion was considered a basic law of human behavior. Individuals differ as to what they consider painful and pleasurable. Although some experiences could be considered universally painful or pleasurable, individuals differ in the priorities assigned to such experiences. For example, food and sex might be considered universal sources of human pleasure. However, some people will indulge their appetite for food even at the risk of losing their sexual attractiveness through obesity, while others will endure the pain of refusing to satiate themselves with food so as to maximize their sexual or physical attractiveness. More generally, individuals may voluntarily postpone or defer opportunities for present gratification to attain an even larger reward in the future. This deferred gratification pattern seemed to be recognized in the utilitarian theory of crime and punishment. The pain of punishment must be set large enough (but not unreasonably large) to offset the pleasure derived from commission of a crime.

Among the classical pioneers in the development of sociological theory, Herbert Spencer perhaps best reflects the basic principles of individualistic utilitarianism in his sociological approach. Although Spencer's is an organic theory, it is not the same type of organic theory as Comte's and Durkheim's. They both stressed the idea that society or social structure transcends the individual; Spencer's approach emphasized the individual as the foundation of the social structure. For him, although society can be analyzed at the structural level, a society's social structure is established to enable its members to achieve their individual interests. This emphasis on the primacy of the individual is also reflected in various versions of the contract theory of society. According to the basic principles of this theory, society is formed as a result of contractual agreements that individuals negotiate with each other as they each attempt to pursue their own needs and interests rationally.

INDIVIDUALIST versus COLLECTIVIST THEORIES OF SOCIAL EXCHANGE

The contemporary exchange theories of Homans and Blau are consistent with the individualistic emphasis of eighteenth- and nineteenth-century British social thought. But the exchange process could be analyzed with a different set of fundamental assumptions.[2] For example, Durkheim's theory of organic solidarity implies an exchange process, even though his theory is not generally considered an exchange theory and certainly did not rest on the individualistic assumptions of British social thought. (In fact, Durkheim criticized Spencer's theory precisely on this account.) Nevertheless, growth in the division of labor and increased levels of specialization imply an increase in the volume of exchange transactions that take place in society. Organic solidarity based on interdependence could hardly be expected to increase otherwise. Even in primitive societies, characterized by mechanical solidarity, there are various forms of simple cooperation that members engage in as they carry out their common tasks. This cooperative behavior implies an exchange process.

Working in the Durkheimian tradition, French anthropologist Levi-Strauss developed a theoretical perspective on social exchanges in his analysis of marriage practices and kinship systems of primitive societies.[3] Without going into detail, we note that primitive societies did not leave the choice of marriage partner up to the individuals directly involved to the same extent that American society does, nor was the field of "eligible" marriage partners nearly as broad as in modern society. Frequently, primitive clans would have specific institutional arrangements for the exchange of women as marriage partners. A common pattern, one that Levi-Strauss analyzed in detail, was for a male to marry his mother's brother's daughter. An alternate and less frequent pattern was for a person to marry his father's sister's daughter. This latter pattern was analyzed by Malinowski for the Trobriand Islanders.

In developing his analysis of the marriage and kinship system of primitive societies, Levi-Strauss distinguished between two different systems of exchange: *restricted* exchange and *generalized* exchange. In restricted exchange members of a dyad are involved in direct exchange transactions, each member of the pair reciprocating the other on a personal basis. In generalized exchange members of a triad or larger group receive benefits from a partner *other* than the one to whom they give benefits. In other words, the exchange is indirect, not one of mutual reciprocity. The difference between the two types can be diagrammed as follows: the restricted exchange involves the pattern $A \leftrightarrow B$, $C \leftrightarrow D$, while the generalized exchange is based on the pattern $A \rightarrow B \rightarrow C \rightarrow D \rightarrow A$.

The restricted exchange pattern, in which two parties are involved in a relation of mutual reciprocity, tends to involve a strong emphasis on balance or equality. Also, there is often a heavy emotional involvement of exchange partners with one another.[4] A social system based on restricted exchanges would be a segmental social structure; this can readily be visualized if the preceding pattern were extended to include more dyadic partnerships. Each dyad is relatively self-sufficient, and there is no overall integration of the various dyads with one another. Extended to a larger system, this type of exchange system would seem to be compatible with an overall social organization made up of relatively self-sufficient families, tribes, or local communities.

In contrast to restricted exchange, generalized exchange contributes to the integration and solidarity of larger groups far more effectively. No dyad can be self-sufficient in this generalized chain pattern of exchange. As a result, there will be relatively less emphasis on *ad hoc* personal negotiation of exchange terms and relatively less concern with short-term equality. Instead, each party's interest will be in the overall operation of the entire system. Such a system can function only if each party is willing to make a contribution without concern for an immediate benefit in return. For example, *A* provides some benefit to *B,* even though *A* does not expect *B* to reciprocate personally. For this type of system to operate effectively, the parties involved must have a relatively high level of trust that others will discharge their obligations, without concern for immediate benefits in return, and that all will eventually receive the benefits to which they are entitled.

Generalized exchange is conducive to a higher level of social integration of the entire system than the segmental type of structure based on restricted exchanges. Specifically, all members of the system are linked together through the exchange process. Also, the generalized pattern should be associated with a higher level of moral development than the restricted pattern. This moral development refers to the willingness of the system's members to fulfill their obligations without concern for their individual interests (at least in the short run) and their trust that others will also conform to these moral requirements. The fundamental image of human nature, the exchange process, and social organization implied by Levi-Strauss' analysis differs from the implications of classical economic thought and British utilitarianism.

In Levi-Strauss' model, the primary purpose of the exchange process is not to enable the exchange partners to meet their individualistic needs. Instead, its significance is that it expresses the individual's moral commitment to the group. The specific form of the exchange, whether restricted or generalized, is not a matter for individuals to decide on an ad hoc basis. The form of the exchange is defined by the overall culture and is institutionalized in the social structure itself, the reality of which transcends the individual and his or her particular needs. Levi-Strauss distinguished between *economic* exchanges (in which individuals' interests are presumably paramount) and *social* exchanges (in which the integration and solidarity of the group are paramount). He explicitly rejects the use of economic or individualistic motives to explain *social* exchanges. Indeed, his own analysis of marriage and kinship behavior was intended as a rebuttal to British anthropologist Frazer's quasi-economic interpretation of primitive patterns of exchange of marriage partners.[5]

The individualistic emphasis of American exchange theory is consistent with the individualism of the American cultural heritage (as noted briefly in Chapter 1). It is interesting to note that the recent origins of contemporary American exchange theory grew out of polemical confrontation between the individualistic and collectivistic orientations. Homans, who is perhaps the foremost American representative of an individualistic approach to the development of social theory, established the rudiments of his perspective in opposition to Levi-Strauss' collectivistic explanation of marriage and kinship patterns. Homans' exchange theory also illustrates the basic strategy and logic that he insists are essential for the development of an *explanatory* social theory (as opposed to merely descriptive concepts).

HOMANS: A BEHAVIORAL APPROACH TO ELEMENTARY EXCHANGES

George Homans was educated at Harvard University and has spent most of his professional life as a member of the faculty at Harvard. Homans' writings are not limited to exchange theory. Indeed, one of his books, which we will discuss, *The Human Group,* deals primarily with the dynamics of groups as social systems. Eventually, his exchange theory will be offered to *explain* the behavior of individuals in groups, as opposed merely to *describing* these behaviors. Although Homans' 1961 book, *Social Behavior: Its Elementary Forms,* is generally regarded as the major exposition of his exchange theory, many of the basic ideas of this work were foreshadowed in his attack on Levi-Strauss' interpretation of primitive societies' marriage customs and his alternative interpretation. This was the major theme of the cross-cultural analysis that Homans undertook in collaboration with anthropologist David Schneider.[6]

Levi-Strauss had argued that the pattern in which a person married his mother's brother's daughter contributed to a higher level of solidarity than the alternative pattern whereby a person married his father's sister's daughter. According to his argument, this higher solidarity accounts for the fact that the former pattern (of marriage of mother's brother's daughter) occurs more frequently in primitive society than the alternative pattern. The reason Levi-Strauss gives for this higher solidarity is that this preferred pattern involved a generalized instead of a restricted exchange. To put this analysis in more general terms, a given institutionalized exchange pattern persists because it is *functional* or beneficial for the society. (This same general strategy, incidentally, whereby social institutions are *explained* in terms of their contributions to the overall solidarity or survival of society, also characterizes contemporary sociological functionalism.)

Homans rejected this functionalist type of explanation. For him, to show that a particular pattern is beneficial for society is not to explain why people actually conform to that pattern. Explanation of behavior requires an understanding of the motives and sentiments of human beings and not of the hypothetical needs or requirements of society. Moreover, there seems to be no way to determine definitively what the functional needs or requirements of society are, especially when it is recognized that a deficiency created by the breakdown of any one institutional pattern is usually followed by the emergence of alternative institutions to replace the one disrupted. Instead of resorting to functional-type explanations, Homans insists that exchange patterns be analyzed in terms of the motives and sentiments of those involved in the transaction.[7]

In the case of the marriage patterns described by Levi-Strauss, Homans argued that the reason for the frequent occurrence of marriage to mother's brother's daughter is simply that the individual feels emotionally closer to his mother than to his father. This is because the father has jural authority over his son, and individuals generally feel a greater social distance from those who have authority over them than from those who are more nearly equal. In contrast, where the alternative pattern of marriage to father's sister's daughter is followed, jural authority is exercised by the mother's brother and not by the father. This alternative pattern is followed by the Trobriand Islanders, as shown in Malinowski's work. In spite of the contrast in form, the same kind of explanation can be offered. This explanation is that the marriage pattern follows the line of the strongest emotional attachment. Homans' examination of the available comparative data was largely supportive of this hypothesis relating marriage patterns and authority structure.

Homans' ultimate explanation for the marriage patterns observed is a psychological-type explanation. Its appeal is to the natural (as opposed to culturally determined) sentiments of people, not to the overall integration or solidarity of society. This emphasis on explanation of social institutions at the level of individual psychology is basic in Homans' approach to theory development. Moreover, since the basic psychological processes of human beings are the same the world over, in spite of numerous cultural variations, the type of theoretical statements developed to explain social institutions or social processes should have universal applicability.

Behavioral Dynamics of Small Groups

The same goal of developing theoretical concepts and principles with wide generality is also evident in Homans' analysis of small group processes in *The Human Group*. There is also a polemical aspect to this work, just as there was in his analysis of marriage patterns and kinship systems. Specifically, Homans argued that much sociological writing is far too abstract to have clear reference to observable empirical data. Sociological concepts such as social institution, role, culture, authority structure, and status are abstract constructs, not observable concepts. As a result, it is frequently difficult to connect the theoretical concepts to any specific observable phenomenon clearly and unambiguously.[8]

Homans chose the small group for his descriptive analysis partly because the group is such a basic unit in practically all other types of social structure and all cultural settings and because involvement in groups is so pervasive in the human experience. There is also the advantage that social behavior in small groups can readily be described in terms close to the level of empirical observations.

There are three primary concepts that Homans uses for describing small groups: (1) activity, (2) interaction, and (3) sentiment. The definitions are close to the everyday life definitions.[9] *Activity* is actual behavior described at a very concrete level. Part of the description of any group should involve simply noting the activities of its members. Individuals or groups can be compared in terms of the similarity or dissimilarity of their activities and of their rate of performance of various activities. *Interaction* is simply any activity that stimulates or is stimulated by the activity of someone else. Individuals or groups can be compared in terms of frequency of interaction, in terms of who initiates interaction for whom, in terms of the channels through which interaction flows, and so on.[10] *Sentiment,* as noted earlier, is not defined merely as a subjective state (as might be expected on a commonsense level) but as an external or behavioral sign of some internal state. The signs, like the internal states they signify, may vary widely. Physiological states, such as hunger or fatigue, positive or negative emotional reactions to some event or some stimulus, feelings of liking or disliking for a fellow group member, these and many other kinds of internal physiological, psychological, or emotional states would be included under the general rubric of sentiment, as long as these internal states are manifested in some type of observable behavior. One important basis for comparison of different individuals or groups is in terms of the general strength (high or low) and direction (positive or negative) of emotional feelings toward other individuals in the groups or the group as a whole.

These three elements—activity, interaction, and sentiment—form an organized whole and are mutually interrelated.[11] That is, activities will have an effect on (and be affected by) interaction patterns and sentiments; interactions will influence and be influenced by activities and sentiments, and sentiments will be mutually related to activities and interations. If any one of these elements changes, the other two will also be likely to change.

The entire set of activities, interaction patterns, and sentiments and their mutual interrelations within a group make up the social system of the group. The range of these mutual interrelations marks the boundary of the group, and beyond this boundary is the environment within which the group exists and to which it must adapt. A full description of the group's environment would include the physical surroundings, the personality patterns and attitudes of the group members that they bring to the group, and the larger organizational or cultural context within which the group functions.

Some of the activities, interactions, and sentiments that occur within the group result from demands imposed on the group from its environment or strategies for adapting to the environment. These particular activities, interactions, and sentiments are referred to as the *external system.* Thus, for example, the members of an industrial work group would have to fulfill the various formal job requirements, comply with organizational rules and regulations to some extent, and make appropriate use of existing technical equipment or supplies simply in order to maintain their membership in the group. The technology involved, as well as the larger organizational structure, would be considered part of the group's environment.

But group members seldom limit their activities, interactions, and sentiments to those imposed by the environment or required for their survival. Instead, they elaborate or expand their activities, interactions, and sentiments over and above survival requirements. For example, members of a work group who must interact to perform their jobs may become close friends and go drinking after work or bowling on the weekends. These additional activities, interactions, and sentiments are referred to as the *internal system*.

The external and internal systems are also linked in a relationship of mutual interdependence, so that if there is a change in one system it will be likely to produce change in the other. For example, if job assignments in a work group are changed so that members work in more scattered locations, the opportunity for convivial interaction will be decreased, and individuals' sentiments toward one another may change accordingly. This would illustrate an external system effect on the internal system. By the same token, social processes that emerge in the internal system may affect the external system. For example, in a junior high school classroom a group of students may engage in horseplay in rebellion against classroom routine; in reaction, the teacher or principal may adopt a style of closer supervision or formulate a new rule that restricts students' freedom and, by implication, the internal system that they may develop.

Many additional concepts of the type traditionally used in sociological analysis can readily be defined in terms of Homans' basic concepts. For instance, the concept of *custom* would refer to activities and interaction patterns that are recurrent.[12] Similarly, a *norm* could be defined as an activity or interaction pattern that is expected to be followed by group members, with positive sentiment expressed toward those who conform and negative sentiment toward those who do not.

In spite of the usefulness of these concepts, there are logical difficulties with them. If we examine their meaning closely, we learn that they are not mutually exclusive. Each consists of some form of activity. Thus interaction is activity that is stimulated by or stimulates the activity of another, and sentiment is activity that indicates some internal state. It seems that Homans has really identified only one basic concept with two different subtypes of that one concept.

To demonstrate the usefulness of this approach, Homans selected five case studies of small groups already available in the literature and reanalyzed them in terms of the basic concepts and principles of his own perspective. The groups selected were: the bank wiring group in the Western Electric plant (which had been observed intensively as part of the series of Hawthorne studies); the Norton Street gang (an urban street corner peer group that had been studied intensively by William F. Whyte); the family system in Tikopia (a small Polynesian island that had been described and analyzed by Raymond Firth); Hilltown (a declining New England community); and the Electrical Equipment Company (a company in which strains and problems in interpersonal relations led ultimately to reorganization). The latter two studies were much larger than the typical small group in small group analysis.

These studies were used as a basis for explicit propositions illustrating the mutual interrelations among activities, interactions, and sentiments in the internal and external systems. The following proposition, for example, taken from Homans' analysis of the bank wiring group, describes the general tendency for informal social relations to emerge within bureaucratic organizations: "If the interactions between the members of a group are frequent in the external system, sentiments of liking will grow up between them, and these sentiments will lead in turn to further interactions, over and above the interactions of the external system."[13] Alternatively, the decline in the social life of Hilltown can be summarized briefly in the following two propositions: "As the frequency of interaction between the members of a group decreases in the external system, so the frequency of interaction decreases in the internal system,"[14] and ". . . a decrease in the frequency of interaction will bring about a decrease in the strength of interpersonal sentiments."[15] Such examples could be multiplied extensively.

The numerous propositions formalized in *The Human Group* are descriptive, not explanatory. That is, they state empirical uniformities in relationships between variables, but they do not attempt to show *why* these uniformities should emerge or persist. Homans attempted to move beyond description toward explanation in the book published 10 years later, *Social Behavior: Its Elementary Forms,* which is usually taken as his first full-fledged exposition of exchange theory. Homans' intention in this latter work was to develop highly general explanatory propositions from which observed empirical uniformities could be deduced.[16] His focus is even more micro than in the earlier book. While the earlier work focused on the group as an organized whole, the latter is explicitly individualistic and reductionist, with group-level propositions being derived from individual-level propositions. Also, by focusing on *elementary* social behavior, Homans explicitly limits himself to face-to-face interaction in which social exchanges are direct, not indirect (or restricted instead of generalized, to use Levi-Strauss' terminology).

Psychological Foundations of Exchange Transactions

Homans builds his exchange theory on a foundation of concepts and principles taken from behavioral psychology and elementary economics.[17] From behavioral psychology is derived an image of human behavior as shaped by differential reinforcement. Homans reviews briefly Skinner's operant conditioning laboratory experiments with pigeons, noting that their random pecking behavior can gradually be shaped by giving the pigeon grain when the appropriate target is pecked so that the frequency of pecking that specific target is increased. In the same way, if the pigeon were administered a painful electric shock for pecking a particular target, the pigeon would learn to avoid that target. The findings from these laboratory experiments with subhuman species are extrapolated by Homans to the real-life social behavior of human beings. In this context, human beings provide positive or negative reinforcement to one another in the process of interaction, thereby mutually shaping one another's behavior.

From elementary economics Homans takes concepts such as cost, rewards, and profits. The basic image of human behavior provided by economics is that human beings are continually involved in choosing between alternative behaviors, with their choices reflecting the various expected costs and rewards associated with alternative lines of behavior. Individuals tend to choose the lines of action in which the ratio of costs and rewards (or profits) will be most favorable.

Although this image of human behavior had been developed to account for economic exchanges in the marketplace, Homans' intent is to expand it to encompass *social* exchanges as well. Thus, for example, social approval as well as money can be seen as a reward, and being in a position of subordination in a relationship can likewise be a cost. The economic concept of reward would parallel the psychological concept of reinforcement, while the economic concept of cost would parallel the psychological concept of punishment. Combining the two perspectives, Homans states his overall goal as follows: "Thus the set of general propositions I shall use in this book envisages social behavior as an exchange of activity, tangible or intangible, and more or less rewarding or costly, between at least two persons."[18]

The concepts used in *The Human Group*—activity, interaction, and sentiment—are incorporated into the exchange theory developed in *Social Behavior: Its Elementary Forms* as descriptive terms. Several additional concepts are also introduced. Two of them, *quantity* and *value,* are presented as variables, which means that they will be the focus of the explanatory propositions developed.[19] *Quantity* refers simply to the frequency with which a particular behavior is emitted for a given time period, or the amount of the behavior in question. *Value* is the degree to which a particular behavior is reinforced or punished. Precise measurement of value independently of quantity is often difficult; it is too easy to make an inference regarding a person's values by noting the frequency with which he or she engages in particular forms of behavior. This means that quantity and value seem to be synonymous at the level of empirical measurement. Homans suggests that one way out of this problem is to examine a person's past experience for clues as to what kinds of behaviors are valuable or rewarding. Nevertheless, the vagueness of Homans' concept of *value* and the difficulties of using it for predictive hypotheses rather than *ex post facto* explanations is a source of criticism of Homans' theory as a genuinely deductive theory.

Deprivation and satiation, investment, and distributive justice are also basic in the explanatory propositions Homans develops. Deprivation is the length of time since a person received a particular reward; satiation is a quantity of reward received in the immediate past that is large enough to satisfy the person so that no more of that particular reward is desired for the time being. Obviously, deprivation and satiation are themselves inversely related.[20]

Investment might seem at first to be synonomous with costs, particularly long-term costs. However, there is a subtle but crucial distinction between these two concepts. Perhaps the best way to conceptualize investment is to consider it as all of the individual qualities and experiences relevant to a particular social encounter but not expended (as costs would be). Age, for example, could be considered an investment, as could seniority in an organizational context. Age or seniority are not actually "spent" in a particular encounter in the same sense that time, say, or money or physical energy might be spent. Even so, such investments usually have a bearing on the ratio of costs and rewards exchanged. In general, it is expected that people's profits (i.e., rewards minus costs) should be higher if their investments are higher.[21] For example, a long-time employee of a business firm is expected to earn a higher wage than a newcomer, even though the jobs of both might be identical.

Other investment qualities would be social rank, knowledge, expertise, and ascribed characteristics such as ethnicity, for example. To illustrate, a skilled surgeon is expected to charge higher fees than a general practitioner. Similarly, a presidential visit to a community entails more elaborate welcoming preparations than a visit by an average tourist. The matter is not so simple in the case of ethnicity, however. In a society with castelike stratification of ethnic groups, it would be expected that members of high-ranking ethnic groups should receive greater profits for a given activity than those in low-ranking ethnic groups. However, in a society based on egalitarian ideals, ethnicity is expected not to have a bearing on an individual's profits. Indeed, affirmative action policies are intended to insure that individuals are not rewarded differentially according to ethnic or racial background. In the end, the qualities or characteristics considered relevant as investment values will depend on the particular cultural traditions and values of the society (or group) in question.

The ratio of investments to profits is involved in the notion of *distributive justice,* as is the ratio of costs to rewards.[22] Distributive justice refers to individuals' judgments regarding the appropriateness or fairness of a particular distribution of costs and rewards. Other things (such as investments) being equal, individuals in an exchange transaction expect that if their costs are high, their rewards should also be high. If investments are not equal, distributive justice requires that those whose investments are higher should enjoy higher profits (i.e., a more favorable cost-reward ratio).

How do individuals arrive at their standards of fair exchange, or an appropriate ratio between costs and rewards or between profits and investments? Part of the answer is in the individual's own past experience. A person who in the past has received a particular level of reward in exchange for a particular level of cost will expect this ratio to prevail in the future, or even to increase if the individual's investments gradually increase. If a person receives *less,* this reduction will be seen as unfair. This helps account for the extreme difficulty any business firm would have in lowering wages and salaries (even if there were no inflation), even though such reductions might be necessary in a declining market to protect existing jobs. The same type of expectation holds for social exchanges (as opposed to economic ones) as well. Thus a husband or wife might complain that "You don't love me like you used to'' if the other partner seems to be even slightly less responsive or appreciative of favors given.

Another source of people's standards of fairness in exchange is based on comparison of their own outcomes with the outcomes of others who are similar in some respect. The bases for such comparisons may vary for different individuals or different groups. Characteristics such as age, expertise, occupational position (and associated responsibilities, authority, etc.), and seniority are common bases for comparison. Whatever the specific bases, individuals expect rough equality in the payoffs (or reward-cost outcomes) received by those who are similar to one another. Thus a person would feel it is unfair to be paid less for a particular job than another who is performing an identical job and is identical in training and seniority. Again, the same principle would apply in social exchanges although, admittedly, determination of precise levels of cost and reward on an objective basis would normally be far more difficult than for economic exchanges.

These concepts are incorporated into a set of basic propositions that form the heart of Homans' exchange theory. These propositions focus on the likelihood that a particular behavior pattern will be enacted, the reaction to the results of that behavior, and the process of choice between alternative behaviors.[23] Briefly, the likelihood that a particular behavior pattern will be enacted increases in direct proportion to the frequency with which that behavior has been rewarded in the past, the value of the reward received, and the similarity of the present situation to past situations in which the behavior in question was rewarded.

For example, with respect to reward frequency, a person is more likely to initiate interaction with someone who is consistently supportive than with someone who is sometimes supportive and sometimes critical. To illustrate the significance of value, a person who dislikes classical music is hardly likely to spend money buying classical albums or attending classical music concerts. Comparison of the present situation to past situations involves the ability to discriminate between situations in which a particular behavior is rewarded from those in which it is not. For example, a person desiring a hot meal will not order it in a bookstore but in a restaurant.

The probability that a particular behavior will be enacted is decreased by high cost (relative to reward received) and by the effects of satiation. The relevance of satiation is obvious with respect to physiological needs such as food and rest; with social rewards, such as social approval, for example, it may not be so obvious. Although most people would probably not reach a point where additional social approval has no value at all, those who receive a large amount of social approval may find that other kinds of rewards become *relatively* more important in the short run. For example, after receiving high grades for an academic term, many students will slack off somewhat from their studies as they attempt to ''catch up'' on social activities.

In contrast to satiation, the effects of deprivation increase the longer the time period since a person last received a particular reward. The higher the deprivation, the higher the value of a particular reward and the greater the likelihood that an effort will be made to obtain it.

An individual's reaction to the rewards received from a particular behavior will be influenced by a comparison of these rewards with those anticipated. This comparison involves the idea of distributive justice, as discussed earlier. If individuals receive less than they anticipated in a given exchange or if they received unexpected punishment, they are likely to become angry and engage in aggressive behavior. In contrast, if they fare better than they expected, they will be pleased and will be likely to provide approval to their exchange partner(s).[24]

In many situations individuals face choices as to which line of behavior to enact. Homans maintains that their choices will reflect both their assessment of the value of the rewards that can be received and their estimate of the chances of receiving that reward.[25] In many situations individuals choose a less rewarding line of action for which the reward is more certain than a potentially more rewarding alternative for which the reward is less certain. (''A bird in the hand is worth two in the bush.'')

Applications of the Basic Exchange Principles

The preceding propositions provide the foundation for analyses of numerous standard sociological concepts such as social rank, normative conformity and innovation, influence, esteem, status, and authority. In many cases experimental studies are cited to provide empirical support for the basic propositions. For example, the process of social influence typically reflects the ability of one person to reward another for compliance. One such reward is social approval, or expressions of positive sentiment toward the other person. This is why individuals who like one another are able to influence one another.[26]

Moreover, groups in which all the members like one another (or groups that are fairly cohesive) should show high rates of conformity to group norms, since such conformity is rewarded by the approval of fellow members. By the same token, groups that are low in social cohesion should show lower rates of normative conformity and thus greater heterogeneity of individuals' activities.[27] This pattern of low cohesion and low conformity is likely in groups whose members have numerous alternative sources of social approval outside the group. Because of such outside sources of approval, the cost of conformity within the group increases (since costs include alternatives foregone by a particular choice) and, as a result, expressions of social approval within the group would be low.

Some groups are characterized by competition and conflict instead of cohesion or apathy. In such groups, exchanges would include impositions of punishment or cost as well as positive reinforcement. This may be indirect or direct. If rewards cannot be shared and are in scarce supply, individuals may be expected to compete or to be in conflict with one another rather than cooperate, since cooperation would not only increase one's costs but also decrease one's reward. In contrast, cooperative behavior may be expected when rewards are greater or costs lower than would be possible through individualistic activity. The rewards need not necessarily be shared equally; the only requirement is that each person's reward-cost ratio be more favorable than it would be through individualistic competitive activity.[28]

Individuals in a cooperative group receive social approval in exchange for contributing to group goals. However, social approval is not a very scarce reward or very costly for others to provide. For this reason individuals whose contributions are extremely valuable and in scarce supply will be rewarded with esteem, or a higher-than-average level of social approval.[29] To some extent, individuals grant esteem to others whose activities are considered valuable even though they may not benefit personally from these activities. This would indicate a general commitment to standards of distributive justice.

Exchange theory is not limited to dealing with relationships between people who like one another or find their shared activities mutually rewarding. Individuals may interact with others they do not like, even though the level of dislike might actually increase as interaction continues. This pattern can readily be explained in terms of the costs of avoiding interaction.[30] If these costs are great enough, the individual will continue to interact in spite of the lack of positive sentiment. Many examples of this phenomenon could be noted; an employee may intensely dislike a boss but continue to interact simply because another job cannot readily be found with all the benefits of the present one. In such a situation, the individual's choice is simply the lesser of two evils; it reflects a choice for a lesser cost instead of a greater cost.

When individuals make choices from among alternative interaction partners, what factors influence their choice? Specifically, are individuals more likely to choose others who are similar to them in terms of status, or are they likely to choose others who are higher or lower.[31] This would be influenced to some extent by the individual's own status. In many cases, however, individuals choose others who are similar to them in status and in other respects as well. Persons who are similar should be able to provide social support for one another at relatively low cost. In addition, interaction between equals does not entail the cost of being in a subordinate position for either partner or the risk of status loss. Being in a subordinate position would result from interacting with a higher-status person, and losing status with one's peers could result from being associated with a lower-status person. On the other hand, persons who share a relatively high status may avoid interaction with one another if they are competing for dominance, and low-status persons (for whom the risk of status loss would be minimal) may seek to enhance their status by being associated with someone of higher status.

In groups or social relationships that are task oriented rather than sociable, we should expect relatively more interaction *between* status levels. For one thing, if a person's high status is based on above-average knowledge relevant to task accomplishment, we should expect lower-status persons to interact with these higher-status persons in order to benefit from their knowledge. In such a situation, the reward of task accomplishment would offset the subordination involved in the encounter. Moreover, we should expect the higher-status person to initiate interaction to the entire group more than the lower-status person. Communicating to the entire group is less costly than responding individually to each lower-status person who solicits advice or help. Also, in many cases the lower-status person probably would experience less subordination as a member of a group receiving help from a higher-status person than by soliciting help on an individual basis.

Being able to contribute constructive advice in a task-oriented group is not the only source of high status, however. Status is a multidimensional concept. Homans offers a general definition of status as ''the stimuli a man presents to other men (and to himself).''[32] There may be several characteristics that indicate a person's rank, esteem, or authority. Some of these will be ascribed, such as family, racial, or ethnic background. Other characteristics will be achieved, such as a person's educational attainment or physical skills. Some of these characteristics would be relevant as investments in an exchange transaction. But whether ascribed or achieved, the fact that there may be several such characteristics leads to an interesting question regarding status congruence or consistency. Briefly, to what degree are an individual's various status characteristics consistent with one another in establishing his or her rank? Equally important, what effect does status consistency or inconsistency have on an individual's interaction patterns and the reactions of others?[33]

If an individual is *consistently* higher or lower than a second individual on all relevant status characteristics, that person should be described as having high status congruence. In contrast, if an individual is higher than another individual on some characteristics but lower on other characteristics, this would indicate incongruence or inconsistency of status. One of the main effects of status incongruence is that it reduces an individual's security or certitude in social relations. There is uncertainty as to whether others will respond in terms of the relatively low-status characteristic or in terms of the relatively high-status characteristic. For example, given the traditional sex-role stereotypes of our society, a female physician would, at least in many social circles, face the problem of social insecurity. Will others respond to her in terms of her sexual identity as a woman? Or will they respond in terms of her professional status as a doctor? Or will the ranking of the two status characteristics be averaged, so that she enjoys higher esteem than most women but not as much esteem as most doctors?[34]

Since status incongruence produces social insecurity, it could be considered a cost, and efforts to reduce incongruence would, if successful, be rewarding. In the short run, such efforts may involve developing a style of presentation of self so that the high-status instead of the low-status characteristics are emphasized. In the long run, the desire to reduce status incongruence may even lead to efforts to change the basis for evaluation of a person's rank; for example, the women's liberation movement represents an effort to eliminate sexual identity as a basis for differential job assignment, pay, and promotion. If these efforts are not successful, the individual is likely to be dissatisfied in social relationships and to feel that he or she is the victim of injustice.

Although Homans' analysis discusses mainly face-to-face behavior involving a direct exchange of costs and rewards, the last chapter of *Social Behavior: Its Elementary Forms* launches into a discussion of the contrast between elementary social behavior as subinstitutional behavior versus institutional behavior.[35] One of the most important differences between elementary (or subinstitutional) behavior and institutional behavior is that the latter is much more complex, with many exchanges being indirect instead of direct. Also, institutional behavior involves greater usage of *general* reinforcers (such as money) that are subsequently exchanged for primary reinforcers to meet individuals' basic needs. Nevertheless, Homans insists, social institutions do not persist of their own built-in dynamic independently of elementary social processes. They are continually dependent on the dynamics of elementary social behavior whereby individuals attempt to satisfy their needs as human beings (and not as members of some social institution or society). It follows that if conformity to institutional norms should become less rewarding or more costly, rates of social deviance should be expected to increase and, ultimately, the institutional patterns themselves may be expected to change.

JOHN THIBAUT AND HAROLD H. KELLEY: EXCHANGE THEORY APPLIED TO DYADS AND GROUPS

Thibaut and Kelley developed an exchange theory perspective in which they contrasted the exchange processes manifested in dyadic relationships with those manifested in groups.[36] Some of the ideas that they developed in *The Social Psychology of Groups* will be noted briefly. To begin, every individual, either alone or in a social encounter, has a repertoire of potential behaviors that *could* be enacted. A choice of any one behavior or set of behaviors from this array will, of course, reduce or eliminate the possibility of enacting other behaviors. In an interaction sequence or social relationship, the behavioral repertoires of two or more persons can be combined to form the total array of joint behavioral or interactional opportunities.[37]

What determines which of the various behavioral or interactional possibilities will actually be enacted by the members of the dyad? The answer is the rewards and costs anticipated or experienced in connection with these behaviors. Individuals choose the behaviors that they anticipate will result in the most favorable reward-cost outcome. In a dyad (or larger group) the actual combination of behaviors will reflect the outcome evaluations of all of those involved in the interaction sequence. This means that any one person's outcomes will be contingent on the behaviors or reactions of the others involved as well as on his or her own behavior.

The exchange pattern is initiated through a tentative and exploratory interaction process in which potential exchange partners offer samples of alternative behaviors and/or reactions from their respective repertoires until they arrive at a mutually satisfactory combination.[38] This process need not necessarily develop into a mutually satisfactory social relationship. Either or both partners may, after briefly sampling one another's behaviors and reactions, decide to withdraw because of a lack of satisfaction with the anticipated outcomes. This process is particularly visible in the "dangling conversations" that occur at parties or other sociable gatherings. Participants at such gatherings usually go through a series of attempted and aborted conversational overtures before getting into a serious conversation (if they ever do). There are occasions, however, where enduring friendships emerge as the ultimate outcome of what may have been a casual introduction at a party. This would occur if both parties experience a series of favorable outcomes from their various mutual overtures to one another.

What determines the nature or size of the rewards and costs that are exchanged in a social relationship? Thibaut and Kelley emphasize two different types of determinants of rewards and costs: exogenous and endogenous. Exogenous factors are external to the relationship itself, such as individuals' personal and social characteristics (social background, knowledge and skills, etc.) and environmental factors (such as ecological setting or geographical distance).

Endogenous factors emerge within the relationship or are intrinsic to the interaction sequence. For example, as a relationship develops, the parties in the relationship become more knowledgeable about one another's unique preferences and characteristics and, therefore, are able to predict one another's responses more accurately. The result is that it becomes relatively easier to elicit a rewarding response from the other person, and there is a lower level of risk involved.

On the other hand, as a relationship expands, there is the risk that one or both partners will introduce behaviors that interfere with already established interaction patterns. This would be exemplified, for example, in a recently established marital relationship when the husband decides to resume his bachelor habit of reading the newspaper at the breakfast table, much to the distress of his new bride. Also included among the endogenous factors would be the effects of satiation and fatigue; individuals gradually move toward a point where the cost of continued exertion outweighs the continued receipt of rewards.

A person's satisfaction with a given relationship or continuation in that relationship is not solely a function of the *actual* costs and rewards that are exchanged. Like Homans, Thibaut and Kelley emphasize the importance of the process whereby given outcomes are compared against anticipated or alternative outcomes. Two different bases of comparison are distinguished.[39] The first, the *comparison level* (CL), refers to the individual's own standards against which costs, rewards, and outcomes are evaluated. This may be based on previous experience or derived from the individual's perceptions of the outcomes of others (including one's partner, perhaps) who are similar in important respects. Or they may be based on the general cultural expectations of what constitutes a fair exchange. Individuals whose actual outcomes in an exchange transaction or social relationship equal or exceed their comparison level will be satisfied, while those whose actual outcomes fall below it will be dissatisfied.

The second basis, the *comparison level for alternatives* (CL_{alt}), refers to the perceived outcomes available in alternative relationships. This level determines the degree of *attraction* to a given relationship rather than the degree of satisfaction in it. The two comparison levels may vary independently. Individuals may remain in unsatisfying relationships if there are no more favorable alternatives. For example, a person may hate his or her job but still not quit because no better (i.e., less costly or more rewarding) jobs are available. Or individuals may leave relationships with which they are relatively satisfied if they become aware of an alternative in which the outcomes are even more favorable. A relatively satisfied employee who accepts an even higher-paying position elsewhere illustrates this process.

Individuals in relatively satisfactory and stable relationships do not necessarily go through the process of conscious calculation of costs and rewards every time an exchange transaction takes place. Instead, exchange transactions may gradually become more and more routine or automatic. This means that conscious efforts to predict consequences in advance or to evaluate alternative behaviors or alternative relationships so as to maximize outcomes are often absent.[40] For example, employees who are reasonably satisfied with their jobs may not become aware of more attractive alternatives simply because they are not looking. Similarly, marital partners develop certain routines in their relationships without any conscious evaluation or comparison. The process of conscious deliberation should be expected to come into play when the individual must make choices at crucial turning points or if the outcomes of a given routine relationship fall drastically below the individual's comparison level.

Thibaut and Kelley attempt to extend their analysis from dyadic relationships to groups. In a manner somewhat reminiscent of Simmel, they analyze the enlarged range of interactional options available in a triad or a larger group as contrasted to a dyad. For example, three persons will form a triad with genuine interdependence only if the most favorable outcomes of each member are dependent on *both* of the others. If, however, two of the members find interaction with each other to be more enjoyable than interaction involving all three persons, the triad would naturally tend to break down into a dyad and an isolate.[41]

Coalition formation is another social process possible only in relationships involving more than two parties. Coalition formation can occur in a group as small as a triad as well as in large-scale social systems. Coalitions may be expected to be formed between persons who are unable to attain their desired outcomes alone but whose combined actions will insure their success in obtaining these outcomes. There must be a minimal degree of compatibility or congruence between the outcomes of the coalition members. Also, their outcomes must be incompatible or incongruent with the outcomes of those against whom the coalition is formed.

If the outcomes are in scarce supply, so that one coalition member's gain means a loss for the other(s) in the coalition, people should be expected to form coalitions with those whose power or resources available for affecting the outcome are the *least* that are necessary for success. This would result in the least amount of sharing of favorable outcomes. In other words, if an individual has a choice of forming a coalition with someone who is relatively weak or someone else who is relatively strong, either of whom could insure the coalition's success, it would be advantageous to form the coalition with the weakest potential partner. This strategy is based on the assumption that the sharing of favorable outcomes will be proportional to the contributions made.[42]

Another example of the differences in reward-cost outcomes that are possible with increased group size is provided by the situation of a leader or high-status person. Other things being equal, the rewards of being a leader or high-status individual are magnified in a large group. Also, a person whose above-average skill or expertise helps others to maximize their outcomes can increase the number of persons with whom he or she shares this skill or expertise at only slight additional personal cost (at least up to a point). In exchange, there is a considerable increase in the social approval and esteem that he or she receives, simply because there are more people to provide such rewards.

Also, the differentiation between task leadership and socioemotional leadership (which Bales and others have documented) can readily be explained in terms of Thibaut and Kelley's perspective.[43] As groups increase in size, the probability that complex and indirect exchanges will be developed also increases. One effect of this increased complexity is that there may be a lag between the time that an individual incurs the costs associated with the group's activity and the time that a compensating reward is received. As a result, the leader is often in a position of having to impose demands without providing an immediate payoff. Negative feelings toward the leader may develop and, when widespread among the members of a group, such feelings could undermine social solidarity. This decline in solidarity can be prevented by a socioemotional leader who would provide various immediate rewards, such as social approval, emotional support, and tension release. The result is that individuals' attraction to the group will remain high in spite of the negative (or ambivalent) feelings that may develop toward the task leader.

A final example of the changes in social dynamics that results from increasing size is that reliance on an impersonal normative structure increases.[44] The reason is that it becomes more difficult to negotiate the details of exchange transactions to everyone's satisfaction on an *ad hoc,* transaction-by-transaction basis. With the development of impersonal norms, however, such negotiations become unnecessary (or at least relatively less important), since the costs and rewards that everyone experiences are predetermined (to a degree). Moreover, with the emergence of an impersonal normative system, social approval may be given as a general reward in exchange for whatever cost may be involved in normative conformity.

These examples illustrate some of the important differences between exchange possibilities in dyads and larger groups. Peter Blau, the next exchange theorist to be discussed, concentrated on the issue of how larger or macro social structures emerge from the elementary exchanges that occur on a face-to-face basis at the micro level.

EMERGENCE OF MACRO STRUCTURES FROM ELEMENTARY SOCIAL EXCHANGES: BLAU'S EXCHANGE THEORY

Peter Blau received his graduate training in sociology at Columbia University. He has held academic posts at Cornell University and the University of Chicago and eventually returned to Columbia. A large part of his contributions to sociology are in the area of complex organization. Blau's exchange theoretical perspective is important for our purposes because of his explicit effort to show the interdependence between social exchanges at the micro level (such as the face-to-face direct exchanges that Homans analyzed) and the emergence of larger (or macro) social structures. Blau's most systematic exposition of his exchange theory is presented in *Exchange and Power in Social Life*.[45]

Unlike Homans, Blau does not concern himself with basic psychological processes such as reinforcement and the like. Although he recognizes the existence of "primitive psychological processes"[46] that underlie social relationships, his focus is on the structure of associations resulting from exchange transactions. In short, while Homans was a *reductionist* who wished to explain social behavior in terms of elementary psychological processes, Blau is concerned with showing that elementary exchange processes generate *emergent* phenomena in the form of more complex social structures. Thus, for our purposes, Blau's theory provides an ideal transition from the micro to the macro level.

Blau does not claim that the principles of exchange theory explain all interaction. Instead, "Social exchange as here conceived is limited to actions that are contingent on rewarding reactions from others and that cease when these expected reactions are not forthcoming.[47] Such interactions reflect, to a greater or lesser degree, explicit expectations and evaluations of alternative outcomes.

Human beings are not motivated in Blau's model solely by narrow selfish interests. Like Homans, Blau emphasized the importance of social approval as a reward. Even altruistic behavior can be motivated by the desire for social approval. To be sure, this desire reflects the egoistic need to be well thought of by others but, in order to achieve this type of reward, the individual must transcend narrow egoistic impulses and consider the needs and desires of others. Blau even applies his exchange theoretic principles to an analysis of relationships between lovers in a section entitled "Excursus on Love."[48] In such relationships many of the specific exchanges that occur can be seen as symbolic of the emotional attraction of each party to the other, of their mutual attachment to the relationship, and of their desire to induce even greater commitment from the other party. Material items that might be exchanged, such as gifts, are important not for their practical utility or economic worth, but as tangible expressions of emotional commitment.

Intrinsic versus Extrinsic Rewards

Social relations can be classified into two general categories based whether the rewards exchanged are intrinsic or extrinsic.[49] *Intrinsic* rewards are derived from the relationship itself, such as in the example of the love relationship just mentioned. In contrast, *extrinsic* relationships serve as a means for some other reward instead of being rewarding in their own right. In such cases the reward is detachable from the specific relationship and could, in principle, be obtained from any exchange partner. Economic relationships in the marketplace are perhaps the most obvious manifestation of extrinsic relationships.

The distinction between intrinsic and extrinsic exchanges parallels the distinction between social and economic exchanges. The two types contrast in several important respects. One of the major differences is that social exchanges are not subject to deliberate negotiation and bargaining in the same sense that economic transactions are. This is due partly to the fact that the authenticity of many social rewards depends on their *not* being consciously negotiated. Partners in a love relationship or close friends who covertly "keep score" on the frequency or volume of favors exchanged demonstrate thereby a lack of the intrinsic emotional commitment on which such relationships depend. Usually, when one party in an intrinsic relationship has to resort to reminding the other of favors done ("After all I've done for you . . ."), this indicates at least a partial break in the relationship, or at least in the equilibrium or mutuality of commitment. Even for casual acquaintances involved in a *social* exchange, the authenticity and value of social approval or other nonmaterial rewards depend heavily on their *not* being provided simply as an inducement for some other reward. For example, people generally have negative feelings toward the flatterer who provides a great deal of approval to an exchange partner merely to induce that partner to provide some favor. The ulterior motive that is behind such approval undermines its genuineness and hence its value as a reward.

The intrinsically rewarding social bonds manifested in a close friendship and the impersonal economic exchanges in the marketplace illustrate extreme cases of intrinsic and extrinsic rewards. However, the intrinsic–extrinsic distinction should be seen as a continuum, with many relationships reflecting varying mixtures of intrinsic and extrinsic rewards. For example, a group of co-workers or professional colleagues who have worked together for a long time and developed strong friendships with one another would be involved in an exchange of intrinsic rewards in their friendship; yet their association with one another may also enhance their professional career advancement in various ways. Or, a person might associate with a higher-status person partly because of the intrinsic rewards involved in the association and partly because of extrinsic benefits such as the enhancement of one's own status that results from being in the company of a higher-status person. It is often a poignant discovery to a person who has lost status for some reason to learn that many friends and associates were attracted to the high status, not to his or her personal characteristics. On the other hand, it is commonly recognized that only when one is "down" does one discover who one's true friends are. Probably most relationships have varying combinations of intrinsic and extrinsic rewards.

Intrinsic rewards emerge in a relationship as the parties involved gradually come to exchange more and more rewards of various kinds. Ultimately, as a result of this gradual enlargement of the set of rewards exchanged, a relationship takes on a unique character that makes comparison with alternative partners difficult if not impossible and inappropriate.[50] Close friends, lovers, or family members share an extensive and unique set of exchange patterns that, in their totality, are not available from any other source. Thus the total array of rewards exchanged becomes fused with the particular partner with whom these rewards are exchanged. This uniqueness contributes to and helps define the intrinsic character of the relationship.

However, in the initial stages of many intrinsic relationships comparisons between alternative potential exchange partners are often made. This indicates that the initial attraction of exchange partners to one another is extrinsic. That is, the reward desired is not intrinsically linked with any one particular partner. For example, the relationship between lovers or marital partners is certainly based on intrinsic rewards that seem unique to the particular relationship; nevertheless, individuals in our society typically go through a process of comparing alternative partners before gradually becoming attached or formalizing a commitment (as in marriage) to just one. Persons involved in dating are continually assessing and comparing alternative dating partners' sexual attractiveness, personality characteristics, popularity with others, intellectual interests, recreational tastes, and so on. Paradoxically, the process of courtship and mate selection involves a process of comparing alternative partners for a relationship that ultimately precludes comparison.

The transformation of relationships from extrinsic attraction (involving comparison) to intrinsic attraction (in which comparison is not appropriate) would apply most clearly to relationships in which individuals have a certain degree of freedom to choose from among alternative partners. Children in a family, for example, are hardly in a position to compare alternative sets of parents. On the other hand, even in this example, most parents probably hope that their children will eventually love and appreciate them for their own sake and not because of what they do for them. And children often learn that a display of *intrinsic* attachment and appreciation can be effective in securing some *extrinsic* favor from their parents.

Even though relationships between parents and their children might be analyzed in terms of the intrinsic and extrinsic exchanges involved, Blau's theory applies most clearly to relationships of choice. Such choices reflect, either implicitly or explicitly, individuals' consideration of the costs and rewards involved. As Blau says, ''An individual is attracted to another if he expects associating with him to be in some way rewarding to himself.''[51] However, in order actually to reap this potential reward, the individual must provide some inducement to the other person to supply it. Such inducement is provided by offering a reward. In a social exchange this offering of a reward need not be a conscious process. It may involve nothing more than attempting to be friendly rather than hostile in an encounter.

In other words, an individual who is attracted to another will attempt to become attractive to the other individual.[52] This strategy of attracting others by being attractive is so common that numerous everyday examples could be cited. With extrinsic exchanges in the market the effort to be attractive to potential exchange partners (or customers) is often overt and blatant. The merchant whose advertisements promise higher quality at lower cost than competitors is an example. With intrinsic exchanges the process is less blatant and more subtle, but the basic dynamics are the same. A man or woman who is attracted to a potential dating partner will attempt, in various subtle ways, to become as attractive as possible to the other party. This may involve an effort to impress the other person with interesting and enjoyable personality characteristics; it may involve strategies to accentuate attractive physical characteristics; or it may include a display of abundant financial resources. Similarly, persons involved in a developing friendship will attempt to strengthen the friendship by bestowing rewards of various kinds on one another, thereby increasing the willingness of the other person to bestow additional rewards in return.

There is a dilemma, however, in individuals' efforts to be attractive.[53] A person who demonstrates unusually attractive or impressive qualities may inhibit the willingness of others to enter a relationship because of the high cost that they perceive will be required. One cost is that of becoming dependent on another person for a reward that is greater in value than any reward that could be offered in return. Another cost is the subordination in status that results from being compared to the highly impressive person. Thus, ironically, the very qualities that may make a person an attractive associate (the ability to supply relatively high rewards) may inhibit others from seeking to establish a relationship through which those rewards could be gained. For example, a young man may hesitate to approach a very attractive woman because he fears that she must have numerous offers and so would probably turn him down.

To overcome this inhibiting effect of being impressive, a person must demonstrate a willingness to provide high rewards to others at relatively low cost. One way to do this is to attempt to appear approachable as well as impressive. This phenomenon can also be observed frequently in everyday life. An individual who impresses others with some outstanding quality (skills, experience, personality characteristics, etc.) will often, immediately afterward, engage in self-depreciating behavior, or attempt to demonstrate that in spite of these outstanding qualities he or she is really no different from anyone else. A widely publicized and highly regarded example of this strategy was President Carter's walk down Pennsylvania Avenue following his inauguration, whereby he demonstrated that even though he was the president he did not have to flaunt his new position by riding his limousine at the head of the parade.

A person's efforts to be attractive through an appropriate mixture of displays of impressiveness and modesty reveal an implicit awareness of the importance of balance in exchange transactions. Exchanges are balanced when the rewards and costs that are exchanged are roughly equal in value, in the long run if not the short run. The effort to maintain an appropriate balance in exchange transactions reflects the "norm of reciprocity."[54] The norm of reciprocity means that favors done for others should be reciprocated. The reciprocation may take a variety of forms. For example, a person may repay a favor by providing a similar kind of service in return. Or a person may provide a different kind of service that is roughly equal in value to the service received. Or, in the absence of actual favors performed in return, the recipient of a favor should at least express gratitude and appreciation.

In many cases complete reciprocation need not be immediate. Indeed, for *social* exchanges an appropriate time interval between receipt of a favor and reciprocation with an equally valuable favor can provide an inducement for both parties to maintain their relationship.[55] The one who provided the favor has an interest in maintaining it in order to receive an eventual return on the "investment," while the recipient will have an equally strong interest in maintaining the relationship so as to be able to reciprocate eventually and thereby avoid the highly disapproved reputation of seeming ungrateful. Besides, the recipient may wish to receive an additional favor in the future; if so, the ability to induce the other party to provide it is enhanced considerably if past favors are reciprocated.

The maintenance of an appropriate balance in the transactions between exchange partners helps to preserve a state of equality between them. In many cases, however, differences in the needs and/or resources of exchange partners result in imbalance in their exchange transactions.[56] The supplier of benefits that others need but cannot reciprocate will be in a position to demand compliance with his or her influence attempts in exchange for continued provision of such benefits. This effort to explain how power differences emerge from imbalanced exchanges is one of the central themes of Blau's exchange theory and provides the transition between exchange processes at the micro level and macro structures.

Emergence of Power Structures from Imbalanced Exchanges[57]

To understand more fully Blau's model of how power inequalities emerge, let us imagine the situation of a person (individual A) who needs certain services or favors that are available only from one other person (individual B), but who has no resources to offer as an inducement for providing such services or favors. If individual A is unwilling to do without, the only option is to try to persuade individual B to provide the needed service or favor on a unilateral basis (i.e., without receiving a reciprocating service in return). One common way to do this is to request the service with a certain degree of deference and then offer gratitude and appreciation on a lavish scale when it is given. Although one such transaction will probably not in itself lead to inequality in power, even a simple one-time exchange of this sort involves a tacit acknowledgment by the recipient of a certain degree of indebtedness to the supplier of the service.

Now let us assume that individual A wishes to continue receiving benefits from individual B on a regular or continuous basis. At some point, continued expressions of gratitude and appreciation from A will become inadequate as an inducement for B. In addition to B's increasing costs, the reward value of A's gratitude would probably decline due to satiation. Individual A may try to compensate by becoming even more elaborate and lavish in expressions of gratitude. But even these inflated expressions of gratitude and appreciation may eventually become inadequate as an inducement for individual B to continue incurring the increasing costs involved in the unilateral exchange.

Eventually and inevitably, the beneficiary of one-sided generosity must assume a position of subordination, at least if he or she wants to continue the relationship. To assume a position of subordination is to acknowledge one's indebtedness and dependence on the generosity of the other party; it is to recognize one's own inferiority or lesser attractiveness as an exchange partner in comparison with the greater attractiveness of one's benefactor. A status difference emerges as a result of inequality in exchange transactions, with higher status (or esteem) being earned by those who excel in the unreciprocated benefits they provide to their exchange partners.

Differentiation of status is not the only effect of imbalanced exchanges. In some cases, high esteem, like expressions of gratitude and appreciation, may eventually become inadequate as an inducement for the high-status person to continue incurring the costs involved in unilaterally supplying rewards to lower-status persons. At this point, if the lower-status person has become dependent on such unilaterally supplied rewards, the only recourse may be to offer compliance or accept the benefactor's demands for it in exchange for continued provision of needed rewards on a unilateral basis.

The extent of compliance expected will depend on the value of the services or rewards received. A person who does a small favor for an acquaintance on a one-time basis may be satisfied with an immediate expression of gratitude and a general understanding that the favor will probably be returned if needed at some unspecified time in the future. Then, when the favor is returned, the obligation is thereby fulfilled, the small power difference erased, and the relationship balanced. But if large favors are performed unilaterally on a continuous or repeated basis, the obligations thereby created may gradually become so extensive that no single act of compliance will be sufficient to cancel the indebtedness or balance the relationship. In this way, power differences emerge from imbalanced exchanges. Recipients of unilaterally provided favors or services are under an obligation to comply with the wishes, demands, or influence attempts of the providers of such services if they desire to maintain the relationship and continue to receive the rewards involved.

Strategies for Acquiring Power or Avoiding Subordination. In many cases persons who have surplus resources or other potentially rewarding characteristics are eager to offer various services or benefits to others on a unilateral basis. In this way they can enjoy the numerous rewards associated with having high status or power over them. Indeed, a common strategy for attempting to acquire power over others is to overwhelm them with benefits to demonstrate superior status and to create indebtedness.[58] The general process of competition for status and power often involves efforts to provide more rewards to potential exchange partners than others are able to provide.

Numerous illustrations exist that demonstrate how inequalities in exchange transactions create compliance obligations and power differences between exchange associates. The well-to-do community philanthropist and local politician who periodically provides various community services thereby creates an obligation on the part of the community residents to exhibit an appropriate degree of deference and respect and to support his or her political ambitions through votes or other means. In the same way, when large business corporations or other political pressure or interest groups provide extensive financial contributions to candidates for public office, they create obligations in those politicians to adopt favorable policies when elected. There need not be any overt negotiation that might be construed as efforts at influence buying or corruption; the norm of reciprocity is generally understood to be relevant.

In another context, as Blau described in his analysis of informal bureaucratic practices, individuals in a work group who have superior experience or expertise can achieve high informal rank and power by providing consultation services to less experienced colleagues.[59] On a different level, the mother-in-law who seeks to overwhelm the newly married couple with lavish gifts that cannot be reciprocated probably expects to be able to exert some subtle influence on their family life. As a final example, the idea that power is rooted in the ability to supply benefits to subordinates is blatantly revealed in the promises of politicians running for office that if they are given the power of an elective office, they will be able to supply many more benefits to the public (or to various interest groups whom they happen to be addressing) than their opponents.

An individual who does not wish to become subordinate through indebtedness to and dependence on others can adopt a strategy of refusing to accept services or favors that cannot be repaid with services or favors of roughly equal value. The poor but proud person who refuses to accept charitable contributions, the politician who refuses excessively large contributions, the newly married couple who refuse to accept an inordinate amount of largesse from their parents, or the nonconformist who refuses to worry about the approval or disapproval of others demonstrate the strategy of maintaining one's independence through avoidance of one-sided exchange relationships that would lead to subordination.

This strategy of doing without a particular reward is only one of four different strategies that Blau, following Emerson, identified for avoiding indebteness and subordination.[60] In addition, dependence on others can be avoided by acquiring resources that can be used to provide reciprocal services of equal value. This would lead to a relationship of mutual dependence or interdependence instead of a one-way dependency relationship. Another strategy is to obtain needed services from some alternative source with whom reciprocal interdependence can be established. A final strategy is to use force; this may involve actual physical coercion, or it may involve depriving a person of rewards received from some other source. In either case, this strategy is incompatible with voluntary relationships and will often not be acceptable because of legal or moral constraints. Nevertheless, established governments are authorized to use this strategy if necessary. If individuals are unable or unwilling to adopt at least one of these strategies, their only alternative may be to accept a subordinate status in a dependency relation with someone who will provide the needed service or reward in exchange for their subordination and/or compliance.

Emergence of Power Structures in Task Groups. The same process by which an individual acquires power through unilaterally providing rewarding services also applies to groups or larger organizations. In order to trace the dynamics of this process, let us imagine a hypothetical newly formed task group in which the members initially seem to be equal to one another in overall status. How will a power structure emerge in such a group?

Initially, interaction might be disorganized and random. After initial mutual introductions, the patterns of conversation will be likely to go through an exploratory phase in which there seems to be no clear focus or direction. Essentially, as Blau points out, this exploratory conversation involves competition by the members to prove themselves attractive (or more attractive than others) to the others in the group.[61] The process described earlier whereby individuals attempt to strike an appropriate balance between being impressive and being approachable will, of course, be relevant. But a necessary condition for being either impressive or approachable is that the individual have the attention of others. Thus the initial competition is for one another's attention or, more simply, for speaking time.

Out of this random exploratory conversation certain patterns emerge. Some individuals will succeed in their attempts to demonstrate impressive qualities to a greater extent than others. Some may succeed in being more approachable or better liked than others. Since the group is a task group, we might expect that those who emerge as most impressive will exhibit certain abilities or skills or knowledge relevant to the group's task. Gradually, patterns of communication shift so that the most impressive persons succeed in capturing the attention of the entire group more than the others do. If several persons succeed in demonstrating impressive qualities, they may compete with one another for domination in the group. At the same time, those who have lost out in the competitive struggle for high status will begin to compete among themselves for mutual respect and favorable attention by those who are emerging as dominant. Eventually, one person may succeed in standing out as more impressive than any of the others. In effect, leadership results from the potential leader's ability to provide benefits to the others in the group on a unilateral basis or to convince the others that following his or her influence attempts will be more rewarding than any other alternative.

If the leader's ideas are effective in enabling the group to accomplish its task, the group's performance will reinforce the leader's position. Members' compliance will have been rewarded through task accomplishment, and the leader will thereby have a basis for expecting continued compliance in the future. The leader also will be likely to assume the responsibility for distributing the rewards gained through successful task accomplishment and, as any politician who has ever helped secure jobs for friends and supporters knows, this can create additional indebtedness on the part of subordinates.

There may be other kinds of rewards that the leader can use to reinforce power by increasing the group members' individual and collective indebtedness. For example, mere social approval by a high-status person such as a leader is generally considered of higher value than social approval by a lower-ranking person. Also, by virtue of being a leader, a person may be able to augment the resources he or she controls, and these resources can be used to provide favors to subordinates to reinforce their subordination. Since the leader is able to collect payments (not necessarily material) from several subordinates, the total accumulation of resources that becomes available might be extensive. As anyone who has ever collected money for a Christmas present knows, numerous small contributions do add up.

Briefly, a leader's success breeds additional success; the leader's power is augmented by virtue of being the leader. In an extreme case, the leader may thoroughly overwhelm subordinates with lavish benefits of various kinds, thereby increasing their dependence to such a degree that it becomes impossible for them ever to come close to discharging the resulting indebtedness.

This model of how leadership structures emerge is perhaps most evident in groups in which the members find group involvement to be personally rewarding. In contrast, in groups in which members do not share a commitment to any group goals or members choose to use one of the previously described strategies for avoiding indebtedness and maintaining independence, this model would not apply. Everyday life offers examples of groups in which members are not strongly committed to shared goals or would-be leaders are unable to create the obligations of subordinates that would consolidate their leadership role. The result is a leaderless group in which members' activities are likely to flounder and their energy to dissipate for lack of a common focus.

Stabilization of Power Structures. If a leader does emerge, however, there are additional emergent processes that contribute to the stabilization of the leadership structure. These processes consist of the development of shared values and norms that legitimate the leadership structure.[62] The result is that the leader is seen as having a *right* to expect compliance from subordinates, regardless of any specific benefits that might be supplied in return. The leader's position becomes one of *authority,* not mere *power* over needed resources. When this occurs, the leader will be able to demand compliance even when there is a temporary disruption in the flow of rewards to subordinates. This whole process does not occur in a vacuum. From the earliest exploratory conversations to the stabilization of an emergent leadership structure, interaction patterns and exchange transactions will be guided and influenced by the already existing wider cultural context. The normal of reciprocity, for example, does not have to be created anew by each group in which imbalanced exchanged transactions develop. The values and norms that ultimately emerge to stabilize a group's leadership structure are not created on a purely *ad hoc* basis; they will reflect the influence of the wider cultural and institutional context.

The legitimation of a leadership structure through shared values and norms is often essential in enabling a group to move toward long-range goals. Progress in moving toward long-range goals often requires deferment of immediate gratification. A leader whose influence attempts are reinforced by the group's values and norms will be able to persuade members to incur costs in moving toward long-range goals without any immediate payoff except the internal satisfaction and social approval that results from normative conformity. Subordinates themselves may even reinforce the leader's authority by providing social approval to one another for their conformity with the leader's influence attempts.

In a group in which a mutually satisfactory leadership structure has emerged, both the leader and subordinates will have an interest in stabilizing their relationship through legitimating values and norms instead of relying solely on the short-run cost-reward balance of their exchange transactions. The leader will have an obvious interest in stabilizing and legitimating his or her leadership position. By holding legitimate authority, the leader is protected from the necessity of continually having to provide short-term payoffs to members to maintain their indebtedness and willingness to comply. But the subordinates will also have an interest in stabilizing the relationship in order to be protected from excessive demands that might be imposed by the leader and to insure continued receipt of the benefits supplied by the leader. In the absence of restraining values and norms the leader could take advantage of the dependence of subordinates by making demands that they perceive as excessive. Thus values and norms that define the rights and obligations of all involved help protect subordinates from arbitrary or unreasonable demands by the leader or from an arbitrary or unexpected withdrawal of rewards on which subordinates have become dependent.

Legitimation processes frequently break down in groups and organizations;

various types of opposition movements often emerge and are sometimes successful in overthrowing established power structures. These processes, which can also be understood in light of the basic principles of exchange theory, will be dealt with more fully in the following section.

From Imbalanced Exchanges to Macro Structures

The emergence of a leadership structure from imbalanced exchanges and its stabilization by legitimating values and norms means that the leader is in a position to control and coordinate the actions of subordinates in developing a group line of action.[63] The extent of this control will reflect the extent of the subordinates' dependence on the rewards derived from group membership and their commitment to the legitimating values and norms. But, to some degree, the behavior of subordinates will not be entirely in their own behalf but will be directed toward goals set by the leader. To be sure, these goals may well be ones that the group members all accept and that may benefit them all. Or they may be goals that primarily benefit the leader. In either case, the leader is able to insure that the actions of subordinates fit together in a unified or collective group line of action. At this point, the group, not its constituent members, is the interacting unit.

Everyday life offers numerous examples in which the group and not the individual should be seen as the true unit involved in some line of action. For example, a football game obviously involves a highly coordinated team line of action. Even though individual players may strive for outstanding individual performances, the overall line of action is still that of a team. As another example, when labor union officials decide to go out on strike or to accept a contract offer and go back to work, their members' action can only be understood as part of the union's overall line of action. Members do not simply decide on their own whether to strike or go back to work (unless the organizational discipline has broken down).

Is a leadership structure necessary in all cases for the development of a group line of action? Or is it possible for a group line of action to be developed by persons who are equal to one another, with no one being dependent on or indebted to anyone else? There are certainly some situations in which a group can act in a united way even in the absence of a clear power or leadership structure. In a situation demanding immediate attention, such as an emergency, a united line of action may emerge even without a leadership structure. However, for task groups involved in a long-range enterprise, reliance on the spontaneous willingness of all members to do their part is generally a precarious strategy to use. Even if the members all agree on the goal, there is the risk that united action will be undermined by disagreement on strategies to use in accomplishing the goal or by the unwillingness of some members to perform the necessary actions when they need to be performed.

The effects of a lack of a clear leadership or power structure was revealed, for example, in the student demonstrations of the late 1960s and early 1970s. Many students were willing to be mobilized to take part in the excitement of demonstrations directed against various university policies. But mechanisms for developing a consensus in terms of specific goals for negotiation could not be established in many cases. As a result, would-be student leaders were often unable to negotiate successfully with university officials because they were unable to insure that agreements reached with administration officials would be honored by the students. Lack of a clear leadership and power structure meant that no one, in effect, could speak for the students in negotiating with university officials. In contrast, the leaders of well-organized labor unions are able to shut down entire industries through strikes, even when many of the union members prefer not to strike.

The difficulties that egalitarian groups would face in developing a group line of action can be considerably overcome by the emergence of a clear leadership structure. By controlling resources used to provide rewards to members and by appealing to their normative commitments, the leader is able to overcome (to a degree) the fragmentation and conflict that would result if members found it impossible to agree or unwilling to do their part to construct the group line of action.

If there are two or more groups in which an established leadership structure has emerged, the stage is set for the two groups to interact with one another as units (assuming that an appropriate reward-cost outcome can be established). In this type of situation the groups, not the individuals who happen to belong to them, are the interacting units. Indeed, over a period of time there may be turnover in the group's membership, even though the group's line of action is maintained. Although the group can only act through its members, the members would be acting not as individuals but as members of the group. This essentially is the basis for the emergence of macro structures. As an elementary definition, a macro structure is a structure made up of groups; a micro structure consists only of individuals.[64]

Interaction and exchange patterns that develop between groups parallel in many respects the same processes that occur between individuals. Groups (or, more accurately, individuals acting on behalf of groups) compete with one another in developing strategies for appearing attractive to potential associates (individuals or other groups). Out of this process balanced or imbalanced exchange transactions will eventually emerge. If the exchange between two or more groups is balanced, relations of reciprocal interdependence will be established. If the exchange relations are imbalanced, differentiation of status and power will emerge. If a dominant group is able to achieve power and dependency relations with one or more subordinate groups, the stage is set for a higher-level combination of groups. That is, the leader of the dominant group can control the various subordinate groups and weld them into a larger unity to develop a coherent line of action with this large collectivity. Thus the subordinate groups may, in essence, become subgroupings within a larger association.

Groups combined in this way may subsequently develop their own exchange patterns. These exchanges may be controlled to some extent by the leader so as to contribute to some overall organizational objective. The nature of such exchanges would be related to the division of labor that is established. Also, additional subgroup exchanges may emerge over and above those required by the leader, as Homans implied in his discussion of the dynamics of the internal system of groups.

Subgroup formation within an association is not limited to associations made up of already existing groups. Any increase in the size of an association, whether based on recruitment of more individuals or by the addition of more groups, will inevitably be followed by increased subgroup formation. This internal structure reflects the outcome of the various internal exchange transactions, which may lead to status differentiation and perhaps some form of division of labor. In addition to these internal exchanges, some subgroups may engage in transactions on their own account with individuals or groups outside the organization. One possibility for such external exchanges is with subgroups in other associations that are similar in status or organizational function. This sets the stage for the emergence of new groups or associations. For example, the secretaries employed in bureaucratic organizations (at one or several hierarchical levels) may develop their own exchange transactions across organizational boundaries and even a national association to promote their own interests.

The general image of a large, complex society implied by Blau's model is that it consists of an elaborate network of associations that are based on exchange transactions, some direct and many indirect, many of which involve varying degrees of imbalance. The complexity of the exchange networks in a large, urban-industrial society practically defies description. Large-scale, complex bureaucratic organizations dominate almost all institutional sectors of society. In addition, there are organizations made up of other organizations, organizations that overlap and crosscut other organizations at various hierarchical levels, myriad subgroupings of various interest groups within practically all large organizations, and interstitial groupings that link different organizations. Practically every conceivable interest is represented by some type of organization that has complex linkages with other groups or organizations whose interests overlap or are related in some way. Practically every recognized social problem has stimulated the emergence of a variety of public and private agencies, many of which establish various kinds of relationships with one another and with numerous other associations. In short, modern society is honeycombed with various overlapping and interpenetrating organizations. To the extent that these organizations are capable of concerted or collective action, they rest, in the final analysis, on exchange processes, specifically imbalanced exchanges with resulting power and dependency relations.

Power Structure Legitimation versus Opposition. The legitimation of a power structure does not guarantee that members will continue indefinitely to be completely satisfied with the leader or eager to conform to any demands that the leader might make. Power structures are frequently resisted and even overthrown. This is true both in small-scale groups and large-scale complex associations. In the long run, structures of power and authority rest on a favorable reward-cost outcome for all involved. If the reward-cost outcome is consistent with the expectations of all involved or if the outcome is more advantageous than could be obtained elsewhere, the members will be likely to perceive the leader as fair and to continue the exchange patterns that have emerged. But if the reward-cost outcomes become less favorable or participants' expectations change, members may be expected to resent or resist the leader's demands or be dissatisfied with the rewards received for their compliance. This may lead to the formation of an opposition movement and, in an extreme case, to the overthrow of the existing power structure.[65]

Numerous processes could adversely affect the reward-cost outcome of subordinates and lead them to perceive the leader as unfair. For example, the leader may actually increase the demands made on subordinates following establishment of a strong dependency relation on their part. Or the leader's demands may remain constant, but members of the group may become satiated with the type of reward that the leader supplies, and the reward-cost ratio becomes relatively less attractive. Or members may eventually feel that their past compliance with the leader's demands is sufficient to discharge their obligations and that no further compliance should be expected. Or, finally, members may become aware of other groups in which the reward-cost outcomes are more favorable and feel disadvantaged by comparison. Power structures are precarious and potentially unstable. Values and norms may reinforce a particular authority structure, but members' willingness to conform to values and norms rests in the long run on a favorable reward-cost outcome.

If a leader exerts power in a way that changes the reward-cost outcomes of members to their disadvantage, the members will be likely to perceive the leader as unfair. If this perception is widespread, it may stimulate the emergence of opposition movements intended to change the leadership structure. Not all dissatisfied members would be likely candidates for participating in opposition movements. Some may simply leave the group and join alternative groups in which a more favorable reward-cost outcome may be obtained. Some may be reluctant to take part because they fear that the potential costs of failing to change the leadership structure would outweigh any gains that might be made. But if the leader's exercise of power becomes sufficiently oppressive, a growing number of subordinates will become willing to explore strategies for opposing the leader's demands, replacing the leader, or changing the leadership structure. There will be wide variation in the goals that emerge within opposition movements, from mild reforms within the existing leadership structure (with or without replacement of leadership personnel) to revolutionary overthrow of the existing structure and establishment of new procedures for selecting leaders.

The relationship between legitimation mechanisms and opposition mechanisms can be seen as one of more or less continuous dialectical conflict.[66] The emergence of strong leadership structures invariably creates the conditions in which opposition movements are likely to be formed. One reason for this dialectical pattern is that a strong leadership structure rests, as we have seen, on resources the leader controls that can be used to reward subordinates for their compliance. But, to the extent that the leader is able to increase the resources at his or her disposal, the leader is likely to arouse dissatisfaction on the part of subordinates who would like to see these resources distributed more generously. This is especially likely if the leader's abundant resources have been accumulated at the expense of contributions provided by subordinates through their compliance.

The social dynamics involved in the emergence of an opposition movement are similar to those involved in the emergence of the leadership structure in the first place. That is, those who are dissatisfied or feel oppressed will begin by communicating with one another in an exploratory fashion, offering alternative goals and strategies, evaluating these alternatives, and so on. Ultimately, certain individuals emerge as leaders on the basis of their ability to convince others that their ideas will prove more effective (or rewarding) than the ideas of others in bringing about desired changes. If the opposition movement is able to make progress in redressing grievances or replacing the leadership structure, this will reinforce the emergent opposition leader's position.

In other words, the ability of dissatisfied subordinates to unite in opposition to the existing leadership structure will depend on the emergence of their own leadership structure. This, in turn, will depend on imbalanced exchanges whereby the emergent opposition leader is able to create dependencies and obligations on the part of others involved in the opposition movement. In the long run, if an opposition movement fails to generate a leadership structure, the result will be the inability of dissatisfied members to act consistently as a unit. The refusal of totalitarian governments to tolerate the organization of opposition parties can be explained in terms of their awareness that unorganized opposition is not very effective.

Just as the initial leadership structure was stabilized by the emergence of legitimating values and norms, so also is the opposition movement reinforced by the development of opposition ideals. This opposition ideology is particularly important for neutralizing the conservative influence of the legitimating values and norms. Many of those involved in the opposition movement may have previously internalized the legitimating values and norms; as a result, they may feel ambivalent about their participation in an opposition movement. An opposition ideology, however, can insure participants in the opposition movement that their efforts to promote change are not undertaken for narrow, selfish interests but are consistent with high moral principles. Failure to strive for change may be criticized as cowardly acquiescence to an unjust system. Moreover, whether or not the opposition movement is completely successful, it may serve a positive function by helping to stimulate renewal or reform of the existing values and norms or even by promoting new values and norms that would legitimate improved reward-cost outcomes for subordinates.[67]

The Process of Institutionalization in Large-Scale Macro Structures. Reliance on abstract values and norms, both in legitimating existing organizational patterns and in supporting opposition movements, may be evident within small-scale systems, but these processes are much more fully developed in larger and more complex systems. Such processes are probably not as critical in small-scale systems because of the opportunity for immediate and direct negotiation of costs and rewards to be exchanged. Large-scale systems, in contrast, are more likely to involve complex series of indirect exchanges between individuals or groups who may not even be in direct contact with one other. Thus internalization of the appropriate values and norms becomes much more crucial for shaping behavior and interaction patterns than exchange agreements negotiated on a direct *ad hoc* basis.

Both of the characteristics of large-scale associations just identified—extensive reliance on abstract values and norms and increased proportion of indirect exchanges—may be seen as emergent phenomena. That is, these characteristics may be only minimally developed, if at all, in small-scale exchange systems, but they are essential for the routine operation of large-scale exchange systems. This is an important emphasis in Blau's theory. Even though large-scale associations rest on elementary exchange processes, they also exhibit certain emergent properties or characteristics, the effects of which may seem to outweigh the dynamics of the small-scale processes of individuals' direct exchange transactions.

Commitment to abstract values and norms may help to insure conforming behavior, even in the absence of any specific payoff in the short run (except perhaps the reward of self-approval or social approval from others). In the long run, other rewards in addition to social approval are no doubt essential, particularly if conformity is very costly. Thus, for example, even though in our society social approval is provided to those who work, probably few would perform their jobs regularly in the absence of a regular paycheck. Blau identified four different types of social values involved in social transactions in complex structures. These are: "particularistic values as media of solidarity, universalistic values as media of exchange and differentiation, legitimating values as media of organization, and opposition ideals as media of reorganization."[68] The latter two types have just been discussed. In complex systems, particularly total societies, opposition values may be more or less permanently institutionalized in the form of opposition political parties instead of emerging on an *ad hoc* basis in response to particular grievances.

The distinction between particularistic values and universalistic values is related to the distinction between intrinsic and extrinsic rewards discussed earlier. Intrinsic rewards are attached to a particular person, while extrinsic rewards are not so attached and can be obtained from a variety of alternative sources. In addition, intrinsic relations are ends in themselves rather than means to some other end, while extrinsic relations are means to some other end. On a larger scale than face-to-face relationships, particularistic values create feelings of solidarity and integration between persons who share certain common characteristics. These characteristics may include racial or ethnic background, similar status or occupation, common religion, residence in a particular community, or shared interests of various types. The sharing of similar characteristics distinguishes between in-group individuals and outsiders. Even in the absence of direct, face-to-face interaction, those who share particularistic values will feel a bond of solidarity against outsiders on this basis. Moreover, interpersonal attraction leading to personal relations should be expected to be strong, since persons who share similar characteristics can readily exchange approval and social support.

In contrast to particularistic values, universalistic values mediate exchanges between persons who are dissimilar. Such values should be expected to increase in importance as the division of labor expands, since growth in the division of labor promotes heterogeneity. By definition, universalistic values transcend the various distinctions reflected in particularistic values. They provide the framework for an overarching unity between groups that may be dissimilar. At the highest level of development, universalistic values appeal to a common humanity that is shared not only by the various heterogeneous groups within a pluralistic society but by all human beings everywhere, regardless of nationality or cultural background.

Universalistic values are particularly important for the maintenance of complex networks of indirect exchange. In complex networks of this type, universalistic values promote diffuse feelings of interdependence with, and obligations toward, a wide range of different types of persons who may not even be known personally. For example, the general desire of many idealistic young people to be involved in careers that provide service to others is one manifestation of universalistic values.

Another distinctive emergent property of large and complex exchange networks is that the ratio of indirect to direct exchanges increases significantly. In many cases it is possible to identify lengthy chains of exchange transactions through which costs and rewards are transferred. In such a network, individuals participate in complex relationships of mutual interdependence with many others who are widely separated in time and space and who do not even have personal knowledge of one another. Such chains might be identified by tracing the flow of money or material resources. For example, employees in a business firm are assessed payroll taxes by the Internal Revenue Service; this money may then be allocated through the Department of Housing and Urban Development to local government officials in an urban area; these officials may use this money to hire recent social science graduates to engage in community organization activities through which various services are delivered to clients in need. This particular chain can be seen as an indirect exchange extending from the taxpaying employee to the client. The employee with whom this particular chain started really has little choice in the matter of who is the ultimate recipient of tax contributions.

To the extent that the various exchange patterns of a complex structure are supported by internalized values, we can say that these patterns have become *institutionalized*.[69] In addition to this subjective dimension of institutionalization, there is also an objective dimension. Established exchange patterns that are repeated over the course of many generations exist independently of the particular individuals who become involved in them. The members of each new generation initially confront these established exchange networks as an objective reality existing independently of any individual calculation of costs and rewards. These recurrent exchange patterns become routinized and formalized as established procedures to be followed. Perhaps the clearest manifestation of the objective existence of such established procedures is their codification in written documents, such as the legal codes. For institutionalized exchange patterns incorporated in established customs or laws, it is obvious that individuals do not have completely open options for evaluating whether or not to comply on the basis of a subjective calculation of costs and rewards. If the socialization process is effective, the members of new generations eventually internalize the supporting values and norms so that conformity to established procedures becomes rewarding. But the point to be noted is that objective formalization or codification of established exchange patterns is an emergent process that is far more crucial for large-scale macro structures than for micro structures.

In large-scale systems such as total societies the maintenance of established relationships and exchange procedures is also dependent on the active support of dominant groups. Such groups naturally have a strong interest in preserving the exchange networks within which they enjoy a dominant position. As a result, their power to control resources and exert influence on less dominant groups is used to reinforce established institutional patterns. Because dominant groups are often in a position to control the terms of exchange, the array of options available to subordinate groups to negotiate favorable terms of exchange are limited to varying degrees. In the extreme case, subordinate groups may be faced with the simple option of complying with the demands of more powerful groups or not surviving.

The process of institutionalization is extremely important for the maintenance of large and complex macro structures such as total societies. To summarize this process, we quote Blau.

> Three conditions, therefore, must be met for aspects of social structures to become institutionalized, that is, to be perpetuated from one generation to the next. Patterns of organized community life must become formalized and part of the historical conditions that persist through time, the social values that legitimate these patterns must be transmitted in the process of socialization, and the society's dominant groups must be especially interested in the survival of these patterns.[70]

The crucial significance of this process of institutionalization is one of the chief differences between the dynamics of social exchange in large, complex macro structures and in face-to-face encounters between individuals.

Summary

In this chapter we have traced the major principles of exchange theory from Homans' emphasis on primary exchanges in face-to-face encounters to Blau's efforts to build on this elementary process by showing that such exchanges are the foundation for large, complex institutional structures characterized by complex patterns of indirect exchange. Thibaut and Kelley's contrast between exchange processes in dyads and groups provided an intermediate step in the transition from micro processes to macro structures.

Homans' exchange theory was built on a foundation of individualistic assumptions derived from behavioral psychology and elementary economics. Individuals' behavior is seen as shaped by positive and negative reinforcement; individuals' choices from alternative behaviors reflect their expectations of a favorable reward-cost ratio. These expectations are influenced by past experience and by observation of the reward-cost outcomes of others who are similar. Whether individuals are pleased or angry with the outcomes of their behavior will be based on a comparison of these outcomes with those expected. Homans' insists that individual-level propositions are essential for explaining social behavior as opposed merely to describing it. The concepts and propositions that form the foundation of Homans' theory are used to try to explain face-to-face interaction and group dynamics. Standard social processes such as exercising influence, normative conformity and innovation, cooperation and conflict, and status concerns are analyzed in terms of Homans' exchange theoretic propositions.

Micro-level concerns are also evident in the exchange theory of Thibaut and Kelley. They trace the process whereby exploratory interactional overtures gradually become routinized on the basis of favorable reward-cost outcomes of all parties involved. Although the participants in established relations do not necessarily go through a process of conscious calculation each time a transaction occurs, an unfavorable shift in reward-cost outcomes or the appearance of a more favorable alternative can stimulate individuals to reevaluate existing relations. One of the major reasons for a shift in the reward-cost outcomes is an increase in the number of persons involved in a transaction. Thibaut and Kelley focus on the contrast between exchanges in dyads and those in larger groups.

Blau's exchange theory reflects an effort to move from the micro level to the macro level. At the micro level, Blau distinguished between intrinsic and extrinsic rewards, with the exchange of intrinsic rewards subject to certain normative constraints prohibiting explicit bargaining over costs and rewards and discouraging overt concern over personal payoffs. In addition, Blau pointed to the paradox that people often refrain from initiating interaction with those who could provide outstanding rewards because they want to avoid the subordination that would be involved in such a relationship.

When individuals are unable or unwilling to avoid being part of imbalanced exchange relations, the stage is set for the emergence of power structures. Persons who supply rewards on which recipients become dependent and that they cannot reciprocate are able to demand compliance in exchange. An individual who achieves power over others by controlling reward resources on which they have become dependent is able to construct a group line of action in relating to other individuals or groups or in moving toward accomplishment of a group goal. The development of group lines of action is the basis for the emergence of macro structures.

There are several emergent properties that macro structures exhibit that distinguish them from micro structures. Blau stresses the importance of the emergence of shared values and norms. Several different types of values and norms were discussed: legitimating values, opposition values, particularistic values, and universalistic values. In large-scale, complex systems such as total societies, such abstract values become relatively more important than immediate rewards for maintaining established exchange patterns. This is because many of these patterns are indirect, not direct. Although personal payoffs are always important, people are often willing to delay immediate gratification of some needs in the interest of conforming to shared values and norms and earning the social approval that results from such conformity. In general, the social dynamics involved in the process of institutionalization are crucial for explaining large-scale macro systems; in contrast, these processes are relatively less important than personal payoffs at the micro level of face-to-face encounters.

In terms of the levels of social reality identified earlier, our overview of exchange theory was initiated at the individual and interpersonal levels. This concern with the micro level of social reality is comparable to symbolic interaction theory and to Simmel's theoretical approach. However, with Blau's theory, we moved from the interpersonal level to the social structural level. Although large-scale social structures are comprised of interpersonal exchange patterns, they also exhibit emergent properties that differentiate them from interpersonal exchanges at the micro level. In addition, Blau's emphasis on the importance of mediating values in large-scale macro structures provided a secondary emphasis on the cultural level of social reality. In the next two chapters our primary concern will be at the social structural level.

Footnotes

1. See George C. Homans, *The Human Group* (New York: Harcourt, Brace and Company, 1950), p. 38, and *Social Behavior: Its Elementary Forms* (New York: Harcourt, Brace, and World, 1961), Chapters 2 and 3, especially pp. 33-34.
2. The following discussion of the contrast between the individualistic approach and the alternative collectivist approach draws heavily from the analysis by Peter Ekeh, *Social Exchange Theory and the Two Sociological Traditions* (Cambridge, Mass.: Harvard University Press, 1975).
3. Claude Levi-Strauss, *The Elementary Structures of Kinship* (Boston: Beacon Press, 1969).
4. Levi-Strauss' recognition of the distinctive characteristics of dyadic relations is reminiscent of Simmel's discussion of the uniqueness of the dyad.
5. For a brief overview of the differences in perspective among the leading early anthropologists, see Jonathan Turner, *The Structure of Sociological Theory*, rev. edition (Homewood, Ill.: Dorsey Press, 1978), pp. 204-212.
6. George C. Homans and David M. Schneider, *Marriage, Authority, and Final Causes: A Study of Unilateral Cross-Cousin Marriage* (New York: Free Press, 1955).
7. For an enlightening account of the development of Homans' thinking along this line, see his Autobiographical Introduction to George C. Homans, *Sentiments and Activities* (New York: Free Press of Glencoe, 1962), pp. 1-49; see especially pp. 22-35.

8. Homans, *The Human Group,* pp. 10–23.
9. Ibid., Chapter 2, "The Elements of Behavior."
10. The interaction patterns of a group can readily be mapped by means of a sociometric diagram, as demonstrated by Moreno. See J. L. Moreno, *Who Shall Survive?* (Washington, D.C.: Nervous and Mental Disease Publishing Company, 1934).
11. For example, see ibid., p. 87. This point is repeatedly made throughout *The Human Group.*
12. Ibid., pp. 28–29.
13. Ibid., p. 112.
14. Ibid., p. 390.
15. Ibid., p. 361.
16. Homans, *Social Behavior: Its Elementary Forms,* Chapter 1, "Introduction."
17. Ibid., pp. 12–13, Chapter 2, "Animal Behavior," and Chapter 3, "Human Exchange: Terms."
18. Ibid., p. 13. Incidentally, in spite of the apparent rough overlap between the concepts from psychology and those from economics, there are some noteworthy differences between the implications of the operant conditioning model and the economic model. For one thing, behavioral psychology tends to focus on the here and now (or the past) instead of on the future, with individuals' behavior explained in terms of current environmental stimuli and current reinforcements, compared with past reinforcements. In contrast, economics tends to emphasize the importance of a future orientation, with momentary payoffs or pleasure frequently subordinated in the interest of long-range goals. This is not to say that the two perspectives are contradictory. Individuals may differ in terms of whether they usually give priority to immediate reinforcement or to long-range profits. Another difference in the implications of the two theoretical approaches is that the operant conditioning model does not explicitly deal with covert or subjective processes, such as the subjective weighing of alternatives or the making of choices based on predictions of future outcomes. For a discussion of these and related issues, see Ekeh, op. cit., pp. 111–119.
19. Homans, *Social Behavior: Its Elementary Forms,* pp. 36–49.
20. Ibid., p. 19.
21. Ibid., pp. 235–247.
22. Ibid., pp. 72–78.
23. Homans, *Social Behavior: Its Elementary Forms,* rev. edition (New York: Harcourt, Brace, Jovanovich, 1974), pp. 15–50.
24. Ibid., pp. 37–40; see first edition, p. 75.
25. Ibid., pp. 43–47.
26. Homans, *Social Behavior: Its Elementary Forms,* 1st edition, Chapter 5, "Influence."
27. Ibid., Chapter 6, "Conformity."
28. Ibid., Chapter 7, "Competition."
29. Ibid., Chapter 8, "Esteem."
30. Ibid., pp. 186–187.
31. The relation between interaction patterns and status is dealt with in several contexts throughout Homans' book. See, for example, Chapter 9, "The Matrix of Sentiment," and Chapter 10, "Interaction."
32. Homans, *Social Behavior: Its Elementary Forms,* 1st edition, p. 149.

33. Ibid., pp. 248–255.
34. It may be recalled that Weber also recognized the multidimensional nature of a person's position in the stratification system of society with his threefold distinction among class, status, and power. Weber's focus was more on the macro level than Homans'; Homans did not deal explicitly with the broad structural bases for individuals' positions in the stratification system of society.
35. Ibid., Chapter 18, "The Institutional and the Subinstitutional."
36. John W. Thibaut and Harold H. Kelley, *The Social Psychology of Groups* (New York: Wiley, 1959).
37. Ibid., pp. 10–14.
38. Ibid., Chapter 5, "Forming the Relationship."
39. Ibid., pp. 21–24, 80ff., 100ff.
40. Ibid., pp. 28–29.
41. Ibid., pp. 191–194.
42. Ibid., pp. 205–219.
43. Ibid., pp. 278–286. Bales' analysis of small groups will be portrayed in the following chapter.
44. Ibid., Chapter 8, "Norms and Roles."
45. Peter M. Blau, *Exchange and Power in Social Life* (New York: Wiley, 1964). Blau has also done considerable work in the area of complex organization; indeed, some of his exchange theoretical principles were developed initially in a case study of a bureaucratic organization. One major pattern he analyzed was the emergence of an informal power and status structure from social exchanges that took place between more and less experienced co-workers. See Peter M. Blau, *The Dynamics of Bureaucracy* (Chicago: University of Chicago Press, 1955). More recently, Blau has devoted himself to the social structural level of analysis, studying characteristics of the structure of organizations (size, structural differentiation, etc.) as opposed to the dynamics of the interaction patterns of the participants. See Peter M. Blau and Richard A. Schoenherr, *The Structure of Organizations* (New York: Basic Books, 1971), and Peter M. Blau, *On the Nature of Organizations* (New York: Wiley, 1974).
46. Ibid., p. 19.
47. Ibid., p. 6.
48. Ibid., pp. 78–85.
49. Ibid., pp. 33–37ff.
50. Ibid., p. 38.
51. Ibid., p. 20.
52. Ibid., p. 38ff.
53. Ibid., pp. 43–50.
54. See Alvin W. Gouldner, "The Norm of Reciprocity," *American Sociological Review*, Vol. 25, April 1960, pp. 161–178.
55. This and several interrelated issues of intrinsic or social exchanges are discussed in Blau, op. cit., pp. 88–106.
56. Ibid., pp. 25–31.
57. This entire section draws heavily from ibid., Chapter 5, "Differentiation of Power."
58. Ibid., pp. 106–112.
59. Blau, *The Dynamics of Bureaucracy*.

60. Blau, *Exchange and Power in Social Life*, pp. 118–125. See also Richard M. Emerson, "Power-Dependence Relations," *American Sociological Review*, Vol. 27, February 1962, pp. 31–41.
61. Blau, *Exchange and Power in Social Life*, pp. 125–132.
62. See ibid., Chapter 8, "Legitimation and Organization."
63. Ibid., pp. 213–220.
64. Ibid., pp. 283–284.
65. The following material relies primarily on ibid., Chapter 9, "Opposition."
66. This and other forms of dialectical conflict are discussed in the final chapter of *Exchange and Power in Social Life*, Chapter 12, "Dialectical Forces."
67. Ibid., pp. 301–309.
68. Ibid., p. 265.
69. See ibid., pp. 273–280, for a discussion of this process.
70. Ibid., p. 276.

Questions for Study and Discussion

1. Contrast relationships involving restricted (or direct) types of exchange transactions with those involving generalized (or indirect) types of exchange transactions and give some examples of each type.
2. Do you agree or disagree with the argument that large-scale institutional structures are based on interpersonal exchange transactions? Explain your answer. In what ways do large-scale institutional processes differ from direct, face-to-face exchanges?
3. Identify some custom or normative pattern that is undergoing widespread change in our society; identify the costs and rewards of complying with the traditional pattern as opposed to adopting an alternative pattern.
4. What are the costs and rewards of being in a leadership position in a group as opposed to being in a subordinate position?
5. Can you identify any behaviors or social relationships to which the basic principles of exchange theory do not seem relevant? Can self-approval serve as a substitute for social approval in the long run?

CHAPTER 10

Integration and Social Order in Society: The Functional Approach

Imagine a forum or panel discussion that includes a conservative clergyman, a high-ranking military officer, a civil rights leader, a high-level corporation executive, a liberal congressional representative, a top union official, a member of a left-wing student group, and an ordinary citizen. These participants are asked to diagnose our society in terms of its overall well-being and where it seems to be headed.

If we were to analyze the arguments offered in such a discussion, we would undoubtedly detect significant discrepancies in the basic assumptions of what constitutes the strength and well-being of a society. There may be agreement on general platitudes, such as the need to pursue peace and the well-being of all citizens but, beyond this, the differences in perspectives and priorities would undoubtedly generate heated discussion.

We will not analyze these various arguments or take a partisan position; instead, our goal is to draw attention to the needs and requirements of society, as opposed to individuals' needs. Some people might argue that the overall welfare of society is best served by attending to the welfare of all its citizens. Nevertheless, participants in our hypothetical discussion would have to transcend individual concerns and problems in order to assess the state of society.

This chapter concentrates on the societal or social structural level. We will deal with basic questions such as what holds the society together, how the foundations of social order are maintained, and how individuals' actions contribute to larger social outcomes that may or may not be consciously intended but that affect society's well-being.

A focus on the societal level is implicit in many public policy debates concerning the long-range consequences of alternative policy decisions. For example, public programs to reduce poverty may have numerous social consequences, some beneficial and some not, in addition to achieving their intended goal. These additional consequences may include increased proliferation of government bureaucracies, increased opportunities for white-collar crime and corruption, and increased middle-class frustration with rising taxes, rising inflation, or both. Also, if such programs raise the aspirations of the poor, the result may be increased frustration on their part, even though there may be improvement in their actual situation. Once these possible unintended consequences are recognized, the issue becomes more complex than whether or not to eliminate poverty. It involves efforts to weigh the various social consequences (beneficial and harmful) and judge whether or not the potential benefits outweigh the various negative consequences.

Functional analysis provides a framework for examining these social policy dilemmas. Although functionalism is an abstract and highly general perspective, it involves essentially an effort to deal with the following general questions. What basic functional requirements must be fulfilled for a society, or any social system, to survive as a viable system, and how are these functions fulfilled? These questions are basic in Parsons' functional perspective. Also, for any given widespread pattern of behavior, what are the overall social consequences or effects on the larger system in which that pattern is involved? Practically any behavior pattern, conforming or deviant, any custom or norm, any broad policy decision, any cultural value can be analyzed in functional terms. That is, it can be analyzed in terms of its overall social consequences, even though many of them may be unintended or unrecognized. These social consequences are often evaluated as to whether they contribute to the strength or well-being of the society (or some other system) or whether they undermine it. This goal of evaluating the social consequences of individuals' behavior patterns is basic in Robert Merton's functional perspective.

It is important to distinguish between *social* consequences of some behavior pattern and *individual* consequences. Although functional theory deals primarily with the social structural level, functionalists need not limit themselves to this level. The early British anthropological functionalists (e.g., Malinowski) emphasized that dominant institutional patterns persist because they are functional in meeting individuals' basic and recurring needs. Parsons, the leading representative of American functionalism for many years, dealt explicitly with the interrelationships among the individual personality, the social system, and the cultural system. His earliest work was comparable to Weber's in focusing on the level of individuals' social action. (His concentration on the social system came somewhat later in his career.) Overall, however, the emphasis in functionalism is on the requirements that must be met for some social system (such as the society itself) to endure, not individuals' needs.[1]

For many years functionalism has been the most highly developed and dominant theoretical perspective in American sociology to concentrate on the social structural level, particularly as it reflects shared normative patterns. Major attention is given to broad institutional patterns and the complex interrelationships between social institutions. Individual behavior is seen as shaped by these institutional patterns through the various mechanisms of socialization and social control. Individuals' actions must fulfill institutional requirements. Partly as a result, the standard or recurrent aspects of individuals' behavior are emphasized as opposed to the unique or idiosyncratic elements.

Durkheim is generally considered the major classical theorist in developing functionalist analysis. His overriding concern with the general problem of social integration and solidarity is paralleled in contemporary functionalism, as is his effort to show the interrelationships between "social facts" as opposed to individual facts. His discussion of how normative breakdown contributes to an increase in suicide rates, his analysis of the social consequences of the division of labor on forms of solidarity, and his portrayal of the effects of religion in reinforcing social solidarity might be cited as classic examples of functional analysis.

Additional examples of functional analysis can be gleaned from some of the other classical European theorists. Weber, for example, explored the various unintended social consequences of the Protestant ethic and the effects of increasing bureaucratization. Simmel noted the social effects of intergroup conflict in promoting solidarity within the group. Comte analyzed traditional religion in terms of its effects in promoting solidarity. Marx, always sensitive to the paradoxes that pervade social life, argued that as capitalists compete with one another in pursuit of higher profits, they inevitably contribute to recurrent economic crises and the eventual demise of the capitalist system.

The emphasis in functionalism on objective social consequences that may or may not be intended or anticipated contrasts sharply with the primary emphasis of symbolic interactionism. Symbolic interactionists stress the ability of human beings to predict and control the future, at least to a significant degree at the micro level, so that their needs and goals can be fulfilled. Even though absolute predictability of the consequences of one's own action or the reactions of others is never possible, the overwhelming emphasis is on the process whereby individuals construct their various lines of action in the light of their plans for the future. Nevertheless, some functionalists, notably Parsons, also emphasize the importance of understanding individuals' subjective orientations, including definitions of situations and individual needs and goals.

Functionalism and exchange theory contrast in the level of analysis on which they focus (macro versus micro) and in terms of the basic underlying assumptions regarding the individual and the nature of social reality. American exchange theory tends to reflect an individualistic orientation. The individual is primary, and society (or any other social structure) is seen as emergent from interpersonal exchanges reflecting individuals' private interests. Even altruistic behavior or love reflects individuals' needs for social approval, social acceptance, and emotional support. In contrast, functional theory gives priority to society. Society precedes the individual, and the individual is formed and molded as a social personality in the context of the social milieu. Even individuals' personal interests reflect the "collective conscience" or overall value system of the society.

To make the transition from exchange theory to functionalism, recall that one of Blau's principal goals was to explain the emergence of large-scale social structures from elementary exchange principles. In contrast, functional theory tends to begin with already existing structures. Primary emphasis is on attempting to understand the social dynamics necessary for its maintenance. For example, in analyzing a society, emphasis is placed on the mechanisms whereby social institutions are integrated with one another to maintain the existing social order.

Functional analysis is also relevant to an understanding of the processes of social change, particularly orderly change. Indeed, the notion of institutional interdependence implies that if change occurs in any one institution, it will generate change in other institutions. Nevertheless, whether the goal is to understand social order or to deal with social change, it is the ongoing operation of a social system, not its emergence or development, that is the central concern of functional analysis. This emphasis is very much in evidence in Parsons's theoretical model of social systems.

PARSONS: FROM SOCIAL ACTION TO SOCIAL SYSTEMS

Parsons has been the leading representative of the functional approach in American sociology for many years, but his earliest focus was comparable to that of Weber in its focus on individual action as the basic unit of sociological analysis. Many sociologists see a sharp break between Parsons' early social action theory and his later structural-functional analysis of social systems.[2] The position taken here, however, is that although there was a shift to a different level of analysis, Parsons' functionalist perspective on social systems actually builds on the foundation of his earlier social action theory. Many major new ideas were added over the years as Parsons gradually made the transition from social action theory to social systems theory. Moreover, there are some differences in emphasis and perhaps some inconsistencies between Parsons' social action perspective and his social systems perspective. But there is still a high degree of continuity.

Parsons has consistently dealt with social reality from a very broad perspective that is not limited to the social structural level. He frequently refers to his approach as a general theory of action. The social system is just one of the systems included in the overall perspective; the personality system and the cultural system are analytically distinct systems that are also included, as is the behavioral organism. In the final analysis, social systems are made up of individuals' social actions. For this reason we will consider the basic ideas of Parsons' early social action theory before dealing with his functional analysis of social systems. But, first, it will be helpful to note some relevant highlights of Parsons' life and intellectual development.

Biographical Highlights of Parsons' Career

Talcott Parsons was born in 1902, the son of a Congregational minister.[3] In his undergraduate education at Amherst College he majored in biology. His career interest at that time was medicine. He also had some exposure to social thought and economics, which he subsequently pursued through graduate work at the London School of Economics. After a year in London, Parsons went to Heidelberg, Germany, where he became acquainted with German sociology, particularly the work of Weber and Marx. Weber's influence was the stronger of the two; later, Parsons would introduce Weber to American sociology and incorporate many of his central ideas into his own theoretical perspective. In 1927 Parsons achieved a doctorate from the University of Heidelberg; his dissertation dealt with the ideas of German social science, especially Weber, Werner Sombart, and Marx, on capitalism.

Except for a 1-year period in which he taught at Amherst prior to completing his doctoral work, Parsons' professional career was spent at Harvard University. He began teaching economics there, but soon became a charter member of Harvard's Sociology Department. Later he organized the Department of Social Relations and was its first chairman. The Department of Social Relations was made up of an interdisciplinary faculty, and Parsons' involvement in such a group may perhaps be seen as part of the stimulus for him to develop a comprehensive general theory of action rather than a more narrow sociological theory.

Parsons' early interest in biology no doubt helped influence the approach he eventually took in analyzing social systems. The important book by biologist Walter Cannon, *The Wisdom of the Body,* published in 1932, demonstrated to Parsons the importance of viewing biological organisms as systems made up of interrelated parts that function together to maintain the health and internal equilibrium of the organism. In addition, Parsons discovered the systems approach of Italian sociologist Vilfredo Pareto. Although Pareto's initial interests were in economics, his focus differed from the British utilitarian economic theorists in that he was interested in the general institutional setting of economic processes, not the abstract analysis of purely economic variables operating as though in a social vacuum. When Pareto turned from economics to sociology, he developed a systems approach that dealt with the process whereby equilibrium is maintained or restored between the various elements that make up society, and between society and its environment. In Parsons' mind it became clear that there are certain parallels between biological organisms as systems and societies as systems. Parsons' interest in Pareto was encouraged by his association with Harvard biochemist L. J. Henderson, who had also influenced Homans' thinking on the interdependence of elements in the social systems of small groups.

Parsons' position in American sociology is unique. His influence has been enormous, especially during the 1950s and early 1960s, when functionalism was the dominant theoretical perspective. Many of the students he trained have become leading representatives of American sociology and have expanded and developed the functional approach in various ways. Sociologists who do not consider themselves functionalists can hardly ignore or avoid Parsons' dominant influence. Even opponents of functionalism, and of Parsons' particular version, must defend their theoretical perspectives in opposition to functionalism, and these opposing theories have no doubt been sharpened and developed considerably in the polemical confrontation with functionalism.

Ironically, however, there is little continuity between Parsons' work and that of earlier American sociologists such as Mead and Cooley. It is probably not surprising that Parsons, a Harvard faculty member, would not look to the American Midwest and the emerging Chicago school for inspiration and guidance. The fact that Parsons acquired his graduate education in England and Germany no doubt helps to account for the fact that his point of departure was European social thought. Indeed, one of his major contributions to American sociology was to promote the theories of European theorists such as Weber, Durkheim, Pareto (in Parsons' early work), and Freud (somewhat later). Parsons' own theoretical perspective is built solidly on the foundation established by these classical European theorists and incorporates many of their essential ideas.

Also, Parsons' insistence on developing an abstract and comprehensive theory resembles the European approach more than the American approach. Parsons has described himself as an "incurable theorist."[4] More than any other American sociologist he has devoted himself to the development of a highly abstract and general theory, disdaining for the most part the more mundane work of gathering and analyzing empirical data. He has analyzed certain empirical phenomena, such as the medical profession,[5] the McCarthy era in American politics[6] or, more recently, American universities.[7] Even these substantive areas are analyzed in an abstract, *ex cathedra* style instead of being based solidly on systematically gathered empirical data.

This propensity for theorizing contrasts sharply with the strong empirical bent of most American sociology from the earliest days to the present. Even though Mead's theoretical perspective, for example, was fairly abstract, the general Chicago school was characterized by a continuous interplay between theory development and immersion in the rich fund of real-life data provided by the Chicago environment. Moreover, much early American sociology reflected a strong concern with the various social problems that developed in the wake of rapid industrialization, urbanization, and immigration.

The major theoretical perspective implicitly accepted by the pioneers in American sociology was some form of social Darwinist evolutionary theory. Various efforts to promote social reform were justified in terms of a general theory of evolutionary progress. On the other hand, skepticism toward these reform efforts were expressed by those who insisted that long-range social progress results from the inevitable clash between the strong and the weak and the eventual triumph of the strong. Aside from these low-level evolutionary theories justifying or opposing social reform efforts, theory development was definitely not the strong point of American sociology. This was the background in which Parsons, not really in tune with American sociology, initiated his professional career by attempting to develop a general theory of action.

In more recent years, as American sociology has become firmly established, the practical concern with social problems has diminished. Many sociologists continue to be interested in analyzing or alleviating social problems, but this concern no longer dominates the profession. It has become an important subfield. For the profession as a whole, gathering and analyzing empirical data, particularly quantitative data, are major preoccupations. Abstract and general theorizing has a much lower priority than "theories of the middle range" (to use Merton's phrase[8]) directed toward specific areas of concern.

Thus Parsons stands outside the mainstream of American sociology in his sustained interest in highly abstract comprehensive theory even while exerting a dominant influence on American sociology. During the second half of the 1960s and during the 1970s, however, Parsons' influence has declined. Perhaps partly as a result of the social and political turmoil of the late 1960s and early 1970s, numerous competing theoretical perspectives, such as radical sociology and various versions of conflict theory, have arisen to challenge the underlying image of social reality implicit in functional theory.[9] Also, symbolic interactionism is frequently promoted as a major alternative to functionalism even though, as noted earlier, its concentration is at the micro level. In view of Parsons' long-term dominance of the mainstream of American sociology, we will look briefly at some of the major ideas of his social action theory before examining his functional analysis of social systems.

The Voluntaristic Theory of Social Action

Parsons developed his theory of social action through an intensive critical analysis of the nineteenth-century European social theorists Alfred Marshall, Vilfredo Pareto, Emile Durkheim, and Max Weber. Essentially, his argument was that these four theorists ultimately converged, in spite of different starting points, in pointing to the essential elements of a voluntaristic theory of social action. Parsons conceived his contribution as identifying these crucial elements and integrating them in a more general theoretical perspective. This was the major goal in Parsons' first book, *The Structure of Social Action,* published in 1937.[10]

The Structure of Social Action introduced much classical European sociological thought to American sociology. Other American scholars had also introduced various European social theorists to American social scientists, but no other American sociologist provided such detailed and comprehensive secondary analyses of the important nineteenth-century European social theorists, and none attempted to integrate such divergent theories in a comprehensive and systematic theoretical framework.

Parsons' analysis makes extensive use of the means-ends framework. In its barest essentials, Parsons' contention is that: (1) action is goal directed (or has an *end*); (2) action takes place in a situation, where some elements are given while other elements are utilized by the actor as *means* to the goal; and (3) action is normatively regulated with respect to the choice of ends and means. In short, the act is seen as the smallest or most fundamental unit of social reality. The basic components of the unit act are ends, means, conditions, and norms. The means and the conditions of action differ in that the actor is able to manipulate means in an effort to move toward the goal; the conditions are the aspects of the situation over which the actor has no control.

These ideas on the nature of social action are consistent with our common sense and everyday experience. No doubt most people would recognize their own actions as goal directed and normatively regulated, and most would recognize that the situation in which action occurs is also important. The significance of Parsons' analysis does not lie in the new light it sheds on common sense or everyday experience but in the fact that it provides a bridge for reconciling opposing and one-sided theoretical positions.

Positivism versus Idealism. In effect, Parsons' theory is a synthesis between the opposing viewpoints of positivism and idealism.[11] Of the four theorists analyzed, Marshall, Pareto, and Durkheim start from a positivist position, while Weber starts from the general context of German idealism. In each case, however, Parsons contends that these theorists each moved toward a recognition of the validity of the opposing position. Parsons saw his analysis as a synthesis between positivism and idealism.

Positivism is not a unified theoretical or philosophical position. Parsons emphasized the distinction between the utilitarian branch of positivism and an antiintellectual branch. In both branches, however, positivism stresses the scientific method as the key to explaining human behavior, thereby implying a deterministic model of human behavior. In Parsons' terms, this emphasis on the scientific method, with its deterministic assumptions, implied that behavior was simply a function of the situation. The major shortcoming was that the normative orientation governing the choice of means and ends was ignored.

The utilitarian branch of positivism was heavily developed in British social thought, particularly in economic theory. This is why Parsons analyzed the work of Alfred Marshall, an economist who pioneered in the development of marginal utility theory. British economic theory and social thought tended to be highly individualistic and to assume a rational model of human behavior, with human beings seen as analyzing and evaluating their environmental situation in terms of a rational means-end schema. Thus, for example, human actions are calculated to maximize pleasure and avoid pain or, in the case of the economic behavior of a businessperson, to maximize profits and minimize costs.

In criticizing the utilitarian perspective, Parsons points out that a great deal of human behavior can be seen as part of a complex and lengthy chain of means and ends. At every link in such a chain, decisions have to be made in the selection of means and ends. The criteria for making such decisions cannot be explained on a strictly positivist basis. Moreover, in many cases the ends of a particular line of action are not ultimate ends but intermediate links in the chain that serve as means for some additional end. In the final analysis, ultimate ends cannot be explained on a scientific basis or in terms of a rational model of human behavior. The utilitarian theorist is forced to make certain basic philosophical assumptions that are not tenable within a strict positivist framework. Such assumptions include the idea that the ultimate ends of different individuals vary on a random basis or that there is a natural identity between the ends of different persons, based perhaps on universal characteristics of human nature.

Parsons argues that the utilitarian model of rational action fails to maintain the analytical distinction between the *ends,* the *means,* and the *conditions* of action. Instead, action is explained simply in terms of the opportunities or constraints provided by the situation. This involves manipulating the aspects of the situation that can be employed as means or adapting to the aspects of the situation that cannot be manipulated. The major deficiencies of this model are its failure to explain the actor's *ultimate* ends of action, its failure to deal with the actor's standards on the basis of which means and ends are selected, and its inadequacies in analyzing the interdependence of different individuals' actions in a complex system, particularly the common orientations of those involved in a social system toward certain shared ultimate ends or values.

Parsons also identified an antiintellectual branch within the positivist tradition. This branch is probably more frequently associated with the positivist label than the utilitarian branch because of the strong emphasis of many positivists on environmental determinants of behavior and their neglect of subjective processes. The subjective processes included in the utilitarian model (such as choice of means based on subjective prediction of their outcome in achieving goals) were excluded from the antiintellectual positivist model.[12] Behavior was explained solely in terms of the situation, including the material environment and biological heredity. This model suffers from the same deficiencies as the utilitarian model. Indeed, it is even more deficient because of the failure to deal with subjective evaluation or selection of means and ends at any level.

Opposed to the general positivist orientation (whether utilitarian or antiintellectual) is the idealistic tradition. This orientation was especially strong in Germany when sociology was being developed. Within the context of this tradition, many German social theorists stressed the importance of grasping the total cultural ethos of a society, its ideals and values, its norms, and its general spirit (*Geist*) as the only valid way to gain understanding of it. Individuals' actions and institutional patterns make sense only in terms of the way in which they embody and express this general world view.

In Parsons' frame of reference the idealistic tradition emphasizes, in a way that the positivist tradition does not, the crucial importance of the normative orientation of action. The major shortcoming of this approach is that it ignores the influence of the situation within which action takes place. The idealistic perspective interprets human action simply as a kind of emanation of cultural ideals and values; it fails to recognize the analytical significance of the obstacles and constraints presented by the material environment and by biological characteristics. Cultural values do not actualize themselves automatically; human energy must be expended in confronting and overcoming obstacles and in manipulating the aspects of the situation that can be manipulated in order to implement abstract cultural ideals and values. In the process the ideals and values may be comprised and diluted instead of being manifested in a pure form.

In spite of this compromise, cultural ideals and values are still analytically significant for giving direction to individuals' actions and for providing cohesion for those involved in a social system. The constraining influence of the situation can readily be appreciated when we consider that the most idealistic forms of behavior, such as altruistic behavior, frequently require a certain level of material resources and the expenditure of human energy. Scarcity of material resources and physiological fatigue can prevent or inhibit the expression of such ideals.

Parsons' secondary analyses of Marshall, Pareto, Durkheim, and Weber can best be understood in the light of the basic conflict between positivism and idealism. It is not necessary to follow the details of Parsons' arguments. Nevertheless, a few salient points should be noted. Marshall, like other British economists and like utilitarian thinkers, emphasized the rationality of human behavior, particularly as reflected in individuals' choice of means in achieving their particular ends. However, subjective processes are not really accorded analytical independence according to Parsons; they simply mirror the external environment so as to enable the individual to adapt to it.

Even more significantly, Parsons attempted to show that the subjective process of evaluating and selecting means on a rational basis is not really the only type of subjective phenomenon that Marshall implicitly included in his model. Individuals' wants and the actions resulting from them imply a noneconomic value commitment that cannot be explained in terms of economic factors or within the overall utilitarian model. For one thing, even rationality itself reflects more than simply a means for maximizing individual pleasures or economic rewards. The obligation to be rational is itself a transcendent ethical value.[13] Rationality becomes, in Marshall's thought, the key to the particular kind of character development that is consistent with the free enterprise economic system and an individualistic type of social order. According to Parsons' analysis, the kind of activities promoted by the ethical obligation to be rational are very similar to the kind of activities that Weber saw as being promoted by the Protestant ethic.[14]

Pareto's Rejection of the Rational Model. In contrast with Marshall, Pareto reflects the antiintellectualist branch of positivism. Pareto, an Italian social theorist, had earlier been an engineer whose training was primarily in the physical sciences and mathematics. Later he became interested in political and economic questions; this led to his becoming an economist. However, instead of believing in a rational model of human behavior, Pareto insisted that a great deal of human behavior is "nonlogical."

Pareto distinguished between nonlogical and logical action on the basis of whether or not an intrinsic connection can be demonstrated between the means that an actor employs in order to achieve certain ends and the actual achievement of these ends. This involves an objective, scientific criterion. To the extent that the actor is subjectively aware of this objective, intrinsic linkage between the means used and the ends anticipated, his or her action would be logical. Thus, for example, a farmer who uses a particular formula of fertilizer to grow bigger cabbages would be engaged in logical action (assuming the appropriate formula is chosen). In contrast, staging a rain dance to insure adequate rainfall would be nonlogical.

To the extent that economic action is logical (or rational), the concepts and propositions of economic theory are applicable. Pareto's ultimate interests, however, following his shift from economics to sociology, were not in economic or other types of logical actions but in nonlogical action. Implicitly, he was aware that economic action is embedded in an institutional setting that, to a large degree, reflects sentiments and not rational calculation of means and ends. This institutional setting had never been adequately dealt with in classical economic theory; this is why economists must qualify their general assertions by noting: "If people's behavior were completely rational. . . ." The obvious implication is that sometimes it is not.

Pareto's overall theory rests on the premise that a great deal of human behavior is nonlogical and reflects sentiments or states of mind rather than rational calculation of means and ends. Nevertheless, people develop various kinds of explanations or justifications for their nonlogical actions, thereby making such actions *seem* to be rational. The underlying sentiments that are the *real* source of the motives for people's actions Pareto refers to as the *residues,* while the various explanations or justifications that people offer as the reason for their actions he refers to as the *derivations*. This distinction between people's real motives and the justifications they offer is frequently considered one of Pareto's most distinctive insights.

This does not mean that the individual actor is necessarily cynical (even though Pareto might be) or deliberately rationalizes actions to mask true motives. To assume such a process is to impute greater rationality to human action than Pareto intended. Individuals are often sincere in their beliefs regarding the logical connection between their actions and the theoretical explanations they offer to justify them.

Another category of nonlogical action, one very important in Parsons' framework, is *non*rational or *non*scientific instead of *ir*rational or *un*scientific. That is, the justifications or theoretical explanations of actions that a person might offer are nonempirical, or beyond the realm of scientific or rational explanation. As Parsons points out, such explanations are "unverifiable, not 'wrong.' "[15] This would be the case, for example, when the end that is sought is a subjective end, not an objective empirical end. To illustrate, if a person engages in certain meditation rituals in order to obtain a sense of peace of mind or union with a divine power, the ultimate criterion for evaluating such an action is the individual's subjective experience, not logical or scientific proof. In the case of the rain dance, participants might indeed experience a strengthening of their confidence in the face of uncertainty; in this case it is the subjective experience, not the objective empirical result of the rain dance, that is the real reinforcement motivating its participants.

Another important category of nonscientific or nonlogical action is action that expresses ultimate ends. Ultimate ends are, by definition, not directed toward the achievement of other ends but are valued for their own sake. Such actions cannot be evaluated in terms of the ordinary scientific criteria of rationality. They must be evaluated on the basis of whether they adequately and appropriately express, on a symbolic level, individuals' subjective commitment to the particular ultimate ends that are involved. Parsons emphasizes the importance of the contrast between the "intrinsic rationality" connecting means and ends in a scientific context and the *symbolic* association between an action and the ultimate ends that it expresses in the category of *non*scientific action.

The ultimate ends of action are not random, contrary to an implicit assumption of utilitarian theory. Pareto identified several types of widely shared residues (sentiments or states of mind) that are mainifested in action. One important implication is that there is a definite patterning involved. This patterning is revealed, for example, in Pareto's frequently cited discussion of the "lions" and the "foxes" in the circulation of political elites. Briefly, this model portrays a cyclical tendency in the political power structure. Those in power who are conservative (or have a large concentration of "persistence" residues) and whose power is backed up by force or the threat of force (the "lions") are gradually undermined by those who are innovators (or have a large concentration of the residue of "new combinations") and who use fraud rather than force to promote their interests (the "foxes"). Once the innovators are successful in achieving power, there will gradually be a shift to a more conservative strategy (reflecting changes in the underlying residues), and the stage is set for the cycle to be repeated. The conservatism of those with strong "persistence" residues reflects, among other things, a strong commitment to traditional values and norms or traditional ultimate ends. Thus the period of their dominance tends to be characterized by a strong emphasis on faith in traditional religious beliefs and values.

Although the ruling elites at different stages in the cycle differ in terms of their emphasis on common ultimate values and norms, Parsons underscores Pareto's recognition of the importance of these shared ultimate ends, particularly on the part of conservative elites. For him, this represents a major movement away from the utilitarian assumption of randomness of ultimate ends and toward Durkheim's analysis of the common collective consciousness (or conscience) shared by the members of society.

Durkheim's Transition to Sociological Idealism. Durkheim, the third theorist analyzed by Parsons who started from a positivist foundation, differs from Marshall and Pareto in his rejection of an individualistic model of action. His strong emphasis on the social environment was developed partly in opposition to the British individualistic approach as manifested by Spencer. Durkheim's positivist emphasis is equally strong, especially in the earlier part of his career. His emphasis on social facts, treating social facts as things, and explaining social facts scientifically in terms of other social facts is clearly in the positivist tradition.

Parsons attempts to show that Durkheim moved away from his positivist position during his career to a position approaching sociological idealism. Durkheim's earliest emphasis was on the external constraints imposed by the social environment. These constraints are taken into account as individuals pursue their various ends, much like the objective facts of the physical environment are also taken into account. The implicit model of human nature is that human beings act rationally in taking social constraints, such as legal codes, into account in planning their own actions.

Later, in developing the concepts of the collective conscience and collective representations, Durkheim treated social factors not simply as a set of external facts that the individual takes into account but as a set of ideas, beliefs, values, and normative patterns that individuals subjectively share with others in their group or with the overall society. His analysis of anomie and of the significance of Protestant-Catholic differences in suicide rates shows that the individual's emotional or psychological well-being is clearly dependent on a subjectively meaningful involvement with others who share a common set of values and normative patterns. By this point in Durkheim's career, social factors are clearly more than simply part of the external environment with which the individual must cope in pursuing personal interests. Instead, the very nature or content of an individual's interests will reflect the shared values and norms of the group.

The final stage in Durkheim's transition from a positivist to an idealistic position was represented by his analysis of religion. The positivist emphasis is still present, even at this stage, in the conviction that there must be an objective reality to which religious beliefs correspond. This reality, as pointed out earlier, is the reality of society itself. Religious beliefs express this reality in symbolic form and, more important, religious rituals reinforce and strengthen the emotional bonds between the members of society on which the reality of society is ultimately based. Durkheim's analysis of religious ritual is far more systematic than Pareto's but, as Parsons shows, both recognized that ritual actions are significant because they give symbolic expression to the ultimate ends, the shared values and norms, of a group or society. These ultimate ends or values cannot be dealt with adequately in terms of a rationalistic or positivistic theory. They transcend the criteria of rationality or empirical proof.

To sum up Parsons analysis thus far, Marshall, Pareto, and Durkheim each moved toward a voluntaristic position in which the importance of the normative orientation and shared ideals was recognized. Weber, however, is the theorist who demonstrated most systematically the possibilities for incorporating cultural ideals and norms in a model of behavior that also recognizes the importance of the material and social situation within which behavior takes place. Both emphases—the normative orientation and the situational context—must be incorporated in any general theory of action. The normative orientation gives direction to individuals' choices of means and ends, while the situational context provides opportunities and sets constraints for individuals' actions.

Parsons intended for his voluntaristic theory to incorporate the valid insights of all the theoretical positions that he reviewed. Specifically, individuals do have certain options for making choices with respect to means and ends (as the utilitarians emphasized); their choices are heavily influenced by the environment (as the antiintellectual positivists insisted), and their choices are regulated by shared norms and values (as the idealists stressed).[16]

Subjective Orientations in Social Relations: The Pattern Variables

Parsons' general theory of social action stressed the subjective orientations that govern individuals' choices. These choices are normatively regulated by shared values and normative standards. This applies to the goals individuals select and to the means used to achieve these goals. Even the meeting of basic physiological needs is normatively regulated.

These basic principles are presumably universal and govern all types of human behavior, regardless of specific social or cultural context. Although a solid foundation of universal principles is important as a starting point, the ultimate goal for any scientific theory is to explain *variations* in the phenomena under consideration. To this end it is important to adopt some strategy for identifying the basic elements of which the phenomena are composed and to develop a set of categories for classifying different types of cases. Specifically, what are the basic ingredients of individuals' subjective orientations? To what extent do these elements vary? What are the different types of subjective orientations that can be identified in this way? How do the subjective orientations of different individuals fit together or lead to interdependent actions that form a social system? Such questions were dealt with by Parsons in collaboration with Edward A. Shils and other colleagues in a 1951 book, *Toward A General Theory of Action*.[17] The question of how individuals' orientations and resulting actions fit together in a social system was addressed more fully by Parsons in *The Social System* (also published in 1951).[18]

A large part of the analysis in *Toward A General Theory of Action* involved the development of various categories and classification systems for analyzing individuals' subjective orientations. Among these classification systems the *pattern variables* are perhaps the most widely known and frequently cited. The pattern variables, however, must be seen within the context of Parsons' more general framework. In the general framework, an actor's orientation consists of two basic elements: the *motivational* orientation and the *value* orientation.[19] The motivational orientation refers to the actor's desire to maximize gratifications and minimize deprivations. One aspect of this concern is the effort to balance immediate gratification needs with long-range goals (which often requires deferring gratification). The value orientation refers to the normative standards that govern an individual's choices (of means and ends) and priorities with respect to different needs and goals.

Each of these elements of an actor's orientation is further subdivided into three different dimensions, each of which is present (to varying degrees) in any individual's orientation. These dimensions are as follows.

1. Motivational orientation.
   a. Cognitive dimension.
   b. Cathectic dimension.
   c. Evaluative dimension.

2. Value orientation.
   a. Cognitive dimension.
   b. Appreciative dimension.
   c. Moral dimension.

The cognitive dimension of the *motivational* orientation refers essentially to the actor's knowledge of his or her situation, especially as this relates to personal need-dispositions and goals. This dimension reflects the basic human ability to discriminate between different stimuli and to make generalizations from one stimulus to another. The cathectic dimension of the motivational orientation refers to the affective or emotional response of an actor to his or her situation or to various aspects of it. This also reflects the individual's needs and goals. In general, individuals have a positive emotional response to elements of the environment that provide gratification or can be used as means in the achievement of goals and a negative response to aspects of the environment that involve deprivation. The evaluative dimension of the motivational orientation refers to the basis (or bases) of an individual's choice between alternative cognitive or cathectic orientations. Individuals always have multiple needs and goals and, for most if not all situations, multiple cognitive interpretations and cathectic responses are possible. The criteria whereby individuals select from these alternatives is the evaluative dimension. To illustrate, a plate full of calorie-rich food can be interpreted as a feast to be enjoyed or as a cause of obesity to be avoided; which response is chosen will reflect the relative priority of the need-disposition for satisfying one's appetite for food or the need-disposition for controlling obesity.

The three dimensions of the *value* orientation may seem equivalent to the three dimensions of the *motivational* orientation. However, Parsons insists on maintaining the distinction between them, arguing that even though interdependent, they may vary independently.[20] The principal difference is that the components of the value orientation refer to general normative standards, not specific orientational decisions. Thus the cognitive dimension of the value orientation refers to the standards used in accepting or rejecting various cognitive interpretations of the situation. Scientists, for example, would not accept magical explanations of natural phenomena. Similarly, the appreciative dimension refers to standards that are involved in the expression of sentiment, or affective involvement. Parents, for example, are expected to love their children, but not in a possessive manner that denies them eventual independence. Finally, the moral dimension of the value orientation refers to the abstract standards used to evaluate alternative types of action in terms of their implications for the overall system (either individual or social) in which that action is embedded. The overall value orientation influences the evaluative dimension of the motivational orientation.[21]

The three dimensions of the value orientation reflect cultural patterns that the individual has internalized. These dimensions can also be used for classifying different aspects of the cultural system.[22] Briefly, the cognitive dimension would correspond to cultural belief systems, the appreciative dimension to the cultural system of expressive symbolism, and the moral dimension to cultural systems of value orientation. In essence, these concepts provide for a kind of parallel analysis of cultural patterns and individuals' subjective orientations. (This concern for developing concepts that can be used to integrate different levels of social reality occurs frequently in Parsons' work.)

Although the cognitive, cathectic, and evaluative aspects are always present in people's orientations, there may be variation in terms of which of these dimensions has priority. If the cognitive dimension has priority, the resulting type of action would be intellectual activity; expressive activity would result if the cathectic dimension has priority; and if the evaluative aspect has priority, the result would be moral action.[23]

Just as the various dimensions of the actor's *orientation* can be systematically classified, so can the various dimensions of the *situation*. The most fundamental distinction is between nonsocial and social objects. Nonsocial objects are further classified into physical and cultural objects. Social objects are either other individuals or collectivities with whom one interacts. The emphasis in Parsons' analysis is orientation toward other individuals with whom one is involved in interaction.[24]

Within this general gramework the *pattern variables* represent five dichotomous choices that an actor must make, explicitly or implicitly, in confronting another person in any social situation. These choices are listed here in the order in which they appeared in *Toward A General Theory of Action*.[25]

1. Affectivity versus affective neutrality.
2. Self-orientation versus collectivity orientation.
3. Universalism versus particularism.
4. Ascription versus achievement.
5. Specificity versus diffuseness.

Affectivity versus Affective Neutrality. This is the dilemma of whether or not to seek or expect emotional gratification from the other person in a social situation. A choice on the affectivity side would mean that the individuals involved would become emotionally involved with one another (or express affection to one another) and provide one another with immediate gratification. High priority would be given to the cathetic dimension. Relations between lovers or between family members illustrate this choice. In contrast, a choice on the neutrality side would mean that the individual avoids emotional involvement or immediate gratification. The relationship between a doctor and patient or between a social worker and client would illustrate this pattern.

Self-orientation versus Collectivity Orientation. This dilemma concerns the interests that are to have primacy. A self-orientation would mean that the individual's own personal interests are to have priority, while a collectivity orientation would mean that the interests of others or of the collectivity as a whole should have priority. That is, the collective moral dimension has priority. To illustrate, business relations are expected to be governed by the individual interests of those involved. In contrast, family relations, relations between close friends, or relations in a church congregation are expected to be governed by shared moral values that may require sacrifice of individual interests.

Universalism versus Particularism. This dilemma concerns the scope of the normative standards that govern a social relationship. The universalistic pattern involves standards that apply to all others who can be classified together in terms of impersonally defined categories. In contrast, the particularistic pattern involves standards that are based on some particular relationship of the other person to the individual actor or on a specific characteristic that both share. This dichotomy was implicit in Weber's comparative analyses of religion. A universalistic religion would be one that attempts to incorporate all human beings, regardless of racial, national, or other distinctions, into a single moral community; in contrast, a particularistic religion, such as a folk religion, would incorporate only the members of a particular community or society and would utilize different normative standards for insiders and outsiders. In American society, the ideal of the equality of all citizens under the law or the prohibition of racial discrimination in education, employment, and housing, are examples of universalistic norms. In contrast, normative patterns that apply, for example, only to members of one's own family, to persons in the same ethnic or racial group, or to persons in one's own age category would be particularistic.

Parsons attempts to show that this dichotomy expresses the dilemma of whether to give priority to cognitive or appreciative standards. The universalistic pattern results from giving primacy to cognitive over appreciative standards, since cognitive standards, by their very nature, are independent of particular relationships. For an employer, for example, the judgment as to whether a potential employee has the requisite skills for a particular job is independent of whether the employer and employee happen to belong to the same race or ethnic group. In contrast, particularistic relationships result from giving primacy to appreciative standards, since they involve a cathectic attachment to those who share some particular bond.[26]

Ascription versus Achievement (or Quality versus Performance). Parsons sees this variable (and the following one) as being different from the preceding three variables in that they concern an actor's perception or classification of others instead of his or her personal orientation. Essentially, others may be perceived and evaluated in terms of *who they are* or *what they do*. The former pattern, ascription, involves treating others in terms of particular qualities or characteristics that define their involvement in some social relationship. Family members, for example, would be treated differently from others simply because of their membership in the family. Similarly, ascriptive qualities such as racial or ethnic background may be taken into consideration as a basis for differential evaluation. In contrast, the achievement pattern involves a focus on overt performances or capabilities. The pattern of career promotions based on merit illustrates this, as does the use of objective measures (e.g., test scores) as the primary basis for determining entry into or graduation from a college program.

Specificity versus Diffuseness. Like the preceding variable, this pattern is also regarded by Parsons as related to perception of the other. Basically, it concerns the scope of an individual's involvement with another person. If mutual obligations are narrow and precisely defined (e.g., as in contractual relations), the pattern would be one of specificity. In contrast, if there is a wide range of gratifications received from or provided to the other, the pattern would be one of diffuseness.

In a relationship characterized by specificity, the burden of proof would be on the person making a demand on another person to justify that demand, while in a relationship characterized by diffuseness, the burden of proof would be on the person on whom a demand is made to explain why it cannot be met. For example, employers in bureaucratic organizations are expected not to make demands on their employees that are outside the domain of their jobs. In contrast, close friends are expected to help one another to the extent possible when the need arises, no matter what the particular need might be.

The pattern variables can readily be related to Tönnies' well-known distinction between *gemeinschaft* and *gesellschaft* types of social relations, or even seen as basic dimensions of Tönnies' typology. The pattern variable choices associated with Tönnies' dichotomy are as follows.

Gemeinschaft	*Gesellschaft*
Affectivity	Affective neutrality
Collectivity orientation	Self-orientation
Particularism	Universalism
Ascription	Achievement
Diffuseness	Specificity

However, Parsons insists that the pattern variables may vary independently; there is no logical necessity why they should always cluster in the manner suggested here. Because these variables are analytically independent, a comprehensive theoretical typology of social relationships could be created by cross-classifying each variable with all of the others. The resulting set of thirty-two types would probably be too complex and unwieldy to be used practically in sociological analysis. Also, many of the cells in such a typology would probably be empirically empty.

Nevertheless, recognizing the analytical independence of these various dimensions of social relations makes some interesting comparisons possible. For example, relations between clerks and customers in a large supermarket and between welfare workers and clients would probably both be classified as *gesellschaft* relations. But in terms of Parsons' pattern variables they differ in the self versus collectivity orientation. Supermarket relations reflect a self-orientation, while the welfare worker is expected to give primacy to the needs or interests of the client and not to personal interests. Thus the pattern variables provide tools for analysis of social relations that are intermediate between the extreme *gemeinschaft* and *gesellschaft* types.

The pattern variables are relevant for synthesizing analysis at different levels of social reality. Perhaps the most obvious level to which they apply is the interpersonal level. That is, they refer to subjective orientations that govern individuals' choices in relating to other persons. In addition, the pattern variables are relevant for analyzing the social structural and cultural levels of social reality. Parsons is insistent on this point. He shows how each pattern variable would apply at the personality level, the social system level, and the cultural level. At the personality level, the pattern variables would refer to alternative need-dispositions; at the social system level, they would refer to alternative role expectations; and at the cultural level, they would refer to alternative value orientations.[27]

One implication of this interdependence is that the orientations that individuals express in their various social relationships reflect the influence of shared values and norms. These values and norms are internalized in individuals' personality systems, giving direction and order to their need-dispositions and thereby shaping their actions. This concept of need-disposition does not refer to innate drives or unsocialized needs but to socially acquired needs or goals. Basic biological needs (for food, sexual gratification, etc.) may be included, but they are inevitably shaped by the culture.

This is not to imply that people's social behavior always conforms fully with the cultural value orientations. There may be incongruence, to a greater or lesser degree, between the cultural value orientations and the individual's own need-dispositions. For example, the pattern of universalism, achievement, and neutrality in a bureaucratic organization may be threatened by the emergence of friendships or by the influence of particularistic ascriptive qualities such as ethnic or racial background. On a more general level, most of us have no doubt felt the tension on numerous occasions between our personal desires and impulses and the demands or expectations of others with whom we are involved. These considerations lead to some interesting questions regarding the extent of tolerance for varying degrees of inconsistency among cultural values, role expectations, and individuals' need-dispositions. Related to this are the processes or mechanisms that insure a minimal degree of congruence among these three different levels.

Parsons does not treat the pattern variables simply as a list of completely independent variables. Instead, selected pairs of pattern variables are grouped together and cross-classified to yield a typology. One primary basis for distinguishing between different pattern variables is whether their focus is the individual's *own* orientation or attitude toward others or whether it is on the individual's perception and classification of the others themselves. The individual's own attitudes reflect his or her *motivational* orientation, while the individual's perception and classification of others is seen as related to the *value* orientation that defines the social structure.

The pattern variables used to identify individuals' *motivational* orientation yield the typology of need-dispositions displayed at the top of the following page. Segmental gratification is the need for specific gratification not involving diffuse emotional entanglement with the other who provides such gratification. The desire for service in a restaurant is one example. If a specific action involves disciplined postponement of gratification (neutrality) combined with a sensitivity to the response of another person to that specific action, the response desired is approval. For example, a student desires approval from a teacher for the specific

Value Components of Need Dispositions

	Affectivity	*Affective Neutrality*
Specificity	Segmental gratification	Approval
Diffuseness	Love	Esteem

Adapted from Fig. 3 in Parsons and Shils, *Toward A General Theory of Action*, p. 249.

action of studying hard to earn high grades. The need for love is a need for a diffuse social involvement that will be emotionally gratifying. Individuals who are in love provide each other with many intrinsically gratifying activities and responses. The need for a positive response from others for a wide array of activities that do not involve immediate gratification is the need for esteem. Immediate gratification or emotional involvement is not necessary for a person to recognize the outstanding achievements of another person. In other words, we need not love those whom we respect.

Similarly, the pattern variables used to identify the *value* orientations of social systems yield the typology of role expectations displayed below. The first of these types, the *universalistic ascriptive* pattern, would involve an orientation toward the use of universalistic norms in relating to individuals on the basis of certain distinctive qualities they possess. An example might be the treatment accorded senior citizens by virtue of their age. The *particularistic ascriptive* pattern would involve relating to another in the light of certain ascriptive qualities that have a bearing on the specific relationship. Kinship relations are perhaps the most common example. The *universalistic achievement* pattern would involve evaluation and treatment of others according to their achievements in terms of

Value Components of Role Expectations

	Universalism	*Particularism*
Ascription	Expectation of conformity with universal norms	Expectation of orientation by virtue of particular prior relationship
Achievement	Expectation of successful accomplishment	Expectation of obligations of particular relationship or membership

Adapted from Fig. 4, Parsons and Shils, *Toward A General Theory of Action*, p. 251.

universalistic norms. Finally, the *particularistic achievement* pattern would involve an orientation based on an individual's achievements, evaluated in light of a particular relationship. Evaluation of fellow members of a religious group in terms of the distinctive ethical patterns of that group is an illustration.

This typology of role expectations can be used to distinguish between the value systems of entire societies.[28] Thus, for example, the dominant value system of American society is that described by the universalistic achievement pattern. In contrast, the universalistic ascriptive pattern could be illustrated by the pre-Nazi German value system. Parsons attempts to show that the strong emphasis on status, the authoritarian tendencies, and the stress on collective political action are all consistent with this pattern. The particularistic achievement pattern fits the classical Chinese value system. This accounts for the strong emphasis on family and community ties and the priority given to traditional values. The particularistic ascription pattern corresponds roughly to the Spanish-American value system. Again, there is a strong emphasis on the family network, but with expressive activities given greater priority than conformity to any abstract value system.

The typologies just reviewed do not exhaust Parsons' use of the pattern variables. They should suffice, however, to demonstrate his approach. Indeed, in much of Parsons' work, developing theory through the identification and cross-classification of variables to arrive at various classification systems is a favorite strategy.

The pattern variables represent a major advance beyond the early analysis of the general characteristics of voluntaristic social action. However, the pattern variables in themselves do not provide anything more than the basis for a set of categories. Classifying phenomena in terms of a set of categories may be a first step in scientific analysis, but it does not accomplish the goal of providing a satisfactory *explanation* of that phenomenon. The next step, therefore, is to try to explain *why* the various pattern variables assume the values that they do. This question leads to an analysis of the basic needs of individuals and the functional requirements of social systems.

The Strategy of Structural-Functional Analysis

The discussion of the pattern variables stressed the individual actor. These variables were seen as tools for analyzing the different types of individual orientations toward the others involved in a relationship. These others also have their own orientations. Thus the dynamics of a social relationship will reflect the mutual orientations of two or more persons toward one another instead of the orientation of just one person. This is implied in the concept of *interaction*. All the parties involved will presumably be interested in improving their overall gratification-deprivation balance. The initiation and maintenance of a social relationship will depend on their success in doing this, just as implied in the exchange theory perspective on the reward-to-cost ratio. The specific manner in which gratification is sought in a relationship will be governed by the normative standards and value orientations of the particular culture.

In addition to the individual needs satisfied through interaction, there will also be additional requirements that must be satisfied if the relationship itself is to endure. Such requirements include, for example, maintaining compatible mutual orientations (not only in terms of general cultural values and norms but also in terms of specific role expectations) and developing ways to resolve conflicts that might emerge. All social systems, from the simplest dyadic relationship to a complex society, must meet certain minimal requirements if they are to survive or maintain their identity and structure as ongoing systems.

Identification of the various functional requirements faced by social systems, particularly societies, was a major concern of Parsons in much of his work.[29] Since social systems are made up of individuals, one general requirement is to insure that the basic needs of their members are met. Concern for the way individuals' needs are met within the context of social systems and an emphasis on the functional requirements of social systems as such are interrelated and interwoven in Parsons' work.[30] The pattern variables are relevant to the analysis of functional requirements because they are used to describe and categorize the general structure of the social relations through which these various needs are met. This is why Parsons' approach is referred to as structural-functional theory. The basic strategy of this approach is to (1) identify the basic functional requirements of the system in question, and (2) analyze the specific structures through which these functional requirements are fulfilled.[31]

Making the transition from individuals' actions to social structure requires explicit clarification of some additional concepts. The concept of *role,* discussed earlier in connection with the pattern variables, refers to the organization of actions in a specific type of interactive relationship. Two dimensions of roles may be distinguished: responsibilities and rights. The actions that an individual is expected to perform are the responsibilities of a role; the actions or responses of others constitute the rights. The concept of role is linked with the concept of status. In this usage, status refers merely to a person's position in an interactive relationship, not to the prestige allocated to a person. Roles or, more precisely, status-roles, are the most elementary units of social structure and, in Parsons' terms, are "the primary mechanisms through which the essential functional prerequisites of the system are met."[32]

Just as "unit-acts" are organized into roles, roles are organized into larger units referred to as *institutions.* As Parsons said, "An institution will be said to be a complex of institutionalized role integrates which is of strategic structural signifi- cance in the social system in question."[33] This definition of institution should be distinguished from the popular idea of institution as a social organization. The concept does not refer to any particular organization, but to a set of types of roles and their associated normative patterns that have a crucial bearing on a particular functional problem. Thus, for example, the economy as an institution is clearly distinct from a particular business firm. Even though the economy can be considered a single institution, it actually consists of a whole set of more specific institutional patterns such as private property, freedom of occupational choice, and the like.

Parsons uses the concept of *collectivity* to refer to a specific social organization. Thus a collectivity is a set of particular positions whose occupants interact with one another (directly or indirectly) in terms of their various roles; an institution is a more abstract set of role types and their associated normative patterns. As Parsons explains the distinction, "A collectivity is a system of concretely interactive specific roles. An institution on the other hand is a complex of patterned elements in role-expectations which may apply to an indefinite number of collectivities."[34] For example, a business firm and a labor union would each be a collectivity; the pattern of collective bargaining in which they engage would be an institution, or at least one of the institutional patterns of the economy.

The Functional Requirements of Societies. Recall that the pattern variables can be applied at the individual and cultural levels as well as the social structural level. One basic type of functional requirement is to insure a minimal degree of congruence between these different levels. Perfect integration would be realized if a given action would simultaneously reflect the individual's own need-dispositions, the expectations of role partners in an interactive relationship, and the general value commitments shared by the individual and his or her role partners. Perfect integration of all three levels is seldom if ever achieved. Yet there must be some minimal congruence or the social system presumably could not endure.

A major goal of Parsons' functional analysis was to investigate the processes or mechanisms that produce this congruence. The concepts of *internalization* and *institutionalization* are crucially significant in this connection. Internalization is the process whereby cultural value orientations and role expectations are actually incorporated into the personality system. This means that the individual's need-dispositions are shaped or influenced in a major way (but not completely determined) by these value orientations and role expectations. To quote Parsons, "It is only by virtue of *internalization* of institutionalized values that a genuine motivational integration of behavior in the social structure takes place, that the 'deeper' layers of motivation become harnessed to the fulfillment of role-expectations."[35]

Internalization refers to the personality system; institutionalization refers to the social system. If individuals' internalized value commitments lead consistently to actions that fulfill the expectations of others and elicit approving responses on their part, such values and the resulting actions are institutionalized. This would be most likely to occur if the others share the same general value commitments. On this point,

Parsons said "In so far as . . . conformity with a value-orientation standard meets *both* these criteria, that is from the point of view of any given actor in the system, it is both a mode of the fulfillment of his own need-dispositions and a condition of 'optimizing' the reactions of other significant actors, that standard will be said to be 'institutionalized.' ''[36]

In addition to the need for congruence among the personality, social, and cultural systems, there are additional functional requirements that can be identified *within* these different systems. For example, at the level of the individual personality, some attention must be given to maintaining a certain degree of equilibrium between competing need-dispositions. This need can be readily appreciated when we consider that individuals face the problem of allocating their time and energy and other scarce resources in dealing with multiple needs. Resources spent satisfying one need are likely to entail deprivation with respect to other needs.

Similarly, the pattern of role expectations in the social system must be compatible with certain minimal needs for order and integration. At the very least there must be mechanisms for dealing with the Hobbesian problem of avoiding the "war of all against all." But beyond this there must be procedures for insuring a minimal degree of cooperation and establishing a minimal degree of congruence or compatibility between the roles of different persons. There must be mechanisms for solving the recurrent problems of allocation of facilities, rewards, authority, and power and for integrating the various types of action into a system. At the level of the cultural system there is the need to establish or maintain a minimal degree of consistency or symbolic congruence. Presumably a value system or cognitive orientation would be undermined if opposing values or cognitive orientations were given equal validity.[37]

Some of the specific functional requirements of societies grow out of the exigencies of human nature and the necessity for human beings to adapt to their material environment and to interact with one another in order to survive. As biological organisms human beings have certain needs such as food, shelter, and sexual gratification. Many of these basic needs require some sort of processing of basic environmental resources. In addition, because of the relatively long period of helplessness and dependency of the human being in infancy and childhood, procedures must be established to provide the necessary care. Moreover, since human behavior is not "preprogramed" through genetic makeup or other biological characteristics, there must be mechanisms of socialization to insure that the members of each new generation internalize the cultural patterns necessary for guiding and regulating their behavior.[38]

The socialization process is never so complete that the individual's need-dispositions correspond fully with the role requirements and value orientations of the society. There is always likely to be some degree of strain or tension between culturally prescribed behaviors and individuals' needs and impulses. In many cases the result is some type of deviant behavior. Since some forms of deviance may threaten to disrupt the established integration or equilibrium of the social system, mechanisms of social control must be developed to deal with it.[39]

The desire to avoid negative sanctions may be effective in motivating persons *not* to engage in disruptive behavior. On the positive side, provision must also be made to reward those who conform to the values and norms by fulfilling their various role requirements. In order to stimulate the effort needed to make the necessary contributions, the reward system must in some manner reflect the differential contributions of different persons in society, with the greatest rewards going to those who make the most valuable contributions. Moreover, most societies must relate in some way to other societies. At the very least there is the need for territorial defense. In addition, there may also be various kinds of trade or diplomatic relationships. This requires some form of territorial organization. Such an organization is also needed to deal with internal conflict; ultimately, this involves monopolizing the use of coercive power within society. Finally, in view of the crucial importance of shared cultural values for maintaining social order, there must be mechanisms to establish and reinforce commitment to these values.

Necessary Institutional Structures of Societies. Investigation of the mechanisms for fulfilling the functional requirements identified here should lead to the identification of certain types of structures that may be expected to exist in some form in any society. Parsons identifies the following such structures.[40]

1. *Kinship Structures.* These structures are concerned with the regulation of sexual expression and the care and training of the young.
2. *Instrumental Achievement Structures and Stratification.* These structures channel individuals' motivational energy in the accomplishment of tasks necessary for maintaining the overall welfare of society in accordance with the shared values. A principal strategy for insuring adequate task motivation is to provide rewards to people in proportion to their contributions. This is how Parsons links the stratification system with instrumental achievement. In America (and other modern societies) the occupational structure channels instrumental achievement activities. The distribution of money, prestige, and power are coupled closely with the occupational structure.
3. *Territoriality, Force, and the Integration of the Power System.* All societies must have some form of territorial organization. This is necessary both for controlling internal conflict and for relating to other societies. More simply, all societies must have some form of political organization.
4. *Religion and Value Integration.* The importance of shared values has been repeatedly emphasized. The problem of defining these values and reinforcing commitment to them is closely linked with the religious institution.

Religion has traditionally provided the general framework of symbolic meaning in terms of which society's value system acquires ultimate significance. In other words, the basic world view of society is linked with its religious structures. This world view provides the general framework for the basic cognitive orientation as well as the system of expressive symbols shared within a society. That is, basic beliefs and sentiments typically are shaped by the religious heritage.

In line with the differences in the type of contributions that each of these structures makes to society, there will be corresponding differences in the pattern variables manifested in them. For example, kinship systems will be characterized by affectivity, particularism, ascription, and diffuseness. Instrumental achievement structures, in contrast, are more likely to reflect affective neutrality, universalism, achievement, and specificity. However, the extent to which these variables are involved in instrumental achievement will be heavily influenced by the degree to which the instrumental achievement structures are structurally segregated from the kinship system. If instrumental achievement is carried out within the context of the kinship system (as in many primitive societies), these patterns would be seriously undermined by the conflicting dynamics of kinship ties.

In addition to the structures through which basic universal functional requirements of social systems are met, there are additional requirements dictated by the nature of a particular social structure. As noted earlier, societies differ in terms of which values have priority. This priority will be reflected in the dominance of a particular structure. Other structures will then face the requirement of adapting to this dominant structure. For example, in America great emphasis is placed on the universalistic achievement pattern. This emphasis is manifested most fully in the occupational structure. Because of the strategic importance of the occupational system, other structures, such as religious structures and kinship, have a lower priority and are obliged to adapt to the demands of the occupational structure. Thus, for example, an explicit focus on religious activities, religious experience, and the like is temporally segregated to one day of the week. This is well understood by the clergy, whose parishioners plead occupational commitments for their lack of more extensive church involvement. At the same time, religious structures may provide the basic underlying foundation for much "secular" behavior in the occupational structure. For example, honesty is recognized as a religious virtue as well as "the best policy" in business.

Similarly, the kinship system must adapt to the demands of the occupational system. Throughout the bulk of the working day, occupational commitments rather than family commitments come first for most employed persons. Moreover, the structure of the modern nuclear family is compatible with the need for a certain degree of freedom for individuals to be mobile in response to occupational demands and opportunities. Individual mobility would be severely constrained if families or kinship structures were organized in terms of an extended family. At the same time, there are situations in which family obligations take priority over occupational commitments.

The American educational system may also be seen as a structure that fulfills a derived or secondary functional requirement. The occupational system requires a steady supply of new recruits who have the appropriate skills and knowledge and the basic motivational commitment to the universalistic achievement pattern. Since families and kinship relations are organized according to the particularistic ascription pattern, it would be difficult if not impossible to provide the necessary universalistic achievement training within the context of the family. Thus the educational system is a transitional link between the family's particularistic ascriptive value system and the universalistic achievement value system of the occupational structure. The educational system also provides the basic skills and knowledge needed for meaningful participation in society on a more systematic basis than families.

School attendance laws help solve the problem of providing supervision for children and young people and structuring their time in lieu of being involved in productive activities within the context of the family. With the separation of productive activities from the family context, a vacuum is created in terms of meaningful activities and adequate supervision for children and young people. The educational system helps to fill this need. However, since parents do not relinquish to the school system complete responsibility for caring for and training their children, there must be strategies and procedures developed to insure at least a minimal degree of cooperation or congruence between school personnel and families. Organizations such as parent-teacher associations can be seen as being established precisely for this purpose.

To summarize Parsons' strategy of functional analysis thus far, social structures and human action reflect both basic value orientations (which may vary for different societies) and the necessity to adapt to the environment. This necessity gives rise to certain universal functional requirements. For societies to survive, specific types of structures must be developed to meet these requirements. Moreover, once a given value orientation and structural pattern are institutionalized, there will be various secondary functional requirements. This may lead to the emergence of additional structures. Overall, there will have to be at least a minimal degree of integration between the various institutional structures of a society.

Development of the A-G-I-L Framework

Up to this point the stress has been on total societies. However, in a series of works in the 1950s, Parsons and his colleagues gradually modified the strategy for functional analysis reviewed here and extended it to cover all social systems, including dyadic relations, small groups, families, and complex organizations as well as total societies. This modified form differs from that just presented in that it is more general and more systematic in identifying universal functional requirements of all types of social systems (as well as all types of societies) and more abstract in analyzing the dynamic interrelations between the component parts (or subsystems) of the system in question.

The revisions resulted partly from Parsons' collaboration with Robert F. Bales, a Harvard colleague who had done extensive work in monitoring and analyzing small-group processes in a laboratory setting. Bales had discovered that the small task groups he observed invariably went through a series of predictable phases during the course of a typical group meeting. These phases were documented by means of twelve categories that were developed to record every discrete communicative act or reaction exhibited by each member of the group. These categories were divided into two broad areas: the instrumental task area and the socioemotional area. Within the task area there were separate categories used to record *requests* for information, opinions, and suggestions and to record *presentation* of information, opinions, and suggestions. Within the socioemotional area there were categories for recording positive actions such as showing agreement, showing tension relief, and showing solidarity and for recording negative actions such as showing disagreement, showing tension, and showing antagonism.[41]

Each type of action was seen as related to certain recurrent problems faced by the groups: problems of orientation, evaluation, control, decision, tension management, and integration.[42] The various phases the groups went through during a meeting seemed to result in a kind of equilibrium as the group dealt successively with each of these various recurrent problems. Thus, for example, at the beginning of a meeting the members needed to develop a common orientation toward one another and toward the task facing them. The early stages of a meeting were spent in requesting and providing information. Once a common orientation is established, the group is ready to deal with its specific task. This will involve sharing or requesting suggestions and opinions and evaluating those offered, interspersed with statements of agreement or disagreement. The group then moves on to the decision phase, which is followed by social control to insure a sufficient degree of consensus. Toward the end of a typical meeting there is frequently a sharp rise in the proportion of interaction in the socioemotional area, such as showing tension relief through joking or showing solidarity. This phase is crucial for the integration of the group, particularly since various types of strains and tensions frequently build up during the earlier, task-oriented phases.

At first glance, Bales' micro-level investigation of small groups in the laboratory might seem quite far removed from Parsons' highly abstract analysis of pattern variables and the functional requirements of total societies. On closer examination, however, it is evident that the phases of Bales' small groups can be analyzed in the same way as the basic institutional structures of the overall society. In both cases these phenomena can be seen as contributing to the fulfillment of certain fundamental functional requirements of their respective systems. In other words, just as the functional requirements of societies give rise to particular institutional structures, the functional requirements of Bales' small groups give rise to certain predictable phases in the meetings of these groups.

It is in this context that the famous A-G-I-L framework for analyzing universal functional requirements of all social systems is developed.[43] Along with the pattern variables, the A-G-I-L schema is perhaps Parsons' most well-known and frequently cited theoretical contribution in American sociology. Essentially, the A-G-I-L schema refers to a set of four basic functional requirements that all social systems must fulfill. These requirements are as follows:

A—Adaptation. This refers to the necessity for social systems to deal with their environment. Two dimensions of this problem may be distinguished. First, there must be "an accommodation of the system to inflexible 'reality demands'" imposed by the environment (or, to use Parsons' earlier terminology, to the *conditions* of action). Second, there is the process of "active transformation of the situation."[44] This involves manipulating the aspects of the situation that can be manipulated as means for the accomplishment of some goal. However, the procurement of means must be kept analytically separate from goal accomplishment, inasmuch as any given set of means may be used to attain a variety of goals. The environment, as noted, will include the physical as well as the social environment. For a small group, the social environment would include the larger institutional setting within which the group operates. (In the case of Bales' small groups this would include the academic setting.) For larger systems, such as total societies, the environment would include other social systems (e.g., other societies) and the physical setting.

G—Goal Attainment. This functional requirement grows out of Parsons' contention that action is goal directed. At this point, however, our concern is not with individuals' personal goals but with the shared goals of the members of a social system. In either case the goal achievement represents a kind of intrinsically gratifying culmination of action following the preparatory adaptive activity. In terms of the mean-ends schema, achievement of the goal is the *end*, while the adaptive activity that has gone before is the *means* for realizing this end. At the individual and social system levels there are numerous goals that might be desired. Thus the goal attainment functional requirement will necessarily include the making of decisions regarding the relative priority of a multiplicity of goals.[45]

I—Integration. This requirement has to do with the interrelations between the various members of the social system. In order for social systems to function effectively as a unit, there must be at least some degree of solidarity among the different individuals involved. The integrative problem refers to the need to insure that the appropriate emotional attachments that result in solidarity and willingness to cooperate are developed and sustained. These emotional bonds must not be contingent on benefits received or on contributions made to individual or collective goal attainment. Otherwise, social solidarity and willingness to cooperate would be much more precarious, since they would be based solely on individuals' personal self-interests.

L—Latent Pattern Maintenance. The concept of latency indicates a suspension of interaction. Members of any social system are subject to the effects of fatigue and satiation and to the demands of other social systems in which they may be involved. Therefore all social systems must provide periods when the system is temporarily disbanded and members are not expected to act or interact as system members. In Bales' small groups this was obviously the period of time between meetings. However, during this period members' commitment to the system must remain intact so that at the appropriate time system roles can be reactivated and system interaction resumed. In some cases special mechanisms may be developed to help restore motivational energy and to renew or reinforce commitment to its cultural patterns. For large-scale systems, such as total societies, this may take the form of collective rituals (e.g., holiday celebrations). Such activities may be seen as symbolic expressions of members' continuing attachment to the system.[46]

A-G-I-L Phase Movements. The four fundamental functional requirements described in Parsons' A-G-I-L schema provide the framework for an analysis of predictable phase movements. These apply in the small groups observed by Bales and in any social action system. The sequence is initiated by the appearance of some type of tension. A tension may be seen as a discrepancy between the current state of a system and a desired state or as lack of a favorable gratification/deprivation balance. This tension stimulates adoption of some particular goal and activates motivational energy directed toward its accomplishment. Accomplishment of the goal provides gratification, thereby resolving or reducing the initial tension.

Before a goal can be accomplished, however, there must be a phase of adaptation to the exigencies of the situation in which energy is mobilized and the means necessary for goal achievement are procured. During this phase, gratification must be deferred. Also, in the case of a social system there must be at least a minimal degree of solidarity among the members so that the system can move as a unit toward goal accomplishment. But the demands for disciplined task performance made on group members in moving toward the system's goals will often undermine emotional solidarity. Thus the goal attainment phase is typically followed by an emphasis on integration, in which overall solidarity is reinforced independently of any concern for instrumental task accomplishment. This phase, in turn, is followed by the stage of latent pattern maintenance. In the case of a small group, this final phase may actually be initiated at the end of the group meeting, when members remind one another of the next meeting date and indicate their willingness to include the next meeting in their individual agendas.

Here is how Parsons and his colleagues portray these phase movements:

> The phases which we have described are not merely descriptions of different possible states of systems. There are determinate dynamic relations among them, in consequence of the one way flow of motivational energy. There is a general tendency for systems to move towards the G (goal-attainment) phase through either the A (adaptive) phase or I (system-integrative) phase. The system-economy necessitates, after prolonged action in one phase, a shift to another phase to reestablish the balance of the system and to meet the system problems which had been disregarded while the system was in the former phase.[47]

This latter point is part of the explanation of phase movements. Action cannot go in all directions at once; hence it is necessary to concentrate on one system requirement at a time.[48] The entire process suggests an image of social systems as maintaining a *dynamic* equilibrium as opposed to a static state. However, the process will not necessarily operate in real life as neatly as suggested here, partly because new disturbances, or new sources of tension, may be introduced prior to completion of a cycle. Thus a system may be at one stage in the cycle with respect to one particular goal and at another stage in the cycle with respect to a different goal.

The four basic functional problems are seen not just as phases that characterize the dynamics of small task groups, but as "fundamental dimensions of action space."[49] In larger systems, such as total societies, the types of action relevant to these four functional problems may be seen as analytically distinct subsystems. Thus, for example, all the actions or institutional structures relevant to the adaptive problems would constitute the adaptive subsystem; all the actions or institutional structures relevant to goal attainment would constitute the goal attainment subsystem, and so on.[50] This idea of subsystem leads to a consideration of boundaries among the four subsystems and of *input* and *output* transactions across the subsystem boundaries. These internal transactions are represented in the following diagram.

Interchanges among the Functional Subsystems of the Social System.

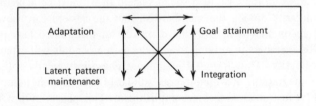

The social system as a whole is also involved with interchanges with its environment. The environment of the *social* system includes the physical environment, the personality system, the cultural system, and the behavioral organism.[51]

The reason for considering the behavioral organism part of the environment is that the basic constituent units of social systems are status-roles (as pointed out earlier). Individual persons are involved in any social system as ''personalities in roles'' and not in terms of their totality as human beings. Moreover, any particular social system is likely to involve only a segment of the personality systems of its members. The roles or other personality aspects that are not activated in a particular system would thus be part of the environment of that system. Similarly, the cultural system is also considered part of the environment in an analytical sense; the degree to which cultural patterns are actually institutionalized in a social system in the sense of guiding behavior and interaction patterns is always a matter of degree.

Hierarchy of Cultural Control. The various systems of action just identified are seen as standing in a hierarchical relationship; they are also interpenetrating and overlapping. Thus the cultural system provides the basic value orientations and normative patterns that are institutionalized in the social system and internationalized in its members' personality structures. Norms, in turn, are crystalized in specific roles in the social system that are also incorporated into the personality structures of the members of the system. The behavioral organism provides the basic energy manifested in role performances in the social system.

Since 1961, Parsons has treated the relationship among these various systems of action in terms of cybernetic control based on information flow from the cultural system to the social system to the personality system to the behavioral organism.[52] The energy manifested in action flows in a reverse direction, deriving ultimately from the behavioral organism. This hierarchical arrangement can be diagrammed as follows.[53]

Hierarchical Relations Among the Systems of Action

Hierarchy of Control	Hierarchy of Conditioning	Systems of Action
Information flow	Energy flow	
		Cultural system
		Social system[a]
		Personality system
		Behavioral organism

[a]The A-G-I-L perspective deals primarily with this system, although it could be applied to the other systems of action as well.

As an analogy to this process, we might note how a thermostat controls a heating or air-conditioning system. The thermostat could be considered a simple information system engineered to detect discrepancies between the desired temperature and the temperature of the surrounding air. Although the energy in a thermostat is very low, the thermostat exerts control over a high-energy system such as a furnace or air conditioner. At the same time, this high-energy system has to operate within certain built-in constraints. If the building within which it is installed is too large for its capacity, the thermostat would be unable to transcend this limitation.

The same processes operate in systems of social action. Culture provides the basic orientation that controls behavior, but this control must always be exerted within the constraints imposed by the lower-level systems. Thus, for example, the cultural ideal of equality would be constrained in Parsons' theory by the social system requirement that rewards be distributed in proportion to the value of contributions made so as to stimulate motivation for making valued contributions. Similarly, the cultural ideal of a close-knit, *Gemeinschaft*-type community is limited in large systems by the time and energy requirements necessary for establishing and maintaining the relationships required for such a system.

The various systems of action are also related to the four functional requirements identified by the A-G-I-L- schema. The relationships among general systems of action and functional requirements are as follows:[54]

Systems of Action	*Functional Requirements*
Cultural system	Latent pattern maintenance
Social system	Integration
Personality system	Goal attainment
Behavioral organism	Adaptation

Latent pattern maintenance is associated with the cultural system because this function stresses the cultural values and norms institutionalized in the social system. The problem of integration concerns the interrelationships between various units in the social system. Goal attainment is related to the personality system in that social system goals reflect the convergence of individuals' goals and give direction to them in accordance with shared value orientations. This linkage between goal attainment and personality systems reflects Parsons' perspective that action is always goal directed. Finally, the nature of the adaptive problem is determined largely by the biological characteristics of individuals as behavioral organisms with certain basic biological requirements that must be fulfilled for them to survive.

The A-G-I-L Framework Applied to Society

Our primary concern is with the social system, not the remaining systems in the general theory of action. Parsons' A-G-I-L model can be used to analyze the interrelations between the major institutional patterns of larger social systems, such as total societies. In collaboration with Neil J. Smelser, Parsons used the A-G-I-L framework for an intensive analysis of the economic system, including internal processes of the economy and other social institutions.[55] In this analysis and in Parsons' subsequent writings,[56] the economic system was seen as the institution that has primary responsibility for fulfilling the *adaptive* functional requirement for the society as a social system. It is through the economic institution that natural resources are transformed into usable facilities and allocated for a variety of personal and collective goals, including, for example, the meeting of individuals' basic biological needs as behavioral organisms (food, shelter, etc.).

Similarly, the fulfillment of the *goal attainment* process centers in the polity, or the political system. Societal system goals are analytically distinct from individuals' personal goals or the goals of various collectivities within society. Individuals' goals relate to societal goals primarily through their citizenship role. For large-scale and complex societies, however, the major decisions regarding societal goals will be influenced more by collectivities than by "individuals as citizens." Political parties and interest groups are two types of collectivities that have an influence on the determination of societal goals. Ultimate authority (and power) for defining society's goals is exercised by government (at various levels) and through various specific agencies or organizations. The process of arriving at a decision as to what the goal priorities will be is a complex process, involving all the political strategies of struggle and conflict, negotiation and compromise that political scientists have analyzed. Once a decision is reached, however, the goal attainment process will involve the mobilization of material and human resources to achieve these goals. Thus taxes are levied, material resources are purchased, and individuals are recruited for achieving the desired goal state.

The *integrative* functional requirement does not correspond as neatly to any particular institutional structure as clearly as the adaptive and the goal attainment requirements. Integration, it will be recalled, refers to the requirement for a minimal degree of solidarity so that members will be willing to cooperate with one another and avoid disruptive conflict. This does not necessarily mean the elimination of all conflict. But, when conflict does occur, it must be carried out within some sort of regulatory framework and not be allowed to degenerate into the "war of all against all." Parsons identifies the legal system and the overall system of social control as the principal mechanisms that deal specifically with the integrative problem.[57]

The legal system and social control structures deal mostly with the external regulation of behavior and with responding to breakdowns that occur. On a more positive note, all of those normative patterns, such as customs of tact and courtesy, which individuals follow in their interpersonal relationships help contribute to social integration. In addition, religious institutions have a bearing on the integrative function in their promotion of altruistic sentiments that, even though not fully manifested in everyday life, nevertheless help to restrain egoistic impulses. Many of the norms governing interpersonal relations are strongly reinforced by religious beliefs and sentiments as moral duties. Parsons recognizes this larger and more positive meaning of integration when he points out that the integrative problem has traditionally been the primary focus of sociological theory.[58]

Promotion and reinforcement of commitment to moral values is also associated with the *latent pattern maintenance* function. At the societal level, the idea of pattern maintenance refers to the need to maintain the basic values and norms shared by the members of society. As with the integrative problem, there is no single institutional structure that fulfills the latent pattern maintenance function. The religious institution is relevant because of its stress on helping to formulate ultimate values and to promote and reinforce commitment to them.

In addition, the family institution is also relevant for its contributions to the latent pattern maintenance functional requirement. The earliest socialization of the child typically takes place within the family. Moreover, although this function is shared with the school system, the family continues to be important in the socialization process throughout childhood and adolescence. The educational system is another major structure contributing to the pattern maintenance function by helping to socialize the ''new recruits'' of each new generation. The socialization process is essential for preserving cultural patterns from one generation to the next.

The family is also relevant with respect to the notion of latency. The family provides a setting for its members to retreat from the demands of their societal involvements. Occupational roles, which are the major vehicle for societal involvement, are typically suspended or ''deactivated'' within the context of the family. Tensions and fatigue that are built up during the course of performing one's occupational role are alleviated by time spent in rest and relaxation at the end of the day and on weekends and vacations. The result of this ''tension management'' is the replenishment of motivational energy for eventual resumption of occupational (or other societal) tasks. In addition, the family is a system and therefore has its own adaptive and goal attainment tasks to perform. However, our focus now is on the societal system, so the family as an institution is analyzed in terms of its contributions to the fulfillment of societal functions instead of as a system in its own right.

The preceding discussion is summarized in the following table.

Institutional Structures and Functional Requirements

Adaptation Economy	Goal Attainment Polity
Latent Pattern Maintenance Family Religion Education	Integration Legal system Social control Interpersonal customs and norms Religion

The linkages shown here between particular institutional structures and particular functional requirements are not as clear in the empirical world as this table would imply. In actuality, any social institution may contribute to some degree to the fulfillment of any of the functional problems. For example, business corporations are involved primarily in the economic system; yet, as collectivities that are part of the overall society, they may influence the political process of defining societal goals. For example, manufacturers of military supplies may seek to increase the priority given to national defense, as suggested by the idea of the "military-industrial" complex. Also, even though families are part of the latent pattern maintenance subsystem, they also perform economic functions (e.g., consumption) involving adaptation to the environment. Nevertheless, this table does portray the principal functional contributions of the institutional structures shown.

Still another complication arises from the fact that each of the institutional structures identified (or any constituent collectivity) may also be seen as a system in its own right. In this case the larger system of which it is a part will be part of the environment. Each institutional structure faces its own particular problems of adaptation, goal attainment, integration, and latent pattern maintenance. For large-scale institutional structures (e.g., bureaucratic organizations) there may be differentiated subsystems (such as divisions or departments) devoted to these various functional requirements. These subsystems will also have their own functional requirements as systems in their own right. Theoretically, this process of identifying various levels of systems or subsystems could be carried all the way from the overall society and its major institutional structures to the micro level of small groups and interpersonal relations. In practice, however, this would be complex and unwieldy. For most practical purposes it is sufficient to identify perhaps three levels: (1) the system of reference; (2) the larger system of which it is a part; and (3) the subsystems of which it is composed. The basic model can be diagrammed as follows:

Subsystem Functional Requirements.

A — Adaptation   G — Goal attainment

L — Latent pattern maintenance   I — Integration

Subsystem Interchanges. The dynamics of the system can be portrayed in terms of input and output transactions across the subsystem and subsubsystem boundaries. The specific inputs and outputs that move across the boundaries will differ at different levels but, if the model has *general* applicability to a variety of types of systems, we should expect some comparability between the inputs and outputs of different types and levels of systems. One common feature of different types of social systems is the fact that the interchanges across the boundaries of the different subsystems are symbolically mediated.[59] This is not to say that these interchanges are limited to symbolic meanings as opposed to material objects. For any system involved in action (as opposed to simply talking) there may be an exchange of physical or material objects. However, the significance of the objects exchanged lies in the symbolic meaning attached to them. For example, material objects such as money may serve as means to be used for goal attainment or as rewards for role performance, depending on the symbolic meaning attached to them.

This idea of subsystem interchanges can be applied at different levels. At the level of the overall society, interchanges can be identified between the various institutions of society, such as the polity and the economy, or the family and the economy, and so on. Interchanges can also be identified within institutions. To illustrate, within the economy there are interchanges between different sectors, such as those between banking and manufacturing. Or, within a particular business firm, interchanges can be identified between the different divisions or departments of the firm. Much of Parsons' and Smelser's analysis of the economy centered on identifying key decisions that affect institutional and subinstitutional interchanges.[60] If the subsystem interchange process could be carried to the lowest possible level within a social system, it would take the form of an exchange transaction between role partners who would presumably be acting on behalf of collectivities or larger institutional structures. The dynamics of the exchange process as analyzed in Chapter 9 would apply at this level, even though the exchange pattern may be heavily influenced by the exchange partners' control of large-scale institutional resources of various kinds.

Media of Exchange Between Subsystems. In analyzing the relationships between the economy and other subsystems of society, Parsons and Smelser developed the idea of a double interchange across subsystem boundaries that is made through generalized media of exchange.[61] Perhaps the most common example of a generalized medium of exchange is money. The significance of money is not its intrinsic or physical worth but its symbolic significance as representative of a certain amount of economic value.

To illustrate the double interchange process, let us consider the interchange between families or households (as part of the latent pattern maintenance system) and the economy. One or more household members is involved in the economic system through an occupational role. Thus there is an output of labor services (defined broadly) from the L system to the A system. This output is reciprocated not by the actual goods and services needed for household consumption but by money. This money (received in the form of wages or salaries) is then used in a *second* type of interchange with various economic structures, particularly retail establishments.

Thus, the A subsystem ultimately provides an output to the L subsystem in the form of goods and services in exchange for an input of labor services.

If *money* is the generalized medium of exchange involved in economic transactions, are there also other media of exchange that are associated with the various other subsystems? Parsons suggests that there are. The medium of exchange involved in the goal attainment subsystem is *power*. In many ways power is comparable to money. It can be transferred from one unit to another; it can be used for a variety of collective purposes and, as we know from our discussion of Blau's model, it can be involved in exchange transactions.[62] Although the concept of media of exchange is not as fully developed for the other two functional subsystems, Parsons suggests that *influence* (as opposed to power) is a generalized medium of exchange that is relevant to the integrative subsystem,[63] and that *value commitments* are generalized media for the latent pattern maintenance system.[64]

Influence is often linked with social approval (which was discussed in Chapter 9 as a medium of exchange). In fact, approval is often provided as the reward for voluntary compliance with influence attempts. A social system in which there is a high level of exchange of social approval would be one in which solidarity or social integration is high. In addition, conformity to mutual influence attempts would also be high, reflecting the high level of emotional attachments and mutual concerns.

Similarly, it would seem that value commitments are closely linked with the concept of prestige. Members of a social system who share a particular set of values frequently consider those who are above average in their achievement or fulfillment of these values as having high *prestige* or respect. In contrast to social approval, prestige (or symbols thereof) cannot be equally shared or its meaning would be undermined. Certainly, however, the process whereby persons (or groups) are singled out for special recognition for outstanding achievements that reflect their shared values may be expected to reinforce the commitments of others involved in the system to these values. Indeed, such occasions may be seen as providing opportunities for ritualistic reaffirmation of the values. Numerous everyday examples could be offered, ranging from the selection of outstanding students for inclusion on the honor roll to honoring an employee for long seniority to awarding military honors to those who exhibited courage in the face of danger. Prestige, in short, might be considered a generalized medium for rewarding above-average role performances, just as social approval is an appropriate reward for adequate role performances.

Structural Differentiation and Social Change

Because of its high level of generality, the A-G-I-L model can readily be used for comparing different types of systems or different stages in the history of a society. A key issue in any comparative analysis is the extent of structural differentiation between different units (or subsystems) performing the four functional requirements. Even in Bales' small groups, there were occasions when elementary role differentiation would occur between the task leader and the expressive leader. (This same type of differentiation has already been noted in connection with Thibaut and Kelley's exchange theory.) The task leader would encourage the group to accomplish the adaptive tasks in coping with the environment and moving toward goal accomplishment; the expressive leader would specialize in the socioemotional area of maintaining the integration or solidarity of the system.[65]

This same basic idea was subsequently used in Parsons and Bales' analysis of the internal structure of families.[66] Specifically, they attempted to show that the father's role and the mother's role in the socialization of the child are differentiated; the father specializes in the instrumental task area and the mother in the socioemotional area. This distinction may be less common today as a result of the influence of the women's liberation movement and the resultant blurring of distinctions between male and female roles.

The issue of structural differentiation is even more crucial in analyzing total societies.[67] (Durkheim had dealt extensively with this issue, as noted in Chapter 5.) Societies with low differentiation have a limited number of different types of structures, and these structures fulfill several functional requirements. For example, the extended family was the major structure in primitive societies, and its responsibilities included economic production, political functions, performance of religious rituals, and education of the young. All four of the basic functions were met in a single type of structural unit, much like Bales' small groups.

In contrast, modern urban-industrial societies, characterized by an extensive division of labor, exhibit a high degree of structural differentiation. This means simply that different types of structures specialize in the performance of different functional requirements. Historically, this has involved the removal of various functions from the family institution to more specialized institutions. Some examples include the transfer of productive functions to specialized structures (such as factories) in the economic institution and of many aspects of the socialization and education process to the educational establishment. This process has left the family as a more specialized institution. Its major remaining contributions include socialization of the young (a responsibility shared with schools), provision of sexual gratification, and fulfillment of tension release and socioemotional support functions.[68]

Another example of differentiation would be the structural separation of religion (as part of the latent pattern maintenance system) from the state (as part of the goal attainment system).[69] Such a development offers numerous possibilities for analysis. For one thing, the political organization of society is no longer fused with the maintenance of basic value commitments. To be sure, society's general value orientations still serve, even in a differentiated system, as an important source of legitimacy for the political system and a major influence on the formation of societal goals. However, structural differentiation means that the political structure is more "on its own," unable to take it for granted that the basic value commitments and religious beliefs of the members of society will "automatically" translate into support for the existing political structure or political policies.

The religious institution, for its part, is also on its own and must survive without political support. At the same time, this structural independence provides the religious establishment with "room to stand" in criticizing the political establishment or political policies in light of religious values and challenging it to strive for a fuller realization of these values in the society. This implies increased tension between the religious institution and the political establishment. It also implies that religious values can become a major catalyst for social and political change. Finally, differentiation between religious and political organizations means that religious bonds can transcend political boundaries. This enhances the possibility for universalistic religions to develop the idea of a universal moral community that includes all people, regardless of nationality.

The process of structural differentiation has been a key element in Parsons' analysis of long-range social change at least since *Economy and Society,* the 1957 book written with Smelser. Nevertheless, Parsons' overall emphasis on social order and equilibrium has been so strong that critics have frequently accused him of failing to deal adequately with conflict and change. Perhaps partly in response to his critics, Parsons' more recent works have stressed the dynamics of social change.[70]

Essentially, Parsons' efforts to deal with social change led to the development of a modern evolutionary theory that combined certain themes that had earlier been developed by Spencer (increased heterogeneity of social structure), Durkheim (increased specialization and growth in organic solidarity), and Weber (increased rationality as reflected, for example, in bureaucratization). The overall direction of evolutionary change is defined by the process of structural differentiation and related developments that facilitate this general process. Some of the specific interrelated developments that Parsons identifies include: (1) emergence of a stratification system as a dimension of social structure separate and distinct from the kinship organization; (2) cultural legitimation of emergent political structure; (3) bureaucratic organization; (4) a money system and impersonal market network; (5) a framework of universalistic norms; and (6) patterns of democratic association. These processes are treated as "evolutionary universals"; they are significant because they enhance the adaptive capacity of society. This means that societies in which such patterns evolve are able to make more effective use of their material and human resources and thus are better able to survive and meet their functional requirements than societies in which such patterns fail to emerge.

These specific "evolutionary universals" were subsequently incorporated into a set of four "developmental processes" that were linked with the four functional subsystems as specified by the A-G-I-L model.[71] These processes and their linkages with the A-G-I-L model are as follows.

Adaptive upgrading: Adaptation.

Differentiation: Goal attainment.

Inclusion: Integration.

Value generalization: Latent pattern maintenance.

In this listing, *adaptive upgrading* is linked specifically with the function of adaptation. In this sense the process of adaptive upgrading centers on the increased efficiency and productivity that is made possible in the economic system through specialization and technological development.

The process of *differentiation* is linked with goal attainment in this list even though it is not limited to the political system (which, it will be recalled, is the primary institution responsible for goal attainment). Differentiation applies to political structures, both in terms of their differentiation from other institutional structures and in terms of their internal differentiation (as, for example, the differentiation among legislative, executive, and judicial functions of government into different structures). Goal attainment or political functions are not limited to government, however. Instead, there is political aspect to all social systems. Differentiation is associated with this political dimension in that this process involves the establishment of various collectivities oriented toward a variety of collective goals. Indeed, Parsons defines complex organizations in terms of the primacy of their orientation toward the goal attainment process.[72]

The differentiation of social structures into specialized collectivities and roles poses a problem of integration of these various structures into some larger system. The developmental process of *inclusion* prevents differentiation from leading to fragmentation. Of special significance in this regard is the establishment of the principle of organizing society (and other structures within it) on a democratic basis and of extending the right to vote and to participate as citizens to more and more of those included within the territorial boundaries of society. These processes are seen as enhancing the loyalty of society's members to the societal community as such, independently of other loyalties based on ascriptive bonds (race, ethnicity, etc.) or other associational involvements.

Finally, the developmental process of *value generalization,* which is associated with the latent pattern maintenance functional requirement, refers to the tendency (which Durkheim had pointed out) for shared values to become more abstract as the degree of differentiation increases. Simple societies with a low degree of differentiation may be united by specific normative patterns shared by the entire society. But specific norms cannot be the basis for unity in a complex and highly differentiated society, since norms necessarily will differ for different collectivities, different roles, and different types of situations. Thus specific values that can only apply to highly specific normative patterns are gradually replaced by value orientations that are much more abstract and general and that can provide the ultimate legitimation for a great variety of different normative patterns.

Parsons' general evolutionary model is applied primarily to the long-range historical development of modern Western societies. He starts with primitive societies and then moves on to the "historic" intermediate empires of China, India, the Islamic empires, and the Roman empire. Israel and Greece are treated as "seed-bed" societies that produced elements that later fostered evolutionary developments in other societies. This evolutionary process culminates in modern urban-industrial capitalistic democracies.[73] The following quotation from Parsons' concluding remarks in analyzing the United States summarizes his application of his evolutionary model.

> The United States' new type of societal community, more than any other single factor, justifies our assigning it the lead in the latest phase of modernization. We have suggested that it synthesizes to a high degree the equality of opportunity stressed in socialism. It presupposes a market system, a strong legal order relatively independent of government, and a "nation-state" emancipated from specific religious and ethnic control. The educational revolution has been considered as a crucial innovation, especially with regard to the emphasis on the associational patterns, as well as on the openness of opportunity. Above all, American society has gone farther than any comparable large-scale society in its dissociation from the older ascriptive inequalities and the institutionalization of a basically egalitarian pattern.[74]

Parsons has frequently been criticized for failing to give sufficient attention to conflict and social change. Perhaps his critics are reacting partially to the conservative and patriotic ideological implications of his theory.[75] The preceding quotation certainly reflects such an ideology in the glowing image of the overall institutional structure of modern American society as the culmination of the evolutionary process thus far. Certainly persuasive arguments could be made for an alternative interpretation that paints a far less benign picture.

But even though Parsons' major concerns centered on explaining the foundations of social order, his theory can also be applied to social change and conflict. The ideas just discussed concerning structural differentiation and related developmental processes demonstrate the relevance of Parsons' approach in dealing with social change. As far as conflict is concerned, the general idea of functional requisites, when applied not only to society itself but to various social systems within it, provides ample opportunities for analyzing conflict. Indeed, highly differentiated societies are rife with possibilities for conflict. Every institution or collectivity or other type of subsystem in society (including each constituent personality) may be considered as a system in its own right, each with its own goals and its own needs to adapt to an environment in which resources may be scarce. Even though on one level the various subsystems (institutions, collectivities, etc.) of a society may be considered as integrated into an overarching system, on another level the larger system may be considered part of the environment to which the constituent subsystems must adapt.

Moreover, even though there may be widespread high commitment to the general value orientations of the society, there are always possibilities for disagreements between various parties in interpreting the values as far as their specific behavioral implications for their particular roles and particular situations are concerned. In short, while Parsons did not stress the process of conflict, this process can be dealt with in his theory. The basic implication of Parsons' approach is not that societies can ever eliminate conflict, but that conflict in any type of integrated system will be carried out within a framework of values and legal norms that regulate the conflict.

MERTON AND MIDDLE-RANGE FUNCTIONALISM

Probably few American sociologists would dispute the claim that Parsons is in a class by himself. From his voluntaristic theory of action in the 1930s to his evolutionary theory of the 1960s, Parsons has doggedly pursued the goal of developing a comprehensive theoretical system that would be sufficiently general and abstract to apply to all types of action in all types of social structure and all types of cultural settings. The enormity of this goal is amply evident even from this selective review of his major works. In its totality his work is in the same tradition as that of the great system builders of nineteenth-century European sociology. Although we have concentrated on his structural-functional analysis of social systems, the image of social reality that he created includes systematic analyses at the individual (personality) level as well as the cultural level.

During the years that Parsons has been at work building his "grand" theory, most American sociologists have pursued far less grandiose goals. One reason for this is the desire to link theory development with empirical research more closely than is currently possible with Parsons' abstract and comprehensive theories. Although selected parts of Parsons' work have been used in empirical research, the theoretical framework as a whole seems to be more of an elaborate interpretive model, with numerous sets of categories for classifying various aspects of social life, than a theory that provides a foundation for specific predictive hypotheses.

Merton is one of the leading contemporary sociologists who is critical of Parsons' abstract, grandiose style of theorizing. He was one of Parsons' earliest students at Harvard University, where in 1936, he received his Ph.D. Since the early 1940s Merton has been on the faculty of Columbia University. While there he collaborated extensively with Paul K. Lazarsfeld in numerous empirical research projects for the university's Bureau of Applied Social Research. Overall, his work reflects a greater sensitivity to the dynamic interrelations between empirical research and the theorizing process than does Parsons' work. On the theoretical side, however, Merton's work has earned him the distinction of being one of contemporary sociology's leading functional analysts whose approach provides a clear alternative to Parsons' style of theorizing.

Merton argues, eloquently and persuasively, that sociologists would make far more progress in advancing their discipline by developing "theories of the middle range" instead of grand theories, at least at the current stage of maturity of the discipline. Middle-range theories are defined as:

> theories that lie between the minor but necessary working hypotheses that evolve in abundance during day-to-day research and the all-inclusive systematic efforts to develop a unified theory that will explain *all* the observed uniformities of social behavior, social organization and social change.
>
> Middle-range theory is principally used in sociology to guide empirical inquiry. It is intermediate to general theories of social systems which are too remote from particular classes of social behavior, organization and change to account for what is observed and to those detailed orderly descriptions of particulars that are not generalized at all.[76]

The Basic Strategy of Middle-Range Functional Analysis

For Merton, the functional approach is not a comprehensive and unified theory but a strategy for analysis. This strategy provides a starting point and a guide, but the middle-range theories developed from this starting point should be able to stand on their own merits, supported by appropriate empirical data. Ultimately, perhaps, these various middle-range theories might be incorporated into some larger theoretical framework, but the real test for a middle-range theory is whether or not it can be used to generate predictive hypotheses that can be empirically tested in a variety of contexts and whether or not it satisfactorily explains uniformities in relationships between variables observed in a variety of contexts. The results of middle-range theories may be consistent with insights gleaned from a functional theoretical orientation or other abstract theoretical orientations. But this is not the crucial test. The crucial test for a theory is whether it can be used to generate empirical hypotheses. And unless the middle-range theory is logically derived from the general theory, the general theory, even if consistent with the ultimate empirical results obtained, is superfluous.

Merton introduced several qualifications and exceptions to some of the implicit assumptions functionalists seem to have adopted. These are included in his "paradigm" for functional analysis which, essentially, provides a checklist of questions that functionalists should keep in mind in their investigations.[77]

Like Parsons, Merton stresses the recurrent or standardized actions that bear on the maintenance or survival of some social system in which they are embedded.[78] Unlike Parsons, however, Merton is not concerned with the subjective orientations of the individuals engaged in such actions but with their objective social consequences. Merton insists on maintaining a sharp distinction between subjective motives (purposes or orientations) of individuals and the objective social consequences that flow from their actions. Whether or not the objective social consequences enhance the ability of the social system to survive is independent of individuals' subjective motives and purposes. Although Parsons recognized that individuals' motives may be oriented *consciously* toward fulfilling their various need-dispositions instead of meeting the functional requirements of some social system, his emphasis on the congruence between individuals' need-dispositions and social system role requirements leads to a blurring of the distinction between motives and objective consequences, which Merton emphasized.

For example, one basic requirement of a society is that its members replenish their numbers through reproduction; yet, when members of a society have children, it is doubtful that they are motivated by any conscious desire to insure the long-range survival of society. Their motivations are more personal; they may include the desire to express love, to experience sexual gratification, to conform to social customs, and to experience the emotional satisfaction of having children. Similarly, in engaging in religious rituals, individuals are probably not motivated by any desire to fulfill the latent pattern maintenance function or even to enhance solidarity; instead, their motives are personal ones, such as fulfilling their religious duties, attaining salvation or peace of mind or, again, conforming to established customs. The distinction between motive and function or social consequence can be represented in the following diagram.

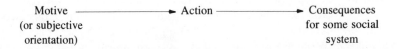

This distinction between motives and functions is expressed in Merton's contrast between *manifest* functions and *latent* functions. To quote Merton, "*Manifest functions* are those objective consequences contributing to the adjustment or adaptation of the system which are intended and recognized by participants in the system; *latent functions*, correlatively, [are] those which are neither intended nor recognized."[79]

Moreover, Merton warns, sociologists employing functional analysis should not assume that all the standardized patterns of action necessarily have consequences that are beneficial for the system or fulfill its functional requirements. Many actions may have consequences that are *dysfunctional* or that "lessen the adaptation or adjustment of the system."[80] A third alternative is that the consequences of many types of actions may be irrelevant as far as the survival or well-being of the system is concerned; in other words, they are nonfunctional.

Analysis of dysfunctions may involve either a short-term or long-term time frame. Some types of action may have dysfunctional consequences in the short run; in other cases there may be a long time interval before the dysfunctional consequences accumulate to the point where the adjustment or adaptation of the system is undermined. For an example of short-term consequences, actions or experiences that promote great solidarity within a particular segment of society may, at the same time, promote tensions and conflicts with other segments, thereby undermining the solidarity of the overall society. The long-term perspective could be illustrated in analyzing certain long-range dysfunctions of technological progress, such as increased pollution of the environment, depletion of natural resources, and increased risk of nuclear war or nuclear blackmail. The question of whether the social consequences of a given action are functional or dysfunctional is always an empirical question and cannot be settled by abstract *a priori* theorizing.

Many actions have consequences that are relevant for numerous social systems in which they are embedded. These multiple consequences must be explored and evaluated in terms of their functional significance for each system in which they are embedded. This is illustrated in the preceding example of in-group solidarity within a limited segment of society that, at the same time, undermines the solidarity of the overall society. Numerous cases of this type could be identified involving, for example, religious groups, ethnic groups, occupational groups, and social classes.

Durkheim's functional analysis of religion can readily be criticized in this context. By studying how common beliefs and rituals promote solidarity, Durkheim ignored the role that religion can play in undermining solidarity and promoting conflict in societies that are divided along religious lines. Indeed, in such situations it would seem that the stronger the solidarity within a religious in-group, the greater the tension and the probability of conflict between the religious in-group and other religious groups in society. Such tension and conflict would be especially likely if there is fundamental disagreement between the various religious groups on basic beliefs and values. On the other hand, strain and conflict may be minimal if the different groups share certain fundamental beliefs and values. The American pattern of denominational pluralism rests on a foundation of widely shared beliefs and values, thereby making possible extensive cooperative or ecumenical relations.

Moreover, given the multiple conflicting interests of different groups and organizations in a complex society and the scarcity of resources, patterns of adaptation that are functional for one group or one segment of society may be dysfunctional for others. For example, installation of labor-saving machinery in industrial plants may be functional in terms of enhancing the profits of the owners but dysfunctional for the working class in terms of increasing unemployment. Similarly, labor strikes that result in high wage settlements are presumably functional for labor unions and their members, but dysfunctional for stockholders and consumers, at least in the short run. Such examples of multiple consequences for different segments of society are so numerous and pervasive in social life that the very idea of analyzing actions in terms of their contribution to the functional requirements of the *overall* society begins to look tenuous.

Certainly there are some functional requirements that apply to society as a whole. Merton, however, is far more cautious than Parsons in attempting to identify these universal functional requirements. One logical problem in this connection is the problem of tautological explanation, which is a pseudo-explanation. In functional theory it is asserted that established social structures or institutional patterns exist because they contribute to the functional requirements of society; then the proof offered for such assertions is simply that society is surviving. This type of explanation is not really an explanation but an *ex post facto* interpretation. The most that Merton is willing to offer by way of a specific statement of functional requirements in advance of empirical observation is that there must be a net balance of functions over dysfunctions.

Even if functional theorists could identify specific functional requirements, this does not provide any clear basis for predicting that these requirements will be met in any particular fashion. There may be a variety of ways in which such requirements could be fulfilled. This gives rise to the concept of functional alternatives (or substitutes). No structure should be assumed on an *a priori* basis to be indispensable for fulfilling a particular functional requirement; alternative structures might be able to fulfill a given requirement just as effectively. The question of how wide the range of functional alternatives might be or, more broadly, how much variability is possible in social structures, cannot be decided on an *a priori* basis but must be subject to careful empirical investigation.

If we use religion as an example again, to argue, as Durkheim clearly implied and as Parsons strongly suggested, that religion is essential for maintaining the integration or solidarity of society is to confuse a functional requirement with a specific structural requirement. The same function of promoting solidarity and integration might be fulfilled by means of a secular value system or even by means of conflict with other societies. Of course, if religion is *defined* in terms of its contributions in promoting solidarity (as Durkheim defined it), *any* structure or mechanism that promotes solidarity could, by definition, be considered a religion. However, this probably stretches the definition of religion too broadly. Merton does not intend to imply that possibilities for structural variation are unlimited. But the existing structure of any particular system is certainly not the only structure possible for fulfilling the system's various functional requirements.

Moreover, functional analysis need not necessarily be limited to investigating the mechanisms that promote stability or preserve the existing structure of a system. To be sure, a great deal of Parsons' functional analysis was intended to explain stability and social order. In addition, the early functional analyses of primitive societies carried out by cultural anthropologists attempted to show that various customs and institutional patterns contributed to the integration and stability of their respective societies.[81] A better strategy, however, is to recognize that whether the objective consequences of particular patterns of action or institutional structures contribute to solidarity or undermine it—whether they promote stability or change— is an empirical question that cannot be answered on an *a priori* basis but only as a result of empirical investigation.

Latent Dysfunctions, Social Problems, and Social Change

The concept of dysfunction is extremely useful in developing a functional approach to social problems and social change. Dysfunctional consequences lessen the adaptability of the system and may eventually lead to overt strain and disruption. One possible result of the accumulation of dysfunctional consequences is that compensating structures may be established to neutralize or eliminate them. This would, in essence, mean structural change. The establishment of these new structures may eventually generate their own dysfunctional consequences, which may stimulate additional structural change, and so on indefinitely. For example, many government agencies can be seen as structural adaptations to the accumulations of latent dysfunctions that become defined as social problems. At the same time, many would see the proliferation of overlapping government agencies as producing their own dysfunctions in the form of increased regulation of individuals' decisions and activities, heavy financial cost, inhibition of individual initiative, and the like.

The distinction between functional and dysfunctional consequences can be used most effectively when combined with the distinction between manifest and latent functions. Numerous instances could be cited in which the manifest functions or overt purposes of some line of action or institutional structure are consciously intended to be beneficial to the system or a specific segment thereof or to oneself. In addition to these manifest functions (which may actually be fulfilled as intended) there are often unintended by-products that are dysfunctional, either for the same system or for some other related system.

For example, minimum wage legislation is intended to be beneficial to those at the bottom of the occupational hierarchy. However, it can be argued that one unanticipated by-product of such legislation is that potential employers of low-skill laborers increase their level of automation; the result is a rise in the unemployment rate. Whether, on balance, the positive consequences outweigh the negative consequences or not is a matter for careful evaluation considering our basic value commitments as well as our objective sociological analysis.

Recognizing the unanticipated dysfunctional consequences of patterns of social actions underscores a paradoxical dimension to social life that is often associated more with dialectical analysis than functional analysis.[82] (Recall from the discussion of the Marxist perspective that the general strategy of dialectical analysis involves an effort to deal with the internal contradictions built into a given social structure.) This paradoxical dimension is the contradiction between people's intentions and the objective social consequences of their actions. In some cases the objective consequences are not only dysfunctional but are actually the exact opposite of the effects intended. Such dysfunctional consequences are often the result of the aggregation of individuals' actions on a broad scale in society.

For example, attending college has traditionally been one of the major avenues for upward mobility in American society. Over the past several years the number of young people attending and graduating from college has increased tremendously. This increase has been partially supported by government programs that provide grants, scholarships, and guarantees of low-interest loans. The development of such programs is consistent with the high value placed on education as a means of upward mobility and for its own sake. The individual college student will presumably be motivated by one or more of several motives, including the desire to expand intellectual horizons, to achieve the prestige associated with a college degree, to enter a career with greater promise of upward socioeconomic mobility than would otherwise be possible, or perhaps even to please parents or be with friends who are going to college.

If these various individual goals are fulfilled they would be *intended individual effects*. There may also be some individual effects that are *not* intended. For example, college education may promote a more liberal social or political outlook or stimulate a change in career goals. In addition, when there is a significant increase in the number of young people enrolling in and graduating from college, there are bound to be some wide-ranging *social consequences*. Some of these social consequences may be anticipated by education policymakers if not by individual students. For example, rapid increases in enrollment create short-term strains on existing facilities and personnel, thereby necessitating increased expenditures to meet this deficiency. Other social consequences are likely not to be anticipated. For example, the various pressures associated with rapid growth may lead to a deterioration of educational quality.

Some of the wide-ranging social consequences may undermine the ability of individuals to achieve their personal objectives. For example, one could argue that as more and more young people graduate from college, the social and economic value of a college degree is likely to decline. This is reflected in the fact that having a college degree no longer carries as much prestige as it once did, nor does it provide guaranteed access to a prestigious career with a good salary and prospects for steady promotion. Indeed, the experience of many college students suggests that finding any job at all is difficult.

There is irony in this type of analysis. Certainly no student wants to contribute to the decline in the social and economic value of a college education. Nevertheless, this could be one of the unintended results of the tremendous increase in the number of individuals graduating from college. Paradoxically, therefore, the consequences of thousands of individual decisions to attempt to improve one's lot in life by attending college might well be that the effectiveness of college as the key to a better life is actually undermined.

The same type of analysis could be applied to our national dependence on the Middle East for the energy resources necessary to maintain our economic system and life-style. At no point in our nation's history did our political leaders make a conscious decision to increase our country's vulnerability to the volatile and unstable political climate of the Middle East. Yet the results of thousands of individual decisions by business leaders, government officials, and private citizens have had precisely this effect. The various motives or intentions underlying these decisions are of interest perhaps, but they are not really relevant as far as assessing the social functions of such decisions are concerned. Aside from the general goals of maintaining continued economic growth and insuring maximum financial profits, one of the goals sought in the past transition of many industries and power plants from coal to oil has been to avoid the environmental pollution resulting from the burning of coal. National policy encouraged this transition from coal to oil for this reason. With the benefit of hindsight, we now realize the national vulnerability that this policy has helped to bring about and so are faced with the pressures to convert back to coal to the extent feasible.

The general principle that this type of analysis suggests is that understanding individuals' subjective orientations and conscious motives or intentions provides at best a limited picture of the dynamics of our social world. Individuals' actions have far-reaching and long-lasting social consequences of which they may be completely unaware. Even though unintended, however, these consequences become part of the world to which individuals must subsequently adapt. In many cases the constraints and problems that individuals confront in attempting to adapt to their environment are a product of their own previous activities. Thus we live in a world of our own making, even though we often experience this world as beyond our control or with a design not of our choosing.

Although our emphasis has been on the unintended or latent dysfunctions or problems that result from human actions, many positive functions beneficial to society or to ourselves as individuals result as the unintended by-product of activities directed toward other ends. Indeed, the survival of many of our basic social institutions no doubt results largely as a latent function and not a manifest function. Probably most of us are consciously oriented toward far more personal and mundane concerns than insuring the long-range survival of social institutions.

This general strategy of functional analysis suggests a view of social processes that is far more sophisticated than one that stresses individuals' subjective orientations or that assumes that existing social structures can be adequately explained by their contribution to the fulfillment of the functional requirements of society. Merton charges that a great deal of functional analysis fails to consider the various reservations and qualifications suggested by the concepts of latent functions, dysfunctions, functional alternatives, and the like.

Specifically, Merton identifies three "prevailing postulates," drawn primarily from early anthropological studies of simple primitive societies, which he insists are unwarranted, particularly in large complex societies.[83] First is the postulate of the "functional unity of society." Essentially, this is the assumption that the various structures and institutionalized patterns of action are all harmoniously interrelated and contribute to the integration and solidarity and other functional requirements of the overall society. The idea of dysfunctions and of nonfunctional consequences can be used to refute this assumption. The second unwarranted postulate is the "postulate of universal functionalism," according to which "*all* standardized social or cultural forms have positive functions."[84] The idea of dysfunctions and of nonfunctional consequences can also be used to refute this assumption. The third postulate Merton criticizes is the "postulate of indispensability."[85] This is the assumption that particular structures or institutional forms that fulfill a functional requirement must be indispensable. The idea of functional alternatives can be used to refute this notion.

In summary, as a strategy for empirical investigation, functional analysis involves concentrating on the objective consequences of institutionalized patterns of action, whether or not these consequences are consciously intended. These consequences are evaluated in terms of whether they are functional, dysfunctional, or nonfunctional for the various systems in which they are embedded. It must be fully recognized that actions may be functional for one system in which they are embedded and dysfunctional or nonfunctional for others. In addition, attention must be directed to the possibility for functional alternatives in different types of social systems and to the nature of the responses that are made to dysfunctions and the social consequences of these responses.

Examples of Middle-Range Functional Theories

Overall, Merton's work does not provide an abstract analysis of functions or dysfunctions, either manifest or latent. Instead, it manifests his preference for middle-range theory focused on specific and limited problems. Most of his well-known book, *Social Theory and Social Structure*, is devoted to a series of middle-range theories on a variety of topics. These theories stand on their own, however, without making extensive use of the terminology of functional analysis and without being clearly related to one another.

Social Structure and Anomie. Merton's well-known theory of anomie and deviant behavior may be noted briefly as an example of a middle-range theory.[86] His basic contention is that anomie and deviant behavior in American society result from certain strains in the social structure. Specifically, there is a discrepancy for certain segments of the population between the material and occupational success goals that our culture emphasizes and the institutional means provided for achieving these goals. Briefly, the American culture encourages all the members of society to aspire to occupational and financial success, regardless of their social and economic class background. The Horatio Alger story of "rags to riches," the cultural symbol of Abraham Lincoln's journey from a log cabin to the White House, the saga of poor immigrants who gradually moved up the socioeconomic ladder in the "land of opportunity," and the idolization of the "self-made" person all express the same general goals that people are encouraged to internalize and pursue.

But, at the same time, the legitimate opportunities for achieving materialistic success goals are not equally distributed to all segments of the population. Some segments do not have access to the legitimate means for achieving these goals in the culturally approved way. The results of this discrepancy is anomie and various forms of deviant behavior. In other words, the discrepancy between goals and means is dysfunctional for the segments of the population for whom such a discrepancy exists, and the consequence of the discrepancy is often some form of deviant behavior.

Whether the deviant behavior is dysfunctional for society is a separate question, however. Merton's theory has often been used in connection with efforts to explain crime and delinquency, in which case it is generally assumed that deviance is dysfunctional for society. However, some forms of deviance, such as inventing a new product or providing a new kind of service, may turn out to be functional for society (or segments thereof) as well as for the deviant. In addition, deviance may stimulate various forms of social change designed to improve the distribution of opportunities for success.

The Bureaucratic Personality. A good example of the counterproductive or dysfunctional type of consequence is provided by Merton's analysis of the bureaucratic personality.[87] As sociologists have often emphasized since Weber, bureaucratic organizations place a heavy emphasis on conforming to formally established rules and procedures. This is necessary (or functional) to insure continuity, reliability, and coordination in accomplishing organizational goals. However, Merton argues that one dysfunctional consequence of the extensive reliance on rules is that bureaucrats may eventually come to see conformity to the rules as an end in itself and, as a result, they may lose their capacity to respond flexibly to new situations. In some cases, the effect of this inability to adapt or modify (or even ignore) rules to fit new situations is that the achievement of the primary goals of the organization is undermined. Here, therefore, is a situation where an institutionalized pattern has both functional and dysfunctional consequences for the same system, depending on the type of situation being confronted. Often, however, the clients of a bureaucratic organization bear the brunt of bureaucratic rigidity.

Reference Group Theory. Another example of a middle-range theory that draws on the strategy of functional analysis is that of reference group theory.[88] Reference groups are the groups with which an individual identifies as a basis for self-evaluation, comparison, and normative guidance. Such groups need not necessarily be groups of which an individual is a member. The idea that individuals' self-concepts and attitudes are derived from the group(s) with which they identify is not original with Merton. Mead's concept of the "generalized other" carried much the same implication. Also, the idea that individuals' satisfaction with their situation is based on comparing their situation with that of others is dealt with in exchange theory in the effort to explain how people evaluate their reward-cost outcomes. The distinctive contribution of Merton's reference group theory is the conceptual distinc-tion he draws between *membership* groups and *reference* groups.

In many cases individuals' reference groups are groups of which they are members. Such persons would be likely to conform to the group's norms and to use the group's standards as a basis for self-evaluation. They would be satisfied or dissatisfied according to whether their situation is better or worse than that of fellow group members. This principle was used to explain data that had been reported by Stouffer and his colleagues in *The American Soldier* on satisfaction with promotion rates in different branches of the military service. These findings initially seemed to be puzzling. In the military police promotion rates were very low, but individuals were not greatly dissatisfied with their chances for promotion. In contrast, promo-tion rates in the air corps were high, but individuals were dissatisfied with their chances of promotion. This paradoxical finding is understandable when we realize the effects of the differential promotion rates on servicemen's expectations. Briefly, the rapid promotion rates in the air corps led to an expectation of being promoted rapidly and subsequent disappointment with failure to be promoted as rapidly as expected. In contrast, the low promotion rates in the military police led to low expectations for promotion and thus to low levels of disappointment.[89]

In other cases, however, individuals may be oriented toward the standards and normative patterns of groups to which they do *not* currently belong. This may help to account for deviance from the normative patterns of membership groups. In-group solidarity would be threatened if a large proportion of the members identified primarily with outside groups. Although this may be dysfunctional from the standpoint of the group in question, it may be quite functional in an open society in encouraging and facilitating social mobility. In many cases individuals identify with groups to which they do not currently belong but that they expect to join someday. Merton contends that this process is functional in facilitating *anticipatory socializa-tion*.[90] That is, individuals learn the normative patterns and standards of groups that they expect to join by identifying with these groups prior to the actual joining. Such a process should make the process of integration into the new group easier.

These examples of middle-range theories illustrate Merton's style of analysis.[91] Middle-range theories are difficult to summarize because, by definition and design, they are not developed to fit into a comprehensive theoretical framework. Instead, each theory stands more or less on its own. The one thread that can be identified in all of Merton's work is a concern for demonstrating the social (and sometimes the psychological) consequences (or functions) of various behavior patterns, particu-larly those that are unintended, to which individuals must subsequently adapt.[92]

The general style of middle-range theorizing is perhaps the dominant style in the various substantive fields of sociology. Sociologists working in diverse fields such as complex organization, family, deviance, social psychology, social stratifi-cation, sociology of religion, and political sociology tend to emphasize particular theories relevant primarily to the particular field. Although some aspects of more general theoretical approaches are used in these substantive fields, major concern is given to the development of particular theories that are closely linked with appropriate empirical data.

The contrast between Merton's and Parsons' versions of functional analysis may be summed up by noting that Merton was not interested in developing a highly integrated "grand theory" of how universal functional requirements are fulfilled but in using functional analysis as a point of departure for raising empirical questions regarding the objective social consequences of recurrent patterns of action. Moreover, Merton explicitly and consistently stressed the social structural level of analysis more than Parsons did. This point applies particularly to his codification of the procedures of functional analysis. The various middle-range theories that he developed frequently incorporate concepts from the individual level (such as motivations, attitudes, and expectations) and from the cultural level (such as cultural values). Parsons, in contrast, was more explicit in attempting systematically to link the social structural level with the cultural level on the one hand and the individual level on the other throughout his theory, even though the social system was his primary concern also.

Summary

This chapter has been devoted to a presentation of the major contributions of two of the leading representatives of functionalism: Talcott Parsons and Robert K. Merton. Parsons' earliest work was devoted to developing a voluntaristic model of social action based on his synthesis of the theories of Marshall, Pareto, Durkheim, and Weber. Basically, Parsons argued that these theorists had established the foundations for reconciling the opposing views of positivism (including both utilitarianism and an antiintellectual branch that emphasized the nonrational foundations of social action) and idealism.

A basic principle in Parsons' overall theory of action is that it is both goal oriented and normatively regulated. Alternative orientations toward goals and norms were incorporated in a set of five pattern variables that describe the choices individuals must make, either implicitly or explicitly, in any social relation. These pattern variables provide a framework for simultaneous analysis of cultural values, social system role expectations, and personality need-dispositions. The alternative choices provided by the pattern variables represent an elaboration of some of the basic dimensions implicit in the gemeinschaft-gesellschaft dichotomy or the primary group-secondary group dichotomy.

The next general area of concern was to determine the basic functional requirements of societies and the structures through which these requirements are met. One general requirement suggested by the pattern variable analysis was that of insuring congruence among cultural values, role expectations, and personality need-dispositions. Other basic requirements grow out of the need to satisfy individuals' basic biological requirements and to adapt to the physical environment and to one another. At the societal level, these functional requirements are met through various social institutions.

Parsons and his colleagues extended the strategy of functional analysis so it could be applied to any micro-level or macro-level social system. Out of this effort the A-G-I-L model was developed. Briefly, this model refers to the need for any social system to fulfill the functional requirements of adaptation, goal attainment, integration, and latent pattern maintenance. Overall, social systems are seen as under the control of cultural values and norms, with the basic energy manifested in action supplied by the behavioral organism.

The emphasis in Parsons' structural-functional analysis is on the mechanisms that promote stability and order in social systems. Eventually, Parsons turned his attention to an analysis of broad historical change by developing an evolutionary model that focused heavily on the process of structural differentiation. This and related changes are seen as occurring in an orderly fashion and as insuring continued social progress.

Parsons' style of developing theory on a grand scale was criticized by Merton, who preferred a more modest strategy of developing middle-range theory. For Merton the strategy of functional analysis involved identifying and analyzing the objective social consequences of selected patterns of behavior. These consequences may be either manifest or latent. They may be beneficial to the system in which they are embedded or dysfunctional or irrelevant as far as functional requirements are concerned. If a given institutional pattern is beneficial in terms of meeting a social system need, this does not mean that this pattern is indispensable; such a requirement could be met by alternative means. Overall, Merton's concern is not with establishing functional requirements on an *a priori* basis but with evaluating the consequences of established patterns of behavior for the system in which they are embedded. We stressed situations in which latent dysfunctions gradually accumulate to the point where they are defined as social problems and stimulate social reform efforts.

A great deal of Merton's substantive work illustrates the development of middle-range theory. We have briefly reviewed his theory of social structure and anomie, his theory of the bureaucratic personality, and his reference group theory. Middle-range theorizing is also widely manifested in the various specialized substantive fields of sociology.

In spite of the fact that both Parsons and Merton warn against assuming complete integration of social systems, the basic image of social reality that most sociologists derive from the functional perspective is that of a system integrated on the basis of shared values and exhibiting more or less harmonious interdependence between its various "parts" (institutions or other subsystems). Also included in this image is the idea that the system includes various mechanisms to maintain its equilibrium and enhance its ability to survive in its environment. There is also the implication, strongly developed in Parsons' work, that individuals are sufficiently well integrated into the system that a fairly close correspondence exists between their needs and the functional requirements of the system. This correspondence is insured by the various mechanisms of socialization and social control. Overall, this image seems to downplay or deemphasize the pervasiveness and the inevitability of conflict as well as the processes within social systems that generate social change. Accordingly, Chapter 11 will discuss several theories in which conflict is given a much more central place.

Footnotes

1.   For a brief summary discussion of this contrast, see Mark Abrahamson, *Functionalism* (Englewood Cliffs, N.J.: Prentice-Hall, 1978), especially pp. 22–31. This book pro-

vides a short overview of the functionalist perspective and a review of some of the criticisms and specific applications of this perspective.

2. For example, in *The Nature and Types of Sociological Theory* (Boston: Houghton Mifflin, 1960), Don Martindale classifies Parsons' early work in the "social action" branch of the school of "social behaviorism," while his later works are classified in the "macro functionalism" school (pp. 421–425, 484–490, 493–499). See also John Finley Scott, "The Changing Foundation of the Parsonian Action Scheme," *American Sociological Review*, Vol. 28, October 1963, pp. 716–735.

3. The biographical highlights and intellectual influences on Parsons that follow are drawn mostly from Edward C. Devereux, Jr., "Parsons' Sociological Theory," pp. 1–63 in Max Black, ed., *The Social Theories of Talcott Parsons* (Englewood Cliffs, N.J.: Prentice-Hall, 1961), especially pp. 3–7. For an autobiographical statement, see Talcott Parsons, "On Building Social System Theory: A Personal History," *Daedulus*, Vol. 99, Fall 1970, pp. 826–881.

4. See the dedication in Talcott Parsons, *The Social System* (New York: Free Press, 1951).

5. Ibid., Chapter X, "Social Structure and Dynamic Process: The Case of Modern Medical Practice," pp. 428–479.

6. See Talcott Parsons, *Structure and Process in Modern Society* (New York: Free Press of Glencoe, 1961), Chapter VII, "Social Strains in America," pp. 226–247.

7. See Talcott Parsons and Gerald M. Platt, *The American University* (Cambridge, Mass.: Harvard University Press, 1973).

8. Robert K. Merton's middle-range approach will be discussed in detail in due course.

9. Several conflict-oriented theoretical perspectives will be presented in Chapter 11.

10. Talcott Parsons, *Structure of Social Action* (New York: McGraw-Hill, 1937).

11. For a concise overview of the major schools of thought that Parsons attempted to integrate in his voluntaristic theory, see Devereaux, op. cit., pp. 7–20. The discussion that follows differs from Devereaux's, however. Devereaux distinguished among (1) utilitarianism and economic theory, (2) positivism, and (3) idealism. The discussion that follows is based on Parsons' treatment of utilitarianism as one branch of positivism. This rationalistic branch is contrasted with an antiintellectual branch of positivism in Parsons' discussion.

12. The utilitarian treatment of subjective processes was not inconsistent with the positivist emphasis on the deterministic influence of the environment. One of the implications of the rationalistic assumptions of utilitarianism is that subjective processes merely mirror the situation; they do not exert an independent influence on behavior. The actor perceives the environment, notes the opportunities and constraints that it offers, and acts in such a way as to promote personal interests. Any departures from rationality (such as the use of means that fail to accomplish the desired ends) are treated simply as a result of ignorance or error.

13. Parsons, *Structure of Social Action*, p. 164.

14. Ibid.

15. Ibid., p. 202.

16. The synthesis between these three schools is stressed in concise form by Devereaux, op. cit.

17. Talcott Parsons and Edward A. Shils, eds., *Toward A General Theory of Action* (New York: Harper & Row, 1951).

18. Talcott Parsons, *The Social System* (New York: Free Press, 1951).

19. Parsons and Shils, op. cit., pp. 58–60.

20. Parsons, *The Social System*, pp. 13–15.

21. Parsons and Shils, op. cit., p. 71.

22. This idea is more fully developed by Parsons in *The Social System*, p. 57 and Chapters 8 and 9.

23. Parsons and Shils, op. cit., p. 75.

24. Ibid., p. 58.

25. Ibid., p. 77.

26. Ibid., pp. 85–86.

27. Ibid., pp. 80–84.

28. See Parsons and Shils, op. cit., pp. 184–185, and Parsons, *The Social System*, pp. 180–200.

29. This is also a major concern of many other theorists in the functionalist school, many of whom have been heavily influenced by Parsons. For an example, see Marion J. Levy, *The Structure of Society* (Princeton, N.J.: Princeton University Press, 1952). Levy identified four conditions that must be avoided in order for a society to survive. These are: (1) biological extinction or dispersion of the members; (2) apathy of the members; (3) war of all against all; and (4) absorption of the society into another society.

30. Parsons' earliest systematic development of the structural-functional approach is in his 1951 book, *The Social System*.

31. The need for adopting this type of approach was expressed by Parsons as early as 1945. See Parsons, "The Present Position and Prospects of Systematic Theory in Sociology," Chapter XI in *Essays in Sociological Theory* (New York: Free Press, 1949), pp. 212–237.

32. Parsons, *The Social System*, p. 115.

33. Ibid., p. 39.

34. Ibid.

35. Ibid., p. 42 (emphasis added).

36. Ibid., p. 38.

37. This emphasis on congruence and consistency has often been subjected to criticism. For example, Gideon Sjoberg suggests that social systems are actually characterized by contradictory functional requirements involving inconsistent values. To illustrate, a social system may place a high value on equality at the same time that it also places a high value on stratifying people in society according to their achievements (or some other criterion). Moreover, both values may correspond to basic requirements of the system. He recommends that the dialectical strategy of analysis can help direct attention to such internal strains and conflicts. See Gideon Sjoberg, "Contradictory Functional Requirements and Social Systems," pp. 339–345 in N. J. Demerath, III and Richard A. Peterson, eds., *System, Change, and Conflict* (New York: Free Press, 1967).

38. Parsons devotes considerable attention in *The Social System* to the various mechanisms of socialization (see Chapter VI).

39. Parsons also devotes considerable attention to this subject of deviance and social control. See *The Social System*, Chapter VII.

40. Discussion of the following structures is drawn from Parsons, *The Social System,* pp. 153–167. By way of comparison, Levy's structural-functional analysis identified the following as basic universal requirements for all societies: provision for relationship to the environment and for sexual recruitment, role differentiation and role assignment, communication, shared cognitive orientation, shared articulated set of goals, the normative regulation of means, the regulation of affective expression, socialization, the effective control of disruptive forms of behavior, and adequate institutionalization. See Levy, op. cit., pp. 151–197.

41. Talcott Parsons, Robert F. Bales, and Edward A. Shils, *Working Papers in the Theory of Action* (New York: Free Press, 1953), p. 112.

42. Ibid.

43. The A-G-I-L framework is used in almost all of Parsons' subsequent writings. In *Working Papers in the Theory of Action,* Parsons, Bales, and Shils applied this model to the small laboratory groups studied by Bales. For a brief summary statement of the four functional problems applied to society, see Talcott Parsons, "An Outline of the Social System," pp. 30–79 in Talcott Parsons, Edward Shils, Kaspar D. Naegele, and Jesse R. Pitts, eds., *Theories of Society,* 1-vol. (New York: Free Press of Glencoe, 1961), especially pp. 38–41.

44. Parsons et al., *Working Papers in the Theory of Action,* p. 183.

45. Ibid., p. 184; also p. 88.

46. This function of collective rituals in reinforcing commitment to shared values and normative patterns was central in Durkheim's analysis of religion. Recall from Chapter 5 that the sociological significance of religious rituals is that they strengthen individuals' emotional bonds to the group and their commitment to the shared moral values that are the foundation of the group's social order.

47. Ibid., pp. 187–188.

48. This point should be emphasized in rebuttal to those critics who assert that Parsons limits his analysis to functional requirements that are mutually compatible and that can therefore be accomplished through cooperative action with minimal strain. This recognition of multiple functional requirements certainly leaves open the possibility that some functional requirements may have to be suppressed while attention is directed toward other functional requirements. Compare footnote 37.

49. Ibid., pp. 63–109.

50. This identification of functional subsystems was first developed systematically in Talcott Parsons and Neil J. Semlser, *Economy and Society* (Glenco, Ill.: Free Press, 1956). It should be understood that the concept of functional subsystems does not necessarily apply to any specific empirical structure. The identification of subsystems includes all of the mechanisms, structures, and institutional patterns that are relevant for the particular functional requirement involved.

51. See Parsons, "An Outline of the Social System," op. cit., p. 36, and Talcott Parsons, *Societies-Evolutionary and Comparative Perspectives* (Englewood Cliffs, N.J.: Prentice-Hall, 1966), pp. 10–16.

52. Parsons, "An Outline of the Social System," op. cit., pp. 37–38.

53. The following diagram is adapted from Talcott Parsons, *Societies-Evolutionary and Comparative Perspectives,* Table 1, p. 28.

54. Ibid.

55. Parsons and Smelser, op. cit.
56. See Parsons, "An Outline of the Social System," op. cit. The discussion that follows draws heavily from this source and from Parsons and Smelser, op. cit., Chapter 1 and Chapter 2, pp. 46–70.
57. Parsons, "An Outline of the Social System," p. 40.
58. Ibid., pp. 40–41.
59. Parsons, Bales, and Shils, *Working Papers in the Theory of Action*, pp. 31–62.
60. Parsons and Smelser, op. cit.
61. Ibid., pp. 70–85.
62. Talcott Parsons, "On the Concept of Political Power," Chapter 14 in *Politics and Social Structure* (New York: Free Press, 1969), pp. 352–404.
63. Parsons, "On the Concept of Influence," Chapter 15 in *Politics and Social Structure*, pp. 405–438.
64. Parsons, "On the Concept of Value-Commitments," Chapter 16 in *Politics and Social Structure*, pp. 439–472.
65. Parsons, Bales, and Shils, *Working Papers in the Theory of Action*, pp. 245–250.
66. Talcott Parsons and Robert F. Bales, *Family, Socialization and Interaction Process* (New York: Free Press, 1955).
67. See Parsons, "An Outline of the Social System," op. cit., pp. 44–60, and Parsons, *Societies-Evolutionary and Comparative Perspectives*, pp. 18–25.
68. Parsons and Bales, op. cit. See also Ernest W. Burgess, Harvey J. Locke, and Mary Margaret Thomes, *The Family from Institution to Companionship* (New York: American Book, 1963), for a similar type of analysis.
69. Talcott Parsons, "Christianity and Modern Industrial Society," pp. 385–421 in *Sociological Theory and Modern Society* (New York: Free Press, 1967). See also Parsons, *Societies-Evolutionary and Comparative Perspectives*, pp. 96–102, for a discussion of this process in the case of ancient Israel.
70. See Talcott Parsons, "Evolutionary Universals in Society," pp. 490–520 in *Sociological Theory and Modern Society; Societies-Evolutionary and Comparative Perspectives*, and *The System of Modern Societies* (Englewood Cliffs, N.J.: Prentice-Hall, 1968). The following paragraph summarizes Parsons' "evolutionary universals" briefly.
71. Parsons, *The System of Modern Societies*, pp. 10–28, especially p. 11.
72. See Parsons, "A Sociological Approach to the Theory of Organizations," pp. 16–58 in *Structure and Process in Modern Society*, especially p. 18.
73. Parsons, *Societies-Evolutionary and Comparative Perspectives* and *The System of Modern Societies*.
74. Parsons, *The System of Modern Societies*, p. 114.
75. For a recent thorough criticism of Parsons' sociology for its implicit social and political conservatism, see Alvin W. Gouldner, *The coming Crisis of Western Sociology* (New York: Basic Books, 1970).
76. Robert K. Merton, *Social Theory and Social Structure*, enlarged edition (New York: Free Press, 1968), p. 39, emphasis added.
77. Ibid., pp. 73–138.
78. Ibid., pp. 75–76.
79. Ibid., p. 105.

80. Ibid.

81. In spite of this one-sided analysis, the functional interpretation represented an important breakthrough because it was opposed to the view that many primitive customs were mere survivals (i.e., cultural or institutional leftovers from an earlier evolutionary stage).

82. See Louis Schneider, *The Sociological Way of Looking at the World* (New York: McGraw-Hill, 1975), for a perspective that is clearly in the functionalist tradition and repeatedly emphasizes the ironies and paradoxes in social life that sociologists have uncovered.

83. Ibid., pp. 49–91.

84. Ibid., p. 84, emphasis added.

85. Ibid., p. 86.

86. Merton, "Social Structure and Anomie" and "Continuities in the Theory of Social Structure and Anomie," Chapters VI and VII in *Social Theory and Social Structure,* pp. 185–248.

87. Merton, "Bureaucratic Structure and Personality," Chapter VII in *Social Theory and Social Structure,* pp. 249–261.

88. Merton, "Contributions to the Theory of Reference Group Behavior" (with Alice S. Rossi) and "Continuities in the theory of Reference Groups and Social Structure," Chapters X and XI in *Social Theory and Social Structure,* pp. 279–440.

89. Ibid., pp. 288–295.

90. Ibid., pp. 319ff.

91. Other middle-range theories developed by Merton in *Social Theory and Social Structure* include patterns of influence flow between "local influentials" and "cosmopolitan influentials," the "self-fulfilling prophecy" applied to in-group and out-group relations, the effects of the Puritan ethic in promoting scientific inquiry, audience responses to mass media propoganda, and others.

92. For some laudatory evaluations of the impact of Merton's various theoretical contributions to sociology, see Lewis A. Coser, ed., *The Idea of Social Structure: Papers in Honor of Robert K. Merton* (New York: Harcourt Brace Jovanovich, 1975).

Questions for Study and Discussion

1. In what ways are the functional requirements of society based on the fundamental biological characteristics of human nature? Distinguish between universal functional requirements based on universal human needs and the specific requirements of a modern urban-industrial society.

2. Do you think that Parsons' emphasis on functional requirements that all societies must meet undermines his earlier voluntaristic theory of social action? Why or why not? How does Parsons avoid a deterministic view in his functional theory?

3. Select a social system with which you are familiar such as a social club, work group, bureaucratic organization, class, family, nation, or some other system. Analyze this system in terms of the pattern variables governing social relations within it, its specific functional requirements in terms of the A-G-I-L model, and the strategies whereby these functional requirements are met.

4. Contrast Parsons' views on functional requirements with Merton's middle-range functional theory. What are the advantages and disadvantages of each of these approaches?

5. Why is the concept of latent functions or latent dysfunctions so crucial in Merton's approach? How does this emphasis differ from the emphasis in symbolic interaction theory and exchange theory on people's conscious intentions? To what extent can this concept of latent functions (and dysfunctions) be used in evaluating public policy?

CHAPTER 11

Conflict and Social Change

Sometime in the future you could be asked, as a person with some sociological training, to be a consultant in dealing with an organizational conflict. Representatives of top management would brief you on the details and would assure you of a substantial fee if you could make recommendations that would resolve the conflict. You would be told that major conflicts have persisted for some time, despite management's efforts to deal with them, and that both morale and organizational effectiveness are seriously undermined. Your task would be to talk with people throughout the organization to learn their complaints and grievances, sort out the various issues, and decide on a plan to reduce, if not eliminate, the conflict.

How would you approach this challenge? Would you have some basic idea as to how organizations should *normally* function? Would you see conflict as a symptom of organizational disease or abnormality that you, the organization expert, should root out? Would your goal be the elimination of conflict? Or, if complete elimination is not possible, whose interests or ideas would have priority in any settlement that you propose? In spite of your determination to be fair, you would probably find that the basic ground rules established by management would make it unrealistic for you to propose major reductions in management's authority or privileges.

To most leaders of any organization, it is easy to see organizational conflict as a kind of dysfunction or abnormality. For them, the image of a normal organization is one in which members are highly motivated to help fulfill the organization's goals. In this image the members willingly comply with the leader's influence attempts and eagerly cooperate for the good of the organization. The leader or management is expected to establish organizational policy, make administrative decisions, coordinate the activities of the organization's members, and promote the willingness of members to cooperate in achieving the organization's goals.[1] In this model the eruption of conflict signals a disruption in the ongoing routines of the organization, and conflict resolution (or crisis management) is seen as diverting management from its proper function of decision making, coordination of tasks, and promotion of cooperation.

Some sociologists share the "everyday life" image of social reality where conflict in social life is abnormal. In Chapter 10 we examined Parsons' elaborate effort to explain how societies manage to avoid the Hobbesian problem of the "war of all against all" and to fulfill the functional requirement of maintaining stability and social integration. His explanation stressed shared value orientations.

Parsons recognized that no social system is perfectly integrated. There is always the possibility of discrepancies in the priorities assigned to different values, conflicting interpretations of the shared values as they apply to particular situations, role conflict, ambivalent or negative motivations, tension between individuals' needs and culturally prescribed roles, and inconsistency in individuals' expectations of one another. Nevertheless, Parsons' overwhelming emphasis is on the social processes that maintain a stable social order and promote social integration.

In view of this overwhelming emphasis on equilibrium, integration, and solidarity, it is not surprising that Parsons' theory neglects the process of social conflict. The basic implication of his theory is that conflict is symptomatic of tension or strain that the system must solve to maintain its equilibrium. The needs or interests of the individuals experiencing strains are consistently subordinated to the requirements of the overall system for maintaining its equilibrium and the stability of its social order.

Parsons' persistent neglect of social conflict and the effects of conflict in promoting social change has stimulated a barrage of criticism and efforts to develop alternative theories.[2] This chapter will present the major concepts and principles of some leading contemporary conflict theories. Although conflict theory is generally regarded as opposed to functional theory, particularly Parsons' version, the primary concern of this chapter will not be to review and evaluate criticisms of Parsons' perspective. The positive theoretical contributions of the alternative conflict theories, not the shortcomings of Parsons' functional theory, will have priority.

Conflict theory is not a unified or comprehensive theory. For this reason, perhaps, the term "conflict theory" is a misnomer. The major common denominator of the various conflict theories is a concern for recognizing and analyzing the pervasive presence of conflict in social life, its causes and forms and, in many cases, its effects in generating social change. This focus has been sharpened since the 1950s by the opposition of various conflict theorists to Parsons' one-sided emphasis on value consensus, integration, and solidarity.

No single conflict theory in contemporary American sociology equals the scope of Parsons' theoretical framework in terms of comprehensiveness and generality. Whether or not this is a disadvantage depends on one's idea of what a sociological theory should be. For those who follow Merton's preference for middle-range theories, the lack of a comprehensive theoretical framework designed to have universal applicability at a highly abstract level is an advantage, not a disadvantage, at least at the current stage of theoretical development in sociology.

For our purposes, conflict theory is the second major contemporary theory that emphasizes the social structural level of social reality instead of the individual, the interpersonal, or the cultural levels. (Functionalism also focused on the social structural level.) As with functional theory, some important implications of conflict theory extend to the various other levels of social reality. The interpersonal level especially can readily be analyzed in terms of many of the principles developed in conflict theory. In our everyday experiences we certainly encounter interpersonal conflicts at the micro level. However, the emphasis is on the social structural sources of social conflicts, including those that occur on a face-to-face basis. For example, the conflict that might occur between a working-class employee and a supervisor in a bureaucratically organized business firm may not be primarily a reflection of their personal animosity toward one another so much as a reflection of the discrepancy or opposition between their interests as determined by their respective positions in the business.

Similarly, conflict theorists are not necessarily uninterested in cultural values and norms. However, they are more likely to see values and norms as ideologies that reflect the efforts of dominant groups to justify their continued dominance. In a manner reminiscent of Marx, they seek to unmask the various divergent and opposing interests that may be obscured by the appearance of value and normative consensus. When consensus on values and norms prevails, conflict theorists would be suspicious that this reflects the control that dominant groups within society exert over the various communication media (such as the educational establishment and the mass media) through which individuals' consciousness and ideological commitments are formed. Parsons' notion that normative consensus reflects individuals' voluntary moral commitments would be seen by conflict theorists as incredibly naive or as implying ideological support for the existing social structure, particularly the power structure.

Conflict theory did not begin with opposition to Parsons' structural-functional theory. Among the pioneers discussed in Part Two, Karl Marx is considered the major (and most controversial) figure to try to explain the sources of conflict and the effects of conflict in promoting revolutionary change. The process of conflict is also a central element of Weber's theory. This is often overlooked by those who see Weber's emphasis on the influence of religious ideas as a repudiation of Marx's materialistic emphasis. Instead, Weber recognized that religious ideas themselves may be a source of conflict. Moreover, he was aware that religious ideals may serve to legitimate the social position of dominant groups in society.

Although Weber was less deterministic and more sophisticated than Marx in his analysis of conflict, he actually enlarged the domain within which conflict issues may emerge. Like Marx, he recognized the importance of conflict over economic issues; in addition, he showed that struggle or conflict also takes place with respect to the distribution of prestige or status, as well as political power.

Simmel also dealt explicitly with the process of social conflict. Unlike Marx and Weber, he stressed the micro level. His basic emphasis was that conflict is one of the basic forms of interaction and that actual or potential conflict pervades practically all forms of social interaction. (Among the conflict theorists to be discussed in this chapter, Coser's conflict functionalism builds explicitly on Simmel's approach.)

THE LEGACY OF MARX AND THE PERSPECTIVE OF CRITICAL THEORY

Marx's theory provides a kind of intellectual watershed so that social theorists since Marx can readily be classified according to whether they take a Marxist or non-Marxist approach (not all conflict theorists are necessarily Marxists). Whether or not a theorist agrees with Marx's position, there are certain aspects of social reality that he emphasized that any adequate or well-rounded theory cannot ignore. Among these, recognition of the class structure of society, of the opposing economic interests of persons in different classes, of the profound influence of economic class position on individuals' life-styles and forms of consciousness, and of the effects of class conflict in generating social structural change are perhaps the most important.

Beyond these basic points there are disagreements. For example, Marx emphasized the economic foundation of social classes, particularly ownership or nonownership of the means of production, but many contemporary theorists, following Weber, take a multidimensional and less deterministic approach in explaining the stratification system of society. Even more controversial is the idea of a basic two-class system that Marx used in much of his analysis, especially in his prediction regarding the growth of a larger and larger gap between the bourgeois and proletarian classes. Related to this is Marx's prediction of the impending proletarian revolution, and the implicit assumption that major social structural change cannot be achieved except through revolution.

Most contemporary theorists see the class system of capitalist societies as much more complex than Marx envisioned, particularly in view of the growth of the middle classes and the rise in wages of the working class. Moreover, contemporary theorists are much more likely than Marx to see numerous possibilities for significant structural change within the capitalist system far short of violent revolution. However, Marx's dialectical mode of analysis, even though not necessarily used in the same fashion that Marx used it, has nevertheless sensitized numerous contemporary theorists to recognize the numerous internal contradictions and conflicts that are built into the social structure.[3] Social change is widely recognized as a result of efforts to reconcile such contradictions and conflicts.

Marxist Philosophical Assumptions

Marx's philosophical position was interwoven with much of his sociological and economic analysis. The philosophical aspects of his thought center on his efforts to unmask society's value systems, belief patterns, and forms of consciousness as ideologies reflecting and reinforcing the interests of the dominant class, often in a distorted form. Although cultural orientations are not completely determined by the economic class structure in his view, they are heavily influenced and constrained by it. Marx's emphasis on the primacy of material conditions as mediated by society's class structure limits the independent influence of culture on individuals' consciousness and behavior.

Sociologists today recognize the importance of ideology and the relationship between ideological commitments and position in the economic class structure.[4] However, non-Marxist sociologists today would probably not go as far as Marx in trying to explain forms of consciousness in terms of economic structure and class position. For non-Marxists the relationship between subjective consciousness and socioeconomic structure is more complex and more variable than implied by Marx. At the least, the question of the relationship between individuals' beliefs and values on the one hand and the socioeconomic structure on the other is an empirical question and not one to be decided on a philosophical basis.

In contrast, for Marx, the adequacy or validity of a person's beliefs and values was decided partly on a philosophical basis. This is reflected in his distinction between ''false consciousness'' and ''true consciousness.'' It was inconceivable for Marx that working-class individuals could have their human needs fulfilled through their work or that they could express any kind of ''true'' humanistic values in their work. Therefore, if a worker seemed contented, fulfilled, and unwilling to engage in protest and revolutionary struggle, this was taken as evidence of false consciousness. This means that such a worker is alienated or estranged from himself or herself and his or her human needs.

Lack of overt revolutionary struggle need not necessarily indicate false consciousness in itself; it could be that the material conditions are not right for such activities. Even so, working-class individuals certainly should not be expected to be satisfied with their class position or their work if they know what their true needs and interests as human beings are.

Marx's analysis of alienation also reveals his philosophical position. Essentially, this concept refers to feelings of estrangement, particularly those resulting from lack of control over the conditions of one's own life. Marx identified four different types of alienation: alienation from the process of production, from the products that result from individuals' activity, from other human beings, and from oneself.

Alienation can be empirically measured if it refers only to individuals' own subjective feelings of estrangement from self or others or lack of control over the conditions of their lives.[5] But Marx went beyond this. He identified the objective conditions of the working class, and of their capitalist employers, as inherently alienating, without regard to their own subjective reactions to their conditions. Even though his arguments may be persuasive, particularly within the context of factory life in nineteenth-century England, they go beyond the empirical level, revealing Marx's own values and philosophical premises regarding human nature and basic human needs. Similarly, the distinction today between Marxists and non-Marxists reflects differences in underlying philosophical positions and basic assumptions that cannot be proved or disproved empirically. Such assumptions underlie opposing interpretations of empirical data.

Sociopolitical Context of the Growth of Critical Theory

The philosophical and humanistic implications of Marx's perspective form a large part of the foundation of contemporary critical theory. Critical theory emerged in the 1930s among a group of intellectuals centered in the Institute for Social Research at the University of Frankfurt in Germany. Some of the major figures of the "Frankfurt school" (as this group was called) at that time included Horkheimer, Adorno, Marcuse, and Fromm. The growth of fascist ideology provided the immediate historical background; by the middle of the 1930s the Nazi threat effectively disrupted the institute and many of its members fled to America. Some eventually returned to reestablish the institute. One of the leading spokespersons of the Frankfurt school since the 1960s is Jürgen Habermas; he was too young to have taken part in the 1930s, however, and was not among those who migrated to America at that time. The members of the Frankfurt school in the 1930s experienced the rise of Nazism as a major source of intellectual and social repression, and this threat stimulated a strong interest in the Marxist themes of social criticism and human liberation. These themes are central to contemporary critical theory.[6]

For the most part, except for the work of Fromm and Adorno, critical theory had only a limited impact on American sociological theory prior to the middle of the 1960s. Fromm's work on the willingness of people to sacrifice their freedom for the sake of security had been a popular source of social criticism for some time.[7] Also, Adorno's analysis of the authoritarian personality and his efforts to measure authoritarian tendencies empirically is well established in American sociology.[8] In neither of these cases, however, was the link to the broader perspective of critical theory systematically developed in American sociology.

In the second half of the 1960s, however, the influence of critical theory on

American sociology increased significantly; the insights and perspective of critical theory were incorporated into various "new left" or radical sociological frameworks.[9] In particular, the works of Marcuse became influential;[10] his *One-Dimensional Man* provided a perspective for analyzing how the modern technological-bureaucratic society systematically shapes and molds the consciousness and world view of modern people in such a way that the full development of human nature is frustrated and repressed. More recently, Habermas' work has become more widely known, particularly his emphasis on the importance of free and open communication as a necessary condition for emancipation from conditions of sociopolitical domination.[11] (This emphasis on the connection between communication and social structure is reminiscent in many ways of Mead's early symbolic interactionist perspective.) Still another component of the growth in influence of critical theory on American sociology in the late 1960s and the 1970s was the increased availability and popularity of Marx's own early humanistic writings.[12]

The surge of interest by American sociologists since the middle 1960s in a critical theoretical perspective can readily be related to the various protest movements and the extensive social turmoil that erupted in America during these years.[13] These protest movements were associated initially with the civil rights struggle and later with opposition to the Viet Nam war. Ultimately, the sociopolitical issues were broadened to include abuses and misuses of power by those in government and other institutional authority positions, excessive bureaucratization and unresponsiveness of bureaucratized institutions to human needs, excessive emphasis on materialism and a consumption-oriented life-style, blindness to the effects of technological progress and material consumption in polluting the environment and destroying the ecological balance of nature, and a domineering posture in international relations with insufficient sensitivity to the hardships and struggles of those in technologically underdeveloped societies. For some, these issues were combined with a search, or at least a yearning, for an alternative life-style and alternative institutions based on a radically different type of consciousness or world view. This alternative consciousness would place a much lower priority on occupational achievement in a bureaucratic-technocratic system, on continued technological progress and expansion of material consumption, on secondary and manipulative social relationships, and the like.

Subjective Consciousness and Forms of Domination

In the 1930s the Frankfurt school interpreted the rise of fascism as a natural outcome of the inherent dynamics of capitalism. For them this represented a much stronger and more pervasive form of domination than even Marx had envisioned. In contrast, the American sociopolitical structure seems more pluralistic and tolerant. However, contemporary critical theorists would emphasize that beneath this superficial appearance of pluralism and tolerance there is an equally pervasive and much more subtle form of domination that is manifested in the prevailing cultural orientations through which individuals' subjective consciousness is formed. This type of domination involves the subtle shaping of world views and forms of thought rather than explicit or external political control. Nevertheless, the ultimate effect is similar in that it promotes the stability of the capitalist system and reinforces its power structure.

Fulfillment of human needs that cannot readily be incorporated into the structure of the system are generally given lower priority, even when many of those heavily involved in the system experience considerable psychological frustration as a result. The relative priorities of social system maintenance needs versus human fulfillment needs is perhaps revealed most clearly in the willingness of people to conform to the demands of their occupational roles in striving for career success, even when this involves sacrificing many human needs, such as the need for personal autonomy.

The more subtle and pervasive forms of domination that characterize a mature capitalist society become possible largely because of the tremendous expansion of the productive capacity of the capitalist system. Although Marx had envisioned such expansion, he did not foresee that it would be partly used to raise the general level of material affluence of the working class or to create a large middle class who are also deprived of any significant control over the means of production. (Instead, as described earlier, his general view was that the lot of the working class would gradually become more and more desperate.)

The effect of material affluence is to promote tacit, widespread satisfaction with the status quo. Although Marx had predicted that the steadily increasing economic hardships and misery of the working class would stimulate their desire to revolt, the critical theorists perceive that a large part of the population (including the working class) have become passive and lethargic, more eager to support the status quo and insure their security and continued material affluence than to run the risks of engaging in revolutionary struggle to bring about needed social changes.

The willingness of the masses of people to accept or support the capitalist power structure reflects more than just their perceived economic dependence on its maintenance, however. In addition to this externally imposed economic domination, there is also an internally imposed domination of consciousness that occurs because the entire culture is permeated by the kind of logic and world view intrinsic to the capitalist mode of production and organization. The logic involved is that of technical efficiency or, to use Weber's term, instrumental rationality. It involves a manipulative and exploitative approach not only with respect to nature and material objects but also in social relationships. A world view or cultural *Gestalt* dominated by this logic tends to repress or ignore the human needs, values, or sentiments that cannot readily be integrated with the requirements for maintaining the capitalist system or be dealt with in terms of the logic of instrumental rationality.

Moreover, through the various instruments of mass indoctrination and persuasion (such as the educational establishment, advertising and mass entertainment, and nationalistic political appeals), new needs are continually created that insure that people will continue to be motivated to perform the kinds of roles necessary for the maintenance of the capitalist system (e.g., the roles of responsible employee, successful consumer, or loyal citizen). In addition to the need for consumer goods, individuals' psychological needs for security, belonging, recognition, and the like are shaped and exploited so as to promote their willingness to conform to the requirements of the system and support its maintenance.

The political structure of the state plays an even larger and more pervasive part for the critical theorists than for Marx in maintaining the stability of the capitalist system. In Marx's theory the main function of the state was to protect and reinforce the interests of the capitalist class. For the critical theorists the state serves this function plus the function of creating and manipulating symbols of political legitimacy and of linking these symbols with the overall cultural world view. In this process the political system exerts a major covert influence in shaping the overall world view.

To be sure, other institutions, such as the educational establishment, scientific and professional organizations, and the mass media, may be more actively involved than government in cultural creativity and diffusion. These institutions may have considerable autonomy to develop according to their own logic, free from overt political control. Nevertheless, such institutions must operate within a regulatory framework established by government. Thus the political system serves the causes of both economic domination and cultural domination. The result is that individuals' consciousnesses are shaped and molded to insure their political loyalty and conformity to the requirements of the system.

There is a fundamental contradiction between government regulation and control and the classical liberal ideal of maximum individual freedom. As society becomes more and more complex, it becomes necessary for government regulation or domination to be extended into more and more sectors of social life. The result is that individuals find their freedoms more curtailed. This imposes an additional burden on the system of political legitimation. The mechanisms of legitimation appropriate to minimal government interference in other social institutions prove inadequate for legitimating increased government interference. This creates the crisis in legitimation recently analyzed by Habermas.[14] The response of the political authorities to this crisis is to attempt to strengthen their domination and influence over the various cultural symbols of political legitimacy. The ultimate result is additional curtailment of human freedom. Although such a system seems to be open to ameliorative reform, fundamental change that would make the system more responsive to the human needs of its members is virtually impossible short of revolution.

The Critical Perspective and Psychoanalytic Theory

The critical theorists' analyses of the various forms of domination draw not only from Marx's views on false consciousness and the stabilizing effects of ideological illusions but also from Freud's psychoanalytic theory. Fromm in particular used the psychoanalytic perspective to attempt to explain the apparent willingness of people in a mass society to sacrifice their freedom for the sake of security.[15] Marcuse attempted to integrate the central insights of Freud with those of Marx.[16] In his *Eros and Civilization* the Freudian concept of repression is used in place of Marx's concept of economic exploitation to explain the new and more pervasive forms of domination that had developed within the modern system.

For Freud this concept of repression reflected the inevitable tension and conflict between the individual's natural instincts and impulses and the requirements of organized social life, especially in a complex civilization. These requirements are internalized through the socialization process so that the conflict between the individual and society becomes an internal psychological conflict. This conflict is conceptualized in terms of the well-known distinction among the id, the ego, and the superego. The id includes the natural unsocialized needs and impulses of the individual, but the ego and superego represent the reality demands and justifying moral codes, respectively, that emerge in the course of social life and insure its maintenance. Thus the natural needs and impulses of individuals are repressed, and the basic energy that would otherwise be spent in spontaneous fulfillment of these needs is channeled into forms of behavior that fulfill the requirements of organized social life. Freud himself did not limit this model to the capitalist type of social system, but the critical theorists saw Freud's model as particularly relevant for explaining psychologically the dynamics of the various forms of domination prevalent within this type of system.

Critical Theory and the Phenomenological Perspective

The phenomenological perspective is also relevant to the image of social reality developed by the critical theorists. Phenomenology as a philosophical position can be traced back to the distinction that German philosopher Immanuel Kant made between our *perception* of objects in the external world and the nature or essence of such objects in themselves. The implication of this position is that we can never have absolute knowledge of the nature of objects in themselves (or their true essence), since our perception of objects will always reflect the subjective categories of our perceptual framework. It is important to emphasize that these perceptual categories belong to our subjective consciousness, not to the external world of objects as such. Although our concern is not with the philosophical implications of this distinction, it was crucial for subsequent developments in philosophy and sociological theory.

For our purposes, the important point is that our perception of the external world, including the world of physical objects and also the social world, is necessarily a limited and partial perception and reflects our subjective perspective in much the same way that the color of the lens on a pair of sunglasses will determine the color of the world that the wearer sees. To simplify, what we see greatly depends on what we have been trained to seek. Moreover, when a particular set of perceptual categories or a particular form of subjective consciousness is widely shared by the members of a society, the result will be that each person's limited and perhaps biased perspective will be socially reinforced, and alternative or competing perspectives will not be likely to develop. In this way the forms of consciousness created and reinforced within a particular cultural tradition seem to be objectively valid or to correspond adequately and accurately with the external reality of the social world.[17]

But, as we saw earlier, according to the critical theorists, the creation and diffusion of culture is dominated, indirectly if not directly, by the economically and politically dominant capitalist class. The result is that the underlying forms of consciousness help to maintain the structure of the capitalist system and reinforce the patterns of domination within it. This process occurs at a deeper level of consciousness than the one involved in efforts to develop rational arguments in support of a particular ideological position. This deeper level includes the basic image of human nature and social reality and the fundamental assumptions that form the underlying foundation for the development of ideologies.

This phenomenological approach is consistent with the symbolic interactionist perspective developed by Mead. Unlike the critical theorists, however, Mead did not emphasize the influence of underlying forms of consciousness in providing implicit support for the power structure or the prevailing forms of domination in society. His emphasis was on the basic principle that we perceive and respond to objects in our environment in terms of their symbolic meaning, which is socially constructed through communication and is incorporated into the basic subjective perceptual categories of our mind. Specifically, Mead was interested in showing how the use of symbols enables us to adapt to our environment instead of explaining how power structures rest on psychological repression. However, Mead and the critical theorists share the basic insight that our perception of the world, particularly the social world, is influenced profoundly by the structure of our subjective consciousness, which is developed through interaction and communication.

In addition, the critical theorists, particularly Habermas,[18] share with Mead a pragmatic approach to knowledge in which knowledge is linked with action. The goal of critical theory is to transcend the prevailing forms of knowledge by becoming aware of their inhibiting and constraining effects on human action. This enlightenment can have a liberating effect that enables people to act autonomously in fulfilling their human needs. Philosophical or theoretical speculation for its own sake is subordinated to the practical problems of achieving liberation or emancipation from repressive forms of consciousness and from the reinforcing external structures of social and political domination.

Critical theory is highly philosophical, as the preceding overview reveals. Except for Adorno's efforts to measure the authoritarian personality pattern, critical theorists tend to be disdainful of the strong American emphasis on empirical measurement. They regard most efforts to operationalize variables for the purpose of empirical measurement as a superficial enterprise that fails to uncover the fundamental underlying structure of individuals' subjective consciousness at its deepest levels. Indeed, they would see the overriding concern of many American sociologists with sophisticated methodological techniques as another manifestation of the logic of instrumental rationality, linked with manipulation and control, that dominates the consciousness of modern industrial society.

In contrast to this strategy of superficial empirical investigation, the basic strategy of the critical theorists is to examine and evaluate critically prevailing institutional patterns and ideologies or forms of consciousness from the perspective of fundamental human needs for autonomy, self-development, and the like. In modern capitalist societies, such an analysis would reveal that basic human needs are repressed or subordinated in the interest of maintaining the established social structure. The ultimate goal of critical analysis is to promote emancipation or liberation from various forms of domination, both external political domination and internal domination of forms of consciousness. This is unlike Parsons' major emphasis in his structural-functional theory; for the critical theorists, human needs for autonomy and fulfillment, not functional requirements for maintaining the structure of the social system, should have top priority in the development of sociological theory.

MILLS' CRITICAL ANALYSIS OF THE AMERICAN POWER ELITE

The growing popularity of critical theory in American sociology since the middle of the 1960s has been accompanied by a decline of interest in functional theory, particularly as elaborated by Parsons. In the relatively stable period of the 1950s, however, functionalism was the dominant theoretical orientation in American sociology. But even then there were those who had serious reservations about the functionalists' emphasis on shared values as a basis of solidarity and stability and the overwhelming emphasis on functional equilibrium and integration. This was seen as leading to a corresponding theoretical neglect of conflict, exploitation and coercion, and continual internal pressures for change in social systems.

C. Wright Mills was perhaps the most influential critic of functionalism during that time period. Born and reared in Texas, Mills received his Ph.D. from the University of Wisconsin and spent most of his professional life at Columbia University. He died in 1962. His earliest interests were in pragmatic philosophy and Mead's symbolic interactionist social psychology, but these interests were eventually overshadowed by his critical analysis of American social structure. To be sure, Mills was not merely interested in refuting the functionalist image of social reality but in developing his own alternative perspective. However, Parsons' structural-functional model could hardly be ignored in the context of the 1950s. Accordingly, Mills devoted one chapter of his book, *The Sociological Imagination,* to a biting and somewhat sarcastic criticism of Parsonian "grand theory."[19]

In criticizing functional theory, Mills emphasizes the abstract and wordy jargon and the excessive concern for elaborating theoretical categories that cannot be clearly connected with specific empirical phenomena. A large part of his attack on Parsons' grand theory involved translations of excessively wordy sections of Parsons' *The Social System* into simpler and more concise language. The general tone of his criticism is revealed in the following description of *The Social System.* "It is only about 50 percent verbiage; 40 percent is well-known textbook sociology. The other 10 percent, as Parsons might say, I am willing to leave open for your own empirical investigations. My own investigations suggest that the remaining 10 percent is of possible—although rather vague—ideological use."[20]

The charge concerning the ideological uses of Parsons' theory, although made in a backhanded way, is probably the most significant considering Mills' views on what the major goals of sociology should be and his perspective on the American social structure. If we contrast his approach with functionalism, some fundamental differences in priorities become evident. For Parsons, the primary concern of sociology should be to identify the various mechanisms or structural arrangements through which the basic functional requirements of the social system are fulfilled. Individuals' needs are shaped in the socialization process so they will correspond to social structural role requirements and basic cultural value orientations. The functional requirements necessary for maintaining the system have priority over individuals' needs.

In contrast, Mills' approach assigns a much higher priority to individuals' needs. One of the major themes in *The Sociological Imagination* is that sociological analysis should be devoted to showing the connection between individuals' personal troubles and larger social issues rooted in the basic structure of society. Individuals' personal problems, whether they are material problems such as unemployment or poverty or psychological problems such as meaningless work or alienation, can generally be shown to have roots in the structure of society.

Although Mills' philosophical treatment of basic human needs is not as elaborate as that of the Frankfurt school, his approach is similar. This similarity consists of his willingness to examine the existing social structure *critically* in light of its repressive and frustrating effects on individuals. Specifically, for example, he was similar to Mannheim in pointing out that growth in the formal rationality of social structures, as manifested in large-scale and complex bureaucratic organizations, leads to constriction in individuals' freedom and loss of their substantive understanding of the overall dynamics of the organizational structures in which they are involved.[21] In other words, individuals participate in highly rational systems but without being fully aware of how their particular roles fit together in the overall structure.

Mills' fundamental image of social reality was influenced by several different sources or schools of thought, including Weber, Mannheim, Marx, Mead and the pragmatic and symbolic interactionist tradition, and American social critic Thorstein Veblen.[22] Mills' writing style at many points resembles the sarcastic and debunking style of Veblen, particularly his descriptions of various middle-class lifestyles.[23] For our purposes, however, Mills shares with Weber and Marx a central concern with forms of domination and the social dynamics involved in the relations between those who have power and those who do not. Weber's influence was the more important of the two, however.[24]

Mills did not accept Marx's argument that property ownership alone is the basis for power. Instead, he adopted Weber's threefold distinction among economic class, political power, and status as alternative bases for stratification. His primary emphasis was on the power structure, not on property ownership or claims to high prestige. He stressed the institutional basis for power provided by centralized bureaucratic organizations. Those who occupy the top positions in the major institutional orders of society constitute the power elite.

In Mills' perspective, those who are economically dominant and those who are politically dominant share a wide range of interests and therefore collaborate extensively in maintaining their dominance. Moreover, these economic and political elites can readily lay claim to high prestige and can obtain the support of various public celebrities at the top of the prestige hierarchy. Thus, although Weber's three types of social stratification—economic, political, and prestige—are analytically distinct, Mills' analysis demonstrates an empirical tendency for them to overlap considerably or at least to be mutually supportive and consistent.

Mills' 1956 *The Power Elite* is an analysis of the power structure in American society.[25] His central thesis is that those who occupy the top positions of the economic, military, and political institutions—the "corporate rich," the military "warlords," and the "political directorate"—form a more or less integrated and unified power elite whose key decisions determine the basic structure and direction of American society. Their decisions shape the lives of all those who are lower in the power hierarchy. The decisions and activities of those who belong to this upper stratum reflect their interests in maintaining their dominance instead of indicating a genuine concern for the welfare of ordinary citizens. However, this does not mean that they are consciously aware of the conflict between their interests and the overall welfare of society. They simply identify their own interests with those of society.

Mills does not claim that there is a conscious conspiracy among the economic, military, and political elites, or that they always completely agree among themselves or share exactly the same interests. The interdependent and interlocking nature of these elite circles results from certain social structural factors with readily identifiable historical roots and from certain social psychological factors resulting from their common backgrounds and social experiences. The most important social structural factors are the tremendous size and high degree of centralization of the economic, military, and political institutions. The large size of these institutional orders means that the top-level decision makers in each of them must consider the others. None is isolated from the others, and each can facilitate or hinder the others in carrying out their various projects. The high degree of centralization means that the decisions and actions of those at the top of power hierarchy in each institution will have major and wide-ranging ramifications, both within the institution and for the overall society in which it operates.

Both large size and high centralization depend on the modern technology of production, administration, and communication. As Mills states:

> From even the most superficial examination of the history of western society we learn that the power of decision-makers is first of all limited by the level of technique, by the *means* of power and violence and organization that prevail in a given society. In this connection we also learn that there is a fairly straight line running upward through the history of the West; that the means of oppression and exploitation, of violence and destruction, as well as the means of production and reconstruction, have been progressively enlarged and increasingly centralized.[26]

Historical Development of the American Power Structure

This picture of mid-twentieth-century American society contrasts sharply with earlier periods of history.[27] Immediately after the American Revolution, there was a fairly cohesive power structure whose members were also among the intellectual elite. Its scale of operations at that time was much smaller than that of the mid-twentieth-century power structure. The dynamic development of American society in the first half of the nineteenth century, particularly the emergence of the Jacksonian version of democratic equality and the rapidly expanding development of the American frontier, resulted in a partial breakdown of the unity of the power elite and in the development of a decentralized system. During this period, the economic structure consisted mostly of small businessmen and farmers, none of whom was in a position to have a major impact on the system as a whole. The general structure and dynamics of the system emerged from the interplay between the results of numerous individual decisions and actions, with little conscious coordination or integration of the system as a whole. This *laissez-faire* system seemed to be governed by natural forces beyond the conscious control of anyone.

Similarly, political power was extremely limited and highly decentralized. The power of the federal government was remote from most citizens, and resistance to expansion of federal power was justified in terms of the *laissez-faire* ideology. The decentralized political power of states and local communities was utilized to provide needed services that could not readily be provided on a private basis. Moreover, the military establishment was only minimally developed, partly because of geographical isolation from any other society that could pose a serious military threat.

This fragmented and decentralized power structure began to change in the economic sector following the Civil War. The second half of the nineteenth century witnessed the beginning of the growth of large-scale business corporations guided by the ruthless and exploitative captains of industry who seized the expanding opportunities to strive for wealth and economic dominance. As their enterprises expanded, many small business enterprises were gradually eliminated in the competitive struggle. Small entrepreneurs were either absorbed into the growing corporations or were obliged to work for them for the sake of their personal economic survival.[28] (This expansion and centralization of capitalistic enterprises had been predicted by Marx.)

The opening years of the twentieth century witnessed a corresponding growth in the concentration of federal political power. Initially, this expansion was necessitated by American involvement in World War I. However, the end of the war was not followed by a return to the previous decentralized structure. Then, the eruption of the economic crash and the Great Depression in the 1930s stimulated additional enlargement and expansion of the central government. The depression signaled a major breakdown in the self-regulating character of the economic system and brought forth extensive demands that government do something to restore the equilibrium of the economic system and bring a return to economic prosperity. The result was the development of the various government programs associated with the New Deal.

This development is a major watershed in the history of the federal government. No longer would the government play primarily a neutral role so that private economic interests could be pursued on a *laissez-faire* basis. Instead, with the establishment of the various New Deal programs, government became a much more active partner in regulating and guiding the economic system through fiscal policies and various programs established to deal with social problems neglected by the private sector. The result was tremendous expansion in the size and influence of the federal government and concentration and consolidation of its power.

American involvement in World War II, which immediately followed the Great Depression, stimulated the enormous expansion and consolidation of the third major codominant circle of power: the military. Although formally under the control of the civilian political system, the unprecedented expansion of the military system brought about by American involvement in the war inevitably resulted in the military achieving virtually a coequal status with the political and economic power structures. Indeed, the close alliance established between the military structure and business corporations involved in manufacturing military equipment and supplies enabled the military-industrial complex to exert a domineering influence on American political policies.

The strength and pervasiveness of this influence was clearly revealed in the years following the end of the war. The end of the war was not followed by military demobilization; the country remained on a more or less permanent war footing that ultimately was justified in the Cold War ideology of the 1950s. Although Mills had died before the outbreak of the Viet Nam war, his perspective on the American power structure would lead us to evaluate that long, painful, and unproductive struggle as a result of the commanding influence of the military-industrial complex, a concept he introduced to President Eisenhower.[29]

Moreover, the three dominant institutional orders are by no means independent of one another. Their decisions and actions are interdependent and interlocking in numerous ways. Those in the top command positions of each institutional order consider one another's interests and policies and sometimes actively work together in establishing national policy. As Mills explains:

> As each of these domains becomes enlarged and centralized, the consequences of its activities become greater, and its traffic with the others increases. The decisions of a handful of corporations bear upon military and political as well as upon economic developments around the world. The decisions of the military establishment rest upon and grievously affect political life as well as the very level of economic activity. The decisions made within the political domain determine economic activities and military programs.[30]

Social Bonds Among the Elite

The interpenetrating and interlocking nature of policies and activities in the three dominant institutional orders results from social psychological as well as social structural factors. Mills pointed out that those who occupy the top command positions in these orders come from similar social backgrounds and share similar world views. One major bond is that they all tend to be very rich. The wealth may be inherited or it may result from investments or from occupancy of a high-level executive position in a gigantic business corporation. Along with wealth, there is also the common bond of high prestige (which typically accompanies wealth) and high power. Many of those in the top command posts come from old families that have traditionally enjoyed high status, have married members of these old families, or have social acquaintances among them. In addition, they have generally had the same kind of educational background, usually in one of the high-prestige Ivy League schools; they are likely to belong to one of the traditionally high-prestige Protestant churches; and they intermingle with one another frequently in various clubs and associations and social cliques.

In addition, those who belong to the power elite frequently move back and forth between the top of one institutional order and another. Perhaps in Mills' time the most dramatic example is the case of General Eisenhower, who became President Eisenhower. Numerous similar top-level institutional interchanges could be cited; Mills lists several typical cases: ''the admiral who is also a banker and a lawyer and who heads up an important federal commission; the corporation executive whose company was one of the two or three leading war material producers who is now the Secretary of Defense; the wartime general who dons civilian clothes to sit on the political directorate and then becomes a member of the board of directors of a leading economic corporation.''[31]

But, in spite of their extensive and overlapping personal and institutional contacts, Mills insists that the powe elite is not a closed or static clique with a completely unified set of policies. Some of those who belong to this upper stratum may be close personal friends, but many will be only casual acquaintances or will know each other only by reputation. Different kinds of projects or issues will bring together different sets of individuals. On some issues there may be disagreement that results in coalition formation and opposition. Occasionally, too, promising new members will be recruited from the middle ranks of power. In short, the power elite is not a single monolithic network with closed boundaries, but a series of overlapping and intersecting networks with partially permeable boundaries. But Mills' emphasis is on the unity of those in the top strata and on the institutional and social psychological bonds that set them apart from those lower in the various institutional power hierarchies.

Mass Media and Mass Society

Mills criticized the frequently held view of the American power structure as an amorphous and pluralistic structure.[32] According to the pluralistic image, there are numerous largely autonomous centers of power in American society, no one of which is large enough to dominate the others. Each holds the others in check, and the overall direction of sociopolitical policy results from negotiation and compromise between those in the various power centers. There may be coalitions formed on particular issues but, if a coalition does achieve dominance, it is usually temporary and precarious. Overall, the various power centers are in a state of balance in which no one center is able to be dominant for very long or on all issues.

Mills maintains that the balance theory of a pluralistic power structure characterizes the middle levels of power and not the top levels. The attractiveness of the balance theory is due partly to its congruence with American democratic idology; also the activities and decisions of the power elite are not necessarily always widely publicized. Indeed, it would be in the interests of the power elite to minimize public visibility of their dominance and to promote widespread acceptance of the balance theory.

The majority of the population have very little impact, even on the middle levels of power. Mills' image of the vast majority beneath the middle level is that it consists of a fragmented, passive, and inarticulate mass society whose members are not organized and thus cannot have any significant impact on public policy. The emergence of mass society results largely from the influence of the mass media. The mass media are not conducive to informed dialogue between various sectors of the public but to a one-way flow of information. Thus the members of mass society are passive in the communication process. Moreover, because most members of society have very limited firsthand knowledge of national social issues and because their informed dialogue with one another on social issues is so limited, the mass media are able to manipulate public opinions and attitudes through distorted and simplified presentations of public issues.

Those in the power structure are able to take advantage of this situation by using the mass media as a means of indoctrination and persuasion. Thus their decisions and actions may be presented or justified to the public in such a way that they seem to be consistent with democratic principles and American traditions. Moreover, the power structure is tacitly supported by a distorted conservative ideology, promoted by the mass media, that justifies or legitimates the sociopolitical status quo. Beyond this, the media exert a major influence in diverting people's attention from sociopolitical issues by helping to fill their leisure hours with escapist forms of entertainment.

The sharp contrast between Mills' image of American society, particularly the power structure, and that of Parsons should be clear. Parsons viewed the political institution as contributing to the basic functional requirement of collective goal achievement. The political structure is essential for making basic decisions on behalf of society regarding shared goals and mobilizing support and resources for achieving these goals. Ultimate legitimation for these collective goals is provided by the basic value system to which all members of society are committed. In contrast, Mills' analysis views the decisions of the political power structure and the acquiescence of the public at large in an altogether different light. He sees the primary goal of those in the power structure as preserving their dominance and promoting their own interests, independently of active public input. Public involvement consists primarily of passive acceptance of the power elite's dominance, due mostly to the indoctrinating influence of the mass media.

POWER ELITES AND THE "IRON LAW OF OLIGARCHY"

Mills' analysis of the American power structure is consistent with the organizational processes described by German theorist Robert Michels as the "iron law of oligarchy."[33] Born in 1876, just 12 years after Weber, Michels knew Weber personally and, like Weber, was interested in the dynamics of large-scale, complex organizations. Briefly, Michels' concept of the iron law of oligarchy refers to a general tendency for power to become concentrated in the hands of an elite whose decisions and activities gradually become oriented more toward maintaining their power than promoting the interests of the rank and file.

Michels examined this process within the context of political parties and labor unions rather than the overall society. However, the results are comparable to Mills' analysis of American society. The organizations Michels analyzed, like the American political system, were established as democratic organizations to further the interests of their members. However, these interests gradually become subordinated to the interests of those in the leadership structure in consolidating their power and maintaining their elite positions. Paradoxically, therefore, in spite of their democratic ideology, the actual structure of democratic organizations tends to be transformed to an oligarchical form.

The organizational dynamics that result in this transformation originate in the establishment of paid leadership or administrative positions. The organizational decision to have a full-time leader or administrator signals the unwillingness or the inability of the organization's members to share organizational responsibilities among themselves on a part-time or volunteer basis. If the organization is relatively small, the degree of social distance between the leader(s) or administrator(s) and the rank and file would be fairly low, and the members could, if they choose, make their interests known to the leader and monitor the leader's performance.

But, if the organization grows, the social distance between the rank and file and the leadership or administrative structure will inevitably increase. This means that it becomes more difficult for the average member to exert influence on organizational policies or the leader's decisions. This is partially because of the logistical problems of having a large membership actively involved in the formation of a coherent organizational policy or in the day-by-day administrative routines of the organization. Experiments in participatory democracy in large groups have invariably encountered such difficulties. In addition, organizational growth is usually followed by expansion of the number of leaders or administrators. Those occupying such positions are likely to be in frequent contact with one another as they perform their organizational roles. Naturally, therefore, they form their own elite subgroup set apart from the rank and file and oriented toward their own distinctive interests.

In the meantime, as the organization grows and the social distance between the leaders and the rank and file widens, the active interest and involvement of the average member declines drastically, partly because the average members come to feel that their voices will probably not be heard anyway and so withdraw from active participation. When such feelings of powerlessness and indifference become widespread among the rank and file, the result is the emergence of a passive mass without an effective voice in establishing organizational policies or administrative decisions. An extreme manifestation of this pattern is neglect of minimal opportunities for involvement such as voting.

Rampant apathy or indifference makes it possible for those in the leadership structure to consolidate their power and pursue their interests without undue concern for resistance or opposition by the rank and file. However, if an opposition movement should develop, the odds against its success are enormous. For one thing, the incumbents of the power structure are at the center of the communication system and so are able to control the information flow to justify their policies and action to the general membership. Such public relations strategies help to undermine people's motivations for becoming involved with the opposition movement.

Those in the power structure may be able to charge their opponents with being uninformed about the total picture of the organization's operations and of pursuing narrow or selfish interests at the expense of the organization. In this connection the very fact of incumbency provides those in power with a certain legitimacy that those involved in opposition movements lack. Because of this legitimacy, the claims of those in power that they are acting in terms of the best long-term interests of the membership are more likely to be believed than the critical attacks of those in the opposition movement. Moreover, those in positions of power are likely to have various resources that they can use to "buy off" potential opponents or to demonstrate their concern for aggrieved segments of the membership. In American presidential politics, for example, the incumbent alone has the opportunity to "act presidential" and to influence many crucial decisions regarding federal expenditures that will benefit various constituencies. Not least among the resources of those in power is the opportunity to recruit (or co-opt) opponents or potential opponents into the elite circle.

The organizational dynamics implied by the iron law of oligarchy does not mean that overthrowing established power structures is impossible. The history of many organizations and societies reveals that power structures are sometimes overthrown and replaced. Nevertheless, enormous odds must be overcome if an opposition movement is to be successful. However, if an opposition movement is successful in overthrowing an unresponsive or exploitative power structure, the new power structure that is established in its place will invariably manifest the same oligarchical tendencies, in spite of any appeal that may have been made to democratic principles in the process of struggling to overthrow the old power structure.

Neither Michels' model of the iron law of oligarchy nor Mills' analysis of the American power structure stressed the process of overt conflict or rapid social change. Both theories explain the stability of social structures. Although Michels emphasized large-scale, ostensibly democratic organizations and Mills emphasized the American society, the basic structural dynamics implied by both are similar. For both theorists, however, the explanation for high stability or equilibrium and lack of overt conflict is radically different from that implied in functional theory, particularly that of Parsons. Functional theory would explain social stability in terms of consensus on shared values and norms, but both Michels and Mills would explain stability and absence of overt conflict in terms of the ability of those in the power structure to impose their will despite potential resistance and to exploit and manipulate public opinion so as to avoid major dissent.

An even more significant difference, however, is that Michels and Mills emphasize clearly the divergence between the interests and goals of those in the power structure and the general public. In contrast, functionalists assume that those in positions of authority pursue collectively shared goals. Ralf Dahrendorf also recognized the divergence of interests between those in the power structure and those subject to their power; in addition, he stressed the conditions that stimulate the eruption of various types of conflict and the effects of conflict in promoting social change.

AUTHORITY RELATIONS AND SOCIAL CONFLICT: DAHRENDORF'S CONTRIBUTIONS

The conflict theory of German sociologist Ralf Dahrendorf has had a strong appeal to American sociologists since the publication of the revised English edition of his major book, *Class and Class Conflict in Industrial Society,* in 1959.[34] Dahrendorf was born in 1929, the same year as Habermas, and so experienced the rise of Nazism in his youth. After World War II, Dahrendorf became heavily involved in West German political affairs in addition to his academic career; he even served as a member of the West German Parliament. His academic influence extended far beyond Germany, and he was eventually appointed director of the prestigious London School of Economics.

Dahrendorf rejected the functionalist emphasis on integration, value and normative consensus, and stability as one-sided; instead, he attempted to ground his theory in an updated Marxist perspective that recognizes the pervasiveness of social conflict based on opposition of class-based interests and the consequences of conflict in generating social change. Unlike the Frankfurt school, however, Dahrendorf did not use the Marxist perspective as a basis for radical cultural criticism. He emphasized instead the social structural level of analysis. Specifically, he criticized Marx's theory of class formation and class conflict as being relevant only to the early stages of capitalism, not to a "post-capitalist" industrial society. His theory is intended to be more general than Marx's, applying either to a capitalistic or socialistic industrial society.[35]

It should be remembered that Marx based his theory of class formation on ownership or lack of ownership of the means of production. Dahrendorf contends that *control* of the means of production and not *ownership* is the crucial factor. In the early stages of capitalism those who owned the means of production exercised control over their use, but this does not mean that there is a necessary or intrinsic connection between ownership and control. As capitalism has developed and gradually been transformed into a "post-capitalist" society, legal ownership of the means of production and effective control have been segregated to a considerable degree. Ownership of the means of production in a postcapitalist industrial society is widely dispersed among many stockholders, while effective control is exercised by professional managers and executives. Although high-level managers and executives may own large amounts of stock in their corporations, their control does not derive from this partial ownership but from their occupancy of positions of authority within the corporation.

This model would suggest that large stockholders who do not occupy positions of authority within a corporation do not have effective control over the corporation.

Such an inference may seem tenuous. However, the control that stockholders have is latent or potential, not active. Latent control can be translated into active control only by influencing or working through the managers and executives who are in the positions of authority within the corporation or by replacing them if necessary. Dahrendorf's focus is the authority structure of industrial corporations rather than ownership patterns.

Dahrendorf sees his theory as broader than Marx's, applying not only to productive enterprises in which owners exercise authoritative control but to any type of "imperatively coordinated association." This term, borrowed from Weber, points to an enduring feature of all types of social organizations or social systems. Dahrendorf's approach rests on the assumption that all social systems are "imperatively coordinated" by means of authority relations. As he says, ". . . authority is a characteristic of social organizations as general as society itself."[36] Authority relations can be observed not only in owner-controlled productive enterprises but in government bureaucracies, political parties, churches, voluntary organizations of all kinds, labor unions and professional organizations, and the like. The relation between the owners of the means of production and the nonowners who work for them is a special case, or a subtype, of authority relations.[37]

In addition to rejecting Marx's assumption of a necessary linkage between legal ownership and effective control, Dahrendorf identified several other features that distinguish modern industrial (or "post-capitalist") society from the early stages of capitalism that Marx analyzed. These developments, unforeseen by Marx, include increased heterogeneity of the labor force resulting from upgrading the skill requirements for large segments of it; the tremendous growth of the middle class, many of whose members actually participate in exercising delegated authority; increased social mobility between classes; growth of political equality and enlargement of the meaning of political citizenship rights; increased material affluence for larger and larger segments of the population, resulting partly from improved wages and partly from income redistribution through tax policy; and establishment of various institutional mechanisms for recognizing and negotiating class conflict issues (such as through collective bargaining). All of these developments underscore the point that the early capitalist society described by Marx was a historically specific type; this means that the details of Marx's analysis cannot be extrapolated to apply to the modern type of industrial society.

Functionalist versus Marxist Implications in Dahrendorf's Approach

Dahrendorf's emphasis on authority structures rather than ownership of the material means of production represents a crucial shift away from Marx's position. For Marx, authority structures, together with their supporting ideologies, reflect differential distribution of power to control the means of production as determined by ownership. Dahrendorf, like Weber, recognizes the importance of the distinction between power (the ability to impose one's will despite resistance) and authority (the legitimated right to expect compliance). Although power and authority may be combined in particular relationships, Dahrendorf's overall concern is with structures of authority, not relations of pure power. In his view control over the means of production reflects the institutionalized authority structure and not dominance based solely on power. As Turner points out, Dahrendorf's emphasis on legitimated or institutionalized authority structures seems more comparable to Parsons' functionalism than to Marx's effort to uncover the real material factors that underlie authority structures and all other institutional patterns.[38]

Also, Dahrendorf's basic assumption that imperative coordination by means of authority relations is a basic feature of all social organization is essentially a functionalist notion. It is comparable to Parsons' assertions regarding basic functional requisites. The real difference between Dahrendorf and Parsons is not that Dahrendorf established his theory on a revised Marxist foundation; the real difference is that Dahrendorf stressed the conflicting interests inherent in any relationship between those who exercise legitimate authority and those subject to it, while Parsons stressed the underlying consensus implied by the very notion of legitimacy. Thus, even though Dahrendorf makes extensive use of Marx's rhetoric and terminology regarding class formation, class consciousness, class conflict, and the like, the basic foundation of his perspective is quite different from Marx's and comparable to Parsons.

Dahrendorf does follow Marx, however, in accepting a two-class model of social structure, at least as far as the dynamics of conflict are concerned. Indeed, the dynamics of conflict are such that on any particular issue there would inevitably tend to be two principle parties to the conflict, with each party on opposing sides of the issue. Moreover, the idea that the distribution of authority is the basis for class formation also leads to a two-class model. In any particular relationship or organization there will necessarily be a clear dichotomous distinction between those who exercise authority and those who are subject to its exercise.[39] This distinction is based primarily not on personal characteristics but on institutionalized and legitimated positions in "imperatively coordinated associations." The roles that individuals play, whether domination or submission, are attached to the positions they occupy.

Dahrendorf does not systematically distinguish between the positions of those at the highest level who exercise authority over an entire association and are subordinated to none and those in the middle levels who exercise authority over some but are subordinate to others. In most of his discussion, however, those who participate in the exercise of authority, even limited authority in the middle ranks, are all included in the dominant class.[40] This would leave only those in the lowest level, who exercise authority over no one, as the subordinate class.

Those who exercise authority and those who are subject to it inevitably have conflicting interests. The interests of the dominant class involve preserving the legitimacy of their dominant position or, in other words, preserving the status quo, at least as far as the authority structure is concerned. The interests of the subordinate class are in challenging the legitimacy of the existing authority structure.[41] These opposing interests are determined by the very nature of the authority structure, not by the personal or subjective orientations of the individuals involved. Indeed, individuals need not necessarily be consciously aware of their class-based interests. This distinction between objective, structurally determined class interests and subjective class consciousness is comparable to Marx's class theory. Dahrendorf rejects the philosophical implications of Marx's notion of "false consciousness," although he recognizes that individuals may not be consciously aware of their objective class interests.[42]

Objective, structurally determined class interests of which individuals are not consciously aware are referred to by Dahrendorf as "*latent interests.*" In contrast, the class interests of which individuals are aware, especially if they are consciously pursued as goals, are referred to as "*manifest interests.*" If interests are latent, they obviously cannot be the basis for group formation. Thus members of an "imperatively coordinated association" who have the same latent interests can be considered a "*quasi-group.*"

For any association there are two primary quasi-groups: those who have positions of authoritative domination and those who must submit to the exercise of authority. If individuals in either quasi-group develop a shared class consciousness (i.e., awareness of common interests) and organize to pursue these interests, the result is the emergence of an "*interest group.*"[43] (The concept of an interest group in this sense is narrower than the ordinary meaning of a group whose members share some type of common interest.) Although the members of a conflict interest group are recruited from the same quasi-group, not all who belong to the same quasi-group will necessarily join a conflict interest group to pursue their class interests. For example, not all members of the working class are members of labor unions. Moreover, there may be more than one interest group competing for members from the same quasi-group.

Emergence of Conflict Interest Groups

One of Dahrendorf's primary objectives was to specify the conditions under which latent interests become manifest and quasi-groups can be transformed into conflict interest groups. These conditions are classified as (1) technical conditions, (2) political conditions, and (3) social conditions.[44] Within each category specific variables are identified that influence the extent of conflict group formation. Under technical conditions, Dahrendorf discusses the emergence of leaders and the formation of an ideology. Both are considered essential for conflict group formation and collective action. No organized group action can take place without some type of leadership and some form of justifying beliefs or ideology.

Under political conditions, Dahrendorf emphasizes the degree of freedom available for group formation and group action. At the societal level, one extreme would be provided by totalitarian governments that rigidly prohibit the establishment of opposition political parties or other types of voluntary associations. At the other extreme, in an open democratic society there is a wide range of tolerance for conflict groups of numerous types to pursue their interests within the broad boundaries of legal constraints and regulations designed to preserve this freedom for all. The same variation can also be observed within particular associations. In some associations formation of conflict groups will be overtly or covertly discouraged if not forbidden, while in others conflict groups are allowed and are expected to have an influence on the decision-making process, at least to a limited degree.

The category of social conditions includes primarily the degree of communication between members of a quasi-group. Conflict groups should not be expected to emerge among people who are isolated from one another due to ecological dispersion or who are unable or unwilling for any other reason to form social ties.

These conditions—leadership, ideology, minimal political freedom, and internal communication—are basic prerequisites for the formation of conflict groups. This suggests that if any one of these elements is missing among the members of a quasi-group, a conflict group will not be formed. These conditions are also seen as variables that may take on different values in different conflict groups. Beyond the minimal level necessary for conflict group formation, leaders and ideologies may vary widely in terms of their capacity to mobilize and stimulate collective group action. Similarly, as noted earlier, the degre of external political freedom may vary widely. Finally, the extent of communication among members of a conflict group and its intensity and frequency may vary for different conflict groups. Variations in communication patterns may reflect variations in the internal solidarity of the conflict group.

These conditions, although necessary for the formation of conflict groups, do not guarantee that a conflict group will be formed. There are also certain psychological or social psychological requirements. One of the most basic of these is simply the requirement that latent interests become manifest. Although this process may be stimulated by conflict group leaders and ideologies and by communication with others in the same quasi-group, it is a conceptually distinct process at the psychological level of individuals' consciousness rather than at the structural level.

Just as the structural conditions may vary in different cases, there may be variation in individuals' subjective awareness of the common interests shared with others in the same quasi-group and in their actions to promote these interests. In many cases individuals may fail to develop "class consciousness" because they anticipate being upwardly mobile. Individuals who believe that they will eventually move out of positions of subordination into positions of domination may be expected to support the legitimacy of the existing authority structure. This belief in the possibility of upward mobility is no doubt related to the openness of the class structure and the degree of mobility that actually takes place. In short, class-based interests are most likely to become manifest in individuals' consciousness and to stimulate class action if the boundaries between classes are impermeable and the mobility rates are low.

Another important factor that influences the likelihood of class consciousness and class action is the degree of consistency of individuals' class positions in different associations. Thus far our discussion has emphasized quasi-groups or conflict interest groups within particular associations. However, individuals typically belong to a variety of different associations (or "imperatively coordinated associations," to use Dahrendorf's terminology). As we saw earlier in our discussion of Homans' exchange theory, individuals differ in terms of the degree to which the various dimensions of their status are consistent or congruent. This idea of status congruence can be extended to individuals' organizational involvements. Some organizational involvements may be a source of high status; others may be a source of low status. Individuals differ in terms of whether their status is consistent or inconsistent in the various organizations in which they are involved.

Some societies may be organized so that there is high consistency in the class positions of individuals in the various associations to which they belong. This means that individuals who are in subordinate positions in one organization will also be in subordinate positions in other associations; similarly, those who are in dominant positions in one organization will also be dominant in other associations. For example, in Marx's theory there is the basic assumption that those who are subordinate in economic organizations are also subordinate in political organizations.

In contrast to this pattern of "superimposition," Dahrendorf identifies the "pluralistic" pattern as one in which there is a much lower degree of carry-over of individuals' class positions in any one organization to other organizations. That is, individuals may be subordinate in one association and dominant in another.[45] Dahrendorf suggests that the higher the degree of superimposition, the greater the probability that class consciousness will be developed and class action undertaken. In such a situation, it is easy for conflict to be carried over from one association to other associations. Such generalized conflicts would both reflect and reinforce the emergence of class solidarity and a common class culture.[46]

Intensity and Violence of Conflict

Dahrendorf also attempted to explain variations in the *intensity* and *violence* of class conflict. Intensity and violence are seen as two analytically distinct dimensions of class conflict. Intensity refers to the "energy expenditure and degree of involvement of conflicting parties."[47] Whether individuals are completely absorbed in a particular conflict or whether the conflict is minor reflects the significance or importance of the outcome to those involved. In contrast to intensity, the concept of violence refers to the means used by the contending parties to pursue their interests.[48] The degree of violence can vary widely, ranging from peaceful negotiation to overt violence involving physical attacks on property or persons. Whether peaceful or violent means are used to attempt to resolve conflicts will depend on the available alternatives. While intensity and violence of conflict may be related, Dahrendorf insists that these variables are conceptually distinct and may vary independently.

Many of the conditions discussed earlier that influence strength of class consciousness and degree of conflict group formation also influence the intensity or violence of the conflict. Two major variables that affect intensity are the degree of superimposition of conflict in different associations and the degree of mobility. In general, intensity will be high (reflecting high energy expenditure and high involvement) if there is a high degree of superimposition. High superimposition means that members of the same conflict groups confront one another in a variety of associational contexts. This occurs because people who are dominant in one association are also dominant in others, while those who are subordinate in one are also subordinate in others. In such a situation the energy invested in conflict in different associations is added together, and the conflict issues themselves coalesce into a broad front that transcends particular associational boundaries. In an extreme case the society as a whole is divided into two large hostile camps, with pervasive conflict absorbing much of the energy of a large proportion of the society.

In addition, the chances for pervasive and intense conflict of this type would be increased if none of the associations involved provides any opportunity for upward mobility. In contrast, as Dahrendorf points out, "As mobility increases, group solidarity is increasingly replaced by competition between individuals, and the energies invested by individuals in class conflict decrease."[49]

The intensity and violence of conflict are influenced by the distribution of rewards, facilities, property, and general social status. Just as authority relations in different associations may be superimposed, the distribution of economic rewards and socioeconomic security may overlap with the distribution of authority. This would mean that those in positions of dominance and those in positions of subordination are also dichotomized in the same way in terms of financial rewards, social status, and general socioeconomic security. If so, this would reinforce the image of a two-class system.

In contrast, the distribution of economic rewards, status or prestige, or property may follow the pattern of a more or less continuous distribution from the top of the scale to the bottom. This distribution need not necessarily be rigidly connected with the distribution of authority. For example, persons may have high financial rewards or high status even though they are not in any position of authority. Or they may have positions of authority without necessarily being wealthy or enjoying a generalized high level of prestige.

If the distribution of economic rewards, social status, and the like follows a more or less continuous distribution, with no clear breaks between different strata, the idea of a two-class system with clear boundaries is arbitrary and fails to reflect the complexity of the situation. Instead, numerous strata could be identified and the dividing line between any two strata would be an arbitrary division. In many cases those who have positions of dominance also enjoy a high level of material and social rewards. However, the degree of overlap between the distribution of authority and the distribution of various economic and social rewards is always an open empirical question.

In general, the greater the overlap or superimposition between the distribution of authority and the distribution of material rewards, economic security, social status, and the like, the greater the intensity of class conflict. Whether violence is also greater with high overlap depends on whether the socioeconomic deprivation of those in the subordinate class is "absolute" or "relative."[50] Absolute deprivation refers to a level of deprivation that falls below a minimal level of subsistence. Relative deprivation, in contrast, is a level of deprivation above this minimal subsistence level. This type of deprivation could be experienced by persons who are fairly affluent and who enjoy a high degree of socioeconomic security but nevertheless enjoy less affluence and security than those above them with whom they may compare themselves.

Dahrendorf suggests that if the socioeconomic deprivation of those in subordinate classes is absolute, class conflict is likely to be violent. In contrast, if the deprivation is only relative, violent conflict is not likely, even though intensity may be high. Intensity would be high if the relative deprivation is superimposed on the authority structure, so that those who are in positions of subordination also suffer from relative deprivation.

For example, in a one-industry town in which management personnel occupy the town's local political positions, serve on the local school board, head local voluntary social or civic associations, hold positions on the boards of trustees of local banks, and live in a well-defined upper or upper-middle class section of town, we would expect the intensity of conflict to be high (assuming that the necessary conditions for conflict group formation are satisfied). Violence would not be high, however, as long as the firm's employees enjoy reasonably good pay and socioeconomic security, are able to look forward to the possibility of promotion in the firm, and are able to participate in local community affairs and be respected for their participation. But if wages are at a bare subsistence level and the chances for getting fired are much greater than chances for promotion, and if the subordinate class is excluded from participation in community affairs and is confined to a dilapidated section of town, we would expect that if conflict occurs the potential for violence would be high. (Note that this prediction seems inconsistent with the predictions from Merton's reference group theory, discussed in Chapter 10, that higher promotion rates generate greater frustration among those not promoted than lower promotion rates because of the effect of high rates on people's expectations; determining the conditions under which each of these predictions holds requires further investigation and analysis.)

Conflict Regulation and Violence

One of the most important variables in Dahrendorf's model that influences the degree of violence in class conflict is the extent to which conflict is explicitly recognized and regulated.[51] Conflict regulation is closely related to the political conditions mentioned earlier that affect class consciousness and conflict interest group formation. At one extreme, those in positions of domination may attempt to deny the reality or the validity of class-based antagonism and conflict, and they may forbid the establishment of conflict interest groups. For example, political leaders in totalitarian societies may prohibit the formation of opposition political parties, or the managers of industrial enterprises may prohibit the organization of labor unions. This may be justified in terms of some type of ideology regarding the deep concern of those in authority for the welfare of their subordinates.

Regardless of how such efforts to suppress conflict may be justified, conflict and antagonism cannot be eliminated; they are built into the very structure of authority relations. Efforts to suppress or deny conflict simply lead to its submergence beneath the surface, where it may simmer and smoulder unrecognized for long periods of time. Periodically, however, submerged conflict erupts into the open. When it does, it usually takes a violent revolutionary form. This is inevitable in view of the lack of channels or mechanisms through which conflicts can be handled within the existing structure. Thus the totalitarian pattern is one in which efforts to suppress conflict are punctuated periodically by violent outbursts of rebellion.

In contrast to this totalitarian pattern, those in positions of domination may explicitly recognize the existence of conflicting interests and provide channels for their expression and negotiation. Paradoxically, the very recognition of conflicting interests leads ultimately to the diminishment of violent manifestations of conflict. Even in systems that are overtly totalitarian, informal (and perhaps officially unrecognized) channels may be developed whereby those in subordinate positions may be able to express their grievances or have their interests taken into consideration by those in power, at least to a degree. Open democratic societies, however, provide the sharpest contrast to totalitarian ones in terms of the explicit recognition of conflicting interests and the development of mechanisms for regulating conflict.

Such regulation, Dahrendorf argues, decreases the likelihood of violence. For one thing, conflict regulation is based on explicit recognition of the reality and the validity of the conflict; that is, both parties are seen as having *legitimate* opposing interests. Also, conflict regulation requires the formation of organized interest groups and the establishment of a common framework for negotiating differences. The organization of interest groups channels and controls the expression of opposition, while the establishment of a framework for negotiation provides a bond between the conflicting parties. An example of the institutionalization of conflict regulation is provided by the collective bargaining procedures established between labor unions and the management of industrial enterprises.

Consequences of Conflict: Structural Change

What are the functions, or consequences, of conflict? A principle function is promotion of social structural change, particularly with respect to the authority structure. Dahrendorf identified three different types of structural change: (1) complete change of personnel in positions of domination; (2) partial change of personnel in positions of domination; and (3) incorporation of the interests of the subordinate class in the policies of the dominant class.[52] Change of personnel, whether complete or partial, would mean simply that persons in the subordinate class enter the dominant class. Either of the first two changes would normally increase the probability that the third change will also occur;[53] however, the third change may also occur without any significant change of personnel. Indeed, it would seem that the more successfully the dominant class can follow the third strategy the less likely the previous two types of structural change will be.

Dahrendorf proposes that structural change varies in terms of how *radical* it is and in terms of how *sudden* it is. These variables, like intensity and violence of conflict, are conceptually distinct and may vary independently of one another. Radicalness refers to the *extent* of structural change, either with respect to the personnel in dominant positions, the policies of the dominant class, or the basic overall relation between classes. Suddenness refers to the speed of structural change. Change may be sudden and radical, or it may be slow and radical. In the latter case, the radicalness may not be consciously experienced as such by those involved because of the long time period in which it occurs; nevertheless, in retrospect, a long-term evolutionary change of major proportions has occurred. Similarly, nonradical changes may be either slow or sudden.

The radicalness and the suddenness of structural change are related to the intensity and violence of class conflict. Dahrendorf suggests that there is a positive relationship between the intensity of class conflict and the radicalness of structural change (even though such radical change need not necessarily be sudden). Similarly, he hypothesizes that the violence of conflict is correlated with the suddenness of structural change. Revolutionary political change would illustrate this type of change.

As noted earlier, Dahrendorf sees his theory of class formation and class conflict as a more general theory than Marx's. Marx's analysis of the early days of capitalism thus becomes a special case of a broader, more comprehensive theory. Dahrendorf points out that class formation and class conflict in Marx's perspective took place under the following historically specific conditions: "(a) absence of mobility, (b) superimposition of authority, property, and general social status, (c) superimposition of industrial and political conflict, and (d) absence of effective conflict regulation. Thus, classes are conflict groups involved in extremely intense and violent conflicts directed toward equally extreme sudden and radical changes.''[54]

Moreover, the changes that have occurred since Marx in these various conditions have had the effect of decreasing the intensity and violence of class conflict. Institutionalized patterns of conflict regulation, increased mobility, increased matetial affluence and socioeconomic security of persons in subordinate classes, and institutional segregation of industrial, political, and other forms of conflict help to preserve the basic structure of authority relations. Overall, then, contrary to the earlier assertion regarding conflict promoting structural change, whether conflict promotes structural change or reinforces the existing structure depends on the extent to which conflict is regulated.

Conflict Model versus Functional Model

Dahrendorf recognizes that his theoretical focus on conflict and social change is a one-sided perspective on social reality. Although this perspective is offered as an alternative to the functionalist emphasis on solidarity, integration, and equilibrium, both the functionalist perspective and the conflict perspective are considered by Dahrendorf as valid but partial perspectives on social reality. Each of these perspectives is one-sided when used alone; both are needed for a more comprehensive picture of social structure than either can offer by itself.

Dahrendorf summarizes the opposing assumptions of functionalist (or consensus or integration) theory and of conflict theory as follows:

Functional Theory

1. Every society is a relatively persistent, stable structure of elements.
2. Every society is a well-integrated structure of elements.
3. Every element in a society has a function, i.e., renders a contribution to its maintenance as a system.
4. Every functioning social structure is based on a consensus of values among its members.

Conflict Theory

1. Every society is at every point subject to processes of change; social change is ubiquitous.
2. Every society displays at every point dissensus and conflict; social conflict is ubiquitous.
3. Every element in a society renders a contribution to its disintegration and change.
4. Every society is based on the coercion of some of its members by others.[55]

These opposing assumptions describe the "two faces"[56] of society. When stated in this form these assumptions are oversimplified and too general, and the contrast between them is exaggerated. As we have seen, Dahrendorf's own conflict theory is not really consistent with the basic assumptions of conflict theory as listed here. For example, in this model, established patterns of conflict regulation contribute to the *maintenance* of the existing authority structure instead of to its disintegration and change. This contradicts the third statement under the conflict theory heading.

Nevertheless, having the two basic models presented in this simplified and exaggerated format clearly underscores the contrast between them. Overall, functional theorists emphasize the social processes that rest on value consensus and contribute to solidarity, integration, and equilibrium. Conflict theorists in general direct their attention to the opposing interests of different persons and groups in the social structure and to the way in which this clash of interests generates continuous social change. Even when the rate of change is minimal, this is explained not in terms of consensus but in terms of the success of the more powerful groups in imposing their will or winning acceptance by the rest of society. The challenge for sociology is to incorporate both perspectives explicitly into a more comprehensive theoretical framework and to identify the conditions in which the functional theory seems most appropriate as opposed to those in which the conflict theory seems most appropriate.[57] The next conflict theorist to be discussed offers one strategy for integrating the opposing assumptions of these two perspectives.

FUNCTIONAL ANALYSIS OF CONFLICT: COSER'S CONTRIBUTIONS

In 1956, 3 years before the publication of Dahrendorf's *Class and Class Conflict in Industrial Society* in English, Lewis Coser, a prominent American soiologist, published *The Functions of Social Conflict;*[58] this title would seem to imply an effort to get to the heart of the opposing implications of functionalism and conflict theory. Coser was born in Berlin, in 1913, but received his Ph.D. from Columbia University. He taught for a while at the University of Chicago, but most of his academic career was spent at Brandeis University. Since 1968, he has held the position of Distinguished Professor of Sociology at the State University of New York at Stony Brook. Overall, Coser's analysis of social conflict can be considered an alternative to Marxist-inspired radical conflict theory perspectives.

As might be expected for a conflict theorist writing in the middle of the 1950s, when functionalism was the dominant theoretical orientation in American sociology, Coser launched his approach with a criticism of the prevailing emphasis on value or normative consensus, order, and harmony. He pointed out that the process of conflict, if dealt with at all, was treated as disruptive or dysfunctional for the overall equilibrium of the system. This one-sided emphasis on harmonious integration based on normative consensus was manifested, he argued, in the general theoretical works of Parsons and also in other areas of American sociology. For example, the growth of the human relations movement in industrial sociology, inspired largely by the series of Hawthorne experiments, was based on the premise that antagonism and hostility between labor and management could be overcome by open communication and other forms of "good public relations."[59]

Coser based his analysis in *The Functions of Social Conflict* on the ideas of Simmel. However, these ideas seem to undergo a subtle shift in Coser's treatment. Simmel's emphasis, it will be recalled, was on the idea that conflict is one of the basic forms of social interaction and that the process of conflict is linked in innumerable and complex ways with alternative forms, such as cooperation. Coser's concern, however, is not so much with the complex and subtle interplay between conflict and other interaction forms at the interpersonal level but with the overall consequences of conflict for the larger social system in which the conflict occurs.

Coser does not disagree with Parsons' concentration on the social system level of analysis, nor does he follow Simmel's suggestion that the sociological analysis should focus primarily on forms of interaction. Coser's overall concern is to demonstrate that conflict is not necessarily disruptive or dysfunctional for the system in which it occurs but that conflict may have some positive or beneficial consequences for the system.[60]

Conflict Between Groups and In-Group Solidarity

The positive functions of conflict are perhaps most clearly evident in the dynamics of in-group versus out-group relations. At the risk of overgeneralizing, social processes emphasized in the functional model might apply to social relations within an in-group, while the social processes emphasized in the conflict model might apply to social relations between the in-group and the out-group.

Moreover, the two processes are often directly correlated. That is, the strength of the internal solidarity and integration of the in-group increases as the degree of hostility or conflict with an out-group increases. The heightened cohesion of a group involved in conflict helps to reinforce the boundary between the group and other groups in its environment, particularly hostile or potentially hostile groups. Within the group there is likely to be decreased tolerance of dissension or fragmentation and increased emphasis on consensus and conformity. Deviants within the group are no longer tolerated; if they cannot be brought into line by persuasion, they are likely to be expelled or subjected to rigid controls.

In contrast, when the group is not threatened by conflict with hostile outgroups, the strong emphasis on cohesion, conformity, and commitment to the group may be relaxed. Internal disagreements may be allowed to surface and be negotiated, and deviants are more likely to be tolerated. Overall, individuals will have greater latitude for pursuing their personal interests.

The functions of external conflict for strengthening internal cohesion and increasing the group's morale are so crucial that groups (or group leaders) may seek to provoke antagonisms with outside groups or to invent external enemies in order to preserve or enhance internal solidarity. This need not necessarily be a conscious process. Whatever their source, perceptions of external threats help promote or preserve internal solidarity, whether or not they are realistic. Even if the threat by a potential enemy is purely imaginary, the enemy may still perform a valuable function for the group by serving as a scapegoat. Indeed, a group's internal tensions and strains may be prevented from undermining the group if they can be projected onto some external source. The result is that group members blame the external enemy for their internal difficulties instead of allowing these difficulties to generate dissension or conflict within the group.

The relationship between the group and an external enemy will vary widely in different circumstances. On the one hand, contact between the potential enemy and the in-group may be minimal or nonexistent, and common characteristics shared with the out-group may be completely lacking. In this case the potential enemy is simply a continual threat, or perhaps a source of indirect competition. On the other hand, there may be some interaction or other bonds between the out-group and the in-group. Some members of the in-group may be perceived as having certain characteristics that resemble those of the out-group, or some may be involved in social relations with members of the out-group. When this occurs, the aggressive hostility felt toward the out-group may be directed toward those in-group persons who have some similarity to out-group members or some bond with the out-group.

Social bonds with the out-group may emerge for a number of reasons, such as the desire to seek accommodation with the enemy instead of pursuing an active and costly struggle. However, those who express such a desire for peace through accommodation are sometimes perceived by the group as traitors, and they, not the out-group, may become the scapegoats. Indeed, any deviant or dissenter, regardless of the nature of the deviance or dissent, could become a scapegoat onto whom the group displaces its frustration and aggression.

Numerous examples of these processes could be cited at various levels of social structure. Anti-Semitism or racial prejudice can readily be explained in terms of the dynamics of in-group versus out-group relations and displaced frustration and aggression. Thus, for many persons, economic frustrations might be blamed on the perceived economic power of Jews, or anxiety over social status might be expressed in terms of opposition to programs designed to expand opportunities for blacks. Wars between nations frequently stimulate heightened nationalism and patriotic fervor, particularly if the perceived threat of the enemy is widely acknowledged. The Viet Nam War does not illustrate this relationship because the Viet Cong in North Viet Nam were not clearly seen by the American public as a real threat. Nevertheless, the patriotic in-group feeling of many Americans was expressed in bitter opposition to fellow Americans involved in the antiwar movement. In World War II, in contrast, patriotism and commitment to victory over the Nazi threat were highly evident. Moreover, the entry of Japan into the war was followed by curtailment of the freedom of Japanese-Americans in this country.

Some groups rely heavily on opposition or conflict to justify the group's very existence. Opposition political parties, for example, are established to engage in conflict with the dominant political party. Similarly, the ideology of religious sects usually involves opposition to the dominant religious establishment or the wider secular society. Such opposition may be expressed in overt conflict or passive withdrawal. In either case, maintaining tension with the surrounding society is essential for preserving the distinctive organizational and motivational patterns of the sectarian organization. This explains why the gradual accommodations of a religious sect's members to the surrounding society is followed by a gradual transformation of the organization from a sectarian organization to an establishment-type of organization such as a denomination.[61] It also explains why sectarian organizations have difficulty maintaining their distinctive characteristics in a tolerant society.

Does external threat stimulate centralization of power within a group? Coser suggests that the answer depends on the nature of the outside threat and the internal structure of the group.[62] If the conflict involves war (or, presumably, physical attack or the threat thereof), and if the group has a high division of labor, centralization of power may be expected to increase. This is inevitable in view of the need for highly coordinated and decisive action in a complex system. The various contributions of those involved in a complex division of labor must be tightly coordinated to produce specific results in a situation where hesitation or indecisiveness can be extremely costly.

The question of whether the centralized power center is despotic or repressive is a separate question, however. Coser argues that a despotic centralized power structure is likely to emerge when there is external conflict and when internal solidarity and cohesion are relatively low. In this type of situation despotic control exerted by those in power represents an effort to shore up group solidarity in the face of an outside threat. This development is not inevitable, however. A group with low cohesion or widespread apathy may respond to an external threat by becoming even more apathetic, by internal fragmentation and conflict, or by disbanding. Presumably, whether breakdown occurs or the growth of authoritarian control emerges will depend partly on the strength of those in power and on the availability of options for leaving the group. Leaving a voluntary organization is relatively easy; leaving one's nation is not so easy.

Repressive control may turn out to be counterproductive in the long run, however. Efforts to exert repressive control are likely to generate increased resistance on the part of group members to the demands imposed on them. In this way a vicious cycle mechanism is set in motion. The leader attempts to tighten control; this stimulates internal rebellion, which stimulates even more repressive controls, and so on. Thus it should not be surprising when the termination of external conflict led by a despotic leader is followed by efforts to launch an internal revolution against the power structure. The chances for success are often minimal, however, particularly if victory in conflict has enhanced the power of the leaders to control resources on which members are dependent.

Conflict and Solidarity within Groups

Thus far we have looked primarily at the functions of conflict with an out-group for enhancing in-group solidarity and promoting group morale. Does *internal* conflict also have positive benefits for the group? Coser's answer is affirmative. Like Simmel, Coser recognizes that all social relationships inevitably have a certain degree of antagonism, tension, or negative feelings. This is true for in-group relations, including close, intimate relationships and segmental, secondary ones. The inevitability of tensions and negative feelings results from the desires of individuals to enhance their wealth, power, prestige, social approval, or other rewards. Since many of the rewards people seek are in scarce supply, a certain degree of competition is inevitable. Even for rewards such as social approval, which are not subject to the same kind of scarcity as material rewards, there will still be the competitive desire to improve one's position in comparison to others, even within a close-knit in-group. Moreover, strains and tensions should be expected in all social relations simply because individuals differ from one another in their needs, personal goals, skills and abilities, and so on.

The important point, therefore, is not whether tension or conflict exists within in-groups or not, but the form that such tension or conflict takes. To a large degree, this will reflect whether conflict is explicitly recognized and negotiated and whether the conflict concerns basic principles or secondary issues in the relationship. On the one hand, members of an in-group may belive that internal conflict on any issue is bad or undesirable and may refuse to acknowledge its existence or validity. On the other hand, members may openly acknowledge their opposing interests, particularly on secondary issues, and establish mechanisms for dealing with them.

Suppression of conflict is particularly common in groups such as families, which are expected to involve emotionally warm and mutually supportive intimate relations.[63] Suppression means that members' opposing interests are seen as illegitimate or inappropriate and therefore must be repressed, not openly negotiated. However, repression of conflict does not eliminate the opposing interests. Thus, without explicit mechanisms for resolving or negotiating opposing interests, the underlying antagonism continues to exist, seething beneath the surface of the relationship, contributing to strain and tension, and sometimes spilling over into other aspects of the relationship. Even though covert, such underlying and repressed conflicts have very real effects on the relationships within the in-group, undermining solidarity and, ultimately, in some cases generating a bitterness that is far too deep and pervasive to be resolved easily, even if a conscious effort is eventually made.[64]

Alternatively, members of an in-group may openly acknowledge their opposing interests and establish mechanisms for dealing with them. This pattern is more likely in secondary relationships rather than intimate ones or for secondary issues rather than basic principles. By definition, secondary relations involve less emotional intimacy and less emphasis on complete consensus. As a result, the acknowledgment of conflict is not so threatening as in intimate relations.

Strategies for dealing with conflict will vary, depending on the size and degree of bureaucratization of the group. In large, bureaucratic organizations formalized procedures may be developed to negotiate differences. An example would be the collective bargaining procedures developed within industrial organizations for negotiating labor-management disputes. In contrast, in small groups or families less formal procedures for settling differences may emerge. In either case, the point is that opposing interests are acknowledged and dealt with openly. In this way each individual's own personal needs and interests are recognized as legitimate and worthy of attention. In many cases the result is enhancement of the individual's commitment to the group and consequent strengthening of group solidarity.

The integrating functions of conflict are evident primarily in groups or organizations in which there is a larger framework of consensus within which the disagreements occur. If the general framework of consensus on basic issues should break down, so that there is no basis for unity in the group, internal conflict may lead to disintegration or fragmentation of the group. However, erosion of underlying consensus on basic issues is less likely if antagonistic feelings and disagreements are dealt with openly instead of being repressed.

Ironically, the presence or absence of overt conflict may be misleading as an indicator of the cohesion and solidarity of the group. Groups in which there is frequent overt conflict may actually have greater solidarity than those in which there seems to be complete absence of conflict. For the latter type of group the overt appearance of complete unity may be masking deep tensions and hostilities. If these erupt they could seriously disrupt the integration of the group.

Any relationship with a heavy emotional investment and a high level of ego involvement is vulnerable to the disintegrating efforts of repressed conflict. Like Simmel, Coser emphasizes that emotionally close relationships are characterized by ambivalent attitudes or by closely interrelated positive and negative feelings. Indeed, the closer the relationship, the more likely it is that occasions will arise that stimulate the emergence of antagonistic feelings or tensions. If members of a relationship or a group rely extensively on one another to meet many of their socioemotional needs, the chances for failure or disappointment will obviously be greater than if they expect less of one another. In contrast, secondary groups, in which social relationships are more segmental in character, will normally provide less occasion for the emergence of tension or hostile feelings, partly because less socioemotional satisfaction is expected in such relationships.

Even though negative or hostile feelings are inevitable in intimate relationships, open acknowledgment or expression of such feelings is often avoided because of the fear that the solidarity of the relationship will be undermined. As Coser states, "The closer the relationship, the greater the affective investment, the greater also the tendency to suppress rather than express hostile feelings."[65] The result is that hostile feelings build up or accumulate; each episode of suppression adds to their intensity. This danger to the solidarity of the relationship is greater, the greater the emotional involvement or intensity of the members with one another. This model suggests that the long-term stability and solidarity of an intimate or emotionally close relationship may best be insured if antagonistic or hostile feelings are openly acknowledged so that opposing interests can be explicitly negotiated.

Consequences of Conflict Repression

What happens when opposing interests or hostile feelings are repressed? The results will vary, depending on the degree of mutual involvement, the emotional intensity of the relation, the size of the group, and other factors. In general, however, two different consequences of repression might be identified. First, suppression of conflict could lead to termination of the relationship. If the emotional involvement of the members had been high, termination might be precipitated by the eruption of a sudden and intense conflict in which the accumulated tensions and hostilities that have steadily built up in the past break out in a violent rage. In such a situation, the precipitating episode may in itself be trivial; its significance as a triggering factor must be understood against the backdrop of a history of accumulation of repressed hostility. (In other words, the specific triggering factor is "the straw that breaks the camel's back.") In contrast, if the relationship is secondary or segmental in character, termination resulting from repressed conflict may simply involve gradually increased apathy and eventual withdrawal. For example, members of voluntary organizations may simply quit coming to meetings and eventually drop out.

A second possible consequence of conflict repression is deflection of hostile feelings from their real source and development of alternative channels for their expression. Such alternatives are a kind of safety valve through which hostile or aggressive impulses can be expressed in ways that do not threaten or undermine solidarity. For example, interpersonal tensions may be expressed in various forms of wit or jokes. Some examples would be the desire of schoolchildren to pull humorous pranks on the teacher, the use of political leaders as objects for the barbs of comedians, or the widespread popularity of mother-in-law jokes. Or, repressed aggression and hostility may be channeled in competitive games or other rituals. Or, finally, aggression and hostility may be deflected onto convenient scapegoats—either an out-group or deviant persons within the group.

Regardless of its particular form, the safety-valve mechanism benefits the group by permitting release of tensions arising from internal antagonisms and conflicts in ways that will not overtly threaten the solidarity of the group. However, such mechanisms do not allow for the explicit acknowledgment of conflict or realistic negotiation of the basic underlying differences responsible for it. The underlying tensions and hostilities remain beneath the surface appearance of solidarity and cohesion.

Realistic versus Unrealistic Conflict and Social Change

Coser makes a crucial distinction in this connection between "realistic" and "nonrealistic" conflict.[66] Realistic conflict is a means to a specific end, the attainment of which would presumably remove the underlying causes of conflict. In contrast, nonrealistic conflict involves the expression of hostility as an end in itself. Realistic conflict is directed toward the object of the conflict; nonrealistic conflict involves deflection from the real object of conflict. Conflicts are more likely to be realistic rather than nonrealistic if the validity of opposing interests is explicitly acknowledged instead of denied and if such opposition leads to negotiation of differences instead of suppression.

Realistic conflict is often a major stimulus for social change.[67] Such change may be beneficial to the system by enabling it to cope more effectively with changes in its environment. Or, change may result in a greater responsiveness to the individual needs of the members of the system; in this case their commitment to the system is likely to be enhanced.

Whether or not solidarity and change are positively correlated will reflect the degree of flexibility of the group in coping with conflict. Groups with a rigid structure are likely to attempt to suppress conflict and to resist pressures for change. Ultimately such pressures may build up to a violent revolution that results in radical structural change. On the other hand, groups that tolerate dissension and respond positively to pressures for change are more likely to exhibit gradual evolutionary change *in* the structure of the system instead of violent revolutionary change *of* the structure of the system. Overall, permitting realistic conflict and developing procedures for dealing with it help maintain the dynamic vibrancy or vitality of the system and prevent it from degenerating into a rigidly ossified system incapable of responding to pressure for change or to its members' individual needs.

The positive functions of conflict in stimulating needed social change is even extended by Coser to cases of violent conflict.[68] At the very least, violence is an indicator of deprivation; this is reflected in the fact that illegitimate violence occurs disproportionately among those at the lower end of the socioeconomic class structure.[69] Even though resorting to illegitimate violence might be deplored on a moral basis, its occurrence, like a fever or sharp pain, can be a "danger signal" to alert the members of society, particularly those in the power structure, to grievances and hardships suffered by those who are deprived from a fair share of material or other social rewards. (Definitions of a "fair share" will vary, depending on the expectations of those involved and on the general values of the society at large.) As noted earlier, if there are no established procedures for recognizing and negotiating opposing interests, violence may be the only option that deprived segments of society have for making their voices heard.

Within an opposition movement commitment to violence as a strategy for promoting social change can have strong integrating and solidifying effects. Actual engagement in violent acts to oppose a repressive power structure is inherently risky. Those who are willing to take such risks demonstrate the full measure of their commitment to the opposition movement. Moreover, success in the commission of violent acts can be an alternative measure of achievement, increasing the self-confidence of participants and inspiring others to demonstrate their commitment in equally dramatic ways.[70] The result is increased solidarity of the opposition movement as participants transcend their personal security and personal interests in order to pursue their cause.

As a stimulus for social change, however, the impact of violence extends beyond the internal solidarity of those involved in it. Violence also demonstrates to the rest of society, particularly the power structure, the seriousness of the participants' commitment to the struggle for social change, thereby adding credibility to their demands. Indeed, once the threat of violence is clearly established, those involved in an opposition movement may not necessarily have to resort to it in order to have their claims and their demands taken seriously. This point is particularly relevant when the opposition movement itself is split into an extremist faction bent on violence and a moderate faction committed to peaceful compromise. Even though the moderates may disagree with the extremists, the moderates may be reinforced in their demands for change by the threat offered by the extremists. In effect, the moderates are in a position of insisting that unless needed changes are made, they will no longer be able to prevent the extremists from pushing even more extreme demands by violent means.[71]

Many of these principles can readily be illustrated by the 1960s civil rights movement. Although Dr. Martin Luther King, the leader of the civil rights movement in its early days, was committed to using nonviolent means to pursue the goals of freedom and equality for blacks, the frequent summertime riots in urban ghettoes added a strong note of urgency to the demands for change. Many of the various federal programs developed during the late President Johnson's administration were undoubtedly a response to these pressures, including the threat of violence. Although his "Great Society" programs are generally acknowledged as having failed to fulfill the promise of complete socioeconomic equality, they at least demonstrated that the problems of racial discrimination and inequality of opportunity were officially recognized and that basic changes in the laws and social structure of American society were needed. In retrospect, it would seem that the limited gains in legal codes, education, employment, and the like resulted in no small part from the massive protest demonstrations and forceful demands for change. Besides peaceful demonstrations, the threat of violence was included in the overall picture.

Conflict as a Stimulus for Intergroup Integration

Changes often occur in the nature of the relationship between the in-group and other groups as a result of conflict. As noted, conflict often reinforces the boundary between an in-group and out-group and promotes an effort to shore up the solidarity of the in-group. In addition, if the conflict is a prolonged one, social bonds may gradually be developed between the contending parties themselves. One such bond would be the establishment of norms and procedures to regulate the expression of conflict. The collective bargaining procedures developed for labor-management negotiations is a major example. In international relations, even wars have traditionally been regulated by shared understandings regarding appropriate forms of warfare. Moreover, the termination of war is frequently followed by the establishment of treaties between the nations involved.

Another type of bond is provided by the emergence of shared symbols of victory or defeat. As Coser points out, violent conflicts are usually terminated long before the defeated party has lost absolutely all power to continue the fight.[72] Prior to complete exhaustion, the losing party typically makes some overture indicating a desire to establish peace. Such overtures will lead to termination of hostile action, however, only if their meaning is shared. For example, the white flag of surrender waved by the losing party will signal the winning party to terminate its drive for complete and total domination only if the symbolic meaning of the white flag is the same for both parties. Numerous events can symbolize victory or defeat. The emergence of shared understandings of the symbolic meaning of such events is an important bond between the contending parties because it facilitates the termination of the conflict before either party has to pay the ultimate cost involved in complete and absolute domination of the other.

In addition, conflict often stimulates a search for alliances with other groups.[73] In some cases antagonisms between different groups may be overcome as these groups band together in a coalition against a common enemy. Whether such a coalition evolves into a highly unified and solidary group will vary, depending on the cultural similarity of its members, the number of common interests, and the degree of repressive resistance to change that is encountered in the opposing group.

The emergence of deep and abiding cleavages between hostile camps results when many common interests and values are shared within each camp and when the opposing interests of each camp are suppressed. In this type of situation, the pervasive hostility between the opposing camps is likely to be expressed in nonrealistic conflict. In contrast, when there is considerable diversity of interests and values represented within a coalition and when the opposing groups are willing to recognize and negotiate conflicting interests, cleavages are less sharply drawn and conflict issues are more likely to involve specific realistic goals.

The American pattern of "limited purpose" interest group formation reflects this latter form of conflict. Typically, individuals in American society have limited or segmental involvement in several different interest groups or limited purpose organizations. Within each group or organization, in addition to the shared interests expressed in the goals of the organization, there are likely to be diverging interests. Some of these interests might be represented in other opposing organizations, and the overlapping membership of these organizations provides at least a limited basis for unity between them. Thus lines of conflict are not parallel or congruent; they crisscross and intersect one another in innumerable complex patterns.

To the extent that conflicting interests are explicitly recognized and openly dealt with, the overall society might seem to be pervaded by continual conflict on numerous issues. However, these conflicts are limited in nature and so do not lead to the formation of deep and pervasive hostility between clearly defined and permanent conflict groups. Instead, the overall society is knit together by crisscrossing lines of limited conflict. Although conflicts are expressed in a multiplicity of various interest groups and associations, individual involvement in such organizations usually is limited or segmental in nature. The result is that conflict does not undermine the solidarity of the overall society; it helps to promote it.

INTERACTIONAL DYNAMICS OF CONFLICT: COLLINS' THEORETICAL SYNTHESIS

The theoretical perspectives on conflict of Mills, Dahrendorf, and Coser have limited focuses. Mills explicitly limited his analysis to the interlocking and mutually supportive character of the power elite at the apex of the business, military, and political institutions of American society. Dahrendorf and Coser offer more general perspectives that are not limited to any one particular society. However, Dahrendorf specified "imperatively coordinated associations" as his major unit of analysis and restricted his focus to conflicts between hierarchical levels over the distribution of authority. This means that his model is *most* appropriate for handling conflicts within bureaucratic organizations or bureaucratically organized societies. Similarly, Coser's principle concern was not to develop a comprehensive theory of conflict but to show that conflict may have positive functions for a group or society instead of being disruptive or undermining solidarity, particularly if conflict issues are recognized and dealt with openly instead of being suppressed.

Moreover, all three theorists stressed the social structural level of analysis and not the interpersonal. There are implications for the interpersonal level as well as for the individual level. Coser's heavy reliance on Simmel results in frequent reference to interpersonal processes at the micro level, particularly in his discussion of intimate relations. Dahrendorf and Coser refer frequently to variables or processes at the individual level. Both, for example, deal with intensity of emotional involvement in a conflict group. Also, Dahrendorf stressed individuals' conscious awareness of common class interests as a variable in conflict group formation. Finally, Mills' portrayal of the American power elite dealt with interpersonal interaction that occurs between those who occupy the top positions in the economic, political, and military ruling circles. In short, micro-level processes at the interpersonal and individual levels are recognized in these theories; however, the principle concern is to develop a theoretical perspective that will apply to the social structure at the macro as well as the micro levels.

In 1975, Randall Collins published *Conflict Sociology*; it was intended as a general theoretical framework for sociology as a scientific discipline and it builds on a micro-level foundation of individuals' real-life behavior and interaction patterns.[74] Collins is the youngest of the contemporary theorists discussed thus far. He was born in 1941, received his undergraduate education at Harvard University, and earned his Ph.D. from the University of California, Berkeley. His academic career thus far has been spent at the University of California, San Diego, and the University of Virginia in Charlottesville.

Social structure in Collins' perspective, whether at the micro level of friendship groups or the macro level of large-scale bureaucratic organizations, for example, consists simply of repeated interaction patterns. The repetition of interaction patterns occurs mostly because human beings are able to remember past interactions and anticipate future ones.[75] Social structure has no *objective* existence apart from these recurrent interaction patterns.

However, social structure does exist as a *subjective* reality in individuals' minds. Collins draws explicitly on the symbolic interactionist (and phenomenological) insight that human beings live in a socially constructed symbolic world. The reality of this world consists of shared subjective definitions and expectations established through interpersonal communication. It follows that individuals' subjective reality is continually renegotiated. A major source of conflict in social life results from the efforts of people to influence or control the subjective definitions of others so as to maximize their personal advantage in interpersonal encounters.

Collins' does not limit himself to the micro level, however. The bridge between the micro and macro levels is provided by a model of stratification.[76] At the micro level, stratification is reflected in relations of dominance and submission. At the macro level, it is reflected in differential control of various kinds of resources by different groups or categories of people. At the micro level, relations of dominance and submission are symbolized by rituals of deference that low-status individuals are expected to adopt as part of their general demeanor when interacting with high-status individuals, even in the absence of overt conflict. Such rituals are manifested even in everyday conversational encounters.

In addition to this analysis of micro-level processes, Collins attempts to explain the social processes of large-scale complex organizations and social institutions. Indeed, his conflict model is more comprehensive than any of those discussed earlier. He does not limit himself to economic conflict, for example, or conflict within bureaucratic organizations. His model can be applied to any institutional area, such as families, religious organizations, scientific-intellectual communities, and economic, political, and military structures. Moreover, Collins' model is relevant not only to modern industrial society but to other societies and previous historical stages as well.

Most of the major theoretical ideas that Collins uses have been encountered in earlier chapters. Essentially, Collins' contribution is a creative and provocative synthesis of several of the key ideas of Weber, Marx, Durkheim, and Goffman. Of these, Weber's influence is the most pronounced. Collins' broad, comparative style of analysis, utilizing information from several different types of society and several historical periods, is somewhat reminiscent of Weber.

Also, Collins uses Weber's threefold distinction among class, status, and power as the foundation for his model of stratification and his analysis of the dynamics of social conflict. Recall that Weber had rejected Marx's argument that economic class (specifically, ownership or nonownership of the means of production) was the sole determinant of a person's position in society's stratification system. In addition to variations in economic position, individuals also vary in terms of the prestige they enjoy and their political power. (Variations in prestige give rise to status groups, while differences in political power are typically expressed in political parties.) Like Weber, Collins' underlying image of human behavior is that individuals strive continually to improve their position in terms of all three dimensions of stratification.

Collins also accepts and enlarges on Marx's emphasis on the importance of material resources for affecting a person's position in the stratification system. Marx had emphasized the distinction between those who own and those who do not own the means of material production. In addition, individuals also differ in their control of the means of ''mental production,'' ''emotional production,'' and violence or coercive power.[77] Marx had recognized the importance of mental production in his analysis of the way that ruling groups develop and promote an ideology that legitimates their dominant position. The means of mental production would include the educational system, for example, and the mass media.

The means of emotional production refer to resources that are involved in generating emotional bonds to the group or society, particularly to those in ruling positions. Traditionally, those who control religious symbols and lead religious rituals dominate in this area. Durkheim's emphasis on emotional solidarity created and reinforced through religious rituals is incorporated into Collins' perspective at this point. For Collins, however, it is important to understand that emotional solidarity created through shared ritual observances does not necessarily occur spontaneously. Nor does participation in rituals completely override individuals' divergent interests. As Collins said, ''The creation of emotional solidarity does not supplant conflict, but is one of the main weapons used in conflict. Emotional rituals can be used for domination within a group or organization; they are a vehicle by which alliances are formed in the struggle against other groups; and they can be used to impose a hierarchy of status prestige in which some groups dominate others by providing an ideal to emulate under inferior conditions.''[78] In societies dominated by a secular instead of a religious world view, the same process occurs with secular rituals, such as patriotic celebrations.

Control over the means of violence or coercive power essentially involves military and police structures. Collins emphasized that the threat of violence or coercion is always a potential element in any conflict. Those who control the means of coercion are able to impose their will on others through the threat of violence. At the same time, individuals generally seek to avoid situations in which they are subject to the coercive power of others, or at least to minimize the amount of coercion to which they are subject. In the final analysis, ideological justification for a given distribution of authority or emotional attachment to the society and its leaders rests on the differential distribution of the means of violent coercion.

For organizations other than the political system of the state, success in maintaining existing authority structures rests ultimately on being able to use the coercive power of the state if necessary. As long as the means of mental and emotional production are used successfully, coercive power may remain latent. However, as demonstrated by the use of military troops to deal with riots, control strikes by labor union members, or enforce school desegregation, for example, this coercive power potential can readily be activated if needed.

Interaction Rituals and Social Stratification

In line with his emphasis on micro-level processes, Collins links Durkheim's emphasis on ritual solidarity with Goffman's analysis of the strategies used in staging interactional performances. As noted in Chapter 8, Goffman's overall concern was to show how individuals attempt to control the impressions they make on others so as to gain social support for their idealized self-concepts. To this end, they seek to manipulate the shared definition of the situation, as well as their actual behavior, so it will be congruent with the self-identities they are trying to project. Material resources of various kinds are important as stage props for the performance.

Because social reality rests on subjective definitions developed through interaction, it is inherently fragile and precarious. Interactional rituals of various kinds help to reinforce the shared definitions of the situation and the identities of those involved, thereby preserving a semblance of order and certainty. These everyday rituals include basic norms of tact and courtesy. Many of these norms involve tacit agreements not to spoil one another's performance or to question one another's identity claims or implicit definitions of the situation, at least not without good reason.

In short, Goffman's overall image of social reality sees social life sewn together by numerous everyday rituals whose cumulative effect is to create and reinforce emotional bonds between people and emotional attachment to the group or society. In Collins' synthesis, even though Goffman did not deal with social structure systematically, especially at the macro level, his analysis of everyday rituals can be reconciled with Durkheim's insight that the reality of society itself rests on emotional bonds of solidarity created and reinforced through rituals. Indeed, as noted earlier, society (or other types of social structure) does not exist as an objective reality but as shared subjective definitions created and maintained through interaction. Durkheim and Goffman emphasized the ritualistic nature of the interaction involved in preserving subjective definitions of social reality.

Collins emphasizes that the micro-level interaction rituals described by Goffman express and reinforce the stratification system of society. For example, those in positions of dominance will naturally be concerned with people's adherence to rituals that dramatize their dominance and preserve and strengthen the emotional attachment of subordinates to the existing social order. Such rituals help to reinforce the legitimacy of the existing distribution of power and authority. Some examples would be the use of titles of respect when addressing one's superiors ("Yes, Sir," "No, Sir," "Your Honor," "Mr. President," etc.) and expressions of patriotic commitment to the society (such as the custom of standing during recitation of the pledge of allegiance).

By the same token, those who are in low-level positions of subordination will develop behavior and interaction styles that express their emotional detachment from the power structure and dramatize their efforts to maintain or enhance their independence and autonomy. Of course, their resources for controlling the definitions of others are less than those of people in high-level positions, and they may be obliged to be submissive in order to survive and meet their needs. But this does not mean that they are emotionally committed to the existing social order in the same sense as those in top-level positions. This is widely recognized among many working-class persons who perform their jobs and show respect for their superiors at the minimum level necessary for getting by, but who certainly do not like their jobs and feel no strong emotional attachment to the organizations within which they work.

Occupation and Authority Relations

Collins emphasizes occupation as the major determinant of an individual's class position. Marx's distinction between those who own the means of production and those who do not is seen as important because it determines the occupations whereby people earn their living. Collins is consistent with Dahrendorf in treating the authority structure with which individuals are involved in their occupations as the most important dimension of their class position and their general subjective outlook or "class consciousness." (The relationship between property ownership and position in the authority structure of an economic organization varies in different circumstances.) The emphasis on authority relations refers essentially to the experience of giving or taking orders. Collins writes, "Undoubtedly, the most crucial difference among work situations is the power relations involved (the ways that men give or take orders). Occupational classes are essentially power classes within the realm of work.''[79]

Unlike Dahrendorf, Collins did not adhere to a two-class model of authority relations. Instead, authority or power relations can be seen as a continuous hierarchical distribution, reflecting the number of persons to whom orders are given. In general, three broad categories of occupational groups are distinguished. At the top of the hierarchy are those who give orders to many persons but take orders from few or none. In the middle level are those who give orders to some but take orders from others. In large, bureaucratic organizations this middle level is extremely broad, with gradations from upper middle to lower middle reflecting the ratio of giving to receiving orders. High-level people in the middle ranks, such as top-level managers, take orders only from those in the top positions and give orders to subordinates who themselves give orders. At the lower middle levels are people such as factory foremen, who give orders to subordinates who actually perform physical tasks instead of giving orders to anyone below. These subordinates, whose involvement in the authority structure is limited to taking orders, constitute the lowest occupational class.

Other important differences are related to the differences in the ratio of order giving to order taking. One additional variable is position in a communication network. Those at the top of an organizational hierarchy tend to be more centrally located within the organization's communication network. In addition, these people are more likely to have wide-ranging social contacts outside the group or organization in which they are dominant. This facilitates their ability to maintain control over resources and to coordinate the various activities of their subordinates. In contrast, those at the bottom of the power hierarchy tend to have a more limited range of social contacts and to be located at the periphery of the communication network. This frequently accounts for their more local, less cosmopolitan orientation. Other differences between people in different occupational classes is the amount of wealth they earn or control and the physical nature of the occupational tasks performed. Those at the lower levels typically earn less money and are obliged to perform the dirtiest, most unpleasant, or riskiest tasks.

Collins argues that the nature of one's occupational position, particularly the experience of giving or receiving orders, carries over into other aspects of life, including one's subjective world view and degree of attachment to the existing social order, one's life style, and the general tone of one's interactional encounters. Those in the highest ruling positions are accustomed to continually receiving deference from their subordinates; thus they tend to be proud, self-assured, and unconsciously domineering in their general orientation. Moreover, such persons tend to insist on ritualistic formalities, especially in their relations with subordinates, since such formalities dramatize their dominant position.

In contrast, the occupational experiences of those at the lowest level give rise to a distinctive working-class culture. Collins describes this culture as "localistic, cynical, and oriented toward the immediate present."[80] Working-class persons usually have little stake in the maintenance of the existing authority structure and so do not feel a strong attachment to the moral ideas that legitimate it or the ritual formalities that dramatize it. They may exhibit the appropriate deference to their superiors when it is demanded, but such rituals do not necessarily carry any emotional commitment. The socioemotional needs of those at the lowest level are met with close personal friends who are usually at the same occupational level. Moreover, since working-class occupations involve greater physical exertion and risk than higher-level occupations, the working-class life-style is likely to emphasize physical toughness and courage. The alienation of working-class persons from the existing social order and its established power structure will be diminished to the extent that working-class persons are able to improve their material well-being or anticipate upward mobility.

The life-style and subjective orientations of those in the middle levels of power will reflect how close to the top or bottom they are. In general, those in the upper middle levels will exhibit patterns similar to those in the top levels, although to a lesser degree. The sharpest break is between the lowest level and the lower middle level. Those in the lower middle level have at least a minimal stake in the existing social structure in that they are able to feel superior to those below them and to issue orders to them on behalf of the organization. However, this stake is tenuous. As a result, those at this level tend to be highly moralistic, to emphasize self-discipline, and to work hard. This life-style confirms their moral superiority over the working class; it is also essential to maintaining their tenuous position and perhaps giving them a chance to move up the hierarchy. The ascetic life-style and moralistic orientation of this class are essentially the same elements that Weber identified as the Protestant ethic. It is no coincidence that Weber was able to show that many of the upwardly mobile pioneering capitalists were attracted to Protestantism.

The Dynamics of Status Groups

In addition to their occupational associations, individuals also establish social relations in the communities in which they live, religious groups to which they belong, voluntary organizations and friendship networks, and so on. These various nonoccupational relations will be influenced by occupational position. For example, the income received through occupation influences the type of community in which one can afford housing; as a result, people at similar occupational levels are likely to be neighbors in their residential community. However, occupational position does not *determine* the nature or extent of one's social involvements off the job. To a considerable degree, social relations off the job reflect individuals' voluntary choices.

What determines the nature of individuals' social relations outside of their occupational involvements? No single answer can be given, but Collins suggests that individuals generally initiate and maintain social relations that enable them to maintain or improve their subjective status as much as possible. This means that individuals choose associates who will accept their self-identity claims and their definitions of social reality; reciprocal social support will have to be provided in exchange. In relations between persons who are of roughly equal status, the exchange of support for one another's identities and definitions of the situation will be reflected in various mutual deference rituals, as shown for example, in the mutual respect that neighbors exhibit toward one another.

An individual's status is always relative to the status of his or her associates, however. Since individuals usually desire to enhance their status as much as possible, they will seek to stage their self-presentations in such a way that others will be obliged to acknowledge their superiority. This staging may involve displays of material resources that symbolize superior status, demonstrations of superior knowledge or skill in some area, conversational references to personal involvement in a network of high-status or high-class persons, or the use of various other resources to support one's claim to a greater degree of deference from one's associates than must be given in return. Groups in which individuals' resources for claiming superior status are about equal may be expected to alternate between the use of rituals that symbolize fraternal equality and those that symbolize friendly status competition. The reason the competition remains friendly is that no one is in a position to claim permanent superiority; a person who is superior in one area or on some occasions may be inferior in other areas or on other occasions. Often, however, the overt friendliness may mask feelings of envy or invidious status comparisons.

Status groups emerge from the efforts of those who share similar characteristics to provide social support to one another and defend their status claims against those who are different. Some of the characteristics that may become relevant for status group formation include age, sex, recreational interests, ethnic background, educational level, religious group membership, and residential community.[81] Essentially, those who are similar on these or other relevant characteristics tend to band together and develop a distinctive orientation and life-style that sets them apart from those who do not share these characteristics. This particular orientation and life-style bolster their distinctive claims for status or prestige in opposition to those who do not share the appropriate characteristics.

For example, if the necessary resources are available, young people will band together in their peer groups to defend their particular interests in opposition to their parents and the older generation and to develop their own distinctive outlook and behavioral style. Similarly, those in low-level occupational positions will support one another in their claims of moral superiority in opposition to the moral corruption of those in the upper class. Religious groups in a pluralistic society distinguish themselves from one another, and each is likely to insist on its superiority to others; if no one group is clearly dominant, this competition may be carried out in a friendly spirit. In the last several years blacks have attempted to establish their particular claim to status distinction in the assertion that "black is beautiful." Finally, the distinctive status claims of those in upper-class positions are expressed and reinforced through distinctive clubs, through restrictions on marriage or other intimate contacts outside the appropriate circle, and through a distinctive life-style that can only be supported by great wealth.

Status groups are not necessarily completely egalitarian. Although all those who belong to a particular status group may claim general superiority to those who do not belong, there are important internal differentiations of power and prestige within status groups. Churches, for example, have their ministers or priests and other hierarchical officials, their highly involved regular attenders and major supporters, and their marginal members; the black community has its leading spokespersons and rank and file; and social circles of sports fans are differentiated in terms of their knowledge and skills.

Individuals' voluntary involvement in various status groups in which they are not dominant rests on their assessment that the personal benefits of belonging outweigh the costs of being in a subordinate position. This assessment is encouraged and reinforced by the ability of status-group leaders to use the various resources of emotional manipulation that they control (e.g., enactment of rituals) to strengthen individuals' emotional attachment to the group and to link group loyalty to identification with the leader. There are numerous variations in the internal ranking system of status groups and the extent to which formalized rituals are utilized to reinforce solidarity. Many churches, for example, would be high on the hierarchical and formal side of the continuum; a clique of close friends in a residential neighborhood would be on the egalitarian and informal side of the continuum.

Applications of the Model

As suggested earlier, Collins' model is applicable both to the micro level and the macro level; however, macro-level processes are based on the micro-level processes instead of being independent of them. Collins applies his basic theoretical principles to both levels. At the micro level, he analyzes conversational encounters, interaction rituals, and family relationships. At the macro level, he stresses large-scale organizations, including the distinction drawn from Weber between bureaucratic and patrimonial organizations. The basic principles of his organizational analysis are applied to political and military structures, religious organizations, and intellectual communities.

Collins' analysis is interlaced with formalized propositions that cryptically express the various relationships between the variables that he discusses. A few examples might be cited merely to illustrate this style: on conversational encounters, "The more people one gives orders to and the more unconditional the obedience demanded, the more dignified and controlled one's non-verbal demeanor";[82] on deference patterns, "The more unequal the power resources and the higher the diversity of communications, the more elaborate the deference rituals and the more complex the standards applied";[83] on sexual stratification, "The greater the concentration of force in the household (rather than at some other political level or organization), the greater the power of men over women in terms of menial labor, ritual deference, and standards of sexual morality. . . ."[84]

At the organizational level, the following examples are noted: "The more one gives orders in the name of an organization, the more one identifies with the organization,"[85] and "The more closely a superior watches the behavior of his subordinates, the more closely they comply with the observable forms of behavior demanded."[86] Michel's iron law of oligarchy might be expressed as follows: "The larger a membership association" and "the more dispersed the members, the greater the tendency to oligarchy."[87] On the means of violence, "The more reliance on *expensive, individually operated weapons,* the more fighting is monopolized by an aristocracy of independent Knights, and the greater the stratification of society,"[88] and "The more reliance on *expensive weapons operated by a group,* the more an army takes the form of a central command hierarchy and a subordinate group of common soldiers."[89] On religious rituals, "The greater the *equality within the ceremonially united group,* the more likely the religion is to emphasize mass participation rituals, signs of membership, and the ideal of group brotherhood."[90] On status-group formation and political power, "The greater the resources for organizing itself as a status group, the greater the political influence of a collection of individuals."[91] This sampling of Collins' formalized propositions has been selected from several larger lists included in the various chapters of Collins' book. The sampling illustrates the style of explicit proposition formalization; in addition, the propositions selected briefly summarize much of the earlier discussion of Collins' overall theoretical perspective.

In concluding this overview of Collins' comprehensive theoretical synthesis, it is illustrative to note that although he recognizes the potential for violence or physical coercion in any conflict situation, most of his analysis centers on the various strategies individuals use to avoid violence or corecive conflict. Many of these strategies involve rituals that dramatize individuals' positions in the stratification system or symbolically express their emotional attachments to one another or to their group or society. As we have seen, those in dominant positions rely on deference rituals from their subordinates, not physical coercion, to reinforce their dominance. Those in subordinate positions develop rituals to express their alienation or lack of commitment to the existing social order, particularly the power structure, rather than engage in violent rebellion. At all levels, various rituals are used to enhance the emotional solidarity of the group or society or to reinforce the moral commitments of members in opposition to other groups or societies. In all cases, however, emotional solidarity or moral commitments should be seen as means whereby individuals, groups, or societies attempt to enhance their resources or their subjective sense of superiority.

Thus Collins' conflict theory comes to a position not wholly dissimilar from Parsons' functionalist perspective. Recall that one of Parsons' overriding concerns was to explain how the Hobbesian problem of the ''war of all against all'' is avoided and social order is established and maintained. Parsons' explanation of social order emphasized shared value orientations. Like Collins, Parsons recognized the importance of expressive rituals in reinforcing individuals' commitment to shared values. Critics of Parsons' functionalist approach often overlook the fact that the degree of congruence between the cultural value orientations and individuals' need-dispositions is always problematic and can never be taken for granted.

Nevertheless, the two theoretical perspectives clearly differ in overall emphasis. Parsons stressed the influence of shared values in shaping individuals' goals and the importance of individuals' moral commitments in motivating them to transcend their narrow selfish interests. In contrast, Collins treats individual interests as primary and as relatively independent of any moral code. Efforts to promote and reinforce moral commitments are seen as strategies whereby individuals attempt to influence one another or insure one another's loyalty. The real motivation underlying individuals' shared values, however, is the desire to maintain or improve their economic position, status, or political power.

Summary

In this chapter several different conflict theoretical perspectives have been presented. Not all of them emphasize equally the process of actual conflict. Instead, considerable emphasis is given to the social processes whereby actual conflict is avoided. Nevertheless, all of these theories have in common a basic image of social reality and fundamental social processes that sets them apart from functionalism.

This fundamental image includes a strong emphasis on: the hierarchical distribution of the members of society in different social strata that reflect differential access to valued resources; the opposing interests of different groups and social classes in society; the ability of dominant groups to maintain their dominance by persuading or threatening to coerce other groups to support the status quo and fulfill the role requirements necessary for maintaining the existing structure of the system; and the opposition of subordinate groups and subsequent conflict as a major stimulus for social change. However, contrary to the widely accepted image of conflict theory as emphasizing social change rather than stability, all the conflict theories we have reviewed devote considerable attention to the processes whereby social stability is maintained.

To a large extent (although not completely) contemporary conflict theory reflects the influence of Marx. In particular, the critical school of theory draws heavily from Marx's philosophical assumptions and utilizes his style of analysis in showing that dominant forms of consciousness express and reinforce patterns of sociopolitical domination. Freedom from such domination and maximum fulfillment of human needs are goals that are strongly emphasized by the critical theorists.

The general style of critical analysis was also manifested in Mills' insistence on identifying the social structural sources of individuals' problems. His analysis of the American social structure, particularly the power elite, represents a sharp departure from both the functionalist perspective and the popular image of the American power structure as one in which pluralistic power centers negotiate and compromise in a democratic fashion to arrive at national policy decisions. Specifically, Mills focused on identifying a power elite at the apex of the economic, political, and military institutional orders.

Mills' picture of the power elite in American society is consistent with the process described by Robert Michels as the iron law of oligarchy, which describes a general pattern for persons in positions of power to give priority to maintaining themselves in these positions instead of meeting the needs of the rank and file of the organizations they lead. This process applies to democratic as well as to authoritarian organizations.

The relationship between those in positions of authority and those in subordinate positions is further developed in Dahrendorf's model of class conflict. Although Dahrendorf starts with a Marxist perspective, the crucial modifications he makes transform it into a model not unlike that of the functionalists in some ways. One of the crucial changes is that Dahrendorf stresses the authority structure of organizations instead of property ownership as the fundamental basis for class formation. Those who exercise authority and those who are subject to it inevitably have opposing interests, whether or not they are consciously aware of these interests. A large part of Dahrendorf's model is devoted to identifying the conditions under which people become aware of their class interests and form class conflict groups to attempt to change the authority structure. The effect of class conflict is structural change. The suddenness and radicalness of structural change are related to the intensity and violence of conflict. Intensity and violence, in turn, are related to several variables that affect conflict group formation. One crucial point in this regard is that explicit acknowledgment of conflict issues and establishment of mechanisms to regulate it reduce its violence.

The importance of open acknowledgment of conflict and of conflict regulation mechanisms is also dealt with in Coser's conflict theory. Coser's major goal was to demonstrate the positive functions of conflict in promoting social integration. Conflict *between* groups promotes internal solidarity within the conflicting groups. Conflict *within* groups prevents the inevitable antagonisms that characterize all social relations from building up to the point that the relationship itself is threatened. Conflict also promotes the development of social ties between groups, including the conflict groups themselves. Conflict can be a major stimulus for social change in Coser's perspective, particularly if the conflict is realistic. In contrast, nonrealistic conflicts may provide emotional release, but they do not deal with the underlying causes.

The final conflict theory presented was Collins' theoretical synthesis between the micro and macro levels of analysis. His general view of social structure, including the stratification system, is that it consists of subjective definitions developed through the interaction process. The material resources used in developing these definitions and persuading others to accept them are differentially distributed. The resulting differential degrees of success in individuals' ability to claim social superiority is reflected at the interpersonal level in their styles of presentation of self. Persons who control resources are able to assume a domineering demeanor in interpersonal encounters. Those who lack control of resources may be obliged to assume a submissive demeanor, even though such a demeanor does not necessarily indicate sincerity in accepting an inferior position. Collins emphasizes the crucial importance of giving or complying with orders in occupational settings as a key factor influencing individuals' orientations toward self and others and toward the normative patterns of the social system. In general, Collins' perspective can deal with conflict at both the micro and macro levels in various institutional settings.

From the standpoint of the overall framework of this book, conflict theory, along with functional theory, emphasizes the social structural level of analysis. As with functional theory, however, it is by no means limited to this level. Critical theory involves an explicit concern with the cultural level in terms of showing how the dominant forms of consciousness reflect and reinforce the social structure. Also, Coser dealt extensively with conflict at the interpersonal level of intimate relations, and Collins built explicitly on a micro-level foundation of subjective definitions developed through interpersonal interaction.

Footnotes

1. The idea that the successful organization leader's principle task is to facilitate and promote cooperation on the part of subordinates in accomplishing organizational objectives is emphasized by Chester Bernard in *The Functions of the Executive* (Cambridge, Mass.: Harvard University Press, 1938). Moreover, the whole human relations approach in organization analysis rests on an image of successful organizational functioning as being based essentially on harmonious cooperation between organizational participants. Needless to say, this approach has been criticized for its promanagement ideological biases and its failure to recognize the pervasiveness of conflict in organizational settings and the positive contributions that conflict can make to successful organizational functioning. Some of these opposing views will be dealt with on a more general level in the pages that follow.

2. Some of these criticisms will be referred to subsequently in this chapter. For some pertinent examples, see David Lockwood, "Some Remarks on 'The Social System,'" *British Journal of Sociology*, Vol. 7, June 1956, pp. 134–146; Ralf Dahrendorf, "Out of Utopia: Toward a Reorientation of Sociological Analysis," *American Journal of Sociology*, Vol. 64, September 1958, pp. 115–127; and C. Wright Mills, *The Sociological Imagination* (New York: Oxford University Press, 1959), especially Chapter 2, "Grand Theory," pp. 25–49. For a relevant sampling of some of the literature, both supportive and critical, on this and other issues involved in functional analysis, see N. J. Demerath, III and Richard A. Peterson, *System, Change, and Conflict* (New York: Free Press, 1967); on this specific issue of conflict versus consensus in social life, see

the papers in Chapter IV, ''Conflict and Consensus.'' See Alvin W. Gouldner, *The Coming Crisis of Western Sociology* (New York: Basic Books, 1970), for a thorough critical analysis of Parsons' functional perspective that goes beyond the point that Parsons failed to deal adequately or systematically with conflict and that underscores the implicit ideological conservatism on which Parsons' theoretical model rests.

3. For an example of an effort to integrate the opposing implications of dialectical analysis and the functional approach, see Pierre L. van den Berghe, ''Dialectic and Functionalism—Toward a Synthesis,'' *American Sociological Review,* Vol. 28, October 1963, pp. 695–705.

4. Contemporary sociologists are indebted not only to Marx for this idea that dominant forms of consciousness serve as ideologies to support the existing social structure and class relations. Another major influence is that of Karl Mannheim, *Ideology and Utopia,* translated by Louis Wirth and Edward Shils (New York: Harcourt, Brace & World, 1936). In Manneheim's perspective Marxism itself can be seen as an ideology used to support or legitimate the interests of the working class in their various struggles with bourgeois capitalists. Thus the same critique that Marx applied to the dominant bourgeois forms of consciousness can also be applied to Marx's own perspective.

5. See Melvin Seeman, ''On the Meaning of Alienation,'' *American Sociological Review,* Vol. 24, December 1959, pp. 783–791.

6. For a brief sampling of the literature in critical sociology, see Paul Connerton, ed., *Critical Sociology* (New York: Penguin Books, 1976).

7. Erich Fromm, *Escape from Freedom,* (New York: Holt, Rinehart & Winston, 1941). See also Erich Fromm, *To Have or to Be* (New York: Harper & Row, 1976). It should be pointed out that Fromm's analysis of contemporary forms of consciousness draws as heavily from Freud and the psychoanalytic tradition as from Marx's social criticism. This linking of Marx and Freud is also reflected in the works of others in the critical school.

8. Theodor W. Adorno, with E. Frenkel-Brunswick, D. T. Levinson, and R. Newitt Sanford, *The Authoritarian Personality* (New York: Harper & Row, 1950). One of Adorno's principle goals was to explore whether the kind of mentality that supported the rise of Nazism in Germany also existed in American society. Numerous empirical studies have been done since Adorno's pioneering work that have investigated the relationship between authoritarian personality patterns on the one hand and anti-Semitism and attitudes toward other minority groups on the other. See, for example, Charles Y. Glock and Rodney Stark, *Christian Beliefs and Anti-Semitism* (New York: Harper & Row, 1966).

9. For some examples see Irving L. Horowitz, ed., *The New Sociology: Essays in Social Science and Social Theory in Honor of C. Wright Mills* (New York: Oxford University Press, 1964); Norman Birnbaum, *The Crisis of Industrial Society* (New York: Oxford University Press, 1969); Norman Birnbaum, *Toward a Critical Sociology* (New York: Oxford University Press, 1971); Thomas B. Bottomore, *Critics of Society: Radical Thought in North America* (London: G. Allen & Unwin, 1967), and Thomas B. Bottomore, *Sociology as Social Criticism* (London: George Allen & Unwin, 1974). C. Wright Mills (honored in the title of Horowitz's reader) was one of the earliest of the critical sociologists in American sociology, and some aspects of his analysis of modern American society will be reviewed in this chapter.

10. See Herbert Marcuse, *One-Dimensional Man: Studies in the Ideology of Advanced Industrial Society* (Boston: Beacon Press, 1966); Herbert Marcuse, *Reason and Revolution* (Boston: Beacon Press, 1960); and Herbert Marcuse, *Counter-revolution and Revolt* (Boston: Beacon Press, 1973). Note that Marcuse draws heavily from Freud as well as from Marx.

11. See Jürgen Habermas, *Knowledge and Human Interests,* translated by Jeremy J. Shapiro (Boston: Beacon Press, 1971), and Jürgen Habermas, *Theory and Practice,* translated by John Viertel (Boston: Beacon Press, 1973).

12. See Erich Fromm, *Marx's Concept of Man* (New York: Frederick Ungar, 1961).

13. An extensive literature has been developed offering alternative interpretations of these developments and the closely related rise of the youth counterculture. For some examples see Theodore Roszak, *The Making of a Counter Culture* (Garden City, N.Y.: Doubleday, 1969); Charles Reich, *The Greening of America* (New York: Random House, 1970); Richard Flacks, *Youth and Social Change* (Chicago: Markham, 1971); Philip Slater, *The Pursuit of Loneliness* (Boston: Beacon Press, 1970); Philip Slater, *Earthwalk* (Garden City, N.Y.: Doubleday, 1974); and Peter Berger, Brigitte Berger, and Hansfried Kellner, *The Homeless Mind* (New York: Random House, 1973).

14. Jürgen Habermas, *Problems of Legitimation in Late Capitalism* (Boston: Beacon Press, 1975).

15. Fromm, *Escape from Freedom.*

16. Herbert Marcuse, *Eros and Civilization* (New York: Vintage, 1962).

17. For a basic statement of this position, see Peter L. Berger and Thomas Luckmann, *The Social Construction of Reality: A Treatise in the Sociology of Knowledge* (New York: Doubleday, 1966). Berger and Luckmann, however, do not deal explicitly with the question of how dominant forms of consciousness reflect and reinforce forms of social and political domination. Their concern is to explain the dialectical relationship between human beings as creators of their social world and the social world as an objective reality to which individuals must adapt. Social institutions and forms of consciousness are reciprocally related in their perspective, but this relationship is a universal one and is not limited to modern capitalist or industrial society.

18. Habermas, *Theory and Practice.*

19. C. Wright Mills, *The Sociological Imagination* (New York: Oxford University Press, 1959), Chapter 2, "Grand Theory," pp. 25–49.

20. Ibid., p. 49.

21. Ibid., Chapter 9, "On Reason and Freedom," pp. 165–176.

22. See Joseph A. Scimecca, *The Sociological Theory of C. Wright Mills* (Port Washington, N.Y.: Kennikat Press, 1977), especially Chapter 3, "Influences on Mills." Scimecca's overview of Mills' major ideas provides an intellectual biography of the development of Mills' theory as an "alternative to both structural-functional and conflict models." The influence of symbolic interactionism on Mills' perspective is manifested primarily in Hans Gerth and C. Wright Mills, *Character and Social Structure: The Psychology of Social Institutions* (London: Routledge and Kegan Paul, 1953).

23. C. Wright Mills, *White Collar* (New York: Oxford University Press, 1956). See also Thorstein Veblen, *The Theory of the Leisure Class* (New York: Modern Library, 1934).

24. In collaboration with Hans Gerth, Mills provided American sociologists with an edited

volume of Weber's work in English translation. See Max Weber, *From Max Weber: Essays in Sociology,* translated and edited by Hans Gerth and C. Wright Mills (New York: Oxford University Press, 1946).

25. C. Wright Mills, *The Power Elite* (New York: Oxford University Press, 1956).

26. Ibid., p. 23.

27. Ibid. See Chapter 12, "The Power Elite," pp. 269–297, for a historical description of the various changes in the American power structure.

28. Mills' analysis of these developments might be compared with the more recent analysis by Charles Reich of the historic transformation from the individualism of Consciousness I to the large-scale corporate and technological dominance manifested in Consciousness II. Reich thought he saw a new third stage of consciousness (Consciousness III) beginning to emerge in the middle of the 1960s among those caught up in the spirit of the youth counterculture. See Reich, *The Greening of America.*

29. See C. Wright Mills, *The Causes of World War III* (New York: Simon and Schuster, 1958), for a sequel to the analysis in *The Power Elite* on the growing dominance of the military institution.

30. Mills, *The Power Elite,* p. 7.

31. Ibid., p. 288.

32. Ibid., Chapter 11, "The Theory of Balance," pp. 242–268.

33. See Robert Michels, *Political Parties* (Glencoe, Ill.: Free Press, 1915).

34. Ralf Dahrendorf, *Class and Class Conflict in Industrial Society* (Stanford, Calif.: Stanford University Press, 1959).

35. Ibid., Chapter 2, "Changes in the Structures of Industrial Societies Since Marx," pp. 36–71.

36. Ibid., p. 168.

37. Ibid., p. 136.

38. Jonathan H. Turner, *The Structure of Sociological Theory,* rev. edition (Homewood, Ill.: Dorsey Press, 1978), pp. 155–158.

39. Dahrendorf, *Class and Class Conflict in Industrial Society,* pp. 165–173.

40. Ibid., p. 55.

41. Ibid., p. 176ff.

42. Ibid., p. 179.

43. Ibid., Chapter V, "Social Structure, Group Interests, and Conflict Groups," pp. 157–205.

44. Ibid., pp. 182–189.

45. Ibid., pp. 213–215.

46. Ibid., pp. 191–193, 201–205.

47. Ibid., p. 211.

48. Ibid., p. 212.

49. Ibid., p. 222.

50. Ibid., pp. 217–219.

51. Ibid., pp. 223–231.

52. Ibid., pp. 232–233.

53. Incorporation of personnel from the subordinate class into the dominant class need not necessarily lead to policy changes that will adequately incorporate the interests of the subordinate class. A major reason for this was discussed earlier in connection with the

iron law of oligarchy. Persons who move up from the subordinate class into the dominant class may shift their priorities to maintaining their new positions of domination instead of promoting the interests of the subordinate class from which they were recruited. Whether or not significant policy change occurs as a result of the incorporation of subordinate class members into the dominant class is an empirical question that cannot be decided on an *a priori* basis.

54. Ibid., p. 245.
55. Ibid., pp. 161–162.
56. Ibid., p. 157.
57. This particular strategy is incorporated into the comparative analysis of societies of Gerhard Lenski. He suggests that the functional model is most appropriate for simple, small-scale societies, while the conflict model is most appropriate for complex, large-scale societies. See Gerhard Lenski, *Power and Privilege: A Theory of Social Stratification* (New York: McGraw-Hill, 1966).
58. Lewis A. Coser, *The Functions of Social Conflict* (Glencoe, Ill.: Free Press, 1956). Coser's long-term interest in the study of social conflict is shown also in *Continuities in the Study of Social Conflict* (New York: Free Press, 1967), published 11 years later and reflecting the same basic approach as the earlier work. (Some of the chapters in this latter book had been published elsewhere previously.)
59. Coser, *The Functions of Social Conflict,* pp. 20–29.
60. Our discussion of the "positive" functions of conflict should not be taken to imply that conflict is therefore good in a moral sense. Instead, our analysis will center on the objective sociological consequences of conflict. Whether these consequences are good or bad in a moral sense is a separate question.
61. This transformation of "sect-type" religious organization to "church-type" religious organizations has been thoroughly discussed in the sociology of religion. This analysis can be traced back to the pioneering work of Ernst Troeltsch, *The Social Teachings of the Christian Churches,* 2 volumes, translated by Oliver Wyon (New York: Macmillan, 1931). In the American context, however, because of our religious pluralism, sect-type organizations evolve into established denominations, not church-type organizations that encompass the entire society.
62. Coser, *The Functions of Social Conflict,* pp. 87–95.
63. Ibid., p. 62.
64. Ibid., pp. 67–72.
65. Ibid., p. 62.
66. Ibid., pp. 48–55.
67. See Coser, *Continuities in the Study of Social Conflict,* Chapter 1, "Social Conflict and the Theory of Social Change," pp. 17–35. Theorists who contrast functional and conflict theories often seem to assume that integration is necessarily associated with stability and conflict with change. (Dahrendorf's discussion of the "two faces" of society, reviewed above, illustrates this assumption.) However, these processes may vary independently. A social system may have high solidarity and integration and still undergo change. This would occur, for example, if there is consensus among the members of the system as to the type of change desired.
68. Ibid., Chapter 4, "Some Social Functions of Violence," pp. 73–92.
69. Ibid., Chapter 3, "Violence and the Social Structure," pp. 53–71.

70. Ibid., pp. 78–81.
71. Ibid., pp. 108–109.
72. Ibid., Chapter 2, "The Termination of Conflict," pp. 37–51.
73. Coser, *The Functions of Social Conflict,* Chapter VIII, "Conflict Calls for Allies," pp. 139–149.
74. Randall Collins, *Conflict Sociology: Toward an Explanatory Science* (New York: Academic Press, 1975).
75. Ibid., pp. 53–56.
76. Ibid., Chapter 2, "A Theory of Stratification," pp. 49–89.
77. Ibid., pp. 58–59.
78. Ibid.
79. Ibid., p. 62.
80. Ibid., p. 71.
81. Ibid., pp. 82–87.
82. Ibid., p. 157.
83. Ibid., p. 216.
84. Ibid., p. 283.
85. Ibid., p. 301.
86. Ibid., p. 307.
87. Ibid., p. 334.
88. Ibid., p. 357.
89. Ibid.
90. Ibid., p. 370.
91. Ibid., p. 386.

Questions for Study and Discussion

1. How would a critical theorist analyze the role of the mass media in modern American society? Would you agree or disagree with the argument that the mass media basically support the political and economic power structure? What evidence would you need to support your position?
2. It is often assumed that conflict promotes social change. Drawing on the various theorists discussed in this chapter, identify as precisely as possible the conditions under which conflict promotes change and the conditions under which it does not. Are there some conditions under which conflict might be followed by increased stability? Explain.
3. In what ways is Dahrendorf's theory a more comprehensive theory than Marx's? From the earlier discussion of Marx, do you think Marx would agree with Dahrendorf's basic assumption regarding the inevitability of authority relations in social organizations?
4. Distinguish between realistic and unrealistic conflict in Coser's model. Under what conditions are each of these types most likely to erupt?
5. How do the norms governing interpersonal relations express and reinforce the differences between people in terms of status and power? Cite some examples of norms that ritualistically reinforce positions of subordination, dominance, and equality. Do such interpersonal rituals help prevent conflict or do they sometimes promote it?

CHAPTER 12

Open Systems Theory:
An Approach to
Theoretical Integration

A major consequence of the recent growth of public interest in ecology and ecological balance is increased awareness of the interrelatedness of different life forms to each other and to the physical environment. Thus, for example, we now know that widespread use of inorganic fertilizers, pesticides, and herbicides in agriculture may have runoff effects that poison or otherwise disturb lakes, rivers, and oceans, so that fish and the health of human beings who eat the fish are endangered. Also, the efforts of large masses of people to escape the pressures and strains of urban life by vacationing in tranquil wilderness areas result in excessive crowding and destruction of their natural tranquility and an increase in the urbanization of nearby areas through tourist-oriented businesses.

Recent years have also witnessed a greatly increased awareness of interdependence in America's international relations.[1] This is manifested dramatically in American dependence on Middle Eastern oil imports. Because of this dependence our society has become vulnerable to the political conflicts and international disputes of that area. Another example of increased international dependence is demonstrated in the large Soviet purchases of American wheat in recent years to make up for deficiencies in their harvest. These examples of international interdependence through trade can have a direct bearing on the activities and life-styles of many American citizens. A decision by an American family to take a short vacation instead of a long one because of the high price of gasoline or the price that Americans pay for bread or other foods can be influenced by Middle East politics or the amount of rainfall in Russia.

This image of the high level of interdependence between human beings and the natural environment and between different societies in different parts of the world has perhaps been somewhat reinforced by the widely publicized pictures of our planet taken from space. From the perspective of space the blue-green image of the Earth is seen as a single entity without boundaries between nations or between human life and the natural environment, a small spaceship set against the background of the vastness of space.

At no previous period in history was it possible to see our world in this way. Combined with our renewed awareness of the fragile nature of the ecological balance and the limits of our natural resources, the image that emerges is that of a single complex system in which no individual, group, or society can remain isolated from the whole; all are interrelated and interdependent. Although the degree of interdependence will vary for different parts of the system, the idea that all human life, as well as other life forms, are intricately linked through common dependence on a single life-support system is widely acknowledged today.

But we need not adopt such a global perspective to recognize the interrelatedness of phenomena. In formal organizations, for example, interdependence is deliberately built into the design of the organizational system. Thus the various departments of a business firm—production, purchasing, accounting, sales, and research and development—are designed to be highly coordinated; one cannot function without the contributions of all the others. In addition, the functioning of a complex organization is interrelated with numerous additional phenomena such as government policies, attitudes toward work of employees, community resources such as transportation, general economic conditions, activities of other organizations in the area, policies of educational institutions in providing appropriate training for organizational roles, and even climate and geographical conditions. It is widely recognized by organization specialists that complex organizations are not self-contained or closed systems but are part of larger, more comprehensive systems.[2]

Interdependence between many different kinds of elements may be illustrated by the development of the social and ecological structure of an urban community. Unlike a formal organization, the development of an urban community is less likely to be by deliberate design. Instead, individual decisions are made so as to take advantage of existing opportunities, and the eventual result is the emergence of a highly interdependent system. To illustrate with a hypothetical example, let us say that a manufacturing plant is built in a small rural village in order to escape the high tax rates of urban areas, to be close to raw materials, or for any number of other reasons. The immediate effect of this decision will be to attract persons looking for employment—initially construction workers and later permanent employees. Thus the population grows. As it does, various opportunities for local businesses expand, ranging from bars and rooming houses for the construction workers to residential developments and retail stores for new residents. Eventually, additional business establishments may be attracted to take advantage of the expanded local market, thus promoting additional population growth. Meanwhile, land prices rise, and local landowners and political leaders decide that selling land for industrial, commercial, or residential development is more advantageous than farming. So they develop an explicit policy of attracting more business. As the one-time small rural village continues to grow, needs for various public services (roads, water and sewer systems, parks, etc.) expand, and offering these services provides additional employment for even more people.

As the community grows, those who can afford to will move away from the congestion to less crowded peripheral areas, leaving their former neighborhood to those who cannot afford to move or to newcomers seeking work. Eventually, the community is characterized by sharp distinctions between working-class neighborhoods and professional-executive neighborhoods. This is followed by differentiation in the businesses serving these neighborhoods. This sketch illustrates the high level of interdependence that emerges among variables such as natural resources, population growth, employment opportunities, land prices, public services, number of manufacturing and retail establishments, and degree of class differentiation of neighborhoods. No one decision involved in this process can be completely isolated from other innumerable decisions.

Even a small-scale system such as a family reveals complex patterns of interdependence between several different kinds of variables.[3] This means, for instance, that the relationship between mother and infant child will be affected by the mother's relationship with her husband, and both may be influenced by additional factors such as relations with neighbors or other relatives, economic resources, and already existing personal attitudes and feelings. Thus, for example, in a traditional family structure where the father works and the mother stays home with the infant, if the father feels frustrated and unable to fulfill his job aspirations, he may express his frustration by behaving in a negative or hostile way toward his wife, who may in turn become discouraged with her family life and fail to provide adequate care and emotional support for their infant.

If this pattern were to continue and the child were to develop behavior problems or become delinquent in early adolescence, this antisocial or delinquent behavior would have to be explained partly in terms of the unsatisfying relationship between the mother and father because of the father's frustrated aspirations. This illustration shows the interdependence between the various relationships within the family. Moreover, in this example, explaining the husband's frustration in his job would also have to take into account the reasons for his unfulfilled aspirations, the nature of his job, and the overall state of the economy as it has a bearing on lack of alternative job opportunities.

ALTERNATIVE THEORETICAL MODELS OF INTERDEPENDENCE

Interdependence between individuals' actions is recognized, implicitly if not explicitly, in all the theories that have been discussed in preceding chapters. Of these theories, functionalism emphasizes interdependence perhaps the most strongly. At the interpersonal level, this is seen in the notion that individual's roles are complementary to one another or fit together more or less harmoniously. This harmonious interdependence results from the common value orientation shared by the interacting parties and from the fact that conforming to one another's expectations fulfills a need disposition of each party. At the institutional level, functionalists tend to emphasize the harmonious interdependence between various social institutions in contributing to the fulfillment of the overall requirements of society as a social system.

Conflict theory also acknowledges the fact of interdependence in social life, even though its explanation seems radically different from that of the functionalists. In general, conflict theorists treat interdependence as a result of the power of those who control resources of various kinds to impose their will on others. This domination is manifested in all the major social institutions, but it is particularly acute in the economic, political, and military areas. Because of their control of various resources, those in dominant positions are able to insure that the actions of others contribute to the maintenance of the structure within which they are dominant. In short, the interests of those in dominant positions and not the values shared by all members of the system explain the patterns of interdependence that exist.

The other two contemporary theories discussed earlier—symbolic interactionism and exchange theory—stress patterns of interdependence in small-scale systems at the interpersonal instead of large-scale institutional levels. Symbolic interactionists explain interdependence as a result of the sharing of common symbols whereby individuals can negotiate their respective actions so they fit together in an organized whole. Individuals consciously take account of one another in planning their own actions. Therefore the actions they construct in performing their roles make sense only in the context of their interrelationships with one another as parts of a larger whole. Although this larger whole may include large-scale systems such as total societies, the emphasis in symbolic interactionism is on micro-level social processes involving face-to-face negotiation.

Exchange theorists, in contrast, explain interdependence as a result of the fact that people depend on one another for various rewards, both material and nonmaterial. In an established exchange network individuals are motivated to provide rewards for others by their desire to receive rewards from others in return. Exchange networks are maintained to the extent that individuals experience reward/cost outcomes with which they are satisfied, or at least more satisfied than with alternative exchange patterns. As we have seen, exchange theory is not limited to the micro level. However, even though macro structures exhibit new emergent processes that are not manifested at the micro level, macro structures are dependent, in the final analysis, on micro-level interpersonal exchanges in which individuals assess their personal reward/cost outcomes.

Symbolic interaction theory is somewhat more general than the other three theories in its explanation of interdependence. Its major focus is on the symbolic medium through which patterns of interdependence emerge and are maintained. The general image of social reality promoted by symbolic interactionists is that its maintenance or change is continually dependent on symbolic communication. The emphasis on sharing common symbols and meanings and on cooperation is comparable to functional theory, but symbolic interactionists are much more likely than functionalists to emphasize the fluid and continually negotiated character of social structures. Nevertheless, the crucial importance of symbolic processes is recognized, implicitly if not explicitly, in all of the theories reviewed.

The notion of interdependence is evidently basic in all of the contemporary theories discussed in the preceding four chapters. Beyond this, each theory reflects a distinctive and limited perspective on the nature of this interdependence. Exchange theory reflects a primary emphasis on individuals' self-interests as the ultimate source of interdependence; individuals are dependent on one another for various rewards. In functional theory, the major source of interdependence is shared value orientations; because of individuals' moral commitments to these shared values, they transcend their narrow personal interests if need be in carrying out actions that are beneficial to the social system in which they are involved. Indeed, individuals' personal interests are seen, for all practical purposes, as virtually equivalent to fulfilling the role requirements necessary for maintenance of the system. Conflict theory, in contrast, bases interdependence ultimately on coercion, or the threat of coercion. This includes physical coercion (or the threat thereof) or, more important, control over scarce resources. These alternative explanations of interdependence—self-interests, moral commitments, or coercion—correspond to Etzioni's classification of formal organizations on the basis of their primary compliance relationships.[4]

Symbolic interaction theory, even though more general than the other theories, also has its limitations. Specifically, it does not emphasize patterns of interdependence that are not symbolically mediated, such as symbiotic relationships of the type that ecologists analyze. Yet human beings as well as other life forms do manifest relationships of this type, partly because they affect the environment in which others act. The example cited in the opening paragraphs regarding environmental pollution is a case in point.

In short, all four of the contemporary perspectives discussed here have a limited view of the nature of interdependence. This statement oversimplifies to a degree. Exchange theorists such as Blau recognize the importance of the influence of emergent values as well as coercive control in the exchange process. Functional theorists acknowledge that the personal needs of the participants in a system are met, to a greater or lesser degree, through exchanges manifested in reciprocal role performances. Functionalists also acknowledge the possibility that there may be strains or conflicts between the needs or functional requirements of different "parts" (individuals, groups institutions, etc.) of the overall system. Conflict theorists implicitly recognize the importance of the exchange process but treat this process as benefiting those who are dominant more than those who are subordinate. Moreover, they recognize that the process of conflict is constrained and regulated in a variety of ways, including shared rules and dominant forms of consciousness (or "false consciousness," in Marx's perspective). Finally, symbolic interactionists are fully aware of the fact that human beings are biological organisms who live not only in a subjective symbolic world that they have constructed but also in an objective material world. It follows, therefore, that there must be some congruence or compatibility between symbolic definitions and meanings on the one hand and the objective physical world to which individuals must adapt as biological organisms on the other. Individuals could hardly survive if their symbolic world were simply a world of "make-believe" that ignored their biological makeup or the hard facts of their environment. Nevertheless, in spite of the danger of oversimplification, these four theories clearly differ in terms of their primary emphases in explaining interdependence in social life.

Could the contrasting emphases of these theories be integrated in a larger, more comprehensive model or theoretical perspective? For example, could individual self-interest, moral commitments, and coercive control be seen as alternative bases for interdependence or as variables that may coexist to various degrees or in various combinations in any relationship or social system? Similarly, could the symbolic and nonsymbolic aspects of human interdependence be interrelated in a more general perspective? A major argument of this chapter is that *general systems theory* (or open systems theory) offers such a perspective. Our discussion of general systems theory will be elementary. Our goal will be to portray systems theory as a general framework that can incorporate many degrees and types of interdependence between the various units (individuals, groups, institutions, etc.) that make up the system.

Although Parsons' structural-functional model of social systems may be seen as one type of system perspective, general systems theory, as used here, is broader than Parsons' theory of social systems and is less definitive in specifying essential system processes. Nevertheless, the dividing line between the functionalist perspective on social systems and the general systems perspective is vague. Moreover, for some sociologists the shortcomings of functionalism, particularly Parsons' version, provide the point of departure for the use of general systems theory as a better alternative.

General systems theory is typically seen as relevant for the macro level of social reality. This is perhaps partly because this perspective is often promoted as an alternative to functionalism. However, the general systems perspective is relevant to any level of social organization, micro or macro. As we will see shortly, Walter Buckley, a major proponent of general systems theory in sociological analysis, made an explicit attempt to incorporate micro- and macro-level processes in the same general framework.[5] In terms of the perspective used throughout this book, this means that systems theory is relevant both for the social structural level of analysis as well as the interpersonal level.

THE BASIC PERSPECTIVE OF GENERAL SYSTEMS THEORY

The central concept of general systems theory is that of *organization* in a broad sense. Essentially, this implies a set of components or elements that are involved in relations of mutual interdependence. Because of this interdependence a change in any one of the constituent elements will have effects, either direct or indirect, on all the others. The significance of these effects will range from insignificant to crucial.

In its broadest sense, the concept of organization applies to the social realm and also to the biological and physical realms. In the work of Bertalanffy, a biologist, general systems theory is recommended as a perspective broad enough to promote a kind of unity among all the sciences—physical, biological, and social—in terms of their basic approach to their various subject matters.[6] This common approach involves a commitment to viewing phenomena in terms of patterns of interdependence between interrelated elements, the organization of which forms a whole.

This stress on organization of parts to form a whole can be contrasted with the traditional scientific approach, which implied that phenomena could best be understood by breaking them down into their constituent components. For example, the traditional scientific strategy used to understand biological organisms was to identify and analyze the various parts that make up the organism, including the different organs, types of tissue, cells, and so on. The ultimate goal was to identify the basic building blocks that composed phenomena. In contrast, systems theory incorporates the notion that the whole is greater than the sum of its parts by virtue of the patterns of organization exhibited in the whole. By concentrating on the individual parts included in the whole, scientists lose sight of their organization or their interdependence. This organization or interdependence manifested in the whole is not reducible to the individual parts that comprise the whole.

Bertalanffy expresses this common emphasis on organized interdependence as follows:

If we survey the evolution of modern science, as compared to science a few decades ago, we are impressed by the fact that similar general viewpoints and conceptions have appeared in very diverse fields. Problems of organization, of wholeness, of dynamic interaction, are urgent in modern physics, chemistry, physical chemistry, and technology. In biology, problems of an organismic sort are everywhere encountered: it is necessary to study not only isolated parts and processes, but the essential problems are the organizing relations that result from dynamic interaction and make the behavior of parts different when studied in isolation or within the whole. The same trend is manifest in *gestalt* theory and other movements as opposed to classical psychology, as well as in modern conceptions of the social sciences.[7]

The reference to biological organisms must not be misunderstood, however. Contemporary systems theory is not a revival of the old organic model, which assumes that social systems are similar to biological organisms in the high level of stable and harmonious interdependence between their component parts. Instead, contemporary systems theory leaves open the question of how closely related the parts of the system are and the nature of their interrelationships. Sociocultural systems are seen as exhibiting distinctive patterns of organization not shared by biological or physical systems.

According to Buckley, one of the leading contemporary advocates of general systems theory for sociology, the distinction between sociocultural systems and other types of systems has not always been clearly recognized. He contrasts the ''process model,'' which he sees reflected in works as divergent as that of Marx, Simmel, Cooley, and Blumer, with the mechanical and organic models of social organization.[8]

The mechanical model emerged from the early efforts to explain human behavior and society scientifically, or as part of the objective world of nature. (Comte had used the term ''social physics'' to refer to the study of society before he coined the term ''sociology.'') Buckley argues that the concepts of *equilibrium* and *inertia* are derived from this mechanical model. The concept of equilibrium suggests a highly stable relationship between the parts that make up the system. Disturbances lead to a redistribution of the parts, which restores the system to its steady state. In the absence of disturbances the system exhibits inertia, or a tendency to maintain its existing structure, much like a pool of water will remain calm unless disturbed by the wind or a rock thrown in it. Buckley notes that Parsons made use of both the equilibrium and the inertia concepts in his effort to establish a stable reference point for analyzing social systems.

The organic model suggests a higher or more complex level of organization than the mechanical model. Both models incorporate the notion of interdependence of parts and maintenance of a steady state. However, the emergence of the organic model reflected the view that societies are not merely mechanical systems but living systems. Thus biology, not physics, is the model for sociology. Among the pioneers in sociology, Spencer was one of several to draw analogies between biological organisms and societies.[9] The popularity of Darwin's theory of biological evolution and the development of social Darwinism to explain social evolution provided major reinforcement for the organic model.

Buckley points out that the organic model actually involves at least two different levels of organization: the level of the individual organism and the species level. Theorists such as Spencer tended to use the individual organism as their basic model for emphasizing the harmonious interdependence between the various "parts" of society. This model is also reflected in contemporary functionalism, even though, according to Buckley, the functionalist concept of equilibrium is really derived from the mechanical model. A more appropriate concept for describing the self-regulating character of biological organisms is *homeostasis*. Homeostasis refers to all the dynamic processes whereby organisms maintain their structure and the internal state necessary for their survival in the face of continuous change and threats of disruption in their environment. The mechanisms for temperature regulation in organisms is an example used by Parsons.

Homeostasis implies a much more dynamic process than equilibrium. There may be continuing, potentially disruptive change in the organism's environment and internal changes within the organism, but homeostatic processes regulate the organism's response to these changes to preserve the basic structure of the system. The tolerance for basic structural change is very narrow and, if the homeostatic processes should break down, the result could be the death of the organism. Parsons' concept of functional requisites is highly relevant in connection with biological organisms perhaps to a greater degree than with social systems.

The emphasis on harmonious interdependence and homeostasis is not so crucial if the species level of organization and not the individual organism is analyzed. At the species level, the concept of the competitive struggle for survival rather than harmonious cooperation is emphasized. This process was emphasized by the social Darwinists. For them social progress depended on this competitive struggle and the resulting elimination of those less fit for survival and the preservation of those most fit. The ecological balance that exists in nature and in human society emerges as an unintended consequence of competition and conflict, not as a result of any built-in homeostatic mechanism.

The *process model* is recommended by Buckley as a more appropriate model for analyzing sociocultural systems. It is more flexible than the mechanical or organic models and does not include any unnecessary or inappropriate assumptions regarding specific functional requirements or the necessity for maintaining a steady state for survival. In addition, Buckley writes, "In dealing with the sociocultural system, however, we jump to a new system level and need yet a new term to express not only the *structure-maintaining* feature, but also the *structure-elaborating* and *changing* feature of the inherently unstable system. . . ."[10]

Buckley describes the basic image of society implied in the process model as follows:

> In essence, the process model typically views society as a complex, multifaceted, fluid interplay of widely varying degrees and intensities of association and dissociation. The "structure" is an abstract construct, not something distinct from the ongoing interactive process but rather a temporary, accommodative representation of it at any one time. These conditions lead to the fundamental insight that sociocultural systems are inherently structure-elaborating and changing. . . .[11]

The distinction between the mechanical, organic, and process models can be summed up by noting the differences in the level of organization that they exhibit.[12] Mechanical systems, unless renewed by outside energy sources, tend to lose organization until they reach a level of equilibrium requiring minimal or no energy for their maintenance. Organic systems (at the individual and not the species level) have a higher level of organization that they preserve within narrow limits through homeostatic mechanisms, in spite of environment changes and disturbances. Preservation of structure through homeostatic mechanisms requires constant inputs of energy, however. The process model applies to systems whose structure continually changes as they adapt to their environment. Specifically, structures tend to be elaborated as improvements are made in patterns of environmental adaptation. Such improvements involve increased utilization of energy and other environmental resources for meeting a continually expanding range of internal system needs.

The general systems model does not include any built-in assumptions regarding the nature of the relationships between the component parts of the system. In terms of the various theories discussed earlier, the relationships may be cooperative or conflicting; they may be based on shared moral values or individualistic interests; they may be coercive or voluntary; and they may be symbolic or symbiotic in nature. In addition, whatever the nature of the relationships, the strength of the relationships may also vary. That is, the component elements may be either highly interdependent or loosely interrelated. These are all empirical questions that cannot be decided on *a priori*.

Environmental Relations

The system as a whole is seen as being involved in various kinds of transactions with its environment. These transactions can be broken down into receiving inputs from the environment and providing outputs to the environment. Changes in the environment may have various effects on the relationships within the system. However, systems vary greatly in terms of boundary permeability, and a system may be able to insulate itself to some extent from certain kinds of environmental disturbance. For example, religious sects may attempt to withdraw as much as possible from the surrounding society, or they may develop various strategies for preventing their members from becoming excessively involved in secular institutions. Similarly, societies invariably develop procedures for monitoring and controlling the flow of people or goods across their boundaries. The contrast between a relatively open society such as the United States and a relatively closed society such as the Soviet Union demonstrates the variable nature of boundary permeability. Within American society the Democratic party is an example of an extremely open system, subject to the influences of numerous constituencies in the society and numerous political pressure groups.

Because of the continual dynamic interchanges between a system and its environment, the boundary between the system and its environment may be arbitrary. As suggested at the start of this chapter, the entire planet could be considered a single system. Alternatively, various nation-states could be considered the major type of system that should be identified for any kind of global analysis. In this case, the environment of any one nation would include other nations. Within a society, various institutions or organizations could be identified as systems in their own right, with the rest of the society considered as the environment. Or, finally, within a complex organization a single department or a single work group could be analyzed as a system, with other departments or the overall organization considered the environment of this smaller-scale system.

One possibility for determining appropriate system boundaries would be to establish a certain minimal strength of relationship between a set of specified elements. Elements whose mutual relations fall below this minimal level would be excluded; those whose mutual relations fall above it would be considered part of the system. Thus, for example, a supervisor of a work group in a factory setting who is not heavily involved in the informal social life of the group could appropriately be excluded as part of this particular system, even though the supervisor would normally interact from time to time with various members of the group. In contrast, a multinational corporation or industry could be considered a single system even though its operations transcend the national boundaries of any one societal system. (A multinational firm may even have its American branch, its European branch, its Japanese branch, etc., as though the societies in which it operates are merely component parts of the larger system.)

This arbitrary criterion, based on examination of the strength of the relationships between parts would probably be inappropriate when applied to a system "part" that performs a specialized function for the system of carrying out a particular type of environmental transaction. In the social realm numerous examples of such boundary roles could be cited. For example, a salesperson may interact far more frequently with customers than with other members of the organization. Even so, it would probably not be appropriate to exclude the salesperson from the organizational system or to consider him or her primarily as part of a different system made up of the various customers. (The latter may be appropriate for certain kinds of analysis.) In general, the task of determining system boundaries may be simplified considerably for many social organizations by using conventional criteria such as geographical boundaries or membership lists.

System Parts

The nature of the component parts that make up a system has been left unspecified deliberately. One reason is that our discussion thus far has dealt with the *general* concept of system, not with any particular type of system. A popular view among many people is that the basic component unit of social systems is the individual person, or perhaps groups of individual persons. However, the involvement of individuals in social systems usually does not involve their total being but only certain segments of their personalities. The degree of involvement will vary for different types of systems and different individuals. Nevertheless, it can be argued that the basic component of social systems is not the individual as such, but individuals' actions and interactions, organized in roles. Thus the units of a social system are not objective entities (such as physical objects) but events. It follows that structure and process cannot be separated because, if the processes of action and interaction that make up the system should cease or change, the system itself would disappear or be changed.

Buckley draws heavily on Mead and the symbolic interactionists in analyzing the nature of the acts and interaction patterns that make up a social system.[13] We recall that individuals' actions are not seen as fixed and automatic responses to environmental stimuli; instead, individuals construct their actions in accordance with the symbolic meaning they attribute to the objects in their environment. This meaning may be highly variable, reflecting individuals' particular goals and plans and manifesting a degree of human creativity. Also, it is the sharing of common symbols and common definitions of objects in the environment that make interaction and joint action possible. Thus the components that make up a social system include interdependent overt *actions* and also shared symbolic *meanings*.

In addition to overt actions and associated subjective meanings, other elements may also be included as component parts of a social system in a broad sense. These additional elements include the material objects and artifacts in the environment, human beings' biological characteristics and other life forms in the environment, and individuals' perceptions, expectations, attitudes, and goals. On the other hand, in a narrower definition of a social system, these elements could be considered part of the environment. Nevertheless, individual subjective factors are particularly important because they influence the meaning attached to objects in the environment and thereby the response to such objects. The degree of congruence among the attitudes and goals and subjective definitions of different individuals varies in different systems, reflecting the degree to which a common culture is shared.

Information Linkages Between Parts

The linkage between individuals and their environment and with one another is essentially an informational linkage, not an energy linkage. As a result of the constant process of individuals' creative adaptation to one another and to their environment, they develop a "cognitive map" that is a subjective representation of the material and social environment. This map will not necessarily be accurate or complete. As social psychologists have repeatedly emphasized, individuals are selective in their perception and interpretation of their environment. Their perceptions reflect their particular attitudes, goals, and subjective dispositions. Moreover, the map is not static; it continually changes in the course of adaptation to the environment. If individuals' inadequate perceptions lead to unsuccessful responses, they will revise their perceptions. For example, a person who shares a secret with an acquaintance and subsequently learns that the secret was not kept will revise his or her perception of that acquaintance as a trustworthy individual and will probably not share secrets with that person in the future. Organized social life involves a sharing or pooling of information derived from the experiences of numerous individuals. Through the learning process (defined broadly), each person's cognitive map will incorporate information derived from symbolic communication with others.

Social systems are not the only type of system to involve informational linkages. A simple mechanical device such as a thermostat may be considered an elementary information system; it continuously monitors air temperature and triggers the heating or air conditioning system to respond when deviations from the set temperature are large enough. Similarly, in biology the genetic structure transmitted through heredity can be thought of as an information system whereby individual characteristics and patterns of development are transmitted unconsciously from parents to offspring. In some nonhuman species specific behavior patterns are genetically determined. The genetic makeup of the human species allows considerable variation in the specific behavior patterns whereby individuals adapt to their environment and to one another. Perhaps partly for this reason sociologists have emphasized the process of information transmission through cultural learning instead of genetic codes. This is beginning to change for some sociologists as a result of the growing influence of sociobiology. Open systems theory can readily incorporate the basic principles of sociobiology as they affect human behavior and cultural patterns.

SYSTEMS THEORY AND THE SOCIOBIOLOGICAL PERSPECTIVE: GENETIC VERSUS CULTURAL INFLUENCES ON HUMAN BEHAVIOR

Current efforts to explain human behavior in terms of biological processes or characteristics are not new. Such explanations were popular in Europe and America throughout the last half of the nineteenth century and the first part of the twentieth, especially in the decades before World War I. This is evident in the strong influence that social Darwinism exerted on American social thought during this time.[14]

Historical Background: Social Darwinism

Essentially, social Darwinism represented an extension of the principles of biological evolution to social evolution. In both the biological and the social realms there was an emphasis on the process of the competitive struggle for survival in an environment in which the resources needed for survival are scarce. In the biological realm the competitors may be individuals or species. In the social realm the competitive struggle may be among individuals or among different groups within a society, among different societies, or among different racial or ethnic populations, each with its own distinctive cultural patterns for adapting to the environment. The outcome of this competitive process is the survival of the fittest. As a result of natural variation, some individuals or groups are better equipped than others to adapt successfully to their environment. Those who are able to adapt most successfully are destined to succeed in the competitive struggle, to reproduce more abundantly than their competitors, and to become dominant. In contrast, those who are unable to adapt successfully are doomed to extinction or subordination.

The differences between those with favorable characteristics and those with unfavorable characteristics are a result of natural variations that are transmitted through heredity. Thus the evolutionary process involves a gradual selection over many generations of those individuals or groups who are able to adapt most successfully to their environment. In the same way cultural patterns that prove to be beneficial in enabling individuals or groups to adapt to their environment are gradually selected over those that are less beneficial. In this way long-term biological and cultural progress is assured.

In America, between the end of the Civil War and the outbreak of World War I, these ideas were used to provide ideological support for policies that encouraged the growth of gigantic business enterprises. The success of these enterprises was viewed as a natural outcome of the normal evolutionary process and as proof of their superior fitness. By the same token, those who failed to achieve success in this competitive struggle or who comprised the lower or subordinate classes in society were considered to be in a position appropriate for their limited adaptive abilities.

A principle implication drawn from this evolutionary model was that there should be no artificial interference with the evolutionary process. This meant that conscious efforts to institute social reforms or regulate the activities of big business enterprises were viewed negatively. The most appropriate policy for government was a *laissez-faire* policy. Even efforts to provide minimal welfare assistance to the poor were suspect because of the effects of such efforts in enabling those who were less fit to survive and reproduce. Although individual acts of charity might be practiced, such behavior was inconsistent with the basic long-range implications of the evolutionary model.

There were dissenting opinions, even in the time period under consideration. Social theorists such as Lester Ward, for example, revised the evolutionary model as it applies to social evolution in such a way as to justify conscious efforts to guide and control the evolutionary process.[15] In his view human intelligence itself is an emergent product of the evolutionary process and thus should be considered as part of nature, not in opposition to it. Human intelligence makes it possible for human beings to shape and control the evolutionary process so as to maximize human welfare instead of relying solely on chance variations or the blind forces of nature as subhuman species do. Recall that Mead also stressed the role that human intelligence plays in the evolutionary process in enabling human beings to cooperate in attempting to achieve shared goals.

The prevailing view, however, was the one that discouraged artificial interference in the natural process of competitive struggle and survival of the fittest. However, there is another type of interference that was regarded by some as consistent with evolutionary principles. A key element in the social Darwinist model is that the characteristics that enable individuals to adapt successfully to their environment, or that prevent them from doing so, are transmitted through heredity. This emphasis on hereditary differences provided the basis for various racist proposals such as the development of ''eugenics'' programs to insure the dominance of ''superior'' races.[16] Beliefs in superior and inferior races also provided ideological justification for European and American efforts to dominate colonial societies. Perhaps the most dramatic of the political implications of social Darwinism was the rise of Nazism in Germany, with its explicit policy of attempting to insure the dominance of the Aryan race.

The belief that personality traits or behavior tendencies are transmitted through heredity is probably still common among many lay persons. Social scientists today, however, generally do not accept explanations of behavior based on heredity. Indeed, since the Nazi era in Germany, most social scientists seem to want to detach themselves as much as possible from any theory that implies the possibility of innate differences among individuals, races, or ethnic groups that could be used as a basis for labeling them as inferior or superior. Instead, differences among individuals or groups are explained by social scientists today in terms of social milieu or cultural conditioning. Lack of success of the disprivileged groups in society is a result of their position in the social structure, not lack of innate ability, according to contemporary social scientific beliefs.

Also, the *laissez-faire* political implications of social Darwinism are not widely accepted among sociologists today. Most of them probably recognize the need for government involvement in regulating a complex economic system, and many are also committed to some form of welfare state policy. These basic changes in social scientists' values and intellectual orientation results in a sharp break between contemporary social theory in America and the earlier social Darwinist period. Contemporary theorists are likely to regard the earlier acceptance of the social Darwinist model as a grievous and embarrassing error, and they are extremely suspect of any theoretical model that relies heavily on inherited biological characteristics. This is consistent with the modern egalitarian ethos of American society.

Biological and Genetic Foundations of Social Behavior

In view of this historical background it is perhaps not surprising that contemporary sociobiological explanations of behavior should seem like a radical new approach for social scientists. Growing interest in recent years in sociobiology has helped to correct the persistent neglect of biological influences on human behavior.[17] In many ways sociobiology is based solidly on the Darwinian principles of how natural variations between organisms give rise to differences in their ability to adapt successfully to their environment and reproduce. Understanding the specific mechanisms whereby beneficial characteristics are transmitted to offspring has been greatly enhanced by modern developments in genetics. This recognition of how natural variations lead to differences in reproductive success does not provide any basis for evaluating different populations as inferior or superior. After all, some characteristics may be advantageous in one environment but disadvantageous in another. Thus there is no basis for drawing racist implications from the sociobiological model.

Recognition of the importance of biological factors is not intended to deny the importance of cultural variations or cultural influences on behavior. Human behavior may be profoundly influenced by biological factors even though specific behavior patterns are not genetically preprogrammed. This lack of specific programming means that biological influences may be manifested in various ways. This flexibility provides ample room for the influence of culture.

However, it is easy for sociologists to exaggerate the extent of cultural variation. From a sociobiological perspective, culture can be seen as a set of strategies that enables human beings to adapt to their environment and to reproduce. These strategies are transmitted to each new generation through the socialization process, not through genetic codes, but the genetic code nevertheless establishes certain conditions or parameters within which the cultural strategies must operate if they are to be beneficial for survival and reproductive success. On a more general level, behavior patterns that are prescribed or proscribed by culture cannot, in the long run, be grossly inconsistent with human beings' biological nature. For example, certain religious groups may encourage fasting for certain people or at certain times of the year, but long-term fasting could never be expected as a required pattern for the majority of people because it would run counter to an obvious biological need. Similarly, cultural values may encourage people to desire freedom from the responsibilities of rearing offspring; however, no population could endure if its members simply refused to reproduce or abandoned their offspring to fend for themselves.

The pattern of reproducing and caring for offspring can illustrate the logic of sociobiological analysis. Given the helplessness of the newborn infant and the need for being socialized, it is imperative that adults (the parents, in most cases) be willing to invest the time, efforts, and material resources needed to care for their offspring until they can survive on their own. The involvement of the mother is crucial. By the time an infant is born, she has already made a major contribution during the period of pregnancy. Moreover, in the absence of modern substitutes, she must continue to provide nourishment from her own body for some time after the infant's birth. The motivation to provide the needed resources and care is supplied not only by cultural prescriptions (''Parents are expected to care for their children'') but also by the emotional satisfaction that parents derive from caring for their children. Indeed, the desire to care for offspring is so widespread that people often assume that there is a parental, or maternal, instinct that is universal in the human species and that would supply the needed motivation even without the social approval that results from conformity to cultural prescriptions.

The sociobiological model does not require an assumption of universal, uniform instincts or biological determinism, however. Instead, a better assumption is that there are natural variations between individuals or among populations with respect to the degree of emotional satisfaction derived from caring for offspring. That is, some experience greater satisfaction than others. If we assume that these differences are somehow linked with genetic variations, the stage is set for a sociobiological interpretation of the desire to care for offspring.

As a starting point, let us assume random variation in the part of the genetic code that is relevant to caring for offspring; that is, some individuals or populations are genetically predisposed to provide thorough care for their offspring, while others are genetically predisposed to abandon them shortly after birth. The result is that those who provide care are likely to rear offspring who will themselves reproduce (thereby transmitting the genes favorable to caring for offspring), while those who abandon their offspring would be unlikely to transmit their genetic characteristics to future generations. Thus, over the long course of evolutionary history, there has been a gradual selection of individuals or populations who are genetically predisposed to find emotional satisfaction in caring for their offspring.

This does not eliminate variations, however; from personal experience we know that some parents experience greater satisfaction in their parental role than others and that some provide optimum care and support for their offspring while others provide only minimal care. Moreover, the natural evolutionary consequences of these differences are probably undermined by various institutional mechanisms to insure that even abandoned children will be cared for by adoptive parents, in orphanages, or through other means. Such institutions represent a cultural elaboration of the basic biological requirement for new offspring to be cared for by adults until they become old enough to care for themselves.

The high cultural value that is placed on fulfilling parental roles thus can be seen as an elaboration of a sociobiological necessity. This is not to say that all elements of culture necessarily reflect genetically determined predispositions or biological necessities. Indeed, cultural evolution may become somewhat detached from its biological base or develop in directions that are inconsistent with genetic predispositions or biological necessities. In the long run, however, the constraints of genetic predispositions or biological needs are bound to be evident, especially in the differential reproductive success of groups that follow different strategies.

It is easy for sociologists to exaggerate the extent of cultural variation. In spite of the wide range of cultural differences exhibited by different societies in different historical epochs, there are certain basic underlying similarities that are simply too significant and too numerous to attribute to chance or to tenuous explanations such as imitation and diffusion. The variations between different cultural systems are mostly variations within parameters set by genetic and biological characteristics. They are possible because of the flexibility built into our genetic code. This flexibility is itself adaptive because it means that we can adjust our responses to the environment in light of changing environmental conditions.

For example, although different societies exhibit considerable variation in specific family forms, no society has managed to endure without the family as a basic unit of social organization. In all societies the nuclear family, consisting of a male and female bonded for reproduction and their offspring, exists as a recognizable social unit. (Some subhuman species also exhibit this pattern to a degree.) In those relatively rare circumstances where efforts have been made to abolish the family, these efforts generally do not succeed in the long run. For instance, the Israeli *kibbutz* system, which might seem initially to be the exception that proves the rule, has not succeeded in eliminating the primordial ties between natural parents and their offspring.[18] This experiment in communal child-rearing has gradually been modified to allow mothers more involvement with their own natural children. In the face of such overwhelming evidence, sociobiologists would insist that the family cannot be merely an arbitrary cultural or institutional creation but must reflect some basic biological or genetic characteristics of human nature.

Numerous other patterns of behavior can be similarly analyzed. Specifically, sociobiologists have examined the establishment of dominance hierarchies within groups, patterns of territorial defense, competition for scarce resources, aggression, altruism (especially toward family and kin), reciprocal exchange of goods and services, and group solidarity as reflecting the possible influence of biological factors that are transmitted through the genetic code. The reason that such behavior patterns are universal (or at least nearly so) is that they give those who exhibit such patterns a survival advantage over those who do not in the process of adapting to the environment.

To be sure, each biological predisposition may be expressed in varied ways in different cultural settings and environments. Aggression, for example, may be manifested in the fights of teenage gangs over their turf, in the battle for superiority between chess contestants, in the rivalry between two cities' professional football teams in the annual superbowl contest, and in the strategies whereby national political and military officials attempt to "preserve the peace" by continually investing in more and more deadly weapons. This does not mean that aggression is necessarily beneficial in all these cases. The only claim that would be made in a sociobiological model is that over the long course of evolutionary history, a certain level of aggressiveness has proved beneficial for survival and reproductive success in many cases. Predispositions for aggressive action thus reflect this biological or genetic heritage, even though specific acts of aggression by individuals need not necessarily be beneficial.

Different societies will vary in the specific institutional mechanisms whereby biologically or genetically based behavior patterns are manifested and in the degree to which they are expressed. Some societies (or some groups within a society) may consciously attempt to eliminate the most blatant forms of aggressiveness, for example, and this strategy may result in limited success. But, in most cases in the long run, such societies should not be expected to survive, since they would be vulnerable to attack by other, more aggressive societies. The risks of unilateral disarmament are widely recognized. Behavior patterns such as those just listed are not only nearly universal in the human species; they are also shared by many nonhuman species, thereby demonstrating that they must have a biological base instead of being arbitrary cultural inventions.

Numerous other widespread behavior patterns can be analyzed in the light of the possible long-term survival advantages that they confer. For example, altruistic behavior toward one's offspring and kin can readily be interpreted as selfishness in disguise, since such behavior helps insure that one's own genetic characteristics will be preserved and transmitted to future generations.[19] Similarly, the establishment of dominance hierarchies is beneficial not only to those who are dominant; those who are subordinate in the group may also benefit because of the care and support that dominant individuals often provide subordinants, and because groups with well-established leadership structures will probably be better able to adapt successfully to their environment than those without a clear organization or leadership structure. This is consistent with Blau's model (discussed in Chapter 9) of the benefits that may result to both leaders and subordinants from the emergence of a power structure.

In general, group solidarity is also often beneficial to individual members and enhances their ability to adapt successfully and reproduce. Such benefits result from the increased effectiveness of groups with a high level of solidarity in adapting to their environment as compared to those without high solidarity. The benefits of solidarity must be weighed against the benefits of individual assertiveness. (This is not a conscious process, of course.) If solidarity is too high, individuals might be so eager to sacrifice themselves for the sake of the group that the probability that they will transmit their own genes to future generations is diminished. The optimum strategy probably requires some type of balance between submitting to the group and asserting one's individual interests. This analysis suggests that the continuing dilemma in social life between the needs of the group and the desires or interests of the individual may be grounded in our genetic or biological characteristics.

A large part of the research and the theorizing stimulated by the sociobiological model is based on subhuman species. As a result, it is perhaps inevitable that sociobiologists would fail to analyze explicitly the distinctive influence of cultural influences on behavior. Specifically, sociobiologists do not concentrate on the question of why one cultural strategy for meeting biological necessities should be chosen over another, except that these strategies reflect the exigencies of adapting to particular environments. Perhaps random variations provide the pool of strategies from which the successful ones are selected.

Also, it is difficult to use the sociobiological perspective as a basis for predictive hypotheses to be empirically tested. The time frame involved in sociobiological evolution encompasses thousands of years. Apparent short-term exceptions to the patterns predicted by the sociobiological model (such as contemporary widespread use of birth control devices or female rejection of maternal roles for the sake of occupational careers) are "explained away" as short-term aberrations that are not necessarily significant in the long run. In the long run such patterns may be selected out or eliminated (as dysfunctional patterns have been in the past) due to the failure of those who exhibit such patterns to reproduce. Or, because of changes in the environment brought about by modern medical and agricultural technology and resulting declines in death rates, cultural patterns that discourage maximum reproduction may prove more advantageous in the long run than patterns that encourage it. In either case, short-term exceptions and fluctuations are not considered relevant for evaluating the long-term implications of the sociobiological model.

Perhaps because of their intense interest in cultural variations and their influence on behavior, sociologists have generally been reluctant to deal explicitly with the influence of biological or genetic factors on human behavior. Except for noting obvious biological necessities such as the need for food, sexual gratification, and shelter, sociologists have usually insisted on trying to explain human behavior solely in terms of cultural conditioning. Such explanations have appeared plausible because of the extremely wide variation of human behavior and social institutions in different societies with different cultural traditions. The underlying assumption seems to have been that such variety would not be possible if biological characteristics shared by all members of the species had any kind of determining influence on behavior. Instead of acknowledging the importance of biological constraints, sociologists have emphasized that human beings can transcend many of their limitations as biological organisms.[20] This capability is expressed most clearly in the growth of technology.

One major exception to this pattern of neglecting the biological dimension is provided by Parsons' explicit acknowledgment of the biological organism as the ultimate source of the energy necessary for action at the individual level and in social and cultural systems (as discussed in Chapter 10). Also, basic to his structural-functional model of social systems is the idea that social and cultural systems must operate within the parameters set by our biological characteristics as human beings. Specifically, for example, the helplessness of the human infant and the lack of specific genetic programming of appropriate responses to the environment means that social systems must establish institutional patterns (such as the family) to care for and socialize the young. In the same way, specific institutional patterns must be established to enable us to meet our biological needs. Although Parsons recognized the importance of the biological parameters of social action, his major emphasis was the way that action in social systems is guided by shared cultural orientations.

The sociobiological model reminds us that our behavior as human beings is as much a product of our biological heritage as our cultural heritage. This basic insight can readily be incorporated into contemporary systems theory because of the explicit recognition of the permeability of system boundaries. That is, sociocultural systems are not closed systems; they receive input from the biological level. Basic biological characteristics or predispositions may reflect information about how to respond to the environment that is unconsciously transmitted through genetic codes. This information will be reflected in some fashion in the nature of the sociocultural systems that we create and consciously attempt to transmit to future generations. This is not to say that our culture is *determined* by genetic codes; instead, genetic codes can be regarded as providing certain general impulses that can be expressed in a variety of specific behaviors. Moreover, cultural patterns that are created may be expected in some cases to have feedback effects on the genetic code by facilitating or inhibiting behavior patterns that would promote survival chances and reproductive success. This concept of feedback will be dealt with explicitly in the next section.

In contrast to genetic codes, the distinctiveness of sociocultural systems lies in the fact that the informational linkages between their component "parts" is symbolically mediated, often consciously. Moreover, the relative lack of genetic programming of *specific* behavior patterns or other kinds of deterministic influences on behavior based on biological factors means that human behavior and patterns of social organization are highly flexible and exhibit considerable variety in terms of their relationships to the environment. In view of this flexibility and variety, the negotiation of common meanings whereby joint responses to the environment may be organized becomes crucial for social systems. This was the emphasis in symbolic interaction theory (discussed in Chapter 8). Such shared meanings comprise a major part of our cultural heritage.

THE FEEDBACK LOOP AND GOAL-DIRECTED BEHAVIOR

The information that individuals need to adapt to their environment and relate to one another is provided on a conscious level through cultural codes and on a subconscious level through genetic codes. Within the general framework established by genetically influenced predispositions and biological characteristics, the specific information necessary for guiding individuals' actions is drawn from both the external material and social environment and from internal states of the individual or the social system. The ability to monitor internal states and to adjust behavior accordingly is crucial for purposive or goal-directed behavior. To begin, individuals are motivated to act in a particular way to meet some need or to achieve some goal. These actions produce certain effects on the environment and on the relationship of the individual or group to the environment. These effects are monitored and evaluated in terms of their relevance for the needs and goals of the individual or group. If an action is successful in meeting a need or achieving a goal, this success will serve as positive feedback that reinforces that action. However, if the consequences of an action deviate from the desired goal state, the negative feedback information regarding this deviation will stimulate corrective action. Maintaining or changing courses of action is dependent on the more or less constant flow of information from the environment regarding the consequences of previous actions. These consequences are compared with a subjective image of desired goal states as a guide for future action.

The feedback process described above may be diagrammed as follows:[21]

Diagram of a Feedback Loop.

Feedback loops such as this are emphasized in systems theory as crucial for self-regulating systems. Numerous examples of this process might be noted. At the individual level, even a simple act such as tossing a basketball into a basket utilizes this process. If the ball is underthrown, for example, the individual will take corrective action on the next attempt by exerting more energy. In the same way, a person who is misunderstood or fails to receive adequate social approval in a conversational encounter will adjust his or her conversation by changing the subject, changing strategies, or seeking new conversational partners.

At the level of a complex social system, similar processes of monitoring feedback and adjusting behavior accordingly can be identified. For example, large business firms engage systematically in market research in which they attempt to evaluate customer satisfaction with products, for example, or public preferences for various types of products. If widespread negative feedback is received, corrective action is taken, either in terms of advertising campaigns or changes in products. Similarly, national political leaders continually monitor public opinion polls and adjust their policies and strategies accordingly. In addition, political policies reflect to various degrees numerous types of feedback, including pressures or complaints from interest groups and statistical data on economic trends. Within a bureaucratic organization, feedback is regularly received by high-level personnel in the form of reports from subordinates, complaints, suggestions, and so on, and organizational policy is influenced as a result. This process sometimes breaks down due to excessive insulation of top-level personnel from their subordinates or their refusal to accept any kind of negative feedback. Regardless of their cause, breakdowns are likely to undermine the ability of the system to adapt successfully to changes in its environment or its internal structure.

Buckley describes the feedback process involved in goal-seeking behavior in social systems in terms of the following five stages:

> 1) A control center establishes certain desired goal parameters and the means by which they may be attained; 2) these goal decisions are transformed by administrative bodies into action outputs, which result in certain effects on the state of the system and its environment; 3) information about these effects are [sic.] recorded and fed back to the control center; 4) the latter tests this new state of the system against the desired goal parameters to measure the error or deviation of the initial output response; 5) if the error leaves the system outside the limits set by the goal parameters, corrective output action is taken by the control center.[22]

Although this description portrays the feedback loop as a formally established procedure in a complex organization, the basic dynamics of this process are applicable to any level of social system, whether formalized in this way or not, or to any other type of self-regulating system. The feedback process could be applied at the biological or genetic level to analyze the dynamics of sociobiological evolution (as discussed in the last section), even though the process would not be a conscious one at this level. The implicit (unconscious) goal in sociobiological evolution is survival and reproductive success. Behaviors that increase the organism's chances of survival and reproductive success serve, in effect, as positive feedback to the genetic characteristics that contributed to such behaviors and increase the chances that these characteristics will be represented in succeeding generations. In contrast, behaviors that fail to contribute to survival and reproductive success can be seen as deviations or errors that will be eliminated in succeeding generations. In short, the basic argument in sociobiology is that genetic variations help to produce variations in behavior; these variations in behavior in turn have a feedback effect on these genetic characteristics by increasing or decreasing the probability that they will be represented in succeeding generations. Although the process is an unconscious one, it nevertheless has the properties of a self-regulating or error-correcting system.

As applied to social systems, the feedback loop can be documented through a variety of research strategies. In all such research, however, it must be recognized that the variables involved in a feedback process may be both independent and dependent variables, depending on what stage of the process is examined. At one stage, a change in some independent variable may be observed contributing to a change in a dependent variable; at a subsequent change, the independent variable itself may be affected by the change in the dependent variable that occurred during the first stage as a result of its influence. The independent variable thus becomes the dependent variable. This suggests that it is important to take the longitudinal dimension into consideration.

Participant observation and ethnographic styles of research lend themselves readily to documentation of the feedback process. Both types of research necessarily have a longitudinal dimension, and both are concerned with the need to view social systems in a wholistic sense. This wholistic view is sensitive to the complex interplay between the numerous different kinds of elements making up a system, with all the constituent elements related to one another either directly or indirectly. Thus, for example, not only does a particular stimulus lead to a specific response, but the response may affect the stimulus, and this change in the stimulus may result in a change in the next response. At the same time, both stimulus and response may be affected by other variables in the system in which they are embedded.

This view clearly is not limited to a simplistic stimulus-response model of behavior. Nor does it assume that behavior is simply a manifestation of internal states such as attitudes or orientations. Instead, the behavioral response to environmental conditions is continually adjusted and readjusted on the basis of a constant monitoring and evaluation of its results. These results include effects on oneself as well as on the material and social environment. The process of continuous adjustment and readjustment among individuals to one another, to changing environmental conditions, and to themselves would seem to necessitate the kind of wholistic and longitudinal perspective provided through participant observation and ethnographic types of research. Such a view is also provided by symbolic interactionism.

Systems theory can readily be used in quantitative as well as qualitative types of research. Such an approach would require that the variables making up the system be defined as precisely as possible so they can be measured in quantitative terms. Standard statistical correlation techniques would then be used to determine the degree to which these variables affect one another. By means of computers, the complex interrelations between numerous variables can be examined simultaneously, or even simulated in the absence of adequate empirical data on all variables. The effects of the feedback process could be detected as a change in the way that a particular independent variable affects a particular dependent variable as a result of its own prior influence on the dependent variable. That is, the independent variable would be observed undergoing change as a result of the feedback from a dependent variable. Again, this suggests that identification of independent and dependent variables is somewhat arbitrary; a better approach would recognize such variables as involved in relations of mutual interdependence.

To illustrate the applicability of systems theory to both qualitative and quantitative types of research, the decision of a particular newly married couple to have a child could be analyzed in terms of the complex interplay of individual motivations and experiences, interpersonal dynamics, and environmental influences that contribute to this decision. Such an analysis could well be a virtual case study of the development of a marital relationship, exhibiting its own unique configuration of elements not shared by any other marital pair. Alternatively, such a decision, when multiplied many times among the members of a population, gives rise to a particular birthrate. A birthrate, in turn, can be seen as a variable in its own right, one that readily lends itself to quantitative measurement and that can be related to other quantitatively measurable variables such as consumer demand for diapers and baby bottles, frequency of participation in public entertainment events, perhaps increased absences of female members of the labor force from their occupations, increased demand for family-oriented housing, and increased demand on garbage disposal facilities. Some of these variables may even have a subsequent effect on the birthrate.

By providing a model for explaining purposive or goal-directed behavior, the feedback process as developed in systems theory avoids some of the difficulties of functional theory in establishing causal relationships. In functional theory an attempt is made to explain social phenomena in terms of their consequences for the social system, for the individual, or for both. This implies that the cause of such phenomena follows its effects in temporal sequence. The usual cause-and-effect sequence is thereby reversed, and functional theorists are often criticized on logical grounds for attempting to show that actions are caused by their consequences.[23] According to many of the critics, a more appropriate strategy is to focus on individuals' motivations and the various internal or external influences that affect them as the only valid strategy for establishing causal relations. But whether the focus is motivation or some other factor, the critics generally agree on the logical necessity of causes preceding their effects, not following them.

The feedback mechanism in systems theory makes it possible to combine functional analysis and motivational analysis without committing the logical fallacy of assuming that a future event can be a cause of a present event. It is not the future consequences that cause present behavior, but the desired goal states, or subjective images of future consequences in the light of present needs and environmental conditions, that stimulate or motivate present behavior. The actual consequences are then compared with the projected consequences, and adjustments in behavior are made accordingly. Thus the consequences, or functions, of behavior patterns, when perceived by the actor(s), influence subjective motivations in terms of reinforcing the behavior or in terms of stimulating change. In a social system individuals perceive the consequences of their own behavior and that of others as well. These consequences are evaluated in terms of both individuals' own personal goals and shared goals, and adjustments are made accordingly. Because of this process, a social system can be conceptualized as a goal-oriented, self-regulating adaptive system.

MORPHOGENIC VERSUS MORPHOSTATIC PROCESSES

Evaluation of feedback in relation to desired goals can have a variety of effects on behavior. At the individual level, whether or not a given behavior is repeated or changed will be influenced by the type of feedback received. In general, we might expect that positive feedback (as manifested in successful goal accomplishment) will reinforce a given behavior or increase the likelihood that it will be repeated. In contrast, negative feedback might be expected to stimulate behavioral change.

However, the reinforcing effect of positive feedback would have to be balanced with the effects of satiation. If a person is satiated by achieving a particular goal, presumably the specific behavior involved in achieving that goal would be less likely to be repeated, at least in the short run.[24] The individual would probably develop a different line of action intended to achieve some other goal. Overall, however, human needs and goals are insatiable; there is always some degree of tension between individuals' aspirations and achievements.

Individuals who are relatively successful in accomplishing their basic survival goals may be expected to develop additional goals and to adjust and elaborate their behaviors accordingly. In contrast, those who live at a subsistence level will have to devote practically all of their actions to physical survival, with little elaboration of behaviors beyond the struggle to obtain the physical necessities. This struggle may be minimally successful, but the level of satiation is still not high enough to permit elaboration of additional types of behavior oriented toward different goals. In short, the extent and type of feedback received will influence whether an individual simply maintains a given behavior pattern oriented toward a specific goal or elaborates behaviors oriented toward an increasing variety of goals.

Similar processes operate at the level of social relations or social organization. Individuals' degree of success in achieving various goals can be facilitated or hindered by the actions or reactions of others. Moreover, individuals' goals are not random, or completely unrelated to the goals of others. The convergence or overlapping of individuals' goals often leads to the emergence of social relations, and such relations, once established, give rise to additional goals. At the very least, if the relationship is beneficial to the parties involved, the additional goal of preserving the relationship would emerge. Moreover, just as individuals may elaborate their behaviors in pursuit of an increasing variety of goals, so may social relationships be expanded to enable the parties involved to pursue an enlarging set of shared goals.

To illustrate, individuals may become acquainted initially because they live near one another or work together. Certain common problems are likely to be faced because of the shared environment. This perception of common problems may lead to tentative efforts at elementary cooperation on certain specific tasks. Initially, this may involve no more than watching one another's homes for suspicious activity by strangers (in the case of neighbors) or covering for one another at work during trips to the water cooler or rest room. If these rudimentary cooperative efforts are successful, additional cooperative tasks may be undertaken. As this occurs, the parties involved may develop additional common interests that lead to new interactions. Thus, let us say, neighbors or co-workers become bowling partners. During this process emotional bonds gradually emerge, and the shared activities become even more salient and rewarding to the parties involved. In this way neighbors or co-workers who were initially casual acquaintances become close friends.

In the case of larger macro-level structures similar processes of elaboration are often evident. At the macro level, however, elaboration often takes the form of structural expansion, not increasing interpersonal involvement. For example, let us assume that a small business firm has been highly successful in marketing a product. The initial response is likely to be enlargement of the size of the work force. Beyond a certain level, however, the work force becomes too large to be supervised by the owner of the business, and an assistant is recruited. If the work force continues to grow, additional supervisory personnel will be needed. As the number of supervisory personnel grows, it eventually will be necessary to recruit additional, higher-level supervisors or managers to supervise or coordinate the supervisors.

Also, as the size of the organization grows, it becomes possible to expand the division of labor, with different persons specializing in different tasks, in an effort to increase efficiency and to take advantage of individuals' different interests and abilities. Growth in the division of labor results in even greater needs for coordination. Also, it becomes necessary to develop a basis for assigning various specific tasks and responsibilities. In short, the structure of the organization expands and becomes more complex. This involves both hierarchical expansion, with authority differentiated among various levels, and horizontal expansion, with various tasks differentiated among various specialists in the division of labor. Ultimately, the owner of the business shifts from direct supervision to general policy formulation and coordination of the overall enterprise.

As the firm expands in this way, new organizational needs emerge. For example, it may become apparent that managers and supervisors are not equipped to recruit or train their subordinates themselves; also, different supervisors gradually may begin to develop inconsistent or contradictory procedures in evaluating and supervising their subordinates, which could lead to morale problems as employees become aware of unequal treatment. In response to such needs, a specialist in personnel management may be recruited and a personnel department established. This department would recruit and terminate employees, develop training programs and motivational strategies, settle employee grievances, formalize promotion policies, and the like. Meanwhile the workers themselves could perhaps attempt to organize to bargain collectively over wages, promotion policies, and working conditions. If successful, rules and procedures for negotiating labor-management disputes will be created; personnel will be designated with responsibility for enforcing such rules; and supervisors will be bound by these rules in their supervisory style.

The purpose of this example is not to describe in detail how organizations grow but to illustrate the process of structural elaboration, which Buckley referred to as *morphogenesis*.[25] Although the root meaning of this term suggests the concept of *beginning of form,* the meaning, in terms of systems theory, does not necessarily refer to the initial beginnings of social structures but to the tendency for social structures constantly to change, especially through elaboration and expansion. According to Buckley, "Morphogenesis will refer to those processes which tend to elaborate or change a system's given form, structure, or state."[26]

The concept of morphogenesis can be applied at either the micro or macro level. Thus the growth and development of a complex organization (like the business firm just cited) and the emergence and growth of friendships (as suggested in the earlier example of how casual acquaintances become friends) are manifestations of morphogenesis. Even at the individual level, the process of morphogenesis can be identified; it would include processes such as acquisition of new skills or new knowledge or the enlargement of one's repertoire of activities to meet a widening range of emergent needs.[27]

The concept of morphogenesis can be contrasted with the concept of *morphostasis*. Morphostasis refers to the various processes or mechanisms that "tend to preserve or maintain a system's given form, organization, or state."[28] To illustrate, a small rural community would be exhibiting morphostasis if its members oppose and prevent population growth for fear of the various problems that rapid growth could bring. Similarly, if a community or society attempts to deal with deviance by suppressing it (through punishment or isolation of the deviant) and is successful, the result presumably would be the preservation of the existing customs and normative patterns. Within complex organizations training programs that indoctrinate the new recruits with established rules and procedures could also be seen as examples of morphostatic processes.

Morphogenesis and morphostasis thus refer to alternative dynamic processes that social systems may exhibit. The question of which of these processes is dominant in any particular system is an empirical question that cannot be decided *a priori*. In most cases there is no built-in necessity for social systems to maintain a particular structural form. Buckley emphasizes this point in his argument for replacing the structural-functional equilibrium model (as developed by Parsons, for example) with an alternative systems model which incorporates explicitly the built-in tendency for structural elaboration and change.

The notion of equilibrium and the closely related notion of homeostasis suggest an image of social systems that emphasizes morphostatic processes to the exclusion of morphogenic processes. When this equilibrium model is combined with the notion of functional requisites (as in Parsons' theory), the apparent implication is that the very survival of a social system depends on the successful operation of mechanisms that maintain its existing form. This image of Parsons' structural-functional model persists among Parsons' critics despite the fact that maintenance of a *particular* structural form is not included among the functional requisites that Parsons identified.[29] Nevertheless, the emphasis in functional theory is on the processes that promote stability and integration; in contrast, Buckley's application of general systems theory emphasizes the inherent dynamic of structural elaboration and change.

THE MORPHOGENIC PROCESS AND DEVIATION-AMPLIFYING FEEDBACK CYCLES

What determines whether morphogenic or morphostatic processes will be predominant in a social system? The answer lies in the nature of the feedback received, either from the environment or from within the system, especially in reaction to deviance. *Deviance* in this connection should be understood not necessarily in the usual sense of violations of moral or legal codes. Instead, it refers to any behavior that departs from the established structural form. Violation of established norms would be included, but so would the development of a new social relationship, the creation of a new department in a bureaucratic organization, the invention of a new tool or new strategy for accomplishing some task, or movement by individuals or groups to a new location. Two different types of feedback can be identified: the *deviation-amplifying* (or positive) feedback cycle[30] and the *deviation-counteracting* (or negative) feedback cycle. These might be thought of as deviation reinforcing or deviation inhibiting, respectively. Deviation-amplifying feedback cycles are associated with morphogenic processes, while deviation counteracting feedback cycles are associated with morphostatic processes.[31]

The concept of deviation-amplifying feedback cycles is extremely useful in analyzing many types of social change. Essentially, such a cycle is initiated when a deviation or variation from an established pattern is reinforced, thereby stimulating further deviation along the same line. The initial deviation may be minor and without major effects on the system. Its significance, however, lies in the fact that it sets in motion a process of cumulative change. That is, the positive reinforcement for the initial small deviation stimulates a slightly larger deviation in the same direction. This additional deviation, if reinforced, is followed by an even larger deviation which, if reinforced, is followed by a still larger deviation, and so on. As these positive effects become more widely known, the enlarging deviations spread among the members of the system. This process may be revealed on a small scale in a family setting in which children "test the limits" of their parents' tolerance for mischief by gradually escalating the forbidden mischief that they try to get away with before their parents finally intervene.

Neither the initial deviation nor the cumulative effects need necessarily be consciously intended. The initial deviation may simply be a random variation. The cumulative process will eventually be influenced by the unfolding needs or conscious goals that emerge among the members of the system. Indeed, constant pressures for innovations or deviation of various kinds are provided by the desires of individuals to improve their well-being, however this may be defined. There is always some degree of tension between the current state of a system and the ideals or aspirations of its participants. This tension creates a constant source of deviation. Perhaps the most common type of tension is that between the demands imposed on individuals by virtue of institutionalized role requirements and the desire of individuals to maximize their freedom and personal autonomy as much as possible. Social change often occurs also as the direct or indirect outcome of individuals' continuous efforts to improve their well-being or position in the system.

Maruyama cites numerous examples of such deviation-amplifying processes. These include "accumulation of capital in industry, evolution of living organisms, the rise of cultures of various types, interpersonal processes which produce mental illness, international conflicts, and the processes that are loosely termed as 'vicious circles' and 'compound interests': ..."[32] Such processes also are experienced widely in everyday life. The example cited earlier regarding growth of a friendship is an example. Similarly, a minor deviation in artistic or musical forms may "catch on," stimulating the gradual rise of a new school of art or music as more artists or musicians imitate the deviation and elaborate its implications in a way that reflects greater departures from the previously established forms.

The "vicious circle" referred to by Maruyama may be illustrated by the emergence of intergroup tensions and hostilities. Members of one group may act in a mildly hostile or threatening way toward members of the other group. The members of the other group respond in a slightly more hostile or threatening manner, reflecting their determination to insure that the first group's behavior will not be repeated. However, the first group is not dissuaded but responds to the response of the second group by even more hostile or threatening behavior. This stimulates an even greater response by the second group. In this way the level of conflict gradually escalates. The initial stimulus may be insignificant in itself; its importance is that it sets in motion a self-perpetuating vicious circle. At the level of interpersonal relations, this process can be observed in the eruption of violent fights from what may have started out as a minor disagreement or simply an exchange of verbal insults.

Deviation-amplifying feedback cycles are involved in the formation of alternative or deviant subcultures by subordinate or minority groups within a society. If two groups differ in terms of their control of resources on which they both depend, the process of conflict is likely to result in one group becoming dominant and the other subordinant. On a societal level, the dominant group may then establish laws designed to protect its interests in opposition to the interests of the subordinant group. Subordinant group members then find it more difficult for them to pursue their interests legitimately. Some of them may adapt by developing illegal strategies. The dominant group responds by establishing or expanding agencies of social control to suppress such behavior, either by punishing or attempting to rehabilitate the guilty people.

In this way, those who belong to the dominant group may gradually come to see the subordinant group as guilty of frequent illegal behavior and generally inferior in various ways. The results of such rejecting and discriminating attitudes is that the subordinant group withdraws as much as possible from contact with dominant group members and develops an alternative life-style, alternative customs, and an alternative morality more suited to their subordinant position. This alternative subculture reinforces the perceptions of the dominant group of the general inferiority of the subordinant group, and the dominant group becomes even more rejecting and discriminating. This, in turn, reinforces the subordinant group in its development of an alternative subculture.[33]

This model of the formation of deviant subcultures as the product of deviation-amplifying feedback cycles is consistent with the labeling theory perspective as developed in sociological efforts to explain deviant behavior. According to this perspective, individuals who are defined in a negative way as inferior or deviant actually incorporate this definition into their self-concepts and subsequently act in a way that expresses this self-concept. In short, defining an individual as deviant reinforces that individual's deviance. It does not matter in this connection whether the identification of a person as deviant is merely for the purpose of punishment or for the more humane purpose of rehabilitation. In either case, attachment of the deviant lable is likely to be a self-fulfilling prophecy because the treatment given to a person so labeled is likely to make it difficult for that person to respond in a way that does not conform to the lable. The same process would apply in the field of education with respect to children who are identified as slow learners or potential behavior problems.

In some cases the initiation of a vicious circle may not result from a single episode but from a series of minor events that gradually build up to a breaking point. The episode that finally triggers the cycle obviously must not be seen as an isolated episode but as the culmination of a series of episodes. Moreover, without the preceding series, the culminating episode would not have the effect that it does. For example, in the eruption of violent conflicts, a person who finally attacks an opponent may have suffered a whole series of insults or other indignities before finally reacting by means of a violent attack in response to what may seem like a trivial incident. Similarly, in an organizational context, structural change is often initiated only after a whole series of problems or challenges that cannot readily be dealt with within the existing structure. For example, a retail establishment would not set up a Customer Complaint Office in response to just one complaint; however, a series of complaints would presumably create a sufficient strain so that a special office of this type would be created.

In contrast to *morphogenic* processes resulting from deviation-amplifying feedback cycles, *morphostatic* processes reflect the effect of deviation-counteracting feedback cycles. As noted earlier, morphostatic processes preserve the existing form or structure of a system. Perhaps the most common sociological example is the process whereby the customs and normative patterns of a closely knit and stable society or community are maintained. In such a system the occurrence of deviant behavior activates various kinds of social control processes, ranging from informal social disapproval to official punishment. Whatever the specific mechanism employed, its effect is to prevent the deviant pattern from continuing or expanding. As noted, however, reactions to deviance may, under some circumstances, have the effect of setting in motion a deviation-amplifying feedback cycle. This would seem most likely in a complex and pluralistic type of social structure in which individuals are not solely dependent on a single closely knit community for meeting all their needs. In the final analysis, whether reactions to deviance succeed in minimizing it or are actually counterproductive in reinforcing it is an empirical question.

Buckley's presentation of systems theory stresses morphogenic and not morphostatic processes primarily because of his effort to distinguish his approach from Parsons' functional approach to social systems. Buckley's critical orientation toward Parsons' functional approach leads him to emphasize the process of structural elaboration and increasing complexity as opposed to the process of maintenance of an existing form.

Nevertheless, in spite of his disagreement with the major thrust of Parsons' functional approach, Buckley notes with approval Parsons' identification of "evolutionary universals" as structural changes that enhance the long-range adaptive capacity of society.[34] These evolutionary universals include, among other processes, increased differentiation and resulting structural complexity, a process very similar to what Buckley refers to as structural elaboration. This process includes expansion in the division of labor which, in turn, results in increased efficiency and effectiveness in adapting to the environment.

Recall that Parsons stressed the structural differentiation of institutions fulfilling the various functional requirements of society. Buckley does not utilize the concepts of specific functional requisites; implicit in his perspective, however, is the idea that social systems with a high adaptive capacity will be more likely to survive in the long run than those with a relatively low adaptive capacity. The increased adaptive capacity resulting from growth in the division of labor can be realized only if mechanisms for coordinating or integrating the various specialized parts are developed. This requirement is implicit in Parsons' identification of evolutionary universals such as cultural legitimation of a political system independent of the family structure and development of universalistic norms. In short, in spite of the difference in emphasis, Buckley's model does not contradict Parsons.

STRUCTURAL ELABORATION VERSUS STRUCTURAL SIMPLIFICATION

Although Buckley emphasized the process of structural elaboration and increasing complexity, social systems may, under certain circumstances, change in the direction of structural simplification. This process is the opposite of structural elaboration. It involves decreasing the degree of centralized coordination and control, reducing the degree of specialization and interdependence, and increasing the autonomy and self-sufficiency of the various "parts" or groups within the system. A major historical example is provided by the collapse of the Roman empire. As the Middle Ages opened, its highly centralized political system was replaced by the emergence of fragmented and independent political entities (such as village communities) that were smaller and less interdependent with one another.

A similar phenomenon has occurred in more recent times in the changes that have taken place in the family in response to the pressures and demands of industrialization and urbanization. The large extended family has declined and been replaced by the isolated nuclear family.[35] This transformation means, in essence, that the patterns of extensive coordination and high interdependence between a wide range of relatives in the kin network have been reduced significantly, and the nuclear family has become relatively more autonomous and self-sufficient. The general process can be seen as one of structural simplification.

Structural simplification is also manifested on a relatively small scale in the various efforts that periodically are made to establish independent and self-sufficient communes within modern urban-industrial societies. Those involved in such efforts make a conscious choice to drop out of the complex and highly interdependent technological-bureaucratic society, with all of its pressures and uncertainties and other problems. They seek to establish an alternative type of community in which members can preserve their autonomy, relate to one another on a more authentic or personal level than is possible with a high degree of specialization, and develop an alternative life-style and alternative values that promise to be more meaningful and satisfying than is possible in a complex technological-bureaucratic society, with its fragmented and impersonal social relations.

Many such efforts to develop alternative life-styles in autonomous communes do not succeed. Among those that do, probably most are, in the final analysis, dependent on resources and some degree of material affluence derived from the wider society. Nevertheless, the effort to form autonomous and independent communities that are isolated and insulated from the wider society can be seen as a manifestation of a desire for structural simplification. Moreover, the success of some independent communities, such as the Amish, demonstrates that it is possible for simple and autonomous systems to be established within the framework of a complex and highly interdependent society.

Structural Elaboration and Tension

What are the reasons behind the process of structural simplification? What are the motivations of those involved in this process? All forms of structural change—indeed, all forms of behavior—reflect efforts to reduce tensions. Tensions result from discrepancies between people's actual situation and their needs and goals.

Therefore the motivation to drop out of a complex and highly interdependent society and to establish a simpler, self-sufficient community is perhaps a response to the particular tensions and strains experienced in a large, complex society.

The need to cope with tensions and strains is a universal need not limited to modern society. Nevertheless, it seems plausible that modern urban-industrial society, with its high level of complexity and interdependence, generates particular types of tensions and strains that differ from the tensions and strains of simpler societies. As a general principle, increased interdependence resulting from structural elaboration implies increased control over the various units (individuals, groups, organizations, etc.) making up the system.[36] This implies a necessary reduction in the autonomy of the individuals or other parts (groups or organizations) that comprise the system.

This increased control does not necessarily mean that complex systems must be governed by an authoritarian or totalitarian leader. However, it does suggest a need to insure adequate coordination of specialized and interdependent parts. Regardless of the particular form that such control and coordination takes or the particular ideology used to justify it, the need to insure adequate coordination will be experienced as a constraint on the autonomy or freedom of the individuals, groups, or other constituent units in the larger system. In short, there will be strong pressures to submit to the discipline required for maintaining the complex structure and to perform specialized roles within the system. For young people, for example, this is reflected in the pressure to choose a career as opposed to drifting or acting impulsively and spontaneously.

A closely related tension might be identified in the psychological effects of a high degree of specialization in the division of labor. Since Marx, it is widely recognized that a high level of specialization in industrial production limits the ability of individuals to develop their full potential as human beings. As Weber pointed out, this same limitation applies equally to specialists involved in bureaucratic administration. The necessity of performing specialized roles is not necessarily experienced by all specialists as a constraint on their autonomy or their full development as human beings. Different occupational specialties vary in terms of the degree of autonomy they provide and the activities they include. For example, a lawyer probably does not experience the constraining effects of his or her specialty to the same degree as a blue-collar worker on an assembly line. Nevertheless, for some people the demands of specialization in occupational roles may be experienced as a constraint on their individual autonomy and personal development.

The tensions resulting from specialization are compounded by the fact that individuals may be unaware (or perhaps only dimly aware) of the overall dynamics of the large, complex system in which they are involved. As social structures become larger and more complex, they eventually reach a point where many of their participants will not be able to maintain an understandable subjective image of the total system and of how their particular roles fit into the larger picture. This means that it becomes more difficult for individuals to achieve a satisfying sense of personal worth in their organizational roles. Although participants may have a general and superficial awareness of the overall structure and goals of the organization, their individual roles are such a small part of the total picture that it is difficult for them to identify emotionally with their tasks or the overall goals of the organization. Instead, their jobs become meaningless routines. Again, the degree to which this general process applies would vary widely for different occupational specialists.

On an even broader level, the members of a large and complex society may experience considerable psychological insecurity as a result of their inability to affect in a significant way, or even to understand, the dynamics or the development of their society. National issues or policies are simply beyond their comprehension. One response is to simplify complex issues. In this case strain may be experienced in the difficulty of interpreting complex issues in terms of a simplified model. Another response is psychological withdrawal. Probably one reason for the low voting rates during elections is the widespread feeling on the part of many that their vote will not really matter.

Structural simplification is one type of response to the various tensions resulting from structural elaboration. Structural simplification also rests on deviation-amplifying feedback cycles. If the tentative processes reflecting simplification are reinforced, this reinforcement stimulates additional simplification. Moreover, these reinforcements become progressively more important as the negative feedback generated within the complex structure increases. This implies, for example, that efforts to develop simpler alternative life-styles should be more numerous during periods of widespread crisis or strain in the larger society.

A Dialectical View of Structural Elaboration and Simplification

These considerations suggest that the positive benefits of structural elaboration are accompanied by certain negative consequences. As noted, the major type of benefit resulting from structural elaboration is enhancement of the adaptive capacity of society (or some other system). This means greater efficiency and effectiveness in exploiting natural resources in the environment in order to meet an expanding range of human needs. The ultimate result is a rising standard of living, or increased material affluence for more people. However, as the economic or material well-being of people increases, certain changes take place in individuals' goals and motivational patterns. As we know from Maslow's theory of self-actualization, individuals whose basic survival needs are met are no longer motivated to the same degree by these needs; new, higher-level needs became dominant.[37] Ultimately, perhaps, a level of satiation is reached with respect to material well-being, or at least material needs become less important and other kinds of needs become more important. (The satiation level for material goods may be increased as a result of advertising campaigns or other influences.)

People's needs and motivations change as a result of the high level of economic security and material affluence made possible in a complex system with a high adaptive capacity. Paradoxically, however, it may not be possible for the new needs to be satisfied within the framework of a complex, highly interdependent social structure. The need for individual autonomy, for example, or for individual creativity or "self-actualization" is inevitably frustrated, at least for many persons, by the inherent dynamic based on specialization, interdependence, and high coordination. Thus the result of the shift in individuals' needs and motivational patterns is a change in the evaluation of the feedback received from continued involvement in a complex, highly interdependent system. Continued improvements in material well-being become less important as positive reinforcement, and continued suppression of needs for individual autonomy, creative self-expression, and the like become more frustrating. In this way the motivation for attempting structural simplification gradually emerges.

This explanation of the psychological costs generated in modern complex society is consistent with the fact that the majority of those who have been attracted to various countercultural protest movements within the past several years have been affluent, middle-class young people, not lower-class young people.[38] Continued enhancement of their material affluence is presumably less important than the desire to develop and express values other than the materialistic values that are dependent on occupational success within the system. For those attracted to various countercultural values, the psychological costs of conforming to the demands imposed by the technological-bureaucratic system are potentially greater than the economic costs that might result from dropping out and exploring an alternative life-style. Similarly, threats to continued economic security and material affluence resulting from inflation, increased energy scarcity, and unemployment result in increased concern of young people with conventional career goals and a decline in interest in creating alternative life-styles.

In addition to the social psychological strains generated within a complex and highly interdependent system, there are also various kinds of organizational strains. As social systems grow in size and expand in structural differentiation and interdependence, the resources that must be devoted to coordination and control of the various specialized parts will necessarily grow accordingly. These resources necessary for organizational maintenance must be balanced against the increased efficiency and productivity that results from an economy of increasing scale.

To illustrate, a large retail establishment can afford to sell products at a lower cost per item than a small establishment because of the larger volume they generate. Nevertheless, maintaining adequate communication among the thousands of members of a gigantic firm who are scattered in many different locations across the nation presents a much greater organizational challenge than maintaining communication and coordination in a small, independent establishment with only a dozen or so members. To be sure, the coordination of large-scale organizations nationwide is greatly facilitated by modern transportation and communication technology. Even so, the cost of such technology must be considered as a coordination or organizational maintenance cost that must be "subtracted" from the increased benefits that occur because of large size, high specialization, and resulting high interdependence.

The question of where the break-even point is with respect to the organizational costs of continued expansion and structural elaboration is, however, an empirical question and probably varies for different types of organizations. Theoretically, the break-even point could be considered the point at which the costs of coordination and control outweigh the benefits that result from continued growth and differentiation in the division of labor. In other words, the process of structural elaboration ultimately reaches a limit beyond which the negative consequences of continued elaboration outweigh the positive consequences.[39] Organizations that go beyond this point presumably would benefit from structural simplification.

Awareness of the disadvantages of excessive size and centralization is one of the major sources of political criticism in modern American society. Many critics argue that government has become too large and too centralized to meet even minimal criteria of efficiency. (This criticism begs the question of how efficiency of government might be determined.) One manifestation of this inefficiency is the proliferation of overlapping and duplicating agencies and programs of various kinds, many of whose participants may be unaware of one another's activities and actually working at cross-purposes.

In summary, in most if not all cases maintenance of an established structure should not be considered a functional requirement for the survival or well-being of the system. The concept of morphogenic processes calls attention to the tendency for sociocultural systems to undergo continuous structural change. We have stressed structural elaboration and structural simplification. The basic mechanism involved in structural change of either type is the deviation-amplifying feedback loop. Its effect is to provide reinforcement for deviations from established forms, thereby stimulating additional deviation in the same direction. Under some circumstances, however, social systems will exhibit morphostatic instead of morphogenic processes. That is, their particular structural forms persist rather than change. The basic mechanism underlying this tendency is the deviation-counteracting feedback cycle.

VARIATIONS IN INTERNAL STRUCTURE

Morphogenesis and morphostasis both imply interdependence between individuals or other units in a social system. Deviation-amplifying or deviation-counteracting feedback cycles incorporate responses from the others involved in the system. There is also feedback from the material environment that individuals take into account in adjusting their behavior. For example, if the temperature in a room gets too hot or too cold, an individual will adjust the windows or the thermostat accordingly. On a broader scale, the growth of technology can be seen as the development of innumerable complex techniques for adapting more effectively to the material environment by learning how to use various resources of the material environment for meeting a constantly growing range of human needs.

Our focus, however, is on feedback and interdependence in a social sense, involving interaction between people and their responses to one another's behavior. The growth of technology reflects a social process in this sense as well as the process of learning how to adjust behavior more effectively in response to feedback from the material environment. Even in the example of adjusting the windows or thermostat, a person may be stimulated to perform such an action by complaints of others in the room about the room temperature.

Interdependence in a social sense is central in systems theory. The underlying image of social reality is that individuals or other types of units are interrelated; the actions of any one part of the system will have effects on other parts. At the micro level, for example, the actions or responses of any one person in a small group are likely to influence the actions or responses of others. The discussion in the last section about the effects of deviance suggests that these effects are not confined to the individual deviant; they have ramifications throughout the system of which the deviant is a part, either by way of stimulating structural change or by way of activating various social control mechanisms.

This basic image of interdependence is shared by functional theorists and conflict theorists. At the societal level, functionalists view the various institutions of society as interrelated with one another so that developments within any one institution are likely to have various effects on others. This idea of interdependence is most fully developed in Parsons' emphasis on more or less harmonious interdependence between institutions whereby the survival and well-being of the overall system is maintained. Conflict theorists take issue with this notion of harmonious interdependence. However, conflict theorists, no less than functionalists, recognize implicitly the notion of interdependence. Marx and his followers, for example, emphasize how the political establishment reinforces the economic structure. And both Marxist and non-Marxist conflict theorists stress the importance of analyzing the nature of the relationship between those in positions of power or authority and those in subordinate positions. The clear implication is that the actions of persons at different levels (of power, authority, economic position, prestige, etc.) are interrelated.

This widely accepted implicit assumption of interdependence must be examined more closely. Some minimal level of interdependence is necessary for considering a collection of units (individuals or other types of units) as a system. This minimal level need not mean that the various units would be unable to survive and meet their needs on their own, nor does it necessarily imply interaction through communication, either direct or indirect. Different units may affect one another by virtue of sharing a common environment, in which case each unit is likely to affect the environment within which other units must act. This would mean that interdependence is symbiotic or ecological, not symbolic or socially constructed. In addition, socially constructed forms of interdependence may involve cooperation, conflict, or varying mixtures of these patterns.

Functional Interdependence versus Functional Autonomy

Beyond the minimal level of interdependence necessary for considering a collection of units as a system, there is a wide range of degrees of interdependence. At one extreme, the interrelations between the units making up the system may be very loose, with the actions of each having only minimal effects on the others or on the overall system. At the other extreme, there may be a high level of interdependence, with the actions of each affecting and being affected by the responses of the others in a major way. As an analogy we might consider the differences in degrees of interdependence between participatns in a golf game and a football game. In a golf game each person's performance is relatively independent of the performance of the others involved. In contrast, the performances of the participants in a football game are highly interdependent; each player is successful in performing his role only if the others are successful in performing theirs.

On a broader scale, a relatively low level of interdependence would be exhibited between the various clans of a primitive society that may inhabit the same general territory but seldom interact with one another. In contrast, the various communities and social institutions of modern society are highly interdependent and could hardly survive, at least in their current form, without innumerable complex interrelations with other parts of the overall system.[40] In short, the degree of interdependence may vary for different systems and thus must be empirically investigated.

This idea of interdependence as a variable was analyzed by Alvin W. Gouldner in a paper entitled "Reciprocity and Autonomy in Functional Theory."[41] One of his key ideas is that *interdependence* between the parts of a system and *independence* of parts are inversely related. That is, the higher the level of interdependence, the lower the autonomy or independence of the parts making up the system. For example, an independent business person or a professional in private practice would normally have a greater degree of autonomy than a member of a large-scale bureaucratic organization. Moreover, even within the context of bureaucratic organization, the faculty of a university, for example, would normally have greater autonomy and less interdependence than the members of a combat unit in the military.

Even within the same system the degrees of participants' dependence on the system will vary. Some participants will be highly dependent on the system for fulfilling a wide range of their needs; others will be less dependent on the system and thus will have greater functional autonomy. Participants in a system will also vary in terms of how much their actions affect others in the system. Some will have a major determining influence on the actions of others but are not themselves influenced to the same degree. As Blau emphasized in his exchange theory, the degree of reciprocity between different participants in the system will vary. This point is implicit in the concept of a structure of power or authority. Those who have high levels of power or authority in a system are able to affect the actions of numerous others in the system to a major degree. In contrast, those at lower levels have much less influence on the actions of others, particularly those at the top, or on the system as a whole.

Gouldner suggests that a major interest of the parts of a system is to maintain or enlarge their functional autonomy. This interest in functional autonomy may conflict with the need to fulfill the requirements of the system or the expectations of those in the system who are highly dependent on the system and whose primary interest is system maintenance or promotion of increased interdependence. As Gouldner states: ''It must then be assumed that parts with some degree of functional autonomy will resist full or complete integration into the larger system. Conversely, the system itself, straining toward integration, can be expected to seek submission of the parts to the requirements of the position they occupy. Consequently, there may be some tension between the part's tendency to maintain an existent degree of functional autonomy and the system's pressure to control the part.''[42] The process of ''straining toward integration'' does not occur automatically; it reflects the efforts of those who control the system and benefit from a high level of interdependence to increase their influence over the members of the system.

Gouldner suggests that this tension between the parts and the whole is reflected in the various theories ''which postulate an endemic conflict between the individual and the society or group.''[43] This conflict is no doubt widely experienced in our society, especially in view of the high value that our culture places on individual freedom. Perhaps the most obvious illustrations of the tension between individuals' needs for personal autonomy and system requirements imposed on them is in their occupational roles and their roles as taxpayers. The degree of autonomy in both cases will vary. Some occupations allow greater scope for individual initiative and independence than others, and some wealthy individuals are able to reduce their tax obligations through contributions or investments. Nevertheless, a certain degree of tension or conflict is generally accepted as inevitable for most persons in these particular roles.

Gouldner cites Everett C. Hughes and Erving Goffman in this connection for their observations regarding various techniques for expressing role distance. Hughes had noted the various techniques whereby individuals attempt to maximize their autonomy in their occupational roles. This is reflected in the efforts of working-class persons to avoid surveillance by their supervisors and in the attempts of professionals to have their professional expertise respected by others. Even in the course of actually performing a demanding role, individuals frequently engage in various side actions that demonstrate that their occupational role is not absorbing their entire personality. An example would be the case of the surgeon who flirts or jokes with the nurses while preparations are being made for an operation. Goffman had noted that various deference rituals often help to maintain a certain degree of social distance between persons and to protect individuals' fundamental rights to privacy and a degree of personal independence.

The desire to maintain or promote functional autonomy applies at both the individual level and various other levels of social structure. For example, work groups or departments within a bureaucratic organization will often attempt to maximize their autonomy and independence from other groups or other departments as well as from top level management; branch offices will often try to establish a certain degree of independence from the central office; and local communities may seek to preserve their autonomy in the face of pressures or constraints imposed by the federal government.

Social systems in which the level of interdependence is fairly low and the functional autonomy of parts is high may be considered a *segmental* type of social structure. That is, the social structure consists of a number of more or less independent, self-sufficient segments, any one of which has only minimal effects on the others or on the overall system. This is the type of social structure identified by Durkheim as based on mechanical solidarity. Recall that societies based primarily on mechanical solidarity have a minimally developed division of labor. As a result, the level of interdependence is low, and any solidarity that exists must be based on a strong "collective conscience," or high similarity in basic beliefs and values. In the absence of a strong "collective conscience," the social structure would have to be considered a fragmented structure with only minimal development as a system.

Although Durkheim's model of mechanical solidarity was based on his analysis of primitive societies, the concept of segmental structures also can be applied to other, more complex societies. For example, small, independent businesses (beauty shops or television repair shops) or local government units would be more segmented from one another than large-scale national corporations or the federal government. To be sure, in a complex society such as ours these segmental structures may be overshadowed or dominated by large-scale organizations with high levels of interdependence. Also, as the segmental structures adapt to the large-scale structures, various patterns of interdependence may emerge between them. Overall, the structure of an urban-industrial society should be considered a highly interdependent type of structure rather than a segmental type. Nevertheless, the various parts of segmented structures in a complex society are less likely to have a major impact on one another than if they were parts of some larger, overarching system.

An implicit assumption that underlies much functional analysis is that equilibrium and interdependence are always related in the same way to one another and are therefore virtually synonymous. However, equilibrium and interdependence are analytically distinct and may vary independently. If a system is highly segmented it is possible for equilibrium to be maintained with only minimal levels of interaction and integration. This is because of the high level of functional autonomy of parts. The actions of each part have only minimal effects on the other parts. In contrast, if a system is highly interdependent, the maintenance of equilibrium would require a much higher level of interaction and coordination between parts. In this type of system excessive functional autonomy of parts could be disruptive to the integration of the overall system.

Morphogenic and morphostatic processes are affected by the degree of segmentation or interdependence of the system. Recall that morphogenesis refers to the processes involved in structural elaboration and change, and that such processes rest on deviation-amplifying feedback cycles. The initial deviance may result from the efforts of one or more parts of the system to increase their functional autonomy or from a disturbance in the system's environment. In either case, the effects of the deviance or disturbance are more likely to spread throughout the system if interdependence is high and segmentation low. In this type of situation, the high interdependence would make the entire system very vulnerable to disturbances in its equilibrium or changes in the actions of its parts. In contrast, if the system were highly segmented, it would be easier for the effects of deviance or other types of disruption to be confined to the part(s) in which they erupt instead of spreading through the system. This suggests that *insulation* between parts, not *interdependence,* may be important as a morphostatic mechanism for maintaining the equilibrium of the entire system.

Gouldner's explanation of the distinction between equilibrium and interdependence is pertinent at this point. He notes:

> One may find, however, a conjunction of low interdependence with high equilibrium where the low interdependence permits a localized absorption of externally induced trauma, thus guarding the remainder of the system elements from ramifying damage. . . .
>
> Conversely, an instance of a conjunction of high interdependence and low equilibrium would seem to be implied in the notion of a "vicious cycle." Here, the very interdependence of elements enables negative feedback cycles to develop with cumulative impairment of the system's equilibrium. From these considerations it seems clear that equilibrium and interdependence may vary independently. . . .[44]

Even within a particular system, different parts will vary in terms of how insulated they are from other parts and, consequently, how much effect they have on other parts. For example, a branch office of a national corporation in a remote location would presumably have less effect on the corporation than a key department or division within headquarters. The parts of the system that are most dependent on high integration would normally be the most concerned with maintaining equilibrium and insuring that the parts perform their roles within the system without deviation. In contrast, the parts of the system that have the highest degree of functional autonomy would presumably be less concerned with the equilibrium of the overall system and therefore would be more likely to generate internal tension by resisting system controls.

As Gouldner explains:

> It would seem reasonable to suppose that those parts in a social system with most functional autonomy can more readily become loci of organized defiance and of effective resistance to system controls.
>
> .... [I]t would also seem consistent to maintain that not all have an equally deep involvement in the resolution of the tensions of the system, or in the mobilization of defenses against these. That is, those parts with least functional autonomy, those which cannot survive separation from a social system, are more likely to be implicated in its conservation than those which can.[45]

Gouldner's discussion of the inherent tension between functional autonomy of parts and system interdependence is consistent with Buckley's argument that generation of deviance is a process intrinsic to sociocultural systems.[46] This argument was developed in opposition to the functionalist assumption that deviance is an abnormal disruption that undermines the solidarity and integration of a "normally" functioning system in equilibrium. Instead, Buckley contends, deviance grows out of processes that are inherent in the system itself.

The irony of this is that mechanisms established to control deviance may actually be counterproductive in that they stimulate an increase in deviance. The reason is that social control efforts may contribute to the emergence of a deviation-amplifying feedback cycle as discussed earlier. Briefly, the effort to control deviance frequently leads to isolation and differential treatment of the deviant. This, in turn, increases the alienation of the deviant and the motivation to continue or to expand deviant behavior in order to assert autonomy.

Also, deviance may have important effects on the system in terms of stimulating social structural change. At the very least, deviance increases the range of behavioral options from which members of the system may choose. In some cases (but not all), the long-range adaptive capacity of the system may be expanded or enhanced as a result of the social change or increased flexibility stimulated by deviance.

In contrast, if the members of a highly interdependent system are unable or unwilling to tolerate change in established patterns or to engage in innovative action, the resulting rigidity of the system may make it extremely difficult to cope with environmental disruptions or internal tensions. This is consistent with Dahrendorf's and Coser's analyses of conflict; as we saw earlier these theorists underscored the importance of explicit recognition and negotiation of conflicting interests as opposed to suppression of conflict. One result of such recognition and negotiation is that the system may become more responsive to its members' needs and more flexible in coping with various disruptions that erupt. It might be hypothesized that tolerance for a certain amount of deviance may be less disruptive to a system in the long run than efforts to repress all forms of deviance. Such a policy, applied to nondisruptive forms of deviance, could readily be justified in terms of the need for functional autonomy on the part of the members of the system. The range of tolerance that could be justified would vary depending on whether the system is highly segmented or highly interdependent.

In summary, the relationship between interdependence versus segmentation on the one hand and equilibrium and deviance on the other suggests that the dynamics of social systems are more complex and variable than is commonly assumed. Specifically, interdependence and equilibrium must be differentiated as analytically distinct concepts, and they may vary independently. Moreover, pressures for interdependence or integration conflict inevitably with pressures for functional autonomy. Pressures for functional autonomy often give rise to deviant behavior. This suggests that the higher the demands made on the parts of the system, the greater will be the pressures for engaging in deviant behavior unless, of course, these demands are compensated by higher rewards. The balance achieved between the opposing pressures of integration and functional autonomy will be related to the degree of interdependence or segmentation of the system. When deviance does occur in a highly interdependent system, its effects will be more widely felt than in a segmented social structure.

Functional Interdependence, Value and Normative Consensus, and Emotional Solidarity

Interdependence is not the only type of bond between members of a social system. Durkheim treated functional interdependence as one of two alternative bases of social integration. The other basis was a strong collective conscience, or a common commitment to shared values and norms. Durkheim recognized, however, that this latter type of solidarity, involving consensus on shared values and norms, tended to be undermined as the division of labor expanded and the level of heterogeneity increased. In other words, increases in functional interdependence lead to a decline in solidarity based on normative consensus.

The contrast between interdependence of specialized parts and consensus on shared values and norms seems at times to be forgotten by contemporary functional theorists. The implicit assumption seems to be that the integration of a social system requires *both* interdependence between specialized parts *and* normative and/or value consensus. Parsons, for example, treats shared values as the essential foundation of social order, even while analyzing extensively the functional specialization of various social institutions resulting from structural differentiation. However, Parsons recognized that the value system of a highly differentiated society must be abstract and that the behavioral implications of the shared values will vary as their meanings are specified for the different institutional sectors and the various roles that make up the system. Further specification is involved in interpreting the implications of the shared values for the different types of situations that individuals confront in the course of performing their roles.

Durkheim also recognized that the "collective conscience" does not disappear with growth in the division of labor; instead, it becomes more abstract. Nevertheless, interdependence and normative consensus may vary independently, and the relative importance of each of these variables must be investigated empirically for different types of systems. It should not be assumed *a priori* that functional interdependence and normative consensus are synonymous processes or that they are necessarily congruent with one another.

To illustrate, people who participate in an economic market as buyers and sellers may become highly interdependent with one another, but they could conceivably have only a minimal degree of consensus in terms of many basic values. Indeed, in a large-scale market system, participants need not even be aware of the basic values or the specific normative patterns of all those involved in the impersonal market exchange network. Similarly, the members of the different departments of a bureaucratic organization are also likely to be highly interdependent, with each person's role linked in some fashion, directly or indirectly, with those of other participants. Yet the degree of consensus may vary greatly and need not necessarily be crucial for the survival or well-being of the system. Indeed, individuals may participate in the system because of their own self-interest (just as they do in the market system), or they may be coerced into participating even though they disagree with the basic values of those who set policy in the organization.

In rebuttal one could argue that an orderly or well-integrated market system or bureaucratic organization must nevertheless rest on the general values and norms that are relevant for regulating or controlling the specific system in question. Participants in the market system are expected to abide by norms such as those involving honesty, fairness in exchange or competition, and compliance with contracts. In a complex society such as ours, numerous laws and regulations explicitly govern many aspects of the market exchange process. Similarly, in a bureaucratic organization it is expected that the behavior of members will be guided by the rules of the organization, that they will contribute in various ways toward the maintenance of the organization, that they will cooperate with one another when appropriate, and so on. At many points in his model, Parsons deals precisely with broad regulatory norms or highly abstract values.

However, consensus on basic values and norms is a matter of degree. Even if high consensus is lacking, it is still possible for a system to be highly integrated on the basis of interdependence among its various parts. Conversely, interdependence may be relatively low, but members of a system may still be highly integrated on the basis of strong commitment to shared values. High consensus on basic values would be more crucial for a religious organization, for example, than for a market system.

Even religious organizations, however, may exhibit considerable variety in the extent to which members are expected to exhibit ideological or normative unanimity. Some religious groups may take considerable pride in their tolerance for differences of opinion, in which case this very freedom for individuals to make up their own minds could be considered the group's shared value.

The relative importance of consensus on values and norms may depend partly on the members' own definitions of what is important as the basic source of their solidarity. If the members themselves feel bound together primarily by shared values and norms, the appearance of even minor disagreements is likely to be perceived as a threat to the group's solidarity. But if consensus on values and norms is not seen by the members as important, a certain degree of dissension need not undermine the integration of the system.

It might be argued that consensus on values and norms is much more crucial for personal relationships, such as those within families or among friends, than in systems in which social relations are more impersonal. Certainly individuals who share the same values and norms might be expected to be attracted to one another on this basis, and the support and reinforcement they provide for one another's values and norms may be an important element in strengthening or maintaining the relationship.

However, it is also true that even close friends may "agree to disagree" on certain basic values and norms, and the maintenance of their relationship may be based more on avoiding controversial topics than on providing ideological support to one another. This is widely recognized in everyday life in the reluctance of many persons to discuss politics or religion with certain friends or acquaintances. In this type of situation there must be some basis for solidarity other than ideological consensus. Naturally, there may be large areas of agreement as well as disagreement. But in addition to ideological consensus, there may be bonds based on emotional attraction growing out of shared experiences or compatible personality patterns.

Solidarity based on emotional attachment is another variable not always clearly differentiated from consensus or interdependence as a basis for social integration. Contemporary functional theorists, including Parsons, seem to accept implicitly Durkheim's emphasis on the crucial importance of the emotional bonds that link individuals to one another and to the group. Although solidarity was explained by Durkheim in terms of shared religious beliefs and moral values, the cognitive dimension is almost overshadowed by the emotional dimension. It is not just the intellectual sharing of beliefs and values but the shared emotional experience generated by religious rituals that Durkheim emphasized as crucial.

This emotional bond is not limited to the micro level of interpersonal attachment. Individuals may also experience a strong emotional attachment to various groups or larger systems (such as a nation), and this bond may persist despite serious disagreements regarding basic values and norms. For example, individuals may feel an emotional loyalty or love for their country even while disagreeing with major policies of the current political leaders or with certain widespread values and norms held by other members of the system. In short, just as consensus must be differentiated from interdependence as a basis for social integration, so also must emotional attachment be differentiated from consensus. Functional interdependence, ideological or normative consensus, and emotional attachment are conceptually distinct variables, and each may vary independently of the others.

The strategy of attempting to disentangle the various concepts implicit in the general notion of social integration so that these concepts can be treated as independent variables is strongly recommended by Percy Cohen.[47] Although Cohen is not a proponent of contemporary systems theory in the same sense as Buckley, his critique of functionalism readily lends itself to a systems approach that emphasizes the highly variable nature of the relationships between the different components of the system. Specifically, Cohen suggests that the general question of what holds society together actually includes a number of distinct questions, each focusing on a different aspect of social integration or social system maintenance.

These questions are as follows, along with the distinctive focus of each.[48]

1. "Why do members of social groups and systems continue to participate in them?" This question deals with the problem of *participation*.

2. "Why do the sections or segments of a social unit, or collectivity hold together," as opposed to splitting apart into different segments? This is the problem of *cohesion*.

3. "Why do members of a social group, quasi-group or collectivity continue to recognize themselves as an entity, distinct from other such entities, and why are they prepared, under some conditions, to act as an entity?" This is the problem of *solidarity*.

4. "Why do the participants in a social system or sub-system of a society adhere to or conform to its norms? These are the problems of *compliance, commitment, conformity,* and *consensus.*"

5. Why do individuals' actions "continue to complement, reciprocate, support or correspond to one another? This is the problem of *mutuality*. A subsidary problem in this category is that of *cooperation.*"

6. "How is it that different sets of activities which occur within a society or sub-system of a society do not obstruct one another, and may even lend support to one another? And how do the different sets of beliefs, symbols, values and sentiments coexist? This may be called the problem of *functional interdependence* or, as it is sometimes called, the problem of *system integration.*"

7. Why does the structural form of a social system exhibit high stability over time? This "final problem is that of social *persistence.*"

Although Cohen makes more distinctions in these questions than we have discussed in detail, the basic import of his approach is that the linkages between the individuals or other types of units in a system are highly variable and may vary independently of one another. To be sure, many of the dimensions listed may be positively correlated in numerous cases. For example, participation, cohesion, commitment, and solidarity may be expected to be highly correlated in many types of systems. However, there is no need to make an *a priori* assumption that the answers to most of these questions are necessarily affirmative. Even a superficial examination of the history of any society or of the contemporary social scene reveals that social systems sometimes fail to insure adequate participation, cohesion, solidarity, conformity, and functional integration. The result presumably would be decline of the system or even its disappearance as a recognizable entity. Total societies are more likely to persist as recognizable entities despite extensive structural change than small voluntary organizations, for example. Nevertheless, the extent to which the previously mentioned problems are dealt with satisfactorily in any particular system is a matter for empirical investigation.

Many of the specific concepts pinpointed by Cohen can be related to our earlier discussion. For example, Cohen's fourth question, which deals with normative conformity, can be related to the contrast among exchange theory, functionalism, and conflict theory. To reiterate, exchange theorists emphasize individuals' *interests* in securing the rewards that result from normative conformity; functionalists stress the importance of individuals' *moral commitments* as a basis for their conformity; and conflict theorists underscore the importance of various forms of direct or indirect *coercion* exerted by those in power. Indeed, mere *compliance* with normative patterns need not necessarily imply moral *commitment* to these patterns and, in a pluralistic society, neither compliance nor commitment necessarily imply a high level of normative or value *consensus* among different segments of society.

Cohen's seventh question, that dealing with social stability or persistence, can be examined in the context of our previous discussion of morphogenic versus morphostatic processes in social systems. Briefly, the assumption that social systems tend to persist is unwarranted without empirical investigation. As emphasized by Buckley, the evidence is just as strong that social systems tend to undergo continual structural change instead of maintaining a particular structural form. It should also be emphasized that this particular question is analytically distinct from the other questions. Persistence of structural forms or structural change can also be explained in terms of self-interests, moral commitments, or coercion.

The questions regarding solidarity, consensus, and functional interdependence (questions three, four, and six, respectively) were also discussed earlier. Following Durkheim, we noted that normative consensus and functional interdependence can be seen as alternative bases for social integration and that the social dynamics implied by these processes may be somewhat incompatible. Moreover, both concepts were differentiated from emotional solidarity as a basis for social cohesion.

In spite of the wide variation in the nature or the strength of the bonds between the members of a social system, Buckley emphasizes one ingredient as essential for any type of social organization or social system. This ingredient is the sharing of a common set of relevant information.[49]

This idea of information linkage is not synonymous with the functionalist emphasis on value or normative consensus. The sharing of information relevant to individuals' interactions with one another or to their involvement in some social system does not necessarily imply that these individuals agree regarding basic values and norms or that they share the same (or any) moral commitments. In some relationships the knowledge or information that interaction partners may share is that they have some basic ideological disagreements. This information may be taken into account by both partners in a conscious effort not to undermine the relationship by introducing controversial topics.

Another example is the case of individuals who conflict or compete with one another and who take one another into account in planning their strategies. In such a situation the relationship may be characterized more by dissension than by consensus; nevertheless, each party may attempt to gain as much information as possible regarding the resources or intentions of the other(s) in order to adjust accordingly.

Essentially, the idea of informational linkages means that individuals' subjective definitions of the situation must be congruent to a degree. Each member of a system will have distinctive definitions and interpretations of the situation. However, to the extent that individuals' actions become organized in some type of social system, these definitions and interpretations will become at least minimally congruent. In everyday life we recognize this process at the micro level when we gradually get to know other persons with whom we are involved better over time. This occurs regardless of whether the relationship is characterized by consensus or dissension, cooperation or conflict.

In short, the material and social environment is gradually mapped through various learning processes in individuals' subjective consciousness. A social system can be considered as being based on the sharing of congruent cognitive maps. The degree of congruence or overlap between the cognitive maps of different persons in a system varies and must be subject to empirical investigation. In everyday life we recognize that we are more familiar with some persons or some organizations than others, and we can usually adapt more effectively as a result.

The crucial element in individuals' shared cognitive maps is their definition of the social structure in which they are involved. Organized social life rests on individuals' subjectively shared definitions of the nature of their relations with one another and of the various roles through which they interact. These subjective images emerge through various forms of interaction and negotiation and are likely to change continually as the interaction process unfolds.

There may be many social consequences of individuals' actions and interactions that they do not anticipate or of which they are not consciously aware. Indeed, many of the distinguishing characteristics of social systems may not be consciously intended or anticipated by their participants. But, in spite of the fact that the relevant information may be incomplete, inadequate, or unevenly distributed among the members of the system, at least a minimal sharing of common information or common definitions of social reality is essential for members of a social system to be able to interact with one another. Since a social system consists of recurrent interaction patterns, the emergence or maintenance of a social system rests on shared information or definitions of social reality.

In view of the fact that individuals' actions or interactions always take place in a material or physical environment, there must also be some congruence in individuals' cognitive maps of this environment as well as the social environment. This is essential for the development of organized social responses to various aspects of the material environment. To a large degree, the growth of the adaptive capacity of society (essentially through technology) is made possible by increased knowledge about the material environment.

The various natural sciences can be seen as a complex set of social activities designed explicitly to enlarge and organize our knowledge of the material environment on a systematic rather than *ad hoc* basis. By improving the cognitive mapping of the environment that is incorporated into the shared subjective consciousness, individuals are better able to predict and control environmental processes in such a way that their needs can be met more fully. In effect, increased knowledge of the environment means that individuals' responses to their environment can be intelligently selected or constructed to enable them to accomplish their various goals instead of being left to chance. Again, this is not to deny that there may be many unforeseen and unintended consequences of individuals' actions on the physical environment and the social structure.

Buckley's emphasis on information linkages between the members of a social system and on the importance of shared cognitive definitions of the situation draws heavily on the symbolic interactionist perspective. This is most clearly revealed in his treatment of society as an "organization of meanings."[50] This emphasis is also consistent with the phenomenological focus on subjective consciousness, particularly intersubjective (or shared) consciousness.[51]

Indeed, phenomenologists almost exclusively stress the subjective consciousness shared by individuals in interaction instead of concerning themselves with the external or objective world that exists independently of individuals' perceptions and subjective experiences. In contrast, Buckley does not limit himself to the subjective level; he attempts to draw attention to the processes whereby the objective or external world (both material and social) is incorporated into, or mirrored by, individuals' subjective consciousness. Nevertheless, Buckley's development of the idea that social structures and social reality in the broadest sense are constructed through symbolic communication and the idea that this reality is represented within individuals' shared subjective consciousness are consistent with both symbolic interactionism and phenomenologically oriented perspectives.

Authority versus Power as Alternative Bases for Normative Conformity and Interdependence

Unlike many symbolic interaction theorists, Buckley's emphasis is not confined to the micro level of interpersonal interaction. He also deals with the complex organization of actions and interaction patterns into roles and large-scale institutional patterns. His emphasis on the tendency of sociocultural systems to undergo structural elaboration resulting in increased complexity as well as increased adaptive capacity is pertinent in this connection because it demonstrates his concern with macro-level analysis.

In addition, the opposing macro-structural implications of functionalism and conflict theory can readily be analyzed in terms of Buckley's discussion of the contrast between power and authority as alternative strategies for controlling or regulating the behavior of members of a social system.[52] Both strategies may be institutionalized in that both may have significant continuing effects in determining the structure of the system and the actions of many of its participants. However, only authority structures can be considered as *legitimate* in that they rest on knowledgeable consensus of their participants and are directed toward the accomplishment of shared group goals.

Buckley underscores the point that institutionalization and legitimacy reflect two different processes. Structures of power that do not rest on the informed consent of their participants should not be considered as legitimate in the full sense of that term, even though they may be institutionalized and supported in the official rules or legal codes. As Buckley explains: "What is suggested . . . , then, is that 'institutionalized power' may be 'legalized,' but 'institutionalized authority' alone is 'legitimized.' And, clearly, 'legalized' and 'legitimized' are, social psychologically, worlds apart."[53] Moreover, "Power . . . does not become sanctioned, legitimized, consensual authority simply by being clothed in institutional forms."[54]

Buckley contends that the distinction between power and authority has not always been clearly maintained in sociological analysis. He treats these two concepts as being at the opposing ends of a continuum. Power is defined as "control or influence over the actions of others to promote one's goals without their consent, against their 'will,' or without their knowledge or understanding (for example, by control of the physical, psychological, or sociocultural environment within which others must act). The mechanisms involved may range from naked force, through manipulation of symbols, information, and other environmental conditions, to the dispensing of conditional rewards."[55]

In contrast, "*Authority* is the direction or control of the behavior of others for the promotion of collective goals, based on some ascertainable form of their knowledgeable consent. Authority thus implies informed, voluntary compliance, which is a definite psychological state, and a coordination or identity of the goal-orientations of controllers and controlled.''[56] If we use Cohen's terminology, we might say that the exercise of authority is associated with subjective *commitment,* while the exercise of power is associated merely with overt *compliance.* Also, one implication of this contrast between power and authority is that power structures involve an uneven distribution of appropriate information, while authority structures involve a higher level of sharing of relevant information.

Although power and authority are defined as being at opposite ends of a continuum, there may be varying mixtures of these forms of institutionalized control or regulation. Individuals in dominant positions in major social institutions may have both power and authority in varying degrees. This would imply that their strategies of domination may be oriented partly toward their own goals and partly toward goals shared by the group or society. The specific priority ranking of individual versus group goals would vary for different persons in positions of dominance in different systems. Leaders of democratic systems cannot ignore completely the needs or goals of their followers, at least in the long run. At the same time, these leaders are also likely to be concerned with their own particular goals as leaders, such as maintaining their leadership positions.

Since the psychological orientations of subordinates are crucial in distinguishing between power and authority, it is possible for a particular structure to be a power structure to some subordinates and an authority structure to others. In other words, some may recognize its legitimacy, while others may not. This is consistent with Blau's distinction between legitimating values and opposition values, discussed in Chapter 9. Both types of values may coexist in a particular structure.

The dynamics of the social processes associated with structures of power differ significantly from those associated with structures of authority. Authority structures reflect the emergence and institutionalization of social relations that are primarily cooperative. Cooperative relations may be elaborated into complex structures that involve constantly increasing numbers of persons and eventually require some form of centralized control and coordination. The key feature of such relationships, whether small and simple or large and complex, is that the goals of the various participants are congruent and mutually compatible. This means that achievement of the goals of each participant is linked with, or perhaps facilitates, the achievement of the goals of the others. In an extreme case, the success of all the participants in achieving their goals would depend on the success of each one; this would mean that no one participant could benefit at the expense of the others. This type of situation would naturally give rise to a high level of consensus and cooperation, with individuals' goals merged into a collective group goal. In contrast, structures of power are more likely to involve competitive or conflictual social relations. This occurs because the success of any one individual will undermine the chances for success of the others. Such situations are extremely common because of the scarcity of the various resources needed for individual goal achievement. Obviously, if individuals' social relations are primarily competitive or conflictual, shared group goals are less likely to emerge. Thus, if a structure of control emerges it will not reflect group consensus but differential control of various resources that can be used to establish power over others.

The institutionalization of power structures (as opposed to authority structures) is inherently precarious and potentially unstable. Since power structures do not rest on a consensual foundation of shared goals, they are vulnerable to resistance or insubordination from subordinates. This does not mean that subordinates are necessarily always involved in active opposition to the power structure. There may be lengthy periods of relative stability during which subordinates are acquiescent and comply passively and perhaps apathetically with demands made on them that they perceive cannot be resisted successfully.

Whether or not subordinates are involved in active opposition to the established power structure, their efforts to pursue their own particular goals are often expressed in various forms of deviance or collective behavior.[57] By definition, collective behavior takes place outside of, or perhaps in overt or covert opposition to, established institutional structures. If the institutionalized structure is designed primarily to protect or promote the goals and interests of those in power, collective or noninstitutionalized forms of behavior may be the only option available for subordinates to pursue their own goals and interests.

Collective behavior may take a variety of forms, from deviant actions such as criminal behavior to the development of organized protest movements oriented toward bringing about change in the power structure. The changes sought may also vary, ranging from mild reforms designed to gain increased benefits of various kinds from those in power to revolutionary protest movements intended to overthrow the established power structure and replace it with a radically different structure. Those in power may respond to protest movements by making concessions to the demands made, in which case their power is likely to be bolstered by becoming legitimated to a degree. Or they may respond by refusing to negotiate in an effort to maintain their own power and privileges. In this case, the demands for change may build up to the point where revolutionary overthrow becomes not only feasible but perhaps inevitable. In either case, collective behavior provides a continual source of innovation and change in social systems, thereby illustrating again Buckley's contention that sociocultural systems are characterized by continual flux and change.

Buckley's discussion of the contrast between authority and power draws on and elaborates Weber's analysis of authority. It will be recalled that Weber had distinguished among traditional, charismatic, and rational-legal authority. Buckley accepts this distinction and suggests that the same three types might also be applied to power structures.[58] That is, established traditions, charismatic personality characteristics, or rational-legal norms may be used by those in dominant positions to pursue their own particular goals in opposition to, or disregard of, the goals and interests of their subordinants.

Buckley's analysis of the dynamics of *power* structures corresponds reasonably well with the basic principles of the conflict model of society; similarly, his analysis of the dynamics of *authority* structures corresponds to the basic image of social reality developed in functional theory. Overall, Buckley's treatment of these two contrasting systems of control is balanced; he does not insist that one is clearly dominant in most systems and the other is of only secondary or minor importance. Instead, he suggests that societies include varying mixtures of power and authority.

The following quotation provides a clue as to Buckley's own judgment regarding the relative priority of power versus authority and, by implication, his preference for a conflict model or a functional model. ''Historically, most societies have been heavily skewed in favor of the power pole, and most of history—especially modern history—can be seen as a struggle toward the authority pole, that is, toward the institutionalization of a process of informed, consensual self-determination of the whole, which we call 'democracy.' ''[59]

This view of the basic democratic trend of modern society is comparable to Parsons'; however, Buckley's explicit recognition of the key importance of power (as opposed to authority) is in marked contrast to Parsons' overall emphasis. Buckley's judgment regarding the basic trend of modern society contrasts with Lenski's perspective.[60] Lenski had suggested that the functional model is perhaps more appropriate than the conflict model for analyzing simple, small-scale societies with minimal structural differentiation and high consensus on basic beliefs and values; in contrast, he suggested, the conflict model may perhaps be more appropriate for complex, large-scale societies with extensive structural differentiation and low consensus on basic beliefs and values. This basic discrepancy suggests the need for avoiding hasty judgments and recognizing explicitly that social systems may exhibit a wide variety of structural forms and may even incorporate opposing or contradictory principles.

Summary

The general systems perspective is relevant for the macro level of large-scale institutional processes and the micro level of interpersonal negotiation of shared meanings. Moreover, the general image of social reality suggested by systems theory is broad enough and open enough to incorporate the opposing models of functional theory and conflict theory and the basic implications of exchange theory and symbolic interactionism. The contrasting explanations of behavior provided by the sociobiological model can also be incorporated.

The basic image of social reality implied by systems theory as developed in this chapter is that it consists of different types of components (environmental, biological, behavioral, subjective, etc.) that are related to one another either directly or indirectly, so that if one element undergoes change the others are also likely to change to some degree. This set of mutually interrelated elements exists in an environment (both material and social), and the survival or maintenance of the system depends on various interchanges with the environment. These environmental exchanges take place across the boundaries of the system. However, the boundaries are not static and, as the system develops or expands, various parts of the environment may be incorporated into the system. In general, Buckley's version of systems theory as applied to the sociocultural realm stresses the inherent capacity for continual improvement in the strategies whereby systems adapt to their environment.

Obviously, the basic imagery of social reality implied by systems theory is general enough that systems theory can serve readily as a broad, comprehensive framework for an eclectic approach to theory development. In Buckley's version this eclectic approach is facilitated because Buckley draws extensively on various sociological perspectives. Specifically, he made use of concepts and principles from symbolic interactionism, exchange theory, functionalism, and conflict theory, among others, most of which were discussed in previous chapters.

Perhaps a key feature of systems theory that makes it so broad and versatile is that the nature and strength of the relationship between the various components of the system are not specified in advance. Instead, there is explicit recognition that the bonds that link the components of the system may vary widely in different systems and undergo continual change within any particular system. As a result, there is wide variation in the social structural forms of different systems.

This does not mean that there are absolutely no stable reference points in the analysis of social systems. Certainly the basic biological characteristics of human beings suggest certain fundamental requirements that must be satisfied in any type of social system, including the needs for nutrition, shelter, sexual expression, and infant care. It would be difficult to imagine a society surviving that did not insure at least minimal satisfaction of these needs. Beyond this, some of the recent work in sociobiology suggests that much human social behavior may have a biological foundation or reflect the influence of genetic factors.

Nevertheless, the absence of specific biological or genetic programming of behavior means that human beings must construct their actions on the basis of learning experiences acquired in the course of adapting to their material and social environment. Since human beings cannot survive in isolation from other human beings (at least on a wide scale), a communication system must be established. This involves the human ability to create and manipulate shared symbols. But even though such basic requirements for survival can be identified, the social structures through which they are met may vary widely.

In comparison to this explicit recognition of the wide variation possible in social structural forms, all of the theories discussed earlier seem limited in terms of the basic, underlying image of social reality that they imply. Specifically, symbolic interaction theory emphasizes interdependence based on symbolic communication at the micro level. The dynamics of macro structures that go beyond individuals' negotiated intentions are neglected, along with symbiotic types of relations. Exchange theory stresses interdependence based on individuals' self-interests, particularly at the micro level. Shared values or coercive control may be relevant, especially in institutionalized macro structures, but the basic image of social reality implied by exchange theory underscores individuals' self-interests. Functionalism and conflict theory, contrasted in connection with the distinction between authority and power, deal with the macro level, but both are one-sided in terms of their primary focus. Functional theory implies that interdependence involves cooperation based on shared moral values, while conflict theory stresses that interdependence reflects coercion or the threat of coercion or control of scarce resources. These different theories may be seen as relevant for particular types of social structures based on particular types of social bonds but, as such, they are not appropriate as *general* models for dealing with the full range of sociocultural reality in the broadest sense of that term.

The history of science in many areas demonstrates that scientific advance sometimes involves the creation of more elaborate or more comprehensive theoretical perspectives or paradigms within which earlier opposing theories can be incorporated as particular or limited types of cases. If general systems theory should prove in the future to be relevant and fruitful in enabling us to expand our knowledge of sociocultural reality and organize it better, this would be consistent with this pattern of scientific advance.

As Kuhn has suggested in his model of scientific development, improvement in scientific paradigms or basic perspectives results when the established paradigm proves unable to account for or explain anomalies or incompatible data.[61] As anomalies (or exceptions to the prevailing paradigm) accumulate, the inadequacy of the prevailing paradigm becomes more and more apparent, ultimately stimulating the development of a new, more comprehensive paradigm that can incorporate both the preceding theoretical model and the increasingly discrepant empirical anomalies.

As we saw in Chapter 2, sociology at its present stage of development can be considered a multiparadigm science.[62] A major reason for this is that the basic images of social reality implied by each of the prevailing paradigms are clearly inadequate to account for more than a limited range of sociocultural reality. Even our everyday life experiences suggest that social life is considerably more complex than implied by the various theoretical perspectives reviewed in earlier chapters. In other words, anomalies to each of the prevailing paradigms are so abundant that they simply cannot be ignored.

In view of the inadequacies of theoretical approaches that are limited to the micro level (as symbolic interactionism and exchange theory tend to be), to processes of harmonious cooperation based on consensus (as in functionalism), or to processes of coercion and conflict (as in conflict theory), it would seem that general systems theory could hold considerable promise for the future of sociological theory. An adequate theory must be able to deal with the complex linkages between the micro level of interpersonal interaction and the macro level of complex institutional patterns. An adequate theory must also allow for input from the biological and genetic levels in attempting to explain people's social behavior and institutional and cultural patterns. It must also incorporate the fact that social relations involve both cooperation and conflict, consensus and dissension, commitment to moral values and pursuit of individualistic interests, and social control based on legitimate authority and control based on coercive power. Finally, an adequate theory must recognize that social systems may exhibit high levels of stability or rapid change, extensive or minimal degrees of interdependence, high or low levels of individual autonomy, and so on. Systems theory seems to offer an image of social reality that is sufficiently comprehensive and flexible to meet this requirement and to provide a framework within which these variations can be investigated empirically. As such, systems theory helps us to recognize the variability and complexity of the sociocultural world.

Acknowledgement of the variety that we encounter in the sociocultural world provides us with a basis for affirming the reality of human freedom. Although we are all conditioned and constrained by the nature of the sociocultural world into which we have been born and socialized, we are the ones who create and sustain that world. We do have choices.

Footnotes

1. On the development of a world economic system see Immanuel Maurice Wallerstein, *The Modern World System; Capitalist Agriculture and the Origins of the European World Economy in the Sixteenth Century* (New York: Academic Press, 1974).
2. This image of complex organizations as open systems was developed in Katz and Kahn's theoretical perspective on organizations. See Daniel Katz and Robert L. Kahn, *The Social Psychology of Organizations* (New York: Wiley, 1966).
3. The idea that the family constitutes a complex system is increasingly recognized by sociologists of the family and family therapists today. See, for example, Jerry M. Lewis, W. Robert Beavers, John T. Gossett, and Virginia Austin Phillips, *No Single Thread: Psychological Health in Family Systems* (New York: Brunner/Mazel, 1976).
4. See Amatai Etzioni, *A Comparative Analysis of Complex Organizations,* revised and enlarged edition (New York: Free Press, 1975). Etzioni's concept of compliance relationships includes the type of power used to control the behavior of subordinates and the type of orientation of subordinates to the exercise of this control. Briefly, the types of power include coercive power, instrumental power, and normative power. The orientations of subordinates may be strongly negative (alienative), strongly positive (moral), or mildly negative or positive (utilitarian). Coercive power would be the primary type implied by conflict theory; instrumental power (i.e., the power to control rewards and punishments) is the primary type involved in exchange theory, and normative power (i.e., the power to control symbols of moral commitment or emotional attachment) is the primary type implied by functional theory.
5. See Walter Buckley, *Sociology and Modern Systems Theory* (Englewood Cliffs, N.J.: Prentice-Hall, 1967). Buckley's presentation moves from the micro level of individuals' actions and interaction patterns to the macro level of large-scale organizations such as bureaucracies and complex institutional patterns.
6. Ludwig von Bertalanffy, "General System Theory," reprinted in N. J. Demerath III and Richard A. Peterson, eds., *System, Change and Conflict* (New York: Free Press, 1967), pp. 115–129. See also Ludwig von Bertalanffy, *General System Theory: Foundations, Development, Applications* (New York: George Braziller, 1968).
7. von Bertalanffy, "General System Theory," Demerath and Peterson, op. cit., pp. 115–116.
8. Buckley, op. cit., pp. 7–23. Much of the discussion in this chapter will rely heavily on the presentation in Buckley's book.
9. Spencer had also emphasized the crucial differences between biological organisms and social systems. See Robert L. Carneiro, ed., *Herbert Spencer: The Evolution of Society* (Chicago: University of Chicago Press, 1967), "Editor's Introduction," pp. xl–xli. See also Chapter 2, "A Society Is an Organism," p. 7. Here a specific distinction is made

between the "individual organism" and the "social organism" in that the units composing the latter are free from one another and dispersed, not bound together in close contact. Unfortunately, not all of those who followed Spencer in using an organic model were as cautious as him in this regard.

10. Walter Buckley, *Sociology and Modern Systems Theory*, copyright © 1967. Reprinted by permission of Prentice-Hall, Inc., Englewood Cliffs, New Jersey, pp. 14–15.

11. Walter Buckley, *Sociology and Modern Systems Theory*, copyright © 1967. Reprinted by permission of Prentice-Hall, Inc., Englewood Cliffs, New Jersey, p. 18.

12. Ibid., p. 40.

13. Ibid., pp. 94–100.

14. One of the principle representatives of the social Darwinist point of view was William Graham Sumner. His best-known work, *Folkways* (Boston: Ginn, 1906), suggests an evolutionary approach to the development of social customs. See William Graham Sumner, *Essays of William Graham Sumner*, 2 vols., edited by Albert G. Keller and Maurice R. Davie (New Haven, Conn.: Yale University Press, 1934). For an overview of the influence of social Darwinism in America, see Richard Hofstadter, *Social Darwinism in American Thought* (Philadelphia: University of Pennsylvania Press, 1944).

15. Hofstadter, op. cit., Chapter IV, "Lester Ward-Critic," pp. 52–67.

16. For some examples, see Francis Galton, *Hereditary Genius: An Inquiry into Its Laws and Consequences* (London: Macmillan, 1869); Karl Pearson, *The Scope and Importance to the State of the Science of National Eugenics* (London: Dulau, 1909); and Lothrop Stoddard, *The Revolt Against Civilization* (New York: Scribner's, 1922).

17. Some examples of works that represent this approach include: Robert Ardrey, *African Genesis* (New York: Atheneum, 1960); Robert Ardrey, *The Territorial Imperative* (New York: Atheneum, 1966); David P. Barash, *Sociobiology and Behavior* (New York: Elsevier, 1977); Konrad Z. Lorenz, *On Aggression* (New York: Harcourt, Brace and World, 1966); Lionel Tiger, *Men in Groups* (New York: Random House, 1969); Lionel Tiger and Robin Fox, *The Imperial Animal* (New York: Holt, Rinehart & Winston, 1971); Edward O. Wilson, *Sociobiology, The New Synthesis* (Cambridge, Mass.: Harvard University Press, 1975); and Edward O. Wilson, *On Human Nature* (Cambridge, Mass.: Harvard University Press, 1978). For an example of an introductory sociology text based solidly on explicit recognition of the biological foundations of human behavior, see Pierre L. van den Berghe, *Man in Society: A Biological View*, 2nd edition (New York: Elsevier, 1978).

18. See Melford E. Spiro, *Kibbutz, Venture in Utopia* (Cambridge, Mass.: Harvard University Press, 1956), and *Children of the Kibbutz* (Cambridge, Mass.: Harvard University Press, 1958).

19. This is one of the major arguments developed by Richard Dawkins, *The Selfish Gene* (New York: Oxford University Press, 1956).

20. See, for example, Louis Schneider, *The Sociological Way of Looking at the World* (New York: McGraw-Hill, 1975), pp. 62–69.

21. Adapted from Buckley, op. cit., p. 173.

22. Walter Buckley, *Sociology and Modern Systems Theory*, copyright © 1967. Reprinted by permission of Prentice-Hall, Inc., Englewood Cliffs, New Jersey, p. 174.

23. The criticism of functional explanations offered by George C. Homans (discussed in Chapter 9), is relevant in this connection. Homans' argument was that causal expla-

nations must refer to the motives of human beings instead of to the alleged consequences of their actions for some system in which they may be involved. See George C. Homans and David M. Schneider, *Marriage, Authority and Final Causes* (Glencoe, Ill.: Free Press, 1955). The literature on the logical pitfalls of functionalism is voluminous. For one example, see Ronald Philip Dore, "Function and Cause," *American Sociological Review,* Vol. 26 (December 1961), pp. 843–853. For a recent summary of the logical criticisms of functionalism and of some oversights of the critics in their characterization of contemporary functionalism, see Jonathan Turner, *The Structure of Sociological Theory,* revised edition (Homewood, Ill.: Dorsey, 1978), pp. 61–68.

24. Recall from Chapter 9 that this type of analysis was employed by Homans in developing his exchange theory perspective.

25. Buckley, op. cit., pp. 58–66.

26. Walter Buckley, *Sociology and Modern Symptoms Theory,* copyright © 1967. Reprinted by permission of Prentice-Hall, Inc., Englewood Cliffs, New Jersey, p. 58.

27. Buckley identifies learning as an example of a morphogenic process. Ibid., pp. 58–59.

28. Walter Buckley, *Sociology and Modern Systems Theory,* copyright © 1967. Reprinted by permission of Prentice-Hall, Inc., Englewood Cliffs, New Jersey, p. 58.

29. The concept of latent pattern maintenance that Parsons identified as one of the four basic functional requirements of social systems does not refer to the need to maintain an existing social structural form but to the need to maintain the basic value orientations of the system and the motivational commitments of its participants. Even this idea can still be criticized on the grounds that values themselves may change. However, the distinction between maintenance of a particular value system and maintenance of a particular structural form is important to remember.

30. See Margoroh Maruyama, "The Second Cybernetics: Deviation-Amplifying Mutual Causal Processes," *American Scientist,* Vol. 51 (1963), pp. 164–179.

31. Buckley, op. cit., pp. 58–59.

32. Maruyama, op. cit., p. 164.

33. This explanation of how deviant subcultures emerge is comparable to the theoretical perspective on deviance developed by Leslie T. Wilkins in *Social Deviance* (London: Tavistock, 1964).

34. Buckley, op. cit., pp. 135–136.

35. See Ernest W. Burgess, Harvey J. Locke, and Mary Margaret Thomes, *The Family: From Institution to Companionship* (New York: American Book, 1963). Also, recall that a similar explanation of contemporary family patterns was developed by Parsons and his associates. See Talcott Parsons and Robert F. Bales, in collaboration with James Olds, Morris Zelditch, Jr., and Philip E. Slater, *Family, Socialization and Interaction Process* (New York: Free Press, 1955).

36. This idea that increased differentiation and resulting complexity result in increased needs for control contrasts with Durkheim's analysis of the effects of the division of labor in promoting individualism and with Simmel's analysis of the increased individual freedom that is possible in a society with numerous segmented social relations. It is true that individual freedom is greater in a highly differentiated complex society in the sense that the range of choices left open for the individual is greater. Thus, for example, individuals choose their occupational careers instead of entering the same occupation as their parents. However, once individuals' choices are made, their actions

must then be coordinated with the actions of numerous other individuals as part of a complex and highly interdependent system. The degree to which individuals have options from which to choose would vary greatly for different segments of the population.

37. See Abraham H. Maslow, *Motivation and Personality,* 2nd edition (New York: Harper & Row, 1970).

38. The preceding analysis of the motivations for structural simplification as expressed in countercultural values might be compared with the perspective on modernity developed by Peter Berger and his associates. See Peter Berger, Brigitte Berger, and Hansfried Kellner, *The Homeless Mind* (New York: Random House, 1973). The basic contention of this analysis is that the various psychological strains of modernity can be traced to the high degree of subcultural pluralism in modern society. Subcultural pluralism has the effect of undermining the general world view that provides individuals with ultimate meaning for their lives. In terms of the perspective suggested here, we might note that subcultural pluralism can be considered a consequence of the high level of structural differentiation.

39. For an intensive empirical study of the various relationships between organizational size, degree of differentiation, and "overhead" costs of administration and coordination, see Peter M. Blau and Richard A. Schoenherr, *The Structure of Organizations* (New York: Basic Books, 1970), especially pp. 310–318.

40. For an example of a well-known community study that underscores the linkages between the local community and the wider society, see Arthur J. Vidich and Joseph Bensman, *Small Town in Mass Society* (Garden City, N.Y.: Doubleday, 1960). This discussion of variations in degrees of interdependence can be related to the discussion in Chapter 9 on exchange theory of the difference between generalized exchanges and restricted exchanges. It will be recalled that generalized exchanges involve a series of indirect exchange transactions whereby persons provide benefits to some but receive benefits from others in the exchange network. Thus the level of interdependence between all the exchange partners is high. In contrast, the restricted exchange pattern involves direct exchanges whereby individuals receive benefits directly from those to whom they provide benefits. In this type of system a particular exchange partnership need not have any links with the wider system; thus the level of interdependence between the various segments in the wider system is low.

41. Alvin W. Gouldner, "Reciprocity and Autonomy in Functional Theory," pp. 241–270 in Llewellyn Gross, ed., *Symposium in Sociological Theory* (New York: Harper & Row, 1959). The following discussion draws heavily on Gouldner's paper.

42. Ibid., p. 255.

43. Ibid.

44. Ibid., pp. 253–254.

45. Ibid., p. 258.

46. Buckley, op. cit., Chapter 6, "Social Control: Deviance, Power and Feedback Processes," pp. 163–207. See especially pp. 166–172.

47. Percy S. Cohen, *Modern Social Theory* (New York: Basic Books, 1968), Chapter 6, "Social Structures and Social Systems," pp. 129–166.

48. The following questions are either quoted or paraphrased from ibid., pp. 129–130.

49. Buckley, op. cit., p. 82. The entire section entitled "Organization and Information," pp. 82–94, is highly relevant in this connection.
50. Ibid., p. 92.
51. See, for example, Alfred Shutz, *The Phenomenology of the Social World,* translated by George Walsh and Frederick Lehnert (Evanston, Ill.: Northwestern University Press, 1967).
52. Buckley, op. cit., pp. 176–205. The following discussion draws heavily from Buckley's analysis in these pages.
53. Walter Buckley, *Sociology and Modern Systems Theory,* copyright © 1967. Reprinted by permission of Prentice-Hall, Inc., Englewood Cliffs, New Jersey, p. 197.
54. Walter Buckley, *Sociology and Modern Systems Theory,* copyright © 1967. Reprinted by permission of Prentice-Hall, Inc., Englewood Cliffs, New Jersey, p. 195.
55. Walter Buckley, *Sociology and Modern Systems Theory,* copyright © 1967. Reprinted by permission of Prentice-Hall, Inc., Englewood Cliffs, New Jersey, p. 186.
56. Walter Buckley, *Sociology and Modern Systems Theory,* copyright © 1967. Reprinted by permission of Prentice-Hall, Inc., Englewood Cliffs, New Jersey, p. 186.
57. Ibid., pp. 136–140.
58. Ibid., pp. 191–192ff.
59. Walter Buckley, *Sociology and Modern Systems Theory,* copyright © 1967. Reprinted by permission of Prentice-Hall, Inc., Englewood Cliffs, New Jersey, p. 186.
60. See Gerhard Lenski, *Power and Privilege: A Theory of Social Stratification* (New York: McGraw-Hill, 1966).
61. Thomas S. Kuhn, *The Structure of Scientific Revolutions,* 2nd edition (Chicago: University of Chicago Press, 1970).
62. See George Ritzer, *Sociology: A Multiple Paradigm Science* (Boston: Allyn and Bacon, 1975).

Questions for Study and Discussion

1. Contrast the concept of morphogenesis with equilibrium and homeostasis. Would homeostasis be comparable to morphostatic processes? Would equilibrium be comparable to the process of structural simplification? Can you think of examples of all three of these processes in social life?
2. Contrast the emphasis in systems theory on information linkages between system parts with the functionalist emphasis on shared values and norms.
3. Select some social system with which you are familiar and indicate whether its members are held together primarily by their individual interests, their shared values or moral commitments, or coercion or control of scarce resources. What evidence would you need to support your position?
4. Distinguish between authority structures and power structures and indicate the type of information you would need to determine whether a given system of social control is an authority structure, a power structure, or both.
5. Distinguish between interdependence based on symbolic communication and symbiotic interdependence resulting from the effects of human actions on the environment and cite some examples of both types.

References and Additional Reading

Abel, Theodore, *The Foundation of Sociological Theory*. New York: Random House, 1970.

Abrahamson, Mark, *Functionalism*. Englewood Cliffs, N.J.: Prentice-Hall, 1978.

Adorno, Theodor W., with E. Frenkel-Brunswick, D. T. Levinson, and R. Newitt Sanford, *The Authoritarian Personality*, 2 volumes. New York: Harper & Row, 1950.

Alpert, Harry, *Emile Durkheim and His Sociology*. New York: Columbia University Press, 1939.

American Journal of Sociology, Durkheim-Simmel Commemorative Issue, Vol. 63, May 1958.

Andreski, Stanislav, ed., *The Essential Comte*. New York: Barnes & Noble, 1974.

Ardrey, Robert, *African Genesis*. New York: Atheneum, 1961.

Ardrey, Robert, *The Territorial Imperative*. New York: Atheneum, 1966.

Aristotle, *Organon: Posterior Analytics*, Book 2, Chapter 11, in Richard McKeon, ed., *Basic Works of Aristotle*. New York: Random House, 1941.

Aron, Raymond, *Main Currents in Sociological Thought*, 2 volumes, translated by Richard Howard and Helen Weaver. New York: Basic Books, 1967.

Barash, David P., *Sociobiology and Behavior*. New York: Elsevier, 1967.

Becker, Carl L., *The Heavenly City of the Eighteenth Century Philosophers*. New Haven, Conn.: Yale University Press, 1932.

Becker, Ernest, *The Structure of Evil*. New York: Free Press, 1968.

Becker, Howard, and Harry Elmer Barnes, *Social Thought from Lore to Science*, 2nd edition, 2 volumes. Washington, D.C.: Harren, 1952.

Bell, Daniel, *The Coming of Post-Industrial Society*. New York: Basic Books, 1973.

Bellah, Robert, "Civil Religion in America," pp. 350–369 in Joseph Faulkner, ed., *Religion's Influence in Contemporary Society*. Columbus, Ohio: Charles E. Merrill, 1972.

Bendix, Reinhard, *Max Weber, An Intellectual Portrait*. Garden City, N.Y.: Doubleday, 1960.

Bendix, Reinhard, and Guenther Roth, *Scholarship and Partisanship: Essays on Max Weber*. Berkeley: University of California Press, 1971.

Berger, Peter, *The Sacred Canopy*. Garden City, N.Y.: Doubleday, 1964.

Berger, Peter, Brigitte Berger, and Hansfried Kellner, *The Homeless Mind*. New York: Random House, 1973.

Berger, Peter L., and Thomas Luckmann, *The Social Construction of Reality*. Garden City, N.Y.: Doubleday, 1966.

Berlin, Isaiah, ed., *The Age of Enlightenment*, Vol. IV in *The Great Ages of Western Philosophy*. Boston: Houghton Mifflin, 1956.

Berlin, Isaiah, *Karl Marx: His Life and Environment*. New York: Oxford University Press, 1948.

Bernard, Chester, *The Functions of the Executive*. Cambridge, Mass.: Harvard University Press, 1938.

Birnbaum, Norman, *The Crisis of Industrial Society*. New York: Oxford University Press, 1969.

Black, Max, ed., *The Social Theories of Talcott Parsons*. Englewood Cliffs, N.J.: Prentice-Hall, 1961.

Blalock, Hubert, B., *Social Statistics*. New York: McGraw-Hill, 1960.

Blalock, Hubert B., *Theory Construction: From Verbal to Mathematical Formulations.* Englewood Cliffs, N.J.: Prentice-Hall, 1969.

Blau, Peter M., *The Dynamics of Bureaucracy.* Chicago: University of Chicago Press, 1955; revised edition, 1963.

Blau, Peter, M., *Exchange and Power in Social Life.* New York: Wiley, 1964.

Blau, Peter M., *On the Nature of Organizations.* New York: Wiley, 1974.

Blau, Peter M., and Richard A. Schoenherr, *The Structure of Organizations.* New York: Basic Books, 1971.

Blumer, Herbert, *Symbolic Interactionism: Perspective and Method.* Englewood Cliffs, N.J.: Prentice-Hall, 1969.

Bottomore, Thomas B., *Critics of Society: Radical Thought in North America.* London: George Allen & Unwin, 1967.

Bottomore, Thomas B., *Sociology as Social Criticism.* London: George Allen & Unwin, 1974.

Boulding, Kenneth E., *A Primer on Social Dynamics.* New York: Free Press, 1970.

Bouma, Gary D., ''Recent 'Protestant Ethic' Research,'' *Journal for the Scientific Study of Religion,* Vol. 12, June 1973, pp. 141–155.

Buckley, Walter, ed., *Modern Systems Research for the Behavioral Scientist.* Chicago: Aldine, 1968.

Buckley, Walter, *Sociology and Modern Systems Theory.* Englewood Cliffs, N.J.: Prentice-Hall, 1967.

Burch, William R., Jr., *Daydreams and Nightmares: A Sociological Essay on the American Environment.* New York: Harper & Row, 1971.

Burgess, Ernest W., Harvey J. Locke, and Mary Margaret Thomes, *The Family from Institution to Companionship.* New York: American Book, 1963.

Campbell, Norman, *What is Science?* New York: Dover, 1952.

Capaldi, Nicholas, ed., *The Enlightenment—The Proper Study of Mankind.* New York: G. P. Putnam's Sons, 1967.

Caplow, Theodore, *Two Against One: Coalitions in Triads.* Englewood Cliffs, N.J.: Prentice-Hall, 1968.

Carneiro, Robert L., ed., *Herbert Spencer: The Evolution of Society.* Chicago: University of Chicago Press, 1967.

Chafetz, Janet Saltzman, *A Primer on the Construction and Testing of Theories in Sociology.* Itasca, Ill.: F. E. Peacock, 1978.

Chambliss, Rollin, *Social Thought.* New York: Dryden, 1954.

Cicourel, Aaron, *Cognitive Sociology: Language and Meaning in Social Interaction.* New York: Free Press, 1974.

Cohen, Percy, *Modern Social Theory.* New York: Basic Books, 1968.

Collins, Randall, *Conflict Sociology: Toward an Explanatory Science.* New York: Academic Press, 1975.

Collins, Randall, and Michael Makowsky, *The Discovery of Society.* New York: Random House, 1972.

Comte, Auguste, *Catechism of Positivism or Summary Exposition of the Universal Religion,* 3rd edition, translated by Richard Congreve. Clifton, N.J.: Augustus M. Kelley, 1973.

Comte, Auguste, *The Positive Philosophy of Auguste Comte,* freely translated and condensed by Harriet Martineau. New York: Calvin Blanchard, 1858.

Comte, Auguste, *System of Positive Polity,* 4 volumes, translated by Richard Congreve. New York: Burt Franklin, 1877.

Connerton, Paul, ed., *Critical Sociology.* New York: Penguin Books, 1976.

Cooley, Charles Horton, *Human Nature and the Social Order.* New York: Schocken Books, 1964.

Cooley, Charles Horton, *Social Organization: A Study of the Larger Mind.* New York: Schocken Books, 1962.

Coser, Lewis A., *Continuities in the Study of Social Conflict.* New York: Free Press, 1967.

Coser, Lewis A., *The Functions of Social Conflict.* Glencoe, Ill.: Free Press, 1956.

Coser, Lewis A., ed., *Georg Simmel.* Englewood Cliffs, N.J.: Prentice-Hall, 1965.

Coser, Lewis A., ed., *The Idea of Social Structure.* New York: Free Press, 1975.

Coser, Lewis A., *Masters of Sociological Thought,* 2nd edition. New York: Harcourt Brace Jovanovich, 1977.

Couch, Carl J., "Family Role Specialization and Self-Attitudes in Children," *The Sociological Quarterly,* Vol. 3, April 1962, pp. 115–121.

Dahrendorf, Ralf, *Class and Class Conflict in Industrial Society.* Stanford, Calif.: Stanford University Press, 1959.

Dahrendorf, Ralf, "Out of Utopia: Toward a Reorientation of Sociological Analysis," *American Journal of Sociology,* Vol. 64, September 1958, pp. 115–127.

Dawkins, Richard, *The Selfish Gene.* New York: Oxford University Press, 1956.

Demerath, III, N. J., and Richard A. Peterson, eds., *System, Change, and Conflict.* New York: Free Press, 1967.

Denzin, Norman K., *The Research Act: A Theoretical Introduction to Sociological Methods.* Chicago: Aldine, 1970.

Denzin, Norman K., "Symbolic Interactionism and Ethnomethodology: A Proposed Synthesis," *American Sociological Review,* Vol. 34, December 1969, pp. 922–934.

Dore, Ronald Philip, "Function and Cause," *American Sociological Review,* Vol. 26, December 1961, pp. 843–853.

Driver, Edwin D., "Self-Conceptions in India and the United States: A Cross-cultural Validation of the Twenty Statements Test," *The Sociological Quarterly,* Vol. 10, Summer 1969, pp. 341–354.

Dubin, Robert, "Parsons' Actor: Continuities in Sociological Theory," *American Sociological Review,* Vol. 25, August 1960, pp. 457–466.

Dubin, Robert, *Theory Building.* New York: Free Press, 1969.

Duncan, Hugh Dalziel, *Communication and Social Order.* New York: Bedminster, 1962.

Duncan, Hugh Dalziel, *Symbols and Social Theory.* New York: Oxford, 1969.

Duncan, Hugh Dalziel, *Symbols in Society.* New York: Oxford, 1968.

Durkheim, Emile, *The Division of Labor in Society,* translated by George Simpson. New York: Free Press, 1964.

Durkheim, Emile, *Education and Sociology,* translated by Sherwood D. Fox. New York: Free Press, 1956.

Durkheim, Emile, *The Elementary Forms of the Religious Life,* translated by Joseph Ward Swain. New York: Free Press, 1947.

Durkheim, Emile, *Moral Education,* translated by Everett K. Wilson and Herman Schnurer and edited by Everett K. Wilson. New York: Free Press, 1961.

Durkheim, Emile, *On Morality and Society: Selected Writings,* edited and with an introduction by Robert N. Bellah. Chicago: University of Chicago Press, 1973.

Durkheim, Emile, *Professional Ethics and Civic Morals,* translated by Cornelia Brookfield. New York: Free Press, 1958.

Durkheim, Emile, *The Rules of Sociological Method,* translated by Sarah A. Solovay and John H. Mueller and edited by George E. G. Catlin. New York: Free Press, 1964.

Durkheim, Emile, *Selected Writings,* translated, edited, and with an introduction by Anthony Giddens. London: Cambridge University Press, 1972.

Durkheim, Emile, *Selections from His Work,* with an introduction and commentaries by George Simpson. New York: Thomas Y. Crowell, 1963.

Durkheim, Emile, *Socialism and Saint-Simon,* translated by Charlotte Sattler and edited by Alvin W. Gouldner. Yellow Springs, Ohio: Antioch Press, 1958.

Durkheim, Emile, *Sociology and Philosophy,* translated by D. F. Pocock. New York: Free Press, 1953.

Durkheim, Emile, *Suicide,* translated by John A. Spaulding and George Simpson and edited by George Simpson. New York: Free Press, 1966.

Eisenstadt, S. N., with M. Curelaru, *The Form of Sociology-Paradigms and Crises.* New York: Wiley, 1976.

Ekeh, Peter, *Social Exchange Theory and the Two Sociological Traditions.* Cambridge, Mass.: Harvard University Press, 1975.

Emerson, Richard M., "Power-Dependence Relations," *American Sociological Review,* Vol. 25, April 1960, pp. 31-41.

Erikson, Kai, "Notes on the Sociology of Deviance," pp. 9-21 in Howard Becker, ed., *The Other Side: Perspectives on Deviance.* New York: Free Press of Glencoe, 1964.

Etzioni, Amitai, *A Comparative Analysis of Complex Organizations.* New York: Free Press, 1961; revised and enlarged edition, 1975.

Flacks, Richard, *Youth and Social Change.* Chicago: Markham, 1971.

Freund, Julien, *The Sociology of Max Weber.* New York: Pantheon, 1968.

Freidrichs, Robert W., *A Sociology of Sociology.* New York: Free Press, 1970.

Fromm, Erich, *Escape from Freedom.* New York: Holt, Rinehart & Winston, 1941.

Fromm, Erich, *Marx's Concept of Man.* New York: Frederick Ungar, 1961.

Fromm, Erich, *To Have or to Be.* New York: Harper & Row, 1976.

Galton, Francis, *Hereditary Genius: An Inquiry into Its Laws and Consequences.* London: Macmillan, 1869.

Garfinkel, Harold, *Studies in Ethnomethodology.* Englewood Cliffs, N.J.: Prentice-Hall, 1967.

Gerth, Hans, and C. Wright Mills, *Character and Social Structure: The Psychology of Social Institutions.* London: Routledge and Kegan Paul, 1953.

Gibbs, Jack P., *Sociological Theory Construction.* Hinsdale, Ill.: Dryden, 1972.

Giddens, Anthony, *Capitalism and Modern Social Theory.* London: Cambridge University Press, 1971.

Glock, Charles Y., and Rodney Stark, *Christian Beliefs and Anti-Semitism.* New York: Harper & Row, 1966.

Glock, Charles Y., and Rodney Stark, *Religion and Society in Tension.* Chicago: Rand McNally, 1965.

Goffman, Erving, *Asylums.* Garden City, N.Y.: Doubleday, 1961.

Goffman, Erving, *Encounters.* Indianapolis: Bobbs-Merrill, 1961.

Goffman, Erving. *Frame Analysis—An Essay on the Organization of Experience.* Cambridge, Mass.: Harvard University Press, 1974.

Goffman, Erving, *Interaction Ritual*. Garden City, N.Y.: Anchor, 1967.

Goffman, Erving, *The Presentation of Self in Everyday Life*. Garden City, N.Y.: Doubleday, 1959.

Goffman, Erving, *Stigma*. Englewood Cliffs, N.J.: Prentice-Hall, 1963.

Gouldner, Alvin W., *The Coming Crisis of Western Sociology*. New York: Basic Books, 1970.

Gouldner, Alvin W., "The Norm of Reciprocity," *American Sociological Review*, Vol. 25, April 1960, pp. 161–178.

Gouldner, Alvin W., "Reciprocity and Autonomy in Functional Theory," pp. 241–270 in Llewellyn Gross, ed., *Symposium in Sociological Theory*. New York: Harper & Row, 1959.

Gross, Llewellyn, *Symposium in Sociological Theory*. New York: Harper & Row, 1959.

Gusfield, Joseph, *Symbolic Crusade*. Urbana: University of Illinois Press, 1963.

Habermas, Jürgen, *Knowledge and Human Interests*, translated by Jeremy J. Shapiro. Boston: Beacon Press, 1971.

Habermas, Jürgen, *Legitimation Crisis*, translated by Thomas McCarthy. Boston: Beacon Press, 1975.

Habermas, Jürgen, *Problems of Legitimation in Late Capitalism*. Boston: Beacon Press, 1975.

Habermas, Jürgen, *Theory and Practice*, translated by John Viertel. Boston: Beacon Press, 1973.

Hage, Jerald, *Techniques and Problems of Theory Construction in Sociology*. New York: Wiley, 1972.

Hall, Edward T., *The Hidden Dimension*. Garden City, N.Y.: Doubleday, 1966.

Hall, Edward T., *The Silent Language*. Garden City, N.Y.: Doubleday, 1959.

Hawkins, Richard, and Gary Tiedeman, *The Creation of Deviance: Interpersonal and Organizational Determinants*. Columbus, Ohio: Charles E. Merrill, 1975.

Heath, Anthony, *Rational Choice and Social Exchange*. New York: Cambridge University Press, 1976.

Herberg, Will, *Protestant, Catholic, Jew*. Garden City, N.Y.: Doubleday, 1955.

Hofstadter, Richard, *Social Darwinism in American Thought*. Boston: Beacon Press, 1955.

Homans, George C., *The Human Group*. New York: Harcourt, Brace, and Company, 1950.

Homans, George C., *Sentiments and Activities*. New York: Free Press of Glencoe, 1962.

Homans, George C., *Social Behavior: Its Elementary Forms*, New York: Harcourt, Brace, and World, 1961; revised edition, New York: Harcourt, Brace, Jovanovich, 1974.

Homans, George C., and David M. Schneider, *Marriage, Authority, and Final Causes: A Study of Cross-Cousin Marriage*. New York: Free Press, 1955.

Hook, Sidney, *Revolution, Reform, and Social Justice*. New York: New York University Press, 1975.

Horowitz, Irving L., ed., *The New Sociology: Essays in Social Science and Social Theory in Honor of C. Wright Mills*. New York: Oxford University Press, 1969.

Hughes, H. Stuart, *Consciousness and Society*. New York: Vintage, 1961.

Jandy, Edward C., *Charles Horton Cooley: His Life and His Social Theory*. New York: Octagon, 1969.

Janowitz, Morris, ed., *William I. Thomas on Social Organization and Social Personality*. Chicago: University of Chicago Press, 1966.

Jesser, Clinton Joyce, *Social Theory Revisited.* Hinsdale, Ill.: Dryden Press, 1975.

Johnson, Harry M., *Sociology: A Systematic Introduction.* New York: Harcourt, Brace and World, 1960.

Kaplan, Abraham, *The Conduct of Inquiry.* San Francisco: Chandler, 1964.

Katz, Daniel, and Robert L. Kahn, *The Social Psychology of Organizations.* New York: Wiley, 1966.

Kinloch, Graham C., *Sociological Theory: Its Development and Major Paradigms.* New York: McGraw-Hill, 1977.

Kuhn, Alfred, *The Logic of Social Systems.* San Francisco: Jossey-Bass, 1974.

Kuhn, Manford, "Major Trends in Symbolic Interaction Theory in the Past Twenty-Five Years," *The Sociological Quarterly,* Vol. 5, Winter 1964, pp. 61–84.

Kuhn, Manford H., and Thomas S. McPartland, "An Empirical Investigation of Self-Attitudes," *American Sociological Review,* Vol. 19, February 1954, pp. 68–76.

Kuhn, Thomas S., *The Structure of Scientific Revolutions,* 2nd edition. Chicago: University of Chicago Press, 1970.

LaCapra, Dominick, *Emile Durkheim: Sociologist and Philosopher.* Ithaca, N.Y.: Cornell University Press, 1972.

Lachmann, L. M., *The Legacy of Max Weber.* London: Heinemann, 1970.

Larson, Calvin J., *Major Themes in Sociological Theory.* New York: David McKay, 1973.

Lefebvre, Henri, *The Sociology of Marx.* New York: Random House, 1968.

Lengermann, Patricia W., *Definitions of Sociology: A Historical Approach.* Columbus, Ohio: Charles E. Merrill, 1974.

Lenski, Gerhard, *Power and Privilege: A Theory of Social Stratification.* New York: McGraw-Hill, 1966.

Lenski, Gerhard, "Status Crystallization: A Non-vertical Dimension of Social Status," *American Sociological Review,* Vol. 19, August 1954, pp. 405–413.

Lenzer, Gertrud, ed., *Auguste Comte and Positivism: The Essential Writings.* New York: Harper & Row, 1975.

Lerner, Daniel, *The Passing of Traditional Society.* New York: Free Press, 1958.

Levi-Strauss, Claude, *The Elementary Structures of Kinship.* Boston: Beacon Press, 1969.

Levy, Marion J., *The Structure of Society.* Princeton, N.J.: Princeton University Press, 1952.

Lewis, Jerry M., Robert Beavers, John T. Gossett, and Virginia Austin Phillips, *No Single Thread: Psychological Health in Family Systems.* New York: Brunner/Mazel, 1976.

Lockwood, David, "Some Remarks on 'The Social System,'" *British Journal of Sociology,* Vol. 7, June 1956, pp. 134–146.

Lorenz, Konrad Z., *On Aggression.* New York: Harcourt, Brace and World, 1966.

Lukes, Steven, *Emile Durkheim: His Life and Work.* New York: Harper & Row, 1972.

Lundberg, George A., *Foundations of Sociology.* New York: Macmillan, 1939.

MacIver, Robert M., *Society: A Textbook of Sociology.* New York: Rinehart, 1937.

Maine, Henry Sumner, *Ancient Law.* New York: Henry Holt, 1906.

Manis, Jerome, and Benard Meltzer, eds., *Symbolic Interaction—A Reader in Social Psychology,* 2nd edition. Boston: Allyn and Bacon, 1972.

Mannheim, Karl, *Ideology and Utopia,* translated by Louis Wirth and Edward Shils, New York: Harcourt, Brace, and World, 1936.

Mannheim, Karl, *Man and Society in an Age of Reconstruction*. London: Routledge and Kegan Paul, 1940.

Manuel, Frank E., *The New World of Henri Saint-Simon*. Cambridge, Mass.: Harvard University Press, 1956.

Manuel, Frank E., *The Prophets of Paris*. Cambridge, Mass.: Harvard University Press, 1962.

Marcuse, Herbert, *Counter-Revolution and Revolt*. Boston: Beacon Press, 1973.

Marcuse, Herbert, *One-Dimensional Man: Studies in the Ideology of Advanced Industrial Society*. Boston: Beacon Press, 1966.

Marcuse, Herbert, *Reason and Revolution*. Boston: Beacon Press, 1966.

Martindale, Don, *The Nature and Types of Sociological Theory*. Boston: Houghton Mifflin, 1960.

Maruyama, Margoroh, "The Second Cybernetics: Deviation-Amplifying Mutual Causal Processes," *American Scientist,* Vol. 51, June 1963, pp. 164–179.

Marx, Karl, *Capital,* 3 volumes, translated by Samuel Moore and Edward Aveling. New York: International Publishers, 1967.

Marx, Karl, *The Communist Manifesto*. New York: Appleton-Century-Crofts, 1955.

Marx, Karl, *Early Writings,* translated and edited by T. B. Bottomore. New York: McGraw-Hill, 1964.

Marx, Karl, *Economy, Class, and Social Revolution,* edited and with an introductory essay by Z. A. Jordan, London: Michael Joseph, 1971.

Marx, Karl, *The Eighteenth Brumaire of Louis Bonaparte,* translated by Daniel DeLeon. New York: International Publishers, 1963.

Marx, Karl, *The Marx-Engels Reader,* edited by Robert C. Tucker. New York: W. W. Norton, 1972.

Marx, Karl, *Selected Writings in Sociology and Social Philosophy,* edited by T. B. Bottomore and Maximilien Ruber, translated by T. B. Bottomore. New York: McGraw-Hill, 1964.

Marx, Karl, and Friedrich Engels, *Basic Writings on Politics and Philosophy,* edited by Lewis S. Feuer. Garden City, N.Y.: Doubleday, 1959.

Marx, Karl, and Friedrich Engels, *The German Ideology*. New York: International Publishers, 1947.

Maslow, Abraham H., *Motivation and Personality,* 2nd edition. New York: Harper & Row, 1970.

Masterman, Margaret, "The Nature of a Paradigm," pp. 49–89 in Imre Lakatos and Alan Musgrave, eds., *Criticism and the Growth of Knowledge*. Cambridge, England: Cambridge University Press, 1970.

Matza, David, *Becoming Deviant*. Englewood Cliffs, N.J.: Prentice-Hall, 1969.

McCall, George, and J. L. Simmons, *Identities and Interactions,* revised edition. New York: Free Press, 1978.

McClellan, David, *Karl Marx,* New York: Viking, 1975.

McClellan, David, *The Thought of Karl Marx*. New York: Harper & Row, 1971.

McClelland, David C., *The Achieving Society*. Princeton, N.J.: Van Nostrand, 1961.

McKinney, John C., *Constructive Typology and Social Theory*. New York: Appleton-Century-Crofts, 1966.

Mead, George Herbert, *Mind, Self, and Society,* edited and with an introduction by Charles W. Morris. Chicago: University of Chicago Press, 1934.

Mead, George Herbert, *Movements of Thought in the Nineteenth Century,* edited and with an introduction by Merritt A. Moore, Chicago: University of Chicago Press, 1936.

Mead, George Herbert, *The Philosophy of the Act,* edited and with an introduction by Charles W. Morris in collaboration with John M. Brewster, Albert M. Dunham, and David L. Miller. Chicago: University of Chicago Press, 1938.

Mead, George Herbert, *The Philosophy of the Present,* edited and with an introduction by Arthur E. Murphy. LaSalle, Ill.: Open Court, 1932.

Mead, George Herbert, *Selected Writings,* edited and with an introduction by Andrew J. Reck. Indianapolis: Bobbs-Merrill, 1964.

Meltzer, B. N., and J. W. Petras, "The Chicago and Iowa Schools of Symbolic Interactionism," pp. 43–57 in Thomas Shibutani, ed., *Human Nature and Collective Behavior.* Englewood Cliffs, N.J.: Prentice-Hall, 1970.

Merton, Robert K., *Social Theory and Social Structure,* enlarged edition. New York: Free Press, 1968.

Michels, Robert, *Political Parties.* Glencoe, Ill.: Free Press, 1949, originally published in 1915.

Mill, John Stuart, *Auguste Comte and Positivism.* Ann Arbor: University of Michigan Press, 1961.

Miller, David, *George Herbert Mead: Self, Language and the World.* Austin: University of Texas Press, 1973.

Mills, C. Wright, *The Causes of World War III.* New York: Simon and Shuster, 1958.

Mills, C. Wright, *The Power Elite.* New York: Oxford University Press, 1956.

Mills, C. Wright, *The Sociological Imagination.* New York: Oxford University Press, 1959.

Mills, C. Wright, *White Collar.* New York: Oxford University Press, 1956.

Mitzman, Arthur, *The Iron Cage: An Historical Interpretation of Max Weber.* New York: Alfred A. Knopf, 1970.

Moreno, J. L. *Who Shall Survive?* Washington, D.C.: Nervous and Mental Disease Publishing Company, 1934.

Nisbet, Robert A., *Emile Durkheim,* Englewood Cliffs, N.J.: Prentice-Hall, 1965.

Nisbet, Robert A., *The Sociological Tradition.* New York: Basic Books, 1966.

Nisbet, Robert A., *The Sociology of Emile Durkheim.* New York: Oxford University Press, 1974.

O'Dea, Thomas F., "Five Dilemmas in the Institutionalization of Religion," *Journal for the Scientific Study of Religion,* Vol. 1, October 1961, pp. 32–39.

Ogburn, William F., *Social Change with Respect to Culture and Original Nature.* Gloucester, Mass.: Peter Smith, 1964; originally New York: B. W. Huebsch, 1922; revised, Viking, 1950.

Ogburn, William F., and Meyer F. Nimkoff, *The Social Effects of Aviation.* Boston: Houghton Mifflin, 1946.

Ogburn, William F., and Meyer F. Nimkoff, *Technology and the Changing Family.* Boston: Houghton Mifflin, 1955.

Park, Robert E., and Ernest W. Burgess, *Introduction to the Science of Sociology.* Chicago: University of Chicago Press, 1921.

Parsons, Talcott, "Christianity and Modern Industrial Society," pp. 33–70 in Edward A. Tiryakian, ed., *Sociological Theory, Values, and Sociocultural Change.* Glencoe, Ill.: Free Press, 1963.

Parsons, Talcott, *Essays in Sociological Theory,* revised edition. New York: Free Press, 1954.

Parsons, Talcott, "An Outline of the Social System," pp. 30–79 in Talcott Parsons, Edward Shils, Kaspar D. Naegele, and Jesse R. Pitts, *Theories of Society.* New York: Free Press, 1961.

Parsons, Talcott, "Pattern Variables Revisited: A Response to Robert Dubin," *American Sociological Review,* Vol. 25, August 1960, pp. 467–483.

Parsons, Talcott, *Politics and Social Structure.* New York: Free Press, 1969.

Parsons, Talcott, "A Short Account of My Intellectual Development," *Alpha Kappa Deltan,* Vol. XXIX, Winter 1959, pp. 3–12.

Parsons, Talcott, *Social Structure and Personality.* New York: Free Press, 1970.

Parsons, Talcott, *The Social System.* New York: Free Press, 1951.

Parsons, Talcott, *Societies-Evolutionary and Comparative Perspectives.* Englewood Cliffs, N.J.: Prentice-Hall, 1966.

Parsons, Talcott, *Sociological Theory and Modern Society.* New York: Free Press, 1967.

Parsons, Talcott, *Structure and Process in Modern Societies.* Glencoe, Ill.: Free Press, 1960.

Parsons, Talcott, *The Structure of Social Action.* New York: McGraw-Hill, 1937.

Parsons, Talcott, *The System of Modern Societies.* Englewood Cliffs, N.J.: Prentice-Hall, 1971.

Parsons, Talcott, and Robert F. Bales, in collaboration with James Olds, Morris Zelditch, Jr., and Philip E. Slater, *Family, Socialization and Interaction Process.* New York: Free Press, 1955.

Parsons, Talcott, Robert F. Bales, and Edward A. Shils, *Working Papers in the Theory of Action.* New York: Free Press, 1953.

Parsons, Talcott, and Edward A. Shils, eds., *Toward A General Theory of Action.* New York: Harper & Row, 1951.

Parsons, Talcott, and Neil J. Smelser, *Economy and Society.* Glencoe, Ill.: Free Press, 1956.

Pearson, Karl, *The Scope and Importance to the State of the Science of National Eugenics.* London: Dulau, 1909.

Reichenbach, Hans, *The Rise of Scientific Philosophy.* Berkeley and Los Angeles: University of California Press, 1962.

Redfield, Robert, *The Folk Culture of Yucatan.* Chicago: University of Chicago Press, 1941.

Redfield, Robert, *The Primitive World and its Transformations.* Ithaca, N.Y.: Cornell University Press, 1953.

Reich, Charles, *The Greening of America.* New York: Random House, 1970.

Reiss, Albert J., ed., *Cooley and Sociological Analysis.* Ann Arbor: University of Michigan Press, 1968.

Reynolds, Paul Davidson, *A Primer in Theory Construction.* Indianapolis: Bobbs-Merrill, 1971.

Riesman, David, *The Lonely Crowd,* written in collaboration with Reuel Denney and Nathan Glazer. New Haven, Conn.: Yale University Press, 1950.

Ritzer, George, *Sociology: A Multiple Paradigm Science.* Boston: Allyn and Bacon, 1975.

Rose, Arnold M., ed., *Human Behavior and Social Processes—An Interactionist Approach.* Boston: Houghton Mifflin, 1962.

Ross, E. A., *Principles of Sociology.* New York: Century, 1920.

Roszak, Theodore, *The Making of a Counter Culture.* Garden City, N.Y.: Doubleday, 1969.

Rubington, Earl and Martin S. Weinberg, eds., *Deviance: The Interactionist Perspective*, 3rd edition. New York: Macmillan, 1978.

Schaff, Adam, *Marxism and the Human Individual*. New York: McGraw-Hill, 1970.

Schneider, Louis, *Sociological Approach to Religion*. New York: Wiley, 1970.

Schneider, Louis, *The Sociological Way of Looking at the World*. New York: McGraw-Hill, 1975.

Schneider, Louis, "Toward Assessment of Sorokin's View of Change," pp. 371–400 in George K. Zollschan and Walter Hirsch, eds., *Explorations in Social Change*. Boston: Houghton Mifflin, 1964.

Schneider, Louis, and Louis Zurcher, "Toward Understanding the Catholic Crisis: Observations on Dissident Priests in Texas," *Journal for the Scientific Study of Religion*, Vol. 9, Fall 1970, pp. 197–207.

Schutz, Alfred, *The Phenomenology of the Social World*, translated by George Walsh and Frederick Lehnert. Evanston, Ill.: Northwestern University Press, 1967.

Schutz, Alfred, and Thomas Luckmann, *The Structures of the Life-World*. Evanston, Ill.: Northwestern University Press, 1973.

Scimecca, Joseph A., *The Sociological Theory of C. Wright Mills*. Port Washington, N.Y.: Kennikat Press, 1977.

Scoville, Warren C., *The Persecution of Huguenots and French Economic Development, 1680–1770*. Berkeley and Los Angeles: University of California Press, 1960.

Seeman, Melvin, "On the Meaning of Alienation," *American Sociological Review*, Vol. 24, December 1959, pp. 783–791.

Shils, Edward, "The Calling of Sociology," pp. 1405–1448 in Talcott Parsons, et al., *Theories of Society*, 1-volume edition. New York: Free Press, 1961.

Simmel, Georg, *The Conflict in Modern Culture and Other Essays*, translated with an introduction by K. Peter Etzkorn. New York: Teachers College, 1968.

Simmel, Georg, *Conflict and the Web of Group-Affiliations*, translated by Kurt H. Wolff and Reinhard Bendix. New York: Free Press, 1955.

Simmel, Georg, *Georg Simmel on Individuality and Social Forms*, edited by Donald N. Levine. Chicago: University of Chicago Press, 1971.

Simmel, Georg. *The Sociology of Georg Simmel*, translated, edited, and with an introduction by Kurt H. Wolff. New York: Free Press, 1950.

Skidmore, William, *Theoretical Thinking in Sociology*. London: Cambridge University Press, 1975.

Skinner, B. F., *Science and Human Behavior*. New York: Free Press, 1953.

Slater, Philip, *Earthwalk*. Garden City, N.Y.: Doubleday, 1974.

Slater, Philip, *The Pursuit of Loneliness*. Boston: Beacon Press, 1970.

Smith, Adam, *The Wealth of Nations*. New York: Random House, 1937.

Sokoloff, Boris, *The "Mad" Philosopher: Auguste Comte*. New York: Vantage, 1961.

Sorokin, Pitirim, *The Crisis of our Age*. New York: E. P. Dutton, 1941.

Sorokin, Pitirim, *Fads and Foibles in Modern Sociology and Related Sciences*. Chicago: Regnery, 1956.

Sorokin, Pitirim, *Social and Cultural Dynamics*, 1-volume edition. Boston: Porter Sargent, 1957.

Sorokin, Pitirim, *Society, Culture, and Personality*. New York: Harper & Row, 1947.

Sorokin, Pitirim, *Sociological Theories of Today*. New York: Harper & Row, 1966.

Spencer, Herbert, *The Evolution of Society: Selections from Herbert Spencer's Principles of Sociology,* edited and with an introduction by Robert L. Carneiro. Chicago: University of Chicago Press, 1967.

Spencer, Herbert, *The Man versus the State.* Caldwell, Idaho: Caxton, 1965.

Spencer, Herbert, *Principles of Sociology,* edited and with an introduction by Robert L. Carneiro. Chicago: University of Chicago Press, 1967.

Spiegel, John P., and Pavel Machotka, *Messages of the Body.* New York: Free Press, 1974.

Spiro, Melford E., *Children of the Kibbutz.* Cambridge, Mass.: Harvard University Press, 1956.

Spiro, Melford E., *Kibbutz, Venture in Utopia.* Cambridge, Mass.: Harvard University Press, 1956.

Spykmann, Nicholas J., *The Social Theory of Georg Simmel.* New York: Russell and Russell, 1964.

Stinchcombe, Arthur L., *Constructing Social Theories.* New York: Harcourt, Brace and World, 1968.

Stoddard, Lothrop, *The Revolt Against Civilization.* New York: Scribner's, 1922.

Strauss, Anselm, ed., *George Herbert Mead on Social Psychology.* Chicago: University of Chicago Press, 1964.

Strauss, Anselm, *Mirrors and Masks: The Search for Identity.* Glencoe, Ill.: Free Press, 1959.

Sumner, William Graham, *Essays of William Graham Sumner,* 2 vols., edited by Albert G. Keller and Maurice R. Davie. New Haven, Conn.: Yale University Press, 1945.

Sumner, William Graham, *Folkways.* Boston: Ginn, 1940.

Swanson, Guy E., *The Birth of the Gods.* Ann Arbor: University of Michigan Press, 1960.

Thibaut, John W., and Harold H. Kelley, *The Social Psychology of Groups.* New York: Wiley, 1959.

Thomas, William I., "Life History," published by Paul J. Baker in the *American Journal of Sociology,* Vol. 79, September 1973, pp. 243–250.

Thomas, William I., *The Unadjusted Girl.* Boston: Little, Brown, 1923.

Thomas, William I., and Florian Znaniecki, *The Polish Peasant in Europe and America,* 2 volumes. New York: Dover, 1958.

Thompson, Kenneth, *Auguste Comte: The Foundation of Sociology.* New York: Wiley, 1975.

Tiger, Lionel, *Men in Groups.* New York: Random House, 1969.

Tiger, Lionel, and Robin Fox, *The Imperial Animal.* New York: Holt, Rinehart & Winston, 1971.

Timasheff, Nicholas S., and George A. Theodorson, *Sociological Theory: Its Nature and Growth,* 4th edition. New York: Random House, 1976.

Tiryakian, Edward A., ed., *Sociological Theory, Values, and Sociocultural Change.* Glencoe, Ill.: Free Press, 1963.

Tocqueville, Alexis de, *Democracy in America.* New York: Knopf, 1945.

Tönnies, Ferdinand, *Community and Society,* edited and translated by Charles P. Loomis. New York: Harper & Row, 1963.

Troeltsch. Ernst, *The Social Teachings of the Christian Churches,* 2 volumes, translated by Olive Wyon. New York: Macmillan, 1931.

Turk, Herman, and Richard L. Simpson, eds., *Institutions and Social Exchange: The Sociologies of Talcott Parsons and George C. Homans*. Indianapolis and New York: Bobbs-Merrill, 1971.

Turner, Jonathan, *The Structure of Sociological Theory*, revised edition. Homewood, Ill.: Dorsey, 1978.

Tylor, Edward B., *Primitive Culture*. New York: Brentano, 1924.

Van den Berghe, Pierre L., "Dialectic and Functionalism: Toward a Theoretical Synthesis," *American Sociological Review*, Vol. 28, October 1963, pp. 695–705.

Van den Berghe, Pierre L., *Man in Society: A Biosocial View*, 2nd edition. New York: Elsevier, 1978.

Veblen, Thorstein, *The Theory of the Leisure Class*. New York: Modern Library, 1934.

Vidich, Arthur J., and Joseph Bensman, *Small Town in Mass Society*. Garden City, N.Y.: Doubleday, 1960.

von Bertalanffy, Ludwig, *General System Theory: Foundations, Development, Applications*. New York: George Braziller, 1968.

Wallerstein, Immanuel Maurice, *The Modern World System; Capitalist Agriculture and the Origins of the European World Economy in the Sixteenth Century*. New York: Academic Press, 1974.

Wallwork, Ernest, *Durkheim: Morality and Milieu*. Cambridge, Mass.: Harvard University Press, 1972.

Warner, W. Lloyd, *The Living and the Dead*, Yankee City Series, Vol. 5. New Haven, Conn.: Yale University Press, 1959.

Warshay, Leon, *The Current State of Sociological Theory*. New York: David McKay, 1975.

Weber, Marianne, *Max Weber: A Biography*, edited and translated by Harry Zohn. New York: Wiley-Interscience, 1975.

Weber, Max, *Ancient Judaism*, translated by H. H. Gerth and Don Martindale. New York: Free Press, 1952.

Weber, Max, *The City*, edited and translated by Don Martindale and Gertrud Neuwirth. New York: Free Press, 1958.

Weber, Max, *Economy and Society*, 3 volumes, edited and translated in part by Guenther Roth and Claus Wittich. New York: Bedminster, 1968.

Weber, Max, *From Max Weber: Essays in Sociology*, translated, edited and with an introduction by Hans Gerth and C. Wright Mills. New York: Oxford University Press, 1958.

Weber, Max, *General Economic History*, translated by Frank H. Knight. London: George Allen & Unwin, 1927.

Weber, Max, *Max Weber on Charisma and Institution Building*, edited and with an introduction by S. N. Eisenstadt. Chicago: University of Chicago Press, 1968.

Weber, Max, *Max Weber on Law in Economy and Society*, edited by Max Rheinstein and translated by Edward Shils and Max Rheinstein. Cambridge, Mass.: Harvard University Press, 1954.

Weber, Max, *The Methodology of the Social Sciences*, edited and translated by Edward A. Shils and Henry A. Finch. New York: Free Press, 1947.

Weber, Max, *The Protestant Ethic and the Spirit of Capitalism*, translated by Talcott Parsons. New York: Scribners, 1930.

Weber, Max, *The Religion of China: Confucianism and Taoism,* translated by H. H. Gerth. New York: Free Press, 1951.

Weber, Max, *The Religion of India: The Sociology of Hinduism and Buddhism,* translated by H. H. Gerth and Don Martindale. New York: Free Press, 1958.

Weber, Max, *The Sociology of Religion,* translated by Ephraim Fischoff. Boston: Beacon Press, 1963.

Weber, Max, *The Theory of Social and Economic Organization,* translated by A. M. Henderson and Talcott Parsons and edited with an introduction by Talcott Parsons, New York: Oxford University Press, 1947.

Weingartner, Rudolph, *Experience and Culture: The Philosophy of Georg Simmel.* Middletown, Conn.: Wesleyan University Press, 1960.

Wilkins, Leslie T., *Social Deviance.* London: Tavistock, 1964.

Wilson, Edward O., *On Human Nature.* Cambridge, Mass.: Harvard University Press, 1978.

Wilson, Edward O., *Sociobiology, the New Synthesis.* Cambridge, Mass.: Harvard University Press, 1975.

Wolff, Kurt H., *Emile Durkheim, 1858–1917.* Columbus, Ohio: State University Press, 1960.

Yinger, J. Milton, *The Scientific Study of Religion.* New York: Macmillan, 1970.

Zeitlin, Irving M., *Marxism: A Re-examination.* New York: Van Nostrand, 1967.

Zeitlin, Irving M., *Rethinking Sociology—A Critique of Contemporary Theory.* Englewood Cliffs, N.J.: Prentice-Hall, 1973.

Zetterberg, Hans L., *On Theory and Verification in Sociology,* 3rd edition. Totowa, N.J.: Bedminster, 1965.

Zollschan, George K., and Walter Hirsch, eds., *Explorations in Social Change.* Boston: Houghton Mifflin, 1964.

Name Index

Riesman, D., 36, 66
Ritzer, G., 50, 52-55, 57, 58, 65, 67,
 567
Ross, E. A., 286
Roszak, T., 503
Rousseau, J., 175
Royce, J., 294
Rubington, E., 340

Saint Simon, 23, 73, 75, 81, 112, 119,
 167
Sanford, R. N., 502
Schaff, A., 159
Schneider, D., 347, 371, 390, 565
Schneider, L., 110, 113-115, 200, 244,
 339, 445, 564
Schoenherr, R. A., 383, 566
Schutz, A., 27, 28, 567
Scimecca, J. A., 503
Scott, J. F., 441
Scoville, W., 238, 244
Seeman, M., 502
Shibutani, T., 339
Shils, E., 443
Shils, E. A., 48, 67, 197, 399, 405, 424,
 442, 443, 444, 565
Simmel, G., 4, 5, 53, 165, 201, 206,
 246-286, 292, 293, 336, 360, 381,
 387, 450, 480, 483, 484, 514, 565
Simmons, J. L., 322, 323, 335, 339
Sjoberg, G., 442
Skidmore, W., 35, 47, 65, 66, 199,
 243
Skinner, B. F., 51, 67, 351
Slater, P., 503
Small, A., 283
Smelser, N., 418, 422, 425, 443, 444
Smith, A., 22, 29, 120, 122, 133, 136
 148, 343
Sombart, W., 205, 389
Sorokin, P., 4, 5, 71, 72, 89-105, 108,
 110-112, 114, 115, 117, 197, 198, 202,
 238, 241, 318, 336
Spencer, H., 4, 14, 18, 105, 113, 133,
 167-170, 174, 175, 179, 198, 199,
 250, 273, 285, 312, 344, 345, 425,
 514, 563
Spiegel, J. P., 337
Spiro, M. E., 564
Spykmann, N. J., 248, 284, 286
Stark, R., 199, 502
Stinchcombe, A., 66

Stoddard, L., 564
Stouffer, S. A., 438
Sumner, W. G., 4, 26, 29, 296, 564
Swanson, G., 201

Tarde, G., 169
Theodorson, G. A., 27, 29
Thibaut, J., 343, 358-361, 380, 383,
 424
Thomas, M. M., 565
Thomas, W. I., 4, 51, 293, 311, 317-319,
 335, 338, 339
Tiedeman, G., 340
Tiger, L., 564
Timasheff, N., 27, 29, 67
Tiryakian, E. A., 114
Tönnies, F., 105, 164, 169, 182, 200,
 206, 243, 248, 403
Troeltsch, E., 285, 505
Tucker, R. C., 158, 159
Turgot, J., 75, 81
Turner, J., 27, 339, 381, 470, 504,
 565
Tylor, E. B., 56, 68

van den Berghe, P. L., 58, 68, 502, 564
Veblen, T., 460, 503
Vidich, A. J., 566
von Bertalanffy, L., 513, 563

Wallerstein, I. M., 563
Ward, L., 520, 564
Warner, W. L., 201
Warshay, L., 45, 66
Watson, J. B., 297
Weber, M., 4, 14, 17, 18, 24, 25, 35, 36,
 51-53, 67, 105, 202-245, 247, 248,
 292, 293, 311, 383, 386-392, 394,
 395, 398, 401, 425, 437, 439, 449,
 450, 454, 460, 469, 491, 495, 497,
 504, 559
Weinberg, M. S., 340
Whewell, W., 65
Wilkins, L., 565
Wilson, E. O., 564
Windelband, W., 213
Wolff, K. W., 198, 284
Wundt, W., 164, 295

Yinger, J. M., 285

Zetterberg, H., 37, 40, 42-44, 66

584

Subject Index

Adaptation, 126, 349, 414-416, 440, 520, 522
  and economic structure, 418-420
  as functional requirement of social systems, 414, 440
Affective-type action, 215
Affectivity vs. affective neutrality, 401, 403-405
Aggression: sociobiological perspective on, 424-425
  unsatisfactory exchange transactions and, 355
AGIL framework, 412-421, 439-440
  applied to task groups, 415, 416
  applied to societies, 418-420
  and social evolution, 425-428
  and structural differentiation, 423-425
  and subsystem interchanges, 422-423
Alienation, 34, 37, 62, 67, 156, 158, 162
  in Marx's theory, 134-139
  ritual expression of, 495-499
  social conditions of, 451-452
Altruism, 14, 88, 74, 75, 85, 86, 90
  sociobiological perspective on, 524-525
Anarchy, 74, 77, 79, 84, 85, 89

Anomie, 61
  and deviance, 437
  Merton's theory of, 436, 437, 440
  and suicide, 185-188
Arbitrator, 269-270
Aristocracy, 16, 75, 121, 132, 141, 142, 272
Ascription vs. achievement, 402-406
Authoritarian personality, 452, 458, 502
Authority structure: in capitalist vs. postcapitalist societies, 468, 469, 477, 478
  class relations and, 470-474, 477-478, 493-495
  effect on interactional dynamics, 490-495
  necessity for, 469, 470
  in occupational groups, 493-495
  vs. power structure, 218-220, 557-560
  as source of conflicts, 468-471, 477, 478, 489, 493-495, 500
  traditional, 221, 222, 229, 240
  types of, 85, 219-225, 228, 229, 240, 361
Axiomatic theory construction, 44, 49

Behavioral psychology, 51, 351

Gestures, 298-301, 326
Goal attainment, 414-416, 440
    functional requirement of social
        systems, 414, 440
    phase movements, 415, 416
    political structure, 419, 420
Government, 22, 23, 86, 154, 168, 453,
    455
Gratification-deprivation balance, 399,
    406
Group formation, 257, 273-278, 360-362,
    471-473
Group solidarity, 480-485, 500, 525
    and conflict, 483-485, 500
    as means of domination, 491, 492
    sociobiological explanation of, 525

Hegelian philosophical analysis, 118, 119,
    159, 211, 251, 296
Hierarchical social organization, 14, 259,
    260
    see also Bureaucracy
Hierarchy of cultural control, 417, 418
Hinduism, 236, 237, 242
Historical materialism, 120, 124-129
Historicism, *see* German historicism
Hobbesian state of nature, 161, 162, 448,
    499
Holy Family, The, 157
Homeostasis, 515, 516, 534
Human Group, The, 348, 352
Human Nature and the Social Order,
    312

Idealism, in Parsons' voluntaristic theory
    of action, 392-395, 397, 398,
    439, 441
    sociological, in Durkheim's theory, 397,
    398
    in Weber's intellectual background, 210,
    211
Ideal type, 36, 211-213, 215, 225, 240
Imbalanced exchanges, 366-377
    basis for informal rank in bureaucracies,
    368, 383
    basis for power structures, 366-370, 380,
    383
    dependency relations, 369, 376
    foundation for macro structures, 372-
    374

Implicit theories, 7, 8, 11, 19, 30, 64
Impression management, 326
    breakdowns in, 329, 330
    frontstage vs. backstage, 328, 329
    for stigmatized persons, 331, 332
    team collaboration in, 328-331
Individualism, 22, 23, 77, 84, 86, 127,
    136
    in American social thought, 15, 25, 26
    Durkheim's analysis of, 163, 177, 179,
    182, 565
    social heterogeneity, 182, 183
    Spencer's emphasis on, 167, 199
Individualistic vs. collectivist social thought,
    285
    see also Social reality, individual level
Industrial development, 86, 132, 152, 207,
    250
Industrial Revolution, 14, 17, 20, 106, 127,
    141, 166, 180, 207
    Marx's analysis of, 134
Inner-worldly asceticism, 232, 235
Institution, 34, 35
    in Parsons' theory, 407, 408
    see also Social institutions
Institutionalization, 377-379, 381, 557-
    559
    authority vs. power structures, 557-560
    defined in Parsons' theory, 408, 409
Integralist perspective, 92, 93
Integration, 404-416, 440
    cultural, 91-93, 102
    functional requirement of social systems,
    414-415, 440
    institutional structures for, 419-420
    and phase movements, 415, 416
    see also Social integration
Intellectual development, stages of, in
    Comte's theory, 78-84, 104, 111,
    196, 202
Interaction, 57, 61, 67, 325-334
    context of, 332-334
    dramaturgic model of, 325-334
    between dramaturgic team members,
    328-331
    effects of stigma on, 331, 332
    forms of, 54, 246, 248, 252, 281, 283,
    286, 336
        examples of, 255-286
        influence of numbers on, 267-273, 281,
        283
        vs. content, 252-256, 281

process, 246, 248
  reciprocal, 248, 255, 256
  rituals, 492-497, 499, 500
    as expressive of stratification systems,
      492-497, 499, 500
    in occupational structures, 495
    in status groups, 217, 218, 492-497
  see also Symbolic interaction
Interdependence, 77, 84, 86, 91, 507-513
  conflict theory, 510-512, 544, 554, 557,
    560-562
  examples of, 507-509
  exchange theory, 510-512, 554, 561
  functional, 543-560
    division of labor, 177, 178, 180-182,
      547, 551
    emotional solidarity, 550-554
    and equilibrium, 547-550
    vs. functional autonomy, 545-550
  in functional theory, 510-512, 544, 554,
    557, 560, 561
  in general systems theory, 513-519
  at species vs. individual level, 514, 515
  symbiotic, 511, 561
  in symbolic interaction theory, 510-512,
    526
Interpersonal attraction, 365, 369, 378
  and particularistic values, 378
Interpersonal exchanges, 342
  balanced vs. imbalanced, 366-368
  as basis for social structure, 343, 362, 366-
    379, 380, 388
  competition in, 368-370
  direct vs. indirect, 351, 361, 362, 378,
    380
  dyads vs. groups, 358, 360-368, 380
  Homans' analysis of, 347-358
    contrasted with functional explanations,
      347, 348
    individual motivations for, 343, 348,
      382
    psychological explanations of, 351-355,
      380
  restricted vs. generalized, 344, 345, 566
  social vs. economic, 346, 352, 363
  supported by legitimating values, 371, 374,
    375, 377-379, 381
Investments, 352, 353, 366
Iron law of oligarchy, 260, 465-468, 498,
  500

Judaism, 236, 242

Labor theory of value, 148-150
Laissez-faire ideology, 136, 462, 520, 521
  in America's cultural background, 133,
    461
  in political economic theory, 22, 132, 148,
    343, 344
  in political policy, 120, 122, 168
  social Darwinist support for, 520, 521
Latent dysfunctions, 433-435
Latent pattern maintenance, 415, 416,
  420, 440, 565
  phase movements, 415, 416
  tension management, 413, 420, 424
Law, repressive vs. restitutive, 177
Leadership, see Authority structure;
  Power structure
Legitimation, 131, 155, 216, 371, 372,
  374-376, 455, 557, 558
Looking-glass self, 312-314

Macro level structures, 5, 372-380
  contrasted with elementary exchange
    processes, 377-379
  emergent properties of, 377-311
  legitimation and stabilization mechanisms
    of, 374-377
  opposition movements within, 374-377
  reflecting imbalanced exchanges, 372-374,
    380
Material culture, 104-111
  inventions in, 106, 107
  lags in, 107-109
  vs. nonmaterial culture, 104, 105
Materialism, historical, 120, 124-129
Marxism, 152, 156, 450-452
  criticisms of, 152-155
Mass media, 455, 464, 465, 491
Means-ends framework, 214-216, 392-
  398
Mechanical solidarity, 176-179, 182, 196,
  243, 547
Mediator, 269-270
Middle-range functional theory, 391, 428-
  440, 449
  vs. Parsons' "grand theory," 428, 429,
    439, 440
Military-industrial complex, 104, 462, 463
Mind: and communication process, 297,
  298, 302
  as emergent in evolutionary process,
    296
  and subjective consciousness, 297, 298

592

Money, 276-278, 422, 423
Morphogenesis, 531-543
  contrasted with homeostasis and
    equilibrium, 534
  contrasted with morphostasis, 534,
    538, 548, 554
  deviation-amplifying feedback cycles,
    535-538
  positive vs. negative feedback cycles,
    531-535
  strains resulting from, 539-541, 566
  vs. structural simplification, 538, 539,
    541-543, 566

Natural law, 12, 18, 23, 24, 76, 77, 132
Natural sciences, 17, 24, 31, 32, 63, 77,
    79
Norm of reciprocity, 366, 368, 371

Oligarche, 260, 465, 468, 498, 500
One-Dimensional Man, 453
Open systems theory, 507-567
  applied to sociocultural systems, 514-
    519
  basic perspective of, 513-519
  vs. sociological theories, 514, 515, 518,
    560-562
  and sociobiological perspective, 519-
    527
Opposition movements, 374-377
  see also Class, conflict; Conflict;
    Conflict interest groups
Organic model of society, 76, 77, 91, 514,
    515
Organic solidarity, 176-182, 196, 243
Other-worldly mysticism, 236

Paradigm, 49-54, 57, 58, 64, 562
  social behavior, 50, 57, 64
  social definition, 50, 51, 53, 57, 64
  social facts, 50-53, 57, 58, 62, 64
Pattern variables, 398-407, 439
  applied to personality, social structural,
    and cultural levels, 403, 404
  related to functional requirements of
    social systems, 407, 411, 412
  used in comparative analysis of social
    systems, 405, 406
Phenomenological approach, 4, 60, 293,
    456, 457
Polish Peasant in Europe and America, The,
    318

Political economy, 24, 27, 122, 123, 132,
    136, 137, 148, 343, 344
Political structure, *see* Authority structure;
    Goal attainment, political structure;
    Govenment; Power structure
Positivism, 16, 23, 72-74, 91, 98, 157, 162,
    167, 171, 211, 439, 441
  in Comte's perspective, 76, 77-86, 89
  in Parsons' voluntaristic theory of
    action, 392-394, 398
  see also French Positivism
Power: as medium of exchange, 423
  strategies for acquiring, 368-369
  see also Power structure
Power Elite, The, 460
Power structure: alternative types of,
    559, 560, 563
  contrasted with authority structure, 218-
    220, 557-560
  and dependency relations of subordinates,
    366-371
  emergence from imbalanced exchanges,
    366-370
  as functional necessity for social systems,
    410, 419
  institutionalization in macro structures,
    377-381
  in macro structures, 373, 374
  mass vs. pluralistic, 464, 465
  Mills' analysis of American, 458-465,
    489, 490, 500
    historical development, 461-463
    social bonds among members, 463, 464
  opposition to, 374-377
    see also Class conflict; Conflict interest
      groups
  political, differentiated from religion,
    424, 425
  stabilization through legitimating values
    and norms, 371, 372, 374, 381
Pragmatism, 25, 26, 293-296, 457
Praxis, 125, 135
Prestige, 53, 217, 218, 423, 491
Primary groups, 312-316
Progress, 26, 67, 71, 72, 75, 77, 88, 89
  intellectual, 78-84
  social, 79, 118
  technological, 104-107
  see also Technological development
Proletariat, 121, 141-143, 145-147
Propositions, 32, 33, 38, 43-45, 47, 49,
    54, 64

Protestant ethic, 53, 216, 230-236, 238
  as stimulus for capitalism, 231, 232, 240
Protestant Ethic and the Spirit of Capitalism, The, 205, 230, 240
Protestantism, 82, 236-238, 244
Psychological reductionism, 164, 170, 351, 362

Rationality, 77, 202-204, 213, 227, 235, 238-240
  functional, 200
    vs. substantive rationality, 243
  instrumental, 214, 215, 225, 454
  value-oriented, 214-216
    vs. instrumental, 214, 215, 225, 454
Rational-legal authority, 224, 225, 240
Reality construction, *see* Social reality, socially constructed nature
Reason, 14, 15, 75, 76, 82, 89
Reference group theory, 200, 293, 437-440, 475
Relative deprivation, 145, 200, 475
Religion, 12, 14, 16, 52, 75, 84, 163, 164, 241
  differentiated from political structure, 424, 425
  Durkheim's analysis of, 188-197
    as source of solidarity, 188-194, 196, 197
  functional analysis of, 410, 411, 419, 420
  of humanity, 73, 74, 86-89
  Marx's analysis of, 129-131
  in modern society, 192-194
  Weber's analysis, 230, 236-238
  see also Protestant ethic; Protestantism
Residues vs. derivations, 395-397
Revolution, 117, 121, 122, 124, 132, 139, 141, 146, 147, 154, 218, 219, 477
  of rising expectations, 21
  scientific, 50
Reward: endogenous vs. exogenous, 359
  intrinsic vs. extrinsic, 363-365, 377, 380
  strategies for acquiring, 365, 366
Role, 35, 56, 308, 310, 311, 404-407
Role-identity, 322-324, 335

Satiation, 352, 354, 359, 375
Scientific mentality, 10-12, 14, 24, 30, 38, 54, 75, 84, 88, 195

as stimulus for sociology, 16-19
Secularization, 114, 235, 236, 238, 240
Self-concept, 293, 303-310, 492
  development in primary groups, 312-315
  deviant, 306, 324
  effects on role performance, 326, 327
  "I" and "me" as dimensions of, 304-306, 323, 324
  and identification with group, 309, 314, 315
  McCall and Simmons' model, 322-324, 335
  measurement of, 320
  stages in development, 306-308
  and subjective definitions, 319
  see also Role identity
Selfishness, 74, 85, 86
Self-orientation vs. collectivity orientation, 401, 403
Sentiment, 74, 75, 83, 85, 395
Situational analysis, 318, 319, 335, 339
  contrasted with stimulus-response model, 318, 319
Small groups, Homans' analysis of, 348-351
Sociability, 254
Social action, 51, 53, 388, 389
  logical vs. nonlogical models, 395-397
  Parsons' voluntaristic theory of, 391-398
  Weber's typology of, 213-216
Social and Cultural Dynamics, 91, 97
Social approval, 352, 355, 356, 370
  as general medium of exchange, 423
  as reward for normative conformity, 371, 381
  as stimulus for altruistic behavior, 362, 388
Social behavior, elementary, 51, 53, 351, 358
Social Behavior: Its Elementary Forms, 352
Social change, 13-21, 82-84, 98, 322, 477, 478
  Durkheim's theory of, 180-182
  in functional analysis, 423-428, 433-435
  linear vs. cyclical model of, 89, 90
  Marx's theory of, 127, 128, 146-148
  in open systems theory, 515, 516, 531-543
  see also Evolution; Social evolution
Social class, 34

subsystem interchanges within, 421-423

Social System, The, 399

Sociation, 252, 253, 256

Society: capitalist, *see* Capitalist society
 complex, 183-185, 274
 industrial, 20, 23, 83, 104, 113, 133, 153, 468, 469
 objective vs. subjective nature of, 62
 positivist, 23, 75, 88
 postcapitalist, Dahrendorf's analysis of, 468, 469
  Marx's view of, 152
 socially constructed, 61, 62
 see also Social organization; Social structure; Social system

Sociobiological perspective, 519-527, 560, 561
 behaviors explained by, 522-525
 compared to Parsons' functionalist perspective, 526-527
 cultural variations, 523-526
 related to general systems theory, 519, 527, 560-561
 social Darwinist background of, 519-522

Sociocultural change, 72, 90, 98-100, 119
 see also Social change

Sociocultural systems as open systems, 514-567
 biological and genetic influences on, 519-527
 boundary permeability of, 516, 517, 527, 561
 components of, 517, 518
 environmental relations of, 516, 517, 561
 equilibrium of, 547-550
 information linkages within, 518, 519, 527, 555, 556
 interdependence within, 515, 516, 518, 519
 morphogenic nature of, 531-538
 segmented vs. interdependent, 547-550
 see also Social system

Socialization, 387, 409, 440, 522

Sociological Tradition, The, 50

Sociology: alternative political orientations, 47-49
 early American, 390, 391
 institutionalized as academic discipline, 165, 166
 of knowledge, 155, 194, 195

as multiple-paradigm science, 50-59, 562

objective vs. subjective orientations, 31, 32, 51

Simmel's conception of, 251, 252, 255, 256

stimulated by rapid social change, 13-16

Solidarity, 12, 34, 85, 161-167, 171, 550, 553, 554
 Durkheim's emphasis contrasted with Marxism, 162
 mechanical vs. organic, 188-194, 547
 religious origins of, 188-194
 threats to, 183-188

Specificity vs. diffuseness, 402, 403, 405

Spirit of reason, 118, 119, 135, 210, 211

State, Marx's view of, 131, 138, 139, 455
 see also Government

Status consistency, 357, 358, 473
 distinctions, 356-358, 367
 groups, 217, 218, 240, 495-498

Stigma, 331, 332

Stratification: and control of means of production, 129, 140, 141, 491, 492
 as functional necessity, 410
 and interaction patterns, 490, 492-498, 500, 501
 multi-dimensional nature of, 219, 240, 241, 460, 491, 492
 reinforced by interaction rituals, 492, 493, 499
 and status group participation, 495-497
 see also Class; Social class

Structural differentiation, Parsons' theory of, 423-425, 427, 440
 see also Division of labor

Structural-functional analysis: with AGIL framework, 412-421
 based on social action theory in Parsons' perspective, 388
 Parsons' strategy of, 406-412
 ideological implications of, 427-428

Structual simplification, 538-543

Structure of Social Action, 240, 392

Subjective consciousness, 52, 60, 126, 302-304
 domination, in modern capitalist society, 453, 455
 see also Social reality, subjective nature of

Subjective definitions, 51, 53, 61-63, 490, 492, 493, 500
efforts to control, 491-497, 500
reinforced in interaction rituals, 492, 493
see also Definition of situation; Social reality, subjective definitions
Subjective meaning, 18, 31, 58, 202, 203, 208, 210, 213, 240, 292
Subjective orientations, 216, 241, 242
vs. objective social consequences, 429, 430 430
and Parsons' pattern variables, 398-406
Subordination, 85, 253, 256-262, 366-370
and conflict, 257-261
in democratic vs. hierarchical organizations, 259, 260, 262
effects on group structure, 257, 258
under individual vs. plurality, 257-260, 281
to principles or laws, 260, 261, 281
Suicide, 163, 175, 185-188, 196, 197
Sultanism, 222
Superordination and subordination, 253, 256-262, 281
Surplus value, 148-150
Symbolic interaction, 291-336
and deviance, 324-325
and subjective thought processes, 301-303
vs. interaction through gestures, 298-301
Symbolic interaction theory, 4, 25, 51, 55, 283, 291-336
contrasted with functionalism, 320, 321, 335, 387
contrasted with psychological behaviorism, 297, 320
explanation of interdependence, 510-512
System of Positive Politics, 74, 87

Taoism, 236, 242

Technological development, 21, 56, 83, 104, 111, 114, 141, 153
and cultural lag, 105-107
as stimulus for establishment of sociology, 14, 17, 19
Tertius Gaudens, 270, 271
Theory: alternative forms of, 44-47
objective vs. subjective approaches to, 31, 32, 51
Theory construction, 5, 32-47, 51, 60, 62, 64, 65
Theory of Social and Economic Organization, 219
Toward A General Theory of Action, 399, 401, 405
Traditional-type action, 215
Tragedy of culture, 278
Triad, 268-271
Twenty Statements Test, 320, 335

Universalism vs. particularism, 401-406
Utilitarianism, 22, 23, 27, 198, 209, 343, 344, 393, 394

Value neutrality, 211
Value orientations, 47-49, 64, 91, 377, 378, 510, 511
in Parsons' theory, 399, 400, 405, 406
Value-oriented rationality, 214-216
Value, use vs. exchange, 149
Variables, 32, 33, 36, 38, 44, 64
independent vs. dependent, 41-43
Verstehen, 18, 45, 66
Violence, 486-488, 492, 500
conditions affecting, 473-477, 498
and conflict regulation, 476-478
consequences of, 477-478
Voluntaristic theory of action, 245, 391-398, 406, 439, 441

Work ethic, 238, 239

Young Hegelians, 118, 119